Child and Adolescent Development for Educators

Child and Adolescent Development
for Educators

SECOND EDITION

Christine B. McCormick
David G. Scherer

THE GUILFORD PRESS
New York   London

Copyright © 2018 Christine B. McCormick and David G. Scherer
Published by The Guilford Press
A Division of Guilford Publications, Inc.
370 Seventh Avenue, Suite 1200, New York, NY 10001
www.guilford.com

Printed in the United States of America

This book is printed on acid-free paper.

Last digit is print number: 9   8   7   6   5   4   3   2   1

Library of Congress Cataloging-in-Publication Data is available from the publisher.

ISBN 978-1-4625-3468-5 (paperback)
ISBN 978-1-4625-3469-2 (hardcover)

About the Authors

Christine B. McCormick, PhD, is Professor in the College of Education at the University of Massachusetts Amherst, where she teaches graduate and undergraduate courses in human growth and development, educational psychology, learning and cognition, and classroom assessment. She was Dean of the College of Education from 2005 to 2016. Previously, Dr. McCormick was a faculty member and held administrative roles at the University of New Mexico and the University of South Carolina. She has served on the editorial boards of the *Journal of Educational Psychology* and *Educational Psychology Review* and is a Fellow of the American Psychological Association. Dr. McCormick is author or coauthor of many publications on a variety of topics in child development and education and has coauthored several textbooks.

David G. Scherer, PhD, is a clinical psychologist and Professor of Psychological and Brain Sciences at the University of Massachusetts Amherst. Previously, he was a faculty member at the University of New Mexico and the University of South Carolina. Dr. Scherer is a family systems theorist and therapist and an advocate for developmental and multisystemically informed treatment models. His research publications and clinical work focus on how adolescents develop autonomy in the family context, how adolescents and parents make important medical and research participation decisions, and innovative models of psychotherapy for troubled and substance-abusing adolescents. Dr. Scherer has taught undergraduate and graduate courses in adolescent psychology; psychology and public policy; professional issues and ethics; psychopathology; and child, adolescent, and family psychotherapy.

Preface

This book addresses the topics in developmental psychology that are of the highest priority for educators—teachers, school counselors, school psychologists, and school administrators. The original vision was spearheaded by Michael Pressley, the first author of the first edition. This second edition continues in the tradition of the first by covering the classic developmental canon while being true to its educational orientation. Our intent was to produce a text that emphasizes empirical research and demonstrates its applicability to applied settings. This is truly a 2018 textbook—not just a revision, but a complete reworking of the first edition. This is a textbook and also a resource that can be useful to students pursuing a career in education.

Our conviction is that adequate knowledge of developmental theory is the keystone to competent educational practice. While the text explores a wide variety of developmental themes, it was written to meet the specific needs of future educators. One of the ways we achieve this objective is by consistently and explicitly illustrating how developmental concepts operate in a variety of educational contexts. The emphasis on applications to educational contexts in this book is informed by both historic and enduring themes in development as well as innovative contemporary theories and research.

The organization of this second edition mirrors that of the first edition, reflecting the research literature in development and education. The research cited in the second edition has been extensively updated. Nearly half of the research citations are new to this edition and emphasize work published in the last decade. Part I of the text, *Theoretical Perspectives in Child Development,* is organized in terms of the major theories of development. Chapter 1 sets the stage by introducing the "Big Ideas" that have shaped the study of development. This is followed by a review of research methods commonly used by developmental researchers, including both qualitative and quantitative approaches to conducting research. In this edition, we condensed the major themes of developmental research introduced in Chapter 1, and these themes are revisited in each chapter summary. Chapter 2 describes the biological foundations of development, with explicit discussion of the biological foundations of academic competence. Given advances in neuroscience, genetics research, and the implications of these advances for educators, this chapter has been considerably updated and presents a sound foundation for anyone working with children and adolescents.

The next two chapters provide different perspectives on cognitive development. Chapter 3 highlights Piaget's theory and contributions evolving from his theoretical framework. For this edition, coverage of Kohlberg's theory of moral development has been shortened, and more contemporary perspectives on moral development have been added. This chapter also introduces the concept of theory of mind and significantly updates the sections on moral or character education and constructivist approaches to education. Chapter 4 focuses on insights in cognitive development derived from information-processing approaches and has been updated to incorporate advances from cognitive science. A substantial discussion of executive function is now included.

The final two chapters in Part I describe theories that emphasize social influences on development: Chapter 5 describes some of the more traditional theories emphasizing social influences of individuals in a child's environment, whereas Chapter 6 describes the theories that emphasize the influence of the surrounding culture on development. In this edition, the section on social learning in Chapter 5 benefits from the inclusion of more examples. The historical influences of Freud and Erikson are also noted in Chapter 5, but this edition incorporates greater detail about identity development, adding new theoretical perspectives on ethnic–racial identity. In Chapter 6, problem-based or team-based learning is analyzed in terms of sociocultural theoretical constructs, and research on intelligent tutoring systems is added to the discussion of expert human tutors.

Part II, *Key Topics in Child Development and Education,* discusses significant topics in developmental research of importance to educators. Typically, these topics are not studied in the context of a particular theoretical perspective and are approached by citing researchers from varying theoretical orientations. Chapter 7 is a comprehensive discussion of language development, including information on bilingualism and deafness. The chapter on intelligence, Chapter 8, includes information on the construct and measurement of intelligence typically provided in a child development text but then adds a treatment of learner diversity designed to be more relevant for future educators. Chapter 9 provides a comprehensive view of the development of academic motivation, a topic that is vital for future educators but not adequately addressed by traditional child development textbooks. Topics added to the discussion of motivation in the second edition include teacher–student relationships, the impact of choice and value, and descriptions of intervention research to enhance classroom motivation. Chapter 10 examines in detail the roles of family and peer relationships in development. Given the proliferation of research in this arena, this chapter is extensively updated, including information on early intervention, social media trends, and social–emotional learning. The implications of theory of mind for social relationships are also analyzed. Chapter 11 explores the role of gender in developmental processes, including the power of gender stereotypes and an analysis of gender-related factors influencing academic performance in math and science. Chapter 12 provides an overview of how educators can recognize and understand student mental health problems—a must for any future educator. Finally, the book concludes with an integrative review chapter where the major concepts presented in the text are combined in a longitudinal view of development. Throughout all of the chapters, explicit connections are made to the overall theme of highlighting work that is most relevant to future educators.

Features of This Book

Chapters 2–12 conclude with a *Chapter Summary and Evaluation* in which the major points of the chapter are briefly reviewed, organized around the themes of the Big Ideas in development introduced in Chapter 1. Key terms are bolded and defined in the text where they appear and are presented again at the end of Chapters 1–12 in a *Review of Key Terms*.

At least one *Applying Developmental Theory to Educational Contexts* special feature appears in all chapters. This feature gives detailed recommendations for applying theory to practice or examples of applications to practice. These examples and recommendations help students make connections between theory and practice as they begin to develop the knowledge base required to generate additional applications. In addition, all chapters contain at least one *Considering Interesting Questions* special feature focusing on an interesting question or issue that was not addressed in the text or not completely developed in the text discussion. This feature is designed to spark interest in students new to developmental topics.

Acknowledgments

Foremost, we would like to acknowledge Michael Pressley as first author of the first edition of this book. We also thank everyone we worked with at The Guilford Press for their encouragement and support in developing this second edition.

Instructors considering this book for course adoption will receive a ready-to-use test bank that includes multiple-choice and essay questions, including questions based on classroom scenarios. The instructor's manual for the first edition was developed by Karen Harrington and served as the starting point for the instructor's manual for the second edition.

Contents

PART II   **Key Topics in Child Development and Education**

Child and Adolescent Development for Educators

PART I

Theoretical Perspectives in Child Development

CHAPTER 1

Introduction to Child Development and Education

This is a book about human development, an interdisciplinary field of study. Human development involves biological transformation: from a single cell to a fetus to an infant and then to a toddler. A child matures into an adolescent, who matures into an adult, who ages and eventually dies. Human development also includes psychological changes—from a newborn who exhibits more reflexes than intentional behaviors to a child whose thinking is more concrete than abstract. In turn, the child becomes an adolescent whose thinking gradually becomes more abstract and hypothetical. Teenagers soon become adults, whose intellectual powers increase across the lifespan in some ways and decline in others. Development also involves social changes— for example, from a newborn experiencing people as sensations to an infant who is attached to his or her caregivers to a preschooler with an expanding social world. The world of peers becomes increasingly important as the child grows older and enters adolescence.

Some basic themes have shaped the study of development and over decades have provided a framework for how to think about developmental theory and research. So, we begin this book with an overview of some of the concepts and movements that have defined developmental science and some of the controversies and uncertainties that surround these ideas.

The Evolution of Developmental Science

How educators and social scientists think about development has evolved over the past several decades. One way to think about the changes in the study of development is to consider to what extent children are dynamic participants in their development and to what extent our environment is actively engaged in forming a person's development (see Figure 1.1).

		Environment	
		Passive	*Active*
Person	*Passive*	"Static" theories	"Linear" theories
	Active	"Transformational" theories	"Transactional" theories

FIGURE 1.1. Thinking about developmental science in terms of person × environment interaction.

Suppose neither the person nor the environment is particularly active in determining the outcome of a person's development. This "static" theory was similar to how some people thought about children and development prior to the advent of developmental studies. Children were simply thought of as "miniature adults" and were not accorded any unique status or thought to be a whole lot different than adults. Fortunately, these kinds of ideas were replaced when educators and social scientists started to study children and how they developed. One type of theory that was fairly dominant in the history of psychology was "linear" theory, which assumed that our environment had a tremendous influence on how we behaved and who we became. Such theories were primarily behavioral or learning theories that assumed that contingencies (i.e., rewards and punishments) that rise from our environment determine how we behave and develop.

As psychology and developmental science matured, new theories emerged that emphasized the active role that children play in their development. These "transformational" theories postulated that development proceeds in an orderly fashion, that people go through stages of increasing complexity in their development, and that the capacities children acquire early in development will affect their later stages of development. More contemporary theories of development tend to be "transactional." They presume that both the environment and the person are active agents in a person's development. These theories of development emphasize that children are a product of their environment but that they also alter their environment. From this perspective, both environment and the person engage in a continuous dynamic interaction in which they reciprocally determine one another. Several such "Big Ideas" have been pervasive influences in both developmental science and education as these disciplines have matured. We will outline the more prominent Big Ideas here and refer to them throughout the book.

Active and Passive Child Influences

As already mentioned, one theme that has garnered a lot of attention is the question of how much a child is an active agent in his or her development. Some theories portray children, including infants, as continually active in their own development (Gopnik, Meltzoff, & Kuhl, 1999; Lerner & Fisher, 2013; Piaget, 1970; von Glaserfeld, 1995). They decide what they will attend to and process, seeking out things that are particularly interesting to them. Educators who subscribe to such theories tend to favor arranging learning environments to stimulate children's curiosity and exploration; they believe that the learning resulting from interactions stimulated by the child's own interests will be especially enduring. Other theories depict children as more passive, learning from stimulation that is presented to them (Rosenshine, 1979). The educator's role according to these theories is to select to-be-learned information, present it to children, and provide feedback and reinforcement.

Our perspective is that children learn in a variety of ways. Some learning results from the active efforts of the child, that is, as a consequence of the child's natural curiosity and interests. Even so, humans have a tremendous capacity to learn without effort or even interest, acquiring much information incidentally. Children learn from observation, and they learn when they are reinforced to learn (Bandura, 1986). The skilled educator knows both how to stimulate children's natural activities and how to devise presentations and provide reinforcements in order to promote learning of important material. The skilled teacher also understands just how much can be learned incidentally from rich experiences and does everything possible to make certain that children experience informative worlds. Children learn through what they read, through what they are encouraged to watch on television, and through interactions with classmates and classroom visitors representing diverse perspectives.

Continuity and Discontinuity in Development

One way to think about human development suggests that people go through gradual changes. One example in nature is a blade of grass growing gradually with no remarkable change in its basic characteristics. Theories like social learning theory (see Chapter 5; Bandura, 1977, 1986) and information-processing theory (see Chapter 4) posit that maturation in behavior and intellect evolve gradually over time; that children's and adults' repertoire of behaviors and their intellect increase as their exposure to and knowledge of the world expand. The result is that with increasing age during childhood and continuing into adolescence a person's behavior becomes more complex and his or her thinking skills increase.

In contrast, there are theories of development that specify particular stages of psychological growth and maturation. One example in nature of development occurring in discrete stages is that of the metamorphosis of a caterpillar into a cocooned pupa and its final emergence as a butterfly. According to theories that emphasize discontinuities and stages in growth, children are fundamentally different depending on their stage, and movement from one stage to another stage is rather abrupt. For example, G. Stanley Hall (1904, 1905) conceived of adolescence as a period of great "storm and stress," brought on by the sudden physical changes that accompany adolescence, whereas Erik Erikson (1968) posited that adolescence brings with it concerns about identity that are not important at all earlier in life (see Chapter 5). Another example is Piaget's (1970) theory of intellectual development, which asserts that children during the grade school years are very concrete in their thinking, with the transition into adolescence accompanied by a dramatic increase in abstract thinking skills (see Chapter 3). So, according to the stage perspective, development proceeds in discrete steps that may seem dramatic or sudden. The developmental change is *abrupt*.

As we work our way through the various types of psychological developments that children and adolescents undergo, we will find elements of both continuity and discontinuity. On the one hand, development is often quite discontinuous. Children and adolescents make progress toward more complex and sophisticated psychological functioning and then quite frequently regress and revert to behaviors and ways of thinking characteristic of previous stages of development. Also, sometimes developmental competencies are specific to particular situations, and children and adolescents might demonstrate a developmental competency in one venue or format but not in another. For example, children often recite the polite and considerate way to act with peers; they know in their minds how they are supposed to behave, but they don't always adopt those behaviors in social situations. Or they may be able to do calculations regarding sports or video gaming, while at the same time not be able to perform well in math class.

On the other hand, while there are discontinuities in development, often they are not as pronounced or as rapid in onset as some stage theories suggest. Educators should be realistic about what to expect from children of particular ages, but they should not be so tied to stage thinking as to ignore inconsistencies with it. For example, although elementary-age children often do have difficulty thinking hypothetically, they can be quite hypothetical when thinking about very familiar topics. If you need convincing, ask a 10-year-old chess expert some hypothetical questions about moves in chess!

Nature and Nurture

Today, most developmental psychologists do not believe that development is primarily due to either *nature* (determined by biology) or *nurture* (determined by experience). Instead, there is clear understanding that development is due to both nature and nurture, both biology and experience (Collins, Maccoby, Steinberg, Hetherington, & Bornstein, 2000; Institute of Medicine and National Resource Council, 2012; Rutter, 2002a, 2002b; Sameroff, 2010; Shonkoff & Phillips, 2000). Biology provides a range of possibilities. Which of those possibilities is realized depends greatly on the experiences available in the environment. Consider what may seem a simple example. A child inherits genes that provide him or her with a biological predisposition for being taller than average. Whether this child achieves this biological potential depends on environmental factors, such as the nutrition available and exposure to severe illness or disease.

Human intelligence provides a good example of how environmental influences act upon the range of biological possibilities. Humans do not inherit genes that result in a specific level of intelligence. Rather, they inherit the potential for a range of possibilities. Whether or not a child's level of intelligence reaches the top end of the range depends on the quality of the environment provided. Researchers debate, however, about how much **plasticity,** or sensitivity to environmental experiences, there is for intelligence (Garlick, 2002; Gottesman & Hanson, 2005; Lewontin, 1974). With considerable controversy, some contend the range is very narrow—that parental intelligence largely determines the intelligence of their children (Herrnstein & Murray, 1994; see also Chapter 8 and Hunt & Carlson, 2007). Others argue that the **reaction range** for intelligence, the range of all possible levels of intelligence given the biological predisposition, is substantially broader (Jacoby & Glauberman, 1995; Martinez, 2000), with some researchers emphasizing human autonomy and the role of individual choice in their analyses (Flynn, 2016). There is no doubt that there is some range and that where a child ends up in his or her particular reaction range is a function of the environment he or she experiences.

Virtually all of the theories of development presented in this book have both biological and environmental components. Some theories are more biological than environmental, and others emphasize environment much more than biology, but all are *both* biological and environmental. The goal of educators should be to make the most of the child's biological potential. That means providing children with consistent high-quality experiences. Biological perspectives can provide insights about when particular types of experiences are crucial as well as insights about the risks of environmental deprivations at particular points in development (see Chapter 2).

Social-Ecological Influences

The environment can affect development in many ways. Sometimes we encounter what we refer to as cohort effects. One kind of cohort effect is the time period we live in, and it can often be an important determinant of our development. Children born in the last few years are growing up in a world surrounded by sophisticated technology, a world that those born in earlier eras never could have dreamed of. As a consequence, they have far more information available to them to guide their development.

Family and extrafamilial relationships also can make an enormous difference in children's development (see Chapter 10). For example, how families communicate and interact with their children has a large effect on children's cognitive and social development. Preschoolers who are in families that verbally interact a great deal arrive at kindergarten with better developed language skills and make faster progress learning to read during the elementary years. Similarly, as children age, their range of social contacts increases, and by the time they become adolescents, peer interactions become more influential, interacting with family influences (Bornstein, Jager, & Steinberg, 2013; Hartup, 1989; Csikszentmihalyi & Larson, 1984). In addition to peer relationships, children have contact with a variety of adults besides their parents, such as neighbors, teachers, and physicians.

A variety of institutions, such as governments, media, religions, and schools, affect the life of the developing child. Federal and state *governments* have a variety of policies that can touch the life of an individual child. Government funds can provide money for prenatal care, children's health care, housing, and day care, all of which impact many children. Governments can pass laws that protect children from abuse or environmental contaminants, such as lead paint, and can enforce those laws. Governments can also fail to provide for the needs of children. Either way, children and their development are affected.

Knowledge that affects children comes from other institutions as well. *Media* outlets like the Internet or television have significant influence on youth (Singer & Singer, 2001). *Religion* is a knowledge-building force in children's lives, with the religious exposure children receive affecting their understanding of the world (Kerestes & Youniss, 2003). The institution most often associated with children's development is *school*.

The theory that integrates the various types of environmental influences on child and adolescent development is Urie Bronfenbrenner's (1979, 1989, 1992) *ecological systems theory* (see Figure 1.2). Bronfenbrenner divides the environment into the following elements: the microsystem, the mesosystem, the exosystem, and the macrosystem. The **microsystem** refers to the child's direct experiences in different contexts such as home or school. The **mesosystem** represents the linkages of two or more microsystems—for example, parent and school interactions or interactions of the family with community or church resources. The **exosystem** includes governments and institutions that regulate mesosystems and can have a significant effect on the child, even though they are removed from the child's direct experiences. For example, the policies of the local school may have an indirect effect on the child. Finally, the **macrosystem** embodies the cultural forces, values, and beliefs acting upon the child and the rest of the ecological system surrounding the child.

An important theme in Bronfenbrenner's ideas is that people are embedded in their ecological contexts and are interdependent of and inseparable from their social ecology. Similarly, Bronfenbrenner emphasizes the reciprocity that exists between different levels of ecological systems: the environment affects the child, and the child also affects the environment. Moreover, even though exosystems and macrosystems are rather remote from the day-to-day activities of individual children and adolescents, they still have a profound effect on them, probably much more than vice versa. Because of these principles, Bronfenbreener asserted that studying human beings and their development required understanding their social contexts and that the only legitimate way to understand human nature was to study humans within their social environments.

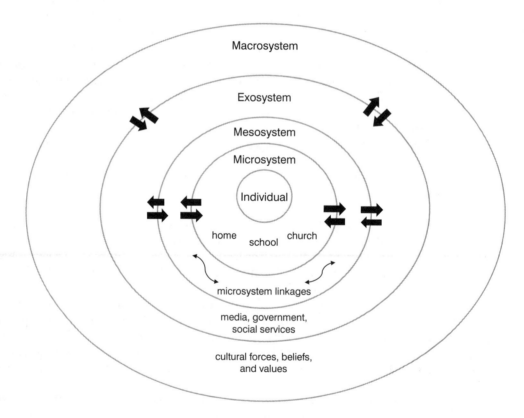

FIGURE 1.2. Bronfenbrenner's ecological systems theory divides the environment into the microsystem, the mesosystem, the exosystem, and the macrosystem, as portrayed in this figure.

Universal and Culture-Specific Development

Many developmental theorists assert that there are universals in development, stages and psychological events that all children everywhere experience (Flavell, 1971). This idea is most strongly evident in developmental theories that emphasize biological influences. At a biological level, the similarities between people from different cultures and races are much more pronounced than the differences. Indeed, from a biological perspective, the similarities between human males and females are much greater than the differences (see Chapter 11). Because of these biological similarities, similarities in physical and behavioral development are inevitable.

Conversely, some developmental theorists emphasize the role of culture in determining development and how development proceeds differently in different cultures (see Chapter 6; Cole & Scribner, 1977; Gauvain & Perez, 2015; Mistry, Contreras, & Dutta, 2013). To the extent that environment makes a difference in development, culture should make an impact on development. The environments children experience in one part of the world can be very different from the environments children experience in another part of the world.

Because development is both biologically determined and a function of environment, there are both universals in development and culture-specific developments. Indeed, evidence of this exists in any school district in the United States. Children in a given classroom may be very diverse both economically and culturally. Nonetheless, these same children are much more similar to one another in their behaviors and competencies than they are to older children or adults.

Summary of the Big Ideas

Development is very complicated, and it is essential that educators appreciate and understand its complexities. Even so, in order to remain manageable, the study of development often requires simplification since individual research studies are always limited in scope (as we will see in the next section on research methods). To emphasize the complexity of human development, we will briefly return to a consideration of the Big Ideas of development outlined earlier in each chapter summary.

Research Methods in Child Development and Education

Since the study of child development is a scientific enterprise, every student of development must have at least a rudimentary understanding of basic research methods. It is also important for educators to be informed consumers of research. Advocates for school reform have emphasized the need for educators to employ evidence-based best practices. To do so, educators need to have at least a rudimentary understanding of how research evidence is gathered. Researchers interested in human development use diverse research methods. One reason for the diversity of methods is that not all problems can be addressed with any one method. A second reason is that some researchers personally prefer some methods over others, perhaps because of their education or their philosophical assumptions. One way to conceptualize research methods is to distinguish between quantitative and qualitative methods.

Quantitative Methods

Quantitative approaches begin with a **hypothesis,** which is a proposed relationship between two or more variables. For example, a researcher may hypothesize that "cooperative learning is more likely to promote achievement in same-sex than mixed-sex cooperative groups." This hypothesis is then tested. Researchers often derive hypotheses from a larger theoretical orientation and/or generate them from previous studies on the topic. The investigations of the hypotheses may in turn lead to revisions and refinements of the theory or, on occasion, the discarding of a theory in favor of a new one inspired by the research results.

After researchers formulate a testable hypothesis, it is operationalized in a study. **Operationalization** refers to the process of defining variables by specifying how they will be measured or manipulated in a study. Thus, for the cooperative learning hypothesis, a cooperative learning situation is specified, perhaps mathematics classes in six fourth-grade, six fifth-grade, and six sixth-grade classrooms, each containing about 30 students. Same-sex cooperative groups are defined as four boys or four girls working together (one each per classroom). Mixed-sex groups are defined as having three boys and a girl (one per classroom), three girls and a boy (one per classroom), or two girls and two boys to a group (one per classroom). Cooperative learning could be operationalized with the teacher urging children in each small group to help one another answer the week's study problems, explaining to each other their rationales for solving problems. Cooperative learning defined in this manner might be studied for 5 weeks, comparing the learning in same-sex and mixed-sex groups with learning defined as the mean performance of each group on end-of-week quizzes over the week's mathematics assignments.

In quantitative investigations, observations are translated into numbers that are then statistically analyzed. There are two main classes of quantitative studies. In **manipulative investigations,** usually called "experiments," researchers control variation by randomly assigning people to one educational treatment or another. **Random assignment** means that before the experiment begins, each student has an equal chance of being assigned to any treatment condition. One way to ensure random assignment of all the students in a class is to pick the names, one at a time, out of a hat. The first name is assigned to condition A, the second to condition B, the third to C, the fourth to D, the fifth to E, and so on.

In **nonmanipulative investigations,** researchers systematically analyze naturally occurring differences between people or settings. Comparisons of different age groups in a developmental study are necessarily nonmanipulative comparisons. We discuss nonmanipulative studies in more detail later in the chapter.

Manipulative Investigations

Often educational researchers compare a new educational intervention to conventional instruction or some other alternative instruction (Campbell & Stanley, 1966). For example, an investigator may compare typical mathematics instruction with mathematics instruction enriched by information about when and where to use the math being learned. A researcher interested in memory strategies may compare the recall performance of students taught to rehearse to learn vocabulary words to those who learned vocabulary words using their own methods. In investigations of reading strategies, the typical comparison would be between reading performances by students taught a strategy (e.g., predicting what will happen next) and those not instructed to use the strategy.

The design for a simple study in which one experimental group is contrasted with a control group contains two conditions. The factors manipulated in an experiment are the **independent variables.** In a simple two-condition experiment, there is only one independent variable: the experimental versus control manipulation.

Independent variables are hypothesized to have effects on particular **dependent variables,** which are the performances measured in the study. Many different types of dependent variables are collected in quantitative studies. These include behavioral observations (e.g., prosocial or aggressive actions), learning measures (e.g., amount of information recalled), performances on standardized tests (e.g., achievement or intelligence tests), and responses to surveys and interviews. Sometimes dependent measures are obtained from secondary sources, such as parents or teachers. For example, parents can provide reports to researchers about the amount of homework done by their children, or teachers can rate the sociability of each of the children in their classrooms.

Research studies are often much more complex than merely contrasting one experimental condition with one control condition. Researchers may be interested in studying several different variables, each of which can be manipulated. For example, if researchers believe that both nutritional supplements and instructional enrichment promote the learning and thinking of young children, they could conduct a factorial study. This study can be set up as a 2 (levels of nutrition) by 2 (levels of instruction) factorial design (see Figure 1.3). In one condition, children receive only the nutritional supplement; in a second condition, children receive the nutritional supplement and instructional enrichment; in a third condition, participants are given only the instructional enrichment; and in the fourth (control) condition, children receive neither the nutritional nor the instructional enrichment. This design permits evaluation of whether nutrition, instruction, or nutrition and instruction combined produce differences in children's performances measured by the researchers—perhaps on learning tasks or on an intelligence test.

How are differences determined in manipulative investigations? For each condition in an experiment, two statistics are particularly important for each of the dependent variables that are collected. One is the **mean** value, which is the arithmetic average of all scores. The second is the **standard deviation,** which is an index of how much, on average, each individual score differs from the mean for the condition. The larger the standard deviation, the more spread out the scores are from the mean. The smaller the standard deviation, the more the scores are clustered around the mean. Thus, the standard deviation is an index of the variation between scores in a condition.

	No instructional enrichment	Instructional enrichment
Nutritional supplement		
No nutritional supplement		

FIGURE 1.3. Design of a 2 (levels of nutrition) by 2 (levels of instruction) study.

How do researchers determine whether or not the differences between means are due to chance? They use the means and standard deviations in statistical tests that produce estimates of the likelihood that the experimental and control means differ at greater than a chance level. These tests determine whether there is a *statistically significant difference*—one that is unlikely to occur by chance—between the means. If there is a statistically significant difference between the experimental and the control group performances, researchers can draw the conclusion that there is a good chance the experimental treatment *caused* the difference in performance. In general, unless there is a 95% chance that the difference is not random (therefore, the chance of an error is 5%—an error rate of $p < .05$), social scientists are reluctant to conclude the difference is real. Often, researchers require even a more stringent standard, such as 99% certainty (an error rate of $p < .01$).

In addition to significance testing as just described, researchers sometimes also calculate the **effect size** that is observed in a study. Why compute effect size if the difference is statistically significant? If a study has a very large number of participants, it is possible for even small effects to be statistically significant. Effect size, however, is not determined by the number of participants in a study. One way to determine effect size is by comparing the size of the difference between the experimental and control means with the size of the standard deviation for the control condition. For example, if the experimental students average 65% on a posttest, with a standard deviation of 15, and the controls averaged 50%, with a standard deviation of 20, the effect size would be 0.75—that is (65% – 50%) / 20. If effect size exceeds 0.8, the difference between the means is usually considered to be large; if effect size is between 0.4 and 0.8, the difference is often described as moderate; and if effect size is 0.2 or less, the difference is considered small (Cohen, 1977). In reading reports of research studies, the informed consumer considers the effect size as well as the statistical significance.

Nonmanipulative Investigations

Some significant developmental questions must be studied using nonmanipulative techniques since random assignment to the variables of interest is not possible. For example, if a researcher is interested in the effects of social class, race, age, or gender on educational achievement, it is impossible to randomly assign students to these socioeconomic or biologically determined categories. People can differ in still other ways, leading to other interesting variables that can predict important outcomes. For example, psychologists have devised tests to classify people as more and less intelligent (see Chapter 8). Intelligence testing remains important to educators because it predicts success in school. Sometimes researchers conduct studies to classify people based on differences in how they process information. For instance, people differ in their use of memorization strategies, reading comprehension processes, and problem-solving tactics. People can be classified as rehearsers, elaborative rehearsers, and imagery users (see Chapter 4). These differences in how students process information also predict memory performance: rehearsers do not remember lists as well as people who integrate list items into memorable mental images.

Researchers also use individual differences in information processing to test theories. For example, suppose a researcher hypothesizes that construction of mental images during reading improves understanding of ideas in the text. If that is true, children who naturally construct mental images while they read should have a better comprehension of what they read. In fact, they do (Sadoski, 1983, 1985). There is a relationship, called a **correlation,** between the two variables, use of imagery and text comprehension. In Sadoski (1983), the correlation between fifth graders' reported imagery and their comprehension and recall of text was +.37. What does this mean?

A **correlation coefficient** is used to summarize relationships between two variables and can range from –1.00 to +1.00. The greater the absolute value of the correlation coefficient, the greater the relationship between the two variables. A correlation coefficient of 0 implies no relationship between the two variables, but the closer the value is to either a –1.00 or a +1.00, the stronger the relationship. For instance, a correlation of .80 (or –.80) is high, .40 (or –.40) is moderate, and .10 (or –.10) is low. When a correlation is positive, it means that high values on one variable are associated with high values on the other variable. For instance, time spent studying is positively correlated with test performance in that more time spent studying for a test is associated with higher test scores. When a correlation is negative, it means that high values on one variable are associated with low values on the other variable. For instance, test anxiety is negatively correlated with test performance in that more test anxiety is associated with lower test performance. So, in the case of the reported correlation coefficient of +.37 reported by Sadoski (1983), the relationship between mental imaging and text comprehension and recall was moderate in size and positive. The fifth graders who reported creating more images while they read comprehended and recalled more text. The presence of a correlation, however, does not prove a causal relationship. For example, in the case of the correlation between construction of mental images and text, recall that it is possible that children who naturally use imagery are more intelligent or deeper thinkers. If so, their greater comprehension could be due to greater intelligence or deeper thinking rather than their use of imagery. Still, many sophisticated statistical analyses use correlational techniques to create complex models showing how variables relate to each. These models increase our understanding of how developmental change takes place.

Summarizing across Quantitative Studies

When a number of individual studies have been conducted on a given topic by different researchers in diverse settings under varied conditions, it can be difficult to summarize what is known about the topic. Researchers who wish to draw conclusions from data generated by multiple studies may employ a technique called **meta-analysis.** Meta-analysis is a statistical technique used to analyze and summarize patterns of results across quantitative studies. Quantitative results across multiple studies are combined to generate an average effect size or to produce a weighted average correlation. Throughout this book, references will be made to a meta-analysis on a given topic (if available), and the magnitude of the effect or the size and direction of the correlations across studies will be discussed. Typically, meta-analyses will yield a d-index, a standardized difference across studies, the difference between the means of groups or experimental conditions on some construct divided by the average standard deviation. A d-index below 0.20 would be considered trivial, between 0.20 and 0.49 small, 0.50 to 0.79 moderate, and 0.80 or higher large (Cohen, 1977). Similarly, weighted correlations less than 0.10 would be considered small, 0.10 to 0.25 small to medium, 0.25 to 0.40 medium to large, and greater than 0.40 large (Roorda, Koomen, Split, & Oort, 2011). How large an effect is important when considering an educational intervention? That depends, and as suggested by Lipsey et al. (2012), the cost (e.g., time, effort, expense) of an educational intervention should always be considered in light of the potential benefits.

Evaluating Quality of Quantitative Investigations

How can the quality of quantitative research be evaluated? A number of characteristics define a good study, described as follows:

• Objectivity of variables: **Objectivity** is the use of measures that are publicly observable and clearly measurable. The number of times teachers assist students is objective data; if researchers ask the teachers why they intervened, the data are more subjective and open to interpretation.

• Reliability of dependent variables: Dependent measures need to be reliable. **Reliability** of a measurement means that if the measurement were to be taken again, about the same score would be obtained. One reason why behavioral measures, objective performance, and standardized tests are more embraced by researchers is that they often are more reliable than other kinds of dependent measures such as surveys, interviews, and adult ratings of children. One way to increase reliability is to combine observations rather than rely on just one observation. Thus, if the dependent variable of interest is learning of text, instead of studying how students learn on text, collect data on three or four texts and combine the performances into a single score. This combined measure will be more reliable than any of the single-text scores.

• "Blind" testing: One way to enhance the quality of a study is to ensure that those collecting the dependent variables are "blind," meaning uninformed, as to key features of the research study. For example, in an experiment, the data collectors should be blind to the participants' assignment to a condition. It helps if participants in the study also are blind to both the hypotheses of the study and to the condition to which they have been assigned. Results can be very different when such precautions are taken. For example, Harrell, Capp, Davis, Peerless, and Ravitz (1981) reported large gains in the intelligence test scores of children with intellectual disability when they were administered large doses of vitamins. Unfortunately, these researchers did not employ blind testing techniques. When others attempted to replicate the outcome using appropriate blinding (i.e., of the researchers testing the children and of the children's families), no effect of vitamin therapy manipulation on the intellectual functioning of children with intellectual disability was found (Smith, Spiker, Peterson, Cicchetti, & Justice, 1984; Zigler & Hodapp, 1986).

• Internal validity: When a study has high **internal validity,** there are no other plausible competing interpretations of the results. A study with internal validity does not have confounding variables (Campbell & Stanley, 1966). **Confounding variables** are variables unrelated to the treatment of interest that may be influencing the outcome. For example, if students taught to use an imagery strategy are led to believe they are being taught this strategy because they are smart, it is impossible to know whether any improvement in performance is due to the imagery instructions. The difference could simply reflect enhanced self-esteem due to the comments about intelligence made to the imagery students. In this case, self-esteem is the confounding variable.

• Discriminant validity: Sometimes general motivational factors are confounding variables. An improvement attributed to an educational intervention may simply be a reaction to novel teaching, owing to increases in student motivation or interest (Smith & Glass, 1987). Perhaps the improvement is due to changes in teachers' expectations that affect student motivation (Rosenthal & Jacobson, 1968). Or maybe the improvement is due to students' awareness that their performance is being used to evaluate the effectiveness of the new instruction (Campbell & Stanley, 1966). To eliminate such explanations, researchers can include variables that should not be affected by the independent variable or be correlated with the nonmanipulated variables of interest. Why? Independent variables are typically hypothesized to affect particular outcomes rather than all outcomes; nonmanipulated variables are typically hypothesized to be correlated with some other variables but not all other variables. If researchers can predict in advance which outcomes measured are affected by an independent variable (and which are not), or which measures are correlated with a nonmanipulated variable (and which are not), the study can produce powerful evidence to support a hypothesis. In that case, the study has **discriminant validity** (Campbell & Fiske, 1959).

- Convergent validity: When researchers use more than one dependent variable and the pattern of outcomes is consistent across the dependent variables, there is said to be **convergent validity** (Campbell & Fiske, 1959) or **triangulation** (Mathison, 1988). For example, suppose that a researcher is studying a method for increasing the amount children read. If the researcher observes the classrooms in the study and records more reading by children receiving the intervention than children not receiving the intervention, the researcher's hypothesis that the factor being studied can increase the amount of children's reading is supported. If the teachers (who are "blind" to which students are receiving the intervention) also rate the amount of student reading and the teacher ratings indicate that the children who are receiving the treatment are reading more, convergent support exists for the researcher's hypothesis. If parents' ratings of the amount of reading occurring at home are also consistent with this pattern, there is additional convergent support of the hypothesis. Three different measures consistent with the hypothesis are better than one measure consistent with it.

- Replicability: **Replicability** is the likelihood of obtaining the same results consistently. Replicability is high when the same results are found on different occasions and low when results differ from occasion to occasion.

- External validity: Studies that have **external validity** resemble the real-life issue the researcher is trying to investigate (Bracht & Glass, 1968). For instance, a study of reading in college students is externally valid to the extent typical college students are reading actual college texts. If the study participants were not representative of college students (e.g., students enrolled in a remedial English class) or if the readings were contrived (e.g., passages written by the researcher rather than from textbooks), external reliability would be reduced.

Qualitative Methods

What are the key differences between quantitative and qualitative approaches to research (Denzin & Lincoln, 2000; Guba, 1990; Hitchcock & Hughes, 1989; Howe, 1988)? Quantitative approaches emphasize hypothesis testing, whereas qualitative researchers are more interested in constructing theories, often based on the perceptions and interpretations of participants in a setting. Whereas quantitative researchers do all that is possible to obtain *objectivity*, qualitative researchers are more comfortable with *subjectivity*. Qualitative researchers often are attempting to develop what is called a **grounded theory,** a theory grounded in data and interpretations of data collected in natural situations (Glaser & Strauss, 1967).

The distinction between quantitative and qualitative methods can be fuzzy in that an increasing number of studies have both quantitative and qualitative aspects (Tashakkori & Teddlie, 2003). One example is an experiment comparing traditional elementary science instruction with science instruction that includes reading of literary pieces related to the science unit (Morrow, Pressley, Smith, & Smith, 1997). In this study, the researchers used both quantitative measures of reading and science achievement (test scores) and qualitative analysis of the differences in the interactions in the two conditions. Mixing of quantitative and qualitative approaches is becoming more common in educational research.

Development of a Grounded Theory

Strauss and Corbin (1998) summarized how to construct grounded theories. Construction of a grounded theory begins with the *collection of data*. Qualitative researchers use a number of approaches to data collection. For instance, the researcher may observe behaviors in a setting of interest. In the case of a researcher interested in constructing a theory of first-grade reading groups, this may mean many visits to first grades to observe reading groups. Alternatively, the researcher may interview many first-grade teachers about what goes on in their reading groups. In some cases, the observations may be made by the participants themselves, perhaps in the form of diaries or daily journals. Of course, the methods of data collection can be combined. Many qualitative studies combine observational and interview data.

Then, the researcher goes through the data, systematically *looking for meaningful clusters and patterns*—behaviors that seem to go together logically. For example, if the teacher pairs off students to read to each other, encourages students to ask one another about difficult words, and suggests that several students read and discuss a library book, these observations suggest a meaningful cluster of activities. The researcher then names the cluster. In this case, "cooperative reading" would be a reasonable category name for this cluster of behaviors.

Analysis of extensive observations and interviews is likely to result in a number of categories. The next objective is to *identify support for the categories* by reviewing the data. The qualitative researcher is always open to—and actually looking for—data inconsistent with an emerging category. Qualitative researchers begin their data analyses early in the data collection. As tentative categories emerge, they look for support or nonsupport of categories. The researchers often take the emerging categories back to those being observed and interviewed and ask them to evaluate the credibility of the emerging categories. This is called **member checking** (Lincoln & Gduba, 1985). Often the subjects of the investigation can provide important refinements and extensions of the categories. As a result of member checking, the researcher may change categories or their names.

Eventually, the researcher has established a stable set of categories based on data collected to date. The task now is to begin to *organize these categories in relation to one another*. For example, the category of "teacher modeling" seems to subsume some of the other categories of behaviors such as teachers' "thinking aloud about how to decode a word," "acting out reading processes," and "acting out deciding to read for fun." Thus, the category "teacher modeling" is higher on an organizational chart than the three categories it subsumes (see Figure 1.4).

Once the researcher has identified categories and placed them in a hierarchical arrangement, more data are collected and old data are reviewed again. For the first-grade reading group example, it could be time to observe some more groups, adjusting the categories and their arrangements in light of new observations, interviews, and so on. The researcher continues to collect and analyze data until no new categories emerge from new observations, no new properties of categories are identified, and no additional adjustments are made to the hierarchical arrangement of the categories.

Once enough data are collected, the researcher begins hypothesizing about causal relationships between the categories of information that have emerged as related to one another. For instance, some reflection on the teacher interviews may indicate that teacher modeling is caused by contemporary teacher education practices. That is, the teachers indicated they were running reading groups as they had learned to run them in their methods classes in college. Alternatively, reflection on the interviews may suggest that teacher modeling is due to tradition. That is, the teachers claimed they were running reading groups consistent with what they had experienced as children. Or perhaps the interviews indicate that teacher modeling is due to in-service resources, since the teachers reported that there had been many in-services on teacher modeling. Teacher modeling is not only caused but also in turn causes reactions. Thus, perhaps students begin to model reading processes to one another. The qualitative researcher evaluates all the various causal possibilities, actions, and reactions, against all of the available data as completely as possible. Those that are supported by the data are retained; those that are not are discarded. This continues until the point of **theoretical saturation,** when all the data are explained adequately.

Eventually, the qualitative researcher must report the data in a way that can be easily understood. The researcher must identify a key category or categories around which to tell the story. These must be in sufficient detail to reflect the richness of the data analysis. This emerging story should be member-checked as well, until there is eventually a tale that seems reasonable to researchers and participants. See the Applying Developmental Theory to Educational Contexts special feature (Box 1.1) for an example of qualitative research.

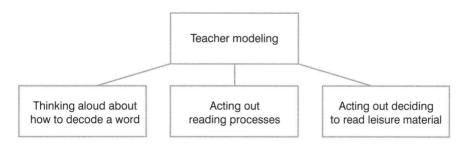

FIGURE 1.4. An organizational chart where the category of teacher modeling subsumes three categories of observations. From McCormick and Pressley (1997). Copyright © 1997 by Christine B. McCormick and Michael Pressley. Adapted by permission.

Applying Developmental Theory to Educational Contexts

BOX 1.1. Difficulties in Communications between Schools and Minority-Group Parents: An Example of a Qualitative Approach

Beth Harry (1992) used a qualitative approach to study potential miscommunications between schools and minority parents, miscommunications that reduce the likelihood of positive relationships between schools and families. Harry focused on the interactions between schools and 12 Spanish-speaking, Puerto Rican American families whose children were enrolled in special education. Such intensive study of a relatively few families is consistent with the qualitative approach to research. She conducted interviews with these families, made observations, and studied the children's school records as part of a large-scale effort to understand how these families interacted with the schools and understood those interactions. Harry alternated between data collection and analyses, changing tactics to take advantage of opportunities that might be revealing. Such flexibility in method is characteristic of qualitative studies. Her findings were quite striking:

1. The U.S. schools seemed impersonal and uncaring to the parents compared to schools they remembered in Puerto Rico. The U.S. schools often made errors in classification of the students in these families, and these errors undermined parental trust. For example, children were "promoted" by mistake and subsequently returned to their previous grade level. Because these parents tended to defer to authority figures, their concerns were not aired. Ironically, the respect of these parents for the professionals they encountered in the school, respect that resulted in the parents not challenging the professionals, increased the lack of trust felt by parents.

2. The written communications from the schools were offputting to these parents, in part because the letters were in English, which required finding someone to interpret them. The letters were also filled with educational jargon embedded in text that was above the readability level of many parents.

3. Parents often felt that they had not received critical information about their children. Sometimes the information had in fact been provided but was not understood. Other times it was provided incompletely. Sometimes the messages were mixed.

4. Many of the parents withdrew from interactions with the school and increasingly felt alienated.

The results of this qualitative study were shocking and led to many changes in how schools communicate with parents since schools recognized that education is more effective when coordinated efforts are made between schools and families. The qualitative research approach can reveal important factors in child development and education.

Evaluating Quality of Qualitative Investigations

Just as it is possible to evaluate the quality of quantitative studies, it is also possible to evaluate qualitative studies and on similar dimensions. The language is different, however (Guba & Lincoln, 1982; Lincoln & Guba, 1985). Thus, rather than worrying about internal validity, qualitative researchers are concerned with **credibility.** The stronger the case that the grounded theory captures the reality of the situation studied, the greater the credibility of the study. Rather than external validity, the qualitative researcher values **transferability,** which is a measure of how representative the setting is. Evaluating transferability means deciding whether the analysis would apply somewhere else, which may require data collection in another setting. **Dependability** is the qualitative researchers' term for replicability. The qualitative researcher must convince others that most people would come to the same conclusions based on the data. **Confirmability** is the term used instead of objectivity. Confirmability is generally high when triangulation occurs in the study—that is, when multiple indicators are used to buttress conclusions.

Specific Approaches to Developmental Research

Without a doubt, the variable most frequently studied by researchers interested in development is age. Since age cannot be manipulated, causal conclusions about effects due to age are not possible. This makes conceptual sense, for age itself cannot cause anything (Wohlwill, 1973). Age can only index potential causal mechanisms, most obviously biological maturation. Thus, walking is not caused by being 9 months of age (or 10 months, or 11 months, or whenever the particular child begins to walk), but, in part, because of motor maturation, which can be indexed by age.

Cross-Sectional Approach

Age differences are sometimes examined at one point in time between different people who differ in age, for example, a study of 5-year-olds, 10-year-olds, and 15-year-olds in which all data was collected in 2018. This is an example of the **cross-sectional approach** to the study of development. One strength of this approach is that data across the entire age range of interest can be collected immediately. This contrasts with the most popular alternative approach to the study of development, the longitudinal approach (Baltes, Reese, & Nesselroade, 1988; Miller, 1987).

Longitudinal Approach

In the **longitudinal approach,** the same people are followed for an extended period of time, for example, from when they are 5 years of age until they are 15. The strength of this approach is that it permits study of *developmental change* rather than only age differences (Wohlwill, 1973). Thus, longitudinal studies provide information about changes within people that cross-sectional studies cannot provide.

Given such an advantage, it might seem that all developmental research should be conducted using longitudinal methods. In fact, there are many more cross-sectional than longitudinal studies. The most important reason is that *it takes much longer to produce information* about relationships between age and behavior using the longitudinal approach. The greater the developmental span of interest to the researcher, the greater the problem. Thus, for researchers interested in cognitive development from middle childhood to old age, a single longitudinal study over this interval would consume more than an entire career!

Besides the longevity of the researcher, the *longevity of the participants* must be considered. In mobile societies, maintaining a sample of participants for any period of time can be a real problem. Even when people do not move, sometimes they choose to discontinue their participation in a study. However, those who are willing to remain in a longitudinal study *may not be representative of the original population sampled.* That is, people willing to undergo repeated testing may be different from people who have a lower tolerance for long-term testing or simply cannot be bothered with continuing in a study. When a large proportion of a sample is lost to a study because they have moved, it is likely that those who did not move were different from those who did. Another concern is that developmental changes in a longitudinal study may be due to *practice effects* with the tests or becoming accustomed to observation by researchers.

Even if there are no practice effects, the measures collected in a longitudinal study may become progressively more problematic as the study continues. For many issues in human development, new (and often better) measures are being developed. Moreover, the hypothesis being studied may be less exciting as a study continues. Hypotheses that seem interesting today may not be so important in the years and decades ahead. Because *a longitudinal study is tied to the measures and hypotheses that were in vogue when the study began*, it is possible that years of effort will produce results viewed as uninteresting or unimportant by the scientific community when the longitudinal study is finally completed.

Longitudinal studies are also *financially expensive* relative to cross-sectional studies. A longitudinal study must be funded for many years before there are definitive outcomes. Typically, research grants are provided for periods of 1–5 years, far shorter than the time needed for longitudinal studies of long-term development. In an environment in which research funds are generally scarce, only the most important longitudinal research questions compete favorably for continuous funding. We stress, however, that some important developmental issues can be addressed only by longitudinal study. Thus, some developmental researchers investigate how certain variables are related to later developmental outcomes in longitudinal studies. See the Applying Developmental Theory to Educational Contexts special feature (Box 1.2) for an example.

Because of the disadvantages of the longitudinal approach described above, many researchers choose to conduct cross-sectional investigations of development. Researchers are aware, however, that the outcomes obtained in a cross-sectional study can be very different from the outcomes obtained in a longitudinal investigation. See the Considering Interesting Questions special feature (Box 1.3) for an example.

Combined Longitudinal and Cross-Sectional Approach

A methodology favored by researchers interested in development across the adult lifespan is to combine cross-sectional and longitudinal methodologies (Schaie & Parham, 1977). For example, if we begin studying samples of 5-year-olds, 10-year-olds, and 15-year-olds today, the result is cross-sectional data (see Figure 1.5). Gather follow-up data on the 5-year-olds and the 10-year-olds in 5 years, who would then be 10- and 15-year-olds, respectively. Add a new group of 5-year-olds at that point. What you will then have in 5 years is longitudinal data on two samples (on the original 5- and 10-year-olds) and a new set of cross-sectional data on 5-, 10-, and 15-year-olds. Then, 5 years later, follow up again, this time seeing the original 5-year-old sample for a third time, revisiting the new 5-year-old sample who would then be age 10, and adding still another sample of 5-year-olds. At that point, you would have 10 years of longitudinal data on the original 5-year-olds, providing longitudinal information on that group for the entire span of development of interest in the study; you would also have 5 years of longitudinal data on the original 10-year-olds (between 10 and 15

BOX 1.2. What Does High School Underachievement Predict?: An Example of a Longitudinal Study

McCall, Evahn, and Kratzer (1992) analyzed data from a study begun in 1965–1966 in the state of Washington. They obtained achievement and ability data on more than 6,000 high school juniors and seniors who spanned the entire range of achievement. The sample included three broad categories of students: (1) overachievers who had better grades relative to their expected ability, (2) ability-consistent achievers whose grades and abilities were consistent, and (3) underachievers whose grades were worse than would be expected on the basis of their ability. Thirteen years later, the researchers located and collected information from many of the original participants—a huge undertaking!

What happened to the underachievers? They continued to underachieve. For example, they made less money as adults than their former classmates who were ability-consistent achievers. Their jobs had less status than the jobs of ability-consistent achievers. They had obtained less postsecondary education than ability-consistent achievers. Underachievers were about 50% more likely than ability-consistent achievers to divorce in the 13 years following high school. Yes, there were exceptions to this general pattern. Underachievers who valued education, came from families that valued education, participated in high school activities, and were confident that they could go on to complete college did seem to catch up after high school, with their incomes, job status, and marital stabilities resembling those of the ability-consistent achievers more than those of the other underachievers. Still, this was a small proportion of underachievers. In general, underachievement in high school predicts future economic and personal difficulties. This type of finding was only possible through longitudinal study. Of course, an immediate question is whether these outcomes might not be cohort-specific. That is, would the same pattern of consistent underachievement be obtained if high school graduates from the early 2000s were evaluated today? We cannot know from the McCall and colleagues (1992) data because they were collected on only one cohort of young adults.

years of age) and from the 5-year-olds added at the second testing (between 5 and 10 years of age). You would have a total of three cross-sectional comparisons between 5-, 10-, and 15-year-olds!

But you have something else: a way to determine whether there are cohort effects. **Cohort effects** refer to children who are born in the same time being influenced by a particular set of historical or cultural conditions. Thus, research results based on one cohort may not apply to others growing up in different times. If there are no cohort effects, then 5-year-old performances should have been about equal at each testing, as should 10-year-old and 15-year-old performances. If there are cohort effects, then there would be differences between the 5-year-old means as a function of time of testing, between the 10-year-old means as a function of time of testing, and between the 15-year-old means as a function of time of testing. To the extent that there are cohort effects, the case strengthens the notion that environmental factors play an important role in determining the behavior being studied. To the extent that cohort effects exist there is an important additional limitation of simple longitudinal studies: outcomes obtained with any particular cohort might not generalize to another cohort. If a single longitudinal sample is studied, the results could reflect development per se or development only at that historical moment. Recall the

Considering Interesting Questions

BOX 1.3. Does Intelligence Decline during Adulthood?: Different Answers as a Function of Methodology

Do you expect to be smarter as you grow older, or do you expect that your intelligence will decline with increasing age during adulthood? Perhaps you believe it will stay the same? For many, the intuitive answer to this question is that intelligence should either stay the same (if intelligence is determined by genetic mechanisms that are insulated from other factors) or perhaps even increase (if experience really is a determinant of intelligence). Data from cross-sectional studies where intelligence tests were administered to groups of adults varying in age across the lifespan, however, indicated that with increasing age after the age of 20, the number of intelligence test items answered correctly declines (Salthouse, 2009; Schaie, 1959).

When intelligence is studied longitudinally, however, the results are very different. In that case, collapsing across all types of items on an intelligence test, intelligence appears not to decline until late in life (Botwinick, 1977; Schaie, 1990, 2013). Yes, a 45-year-old person answers fewer intelligence test items correctly than does a 25-year-old, but there is a cohort effect in that intelligence test items are better matched to the experiences of current young adults than to older adults. That is, differences in educational and cultural experiences found in older and younger adults influence their performance on intelligence tests (Baltes, 1968; Baltes et al., 1988; Kaufman, 1990; Schaie & Labouvie-Vief, 1974). Remember that in cross-sectional studies different people provided the intelligence data at each age level, and thus cross-sectional studies confound age level and the cohort of people providing the data.

In summary, the perspective on the development of intelligence across the lifespan changed entirely once longitudinal data were contrasted with cross-sectional data. The methodology used to study a phenomenon can make a huge difference in the conclusions that are drawn. More nuanced changes in intelligence across the lifespan are discussed in Chapter 8.

Subjects born	Time of testing		
	Now (2018)	5 years from now (2023)	10 years from now (2028)
2003	15-year-olds	Exited study	Exited study
2008	10-year-olds	→ 15-year-olds	Exited study
2013	5-year-olds	→ 10-year-olds	→ 15-year-olds
2018	Not yet in study	5-year-olds	→ 10-year-olds
2023	Not yet born	Not yet in study	5-year-olds

FIGURE 1.5. In this combined cross-sectional longitudinal design, can you find the cross-sectional comparisons? (*Hint:* Look in the columns for three separate cross-sectional comparisons of 5-, 10-, and 15-year-olds.) Can you find the longitudinal comparisons? Can you find the data that allow you to conclude whether a cohort effect is apparent at the 5-year-old level? (*Hint:* Look at each place in the study when 5-year-old data are collected.)

importance of historical moment in determining development, as described earlier in this chapter.

Much more information about development is generated using the combined cross-sectional and longitudinal approach than by either simple cross-sectional or longitudinal methods. Because of the expense and problems associated with the combined approach—basically all the same problems associated with the longitudinal approach plus the additional expense of continuously adding samples with each new wave of data collection—the combined method is rarely used in the study of child development despite its analytical power.

Summary of Research Methods in Development and Education

The two major classifications of quantitative studies are manipulative and nonmanipulative. Random assignment is the key characteristic of a manipulative study. Manipulation of variables, however, is sometimes not possible. The best quantitative studies are simultaneously high on internal and external validity, report outcomes proven to be reliable, and use a variety of objective measures so that triangulation is possible. Sometimes in quantitative studies a relationship between two variables is indicated in a correlation coefficient.

Quantitative research focuses on testing theories using objective techniques. In contrast, qualitative researchers use subjective interpretation to construct a grounded theory that is verified through member checking. The best qualitative studies are credible and produce outcomes that are transferable, dependable, and confirmable. Consult Table 1.1 for a list of questions to consider when reading reports of research.

Longitudinal and cross-sectional approaches to research are specific to the study of development. In the cross-sectional approach, people of different ages are studied at the same point of time. In the longitudinal approach, the same people are studied for an extended period. Although the longitudinal approach allows the researcher to directly study developmental change (and the cross-sectional approach

---

TABLE 1.1. Questions to Ask Yourself as You Read a Description of a Research Study

What research approach was used?
   Quantitative, qualitative, or both?

Depending on your answer to the first question, select questions from the following:
   Is the study manipulative or nonmanipulative?
   Was random assignment used?
   Were any statistical tests significant?
   How large was the effect size?
   Are there any confounding variables?
   Is there evidence of blind testing?
   Are the measures and procedures reliable, valid, and objective?
   Is there evidence of triangulation?
   Can the results be generalized to real-life situations?
   If different age groups are used, is the study longitudinal or cross-sectional?
   Do the data fit the story told?
   Is there evidence of member checking?
   Are the results credible, transferable, dependable, and confirmable?

does not), the longitudinal approach requires a longer investment of time, has a greater likelihood of losing research participants, and is more expensive than the cross-sectional approach. Developmental researchers must always be alert to potential cohort effects, differences due to belonging to a particular *cohort* (a group of people born at the same time) rather than to other factors.

REVIEW OF KEY TERMS

cohort effects Effects due to children born in the same time being influenced by a particular set of historical or cultural conditions.

confirmability In a qualitative study, the point at which multiple indicators all support the same conclusion.

confounding variables Variables unrelated to the experimental treatment that may be influencing its outcome.

convergent validity Consistency of patterns of outcomes across more than one dependent variable.

correlation A relationship between two variables.

correlation coefficient A number, ranging between –1.00 and +1.00, that indicates the size and direction of a relationship between two variables.

credibility The degree to which the grounded theory generated by qualitative research captures the reality of the situation studied.

cross-sectional approach The study of developmental differences carried out by examining age differences among different people at different age levels at one point in time.

dependability In qualitative research, the strength of the argument that most people would come to the same conclusion based on the data.

dependent variables Variables measured to determine the effects of the independent variable.

discriminant validity Pattern of outcome in which variables that should not be affected by the independent variable are not affected.

effect size A measure of the size of a mean difference between experimental and control conditions that allows for comparisons across studies.

exosystem In Bronfenbrenner's ecological systems theory, environmental influences such as media that affect the child but that are removed from the direct experiences of the child.

external validity In a research study, the criterion standard of resembling closely the real-life issue the researcher is trying to investigate.

grounded theory A theory constructed from interpretations of data.

hypothesis A proposed relationship between two or more variables.

independent variables The factors that are manipulated in an experiment.

internal validity In a research study, the criterion of there being no other plausible interpretations of the results.

longitudinal approach The study of developmental differences carried out by following the same people for a period of time.

macrosystem In Bronfenbrenner's ecological systems theory, the cultural influences affecting a child.

manipulative investigations Studies in which researchers control variation by randomly assigning people to one educational treatment or another.

mean An arithmetic average of all scores.

member checking In qualitative research, the practice of taking emerging categories back to those being studied and asking them to evaluate the credibility of the categories.

mesosystem In Bronfenbrenner's ecological systems theory, environmental influences such as school and church that relate microsystems to each other.

meta-analysis A statistical technique to analyze patterns by aggregating data across multiple quantitative studies.

microsystem In Bronfenbrenner's ecological systems theory, the direct experiences of the child in various settings such as home and school.

nonmanipulative investigations Studies in which researchers systematically analyze naturally occurring differences between people or settings.

objectivity The use of measures that are publicly observable and clearly measurable.

operationalization The process of defining variables by specifying how they will be measured or manipulated in a research study.

plasticity Sensitivity to environmental experiences. As used in describing the brain, having fundamental physical properties, such as the size and number of synaptic connections, vary with environmental stimulation.

random assignment A method of ensuring that before an experiment begins, each participant has an equal chance of being assigned to any treatment.

reaction range The range of all possible manifestations of a biological predisposition; the range of possible phenotypes based on a given genotype.

reliability Consistency, as in a test or measure that obtains the same results consistently.

replicability The likelihood of obtaining the same results consistently, as when studies are repeated using the same measures.

standard deviation An index of how much individual scores on a test differ from the mean.

theoretical saturation The point in qualitative research when all data are explained adequately.

transferability In qualitative research, an indication of the representativeness of the setting.

triangulation In research studies, multiple indications of a phenomenon.

CHAPTER 2

Biological Development

B iological factors influence all aspects of psychological life; in fact, some argue that biology and psychology are so blended that it is impossible to separate them (Lickliter & Honeycutt, 2015). The study of how biological factors affect human development has grown dramatically, and with advances in technology and neuroscience, research methodology will undoubtedly continue to expand at a rapid rate. In this chapter, we review some fundamental issues of biological development and their relevance to educators. This information is important for fully comprehending many of the cognitive, socioemotional, and interpersonal issues addressed throughout the book and for understanding how to apply developmental themes to working with child and adolescent students.

Foundations of Neurological Development

Prenatal Neurological Development

The development of the human brain and central nervous system (CNS) begins in the first weeks after gestation and involves a number of intricate steps, each of which forms the foundation for future development and the increasing complexity of the CNS. Any deviations early in neural development can have significant consequences for later pre- and postnatal physiological and psychological development (Martin & Dombrowski, 2008). See the Considering Interesting Questions special feature (Box 2.1) for a discussion of the possible role of prenatal stimulation in promoting children's cognitive development. The human nervous system begins in the developing fetus as a single layer of cells, which thicken to form the *neural plate* (Sadler, 2012; Stiles, Brown, Haist, & Jernigan, 2015). The neural plate differentiates into separate regions shortly after its initial appearance, and as it does so it folds over to form the *neural tube* (Greene & Copp, 2014; Martin & Dombrowski, 2008). The top of the tube

Considering Interesting Questions

BOX 2.1. Does Prenatal Stimulation Augment Children's Cognitive Development?

Over the past few decades, there has been considerable interest in the idea that fetuses can learn prior to being born. This interest has given rise to a large industry of products and advice to prospective parents about how to stimulate fetuses *in utero* to maximize a newborn's cognitive abilities and perhaps optimize the child's musical abilities (the so-called Mozart effect). If all you saw were the claims for fetal stimulation on the World Wide Web, you would assume that prenatal fetal stimulation would certainly lead to advanced brain development in newborns and infants. Alas, the research tells a different story (Swaminathan, 2007). Meta-analytic studies have found no practical differences in the cognitive abilities of babies exposed to music *in utero* compared to those who were not exposed to music.

However, some very ingenious research has determined that human fetuses, particularly those later in a pregnancy and near birth, are receptive to sounds and stimulation and do demonstrate differential responses to preferred sounds and stimuli (Granier-Deferre, Ribeiro, Jacquet, & Bassereau, 2011; Kisilevsky & Hains, 2010; Krueger & Garvan, 2014). As a consequence, infants at birth demonstrate preferences and selective attention for the sounds they like, in particular the maternal voice. In other words, the human near-birth fetus encodes and retains some awareness of the ambient sounds experienced *in utero*. Nonetheless, conscientious researchers have been cautious about overinterpreting these results (DeCasper, Granier-Deferre, Fifer, & Moon, 2011; Lecanuet, Granier-Deferre, & DeCasper, 2005).

In contrast, there is compelling research that maternal stress and emotional state have significant influence on the developing fetus and the subsequent physiological and psychological development of newborns (Baibazarova et al., 2013; Bolten et al., 2013). Prenatal maternal stress has been associated with low birth weight, difficult infant temperament leading to emotional and behavioral difficulties, and poorer cognitive development. Moreover, some of the things that adults do to reduce their anxiety (e.g., cigarette smoking, alcohol ingestion) only make these effects even worse (Mezzacappa, Buckner, & Earls, 2011). In other words, it might be more useful for pregnant mothers, rather than for their not-yet-born child, to listen to Mozart, assuming that would reduce their stress and anxiety.

Although, prenatal stimulation may be a little overhyped, that doesn't mean we should "throw the baby out with the bathwater." The research on fetal awareness suggests that talking with a baby *in utero* may be beneficial. It certainly is useful for establishing a bond and the habit of relating interpersonally to this not-yet-born person; and the more the merrier, fathers and siblings should also be encouraged to talk to and bond with the *in utero* baby. Most importantly, pregnant mothers should be given every opportunity to reduce the stress in their lives.

begins to form into primitive forebrain and midbrain; the hindbrain and beginnings of the spinal cord are formed at the bottom of the tube (Kandel, Schwartz, Jessell, Siegelbaum, & Hudspeth, 2013). Thus, the basic structure of the human nervous system is in place 6–8 weeks after fertilization, corresponding with the end of the embryonic period and the beginning of the fetal period (Huttenlocher, 2002; Stiles et al., 2015). The first behaviors, basic reflexes, appear at this time as well.

Neural progenitor cells (an advanced form of stem cells) begin to create neurons and glial cells around this time. Neurons are nerve cells that are specialized to transmit electrochemical signals in the CNS. Glial cells are the most abundant type of cell in the CNS, and they provide structural and metabolic support for neurons (Lin & Bergles, 2004; Mangin & Gallo, 2011). Neuron development occurs at an extremely rapid rate—thousands of new nerve cells a second (Gotz & Huttner, 2005; Letouraenu, 2008). This proliferation of neuron cell growth is called **neurogenesis.** It is estimated that a mature adult brain has between 80 and 90 billion neurons. If you counted a neuron every second of every minute of every year, it would take about 3,000 years to count all of the neurons in a mature human brain.

These new neural cells migrate to various destinations in the developing brain to genetically predetermined sites using glial cell structures and biochemical signals (Huttenlocher, 2002; Martin & Dombrowski, 2008; Stiles et al., 2015). Most neurons will have been formed and will have migrated to their destinations by birth. During the last trimester of prenatal development, after a neuron has migrated to its appropriate location in the CNS, neurons begin to "differentiate," developing structure and becoming defined as a neuron with a specific function (see Figure 2.1). Neurons grow **dendrites,** which are branch-like extensions of the cell body that transmit impulses toward the cell body from other cells. Ordinarily, each neuron has one **axon**; a stem-like protrusion that conducts impulses *away* from the cell body. Axons contact other neurons at a dendrite, a cell body, or another axon and create a **synaptic connection.** Each neuron can create thousands or tens of thousands of synaptic connections to other neurons resulting in well over 100 trillion synapses in the mature brain.

Neurological Development Following Birth

Compared to other mammals, humans are neurologically immature at birth, and the **cerebral cortex,** in particular, develops substantially after birth (Brown & Jernigan, 2012; Stiles et al., 2015). The cerebral cortex is the outer layer of the brain, and in humans most of it is composed of the neocortex. This "gray matter" (neuron cell bodies have a granular gray appearance) is responsible for consciousness and higher-order cognitive processes such as sensory perception, spatial reasoning, initiation of motor activity, thought, and language, and expands significantly during the preschool years (Brown & Jernigan, 2012). It becomes so large in humans that the brain

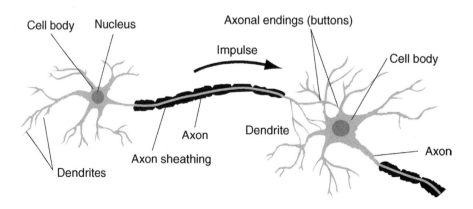

FIGURE 2.1. Axons and dendrites enable nerve cells to establish synaptic connections with other nerve cells.

has to develop folds or grooves called sulci and ridges called gyri to fit inside the human skull.

Neurons take some time to mature, and many are constantly changing as a consequence of a person's interaction with his or her environment. Dendrites start out short, tubular, and unbranched, but lengthen and develop many branches referred to as "arborization," enabling better reception of electrochemical signals from other neurons. Axons also elongate and extend to target cells in other parts of the CNS, equipping neurons with the ability to transmit electrochemical signals to one another. This creation of synapses is called **synaptogenesis,** and it is prolific in early childhood. Some neurons transmit a signal to other neurons that excites or stimulates the subsequent neuron to fire. Other neurons are inhibitory and transmit a signal telling the neurons it connects with to relax and not discharge electrochemically.

The human body is genetically programmed to generate far more neurons than is needed and some of them die off, both pre- and postnatally, through a process of programmed neuronal death called **apoptosis** (Brown & Jernigan, 2012; Martin & Dombrowski, 2008; Naruse & Keino, 1995; Stiles et al., 2015). A significant proportion of the neurons generated before birth have already died by the time of birth, and in some parts of the brain a large portion of the remaining neurons die within a few years after birth (Nikolić, Gardner, & Tucker, 2013). Far from being a problem, this normal loss of neurons is needed for healthy brain development by removing neurons that are not critical to later functioning (Martin & Dombrowski, 2008).

The human brain also overproduces synaptic connections, and just as excess neurons are eliminated, unnecessary synaptic connections are also culled out by a process called **synaptic pruning.** Synapses that are rarely activated are removed, with a great deal of synaptic pruning occurring during the childhood and adolescent years (Huttenlocher, 2002; Spear, 2007, 2010). For example, one explanation for the loss of very early childhood memories is synaptic pruning. Memories that are created before age 3 are rarely recalled, so that the synaptic connections eventually die off. Some believe that second-language acquisition may be more difficult after childhood, reflecting synaptic pruning of connections that mediate learning second languages (Huttenlocher, 2002; see also Chapters 1 and 7). Synaptic pruning during the adolescent years may be more selective. Some evidence indicates that primarily excitatory neural connections are lost, hence altering the ratio of inhibitory to excitatory synaptic connections (Spear, 2007, 2010). It may seem counterintuitive, but the elimination of excess synapses is necessary for the brain and neural networks to function efficiently, and problems with synaptic pruning may be responsible for subsequent learning and mental health problems later in childhood and adolescence (Giedd, Keshavan, & Paus, 2008; Luciana, 2013; Noggle & Dean, 2013; Spear, 2007, 2010).

Maturation of the Nervous System

As children and adolescents age, the CNS matures in some additional significant ways. One of these important developments is the myelination of the nervous system. **Myelination** is the development of a fatty sheath that envelopes an axon (Fields, 2010). This "white matter" (the myelin sheath has a white appearance compared to the gray color of a neuron) covering insulates nerve axons from interference from the electrical conduction in neighboring neurons, which enables faster and more efficient electrical conduction within and between neurons (Bercury & Macklin,

2015). The myelin sheath may also form connections with neurons that contribute to neural signaling (Bercury & Macklin, 2015; Hughes & Appel, 2016; Lin & Bergles, 2004; Mangin & Gallo, 2011; Spear, 2007). In humans, myelination begins before birth and continues robustly through a person's childhood and adolescence (Brown & Jernigan, 2012; Deoni et al., 2016; Paus, 2010), and to a lesser extent into a person's 20s and throughout adulthood (Bercury & Macklin, 2015). In general, CNS myelination occurs first in the inner areas of the cortex and later in the outer areas of the cortex. For example, some outer layers of the cortex involved in learning associations will not myelinate until 4–8 years of age. The myelination of specific brain regions is correlated with cognitive abilities and learning (Deoni et al., 2016; Fields, 2008, 2010; Hughes & Appel, 2016). The importance of myelin becomes especially obvious when it is lost, such as when a person contracts multiple sclerosis (MS). As those with MS experience the degradation of the myelin sheath, they feel numbness, and as the disease progresses they may begin to lose motor control and coordination and ultimately experience cognitive deficits.

Another major brain development that occurs over the course of childhood and adolescence is the evolution of the brain's frontal lobes. This is the part of the brain behind a person's forehead and extending back to just before his or her ears (see Figure 2.2). It's the part of the brain that is most associated with conscious thought, executive skills, cognition, and voluntary movement. Dendritic and synaptic growth and myelin sheathing increase considerably in the frontal lobes during childhood (Huttenlocher, 2002; Klingberg, 2008). As a result, babies begin to develop the motor coordination for crawling and walking, understanding words and concepts, using language, and socializing.

During infancy, frontal lobe development is associated with improved working memory and inhibitory control (Bell, Wolfe, & Adkins, 2007; Fusaro & Nelson, 2009). For example, the human infant's ability to find an object hidden at one of

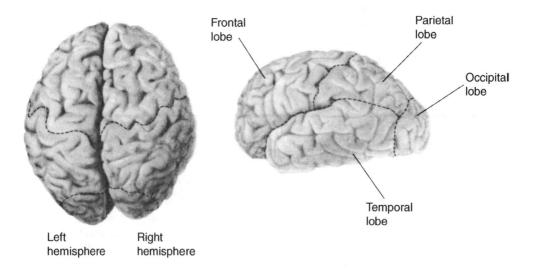

FIGURE 2.2. The human cerebral cortex is divided into left and right hemispheres, which in turn are divided into frontal, parietal, occipital, and temporal lobes. From McCormick and Pressley (1997). Copyright © 1997 Christine B. McCormick and Michael Pressley. Adapted by permission.

two locations (A or B) is a typical test of this ability. In this test, an object is hidden in full view of the infant followed by a delay between the hiding and when the child can retrieve the object. The object is consistently hidden in one place (either A or B) until the child is correct, and then the object is hidden in the other place. Infants under 6 months of age make a classic error called the "A, not B, error." This means they reach to the place where the object was hidden and retrieved the last time rather than where they saw it hidden this time. This error is more likely to occur the longer the delay between second hiding and when the child can retrieve the object. As children grow older, it takes a longer delay to produce the "A, not B, error" (Diamond, 1985). For example, the "A, not B, error" can be induced with delays of 2–5 seconds in 7½- to 9-month-old infants. By 12 months of age, the "A, not B, error" does not occur even with delays of 10 seconds.

Working memory and inhibitory skills are aspects of executive functioning thought to be highly associated with maturation of the frontal lobes (Fusaro & Nelson, 2009). The maturation of the frontal lobes continues into adolescence, when the frontal lobes of the brain become more integrated with the emotion and reward centers of the brain (Casey, Getz, & Galvin, 2008; Johnson, Blum, & Giedd, 2009; Luciana, 2013; Spear, 2013). The maturation of the frontal lobes and the development of executive function skills are particularly important to educators because academic achievement and competence in children and adolescents is highly correlated with their development (Bell, Wolfe, & Adkins, 2007; Fusaro & Nelson, 2009; Spear, 2007, 2010).

The Role of Experience in Postnatal Neurological Development

The mammalian brain is genetically programmed to expect certain forms of experience (Bourgeois, 2001; Markham & Greenough, 2004; Marshall & Kenney, 2009); in fact, normal brain development requires input from the sensorimotor systems. This **experience-expectant** development of neurons proliferates for several months following birth (Marshall, 2015; Marshall & Kenney, 2009; Stiles et al., 2015), particularly in areas of the brain that correspond to perceptual systems, such as the vision system, hearing, or smell, but also in language processing, face recognition, and attachment (Fusaro & Nelson, 2009; Petrosini, Cutuli, & de Bartolo, 2013; Stiles et al., 2015). For example, when light stimulation is encountered, neurons in the visual system are activated and establish synaptic connections with other neurons.

When environmental stimulation is absent or deficient during **critical or sensitive periods,** these experience-expectant neurons fail to develop synaptic connections and eventually are removed through the process of apoptosis. As a result, alternate forms of brain organization develop and may lead to permanent deficits in cognitive abilities (Marshall & Kenney, 2009; Stiles et al., 2015). For the sensory systems, these critical periods occur early in life (Bourgeois, 2001; Greenough, Black, & Wallace, 1987; Horton, 2001; Lichtman, 2001; Tychsen, 2001). For example, if particular visual experiences fail to occur early in development, visual perception is impaired for life, regardless of subsequent remediation efforts. Thus, kittens that were placed in atypical environments and deprived of light for the first 8 weeks of their lives were blind once they were exposed to light (Hubel & Wiesel, 2005). For humans, the critical period for some visual capabilities is considerably longer than 8 weeks. For example, if *strabismus* (a disorder involving poor muscular control of the eyes) is treated before age 5, it produces no long-term impairment (Aslin, 1981). If left untreated, however, strabismus negatively affects the visual system (Anastasiow, 1990). This happens because the sensory organs affected by the strabismus provide inaccurate information that results in the faulty stabilization of the experience-expectant synapses.

A second type of neuronal development is called **experience-dependent.** Experience-dependent neuron development is *not* genetically predetermined to be sensitive to particular types of information (Bourgeois, 2001) and can occur at any time during life (Anastasiow, 1990; Markham & Greenough, 2004; Marshall, 2015; Marshall & Kenney, 2009; Stiles et al., 2015). For example, the types of learning most educators are concerned with involve the creation of experience-dependent synaptic growth. Much like neurons, the development of the myelin sheath also appears to be experience-dependent (Fields, 2008; Makinodan, Rosen, Ito, & Corfus, 2012). Synaptic connections are strengthened by the repeated firing of one neuron and exciting another (Hebb, 1949). As synaptic connections multiply and neurons become more interconnected, they create biological **neural networks** or circuits that are believed to be the foundation of cognitive processes (Arslan et al., 2017; Peterson & Sporns, 2015). As a result, the human brain develops complex neurological patterns of responding to environmental stimuli. Researchers are working to understand and map the neural connections and their resultant neural networks in the human brain in an effort to better understand all of human consciousness and how these neural networks contribute to cognition as well as mental illness and other behavioral and learning disorders (Pessoa, 2014; Power, Fair, Schlaggar, & Petersen, 2010).

The Extent of Neurological Plasticity

Decades ago, scientists believed that brain development was more or less complete by the preschool years; these days we know the reality of brain development is far more complex. Research with laboratory animals and brain-imaging studies shows that the brain is **plastic** or malleable, meaning that the fundamental physical properties of the brain, including its size and the number of its neurons, glial cells, and synaptic connections vary. Neurogenesis, synaptogenesis, apotosis, myelination, and synaptic pruning are all ways in which the brains of children and adolescents are morphing and malleable (Anderson, Spencer-Smith, & Wood, 2011; Johnston, 2009). This plasticity is most evident in early childhood, plateaus in middle childhood as the brain becomes more organized and routinely patterned, and then reemerges during adolescence as the frontal lobes of the brain remodel (Blakemore & Choudhary, 2006; Casey et al., 2008; Fuhrmann, Knoll, & Blakemore, 2015; Johnson et al., 2009; Spear, 2013; Steinberg, 2010; Stiles et al., 2015).

Environmental enrichment does augment brain development. Studies of rodents show that rats that received environmental enrichment in the form of objects to explore, climb, and sniff have an increased brain size and increased number of branches in the dendrites, and thus a greater number of synaptic connections (Johnston, 2009; Markham & Greenough, 2004). Brain-imaging studies of humans have found similar effects (Jolles & Crone, 2012). For example, experienced taxi drivers in London were found to have greater development of a part of their brain responsible for spatial memory and navigation compared to novice drivers or the public (Maguire et al., 2003). Similarly, somatosensory cortex of the brain that is associated with fingers appears to be more developed in Braille readers and stringed instrument musicians (Elbert, Pantev, Wienbruch, Rockstroh, & Taub, 1995; Johnston, 2009; Shonkoff & Phillips, 2000). Furthermore, when a child suffers damage to part of his or her brain, other synaptic connections may take the place of the connections eliminated (or not made) because of the injury (Huttenlocher, 2002; Kolb, Comeau, & Gibb, 2008; Marshall, 2015; Stiles et al., 2015). For example, the auditory cortex is sometimes used for visual processing in children with early deafness, and vice versa for children born blind (Johnston, 2009).

Despite the marvels and adaptability of neurological development in children and adolescents, brain plasticity has its limits (Anderson et al., 2011; Johnston, 2009; Thomas, 2003). Some aspects of neurological (and physical) development seem to occur in nearly all human beings. Waddington (1961) argued that such developments were almost completely genetically determined, or **canalized.** Imagine a ball rolling downhill in a deep trough or canal. A great deal of pressure would be required to move the ball even a little bit up the wall of the canal. Once the pressure ended, the ball would fall back down into the depths of the canal and continue its downward course. Waddington argued that for many developments early in life, genes created something of a canal, with deviation from the canalized path very difficult to produce.

Some aspects of human development seem to be strongly canalized, especially acquisitions early in life. In the case of visual stimulation, infants display a bias for contours or outlines of shapes, which is adaptive since the contour defines the shape (Kellman & Arterberry, 2006). One result of these clear biases in visual perception is that from an early age humans process some types of information more than other types. For example, infants demonstrate a preference for gazing at faces (Frank, Amso, & Johnson, 2014; Kwon, Setoodehnia, Baek, Luck, & Oakes, 2016; McKone, Crookes, Jefifery, & Dilks, 2012; Turati, Valenza, Leo, & Simion, 2005). Biological preparedness is not limited to basic perceptual processing. Humans are also biologically prepared to learn the complex systems of representation that comprise language (Chomsky, 1965, 1980a, 1980b; Tomasello, 2003). The most enduring biological claim about language is Chomsky's contention that all human beings have the competence to acquire language owing to a genetically determined "language acquisition device" in the human mind. The evolution of the neural capacity to perceive and create speech also supports language and the learning of language (Lieberman, 1984, 1989). (Much more about the biological bases of language and language development is presented in Chapter 7.)

A variation on the idea of canalization is the concept of "experiential canalization" in which biology and experience combine to shape development (Blair & Raver, 2012). A child's developing nervous system is more sensitive and reactive to deprivation, neglect, and abuse (Johnston, 2009), and the brain's efforts to adapt do not always lead to positive outcomes (Anderson et al., 2011; Johnston, 2009). Recently, a third model of neuron development, **experience-adaptive,** has gained attention (Marshall, 2015; Marshall & Kenney, 2009). This model of neural development combines elements of the experience-expectant and experience-dependent models and suggests that experiences that a child has at a particular time in his or her development may have effects on brain development and behavior that are more or less permanent. So, for example, a child (or fetus) who experiences malnutrition, neglect, exposure to highly stressful events, or other types of early adversity may develop hormonal and neurological systems that attempt to compensate for this exposure to adversity which in the long run are unhealthy or psychologically and socially maladaptive (Doom & Gunnar, 2013; Esposito & Gunnar, 2014; Gunnar, Doom, & Esposito, 2015; Gunnar & Herrera, 2013; Hostinar & Gunnar, 2013).

The degree to which a child may recover from early deprivation depends on a wide variety of factors, including the timing and duration of the deprivation and/or abuse and the intensity of the efforts to remediate early adversity (Cowell, Cicchetti, Rogosch, & Toth, 2015). This issue is especially relevant to educators because the effects of early adversity may particularly affect attention, memory, learning, and self-regulation. Research to date suggests that much of cognitive development can be caught up if early adversity is arrested, however, children who experience significant early adversity often have significant delays in physical and psychological development and may never recover fully (Anderson et al., 2011; Thomas, 2003)

Patterns of Physical and Motor Development

Development and learning occur through children's and adolescents' exploration of their physical environment, and their abilities to engage their environment are dependent on their physical and motor skills (Adolph & Berger, 2005; Adolph & Robinson, 2015). The development of motor skills initiates a **developmental cascade**; like a chain of dominoes, one event causes subsequent events. For example, the development of visual skills and balance leads to the acquisition of postural skills, which enables reaching and object manipulation, which fosters the growth of perceptual motor skills, attention, and social engagement, which in turn are the foundation of academic learning later in childhood (Adolph & Berger, 2005; Adolph & Robinson, 2015; Brooks & Meltzoff, 2015; Bornstein, Hahn & Suwalski, 2013; Karsik, Tamis-LaMonda, & Adolph, 2014; Rose, Feldman, & Jankowski, 2011; Rose, Feldman, Jankowski, & van Rossem, 2008). And just as was the case with neurological development, delays or inadequacies in physical and motor development can have later effects on cognitive and academic development (Flensborg-Madsen & Mortenson, 2015; Wassenberg et al., 2005). Moreover, there are important cultural differences in parenting practices and in how much and what kinds of movements and activity are allowed or encouraged that have significant effects on the timing and acquisition of motor skills (Adolph & Berger, 2005; Adolph & Robinson, 2015).[*] Hence, an understanding of physical and motor development is crucial for educators.

Physical and Motor Development in Infancy and Childhood

During infancy and throughout childhood, development tends to occur from top to bottom, with the head developing ahead of the trunk. In other words, development is **cephalocaudal,** moving from head to tail. Moreover, until the end of childhood, development tends to be from the center of the body outward. That is, development is **proximodistal,** trunk development coming before the development of arms and legs, which come, in turn, before the hands and feet. However, increases in height and weight are not linear from infancy to adulthood. In general, on the one hand, the rate of change in height and weight tends to be greater in the first 2 years than

---

[*]The developmental milestones described here are applicable primarily to the majority-culture Caucasian Americans.

during the preschool and elementary-grade years. On the other hand, during the adolescent growth spurt, the more distal arms and legs seem to grow at an astonishing rate (Sheehy, Gasser, Molinari, & Largo, 1999), sometimes contributing to some clumsiness and discoordination in early adolescents.

Even more interesting than the physical changes themselves are the changes in what children can do: their *motor development*. Just as general physical development is rapid during infancy, so is motor development (Adolph & Berger, 2005; Adolph & Robinson, 2015; Alexander, Boehme, & Cupps, 1993; Bayley, 1969). For example, one achievement of the first 6 weeks of infancy is the ability to hold the head steady upright. In the first 6 months, babies learn to elevate themselves with their arms while lying on their tummies. They also learn to turn over and to grasp objects. In the second 6 months, infants learn to sit, to crawl, and to stand. By the age of 1½, children can stand and then walk. By age 2, toddlers can scribble, begin to walk upstairs, and jump.

Motor functioning improves strikingly from ages 2 to 6 (Adolph & Berger, 2005; Adolph & Robinson, 2015). Think about the running of a 2-year-old compared to a 6-year-old. Young children run with their feet widely spaced and their running looks more like fast walking (Cratty, 1986). The running of older children is more like adult running, with the feet closer together and the running motion much smoother. Children's jumping also changes greatly in this age span. The 2½-year-old can jump a few inches in the air but cannot coordinate his or her running with jumping, as in a broad jump. In contrast, by age 6, children can jump higher as well as run to a spot and jump forward as in a broad jump. Skills in throwing and catching also develop in this age span. By 6 years of age, children begin to use their whole bodies to throw, step forward as they throw, and begin to make subtle adjustments in the placement of their arms required to catch a moving ball (Roberton, 1984). Although 2-year-olds can scribble, by 6 years of age they can exert greater control, allowing them to print and draw pictures (Morrow, 1989). Improvements in fine motor skills during the course of the preschool years allow children to become more autonomous (Adolph & Berger, 2005; Adolph & Robinson, 2015; Brooks & Meltzoff, 2015; Bornstein et al., 2013; Karsaik et al., 2014). By 6 years of age, children can use both a knife and a fork, dress themselves, and tie their shoes.

Despite this considerable progress, the motor skills of 6-year-olds are no match for those of 11-year-olds. Running, jumping, throwing, catching, and the fine motor skills required for tasks such as writing, drawing, and tool use continue to improve during the elementary school years. Flexibility, speed, accuracy, and strength increase (Adolph & Berger, 2005; Adolph & Robinson, 2015; Thomas, 1984), and with increasing development, coordination of skills increases. For example, skilled catching requires the coordination of running, catching, and jumping. By sixth grade, children can write in long hand and more quickly than when they were younger. Their drawings are much more complex, and they find it much easier to coordinate the skills required to play a musical instrument.

Although there are individual differences in motor competencies from infancy—with some children walking and talking much earlier than others—with increasing age, individual differences become more pronounced. It is easy to spot on the school playground the sixth graders who have better balance and are more flexible, stronger, faster, and more accurate in their throwing. The more athletic sixth graders are often better at a given sport than those who are much older (Ahnert, Schneider, & Bös, 2009).

Puberty and the Adolescent Growth Spurt

One of the most noticeable differences in the rate of change occurs in early adolescence during the **adolescent growth spurt.** This growth spurt tends to occur earlier for girls (between about 11 and 14 years of age) than for boys (between 13 and 16 years of age) (Marceau, Ram, Houts, Grimm, & Susman, 2011; Rogol, Roemmich, & Clark, 2002). Physical growth and development is generally completed by the end of the high school years, with most individuals having reached close to their adult height by the time of high school graduation. In adolescence, motor development continues, but the differences in the motor skills of boys and girls become more apparent (Ahnert et al., 2009; Thomas & French, 1985). By the end of high school, boys are faster, can jump higher and longer, are stronger, and can throw farther. This is one reason why high school physical education classes are more likely to be segregated by gender than elementary school classes. It is important to note that the distribution of athletic abilities for males and females overlaps, so that some females are much more athletic than many males and some males are much less athletic than many females.

Several major physiological changes that occur during adolescence have a distinct impact on the psychology of adolescents. As children enter puberty, increased endocrine activity takes place, particularly in the **hypothalamic–pituitary–adrenal (HPA) axis** and the **hypothalamic–pituitary–gonadal (HPG) axis.** The hypothalamus regulates the pituitary, which controls hormone levels in the body. The awakening of the HPA and HPG axes results in physical growth and body composition changes (e.g., height and weight changes, fat and muscle distribution), increases in strength and physical endurance due to growth in cardiovascular and pulmonary systems, and development of primary and secondary sexual characteristics.

How adolescents respond to the onset of puberty depends to some extent on the sequence, timing, and tempo of pubertal changes. The sequence of puberty is typically divided into three stages and is pretty much the same for all teens. **Prepubescence** starts when these physiological changes are just beginning. Many of the initial changes are subtle and would only be detectable if a person was closely monitoring blood endocrine levels. For girls, the ovaries begin to enlarge and the ova begin to mature, and breast buds begin to appear. For boys during prepubescence, the testes and penis begin to grow. **Pubescence** occurs as the production of sexual hormones increases, resulting in the appearance of pubic hair and the physical growth spurt, the onset of **menarche** for girls and voice changes and facial hair growth in boys. As the pubescent growth spurt tapers off, the adolescent begins **postpubescence.** Although physical changes are slowing, secondary sexual characteristics like facial hair in men and breast development in women continue to mature.

The timing of puberty and its tempo vary considerably across adolescents. Girls mature physically earlier than boys; on average, girls begin puberty around age 10, generally reaching peak growth around age 12. Boys tend to begin growth spurts at about age 12 and have slower but continued growth for longer. The pubertal process occurs over a fairly long duration; for girls, the full manifestations of pubertal changes occur over a period of 3–5 or 6 years; for boys the process lasts a little longer. There is considerable variability in when the adolescent growth spurt occurs (Sheehy et al., 1999). For girls, ordinarily onset of puberty is between 8 (on the early side) and 14 or 15. For boys, puberty can begin anytime between 10 and 16. In developed countries, puberty does appear to be starting earlier than in previous decades. Research on medical records documenting first menses reveal that in 1860–1880 first menses occurred on average around age 14–16 compared to the current 10–12. The age of onset of puberty seems to be dropping for males as well (Steinberg, 2014). One indication is the change of voice that occurs for males. Records of choirs kept for centuries in Europe suggest that voice changes are occurring earlier: from about 18 in the 1700s to about 13 in the 1960s to about 10½ today. Pediatrician records seem to validate this finding, with 2010 data suggesting that boys are entering puberty about 2 years earlier than they did in the 1970s. A variety of theories have been proposed to explain why this is happening. The most likely explanation has to do with improvements in nutrition. There is some evidence to suggest that increased stress, especially family stress, may promote early puberty. Others have suggested that extensive light exposure may be altering hormone expression as well. The most disconcerting reason might be the exposure to endocrine disruptor chemicals that are in furniture, plastics, and food.

Pubertal timing can have an effect on psychological adjustment. Researchers have proposed two hypotheses to explain the influence of timing of maturation upon psychological and social development. The first, the *maturational deviance hypothesis*, argues that adolescents who experience the onset of puberty off-time, either earlier or later than their peers, display more adjustment difficulties than their on-time peers. The second hypothesis, the *early maturational hypothesis*, suggests that developing earlier is especially a problem for girls. In support of the maturational deviance hypothesis, female adolescents who experience puberty off-time (either early or late) generally report more adjustment problems (Marceau et al., 2011), although the effects of later puberty onset are usually not as enduring. In support of the early maturational hypothesis, however, early maturation in girls is often associated with poorer body image dieting, stress and depression related to being unprepared for the social pressures and experiences associated with sexual maturity, and problem behavior such as precocious drug use and sexual encounters (Alsaker, 1992; Flannery, Row, & Gulley, 1993; Ge, Conger, & Elder, 1996, 2001; Ge et al., 2003; Stice, Presnell, & Bearman, 2001). As a result, early-maturing girls are at risk for becoming pregnant and bearing children during their adolescence, which often results in less educational and occupational attainment. Early maturation is generally a positive attribute for boys because it is associated with being perceived as popular, attractive, and poised (Simmons, Blyth, & McKinney, 1983). However, early-maturing boys are also more likely to hang out with older teens and engage in more antisocial behavior. To a large extent, the degree to which pubertal changes will affect an adolescent depends on his or her social environment. Social context can amplify or attenuate the effects of pubertal timing. When the adolescents' social environment (e.g., family friends, school) is positive, stable, and supportive, adolescents experience less psychological upheaval as a consequence of puberty.

Recent research has investigated how sleep and wake cycles change during adolescence. Adolescents develop a change in circadian rhythms called **sleep phase delay** that causes them to want to go to sleep later and wake up later. Most children require 9 hours of sleep, and as children mature into adolescence this number increases. Unfortunately, as this biological need occurs, adolescents are getting less sleep because of social demands and personal choices. So, adolescents sleep less just as their bodies need more sleep; consequently, many adolescents are chronically sleep deprived.

Biological Determination of Individual Differences: The Example of Intelligence

So far we have been focusing on neurological and physiological developments that are universal or common to almost all people. However, there are many individual differences between students that affect their response to instruction, including their intelligence, their personality, and their cognitive style (Jonassen & Grabowski, 2011). Some researchers contend that individual differences of all types are genetically determined (Plomin, Defries, McClearn, & McGuffin, 2000; Plomin, Defries, Knopik, & Neiderhiser, 2013). For example, evidence indicates genetic involvement in the determination of temperament and personality differences (Bouchard & Loehlin, 2001; Kagan, 2010; Markon, Krueger, Bouchard, & Gottesman, 2002), as well as intellectual differences, such as individual differences in learning to read, spell, and understand math (Asbury & Plomin, 2014; Christopher et al., 2013; Gayan & Olson, 2003; Kovas & Plomin, 2007; Plomin & Deary, 2015; Plomin, Kovas, & Haworth, 2007; Plomin & Spinath, 2004).

Intelligence, as an individual difference, has particular import for educators. As early as 1869, Francis Galton argued that blood relationships between geniuses were much closer than would be expected by chance. Galton concluded from these probabilities that genius was inherited. Galton's strong claims about the heritability of genius stimulated interest in individual differences in intellectual abilities. Traditionally, those who studied individual differences in intellectual functioning focused on the conceptualization and measurement of intelligence summarized as an IQ score. (Detailed discussion of IQ scores and their calculation can be found in Chapter 8.) The early years of the 20th century witnessed the proliferation of measures of intelligence (Binet & Simon, 1905a, 1905b, 1905c; Terman & Childs, 1912; Yoakum & Yerkes, 1920). Intelligence tests were developed in the first place because Alfred Binet was trying to find a way to discriminate between normal children and children with intellectual disabilities. Later, Terman believed the tests could also be useful in identifying "feeble-minded" adults. Later still, Yoakum and Yerkes designed tests to select men for officers' training from the pool of military recruits. In general, these early tests made discriminations in ability. The developers of these early intelligence tests believed that the tests were tapping biologically determined differences in functioning.

The study of genetic influence on intelligence has evolved dramatically in recent decades. Initially, behavior geneticists—scientists who study genetic influences on behavior—argued that individual differences in intelligence were due more to heredity than to environment based on the results of twin and adoption studies. Identical twins have the same genes because both children were produced by a division of the same fertilized egg. When identical twins are reared together in the same family, they share similar environments, so the high correlations (review the description of correlation coefficients in Chapter 1) in intelligence between identical twins (usually .80–.90 or higher) are due to both genetic and environmental determinants of intelligence. Sometimes, however, identical twins are reared apart; their genes are identical, but their environments differ. Although the average IQ correlation (around .70) for identical twins reared apart is a little less than that for identical twins raised together, it is still a strong correlation. Another important comparison involves fraternal twins reared together. Since fraternal twins are the product of two different fertilized eggs, they share one-half of their genes and, theoretically, they share a similar environment since they are reared in the same family at the same time. The correlation of IQ scores for fraternal twins (around .60) is less than that reported for identical twins. Researchers used data such as these to calculate the **heritability** of intelligence, or the variation in intelligence that is due to genetic differences, and concluded that roughly half the variability in intelligence is due to genes (Krapohl et al., 2014; Nisbett et al., 2012; Plomin & Deary, 2015; Plomin et al., 2007).

But more recent studies have emphasized that complex traits such as intelligence are the consequence of gene by environment interactions (Asbury & Plomin, 2014; Johnson, Deary, & Iacono, 2009; Mandelman & Grigorenko, 2011; Meaney, 2010; Nisbett et al., 2012) and that hereditability estimates may have limited utility (Moore, 2013; Richardson, 2013). Contemporary genetic studies of intelligence emphasize that the genes we possess, our **genotype,** are inextricably interwoven with our environmental experiences to establish our observable characteristics, our **phenotype.** A relatively new school of genetic studies highlights what is called **epigenetics.** Epigenetic researchers have demonstrated that a person's environment has the ability to alter whether and how that person's genes are expressed and that the expression of a person's genes can, in turn, alter his or her environment (Marshall, 2015; Marshall & Kenney, 2009; McGowan & Roth, 2015; Meaney, 2010; Moore, 2013). These researchers question the use of twin studies that generate heredity correlations for a variety of reasons. To begin with, they assert that the effects of genes cannot be separated from the effects of a person's environment. They also point to significant methodological and statistical limits to twin studies; in particular, they observe that even identical twins reared together have very different environmental experiences and unique subjective assessments of shared experiences. Moreover, contemporary genetics researchers believe that complex human traits and behaviors are not associated with any particular gene, but instead are determined by numerous genes and the result of complex biochemical cellular processes involving DNA (Marshall, 2015; Meaney, 2010; Moore, 2013; Nisbett et al., 2012). Intelligence and cognitive abilities, in particular, appear to be polygenic, with each gene making a small and general contribution to a person's intelligence, which environmental factors then mold into the multifaceted human condition called intelligence (Asbury & Plomin, 2014; Kovas & Plomin, 2007; Krapohl et al., 2014; Nisbett et al., 2012; Plomin et al., 2007).

To summarize, humans inherit a genotype that offers a range of possible biological outcomes. How that genotype is expressed phenotypically depends on the environment and individual experiences. This raises a significant question for educators and education policymakers. To what extent can educational interventions affect intelligence and academic achievement, and how can educators maximize a student's learning potential?

The Effects of High-Quality Environments on Intelligence

The evidence that high-quality environmental manipulations at home and preschool increase measured intelligence, at least in the short term, is compelling (Barnett, 2011). Achieving improvements in IQ and other individual differences seems to work best when environments are nurturing. The greatest gains occur with children who have a predisposition for low IQ either because of their genetic endowment or because of an impoverished social environment (Burger, 2010; Magnuson, Ruhm, & Waldfogel, 2007; Mandelman & Grigorenko, 2011; Tucker-Drob & Bates, 2016). The most effective interventions include teaching parents how to read with and stimulate their children and introducing academically oriented day care to children from economically disadvantaged homes.

There have been a number of small (e.g., Perry Preschool Program, Abecedarian Project) and large-scale (e.g., HeadStart) early education intervention research projects in the United States and internationally (Barnett, 2011; Burger, 2010; Heckman, 2006; Magnuson et al., 2007; Nelson et al., 2007). Generally, these studies have shown that gains in IQ scores are most likely to be observed at the immediate conclusion of an intervention and typically fade several years after the special intervention has ceased, so that the IQ scores of children participating in the intervention are no different than the IQ scores of children who did not participate. This finding has led some to question whether early education intervention programs are beneficial, especially given the intensity of services required and the financial cost of these programs (Asbury & Plomin, 2014; Heckman, 2006; Jensen, 1969, 1992; Locurto, 1988, 1991a, 1991b, 1991c; Spitz, 1986, 1991, 1992). Others believe it is unreasonable to expect children to maintain their intelligence advantages if, as often happens, they return to an environment that lacks additional intellectual stimulation. Educational interventions promoting long-lasting academic competence need to be long-term affairs (Storfer, 1990).

If the intervention advantages provided during the preschool years are continued into the schooling years, intelligence gains are more likely to be maintained and school achievement increased (Magnuson et al., 2007). Some of the strongest evidence in favor of continuing interventions initiated in the preschool years was provided by the Carolina Abecedarian Project (Campbell et al., 2012; Ramey, Ramey, & Lanzi, 2001). This project was aimed at increasing the intellectual competence of children who were at risk for intellectual deficiency because they came from economically impoverished environments. Children in the Abecedarian Project began their participation shortly after birth. Both those in the intervention program and those in the control group were provided nutritional support, family counseling contacts, and medical care. The children in the intervention, however, also attended a high-quality preschool for the entire day throughout the year. Parent meetings were held as part of this preschool program to increase parental awareness of how to stimulate child development and use community opportunities. Was this program successful? In general, the more total Abecedarian treatment received, the lower the failure rate and the higher the IQ at age 12. Moreover, those who had participated in the Abecedarian Project exhibited higher scores on both cognitive and academic measures through the age of 30 (Campbell, Pungello, Miller-Johnson, Burchinal, & Ramey, 2001; Campbell et al., 2012).

It's important to consider too, that intensive, long-term, academically oriented early education intervention programs engender a number of noncognitive skills such as motivation, perseverance, and tenacity in at-risk children (Barnett, 2011; Heckamn, 2006). Providing early learning opportunities for at-risk children instills an appreciation of learning and a desire to learn more, as well as experience with the cognitive, social, and emotional skills necessary for learning at later ages. Consequently, at-risk children who are exposed to early learning opportunities tend to demonstrate better classroom behavior once they enter elementary school, have less youth misconduct and delinquency, require fewer special education services, and graduate from high school more often than peers who did not receive early education intervention. Furthermore, at-risk children who received early education services have been found to have better outcomes when they become adults, including higher income, less need for social welfare services, fewer arrests, and better health behaviors (Barnett, 2011; Burger, 2010; Campbell et al., 2012; Heckman, 2006).

Does that mean biology is not a determinant of intelligence? Not at all. What it means is that children are more likely to approach the top of their reaction ranges for intelligence and academic achievement if they experience a high-quality environment. Humans have evolved to be sensitive to their environments and to respond to them.

Disruptions of Normal Biological Development

Sometimes biological development can go awry. Something happens in the environment that translates into a biological change that has profound, long-term implications for healthy development. Disease and injury are potential dangers from the moment of conception until old age. The study of development has increased understanding about how the timing of such trauma can determine the effects of disease or injury. Developmental psychologists have been especially interested in the effects of biological assaults during the prenatal period because it increases understanding of birth defects that make a difference for the entire life of the affected individual.

Teratogens

A critical period for adverse neurological events is the first 2–3 months of life, which corresponds to neurogenesis, when many new nerve cells are forming and when normal development is dependent on precisely timed biochemical events (Martin & Domborwski, 2008). **Teratogens** are environmental agents that can interfere greatly with normal development by affecting the beginnings of the nervous system. A large number of diseases and chemical teratogens have been identified (Shepard, 1998; Stein, Schettler, Wallinga, & Valenti, 2002). In many cases, prenatal exposure to disease or chemicals will do so much damage to the developing nervous system that normal learning and development can never occur. For example, exposure to rubella during pregnancy can produce extreme cognitive disability as well as a host of other symptoms, such as stunting of physical growth, hearing loss, heart disease and psychiatric illness, in the developing child (Martin & Dombrowski, 2008). Maternal alcoholism can result in **fetal alcohol syndrome,** which is central nervous system damage that can cause learning difficulties and even intellectual disabilities (Martin & Dombrowski, 2008; Mattson, Fryer, McGee, & Riley, 2008). Maternal smoking during pregnancy is associated with low birth weight and expressive language difficulties (Delaney-Black et al., 2000; Martin & Dombrowski, 2008). Children exposed to other chemical teratogens, such as lead and narcotics, experience a range of behavioral and cognitive disorders. For example, heavy marijuana use can produce fetal brain damage that affects later memory, language, and attention (Fried, 2002; Fried & Watkinson, 1990; Martin & Dombrowski, 2008). (See Chapter 8 for additional discussion of the learning difficulties of children who are victims of chemical assaults.) As a general rule of thumb, substance abuse of all sorts during pregnancy is potentially teratogenic (Martin & Dombrowski, 2008). Hence, substance abuse by pregnant women is of great concern.

Although many teratogens are most dangerous during the first trimester of a pregnancy, teratogenic effects, such as the negative effects of smoking on birth weight, can occur after the first trimester. Since teratogens can have negative effects early in a pregnancy as well as throughout the prenatal period, a woman should seek prenatal care as soon as it is clear that she is pregnant.

Malnutrition

Prenatal and postnatal malnutrition can reduce mental competency (Fuglestad, Rao, & Georgieff, 2008; Martin & Dombrowski, 2008). Once again, the timing is important. Greater damage results when malnutrition occurs at critical periods corresponding to rapid development of the nervous system (Fuglestad et al., 2008; Martin & Dombrowski, 2008). Children are especially vulnerable from about 6 months postconception until the second year of life, when neural cell growth via the proliferation of dendritic synapses is rapid (Dobbing, 1974; Frisancho, 1995). Furthermore, because substantial myelination occurs during the middle preschool years (3–4 years of age), this is also a period of great sensitivity to the effects of malnutrition. Children most likely to suffer malnutrition come from lower socioeconomic status (SES) homes. Long-term malnutrition is also common in developing and war-torn countries where many children exhibit lower cognitive development and reduced attentional capacity (Sigman, Neumann, Jansen, & Bwibo, 1989). Diets are not always optimal even in developed countries. It is not unusual for children to have diets deficient in important vitamins, such as A, the B complexes, C, D, and K, or in iron. Cognitive, motor, and a variety of growth problems can result from these deficiencies (Aukett & Wharton, 1995; Martin & Dombrowski, 2008; Pollitt, 1990).

Premature Delivery and Low-Birth-Weight Infants, and Neurological Injury

A number of factors cause babies to be born before they are full term, that is, before they have been in gestation for 38 weeks. The most important one is maternal malnutrition. Also, twins and triplets often are born before full term. Drug use, smoking, and poor maternal health can also contribute to the risk of premature delivery (Martin & Dombrowski, 2008).

Babies born before full term are characteristically low in birth weight relative to full-term infants, who typically weigh about 3,500 grams (7½ pounds). Any infant weighing less than 2,500 grams (5½ pounds) is considered low birth weight. It is not uncommon, because of new technologies, for babies weighing less than 1,000 grams at birth (about 2½ pounds) to survive. Relative to full-term infants, however, very-low-birth-weight infants are at risk for respiratory failure and metabolism problems. In fact, the leading cause of death among preterm infants is respiratory failure. Even when respiratory failure is not fatal, brain damage sometimes occurs due to anoxia. Premature infants are also at risk for intracranial hemorrhage and subsequent intellectual impairment caused by such hemorrhaging. The lower the birth weight, the greater the long-term risk for school failure, retardation, cerebral palsy, blindness, deafness, learning disabilities, and other health problems (Luciana, 2003; Taylor, Klein, & Hack, 2000).

A variety of developmental problems are associated with low-birth-weight babies as they age, including fine and gross motor skill deficits, delayed development of language, poor development of executive functions, and delayed cognitive development and educational progress (Anderson et al., 2003; Luciana, 2003; Rose et al., 2008; Rose, Feldman, & Jankowski, 2011). Pre- and postnatal injury can also reduce mental competency. A common form of injury is **anoxia,** the reduction of the infant's air supply during birth, resulting in a wide range of cognitive and behavioral problems (Caine & Watson, 2000; Martin & Dombrowski, 2008). Fortunately, better fetal-monitoring procedures and widespread dissemination of improved methods of delivery have created the potential for fewer childbirth complications (DeMauro et al., 2013; Serenius et al., 2013; Srinivas, Epstein, Nicholson, Herrin, & Asch, 2010). For example, using ultrasound procedures, doctors can determine when an about-to-be-born baby is in a breech position. A *breech position* is any position except head-first and engaged in the birth canal. In this situation, a Caesarian birth is easiest and safest for both child and mother. Not so long ago, the delivery team only discovered the breech presentation when the baby came into view. Such deliveries took a long time, with great risk of anoxia and hemorrhage due to injury involved in pulling the baby from the womb. Technology, such as ultrasound, is improving the physical and mental health of many newborns. However, access to this level of care is not equally distributed, so that the problems associated with prematurity, low birth weight, and complications at birth continue to be an issue for low-income families and under-privileged children with whom educators work (Krans & Davis 2012).

Biological Risk after Infancy

Traditionally, those who study human development have been more concerned with biological risks during the prenatal period and infancy than later in development. As it turns out, the world remains full of risks for children throughout their development (Bearer, 1995; Croft, 2015; Koger, Schettler, & Weiss, 2005; Trousdale, Martin, Abulafia, Barnett, & Westinghouse, 2010). A variety of common environmental hazards have been identified that are deleterious to children's health and well-being, including exposure to heavy metals (e.g., lead, mercury), chemicals (bisphenol A [BPA, used in plastics], flame retardants [used in clothing and furniture]), pesticides (found in food), and air pollutants and second-hand smoke. There are even concerns about electromagnetic radiation from cell phones.

The risks associated with these dangers vary, but they are usually more serious for developing children than for adults. Children tend to have greater exposure to and absorb a higher proportion of environmental toxins than do adults. Children consume more oxygen relative to their size than do adults, so air pollutants are more dangerous for them. Children are more often on floors where they encounter chemical residues and dust (perhaps 10 times more than adults) (Koger et al., 2005). Children consume more calories relative to their body weight than do adults, so food contamination is a greater risk for them than for adults. Moreover, they tend to have greater exposure to pesticide residues and other food contaminants because they more often consume juices, fruit, milk, vegetables, and water that contain environmental toxins (Koger et al., 2005). Environmental toxins tend to accumulate to a much greater degree in the brains, bones, and organs of developing children than in adults. These toxins, especially the metals, can cause neurological damage, resulting in learning problems, hearing difficulties, slowed growth, headaches, and other difficulties (Chang, 1999; Koger et al., 2005; Phelps, 1999; Stein et al., 2002). While some progress has been made in reducing lead and other environmental toxins, children from poorer neighborhoods and schools still tend to have greater exposure, which causes considerable challenges for impoverished children and families because of the combined effects of environmental and social toxins (Wright, 2009).

Some Unique Aspects of Development Relevant to Educators

Discontinuities in Development

Development in children is typically not continuous. Neurological and cognitive development in particular, rather than changing a little bit at a time at a relatively constant rate, occurs in fits and starts or a 'two or three steps forward, one step back' fashion (Anderson et al., 2011; Fischer, 2008, 2009; Fischer & van Geert, 2014). For example, at about the time infants become less likely to make the "A, not B, error," they have a spurt in brain growth, as shown by measures such as the electroencephlagram (EEG) (Bell & Fox, 1992, 1994, 1997; Cuevas, Swingler, Bell, Marcovitch, & Caulkins, 2012). This growth spurt may be due to increases in the synaptic density in the frontal lobes (Diamond, Werker, & Lalonde, 1994). Fischer (2008, 2009) contends that several brain growth spurts occur between birth and early adulthood, and these growth spurts are accompanied by advances in behaviors and cognition, as summarized in Table 2.1. Throughout this book, we emphasize the idea that the development of skills depends on motivation and emotions as well as physical development and a child's social environment. Fischer has a similar emphasis, noting that emotional development also occurs in spurts, often paralleling the spurts in brain growth (Fischer, 2008, 2009). For example, separation distress (i.e., protests by children when their mothers leave) and fear develop between 4 and 8 months of age (Lewis, Koroshegyi, Douglas, & Kampe, 1997; see also Chapter 10). What is the parallel cognitive advance (see Table 2.1)? For another example, many young children between 18 and 24 months enter the "terrible twos," meaning that they express willfulness and anger when frustrated much more than earlier in their development. What is the parallel cognitive advance (again see Table 2.1)? Considering these parallels, Fischer's perspective on development has the potential for linking neurological, cognitive, and emotional development.

Hemispheric Specialization

The left and right hemispheres of the brain are specialized to perform different functions (refer to Figure 2.2), a feature of the CNS likely shared by other animals (Halpern, Güntürkün, Hopkins, & Rogers, 2005; MacNeilage, Rogers, & Vallortigara, 2009). In humans, the left hemisphere is specialized for processing language, sequential and temporal content, and logical, analytical, and rational reasoning. In contrast, the right hemisphere is better suited for processing nonverbal, visual–spatial content, and simultaneous and analogical information (Pinel & Dehaene, 2009; Springer & Deutsch, 1989). Damage to the left hemisphere results in language disabilities (Bates & Roe, 2001; Foundas, 2001).

Some have argued that Western schooling focuses on developing only one side of the brain: the left hemisphere (Ornstein, 1977, 1978). Many proposals for changes in the educational system have been made in response to this perceived bias in

TABLE 2.1. Levels of Cognitive Development Associated with Brain Growth Spurts

Age	Behavioral-cognitive developments	Examples
3–4 weeks	New, simple reflexes develop	Infant looks at ball moving in front of face; infant grasps cloth placed in hand.
7–8 weeks	Coordination of a few reflexes	Infant hears voice and looks at eyes of speaker; infant extends arm toward ball that he or she sees.
10–11 weeks	Coordination of sets of reflexes	Infant looking at face and hearing voice smiles, coos, nods; infant opens hand while extending arm toward ball.
15–17 weeks	Coordination of reflex actions to produce single, flexible sensorimotor action	Infant looks at ball as it moves through complex trajectory; infant opens hands while extending arm toward seen ball, and in middle of reach sometimes adjusts hands to changes in ball's trajectory.
7–8 months	Coordination of a few sensorimotor relations	Infant grasps ball in order to bring it in front of face to look at it; infant looks at ball to guide reaching for it.
11–13 months	Coordination of sets of sensorimotor actions	Infant moves a rattle in different ways to see different parts of it; infant imitates pronunciation of many single words.
18–24 months	Coordination of action systems to produce concrete representations of objects, people, or events	Child pretends that doll is walking and says, "Doll walk."
3½–4½ years	Coordination of representations	Child pretends two dolls are Mommy and Daddy interacting in parental roles; child understands that self knows a secret and Daddy does not know it.
6–7 years	Coordination of subsets of representations	Child pretends that two dolls are Mommy and Daddy as well as a doctor and a teacher simultaneously.
10–12 years	Coordination of representations to produce abstract concepts	Child understands addition as general operation of joining numbers; child understands that honesty is a general quality of being truthful.
14–16 years	Simple coordination of abstractions	Teen understands how addition and subtraction are opposite operations; person integrates concepts of honesty and kindness into the complex concept of a social lie.
18–20 years	Complex coordination of subsets of abstractions	Young adult understands how operations of addition and division are related through the ways numbers are grouped and combined; person integrates several types of honesty and kindness in the complex concept of constructive criticism.
23–25 years	General principles for integrating systems of abstractions	Person understands moral principle of justice; person understands principle of reflective judgment as knowledge; person understands principle of evolution by natural selection.

Note. From Fischer and Rose (1994). Copyright © 1994 The Guilford Press. Adapted by permission.

educational emphasis. Most approaches encourage more teaching of art, music, and intuitive interpretation in school, presumably to stimulate right-hemisphere functioning. In general, however, there is little support for the theory that instructional activities designed to stimulate one side of the brain over the other are effective (Springer & Deutsch, 1989). In fact, despite the evidence for hemispheric specialization, it is important to keep in mind that the two hemispheres work together. Indeed, some cognitive psychologists feel that the right/left brain distinction is more mythical than real. They suggest that a better way to understand cognitive functioning is the distinction between the upper parts of the brain (top brain; the frontal and parietal lobes) and the anatomically lower parts of the brain (bottom brain; the temporal and occipital lobes) (Kosslyn & Miller, 2013). These studies demonstrate the importance of evidence-based educational practice and the fact that not all educational interventions inspired by biological insights are sound (Fischer, 2009).

Cognitive Capacity Constraints

As awesome as the human brain is in its ability to process and store information, it has its limits. In particular, a number of cognitive processes are rate-limiting steps or "bottlenecks" particularly in visual processing, attention, and memory (Buschman, Siegel, Roy, & Miller, 2011; Cowan et al., 2005; Marois & Ivanoff, 2005; Tombu et al., 2011). Students can only perform tasks that do not require more cognitive capacity than they have available for use. This has led to instructional materials and techniques based on cognitive load theory in which educators endeavor to instruct students without overwhelming their working memory capacities (de Jong, 2010; Paas, van Gog, & Sweller, 2010; van Merriënboer & Sweller, 2005). See the Applying Developmental Theory to Educational Contexts special feature (Box 2.2) for recommendations for helping students cope with short-term capacity demands.

Working memory capacity, a memory store of limited capacity and duration, increases with development (Schneider & Pressley, 1997; see also Chapters 3 and 4). One way to think about short-term memory capacity is to consider the number of pieces of information a student can have active at any one time while working toward some cognitive goal. Consider, for example, what it is like when you hold a telephone number in your memory while you are looking for a way to write it down, or what it is like to sequence ideas in your head as you are trying to write a paragraph on a term paper. Case (1985, 1991) called this limited capacity **executive processing space.**

Executive processing space and speed of processing information increase as children develop because of *practice with familiar tasks* rather than neurological maturation. Consequently, children can perform tasks automatically that once took considerable effort and attention; this automaticity frees up capacity for attention to tasks requiring more effort and attention. Moreover, as described in more detail in Chapter 4, as children mature, they develop more extensive knowledge, which also permits more efficient use of short-term capacity. Thus, with practice, a child has greater functional capacity even if the actual neurologically determined capacity has not increased (Courage & Cowan, 2009; Kail, 2000). So, experiences that increase knowledge permit the more efficient and effective processing of information and thus, the more efficient and effective use of the biologically determined short-term capacity the child has. Clearly, functional capacity depends on both biology and

BOX 2.2. Multitasking and Helping Students Cope with Working Memory Demands

There are limits to our working memory capacity; it's just a fact of life. However, our media-saturated culture is creating ever more entertaining distractions for children and adolescents that further strain their capacities for focused attention and learning. There has been substantial interest in multitasking and the extent to which it might be useful or deleterious to learning. While researchers are just beginning to penetrate the complexities of how media multitasking affects youth, the preliminary results are not promising. It appears that media multitasking has a deleterious effect on attention, working memory, cognition, impulsivity and the ability to delay gratification, and overall academic performance (Baumgartner, Weeda, van der Heijden, & Huizinga, 2014; Cain, Leonard, Gabrieli, & Finn 2016; Courage, Bakhtiar, Fitzpatrick, Kenny, & Brandeau,2015; Uncapher, Thieu, & Wagner, 2016; Wilmer, Sherman, & Chein, 2017).

Unfortunately, teachers are in the unenviable position of having to compete with media distractions and the effects of media multitasking on their students. Furthermore, working memory capacity difficulties are more of a problem with some students, especially younger students, than with others. Teachers can adopt some general tactics to develop their students' capacities for focused attention and working memory development (de Jong, 2010; Dulaney, Vasilyeva, & O'Dwyer 2015; Miller, Woody-Ramsey, & Aloise, 1991; Sweller, 2016):

- Set a good example. Young students admire their teachers and will mirror their behaviors. Even jaundiced adolescent students look to teachers for examples of how to behave and are quick to point out hypocrisy should they observe a teacher engaging in media multitasking after telling students not to do so. Students are unlikely to consider attempting to resist the temptations of technological distractions if they observe their teachers doing it.

- Consider carefully how and when you use media technology for your instruction. Some media may be very useful for teaching, while other times they may only serve to distract students.

- Monitor student media use to assure students are attending to the instructional content rather than surfing the web or checking social networking sites.

- Analyze academic tasks for the capacity demands they place on students. Some students have problems with working memory storage, while others have difficulties with sustaining attention. You will need to use different teaching tactics depending on the source of the problem.

- Simplify complex tasks and break them down into smaller, more consumable, easily accomplished steps that do not tax short-term memory capacity. For example, divide the task of writing a term paper into the following steps: selecting a topic, finding information on the topic, preparing an outline, writing a rough draft, revising the draft, and polishing the final draft.

- Coach and prompt students to help them complete complex tasks. Provide supportive materials (e.g., handouts, questions, prompts, hints) designed to reduce short-term memory load. In short, teachers can engineer materials and the learning environment to reduce short-term capacity demands.

experience! It can also depend on what a teacher does to support students as they attempt to complete complex tasks.

Biological Foundations of Academic Competence

Biological studies offer a tremendous opportunity to expand understanding of important academic competencies. For example, there is a great deal of active research on the brain mechanisms responsible for developing effective reading skills and successful mathematics learning (Fischer, 2009; Katzir, 2009; Katzir & Paré-Blagoev, 2006; Posner & Rothbart, 2005).

Reading

Reading researchers are using biological methods such as brain imaging to better understand reading processes (Goswami, 2008; Hruby & Goswami, 2011; Landi, Frost, Mencl, Sandak & Pugh, 2013; Paulesu, Danelli & Berlingeri, 2014; Shaywitz & Shaywitz, 2004, 2005, 2008; Wandell & Yeatman, 2013). The acts of text decoding and reading comprehension involve a number of neural networks, including attention, vision, and auditory systems and the white matter tracts that connect them (Hruby & Goswami, 2011; Landi, Frost, Mencl, Sandak, & Pugh, 2013; Lebel et al., 2013; Paulesu, Danelli, & Berlingeri, 2014; Shaywitz & Shaywitz, 2008; Vandermosten, Boets, Wouters, & Ghesquière, 2012; Wandell & Yeatman, 2013). Hence, a number of brain regions are active during reading in both hemispheres of the brain.

Some aspects of reading employ left-hemisphere processes more than right-hemisphere processes (Goswami, 2008; Hruby & Goswami, 2011; Houdé, Rossi, Lubin, & Joliot, 2010; Lebel et al., 2013; Paulesu, Danelli, & Berlingeri, 2014; Vandermosten, Boets, Wouters, & Ghesquière 2012). This complements earlier research (Roberts & Kraft, 1989) that studied the electrical brain activity of primary-grade and middle-grade readers (6- to 8-year-olds and 10- to 12-year-olds) as they read material that was slightly challenging for them. For the younger students, most of the comprehension activity occurred in the left hemisphere. For the older students, the activity was more evenly divided between the two hemispheres. Roberts and Kraft suggested that the predominantly left-hemispheric reading by the younger students reflected their focus on decoding during reading. The older students, however, used a range of reading strategies, which resulted in the more balanced hemispheric patterns. What is becoming clear from the neural-imaging research is that, although left-hemisphere functioning is prominent in reading, reading involves a complex coordination of brain functions (Goswami, 2008; Hruby & Goswami, 2011; Lebel et al., 2013; Paulesu et al., 2014).

Dyslexia

Dyslexia is the failure to learn to read despite substantial reading instruction (Shaywitz, Weiss, Saklofske, & Shaywitz, 2016; Shaywitz & Shaywitz, 2014). Estimates of the prevalence of dyslexia vary considerably depending on how it is defined. If being a fluent reader by the middle elementary grades is the criterion for concluding a child is a reader rather than a child with dyslexia, then as many as 17–21% of school-age children are dyslexic (Ferrer et al., 2015). Acquired dyslexia results from some type of brain injury, and developmental dyslexia refers to otherwise normal children experiencing difficulties in reading that are not due to obvious brain injury (Coltheart & Kohnen, 2012). Educators encounter developmental dyslexia much more often than acquired dyslexia. Developmental dyslexia consists of a variety of symptoms (Vellutino & Fletcher, 2005). These include eye-scan patterns that do not match normal patterns; difficulties with spatial orientation, including confusing left and right; and better reading of upside-down text than right-side-up text. The particular symptoms differ from student to student. The most important characteristic is difficulty with word recognition and decoding during childhood, persisting throughout life in most cases (Bruck, 1990; Shaywitz & Shaywitz, 2008; Swanson & Hsieh, 2009).

As early as 2 years of age, dyslexic children experience language difficulties not seen in children who become normal readers (Ferrer et al., 2015; Scarborough, 2001). They produce relatively short utterances and their pronunciations are less accurate. Their receptive vocabularies are not as well developed, and they have more difficulties providing labels for common objects. Thus, dyslexia is part of a general language-processing deficiency as a result of abnormalities in various brain regions (especially in the left hemisphere) and the white matter tracts that connect them (Paulesu et al., 2014; Shaywitz, Mody, & Shaywitz, 2006; Shaywitz & Shaywitz, 2008; Vandermosten et al., 2012; Vellutino & Fletcher, 2005).

Mathematics

The methodological tools that are shedding light on reading processes, especially brain-imaging techniques, are also being used to develop more complete models of how the brain affects mathematical thinking (Ansari, 2010; Houde et al., 2010). As with reading, brain-imaging studies indicate that various brain regions are activated when people engage in mathematical operations. However, in adults, various neural networks in the parietal cortex are especially active mathematical cognition (Ansari, 2010; Houde et al., 2010). However, studies indicate that in young children the frontal lobes and the right hemisphere of the brain are more engaged during numerical tasks leading researchers to conclude that as people age there is a shift from using frontal cortex to parietal cortex and from primary use of the right hemisphere of the brain to use of both hemispheres for mathematical cognition (Ansari, 2010; Houde et al., 2010). This may have implications for how mathematical skills are taught to young learners versus older students.

Chapter Summary and Evaluation

As embryos develop into fetuses, fetuses into infants, infants into young children and adolescents, neurological and physical changes are prolific and have significant implications for how educators work with students of all ages. Children's and adolescents' brains and bodies morph through critical periods of development that, depending on how well they are traversed, can have long-range effects on their cognitive and academic abilities, either for good or for more deleterious outcomes. The research in this chapter that details these issues fit into the framework of the Big Ideas introduced in Chapter 1.

Nature and Nurture

Perhaps the most important idea in this chapter is that a student's genetic endowment and biological constitution interact with his or her social and physical environment to determine his or her developmental outcome and that children and adolescents alter their physical and social environments, creating a dynamic interacting relationship between nature and nurture. The developing nervous system is preprogrammed in many ways (nature), but its development is affected dramatically by environmental agents (nurture). It is important to keep in mind that a genotype has a reaction range of phenotypes associated with it. Phenotypic expression depends on the unique environmental stimulation the organism experiences. Some aspects of development are "canalized," and plasticity declines with age as the brain matures. Consequently, the window of opportunity for some types of intervention may be brief and occur only during certain critical periods. However, children and adolescents have remarkable resilience and capacities for adaptation, and this neurological plasticity provides opportunities for educational intervention and cognitive enrichment. Furthermore, experience-dependent synapses can continue to form throughout the lifespan, extending the time when learning and development can occur.

The environment children experience also depends greatly on the historical era in which they live. The 1,000-gram premature infant now has a chance at life because of modern technology that permits the placement of the premature infant in an environment in which it can survive. Malnutrition is more likely during war than peace, which is one reason why healthy development is more likely during peacetime. Diseases that once ravaged developing children (such as polio and measles) are now very rare because of modern medicine. But modernity has also created environmental pollutants that were not present in earlier eras. *When* one develops does much to determine *how* one develops.

Continuity and Discontinuity

It is also important to keep in mind that development is discontinuous, that neurological, cognitive, and physical development occur in spurts, meaning that the timing of educational interventions can be critical. Moreover, there may be constraints on what a child or an adolescent is cognitively capable of at a given time. Biological research is providing powerful new ways of construing stage-like discontinuities in development. One example is the investigation of discontinuities in brain development and associated growth spurts in cognitive and emotional development described by Fischer and his colleagues. In general, biological analyses make clear that the developing nervous system differs in important ways from the mature nervous system. As research on neurological development and education become more sophisticated, it is critical that educators employ techniques that are evidence-based and to rely on sound educational practices and not momentary fads.

Universal and Culture-Specific

Some perceptual and cognitive developments, such as language acquisition, are probably universal within the human species, occurring in all but the most exceptional circumstances. They are mediated by experience-expectant neurological mechanisms, with their development dependent on appropriate experience during critical periods. Deviation from the canalized perceptual development occurs only in the absence of such experience. Short of raising a child in complete social isolation, human language will develop, although the form and sophistication of language development depend on the richness and particulars of experience (as detailed in Chapter 7). Certain brain structure–function relationships also seem universal. For example, increases in functional short-term capacity with age and central nervous system specialization have been documented in many ways.

Active and Passive Child

Children and adolescents also alter the physical and social environments in which they live. As they develop physical and motor skills and their capacity to interact with their physical environment, they change their physical environment and the way people in their social environment interact with them. As children develop into adolescents, the neurological and physical changes they incur have a pervasive effect on their cognitive, social–emotional, and academic growth. These changes create further opportunities for adolescents to alter their ecology, but they also require the people and institutions in their environment to adapt as well. Some of these changes, in particular, early puberty and changes in sleep patterns, can have negative effects on the adolescent's well-being and educational receptiveness.

REVIEW OF KEY TERMS

adolescent growth spurt A period of rapid physical growth and development during adolescence.

anoxia The reduction of an infant's air supply during birth, which can cause brain injury.

apoptosis Normative genetically programmed neuron death that removes neurons that are not needed.

axon A stem-like part of a cell that conducts impulses away from the cell body.

canalized As used in describing development, when development is almost completely genetically determined.

cephalocaudal Term describing tendency for physical development to move from top to bottom.

cerebral cortex The part of the brain responsible for complex thought processes.

critical periods Time periods of great sensitivity to environmental input.

dendrites Branch-like extensions of the cell body that transmit impulses from other cells toward the cell body.

developmental cascade One event in development that initiates a sequence of other developmental acquisitions.

dyslexia The inability to decode words well despite substantial reading instruction.

epigenetics Changes in gene activity or gene expression likely due to environmental factors.

executive processing space The number of pieces of information a student can have active in memory at any one time.

experience-adaptive neural development A child's experiences at a particular time in his or her development that may have effects on his or her brain development and behavior that are more or less permanent.

experience-dependent synapses Synapses that respond to whatever environmental stimulation an individual encounters.

experience-expectant synapses Synapses that are genetically programmed to respond only to certain kinds of stimulation.

fetal alcohol syndrome Birth defects, such as learning difficulties and mental retardation, caused by damage to the central nervous system as a result of maternal alcoholism.

genotype The genes possessed, which specify a potential range of outcomes.

heritability The variation in a characteristic (e.g., intelligence) that is due to genetic variability.

hypothalamic–pituitary–adrenal (HPA) axis The connections between the hypothalamus, pituitary gland, and adrenal glands that promote physical growth and body composition changes.

hypothalamic–pituitary–gonadal (HPG) axis The connections between the hypothalamus, pituitary gland, and gonads that promote the development of sexual characteristics.

menarche Onset of first menstruation.

myelination The formation of a layer of axon sheathing that permits more rapid firing of axons.

neural networks Neuron circuits that are believed to be the foundation of cognitive processes.

neurogenesis A period of rapid cell growth.

phenotypes The observed outcome of the genotype, or how the genes are expressed.

plastic/plasticity The capacity of the physical brain to be malleable and adapt to changing environmental stimulation and circumstances.

postpubescence The tapering off of puberty as adolescents attain physiological adult status.

prepubescence The initial, typically undetectable, physiological changes that presage puberty.

proximodistal Term describing the tendency for physical development to move from the center of the body outward.

pubescence The beginning of puberty as sexual hormones begin to rise to adult levels.

sleep phase delay A change in circadian rhythm that occurs in adolescents, resulting in adolescents preferring to stay awake later and wake later.

synaptic connections Physical connections between neurons formed through an axon meeting a dendrite, a cell body, or another axon.

synaptic pruning The removal of synaptic connections that are rarely activated.

synaptogenesis The creation of synapses that is particularly prolific in early childhood.

teratogens Environmental agents, such as disease or chemicals, that can damage a developing fetus.

CHAPTER 3

Cognitive Development

Piaget's Stage Theory

No single individual has had as much impact on the study of children's mental capacities as Jean Piaget. Piaget defined many important issues in the development of cognition, and his theory shaped thinking about child development for decades, inspiring a philosophy that continues to influence education. In this chapter, we first describe Piaget's original theory, followed by a description of theories building upon Piaget's ideas referred to as neo-Piagetian theories. Then we present Kohlberg's extension of Piaget's theory to explain the development of moral judgment, followed by a description of moral or character education. We conclude the chapter with a discussion of the constructivist approach to education, for Piaget's theory did much to inspire and inform constructivist educators (Carey, Zaitchik, & Bascandziev, 2015).

Piaget's Four-Stage Theory

Piaget's (e.g., 1983) four-stage theory of development is his most visible contribution to developmental psychology. Think back to the debate between stage-like and continuous views of development described in Chapter 1. According to stage theory, development is uneven, with children fundamentally different in important ways at different times during their development. Rather than making gradual transitions, there are points of rapid development, with abrupt movement from one stage to the next.

In Piaget's stage theory of development, progress through the four stages can occur at different rates, but it is always orderly, taking place in an invariant sequence (Feldman, 2013). Each stage is characterized by the development of new cognitive structures, or schemes. A **scheme** is a coordinated pattern of thought or action that organizes an individual's interaction with the environment. The more advanced stages of cognitive development are associated with more complex and sophisticated schemes, and hence by more advanced and flexible thinking and behavior.

The schemes of infants are simple and action-oriented, such as a scheme of reaching for, grasping, and pulling an object close for careful examination. These first schemes are sensory and motor in nature. Thus, the first Piagetian stage is known as the **sensorimotor stage**. According to Piaget, intelligence during this period consists in the actions of the child on the environment rather than in the child's mind. Piagetians called these actions **motor schemes**.

How do infants acquire sensorimotor schemes? Young infants possess innate reflexes, such as sucking, crying, or grasping. These reflexes serve as the basis for the first motor schemes. For example, infants initially suck their fingers instinctively. Eventually, sucking becomes a strategy for exploring new objects in the environment, a sensorimotor scheme. What are infants likely to do when handed a rattle? Invariably, a portion of the rattle ends up in their mouths. Infants use the sucking response as a strategy, a motor scheme, for interacting with the rattle and other objects in their environment.

The sensorimotor schemes of infancy permit interactions with the environment that eventually lead to the development of object permanence. **Object permanence** refers to a child's understanding that objects continue to exist whether or not the child can see or touch them. Before this acquisition, children act as if objects that are out of their sight no longer exist. Once children acquire object permanence, however, they understand that objects have an existence independent of their perception of them. What do infants do if someone hides a rattle under a blanket? If they have object permanence, they will lift up the blanket to look for the rattle. If not, they'll just look away, seemingly undisturbed by the object's apparent disappearance.

The next stage, the **preoperational stage,** roughly corresponds to the preschool years. Children in this stage have developed cognitive structures called **symbolic schemes** that allow them to represent objects or events by means of symbols such as language, mental images, and gestures. The first evidence of this representational ability is often the display of **deferred imitation**. This refers to children's ability to imitate behavior long after witnessing it. For example, a child who witnessed another child's tantrum at the grocery store last week is capable of imitating the tantrum behaviors today. Another example of representational ability occurs during **symbolic play**. To a child capable of symbolic representation, an empty box can become a castle, and a stick can become a magic wand. The most powerful representational ability is demonstrated in children's use of language, arguably the most powerful symbol system for knowledge acquisition.

Despite the advances evident in preoperational children's thinking due to their use of symbolic schemes, Piaget emphasized the differences between the logic of younger children and that of older children. Preoperational children possess a logic of their own; it is just not the same logic displayed by older children and adults. According to Piaget, preschoolers exhibit **egocentrism,** or unawareness of the perspective of others. They view situations primarily from their own perspective and are unable to understand a situation from another person's point of view. For example, a little girl may have difficulty understanding that her grandma is her mother's mother. How can *her* mother be someone else's daughter? Another example is that preschoolers believe that others view objects in the same way as they do, regardless of the other person's viewing angle. This is why most preschoolers have to be reminded constantly during "Show and Tell" to hold the object so the other children in the class can see it. A high proportion of preschooler speech is described as egocentric since many of their utterances are not social in intent. For instance, preschoolers in conversation often talk all at once, ignoring the speech of others. Preschoolers often do not communicate information to other people very well due to their egocentrism. For instance, preschoolers telling stories tend to leave out important information needed to understand the story fully. Test this out by asking a preschooler to explain what happened on the most recent episode of their favorite television show.

Preschool children are also unable to solve conservation tasks. **Conservation** refers to the understanding that changes in appearance do not equal changes in amount. Preschoolers do not understand that amount can only be changed by adding or subtracting material. For example, preschoolers will claim that the amount of liquid changed because it was poured from a tall, slender glass into a short, wide glass, although they can see nothing was added or subtracted. What is going on to explain this failure in logic? The preoperational children are attending to misleading perceptual cues. They might argue that there is more liquid after pouring because the water is wider after pouring, or they might claim that there is less liquid after pouring because the water is not as high in the glass after pouring. Several years later, when children understand conservation, they offer explanations about how height and width offset one another and about how the amount cannot change when nothing is added or subtracted. Failure to conserve does not mean that preschoolers are completely illogical. Many preschoolers who cannot conserve understand that it is the same water that is transferred from glass A to glass B. That is, they are beginning to understand that the **identity** of the water survives a perceptual transformation. Of course, still less cognitively mature preschoolers do not even understand that identity is preserved following a perceptual transformation.

According to Piaget, preschoolers' thought lacks some of the logical **operational schemes** (operations) that underlie mature thought, which accounts for their errors in conservation tasks (and for the name of the preoperational stage). Operations are cognitive rules. One scheme is the identity function already described. When children completely understand identity, they realize that objects remain the same despite perceptual transformation. A second is **reversibility**. This refers to the understanding that an operation can be undone by reversing it, such as pouring the water back into the tall glass—or by doing so mentally, imagining the water being poured back. A third is **compensation**. This is the recognition that change on one dimension can be compensated for by changes on another dimension. For example, the same amount of water will be higher in a narrow glass than in a wide one.

Having these operational schemes permits conservation. Children with operational intelligence can reason that the amount of water in the wider glass is the same as it was in the taller glass because they can mentally reverse the pouring. They can also point out the reciprocal relationship between height and width of the liquid. Children in either of the next stages of operational intelligence, concrete and formal, are more powerful thinkers than preoperational preschoolers.

During the **concrete operational stage,** which corresponds roughly to the elementary-grade years, children can apply cognitive operations to problems involving concrete objects, but not to problems involving abstract manipulation or hypothetical situations. A hallmark of children in the concrete operational stage is the ability to solve conservation tasks. Thus, if shown two rows of seven buttons lined up evenly, concrete operational children understand that the two rows contain the same number of buttons even when one of the rows is "stretched" so that a greater space lies between individual buttons. This is a number conservation problem. If two balls of clay are the same weight as indicated by a balanced scale, conserving children will predict that the scale will stay in balance even if one of the two balls is reshaped, perhaps flattened like a pancake or rolled into a snake. This is a conservation of mass problem.

Concrete operations permit the performance of other tasks as well, such as **class inclusion** problems. In these problems, children view sets of objects, some of which are subsets of each other, and they answer questions about the subset relationships. For example, if they are given a set of pictures of five cardinals and four robins and asked "Are there more cardinals or birds?," conserving children understand that there are more birds than cardinals. Preoperational children, however, are more likely to respond that there are more cardinals, since there are more cardinals than robins in the pictures they are viewing. In addition, concrete operations permit children to **seriate** items. That is, they can order objects on some dimension, such as shortest to tallest or lightest to heaviest. For example, concrete operators can correctly arrange sticks in order of increasing length.

Students at the **formal operational stage** (beginning with early adolescence) are capable of even more complex problem solving. First, they can handle problems that involve multiple factors. Thus, although concrete operational children can seriate on one dimension, formal operational children can seriate on several dimensions simultaneously. For example, they can correctly arrange sticks in order of color *and* increasing length. Formal operational thinkers are capable of *thinking in possibilities*, meaning that they can generate all combinations of possibilities for a given situation. For example, formal operational thinkers can infer "invisible forces" and thereby solve problems involving such forces. This allows them to solve problems such as how hydraulic presses work given some weights and several presses. Moreover, the thinking of the formal operational adolescent is not closely tied to the constraints of the "real" world. Whereas concrete operators often rely on concrete objects to aid their reasoning, formal operators can discuss complex issues without the concrete props. In addition, the formal operational adolescent routinely utilizes planning, foresight, or *thinking ahead*. Finally, the thinking ability most characteristic of formal operators is *thinking in hypotheses*. The formal operational thinker can survey a problem, formulate all potential hypothetical outcomes, and go about testing the possibilities one at a time.

This characteristic of thinking in hypotheses is a critical component of scientific reasoning. In one of the Piagetian tasks designed to elicit scientific reasoning, the pendulum problem, students are provided three lengths of string and three different weights that they can attach to the string. The students' task is to figure out which factors determine the rate at which a pendulum swings. Usually, the students will conduct one of the following two actions: (1) use one of the strings and try each weight in succession, and (2) use one of the weights and try each string in succession. What students notice is that the speed of swinging varies with the length of the string, but not with the weight. Some students will also systematically vary how much force they use to set the pendulum in motion, and they will note that force is not a critical factor in the speed of the pendulum swing. The students act like scientists in this situation, varying one factor at a time while holding other factors constant. Thus, they are "thinking in hypotheses." In contrast, children who are not in the formal operational stage often proceed in a haphazard fashion, sometimes changing two features at once, such as the size of the weight and the length of the string. See Table 3.1 for a description of another task that elicits formal operational thinking.

TABLE 3.1. A Question That Elicits Formal Operational Thinking: How Might Everyday Life Be Different If We All Had Tails?

College students who were asked this question as part of a classroom exercise generated a variety of responses, ranging from changes in fashion and furniture to changes in religious values and courting rituals. Their responses highlight important qualities of formal operational thought, including thinking in terms of possibilities.

> *Fashion*—tail jewelry, tail braiding, tail ribbons, tail cover-ups
>
> *Furniture*—differences in chairs and beds, hooks to hang by tails
>
> *Sports*—new ball games, new Olympic sports, tail workouts
>
> *Dating*—Do you allow your date to see your tail on the first date?
>
> *Religion*—Are tails displayed? Are there display differences for men and women?
>
> *Politics*—prejudice based on length, color, degree of hairiness of tail

Progress through the Stages

By training and by conviction, Piaget was a biologist who believed in a biological inevitability to the stages, and hence a universality to them (Brainerd, 1978b; Feldman, 2013; Piaget, 1967). The stages build upon one another, with each one a prerequisite for the next. Some individuals, however, move through the stages more rapidly than others, and some do not make it all the way to formal operations.

Initially, Piaget argued that once in a stage, all thinking reflects the underlying competencies characteristic of the stage. Thus, a student who is concrete operational for one task should be concrete operational for all tasks. A later version of the theory permitted "stage mixture" (Brainerd, 1978b; Flavell, 1971, 1972), so that some students might be preoperational for some tasks and concrete operational for others. Other students might be able to attack some problems in a formal operational fashion, while still requiring concrete manipulatives for other problems. **Horizontal décalage** is the term used to describe that students do not master all problems requiring the same logical operations at the same time. For example, children typically acquire conservation of length (i.e., recognizing that the length of a string does not vary no matter how the string is shaped) before conservation of liquid. Moreover, Piaget suggested that individuals reach formal operations in "different areas according to their aptitudes and their professional socialization" (Piaget, 1972, p. 10). Thus, successful mechanics, carpenters, or composers may use formal operational reasoning in their particular specialty but not necessarily in other areas of expertise. See Table 3.2 for a summary of Piaget's four stages of cognitive development.

Mechanisms of Cognitive Change

How did Piaget explain progression through the stages? Piaget (1983) believed that many factors determine developmental change. The first, *maturation*, is biological. As children mature physically, new possibilities for development evolve. Although biological development is necessary for cognitive growth, it is not sufficient for such growth to occur. *Experience* plays a role as well. As children practice new cognitive acquisitions, their experiences with the physical world permit them to learn important regularities. For example, one regularity might be "as the amount of something increases, its weight increases." The *social environment* also plays a role in development.

TABLE 3.2. Summary of Piaget's Stages of Cognitive Development

Stage	Characteristic schemes	Characteristic accomplishments	Characteristic limitations
Sensorimotor stage	Motor	Object permanence	Thinking only by doing
Preoperational stage	Motor Symbolic	Deferred imitation Symbolic play Language	Thinking dominated by perceptions Lack of awareness of others' perspectives Lack of reversibility Lack of compensation
Concrete operational stage	Motor Symbolic Operational–concrete	Class inclusion Seriation Conservation	Thinking only in concrete terms Thinking about only two attributes at once
Formal operational stage	Motor Symbolic Operational–concrete and formal	Thinking in possibilities Thinking ahead Thinking in hypotheses	

The quality of children's social environment at home and school affects the speed of movement through the stages. Environments that provide new experiences and permit practice of new skills facilitate the movement from one stage to the next.

At any given point of development, children understand the world in terms of the cognitive operations they have developed. That is, they **assimilate** new information. Children assimilate when they incorporate environmental stimuli into an existing scheme. For example, a child who sees a girl playing with a dog may be able to assimilate this observation into his or her existing scheme of household pets by thinking, "That girl's dog is her pet just like my collie, Cody, is my pet." If this child walks by a training ground for guard dogs, this new information from the environment cannot be simply assimilated into an existing cognitive structure. Instead, the child must **accommodate** to the new information. Accommodation refers to the modification of existing cognitive structures in response to environmental demands. Thus, the child needs to modify existing schemes about dogs to comprehend that some dogs are not pets but are trained to protect and attack. Assimilation of any stimulus involves accommodation of the learner to the stimulus, although the accommodation can be relatively minor. In the example above, the other girl's pet dog does not look and behave exactly like Cody at home, so assimilation involved some accommodation.

Here's another example to think about. A first grader, who has observed robins and finches in the backyard for years, has little difficulty assimilating a bald eagle into his or her bird scheme when discussing the nation's symbol in first grade. Even though the bald eagle is much larger than the birds in a backyard and a predator unlike the birds typically found in a backyard, assimilation is likely with minor accommodation. This same first grader, however, would have much more difficulty assimilating the penguins observed during the class field trip to the zoo into his or her bird scheme. The child must accommodate his or her bird scheme in response to this very different example of "bird."

Finally, consider how a preoperational child, who lacks the cognitive structures that permit understanding of compensation, responds to a conservation of weight problem. When an experimenter rolls a ball of clay into a sausage shape, the child says it has less clay now than when the clay was in a ball shape because the sausage shape is "thinner." The cognitive structures a preoperational child possesses foster attention to only one dimension in making conservation judgments. If the experimenter continues to roll the sausage out, it gets longer and longer so that the length dimension becomes more salient and less easy to overlook. Some of the time the child responds on the basis of this increase in length, reporting that there is more clay when the clay is in the shape of a sausage than in the shape of a ball. The child eventually notices the inconsistency in responding one way on the basis of length and another way on the basis of width. The result is **cognitive conflict**—that is, the child has increasing difficulty making a conservation judgment based on only one dimension. For example, the child might be thinking, "If I just look at length, I answer one way. If I just look at width, I answer another way. Both answers can't be true."

Piaget used the term **disequilibrium** to refer to the realization that two ways of thinking about the world contradict each other, and thus both can't be true. This realization motivates the resolution of the contradiction through the construction of new cognitive structures. Thus, the child accommodates to the environmental stimulus. Once accommodation occurs, the child's thinking returns to equilibrium. Piaget called this mechanism of cognitive change "equilibration." That is, **equilibration** is equilibrium followed by disequilibrium followed by a new equilibrium that is more powerful because the mind has learned to do more. In the case of conservation, a child becomes a conserver through disequilibration of cognitive schemes that do not support conservation followed by new schemes that permit conservation leading to equilibrium. Cognitive development involves many cycles of equilibrium, followed by disequilibrium, followed by equilibrium at a higher level of competence (Piaget, 1983).

One of the most important ideas in Piagetian thinking is that cognitive conflict occurs most often when children are working on problems that require just a little bit more than they currently know. When children first work on such problems, they have a sense that there is something they don't understand, but that understanding is within reach. Perception of this gap between current knowledge and what needs to be known to accomplish a task motivates cognitive effort to solve the current problem (White, 1959). Some suggestions for applying Piaget's ideas in a classroom are presented in the Applying Developmental Theory to Educational Contexts special feature (see Box 3.1).

Cognitive Conflict and Overcoming Scientific Misconceptions

Science educators in particular have been attracted to the idea that education at its best stimulates cognitive conflict. One of Piaget's (e.g., 1929) most important insights was that people often have ideas about the world that clash with scientific viewpoints. For example, some people believe that inanimate objects, such as the sun, the stars, or a computer are alive! Piaget characterized such **animism** as a symptom of preoperational intelligence. He also believed that with the development of concrete

Applying Developmental Theory to Educational Contexts

BOX 3.1. Piaget in the Classroom

Piaget and his colleagues (Inhelder, Sinclair, & Bovet, 1974) argued that the only educational mechanisms that could produce legitimate conceptual change were those that would mirror natural development via equilibration (i.e., cognitive conflict). How can educators design learning environments so that discovery via equilibration would be likely? Here are some ideas:

- Design instruction so that students are *active participants* in their own learning. Construct learning environments conducive to student exploration. Opportunities for student exploration, especially "hands-on" activities with concrete objects to manipulate, increase the likelihood of learning for both concrete and formal operational students. For example, if the learning objective is for students to understand the principle of compounding interest, ask them to demonstrate their understanding by using Monopoly money.

- Make students *aware of conflicts* between their approaches to problems and features of the problems. Present counterexamples and point out inconsistencies that may lead to disequilibrium. For example, in the case of conservation of weight, you might want to say something like "I see you are thinking about the width of the clay sausage. What have you noticed about its length?"

- *Reduce adult power* as much as possible, encouraging the exchange of points of view between teachers and students and between students and students. Foster student collaboration with peers who have mutual interests and support their working together on classroom tasks.

- Encourage children to think in their own ways rather than to produce the right answers in the right way as defined by a teacher. *Analyze student errors* to gain a better understanding of their thought processes.

and formal operations, children's ideas about what is alive versus what is not alive would reflect conventional thinking about life. A number of studies, many in the 1930s and 1940s, investigated this premise (for a brief review, see Brainerd, 1978b). The results indicated that although animism declined with development from the preoperational to the concrete and formal operational stages, it never extinguished. Animism can persist throughout adulthood.

Science educators have noted that often people have important misconceptions about physical and biological relationships. Although scientific misconceptions in physics have been studied more than other misconceptions (Pfundt & Duit, 1991), people seem to have misconceptions about every scientific arena imaginable. Here are some examples of common misconceptions (Duit, 1991; Woloshyn, Paivio, & Pressley, 1994):

The sun is a living organism—it is an animate object.

One place where water does not exist is in the air.

Molecules in solids are always still.

Plants eat soil and water.

People are not animals.

One way to foster conceptual change and to overcome misconceptions is to induce cognitive conflict through classroom instruction (Vosniadou & Mason, 2012). First, students need to be made aware of their misconceptions. Once students are aware, exposing them to an event that cannot be explained by their erroneous belief system has the potential for producing cognitive conflict. One classroom technique for addressing a misconception might be to first ask students to make predictions based on their current understanding. Then the teacher can present the students with evidence inconsistent with their predictions, perhaps asking students to observe a laboratory demonstration or providing them with data from multiple experiments. The evidence should be accompanied with the scientifically accepted explanation, which can be offered by the teacher or perhaps by peers who do not have the misconception. The intent is for the students to realize the inconsistency between their erroneous belief system and the generally accepted, scientific view. Consistent with Piagetian thinking, such conflict motivates efforts toward conflict resolution and efforts to understand the scientific concept explaining the observed event. That is, conflict motivates efforts toward *accommodation*, setting up the possibility of modification of current cognitive structures and the creation of new ones. How well attempts to induce cognitive conflict work depends on a number of factors such as how open the students are to considering other perspectives, how confident the students are in their misconception, and how well the students can tolerate the ambiguity created by considering the scientific evidence that challenges their belief system (Vosniadou & Mason, 2012).

Misconceptions can be difficult to correct since many scientifically valid ideas initially do not seem as plausible to students as their prior conceptions. For example, Clement, Brown, and Zeitsman (1989) noted that many students find it implausible that static objects exert forces (e.g., a table exerting an upward force equal to the weight of the items on it). Moreover, students often prefer their prior conceptions to the new conceptions offered in school, believing that their own knowledge is consistent with the "real world" even if it is not consistent with what must be learned in school (Dreyfus, Jungwirth, & Eliovitch, 1990). If new knowledge is to prove fruitful, it must prove more useful than the everyday knowledge that the student trusts because it is grounded in experience. di Sessa (2014) argued that the misconceptions of students reveal their underlying "naïve theories" about the universe and that these naïve theories reflect a novice's unstructured knowledge system where knowledge is stored in pieces rather than in a coherent whole. The challenge of fostering the conceptual change required to build scientifically accurate understandings in the context of entrenched inaccurate prior knowledge is formidable.

Some scientific misconceptions are very common, found among a wide range of students. Researchers have had some success overcoming commonly held misconceptions through explicit refutation (van Loon, Dunlosky, van Gog, van Merriënboer, & De Bruin, 2015; Vosniadou & Mason, 2012). For example, preparers of curriculum materials can utilize refutation text—text that contains an explicit refutation of the common misconception as the correct conception is presented. It is not enough, however, to discuss the misconception and correct conception in the same paragraph. Rather, explicit refutation wording such as "This belief, however, contradicts accepted scientific explanation" is required for students to overcome the misconception and learn the scientifically valid concept (Braasch, Goldman, & Wiley, 2013). The knowledge of teachers is critical as well. Students are more successful at overcoming their misconceptions if their teachers not only understand the correct scientific knowledge but are also aware of the common misconception. For example, middle school students whose teachers could identify the popular wrong answer (the common misconception) on multiple-choice questions learned more than students who had teachers who only knew the correct answers but could not identify the common misconception (Sadler, Sonnert, Coyle, Cook-Smith, & Miller, 2013). See the Applying Developmental Theory to Educational Contexts special feature (Box 3.2) for additional recommendations for reducing misconceptions and promoting understanding of science by inducing conceptual conflict.

Evaluation of Piaget's Theory

Does Piaget's stage theory adequately explain what we know today about growth in children's mental capacities? His contribution to our understanding of cognitive development is profound, but many research outcomes generated since the theory was proposed are inconsistent with various aspects of Piaget's theory (Feldman, 2013). For example, some intellectual advances described by Piaget, such as the ability to solve certain abstract logical problems, appear to *develop earlier* than Piaget had described. For instance, when asked to perform a conservation of number task with only three objects, preschoolers as young as age 3 can succeed (Gelman, 1972). Even 5-year-olds can display complex reasoning about relations, such as the correct use of analogies, in conversation with others (Jablansky, Alexander, Dumas, & Compton, 2016). Other acquisitions described by Piaget, such as the conservation of

---

Applying Developmental Theory to Educational Contexts

BOX 3.2. Addressing Scientific Misconceptions through Cognitive Conflict

Suggestions for how teachers can design instruction to address scientific misconceptions of their students include:

- Develop lectures, demonstrations, problems, and laboratory projects that produce cognitive conflict in students by pointing out inconsistencies between students' prior knowledge and to-be-acquired scientific conceptions.

- Model scientific thinking, making it clear to students that their beliefs should be consistent with evidence and that it is not appropriate to "explain away" or ignore evidence inconsistent with their beliefs.

- Act as Socratic tutors, confronting students when they attempt to assimilate scientific concepts to their misconceptions rather than accommodate their current thinking to the scientific idea.

- Encourage the presentation of content in multiple modalities (e.g., verbal, visual, mathematical) that clarify the relationships between the various representations. Fostering the use of different modalities will support the development of more integrated knowledge representations.

- Monitor students' thinking about new to-be-learned concepts using assessments, such as interviews or reflective journals, which can reveal prior misconceptions and encourage conceptual changes in students' thinking.

volume, appear to *develop later* than specified by the theory. And some people never do become as logically scientific, as Piaget contended (Kuhn, Amsel, & O'Loughlin, 1988). In addition, some behaviors reported by Piaget are not manifested in the manner he proposed. For example, Piaget's depiction of preschooler speech as extremely egocentric is not consistent with the many communicative competencies possessed by preschoolers. Preschoolers often do talk with one another and with adults in ways that suggest they do understand the other person's perspective.

Piaget's theory is also *limited in generalizability*. It does not take into account cultural differences, and it only describes the development of normally functioning children. In addition, it accounts for a fraction of lifespan development, rarely mentioning adult development. The highest stage Piaget described, formal operations, is attainable by adolescents. Yes, formal operational competencies can extend with additional experiences in new domains, but no real structural change occurs and no new operations are added during adulthood in Piaget's theory (Piaget, 1972).

Perhaps the most prominent Piagetian idea to be challenged by scientific evidence was the claim that acquisitions such as conservation *could not be taught* and that attempts to do so would invariably disrupt natural development. Researchers had little difficulty establishing conservation using conventional learning procedures such as the following (Brainerd, 1978a; Rosenthal & Zimmerman, 1978):

Simple correction: Give nonconservers repeated trials on conservation tasks, and tell them whether their answers are right or wrong. For example, after pouring liquid from a tall glass into a wide glass, provide positive feedback if a child gives the right answer. Provide negative feedback if a child does not.

Rule learning: Teach the child a rule. For example, when correcting a failure to conserve, tell the child, "I did not add or subtract anything."

Observational learning: Expose the child to a model who performs conservation perfectly. (You will learn more about observational learning in Chapter 5.)

Although Piaget's theory is not completely consistent with our current understanding of cognitive development, its influence on the study of children's thinking has been immense and many educators find the basic principles of Piagetian theory to be useful. In particular, the principle of cognitive conflict is prominent in current instructional models for science and math education.

Neo-Piagetian Perspectives on Development

The shortcomings of Piaget's stage theory led to rethinking the original Piagetian theory. Neo-Piagetian theories attempt to preserve the idea of stage-like movement in development but offer alternative explanations that are grounded in contemporary theory and research.

Case's Theory of Cognitive Development

Building upon work by Juan Pascual-Leone (1970), Robbie Case (1991, 1999) attempted to revise Piagetian theory in light of research establishing that children's ability to manipulate information in short-term memory increases greatly from birth to about age 16. As introduced in Chapter 2, **short-term memory,** often called working memory, is a memory store of limited capacity and duration (see Chapter 4 for a more complete description of short-term memory and working memory). Short-term memory is what we use when we try to hold a telephone number in our head just long enough to dial it. Case's emphasis on the development of short-term capacity to explain developmental changes in thinking abilities differs from Piaget who believed memory changes occurred *as a result of* developmental stage rather than being the *cause of* progress through the developmental stages (Piaget & Inhelder, 1973).

Like Piaget, Case argued that there are four distinct stages of cognitive development, which occur in an invariant sequence. The sequencing is invariant since each stage reflects differentiation, coordination, and consolidation of schemes present in the immediately previous stage. Smaller schemes that were once separate combine to form larger, more powerful schemes. These larger schemes are increasingly coordinated with one another. More powerful schemes that are coordinated with each other permit more advanced performance.

For example, a 4-year-old can draw a human figure that has many of the global features of human beings. A slightly older child can draw a more differentiated figure and do so in relation to a larger scene. Case's explanation is that the drawings of the older child represent a differentiation not present in the younger children, with the parts of a drawing separated into figure (the human) and ground (the larger scene). The 6-year-old's systems for drawing figures and for drawing the larger scene also represent integrations of skills that are not integrated for 4-year-olds. The 6-year-old coordinates these two systems in order to produce the more complete pictures, a complex coordination not likely in 4-year-olds.

How and why does drawing ability improve according to Case's theory? Part of the explanation is *practice*. Only schemes that are highly practiced can be differentiated into new schemes and then integrated with other schemes. Thus, a great deal of practice in drawing global figures is required before there is differentiation of drawing schemes. This practice must occur until the child can automatically perform the behaviors that once took considerable effort and attention.

Although a 4-year-old might have to expend all available working memory capacity (i.e., consciousness) to draw a stick figure, a slightly older child who has drawn many such stick figures can do so automatically. Thus, less working memory is consumed during drawing of global human figures. This frees up some mental capacity for attention to other things, including acquisition of new understandings of how figure and ground can be separated. That is, with increasing automaticity in execution of skills, a child has more functional short-term memory capacity. In general, when more functional short-term memory capacity is available, the quality of thinking is higher.

According to Case's perspective, multiple factors account for developmental increases in short-term memory or working memory capacity.

1. As described in the earlier example of children's drawing, *practicing a procedure makes it more automatic*, with available capacity then used more efficiently, allowing more processes to be coordinated simultaneously and integrated in consciousness.

2. With development, children improve in their ability to *shift their attention rapidly*, getting better at moving between different sources of information and

focusing attention on task-relevant information and ignoring task-irrelevant information.

3. In addition, as *long-term memory develops* and is better organized, information chunks are larger. Preschoolers "chunk" verbal material into single letters; teenagers use whole words and phrases.

In addition to increases in functional short-term capacity due to increases in automaticity, ability to shift attention, and extent and organization of knowledge, the *actual working memory probably increases as a function of neurological maturation.* Because both functional increases and maturational increases in short-term capacity are indexed by age, it is very difficult to determine how much of the increase in apparent short-term abilities is due to functional increases in capacity and how much is due to biological increases. (You will learn more about the development of working memory, long-term memory, and attentional capacity in Chapter 4.)

What suggestions did Case have for developing instruction that is appropriate to the developmental level of the child? In broad terms, Case (1991) argued for beginning instruction with a task the child can understand and perform. The teacher should give feedback about how well the child is performing the task and encourage the child to practice until the task becomes more automatic. Gradually, the teacher increases task demands, taking care to make certain that the more demanding versions of the task do not exceed the child's capacity. Guidance is provided as the child attempts the task, with this guidance and support faded as the child is able to execute the new task independently. The amount of working memory required to execute this new task decreases with practice, as its execution becomes more automatic. Case and his colleagues have investigated such an instructional approach with respect to a variety of tasks, including learning of mathematics and everyday quantitative skills, such as telling time and working with money (see Case, 1991).

Thus, in Case's approach, Piaget's notion of stage development is translated into neo-Piagetian terms. Rather than explaining the superiority of the 8-year-old in relation to the 4-year-old on conservation as a function of acquiring concrete operations, neo-Piagetians explain it as reflecting development of capacity. For example, the 8-year-old is seen as having the capacity to meet the demands of conservation tasks (i.e., paying attention to several dimensions, such as the height and width of a column of liquid, and keeping track of how they co-vary) and 4-year-olds as lacking the required capacity (Chapman & Lindenberger, 1989).

Fischer's Theories of Cognitive Development

Another neo-Piagetian, Kurt Fischer (1980; Bidell & Fischer, 2000; Mascolo, Li, Fink, & Fischer, 2002; Mascolo & Fischer, 2010) recognized that children accomplish many tasks using a variety of skills. For example, preschoolers can solve simple addition problems by using various counting strategies—from counting on fingers to counting quietly to themselves. Particularly important, the skills a child has depends largely on the child's experience in a domain of competence, such as arithmetic. Moreover, different skills are used in different domains. It is hard to imagine an early reading skill that is analogous to counting, just as it is hard to imagine an early arithmetic skill that is analogous to sounding out words. It is difficult to explain such skills in terms of stages of development.

Skills are learned in context, with the specific skills children acquire largely determined by the contexts they experience. For example, children can learn counting strategies as they play house, such as when they count out four of everything to set four places at a table. At first, this skill is very much tied to context, so that the same child might have difficulty doing an abstract task that requires counting by fours. For example, when given 20 checkers, four each of five different colors, the child might not be able to construct four sets with one checker of each color. With increasing experience, however, particular skills are generalized beyond the original contexts in which they are learned and integrated with related skills (Bidell & Fischer, 1992, 2000).

Yet, according to Fischer, a biologically mediated stage-like progression occurs as well. Recall the discussion of Fischer's thinking in Chapter 2. Development depends on brain development, with a series of brain growth spurts that are associated with, and may cause, cognitive and behavioral changes (Fischer & van Geert, 2014). Like Piaget, Fischer believes that development is discontinuous. (Review Table 2.1 if you do not recall these points.) Like Piaget, Fischer views stage-like growth in competence as something that is the stuff of youth—with the last growth spurt occurring at about age 25. The stage-like changes have profound implications for functioning, so that cognitive, behavioral, and emotional shifts occur in parallel.

Moral Judgment: An Approach in the Tradition of Piaget

As a society, we want young people to emerge from school ready to make social, moral, and ethical decisions responsibly and to be prepared to become productive citizens (Wentzel, 2013). A great deal of the most credible theory-driven research on social problem solving was generated in reaction to Lawrence Kohlberg's analyses of moral judgment. In developing his ideas, Kohlberg was profoundly influenced by Piaget's work, including his perspective on moral judgment.

Piaget's Theory of the Development of Moral Reasoning

Jean Piaget's (1965) theory of the development of moral judgment was informed by his observations of children playing games, especially marbles. His observations of children playing games by the rules, children in conflict over rules, children changing rules, and children cheating helped him formulate hypotheses about children's moral understandings. He then tested these hypotheses by asking children to reason about social dilemmas that he presented to them as short stories. For example, one dilemma he posed to children was whether a child who *accidentally* broke 15 cups was naughtier than a child who *intentionally* broke one cup. Piaget proposed two stages of moral development, one reflecting the conceptions about rules held by preschoolers and children in the early primary years (*stage of heteronomous morality*) and the other stage reflecting the thinking of older children (*stage of autonomous morality*).

Children in the stage of heteronomous morality focus on the objective consequences of an action and thus conclude that the child who broke 15 cups is naughtier since that child destroyed more cups. In contrast, children in the stage of autonomous morality make decisions on the basis of the intentions of the actors, therefore concluding that breaking one cup intentionally is much worse than accidentally destroying many more cups. The heteronomous moral child views rules as sacred, as if they were written by the hand of God, never to be reconsidered. In contrast, the autonomously moral child recognizes that the rules have been agreed upon by the players, that they are inventions of people, and that they can be changed if people will it. For example, children who play games such as Monopoly at home may learn that when they play the game at someone else's house other families have different Monopoly conventions, such as the source of the money placed in Free Parking, what deals property owners can make, or even whether or not properties are dealt out at the beginning to make the game shorter. A heteronomously moral child would view such alterations of the official Monopoly rules as almost a sacrilege.

Like all Piagetian stages, this one has an invariant order of development, meaning that a child must manifest heteronomous morality before autonomous morality. As is the case for all of cognitive development according to the Piagetian perspective, equilibration (cognitive conflict) is the main mechanism of cognitive change, facilitating movement from heteronomous to autonomous morality. Children develop an understanding of rules through interactions with peers in the social context, such as playing games (Carpendale, 2009). Game playing with peers can lead to arguments about the rules of the game, perhaps stimulating cognitive conflict about the nature of rules. Such conflicts can be real mind stretchers, moving the child from viewing rules as God-given and inalterable to seeing them as agreements that children can change by a show of hands or a chorus of protesting voices. Piaget's perspective that cognitive conflict was important in the growth of moral thinking would be preserved in Kohlberg's theory, which elaborated and expanded the two stages of moral thinking proposed by Piaget.

Kohlberg's Stage Theory of Moral Reasoning

Kohlberg (1969, 1981, 1984) described the development of moral reasoning as a progression through an invariant sequence of six stages. He developed the stages based on a research tactic similar to that of Piaget. Kohlberg presented moral dilemmas in the form of stories to adolescent boys. One of these dilemmas involved a character named Heinz:

> In Europe, a woman was near death from a special kind of cancer. There was one drug that the doctors thought might save her. It was a form of radium that the druggist in the same town had recently discovered. The drug was expensive to make. He paid $400 for the radium and charged $4000 for a small dose of the drug. The sick woman's husband, Heinz, went to everyone he knew to borrow the money and tried every legal means, but he could only get together about $2000, which is half of what it cost. He told the druggist that his wife was dying, and asked him to sell it cheaper or let him pay later. But the druggist said, "No, I discovered the drug and I'm going to make money from it." So having tried every legal means, Heinz gets desperate and considers breaking into the man's store to steal the drug for his wife. (Kohlberg, 1984, p. 640)

The boys were asked to respond to questions, such as the following, about the moral dilemmas posed by the story:

1. Should Heinz steal the drug? Why or why not?
2. Is it actually right or wrong for him to steal the drug? Why is it right or wrong?

3. Does Heinz have a duty or obligation to steal the drug? Why or why not?

4. If Heinz doesn't love his wife, should he steal the drug for her? (If the boy favors not stealing the drug:) Does it make a difference in what Heinz should do whether or not he loves his wife? Why or why not?

5. Suppose the person dying is not his wife but a stranger. Should Heinz steal the drug for the stranger? Why or why not?

6. (If the boy favors stealing the drug for the stranger:) Suppose it's a pet animal that he loves. Should Heinz steal to save the pet animal? Why or why not?

7. Is it important for people to do everything they can to save another's life? Why or why not?

8. It is against the law for Heinz to steal. Does that make it morally wrong? Why or why not?

9. In general, should people do everything that they can to obey the law? Why or why not? How does this apply to what Heinz should do?

10. In thinking back over the dilemma, what would you say is the most responsible thing for Heinz to do? Why? (Kohlberg, 1984, pp. 640–641)

What mattered in the interview was not whether the boys felt Heinz should steal the drug but the *reasons* they gave for Heinz's actions. These reasons varied from stage to stage (all quotes from Kohlberg, 1984, pp. 49–53, based on Rest, 1968).

The stages of **preconventional morality,** Stages 1 and 2, focus on self-interest in decision making. The reasons given in Stage 1 centered on obedience and avoiding punishment. Staying out of trouble is the concern that is more important than all others for the Stage-1 thinker, exemplified by this rationale in favor of stealing the drug: "If you let your wife die, you will get in trouble. You'll be blamed for not spending the money to save her, and there'll be an investigation of you and the druggist for your wife's death." Of course, a case also can be made that the best way to stay out of trouble is not to steal the drug: "You shouldn't steal the drug because you'll be caught and sent to jail if you do. If you do get away, your conscience would bother you thinking how the police would catch up with you at any minute." The Stage-1 thinker is only worried about protecting him- or herself—avoiding punishment.

The Stage-2 thinker has made only a slight advance: he or she is concerned only about his or her own pleasures. What is right is what brings pleasure to the self. Self-interest comes through clearly in this Stage-2 justification for stealing the drug: "If you do happen to get caught, you could give the drug back and wouldn't get much of a sentence. It wouldn't bother you much to serve a little jail term, if you have your wife when you get out." Self-interest can be used to justify not stealing as well: "He may not get much of a jail term if he steals the drug, but his wife will probably die before he gets out, so it wouldn't do him much good. If his wife dies, he shouldn't blame himself; it isn't his fault she has cancer." By now it should be obvious why Stage-1 and Stage-2 thinking is considered preconventional. An adult offering such justifications would be viewed with dismay by other adults, who long ago rejected such narrow self-interest in decision making.

The stages of **conventional morality,** Stages 3 and 4, focus on maintaining the social order. The Stage-3 thinker is sometimes thought of as displaying "good boy–good girl" thinking, which is concerned with helping and pleasing others. This is conformist thinking in the sense of wanting to go along with the majority. Consider this example in favor of stealing the drug: "No one will think you're bad if you steal the drug, but your family will think you are an inhuman husband if you don't. If you let your wife die, you'll never be able to look anyone in the face again." The concern for the opinion of others comes through in this justification for not stealing the drug as well: "It isn't just the druggist who will think you're a criminal, everyone else will, too. After you steal it, you'll feel bad thinking how you've brought dishonor on your family and yourself; you won't be able to face anyone again."

Whereas the Stage-3 conventional thinker is concerned with the subjective perceptions of others, the Stage-4 thinker is concerned with being in synchrony with the established standards of his or her society. Those in Stage 4 have a deep respect for law and order. The Stage-4 person is concerned with doing his or her duty to country, God, spouse, or whatever else commands allegiance by societal standards. This rationalization in favor of stealing the drug is based on the perception of duty to family members that is expected by society: "If you have any sense of honor, you won't let your wife die because you're afraid to do the only thing that will save her. You'll always feel guilty that you caused her death if you don't do your duty to her." Consistency with the laws of society comes through in this opposition to stealing the drug offered by another Stage-4 thinker: "You're desperate and you may not know you're doing wrong when you steal the drug. But you'll know you did wrong after you're punished and sent to jail. You'll always feel guilty for your dishonesty and lawbreaking."

The highest stages of moral reasoning in Kohlberg's theory, the stages of **postconventional morality,** Stages 5 and 6, are characterized by shared or potentially sharable principles and standards. The Stage-5 thinker views rules and laws in terms of a contract, which is intended to protect the will and rights of others. Those entering into a contract obey rules as part of a social understanding, rather than because of fear of retribution, respect for authority, or sense of duty. If the social purpose for the rules cannot be fulfilled by obeying them, it is all right to dispense with the rules, as reflected in this opinion that favors Heinz stealing the drug: "The law wasn't set up for these circumstances. Taking the drug in this situation isn't really right, but it's justified to do it." The social contract orientation also comes through in this Stage-5 advisement against stealing the drug: "You can't have everyone stealing when they get desperate. The end may be good, but the ends don't justify the means."

Kohlberg contended that progress through the stages is invariant in that to get to Stage 4, one must go through Stages 1, 2, and 3. Achieving Stage 4, however, in no way guarantees achievement of Stages 5 or 6 (nor does achieving Stage 2 assure further progress to Stage 3). A summary view of Kohlberg's six stages of moral reasoning is presented in Table 3.3.

TABLE 3.3. Summary of Kohlberg's Stages of Moral Reasoning

Preconventional morality: focus on self-interest

Stage 1	Focus on obedience and avoiding punishment
Stage 2	Focus on obtaining rewards or pleasure

Conventional morality: focus on maintaining social order

Stage 3	Focus on being a good boy or a good girl
Stage 4	Focus on law and order

Postconventional morality: focus on shared standards and principles

Stage 5	Focus on social contract
Stage 6	Focus on principle

Evaluation of Kohlberg's Theory

Although Kohlberg, like Piaget, proposed a strong stage theory where progress through the stages was orderly and invariant, within-person variability in responding to the Kohlbergian dilemmas was common. Classifying a person into a stage was not clear-cut, and Kohlberg's scoring scheme was revised many times (Dawson, 2002). The content of the dilemmas appeared to influence a person's reasoning, and a given person might offer Stages 3, 4, and 5 responses across the different dilemmas, with stage mixture even for the same dilemma not uncommon (Wark & Krebs, 1996). Moreover, although ample evidence was found for moral reasoning at the preconventional and conventional levels, postconventional reasoning was relatively rare (for a review, see Gibbs, Bassinger, Grime, & Snarey, 2007).

Some critics of Kohlberg's theory, however, were mainly concerned about the emphasis on rationally determined justice as the highest of moral ideals. This focus was perceived to be narrow, reflecting both a masculine bias and a bias toward Western philosophies. For example, Carol Gilligan (1982) argued that females were much more likely than males to consider issues of interpersonal caring and person-to-person connections as they reasoned about moral dilemmas. The differences between reasoning based on *caring versus justice* can be appreciated by examining some responses to the Heinz dilemma presented earlier. Female responses are more likely than male responses to include arguments such as " . . . I think he [the druggist] had the moral obligation to show compassion in this case . . ." (p. 54), " . . . if she [Heinz's wife] dies, it hurts a lot of people and it hurts her . . ." (p. 28), " . . . you have to love someone else, because you are inseparable from them . . . that other person is part of that giant collection of everybody" (p. 57), and "Who is going to be hurt more, the druggist who loses some money or the person who loses her life?" (p. 95). Gilligan contended that analyses of moral judgment using Kohlberg's framework missed the rich diversity of thinking about moral issues. Subsequent research following up on Gilligan's 1992 book indicated that the sex differences described by Gilligan were not large and that both males and females value justice and interpersonal care (see Walker, 2006, for a review). In a meta-analysis of more than 100 studies, Jaffee and Hyde (2000) reported only small differences in the care orientation favoring females and in the justice orientation favoring males. Nonetheless, as a result of the questions raised by Gilligan and the extensive research it inspired, conceptions of morality have broadened to include care, compassion, and concern about the welfare of others (Killen & Smetana, 2015).

The universality of Kohlberg's stages of moral reasoning has also been challenged, particularly for the highest level of postconventional reasoning (Stages 5 and 6). In his review of cross-cultural research (45 studies conducted in 27 countries), Snarey (1985) found evidence for the universality of Stages 1, 2, 3, and 4 but not for postconventional reasoning (Stages 5 and 6). He also reported a bias in favor of middle-class samples living in complex urban societies. Kohlberg's own cross-cultural research revealed little evidence of postconventional reasoning in non-Western villagers. Kohlberg reasoned that village life did not afford the opportunity for the social-perspective taking required to develop postconventional moral reasoning. More recently, Gibbs et al. (2007) analyzed the presence of Kohlberg's stages in data from 75 cross-cultural studies conducted in 23 different countries using different measures, Kohlberg's original dilemmas, and alternative measures developed in the decades since Kohlberg's original work. As in the earlier review, the moral development stage trend was observed at the lower levels, with cultural specificity in moral reasoning found at the higher levels. Gibb et al. (2007) also reported common values (e.g., contract and truth, life and affiliation, property and law) and the relevance of social-perspective taking across the cultural groups. New avenues of research have moved away from assessing the universality of Kohlberg's stages to studying the underlying culture-specific mechanisms, such as customs and belief systems, that influence moral development within specific cultures and racial-ethnic groups (Lapsley & Carlo, 2014).

Other researchers have moved away from the stage theories of Piaget and Kohlberg in favor of *social domain theory* where morality is viewed as one of three domains of social knowledge (see Killen & Smetana, 2015; Turiel, 2015, for reviews). The three domains are *moral* (e.g., issues of fairness, justice, welfare of others), *societal* (e.g., concerns about social conventions, group norms, customs), and *psychological* (e.g., focus on identity, goals, autonomy). According to social domain theory, orientations in all three domains coexist in children and their relative influence in a given situation varies. Killen and Smetana (2015) suggest that the roots of morality can be found in early childhood in the development of awareness of others' welfare, understanding of fairness, and willingness to be cooperative and helpful.

Another approach to studying moral development examines the relationship between moral development and the development of theory of mind. **Theory of mind** refers to knowledge and reasoning about mental states, our own thoughts, feelings, wishes, beliefs, and the ability to attribute mental states to others, with the awareness that the perspectives of others may be different from our own (see also Chapter 10). We can use such understandings to explain and predict the actions of others. Theory-of-mind researchers study the developmental shift from perceiving mental states as copies of reality to something that is more actively constructed internally. For example, researchers studying the development of theory of mind in children are interested in the acquisition of insights such as recognizing that someone can have a "false belief"—a belief that is wrong and doesn't match reality—and coming to the realization that perception is distinct from reality. Children who successfully perform theory-of-mind tasks have developed an understanding that people represent the world in their minds and an awareness that people may have varying perspectives and that they use those different perspectives to interpret experiences (Wellman, 2014).

Wellman and Liu (2004) described a progression in the development of theory of mind in preschoolers. Children become aware that two people can have different levels of desire for the same object before they understand that two people can have different beliefs about the same object. Thus, understanding of the mental state of desire occurs before understanding of beliefs. Children also can perceive that they and another person can have differing beliefs about the same situation before they understand that another person can have a false belief about a situation. Thus, understanding that people have varying beliefs occurs before understanding that some people can have false beliefs.

Theory-of-mind understandings is related to the development of moral reasoning. Killen, Mulvey, Richardson, Jampol, and Woodward (2011) studied the relationship between theory of mind, specifically the concept of "false belief," and the attributions children make about the intentions of moral transgressors. Children in three age groups (3- to 4-year-olds, 5- to 6-year-olds, and 7- to 8-year-olds) were asked to respond to vignettes about an accidental transgressor (a child helping to clean up the classroom who throws out a paper bag not realizing that it contains a special cupcake belonging to another child) and an intentional moral transgression (a child who pushes another child off a swing). Participants were asked a series of questions about the vignettes, including whether the protagonists in the vignettes thought they were doing "something that was all right or not at all right." The children participating in the study were also presented with a false belief theory-of-mind vignette. In the vignette, a child who was playing with markers before recess goes out for recess, and the teacher puts the markers in the cabinet. The participants were asked where the returning child will look for the markers. The children who did not pass the false belief theory-of-mind task were more likely to attribute negative intentions and levy blame on the accidental transgressor (failing to understand the false belief of the classroom helper that the paper bag was empty) and to support punishment of the accidental transgressor. Longitudinal studies have traced the relationship of the development of theory of mind to the development of moral reasoning in preschoolers from infancy to age 5 (Smetana, Jambon, Conry-Murray, & Sturge-Apple, 2012; Sodian et al., 2016).

In their analysis of the current state of moral development research, Lapsley and Carlo (2014) portray the field as being at the crossroads, with the focus of research shifting to the study of topics such as perspective taking, moral emotions such as empathy, guilt, and shame, and the neurobiology related to those emotions. Acknowledging the diversity of interests found in current moral development researchers, Lapsley and Carlo also point to the presence of a "broad interest" in moral and character education (see also Roseth, 2016), a topic taken up in the next section.

See the Considering Important Questions special feature (Box 3.3) for a summary of research on the development of forgiveness, a research program originally inspired by Kohlberg's theory of moral development.

Education and the Development of Moral Judgment

Can students learn to be more sophisticated in their moral reasoning? Can moral education be successful? Kohlberg proposed a model of moral education, sometimes referred to as the **plus-one approach,** where students regularly discuss and reason among themselves about moral dilemmas, including those occurring within everyday school life. The plus-one approach potentially exposes each student to reasoning from one stage beyond his or her current stage of reasoning. That is, each student in the discussion except the most advanced student would have a model who was slightly beyond his or her current functioning; the most advanced student would presumably have the teacher as a model of a higher level of moral sophistication. Kohlberg believed that a plus one-stage discrepancy would be likely to induce cognitive conflict, which in turn would motivate reflection on the new information, reflection that could result in an understanding of the slightly more advanced position. Enright, Lapsley, and Levy (1983) summarized research on moral education that accumulated from the 1960s to the early 1980s and concluded that the plus-one approach to moral education worked well for older students (junior high and high school): The positive effects of plus-one moral reasoning discussions were observed with both short interventions (a single session) and long ones (full semester courses).

The plus-one approach, however, proved to be difficult to implement widely in schools. The types of discussions required demand much of students and teachers.

Considering Important Questions

BOX 3.3. How Does Forgiveness Develop?

Robert Enright and his colleagues (1994, 2001; Ling, Enright, & Klatt, 2011) studied the development of forgiveness by asking students in grades 4, 7, and 10, college students, and adults to respond to modified versions of the types of moral dilemmas used by Kohlberg. The modification involved changing the story so that the lead character was hurt emotionally by the end of the story. For example, in the Heinz story, Heinz was unable to steal the drug from the greedy druggist and his wife died. The students were asked about whether Heinz should forgive the druggist as well as about forgiveness in relation to retaliation, restitution, social pressures, and social harmony. They were also asked about unconditional forgiveness—forgiveness that occurs without getting something in exchange and without external social pressure.

Enright and his colleagues described a developmental progression moving from conditional to unconditional forgiveness, a progression from granting forgiveness in exchange for something to forgiving in response to social pressure to unconditional forgiveness. The participants' answers were classified into six stages (Enright & Human Development Study Group, 1994, Table 1):

- Stage 1: *Revengeful forgiveness.* "I can forgive someone who wrongs me only if I can punish him or her to a similar degree to my own pain."

- Stage 2: *Conditional or restitutional forgiveness.* "If I get back what was taken away from me, I can forgive." Or, "If I feel guilty about withholding forgiveness, I can forgive to relieve my guilt."

- Stage 3: *Expectational forgiveness.* "I can forgive if others pressure me to forgive; I forgive because other people expect it."

- Stage 4: *Lawful expectational forgiveness.* "I forgive because my religion (or other institution) demands it."

- Stage 5: *Forgiveness as social harmony.* "I forgive because it restores harmony or social relations in society." Forgiveness decreases friction and outright conflict in society; it is a way of maintaining peaceful relations.

- Stage 6: *Forgiveness as love.* "I forgive because it promotes a true sense of love. Because I must truly care for each person, a hurtful act on his or her part does not alter that sense of love." The possibility of reconciliation is open, and forgiveness no longer depends on a social context, as at Stage 5.

Enright found a strong relationship between stage level and age, with older participants reasoning about forgiveness at a higher level than younger participants. A modest relationship existed between the level of reasoning about forgiveness and the individual's moral reasoning in general, suggesting some overlap between the two types of reasoning but considerable independence as well.

Participants must be capable of all of the following: open and attentive listening to another's ideas, willing acceptance of corrections by peers, revisions of views in light of ideas from others, development of ideas without fear of rebuff or humiliation from peers, detection of underlying assumptions, ability to ask relevant questions, sensitivity to context when discussing moral conduct, and impartial discussion of issues. Perhaps the complexity of plus-one exchanges explains why moral discussions were not very successful with elementary school students (Enright et al., 1983).

Lapsley and Yeager (2013) argued that although educational interventions based on Kohlberg's theory are not prevalent today, the main features can be found in the identified characteristics of effective schools. These include engaging in class meetings, allowing students to have a voice and giving students choice, encouraging discussions about moral and ethical issues, and promoting the development of connection to schools and teachers. Lapsley and Yeager further maintained that there is no such thing as a values-free education. Schools reflect community values in a variety of ways, including the choice of topics studied, classroom routines and procedures, techniques used in classroom management, the ways student groups are formed, and guidelines for classroom participation. Educators and school systems routinely express goals to produce students of character, who display empathy, self-discipline, and prosocial skills. What moral or character education does is to make the transmission of values that occurs in schools more explicit.

In his review of moral and character education, Berkowitz (2012) summarized research and described effective programs and instructional practices. His list of "what works" included the following: service to others (community service and service learning); moral dilemma discussion; role modeling and mentoring (adults in the community, older peers); fostering of nurturance, trust and high expectations; and implementation of a schoolwide focus on character or moral education. Specific methods to promote moral and character education in the classroom are summarized in the Applying Developmental Theory to Educational Contexts special feature (see Box 3.4).

Constructivist Approaches to Education

Kohlberg and Mayer (1972) proposed a way of thinking about three alternative methods of education. The first, *romanticism*, is based on the belief that the child is naturally good. Education should mostly leave the child alone, allowing natural development to unfold. A permissive educational environment will permit the good in the child to come out and the bad in the child to come under control. Freedom is the prevailing theme in romantic educational settings. Summerhill School, which uses an experimental approach to education based on the ideas of Freud (see Chapter 5), is consistent with the romantic approach.

The second approach, *cultural transmission*, involves direct instruction of the knowledge and values of the culture. If you are in a class in which the professor lectures and you take notes, you are experiencing the cultural transmission model. A significant portion of conventional education in the United States is based on cultural transmission.

The third approach, *progressivism*, originated with the educational philosopher John Dewey (1933). According to this model, education at its best fosters natural

BOX 3.4. Stimulating Socially Responsible Thinking and Behavior

Thomas Lickona (1991) compiled a comprehensive and influential sourcebook on techniques for moral education, articulating a variety of approaches designed to influence moral behavior as well as moral reasoning. Many of Lickona's ideas were also identified by Berkowitz (2012) in his list of "what works" in moral and character education. Lickona's specific recommendations for the classroom include the following:

√ • *Teacher modeling of moral behavior and reasoning.* Teachers who model moral behavior and reasoning are more likely to have students who act in moral ways and can reason in a sophisticated fashion about moral issues.

 • *Guest speakers as additional models.* Teachers should expose students to real ethical models whenever possible. For example, the teacher could invite to class a whistle-blower who exposed wrongdoing at some personal cost.

 • *Use of storytelling and literature.* Students can learn through discussion about the moral dilemmas faced by symbolic models, such as characters found in television, movies, or books.

√ • *Discussion of controversial issues that concern society.* Students can learn that controversial issues are many-sided and complex by discussing them in class.

 • *Use of the curriculum to encourage moral growth.* Teachers should take advantage of any opportunity to teach responsibility. For example, the class's pet rabbit or hamster can be used in many ways for lessons in caring and responsibility. Ethics can be an important theme in the school day.

 • *Direct teaching.* Direct explanations are often effective in changing student behavior. Teachers can make a substantial difference by communicating clearly that values matter.

 • *Asking students to be more ethical in their conduct; explaining why.* Receiving explanations about why antisocial behavior is unacceptable compared to prosocial behavior increases socially acceptable behavior.

 • *Fostering of cooperative learning and cooperation in general.* The ethical and mental health components in a cooperative environment are better than those in a competitive environment.

 • *High expectations.* Teachers can send the message that there are high expectations about the moral, ethical, and civic development of students in the school . . . and then they should actually expect high moral, ethical, and civic responsibility.

√ • *Mentoring and individual guidance.* Development of nurturing and trusting relationships between teachers and students can have a tremendous influence on moral and ethical development.

One movement in moral education, *values clarification*, encourages teachers not to make value judgments about student stances on ethical issues. Lickona rejected this thinking, believing there are some clearly moral and immoral stances that are not controversial at all. He believed teachers should challenge students when they voice ethical positions that are contrary to stances that are acceptable in society—or when they engage in behavior that would be considered unethical by a moral person.

interaction between the child and both the physical and the social environments. Both Piagetian and Kohlbergian approaches to education are progressive. These natural interactions permit the child to construct understandings of the world, with such *constructivist* activities resulting in much more complete understanding than would come from cultural transmission of the same ideas.

According to constructivist theory, a child who constructs an understanding of conservation by playing around with beakers of water will understand conservation better than if the same child were taught the verbal rule, "It is the same amount of water unless water is added or subtracted." But recall the evidence described earlier that conservation can be acquired following instruction.

What might be going on when a child learns to conserve by learning a verbal rule? Perhaps the child does not fully understand the rule when it is expounded, but the rule permits the child to construct relatively quickly an understanding of what is happening as the water is being poured—much more quickly than if the child had to discover the rule through repeated pouring. What might be going on when a child learns conservation by observing a conserving child make judgments about water poured between beakers? Perhaps the child experiences some cognitive conflict between what he or she thought was going on and the conserving child's declarations that the amount of water is the same regardless of which beaker it is in. Observing the conserver exposed the nonconserver to a possibility not hitherto considered, producing some disequilibrium and motivating reflection on the situation and eventual reestablishment of equilibrium. Thus, the possibility exists that knowledge construction can be stimulated by verbal explanations and observational learning opportunities.

Alternative Approaches to Constructivism

There is more than one type of constructivism, although constructivist approaches to classroom practice typically involve social engagement on authentic and meaningful tasks in a supportive context (O'Donnell, 2012). These approaches vary mainly in terms of the amount of instructional support provided by teachers. Some educators describe themselves as "radical constructivists," giving extreme emphasis to the benefits of student discovery relative to learning from instruction. Moshman (1982) refers to this type of constructivism as *endogenous constructivism*–knowledge construction through child-determined exploration much as Piaget had originally depicted constructivism. The endogenous constructivist educator endeavors to provide the child with tasks that are just a bit beyond the child's current competence. Moreover, the endogenous educator encourages students to use what they already know to solve the new problems.

In contrast is *dialectical constructivism*. The dialectical constructivist recognizes the inefficiencies of discovery. The dialectical constructivist educator provides hints and prompts to students as they struggle with problems. That is, he or she provides just enough support so that the child can make progress. The dialectical constructivist educator does not provide full-blown explanations or model particular strategies for problem solving, but rather reminds students about how they might apply what they already know to new problems. Like the endogenous constructivist, the dialectical constructivist educator believes that long-term internalization of problem-solving strategies and mathematical concepts is most likely if students spend time figuring out how and when to apply the mathematical ideas they know. The difference between the two is that the dialectical constructivist is more willing to provide help.

Even more help is provided by *exogenous constructivists*, who believe much more in teaching than do either endogenous or dialectical constructivists. The exogenous constructivist educator provides explanations and models problem solving for students in an effort to give the student a good start on problem solving. The exogenous constructivist educator knows that children do not learn how to problem-solve from teacher presentations. However, if they have watched a presentation carefully, they are in a better position to begin applying the methods explained and modeled, and as they struggle to apply these methods to problems, they construct understanding of the procedures and how to adapt them. The differences in the role of the teacher in these alternative constructivist approaches are summarized in Table 3.4.

Constructivism and Mathematics Education

For decades, mathematics educators have especially embraced constructivist education, emphasizing natural engagement with tasks and the social world (Confrey & Kazak, 2006; Kilpatrick, Martin, & Schifter, 2003). Learning mathematics is constructivist when learners are active and proactive during problem solving—not simply responding to directions given by someone else but doing their own analysis and providing their own interpretations. Knowledge is constructed from experience. Although construction of knowledge can occur when one individual experiments with objects in the world, knowledge construction often involves several people in interaction, bouncing ideas off one another and trying out possibilities together.

Mathematics educators have been conducting evaluations of the effectiveness of constructivist approaches for decades. In a classic study, Paul Cobb and his colleagues (Cobb et al., 1991) compared performance in 10 second-grade classrooms that received problem-centered mathematics instruction consistent with constructivist principles and 8 classrooms that received conventional instruction. Children in the constructivist classrooms solved challenging problems continuously. The students were encouraged to reflect on their problem-solving activities and to construct knowledge about how to solve problems. The problem solving generally took place in interactive, cooperative classroom groups. In these groups, the role of the teacher was to provide support and gentle guidance in the direction of productive problem solving, rather than to provide solutions or explicit instruction about how to solve problems. The experimental curriculum focused on the development of strategies to

TABLE 3.4. Summary of the Role of the Teacher in Alternative Constructivist Approaches

Endogenous constructivism
    Teacher provides challenging tasks and encourages students.

Dialectical constructivism
    Teacher provides hints and prompts.
    Teacher reminds students of what they already know.

Exogenous constructivism
    Teacher provides explanations.
    Teacher models problem solving.

solve addition and subtraction problems. Students were encouraged to believe that success in mathematics was possible through individual and collective efforts.

Did the constructivist approach make a difference in academic performance? It did on state-administered assessments of mathematics achievement as well as on a test of mathematics achievement created by the researchers. Differences favoring the experimental students were especially notable on items requiring application of the concepts covered in the curriculum. Moreover, the students in the experimental classes reported that they valued collaboration more than did control students. In general, constructivist mathematics approaches do seem to promote better understanding of mathematics.

The National Council of Teachers of Mathematics, the primary professional organization for mathematics educators, was so impressed with evidence of the effectiveness of the constructivist approach that they recommended complete revision of the mathematics curriculum to be more consistent with the constructivist model. These *Principles and Standards for School Mathematics* (National Council of Teachers of Mathematics, 2000) have had a great impact on mathematics education reform across the United States. If you were to ask mathematics educators today what good mathematics instruction does, they would tell you that it promotes understanding of mathematical concepts and procedures by encouraging students to construct those understandings. Such understanding is essential if mathematics is to be used broadly and flexibly. These views of mathematical understanding have led to certain assumptions about the teaching of mathematics that are outlined in the Applying Developmental Theory to Educational Contexts special feature (Box 3.5).

Caveats for Constructivist Approaches to Classroom Instruction

Mathematics educators are not the only proponents of constructivist approaches to teaching. Many science educators advocate for constructivist approaches, emphasizing the ultimate goal of teaching students to use the scientific process, to learn how to think like scientists. Some researchers (e.g., Kirschner, 2009; Sweller, 2009), however, have pointed out key differences between scientists and science students. On the one hand, scientists possess coherent, integrated science knowledge and are searching for new knowledge or for new applications of advanced knowledge. Students, on the other hand, are learning basic content in a scientific domain and are unlikely to have the extensive conceptual framework required to "discover" new information. Moreover, think back to the discussion of scientific misconceptions earlier in this chapter. Skilled teachers using constructivist approaches in science classrooms must be alert to the presence of misconceptions so that more inaccuracies are not added to the erroneous knowledge base a student might possess.

Other educators and researchers have pointed out that constructivist approaches to teaching are not equally suited to all learning situations (see Tobias & Duffy, 2009). Consideration must be given to various factors such as the instructional time available, the skills of the teacher, the ultimate goals of instruction, and the domain of learning. Some educators find constructivist approaches to be less effective than more direct instruction, in which students are provided with essential information, full explanations, and refutation of common misconceptions. These educators wonder why teachers would withhold available information from learners and ask them to discover it for themselves (Sweller, 2009). Others point out that decidedly nonconstructivist methods have proven to be very effective. For example, students who are

BOX 3.5. Assumptions about Teaching Mathematics

Look for Piagetian ideas in the following recommendations for teaching practice found in the *Standards* of the National Council of Teachers of Mathematics:

- Learning of mathematics is most successful when it results from children's own mathematical activities—that is, when they construct their own understandings of problem-solving and mathematics concepts rather than when mathematics concepts are taught by a teacher or textbook.

- Often, children can grasp mathematical concepts through manipulatives before they can be grasped symbolically. In general, concrete, incomplete, and unsystematic (informal) learning of mathematics precedes abstract (symbolic), complete, systematic, and formal learning. Formal learning is at its best when it is connected and related to students' informal understanding.

- Instruction should emphasize how mathematical symbols are related to events and relationships in the world, especially events and relationships already understood by the child. For example, relate the mathematical operation of division to sharing, such as when three children share six cookies, with each child receiving two cookies.

- Students should work on word problems from the beginning of mathematics instruction. Word problems place mathematical concepts in real-world situations and require students to map the relationships expressed in the problems verbally to mathematical concepts, symbols, and procedures.

- Mathematics is a means for learning new ways of solving problems. Students should be encouraged to reflect in order to abstract general problem-solving principles and procedures from working particular problems.

- Instruction should support student behaviors likely to motivate appropriate efforts and persistence in learning mathematics. Thus, students should be encouraged to ask questions when a concept or procedure is not understood, to expect errors when doing mathematics, and to relate the mathematics learned in school to everyday life.

- Teachers should question students about how they are solving problems and listen to student answers, since such answers can be revealing about what students understand and do not yet grasp. This is part of the ongoing assessment of student progress in understanding the mathematical ideas they are being taught.

- Students should be encouraged to use technology such as calculators as part of problem solving, since these devices eliminate much of the lower order computational demands of problem solving, permitting students to pay more attention to the higher order, executive decisions.

- Problem solving in small groups is often effective, especially in getting students to explain their reasons for problem solving in particular ways, but also in exposing students to alternative solution methods. Small-group problem solving also permits students to experience the understanding–solving–checking cycle (Polya, 1954a, 1954b). Real mathematics is a social and collaborative enterprise involving talking and explaining and making false starts with other people (Schoenfeld, 1992).

- Teachers should model problem solving, making obvious as they do so that problem solving is not always straightforward, but often involves false starts and consideration of many factors.

Can you detect the Piagetian influence on these recommendations? One example is teaching mathematics to young children using concrete materials. The Piagetian themes of exploration and discovery also pervade the NCTM recommendations. The Piagetian emphasis that instruction should be matched to the child's level of functioning comes through as well, with teachers urged to continually diagnose the child's level of functioning and provide instruction just beyond the current levels of their students.

relative novices in a domain learn better from studying worked examples than from spending an equivalent amount of time problem solving—referred to as the worked example effect (Ayres & Sweller, 2013). Even drill and practice, if well designed, is useful for learning facts and basic procedures. If the goal of learning requires more sophisticated outcomes such as analysis and evaluation, then a constructivist approach may be more appropriate and effective (Fletcher, 2009).

Chapter Summary and Evaluation

Piagetian stage theory continues to have substantial impact on developmental psychology and education. The underlying premise that children think differently than adults and that new ideas emerge from old ones as thinking evolves is powerful today. Most developmental psychologists, however, recognize the limitations of the original four-stage conception of development offered by Piaget. Children obtain some acquisitions much earlier than Piaget proposed, others much later. Moreover, acquisitions such as conservation are much more teachable than Piaget believed. In addition, context matters with respect to cognitive development, with the specific skills a child acquires largely depending on the child's experiences and knowledge about a particular domain.

Neo-Piagetians, such as Case and Fischer, provided alternative explanations to address the shortcomings of Piaget's theory. Case emphasized the role of increases in functional working memory capacity to explain stage-like shifts in development. Fischer focused on the skills children develop in specific domains and argued that qualitative changes in physical development of the nervous system resulted in cognitive, behavioral, and emotional shifts with development.

Building on Piaget's theories, Kohlberg developed a theory of moral reasoning specifying six stages in three levels. Kohlberg's theory engendered extensive research, providing some support for the first two levels of reasoning—preconventional and conventional—but not for postconventional. Citing limited evidence for the invariant sequence and universality of Kohlberg's theory, researchers have moved away from the stage conception to viewing moral development as one of the domains of social knowledge. Moreover, researchers have identified a significant relationship between children's developing theory of mind and their moral reasoning. Ideas derived from Kohlberg's theory and moral development research have inspired a variety of moral or character education programs used in schools.

Piagetian ideas have also had impact on educational thought and practices. For example, inducing cognitive conflict is a valuable technique for countering misconceptions students may hold. The emphasis of constructivist approaches to education on engaging in real-world learning tasks in social contexts creates a learning environment that encourages cognitive conflict leading to better understanding. Constructive educational approaches, differing in terms of the level of teacher support provided, have been adopted widely, particularly in mathematics and science education.

In closing, Piaget studied meaningful learning and a wide range of topics using interdisciplinary approaches. If Piaget was around today, he would be very interested in understanding how children engage with technology in their environment. As suggested by Elkind (2008), it is not too difficult to imagine Piaget sitting on the floor observing a toddler interacting with an iPad!

The frameworks considered in this chapter have broad implications for some of the Big Ideas introduced in Chapter 1. We know much more about development because of Piagetian theory, research inspired by the theory, and other theories inspired by the original framework.

Nature and Nurture

Although the case could be made that Piaget stressed biological unfolding of development over development based on experiences, both nature and nurture were always part of his theory. The role of nurture was especially apparent in Piaget's book *The Moral Judgment of the Child* (1965), where he asserted that many arguments and conflicts with peers were key in stimulating the development of more mature moral thinking. But Piaget took various positions in his writing. Thus, in *Biologie et connaissance* (*Biology and Knowledge*; 1967), Piaget emphasizes biological regulation of development, but stresses the role of the environment much more in *Sociological Studies* (Piaget, 1995). Of course, one way to think about environmental accommodations is that the ability to accommodate was an evolutionary advantage for humans, so that human environmental responsiveness reflects biology. Overall, Piagetian theory is typically thought of as an interactionist theory: biology interacts with environmental input.

Continuity and Discontinuity

The extreme Piagetian stage position has not survived critical scrutiny. The introduction of concepts such as horizontal décalage and stage mixture provided labels for the empirical reality of little stage-like consistency in behavior across tasks. Clearcut stages, with abrupt onsets, are not supported by the research evidence. Neuropsychological research, however, confirms that some discontinuities in development do exist. In particular, spurts in brain growth seem to be associated with cognitive, behavioral, and emotional reorganizations with development. Softer stage conceptions of development, such as Enright's views on forgiveness, are also flourishing. The idea of stage-like development dies hard, perhaps because the idea has some merit.

Universal and Culture-Specific

Both Piaget and Kohlberg believed that they had identified universally experienced stages of development. However, their strong universalist positions were greatly weakened when clear differences as a function of culture and experience were documented in arenas like moral judgment. What may be universal, however, are the mechanisms that account for cognitive development. Cognitive conflict, explanations, and observations make a difference in the development of children growing up in a variety of circumstances.

Active and Passive Child

At the heart of constructivist thinking is the belief that the child is an active self-starter. Some theorists even suggest that when children are taught specific concepts and learn them from direct teaching, they are developing passively. New thinking about constructivism, however, argues that direct explanations and demonstrations can be the beginning of extremely active learning by children.

REVIEW OF KEY TERMS

accommodate In Piaget's theory of cognitive development, the modification of existing cognitive structures in response to environmental stimuli.

animism The belief that inanimate objects are alive.

assimilate In Piaget's theory of cognitive development, the incorporation of environmental stimuli into an existing scheme.

class inclusion The ability to answer questions about subset relationships between groups of items.

cognitive conflict According to Piaget's theory of cognitive development, the situation that occurs when a learner does not have cognitive structures that permit understanding of environmental stimuli.

compensation In conservation tasks, the recognition that change on one dimension can be compensated for by change on another dimension.

concrete operational stage The third stage of Piaget's theory of cognitive development, in which concrete operators can apply cognitive operations to problems involving concrete objects.

conservation Children's ability to realize that the transformation of a substance that changes its appearance does not alter its basic characteristics.

conventional morality According to Kohlberg's theory of moral development, the stages at which individuals focus on maintaining social order.

deferred imitation The ability to represent learned behaviors mentally so that the behavior can be imitated long after it was witnessed.

disequilibrium In Piaget's theory of cognitive development, the realization that two contradictory ways of thinking about the world cannot both be true.

egocentrism The inability to perceive the perspectives of others.

equilibration In Piaget's theory of cognitive development, the process by which a learner constructs new cognitive structures in response to disequilibrium in order to return to equilibrium.

formal operational stage The last stage of Piaget's theory of cognitive development, in which thinkers are capable of complex problem solving and of "thinking in possibilities," "thinking ahead," and "thinking in hypotheses."

horizontal décalage In Piaget's theory of cognitive development, the inability of individuals to master all problems requiring the same logical operations at the same time.

identity In conservation tasks, the realization that basic characteristics of a substance remain the same despite perceptual transformations.

motor schemes Patterns of action used to interact with the environment developed during the sensorimotor stage of cognitive development.

object permanence A child's understanding that objects continue to exist regardless of whether or not the child can see or touch them.

operational schemes The logical patterns of thinking that characterize the concrete and formal operational stages of Piaget's theory of cognitive development.

plus-one approach An approach to moral education in which students discuss moral dilemmas to induce cognitive conflict and growth in understanding.

postconventional morality According to Kohlberg's theory of moral development, the stages at which individuals focus on shared principles and standards.

preconventional morality According to Kohlberg's theory of moral development, the stages at which individuals focus on self-interest in decision making.

preoperational stage The second stage of Piaget's theory of cognitive development, in which thinking benefits from the development of symbolic schemes.

reversibility In conservation tasks, the understanding that an operation can be undone by reversing it.

scheme A coordinated pattern of thought or action that organizes an individual's interaction with the environment.

sensorimotor stage The first stage of Piaget's theory of cognitive development, in which thinking is organized by motor schemes and a major accomplishment is object permanence.

seriate The ability to order objects on some dimension.

short-term memory A memory store of limited capacity and duration; also called working memory.

symbolic play Play that incorporates children's capabilities for symbolic representation so that play objects are used to represent other items.

symbolic schemes Cognitive structures, developed during the preoperational stage of cognitive development, that allow the representation of objects or events by means of symbols such as language, mental images, and gestures.

theory of mind Knowledge and reasoning about mental states, our own thoughts, feelings, wishes, beliefs, and the ability to attribute mental states to others, with the awareness that the perspectives of others may be different than our own.

CHAPTER 4

Cognitive Development
Information-Processing Theory

Although stage models such as Piaget's (described in Chapter 3) once prevailed as the way developmental psychologists characterized the development of thinking abilities, information-processing models of cognitive development and research in the cognitive sciences have commanded much more attention from developmental researchers in the last few decades. A computer metaphor is useful for understanding the information-processing approach to development (Mayer, 2012; Schneider, 2015). Using the computer metaphor, what develops is the hardware, specifically the memory systems and speed of processing, as well as the available software, procedures applied to information to create mental representations, for example, memory strategies. Much like the hard drive of a computer, the human brain has long-term memory stores, which contain our knowledge. This knowledge takes a variety of forms, such as knowledge of factual information, images of things we have seen, and knowledge of how to do things. Much of the time, we are not using the information we have stored in long-term memory. When information from our long-term memory is activated into our short-term memory (analogous to random-access memory [RAM], in computer terms), and then combined with new information being perceived by the senses, that is when thinking occurs.

Memory researchers make a distinction between the constructs of short-term memory and working memory. Short-term memory typically refers to passive storage of information, whereas the construct of working memory encompasses updating or manipulating information as it is being held in a temporary store (Atkinson & Shiffrin, 1968; Baddeley, 1981, 1986; Bauer & Fivush, 2014; Dempster, 1985; Schneider, 2015). Short-term and working memory are usually assessed with "memory span" tasks. A simple assessment of short-term memory would be asking someone to remember a list of numbers (digit span) or a list of words (word span). A working memory task would require someone to manipulate information such as presenting someone with a list of digits and then asking them to recall them in reverse order (backward digit span). In this chapter, we use the terms *short-term memory* and *working memory* somewhat interchangeably.

Consider the following situation. You have just printed out your boarding pass at the ticket kiosk of an airport. You walk toward the gate. You realize that you will need both your boarding pass and a government-issued form of identification (e.g., a driver's license) to pass through security. That knowledge has been in your long-term memory for a number of years, although you rarely think about it. You are now thinking about it in your active consciousness (i.e., your short-term memory) because you are in a setting that cues you to remember this information. You pass through security, and as you do so, the security guard tells you that you can put your identification away. This airport no longer requires an ID check at the gate. You put your ID away, and as you do so, you make a mental note that the procedure at this, your hometown airport, has changed. You have updated your long-term knowledge. Once at the gate, there is a delay, long enough that you will miss your connection. You go to the counter at the gate and ask about other connections you might make. The agent types away at the computer and then begins to read a bunch of options. After about the fourth or fifth one, you say, "Whoa!! I can't keep track of this." That is because your short-term memory, your conscious capacity, has been exceeded. Unless we are doing something to keep information active in memory, we can only hold a few items of information in mind at once. You ask the agent to reread the options, and this time you write down the options as she says them. You are using a strategy to overcome short-term memory limitations.

From the information-processing perspective, cognitive development is about the development of short-term or working memory capacity, long-term knowledge, and the use of strategies (or the ways in which we can plan to acquire knowledge). As portrayed in the anecdote about the airport, the various components of our minds are always interacting as we navigate the world. This is an enormous cognitive accomplishment. In this chapter, we present what is known about the development of working memory capacity, strategies, and the representation of knowledge that allow us to accomplish complex cognitive tasks.

Basic Cognitive Capacities

As mentioned above, **working memory,** the information currently activated in consciousness, is a memory store of limited capacity and duration. When someone holds a telephone number in memory while searching for a piece of paper to write it down (or a list of flight options being rattled off by a harried gate agent), this thinking goes on in working memory. Working memory is active as an author juggles bits and pieces of ideas he or she is trying to combine into sentences and paragraphs.

If a person does not continue to rehearse a phone number, the number will fade from consciousness. If an author is distracted while writing, some of the ideas he or she is juggling will be lost. Moreover, working memory is limited in terms of the amount of information that can be attended to consciously at any one moment. Only so many numbers can be rehearsed at once. Only so many bits of information can be considered before new pieces of information literally seem to push out some of the information already in working memory. Thus, working memory is limited in duration and capacity. You have probably noticed how sometimes other things compete for your limited working memory capacity when you are trying to pay attention in class. Sometimes it's a commotion in the hallway, or the text messages on your phone, or even your own plans for lunch after class, but you probably shift your attention back and forth between the distractions and the task at hand since you find it difficult to hold so many things in memory at the same time.

Developmental Increases in Functional Capacity of Working Memory

Learning and cognition improve with development largely because children's working memory capacity increases (Dempster, 1981, 1985; see also the discussion of working memory in Chapter 2 and the discussion of neo-Piagetians in Chapter 3). Longitudinal research indicates that from age 4 to 17 working memory capacity steadily increases (Schneider, 2015). For example, 4-year-olds may recall two or three digits in a digit-span task in contrast to adults who typically recall six or seven (Cowan, 2014). Fluctuations in working memory capacity have also been observed. For example, Dirk and Schmiedek (2016) asked third and fourth graders to complete working memory tasks on smart phones three times a day for 4 weeks and found that working memory capacity, particularly in the younger children, varied from day to day.

One explanation for the increase in short-term memory capacity is *neurological development*. That is, as the brain increases in size and complexity with maturity, short-term memory capacity expands (Bauer & Fivush, 2014). In this view, the number of available "slots" increase, perhaps one slot every 2 years, as a result of neurological development (Miller, 1956), particularly in the frontal lobes (Alvarado & Bachevalier, 2000; Fabiani & Wee, 2001).

Another explanation for developmental increases in the functional capacity of working memory is the increase in *speed of processing* with age which allows for more efficient use of a limited capacity (Bauer & Fivush, 2014; Cowan, Saults, Elliot, & Moreno 2002). Increased processing efficiency is a result of faster recognition and activation of information from long-term memory. Memory span differences reflect developmental differences in both recognizing span items and speed in saying them (Cowan, 2014; Henry & Millar, 1991; Kail, 1992, 2000; Kail & Park, 1994; Roodenrys, Hulme, & Brown, 1993; Schneider, 2015).

Yet another explanation for increasing short-term memory capacity with development is the number of advantages afforded by a growing knowledge base, particularly since prior knowledge increases the possibility of chunking related information together. One of the most important studies illustrating the power of chunking for memory capacity was conducted by Chi (1978). She compared how well child chess experts and adult chess novices could memorize the position of pieces on a chessboard. Although the children did not perform as well as the adults on a standard memory span task (as would be expected), they did recall more of the chess positions than the adults. In interviews after the experiment, the child experts indicated that they viewed the pieces on the chessboard as interrelated chunks of information, which led to their superior memory performance in comparison to the less knowledgeable adults. Miller (1956) introduced the "magic" number "7 (plus or minus 2)" as the maximum number of chunks of information that could be held in short-term memory at any given instant. Although capacity in terms of chunks is limited, individual differences in working memory capacity can be explained in terms of different-size chunks (Simon, 1974). Thus, an *expanding knowledge base and chunking* provide another explanation for the increase in working memory functional capacity with development (Schneider, 2015).

Working Memory and Academic Performance

Working memory capacity is related to performance on academic tasks, with the correlation between working memory capacity and performance on a variety of academic tasks ranging from .50 to .70 and longitudinal research indicating that working memory predicts performance on reading and math tasks (Alloway & Alloway, 2010; Swanson & Alloway, 2012). In a 4-year cross-sequential study with participants ranging from children in kindergarten to ninth grade, Lee and Bull (2016) found that working memory assessed at an earlier age predicted subsequent performance in mathematics. The relationship between working memory and mathematics performance was stronger at earlier ages, decreasing in older children as they acquired a more extensive knowledge base in mathematics. A meta-analysis of 110 studies found that the strength of the relationship between working memory and mathematics performance varied as a result of mathematics content (e.g., a stronger relationship for performance on word problems) and was strongest for atypical students, those with identified disabilities in math or with some other type of cognitive deficit such as attention-deficit disorder (Peng, Namkung, Barnes, & Sun, 2016). The limitations on mathematical problem solving stemming from working memory capacity can be compensated for by improvements in other academic skills such as reading comprehension and mathematical computation (Swanson & Fung, 2016).

Given the strong evidence of the role of working memory in academic performance, researchers have investigated training methods for increasing working memory capacity. Meta-analyses of dozens of studies reveal that training programs can reliably increase working memory capacity as measured by various memory span tasks (Melby-Lervåg & Hulme, 2013; Redick, Shipstead, Wiemers, Melby-Lervåg, & Hulme, 2015; Schwaighofer, Fischer, & Bühner, 2015). Unfortunately, researchers have yet to document that the increased working memory capacity resulting from training transfers to academic tasks.

What are the implications of working memory capacity for the classroom? Realizing that the amount of information anyone can hold in memory at once is limited and that the younger the child is, the more limited the capacity, teachers need to evaluate the memory demands of classroom tasks (Swanson & Alloway, 2012). When students have difficulty with classroom tasks due to working memory limitations, teachers can support their students by breaking tasks down into parts that are less demanding on memory or by providing external supports that reduce the amount of information the students have to hold in their heads at one time. Teachers can also reduce memory demands by focusing on relevant information, signaling what is important, and resisting the impulse to introduce interesting but tangential information. Teachers should take special note of students who ask for directions to be repeated frequently and should offer additional support for these students. Teachers should also keep in mind that a well-developed knowledge base and practiced use of effective strategies will also reduce demands on working memory.

Allocation and Control of Attention

The voluntary control of attention and the ability to filter out irrelevant information also increase with age (Rustic & Ennis, 2015). How might developmental increases in resistance to distraction increase performance on memory span tasks—and cognitive performances more generally? As the ability to inhibit distracting thoughts increases, more of the short-term capacity is available for the task the child is focusing on (Bjorklund & Harnishfeger, 1990; Harnishfeger & Bjorklund, 1993). Because younger children are more distractible than older children, they are more susceptible to interference from distractions (Brainerd & Reyna, 1989, 1995; Hale & Lewis, 1979; Reyna & Brainerd, 1995). In addition, children with academic difficulties struggle to strategically allocate attention to meet the requirements of a task (Swanson & Alloway, 2012). Moreover, higher levels of anxiety elicit task-irrelevant rumination, which reduces the attentional resources available for the task at hand (Pekrun & Stephens, 2012). Thus, the *increased control of attention* and the ability to inhibit irrelevant information also contribute to developmental increases in functional working memory.

Executive Function

Developmental researchers, educators, and clinicians have begun talking about how various basic cognitive capacities interact to influence a wide range of performances. They utilize the term **executive function** to refer to the higher level cognition necessary for conscious control of actions and thoughts in pursuit of goal-directed behavior (Friedman et al., 2016; Jacob & Parkinson, 2015; Müller & Kerns, 2015). The generally agreed upon key components of executive function include working memory (the active maintenance or updating of information), inhibitory control (the ability to inhibit incorrect or irrelevant responses), and attentional flexibility (the ability to shift focus from one task or response to another). Attentional flexibility is assessed by tasks such as asking children first to sort items under one set of directions (e.g., to organize by color) and then to shift and now organize under a different set of directions (e.g., to organize by size). This attentional flexibility task requires both working memory and inhibitory control—working memory to hold the shifting directions in mind and inhibition of one task when asked to shift to another (Blakey, Visser, & Carroll, 2016).

Executive function increases with development. Studying a large sample representative of the U.S. population, Best, Miller, and Naglieri (2011) found that performance on assessments of executive function improved with age until around age 15, but the rate of improvement slowed down after middle childhood. Executive function is related to academic performance. In a meta-analysis of 67 studies published since 2000 (more than half since 2010), Jacob and Parkinson (2015) provide evidence for the relationship between executive function and achievement in math and reading. The average correlation between executive function and reading tasks was .30 and for math tasks was .31, across a wide age range (from 3 to 18 years of age), using a variety of measures of the subcomponents (working memory, inhibition, and flexibility) of executive function. The relationship between executive function and academic performance was less strong for the youngest students (those ages 3 to 5).

Strategies

Increases in memory capacity and control of attentional processes clearly contribute to cognitive development, but cognitive advances in childhood and adolescence are also determined in part by developmental increases in use of cognitive strategies. This idea is of enormous consequence for educators because it suggests that children's and adolescents' thinking and learning can be improved by teaching them strategies that they do not discover and use on their own.

Definition of Strategies

Strategies are effortful, controllable, goal-directed activities designed to increase performance on a task (Bjorklund, Dukes, & Brown, 2009; Roebers, 2014). Suppose you have to read a chapter for a class. What are the cognitive operations and processes that you must carry out? Of course, you must decode the words, normally by reading the article from first page to last. This is not a strategic activity according to the definition presented here, since decoding the words in order is pretty much obligatory for you to "read" the chapter.

What could you do that would go beyond front-to-back reading? You could employ many different strategies to understand and remember the text better (Pressley & Afflerbach, 1995; Roebers, 2014). Before reading, you could skim the title, pictures, and headings to get a general idea of what the chapter is about. This might lead you to make predictions about what you will be reading. During reading, you might monitor carefully whether your predictions were correct and whether what you are reading makes sense. If it does not make sense, you might reread. Finally, after one reading of the text, you might self-test your understanding of what you read by trying to recall the content of the chapter. You might also look through the chapter, construct a summary, and note which parts of the chapter you did not remember during the self-test.

Teachers should teach their students to use these comprehension strategies when they read. For example, they could teach students to predict what might be in a text based on prior knowledge about the topic, to ask questions while they read (and look for answers), to construct images representing the ideas presented in text, and to test themselves by seeing if they can remember the summary of the text. Many teachers, however, experience difficulty teaching such strategies to their students (Pressley & El-Dinary, 1997; Robertson, 2013). For some, the difficulty stems from the fact that they do not use such strategies themselves when they read (Keene & Zimmermann, 1997). Others find it difficult to allocate time in the school day for strategy instruction and require significant coaching and support to persist in changing their instructional practices (Hilden & Pressley, 2007; Krawec & Montague, 2014; Sailors & Price, 2010). Still, when teachers do teach their students to use comprehension strategies, the students exhibit improvements in their reading comprehension, as captured by a variety of assessments, including standardized tests (Braten & Anmarkrud, 2013; Brown, Pressley, & Van Meter, 1996; Collins, 1991).

In short, many different ways of processing text, beyond simple reading, facilitate understanding and memory of text information. These are strategies. Typically, readers execute strategies consciously and intentionally. Eventually, however, the goal is for readers to carry out these processes more automatically, with great ease and little awareness. Several years of comprehension strategies instruction in elementary school can go a long way toward the development of skilled strategic readers (Pressley et al., 1992). The first step, however, is to understand how strategy use develops in children and adolescents.

Development of Strategy Use in Young Children

Most of the research on the development of strategic competence in children has been conducted by researchers studying basic memory (Bauer & Fivush, 2014; Schneider, 2015). This research has shaped the way educators think about how children learn new information. One of the most common strategies used by children to remember information is **rehearsal,** a strategy of repeating information in order to recall it later. Rehearsal maintains information in working memory, thereby increasing functional short-term memory capacity (Hitch, Halliday, Schaafstal, & Heffernan, 1991). Thus, yet another explanation for the increase in short-term memory capacity with development is the *increase in use of strategies*. See Table 4.1 for a summary of the various explanations for increases in short-term memory capacity with development described in this chapter.

In many research studies investigating children's use of strategies, the children were asked to remember lists of items in a serial recall task. In a typical **serial recall task,** a researcher presents a child with some items to remember: perhaps a row of picture cards, one picture to a card, with the faces turned down. After informing the child that the task is to remember the picture cards in order, the researcher would turn each card face up for a few seconds.

A rehearsal strategy that more advanced learners can apply to this task is known as **cumulative rehearsal** (Barclay, 1979; Butterfield & Belmont, 1977). In this strategy, the learner says the list items over and over in order of presentation. Suppose the pictures are, from left to right, a chair, a dog, a cup, a car, a radio, a book, and a tree. After seeing the picture of the chair, the learner would say "chair" several times. Then, when the picture of the chair is turned face down and a picture of a dog revealed, the learner would say "chair, dog" several times. By the time a picture of a radio is presented, the rehearsal would include saying "chair, dog, cup, car, and radio" as many times as time permits. In contrast, if the rehearsal is not cumulative, the learner would rehearse "chair, chair" . . . with the presentation of the first picture and then "dog, dog" with the presentation of the second picture, and so on.

Use of the more advanced form of rehearsal, cumulative rehearsal, appears later in development (Schneider & Pressley, 1997; Schneider, 2015). Preschoolers and early elementary-age student do not use it when asked to recall a list of words

---

TABLE 4.1. Explanations for Developmental Increase in Working Memory Capacity

- Neurologically determined increases in brain capacity.
- Increases in processing speed and efficiency.
- Increased chunking due to expanding knowledge base.
- Increased control of attention and ability to inhibit distractions.
- Increased and more sophisticated use of strategies.

or a series of pictures. Their most typical strategy is simply to repeat the word or say the name of the picture as it is displayed. This is simple rehearsal without the cumulative quality, and in the case of the presentation of pictures it has also been called a **labeling** strategy (Flavell, Beach, & Chinsky, 1966). Children commonly shift to cumulative rehearsal by the end of the grade school years and this shift is associated with better recall (Flavell et al., 1966; Lehman & Hasselhorn, 2007, 2012; Ornstein, Naus, & Liberty, 1975).

The strategies a person uses are determined largely by his or her personal sociocultural history, with parents and teachers influencing children's use of strategies (Kurtz, 1990; Schneider, 2015). For example, German parents are more likely than U.S. parents to teach learning and memory strategies at home (Carr, Kurtz, Schneider, Turner, & Borkowski, 1989). The German emphasis on teaching strategies is apparent at school as well, with more teaching of learning and memory strategies in German than U.S. schools (Kurtz, Schneider, Carr, Borkowski, & Rellinger, 1990). Naturalistic studies of strategy instruction in U.S. classrooms indicate that children who had been in first-grade classrooms where the teachers talked about memory strategies, asked questions about memory, and made memory demands of their students exhibited better memory skill development in later grades than children who were in first classrooms where memory was not emphasized (Ornstein, Grammer, & Coffman, 2010).

Strategy Use by Preschoolers

Preschoolers are sometimes strategic, at least for some tasks in familiar surroundings. For example, DeLoache, Cassidy, and Brown (1985) hid an object (usually a familiar toy such as a Bugs Bunny or Big Bird stuffed animal) in a living room, with the children watching and aware that later they would have to retrieve the hidden object. In this situation, even 2-year-olds are strategic. Although they played in the living room during the *retention interval* (the time between when the object is hidden and when they must retrieve it), preschoolers frequently looked at the place where the object was hidden. Sometimes, they even pointed to the location and said the name of the hidden object.

These checking-back and simple rehearsal activities are, in fact, memory strategies. Sometimes the object was hidden in the room (e.g., under a pillow); other times it was placed in about the same position, but not hidden (e.g., on top of the same pillow). Only when the object was hidden from view did preschoolers look back at the spot or say the object's name during the retention interval. That is, they used the strategies only when the situation demanded memory.

Sometimes preschoolers exhibit memory strategies that are not yet useful to them (Lange, Mackinnon, & Nida, 1989). For example, Baker-Ward, Ornstein, and Holden (1984) presented preschool children with sets of toys. In both conditions of the study, children played with the toys. In one of the conditions, the directions given to the children only mentioned playing with the toys. In the other condition, the children were asked to remember some of the toys. The addition of this memory demand changed the processing of preschoolers dramatically. The children given the memory instruction played with the toys less. Instead, they looked intensely at the to-be-remembered toys and named them. But even though these children engaged in strategic behavior more than the children who only played with the toys, they did not remember more of the toys.

Thus, preschoolers sometimes are strategic, although their efforts to **encode,** to create durable memories, are not always successful. Even if preschoolers have a memory trace, however, that does not mean they will **retrieve,** or access, the memory trace, later. For example, Pressley and MacFadyen (1983) found that children who learned associations between pairs of items, such as "rock and turkey," using interactive pictures (such as a picture of a turkey sitting on a rock), did not recall more pairs unless they were also given a retrieval cue to "think back to the pictures you saw. . . ." This retrieval deficiency in preschoolers is soon surmounted with development. Unlike preschoolers, kindergarten children do not need retrieval cues to make use of interactive pictures presented at study. Since preschoolers experience retrieval difficulties that do not occur with older children and retrieval processes improve throughout the elementary school years (Ritter, 1978; Schneider, 2015; Sodian & Schneider, 1990), teachers working with young children need to consider how to support the retrieval process for optimal memory performance.

Development of Strategic Competence in the School Years

Although the use of some strategies, especially rehearsal, clearly increases during the elementary school years in Western cultures, use of other, and often more effective, strategies develops slowly (and, for some students, not at all). Consider, for example, how elementary school children tackle *paired-associate learning*, that is, learning associations between two items such as a vocabulary word and its definition, states and their capitals, names of inventors and their inventions, and cities and their products. The most effective strategies for learning paired associates involve elaborations. An **elaboration** is the construction of a meaningful context for the to-be-learned information that can be either verbal or visual. The elaboration to learn a paired associate (e.g., the turkey paired with rock) could be either a verbal elaboration in the form of a meaningful sentence containing both pair members (e.g., "Turkeys have rocks in their gizzards") or a meaningful interactive image (e.g., an image of a turkey scratching at rocks in the barnyard). The research evidence is quite clear. Younger elementary-age children typically do not use elaboration strategies to learn paired associates on their own (Pressley & Levin, 1977a, 1977b), and even many adults fail to use elaboration strategies (Bower, 1972; Kliegl, Smith, & Baltes, 1990; Roebers, 2014; Rohwer, 1980; Rohwer & Litrownik, 1983).

By the end of the grade school years, however, children sometimes elaborate, or in other words, make associations to materials that are more meaningful than paired associates. For example, Chan, Burtis, Scardamalia, and Bereiter (1992) asked children to think aloud as they processed texts about dinosaurs and germs. With increasing age during the elementary school years, students were less likely to rely on superficial understandings and irrelevant associations to text (e.g., associating to a single word in the text) and more likely to relate ideas in the text to one another and to their own prior knowledge in ways that made the ideas more sensible. Even the oldest students, the sixth graders, however, could have benefited from more integration and elaboration.

A pattern of development similar to that observed with elaboration strategies has also been found for strategies requiring students to organize information. **Organization** refers to the process of grouping information into categories or patterns on the basis of relationships or connections. Younger elementary school children are less likely than older elementary school children to organize information in a way that helps them remember the information better but can benefit from instructions designed to promote effective organization (Bjorklund, 2000; Bjorklund et al., 2009; Schneider & Pressley, 1997). Moreover, effective use of organization strategies is also dependent on an increasingly well-developed knowledge base (discussed later in this chapter). See Table 4.2 for a summary of the general trend of strategy development.

Much of the research on strategy development has been cross-sectional, and this research indicates that memory strategy use gradually increases with age. (It might be helpful to review the discussion of the differences between cross-sectional and longitudinal research in Chapter 1.) Longitudinal studies, however, suggest that strategy development may not be so orderly (Bjorklund et al., 2009; Schneider & Ornstein, 2015). In fact, strategy use by an individual student, including the appearance of more advanced strategies, may improve rather abruptly, and more effective strategies do not simply replace less effective ones. That is, students may retain both more and less effective strategies in their repertoires; however, the use of more effective strategies is linked with better recall performance,

It is probably not surprising that many college students do not study effectively and are, in fact, unaware of study strategies that could improve their memory for course material (McCabe, 2010). They fail to use effective memory strategies as well as effective procedures for reading comprehension, writing, and problem solving. College students believe rehearsal to be more critical to learning and studying than the organization and elaboration strategies that college faculty judged to be more

TABLE 4.2. Development of Strategy Use

Early childhood (2–6 years of age)

- Rehearsal strategies
    Primarily labeling, beginnings of simple rehearsal
- Elaboration strategies
    Preschoolers can use if elaborations are provided but need retrieval cue
    Kindergartners can use if provided, no longer need retrieval cue
- Organization strategies
    Can use if provided, constrained by limited knowledge base

Middle childhood (6–11 or 12 years of age)

- Rehearsal strategies
    Simple rehearsal (early elementary school)
    Cumulative rehearsal (by end of elementary school)
- Elaboration strategies
    Can benefit from elaboration strategies but typically don't use them on their own
- Organization strategies
    Begin to use more effectively as knowledge base expands

Adolescence (11–14 years of age to the late teen years)

- Rehearsal strategies
    Cumulative rehearsal continues to improve
- Elaboration strategies
    Can benefit from elaboration strategies; some students may use on their own
- Organization strategies
    Can use effectively as knowledge base expands and becomes more organized

essential to success in their classes (Lynch, 2007). For this reason many campuses now offer study skills courses to students. A main objective of such courses is to teach strategies supporting elaboration and organization of to-be-learned material, which is sensible, given that many strategies can be taught.

Teaching Strategies

As discussed earlier in this chapter, young children often fail to use effective rehearsal strategies when learning lists. It takes only brief instructions, however, to teach 6- and 7-year-olds how to rehearse lists so that they remember them later (Keeney, Cannizzo, & Flavell, 1967). Children in the early school years (kindergarten to third grade) also often fail to make use of the organizational properties of lists, such as categories, that can aid memory. Again, it is easy to teach children to sort lists into categories (Moely, Olson, Hawles, & Flavell, 1969). There have been many demonstrations of teaching children to use memory strategies that they did not exhibit without instruction. We have known for a long time that children can benefit from strategy instruction. Instruction in strategy use, however, is not always enough to turn nonstrategic students into strategy users.

Continued Use of Strategies Following Instruction

Teaching students how to execute a strategy does not guarantee that they will use the strategy in appropriate situations. Students sometimes fail to continue using strategies in situations that are *almost identical* to the ones in which they first learned the strategies. This is called failure to **maintain** strategies. Sometimes students do not apply strategies they have learned to *new* situations and tasks where they could be appropriate. This is called failure to **transfer**.

Why do students fail to maintain and transfer strategies appropriately? First, sometimes students simply do not realize that they could apply a strategy they have learned to a new learning task (Gick & Holyoak, 1980, 1983; Ross, 1984). Second, students sometimes may recognize that a strategy they know is applicable, but their use of it is so mixed up that the strategy is not effective (Harris, 1988). Third, sometimes students do not use a strategy because they do not enjoy using it or do not feel that the gains produced by the strategy are worth the effort (Rabinowitz, Freeman, & Cohen, 1992). Thus, simply teaching a student a strategy in no way assures maintenance or generalization of the strategy (Dimmitt & McCormick, 2012; McCormick, Dimmitt, & Sullivan, 2013).

The possibility that simple strategy instruction did not teach students to recognize when a strategy would be useful stimulated a number of experiments to try to understand how to promote strategy transfer and generalization (Pressley, Borkowski, & O'Sullivan, 1984, 1985). One group of students was taught a strategy for some task. A second group was taught the same strategy for the same task but also was provided information about how the strategy would benefit performance. Knowledge about the potential effects of using a strategy is called **utility knowledge**. The outcome in such experiments was always the same. Students who were informed about the utility of the strategy were more likely to maintain the strategy than students who were not provided the utility information.

To increase the likelihood of strategy transfer, strategy instruction should also include information about when and where the strategy might apply, which is sometimes called **conditional knowledge** (Paris et al., 1983). For example, O'Sullivan and Pressley (1984) taught children in the fifth and sixth grades a strategy to learn associations between cities and the products produced in those cities. Whether the students transferred the strategy to another task—learning Latin words and their definitions—depended on how much information had been included in the instruction about when and where to use the strategy. Utility knowledge and conditional knowledge are examples of metacognition. **Metacognition** is knowledge about and awareness of thinking, including the knowledge of when and where to apply acquired strategies (Dimmitt & McCormick, 2012; McCormick et al., 2013; Winne & Azevedo, 2014). Generally, increasing students' metacognitive understanding about the strategies they are learning increases the likelihood of strategy transfer.

Monitoring Strategy Effectiveness

Suppose that you are taught a new strategy for a familiar task and try it out. How can you know whether the strategy has worked for you, that is, whether it has improved your performance relative to an old approach with the task? If you do recognize the value of the strategy, does it affect your decision to use the strategy in the future? These questions motivated a number of studies on monitoring strategy effectiveness and yielded some surprising but consistent results. Learners, including adults, will often fail to monitor how well a strategy is working as they use it, but they can come to realize that a strategy is effective when they are tested and they can compare how they learned with one strategy versus another (Hunter-Blanks, Ghatala, Pressley, & Levin, 1988; Pressley & Ghatala, 1990; Pressley, Levin, & Ghatala, 1984).

What influence does awareness of differential strategy effectiveness have on decisions to use a strategy in the future? With adults, such awareness results in a strong preference for the effective strategy when confronted with similar learning tasks. With children, especially those in the early elementary grades, awareness of strategy effectiveness is less likely to lead to commitment to the strategy in the future. Indeed, the younger the child, the less likely the child is to monitor strategy effectiveness even when tested and the less likely the child is to continue to use a strategy proven to be effective (Ghatala, 1986; Ghatala, Levin, Pressley, & Goodwin, 1986; Pressley, Ross, Levin, & Ghatala, 1984).

In summary, skilled adult learners use strategies that are well matched to the tasks they are facing. Fortunately, adults and children who do not use strategies can be taught to use them. Sometimes only brief instruction is required. In other cases, longer term instruction is necessary. Effective strategy instruction can be complicated (see the guidelines summarized in Table 4.3). The failure of strategies to transfer beyond training situations is a specific instance of a general conclusion that learning often tends to be tied to the context in which it occurs (see the discussion on situated knowledge later in this chapter). The challenge for instruction is to produce learning that is not bound to specific contexts. The way educators have tackled this challenge is to do long-term teaching, as illustrated by strategy instruction for the academic tasks of writing and reading described in the Applying Developmental Theory to Educational Contexts special features (Boxes 4.1 and 4.2). The constraints of working memory capacity is another issue to consider. Some strategies students use are not effective and other strategies, especially those recently learned, may take up a significant portion of limited working memory capacity and result in lower performance. For example, Swanson (2014) reported that children with math

TABLE 4.3. Guidelines for Strategy Instruction

- Some children learn to use effective strategies on their own. It is important to realize that even if students do not use effective strategies already, they can be taught to use them.

- Be sure to inform students of the *utility* of the new strategy. Describe the potential benefits.

- Be sure students have *conditional knowledge* about the strategy. Describe where and when the strategy is most effective.

- Simply asking students to practice the new strategy is not enough for maintenance and transfer of the strategy. Be sure students *monitor* the effectiveness of the new strategy relative to their own methods by comparing their performance on tests.

- If working with students younger than middle school age, prompt them to think back to their performance using the new strategy, compared to their old performance without the strategy use. Young children often require explicit feedback on their performance in order to realize which strategies are effective.

difficulties and higher working memory capacity benefited from strategy instruction, whereas strategy instruction resulted in decreased performance of children with lower working memory capacity. In other cases, strategy instruction can reduce the effects of a limited working memory capacity. For example, students with lower working memory capacity can take effective notes if they use a supportive notetaking strategy (Bui, Myerson, & Hale, 2013).

Knowledge Representation

Thus far, we have considered two possible explanations for advances in cognitive abilities. One, cognitive development may be due to expanding short-term memory capacity. Two, cognitive development may be due to expanding use of strategies. Now we consider a third possibility, that cognitive development reflects more complete, organized, and accessible knowledge—knowledge stored in long-term memory.

Memory performance is highly dependent on the developing knowledge base. What we know has an enormous effect on what we learn and remember, and what we know increases greatly in the course of development (Flavell, 1985). Researchers have established different conceptions of the nature of knowledge in children, adolescents, and adults. Long-term memory includes representations of everything from the 26 letters of the alphabet and the numbers 1–100, to the concept "mother," and to the knowledge that some animals are more closely related to one another than other animals, to images of dogs chasing cats, to an understanding of what happens when you go to McDonald's, and so on.

Why are there many different conceptions of how knowledge is represented? Some models explain some types of knowledge better than others. For example, in early childhood, you acquired the concept of "mother." You can also access a visual depiction of your mother from a knowledge representation called an "image." Your understanding of the key characteristics of mammals can be represented in a network of related ideas. Connections between ideas may be best described in knowledge representations called "neural networks." Your knowledge of how to behave in

BOX 4.1. Writing Strategies Instruction

Today, in most schools, writing strategies are routinely taught beginning from the early grade school years. Much of this instruction boils down to teaching students to plan, draft, and revise, which is what good writers do (Flower & Hayes, 1980). A number of specific strategies can be taught for each of these phases. Not surprisingly, writing strategies instruction is long term, although it is often possible to observe some benefits after a few weeks or months of some specific type of strategy instruction (Fidalgo, Torrance, & Garcia, 2008; Harris & Graham, 1992; Harris, Santangelo, & Graham, 2010). Successful instruction includes a great deal of explanation and modeling of writing strategies, followed by actual writing in which students are coached in the application and adaptation of the strategies they are learning, described below.

Strategies Addressing the Planning Stage

Because students sometimes do not search their memories thoroughly for everything they might know about a topic either before or while they write (Scardamalia & Bereiter, 1986), strategies that promote more thorough search of memory for ideas can increase the quantity of material written on a topic. For example, Humes (1983) recommended providing sets of question prompts that would stimulate systematic search of memory for relevant content. Thus, if the student were writing about a sequence of events, question prompts might include the following: What happened first? What happened next? Next? What happened last? When did it happen? Where did it happen? Whom did it happen to? Similarly, Bereiter and Scardamalia (1982) provided students with sentence openers such as "One reason . . . ," "Even though . . . ," "For example, . . . ," and "I think . . ." Perhaps the most intuitively obvious prompt to search memory, however, is simply to ask the child who writes a very short essay to "Write some more!," a command that children can internalize and make to themselves if they are taught to do so (Graham, 1990; Graham & Harris, 1987).

Strategies Addressing the Writing Stage

Students can learn to instruct themselves to respond to a series of prompts that elicit the kinds of information found in the type or genre of writing they are attempting. Thus, to write a short persuasive essay, students can be taught to respond to the following four prompts in order: (1) generate a topic sentence; (2) note reasons; (3) examine the reasons and ask if readers are likely to agree with each reason; (4) come up with an ending (Graham & Harris, 1988). A second example is a set of questions for generating a story (Harris & Graham, 1992): Who is the main character? Who else is in the story? When does the story take place? Where does the story take place? What does the main character do or want to do? What do other characters do? What happens when the main character does or tries to do it? What happens with other characters? How does the story end? How does the main character feel? How do the other characters feel?

Strategies Addressing the Revision Stage

Fitzgerald and Markham (1987) taught sixth graders to approach revision as a problem-solving task, one that could be solved by making additions, deletions, substitutions, and rearrangements. Graham and MacArthur (1988) taught students to revise by adding details, examining the clarity and cohesiveness of the paper, and fixing mechanical errors. MacArthur, Schwartz, and Graham (1991) found that peers can be asked to give feedback on the content and structure of the paper.

Instructional approaches that combine strategy instruction for all three stages of writing have been demonstrated to be effective for a variety of ages and types of students, particularly when combined with instructions to self-regulate by setting goals and monitoring progress (see Graham, McKeown, Kiuhara, & Harris, 2012, and Graham & Perin, 2007 for meta-analyses with elementary school students and adolescents, respectively.) Not all college students are skilled writers, and instruction in planning, writing and revising strategies can improve the quality and length of the essays produced by college students as well (MacArthur, Phillippakos, & Ianetta, 2015).

Applying Developmental Theory to Educational Contexts

BOX 4.2. Reading Strategies Instruction

Pressley and his colleagues studied the characteristics of effective strategies instruction for reading comprehension in elementary school programs (Brown, 2008; El-Dinary, Pressley, & Schuder, 1992; Pressley et al., 1992; Pressley, Gaskins, Wile, Cunicelli, & Sheridan, 1991). Students in effective programs typically are taught to *predict, visualize*, and *summarize* as they read. These strategies stimulate active processing of text as students react to text and make associations to background knowledge.

A lesson typically would begin with the teacher reading first, thinking aloud about how the text might relate to prior knowledge. The teacher might make predictions, report images stimulated by the text, or summarize the text while noting consistencies and inconsistencies between text content, text structure, and reader expectations. Then the teacher might invite students to try using the strategic procedures with the text. The students, in reading groups, would take turns reading aloud. Throughout the process, the teacher encourages student interpretations of text and thus exposes reading group participants to a variety of interpretations of text and the processes for constructing and evaluating those interpretations. The teacher never tells students to use a particular strategy, but rather encourages them to be active as they read, choosing for themselves the strategy they need to understand a particular part of the text. The message conveyed is that the student is in control. Students are not learning to take orders from teachers; they are learning to make the types of choices good readers make. Use of strategies over months and years provides opportunities to acquire understanding of where and when to use the strategies and how to adapt them. That is, practice provides plenty of opportunity for metacognition about the strategies to develop.

Pressley and colleagues (1992) refer to this type of instruction as *transactional strategies instruction*, so dubbed because what happens during reading group is codetermined by a teacher and a student in interaction with a text, and the interpretations of the text are codetermined by teacher–student–text transactions (Bell, 1968; Bjorklund, 1989; Rosenblatt, 1978; Sameroff, 1975). Years of transactions involving predictions, questioning, clarifications, visualizations, associations, and summaries are intended to produce independent, successful readers who employ these strategies on their own. In fact, only one school year of such instruction produces substantial gains in reading achievement (Brown et al., 1996).

---

a fast-food restaurant is better characterized by a knowledge representation called a "schema." These different types of knowledge interrelate, with complex, often not very well understood, connections between them.

Researchers build models of how humans represent information in memory, with a goal of enhancing our understanding of how we think, how we learn and why we may forget. It is important to keep in mind, however, that all models are imperfect approximations of human cognition (Shiffrin, 2010). As technological tools became more sophisticated, more complex models have been developed (Rogers & Wolmetz, 2016). Better techniques of brain measurement (PET, fMRI, magnetic resonance imaging, EEG, etc.) have led to new questions. New analytical approaches involving increasingly complicated computation techniques provide glimmers of new answers. But we still don't have "the answer," with some models explaining some observed patterns of recall better than other models. Moreover, the human mind does not always operate rationally, and the human brain is composed of complex, interwoven redundant systems that are difficult to untangle. What we will do is examine different ways to represent knowledge, to model cognitive processes, with the greatest relevance to educational contexts.

Procedural Knowledge

Knowledge can be broadly categorized as being one of two types: **declarative knowledge,** which is knowledge about the world, knowledge *that* something is the case, and **procedural knowledge,** which is knowledge about *how* to do things. Many distinctions between procedural and declarative knowledge exist (Tulving, 1983). For example, procedural knowledge can be demonstrated only by performing the procedure. Evidence of declarative knowledge can come in a variety of forms such as recall, recognition, application to a situation, and association to other knowledge. Procedural knowledge is often acquired only after extensive practice. Declarative knowledge can be acquired after a single exposure. See Table 4.4 for examples of declarative and procedural knowledge.

Procedural knowledge typically starts as declarative knowledge (Johnson, 2003; Neves & Anderson, 1981). In other words, learning how to do something sometimes begins as a verbal description of the procedure. When a sequence of cognitive actions in a procedure is represented declaratively, carrying out the procedure proceeds slowly and requires more of the limited working memory capacity. When first learning an action sequence, we have to interpret each step one at a time. This requires cognitive capacity. With practice, we can execute the procedure automatically. The movement from declarative representation of a sequence of actions to a single procedure is known as **proceduralization**.

Let's say you are learning to use word-processing software. You may begin by reading the directions and spend some time trying to learn the basic steps. Then you struggle to use the program. Initially, you need to cue yourself to take the correct action. For instance, you may say to yourself, "When I want to save a file, I open the file menu and click the mouse on save. If I click close, I better make sure I save

TABLE 4.4. Examples of Declarative and Procedural Knowledge

Declarative knowledge
  Knowing what the Declaration of Independence is
  Knowing the names of all the states and their capitals
  Knowing the formula for computing area
  Knowing what a circle is
  Knowing who wrote *War and Peace*
  Knowing the genus and species of a spider
  Knowing the Pythagorean theorem

Procedural knowledge
  Knowing how to use a computer
  Knowing how to perform mathematical operations
  Knowing how to play basketball
  Knowing how to write
  Knowing how to study
  Knowing how to look up information in the library
  Knowing how to perform a laboratory procedure
  Knowing how to dissect an animal

the file." Gradually, you will need less and less verbal cuing. Eventually, you can write an entire paper without thinking about the word-processing commands. Your knowledge of the processing software has been "proceduralized." At this point, you are no longer using much short-term capacity when you use the word-processing program and you can think more about what you are writing. See the Considering Interesting Questions special feature (Box 4.3) for a description of metacognitive knowledge, another example of the distinction between declarative and procedural knowledge. We now turn to the various ways in which researchers have conceptualized the declarative knowledge base.

Considering Interesting Questions

BOX 4.3. What Is Metacognitive Knowledge?

We introduced the construct of metacognition, the knowledge and awareness of cognitive process, in the discussion of learning and memory strategies. A more fine-grained analysis of metacognition illustrates distinctions between types of knowledge (Schneider, 2015; Winne & Azevedo, 2014). For example, *declarative* metacognitive knowledge refers to being aware that specific information is included in your knowledge base. It also refers to knowledge about your strengths and weaknesses as a learner, knowledge about what is required to succeed on a given academic task, and knowledge of appropriate learning and memory strategies for the task at hand. Metacognitive *procedural* knowledge refers to the ability to correctly implement the steps of a strategy and to monitor and control the learning process. Monitoring includes judgments about how well something has been learned and predictions of future recall. Control processes include selection of strategies and allocation of study time. And, as described previously in this chapter, researchers studying metacognition have also introduced the concepts of *utility* and *conditional* knowledge, knowing "when, where, and why" to apply declarative and procedural metacognitive knowledge.

Declarative metacognitive knowledge develops in early elementary school with substantial increases in adolescence and young adulthood (Schneider, 2010). The development of monitoring accuracy (procedural metacognition) is not as systematic. Young children can exhibit the ability to monitor performance in familiar situations, but even if they are monitoring accurately, they do not possess the requisite metacognitive knowledge or procedural control to implement effective strategies (Dimmitt & McCormick, 2012).

Even successful students, ones who are attending college, display failures in metacognitive knowledge, monitoring, and control. Highly skilled college students effectively calibrate their knowledge in that there is a strong relationship between their metacognition predictions and actual performance. Less skilled college students are often less accurate, often overestimating their knowledge. Fortunately, some aspects of metacognition can be taught. For example, Zepeda, Richey, Ronevich, and Nokes-Malach (2015) conducted a 6-hour intervention with eighth graders teaching them declarative and procedural components of the metacognitive processes planning, monitoring, and evaluation. This relatively brief intervention resulted in better performance on physics problems, compared to a control group who did not receive the intervention. Metacognitive instruction has been demonstrated to be effective at all age levels, including for skilled college learners (McCormick et al., 2013). For example, the comprehension monitoring of college students can be improved and learning can be increased if they understand the likelihood of overconfident judgments of learning and the negative effects of such overconfidence on learning (Roelle, Schmidt, Buchau, & Berthold, 2017).

Concepts

A **concept** is a mental representation of a category of related items (Goldstein, 2015; Klausmeier, 1990). Concepts help us to organize our experiences by allowing us to group similar things together into categories. Otherwise it would be difficult to make sense of the many different things we experience in our environment. Categories increase processing efficiency by enabling us to make assumptions, inferences, and predictions about new information based on past experience with similar items (Gelman & Meyer, 2011; Koenig & Grossman, 2007). For example, your concept of "dog" helps you lump together the Labrador retriever in the neighborhood, the collie "Lassie" from reading books and watching movies and TV reruns, and greyhounds at the race track. When you see an animal coming toward you on the street, you can use your concept of "dog" to decide whether or not the approaching animal is a dog rather than a rat or a lion. Children are very good at noticing essential characteristics of things (such as animals), and they are also very good at learning commonly encountered categories of things (such as dogs) and events in the world (Gelman & Koenig, 2003; Gelman & Meyer, 2011).

Concept Formation

How people classify items into conceptual categories is not completely understood, with many competing perspectives (Goldstein, 2015; Murphy, 2002). Do we create a rule, articulating the defining features of a concept? For example, the defining features of a grandmother are being female and having a child who has had a child. Learning a concept would then largely be a matter of learning its defining features and applying a rule based on those features. For example, a triangle is a closed figure in a plane with three straight sides and three interior angles. Having learned these defining features of a triangle, a student can apply the definition and identify examples of triangles such as a slice of pie or a side of a pyramid.

In contrast to the rule-based perspective, other approaches suggest that we make judgments about concept membership based on similarity (Koenig & Grossman, 2007), but how do we judge similarity? Do we store specific instances of a concept and compare new information to an instance? This is the explanation given by the *exemplar* theory of concepts. Or do we create a summary, a *prototype*, an abstraction based on multiple experiences (Murphy, 2016)?

Prototype theory suggests that people classify concepts on the basis of resemblance rather than by defining features (Rosch, 1975, 1978; Rosch & Mervis, 1975). Prototypes are mental averages of the many instances of the concept previously encountered in the world. Another way of saying this is that conceptual representations are encoded as probability distributions over a large set of attributes (Rogers & Wolmetz, 2016). Thus, typical grandmothers are over 40 and gray-haired. There are also atypical grandmothers who are not as readily classified as grandmothers—for example, a 35-year-old, who had a child at 17, who in turn had a child at 18. Because of its typicality, we easily and quickly classify a robin as a bird, but we less certainly classify a penguin as a bird. We are able to make these classifications because we construct a prototype, or a very typical member of the category. The more an animal resembles this typical bird, the more certainly and quickly we would classify the animal as a bird. We would respond faster to the question, "Is a robin a bird?" than to the same question posed about a less typical example of a bird such as a chicken

(Rips, Shoben, & Smith, 1973; Rosch, 1973; Rosch & Mervis, 1975). People recall more typical category members before the atypical members, and children learn the typical category members first (Goldstein, 2015; Smith & Medin, 1981.)

Which explanation for similarity-based concept identification is more accurate? Do we represent conceptual information through multiple exemplars or through a prototype? The evidence seems to be that we do both. Sometimes we judge the similarity of new information to a specific instance rather than to a generalized concept. Other times we appear to use a prototype in our judgments (Goldstein, 2015; Murphy, 2016).

Networks of Concepts

Our conceptual understandings are related to each other in long-term memory. One conception of how concepts are organized is **semantic networks**. Concepts are nodes in the semantic network, with links between the nodes specifying associations between concepts. Large networks of associations are associated to each node, with many of the associations based on personal experience. Perhaps polar bears are connected to memories of the Antarctic exhibit at a zoo you once visited. Polar bears may also bring to mind Klondike Ice Cream Bars, which have a polar bear on the wrapper. Your knowledge of polar bears is also more general, no longer being tied to particular experiences. For instance, most people have a strong association between polar bears and penguins, sea lions, and walruses, with knowledge of all of these animals associated with knowledge of the Arctic and Antarctic regions of the Earth.

Semantic networks are hierarchically organized. For example, the concept of all living things can be subdivided into animals and plants. Animals can be further subdivided into reptiles, mammals, birds, insects, and so on, each with associated features (such as hair, vertebrate, and warm-blooded for mammals). Mammals can be divided by genus (such as bears, elephants, giraffes, and moles), each with associated features. Each genus is further divided into species (such as bears can be polar, black, brown, speckled, etc.). Each species has its associated features. Consider the animal concept hierarchy in Figure 4.1.

Questions requiring consideration of information at different places in the hierarchy are answered more slowly than questions requiring information coded in nearby nodes (Collins & Quillian, 1969). For example, it takes longer to answer the question "Do birds have skin?" than the question "Do robins have red breasts?," since the feature of red breasts is stored directly with "robins" and the feature of skin is stored with "animals," which is further away in the animal hierarchy.

The associations between nodes are particularly important since activation of any particular part of the network results in **spreading activation** to parts of the hierarchy that are "close" and highly associated with the activated concept (Collins & Loftus, 1975; Goldstein, 2015). Activating some content can make it easier to understand related material. Thus, if the word *stone* is read by a person, followed by the word *rock*, *rock* is recognized more quickly than if *stone* had not been activated, since the activation of *stone* can spread to *rock*, a highly associated concept (Meyer, Schvaneveldt, & Ruddy, 1975; Neely, 1976, 1977). The sentence "The lawyer is in the bank" is understood more quickly if the sentence is preceded by a sentence containing words associated with lawyer and bank, such as *judge* or *money* (Anderson, 1984; McKoon & Ratcliff, 1979).

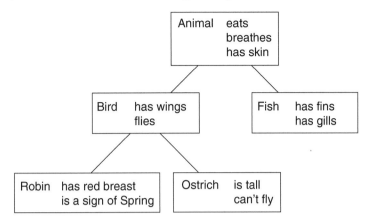

FIGURE 4.1. Sample hierarchical semantic network: animal hierarchy. From McCormick and Pressley (1997). Copyright © 1997 Christine B. McCormick and Michael Pressley. Adapted by permission.

What are the educational implications of semantic networks? Teachers often encourage students to activate background knowledge about to-be-presented material. They may remind students of what they learned yesterday or ask students to think about everyday experiences that are related to the topic at hand. This encourages spreading activation through a hierarchical network that encodes many associations between concepts. For example, a teacher may introduce a lesson on the Spanish Civil War by asking students to consider what they know about the Civil War in the United States. The students could be asked to think about the kinds of tensions and disagreements that lead to civil war. This activation should make it easier to understand new content and its relationship to the activated knowledge.

Sometimes students even reap the benefits of spreading activation while taking a test. For example, consider a student who draws a blank when reading a test question, skips the question, and decides to continue on with the test. Later on, another question on the test activates knowledge the student has. The resultant spreading activation brings to mind the answer to the question the student had skipped. A well-organized semantic network has great advantages!

Development of Concepts and Semantic Networks

Categorization is a primary way of organizing experience from an early age in that infants and very young children spontaneously group similar things (Gelman & Meyer, 2011). Children can also combine concepts into larger representations. Do children have hierarchical conceptual networks that resemble adult networks? In general, even preschool children possess knowledge about hierarchical relations between some of the concepts they know. Infants can abstract categories from presentation of a number of examples of category members (Anglin, 1977; Bomba & Siqueland, 1983; Strauss, 1979), and 2- to 3-year-olds can sort familiar objects into appropriate categories (Carey, 1985; Gelman & Baillargeon, 1983; Horton, 1982; Markman & Callanan, 1983; Sugarman, 1983).

Preschoolers, however, do not always use their knowledge of hierarchical relations. Children often prefer to use thematic relations rather than categories to represent categorizable content (Bruner, Olver, & Greenfield, 1966; Gelman & Meyer, 2011). Thus, when given a group of objects that can be sorted into categories (e.g., tiger, elephant, monkey, giraffe, banana, orange, grapes, apple), preschoolers often sort according to themes (e.g., monkeys eat bananas, elephants and giraffes live in the same house at the zoo, a tiger could eat an apple, Mommy puts oranges and grapes in her fruit salad). Unlike adults, children also *underextend* their use of concepts—using "duck" to refer only to one's pet duck—and *overextend* their use—using "duck" to refer to any bird larger than a robin (Bloom, 1973; Clark, 1973).

Cultural experience affects use of concepts and categories. Specifically, attendance in Western-style schools increases use of hierarchical categorical knowledge (Gauvain & Perez, 2015; Rogoff, 2003). Sharp, Cole, and Lave (1979) found that rural Mexicans without formal schooling classified objects on the basis of functional properties. For example, when given a triad of chicken, horse, and egg, they grouped chicken and egg together as related objects. In contrast, rural Mexicans with some formal schooling used categories comparable to Western-educated adults. They grouped chicken and horse together as examples of the conceptual category of animal.

Connectionist Approach: Neural Networks

In contrast to hierarchically organized semantic networks, the neural network approach suggests that categorical information is represented in multiple layer nets with numerous nodes per layer (Shiffrin, 2010) and the most significant part of the representation is in the connections between units of information (Rogers & McClelland, 2014). **Neural networks** have two basic components (Bechtel & Abrahamsen, 1991; Martindale, 1991; Rogers & McClelland, 2014). First, units of information, called "nodes," can be activated at various levels. If nodes are activated at a high level, we are conscious of what is activated. In general, the nodes are simpler than in concept theories (e.g., single features of letters can be nodes in neural network theory). Nodes can be activated at a low level of strength, outside of "consciousness," and still affect behavior. The second component in neural networks involves the connections between nodes. Two nodes are linked either by connections resulting in simultaneous excitation of the nodes (if one is excited, the other is) or connections inhibiting joint excitement (if one is excited, excitation of the other unit cannot occur). According to neural network theory, learning is the creation of connections and the changing strength or weight of connections. Connections are strengthened by simultaneous activation of nodes in a fashion analogous to strengthening of connections between neurons in the brain (Hebb, 1949). Patterns of activation are distributed over different parts of the brain with considerable redundancy in that a single neuron can be incorporated into the representation of multiple items.

Consider the sample neural network representing knowledge of the letters of the alphabet (Selfridge, 1959). The nodes in this case correspond to features of letters, such as a horizontal bar, a vertical bar, an acute angle, a curve bulging to the right, and a diagonal bar. Suppose a letter is presented to the system, in this case a letter activating the vertical bar and rightward bulge features. Each of these features is strongly connected to the capital letters *P* and *R*, since adults have seen many *P*'s and *R*'s in their lifetime. Each exposure to these letters strengthens the connection between these two features and these capital letters. Thus, the nodes representing both letters are activated. The decision that this is a *P* is reached, however, because a clear signal that the letter is an *R* requires another feature to be activated—a diagonal bar in the lower half of the letter. When the features add up to a *P*, inhibitory signals are sent out from the *P* node to the *R* node, as well as to all other letter nodes.

While children are learning letters, they are building up connections between features and letters. Preschoolers often know the names of the letters before they ever have any idea what the letters look like (Adams, 1990). For example, through listening to the "Alphabet Song," watching *Sesame Street*, playing with refrigerator letters, and reading books on Daddy's or Mommy's lap, a preschooler has many exposures to the name and shape of the letter *P*. With each of these exposures, the connections between the features of the letter *P* and the letter name strengthen. Eventually, features defining the letter automatically activate the letter name. Researchers are studying the correlations between children's conceptual development and their brain functioning to increase our understanding of how the neural networks that support mature thinking develop (Posner, 2001).

Strengthening of connections also explains word recognition (McClelland & Rumelhart, 1981). Consider what happens when the word *EACH* is presented. Connections are activated between the individual features defining each letter and the letters as a group. Connections between each letter and its position in a word are also activated. That is, activating the *E* also partially activates connections with words beginning with *E*. Activating the *A* also partially activates connections with words having *A* in the second position, and so on. For adults who have experienced the set of connections between first-*E*, second-*A*, third-*C*, and fourth-*H* many times before, activation of the word *EACH* and inhibition of other words (e.g., words sharing letters with *EACH*) occur.

What are the implications of the neural network model for educators? In this perspective, knowledge boils down to patterns of connections. The patterns develop slowly as reflected by the incremental nature of learning in that learners must master lower order knowledge before higher-order knowledge. Thus, knowledge of particular letters and associations between patterns of feature activations and their corresponding letter names and sounds must be well established before it is possible to learn to recognize words.

With the advent of brain-imaging techniques and sophisticated data analysis, researchers have been asking whether people actually form mental representations organizing conceptual information into hierarchies as described by Collins & Quillian (1969)? Semantic network hierarchies are efficient in terms of storage space (the number of nodes and associated features), but is memory storage space a major consideration? Are there advantages to storing information more redundantly and distributed across the brain as articulated in the connectionist perspective? Even with the progress technology has brought, the answer is not clear cut.

Concepts are typically learned through multiple experiences over a period of time and appear to be distributed across the brain more in line with the connectionist model (Yee, Chrysikou, & Thompson-Schill, 2014). Yet, some knowledge domains, such as the knowledge of living things in which specific instances share many common features, appear to be represented in ways that are more in line with the hierarchical semantic network model. When we search through our memory of categories, do we use an associative search, with each item recalled leading to retrieval of an associated item? Yes, it appears that something corresponding to an associative search is the most common search process. Yet, for some tasks and for people with extensive prior knowledge, the search is more likely to appear to be categorical in nature (Hills, Todd, & Jones, 2015). Basically, the connectionist models explain a great deal of data generated through sophisticated research techniques, but the more simplistic models, such as the semantic network model, do illustrate some ways in which we store and retrieve information (Murphy, Hampton, & Milovanovic, 2012).

Teaching Concepts

Although children do discover many of the most frequently encountered concepts (Gelman & Koenig, 2003), many others must be taught if they are to learn them, with a variety of ways of doing so (Klausmeier, 1990). A teacher may elect to teach a concept directly, asking students to learn a rule by first presenting the name and definition of the concept, including the defining features of the concept. For example, the defining rule for *square* would be a four-sided figure, with four equal sides and four right angles. Then the teacher might present examples and nonexamples of the concept, since students can learn a concept by seeing examples of what a concept is and what it is not, pointing out the defining features and the irrelevant characteristics of the examples. This approach works best if the examples are presented from easy to more difficult, if examples differ in terms of irrelevant features, and if the teacher points out the similarities and differences between the examples and the nonexamples. Often it is possible to teach abstract concepts by making them more concrete through the use of analogies or illustrations in diagrams or graphs. For example, the concept of "sonar" can be explained as being analogous to the movement detection system used by bats. Braithwaite and Goldstone (2015) examined learning abstract concepts from concrete examples and found that the students with prior knowledge in the content domain learned better when given more varied examples, those that had a wide range of superficial features but shared the underlying structure of the to-be-learned concept. In another study, undergraduate students learned more definitions of fairly abstract psychological terms if they were provided with concrete examples illustrating the concept or generated concrete examples themselves (Rawson & Dunlosky, 2016; Rawson, Thomas, & Jacoby, 2015).

In contrast to this *direct explanation approach*, the teacher can elect a *discovery approach*, presenting examples and nonexamples and asking students to discover the definition of the concept and to determine its defining features and irrelevant characteristics. The students work on this independently or in groups, and the teacher answers questions generated by the students. In a *guided discovery approach*, the teacher supports the students' discovery of the defining features and irrelevant characteristics of the concept through teacher questioning. Innovations in computer program design may lead to advances in supporting the discovery learning experiences of students in school contexts (de Jong & van Joolingen, 1998; Kumar & Sherwood, 1997).

The particular concept learning approach that a teacher uses varies depending on the content being taught and the teacher's teaching philosophy. Learner characteristics are also relevant. McDaniel, Cahill, Robbins, and Wiener (2014) identified individual differences in whether undergraduate students choose to learn concepts using exemplars (instances of concepts) or by rules (abstractions of the underlying similarity). The learning approach appeared to be a stable characteristic or preference of the students, and learners with greater working memory capacity were more likely to use rules.

A major educational implication of the connectionist model is the importance of practice for building and strengthening connections (Annett, 1989). Practice can take many forms. Teachers can help students build connections by providing multiple ways to practice in a variety of ways. For example, mental practice can be effective (Feltz, Landers, & Becker, 1988), and practice tests help strengthen connections (Glover, 1989; McDaniel, Agarwal, Huesler, McDermott, & Roediger, 2011; Roediger & Karpicke, 2006). Whenever possible, teachers should provide feedback with practice so that students have information on what they need to learn (Butler & Roediger, 2008; Lhyle & Kulhavy, 1987). Teachers can encourage students to space out their practice (**distributed practice**) rather than cramming all their practice into one long episode (**massed practice**). Distributed practice is more effective than massed practice, even for young children (Benjamin &Tullis, 2010; Simon, 2013; Son & Simon, 2012; Toppino, Kasserman, & Mracek, 1991). Connectionist theories clarify what is meant by the idea that "practice makes perfect." What practice does is make connections and strengthen them.

Finally, methods of teaching concepts, particularly conceptual knowledge in mathematics, are influenced by culture (Rittle-Johnson, Schneider, & Star, 2015). Should conceptual learning precede procedural learning? In other words, should the abstract general principles be taught before the series of steps used to solve a mathematical problem? Educators in the United States typically emphasize conceptual learning before the learning of procedures. Educators in Asian countries, however, believe that practicing procedures is a route to conceptual understanding. In a review of the research evidence, Rittle-Johnson et al. concluded that the relationship between procedural skill (computations) and conceptual understanding was bidirectional, each supporting the other.

Images

Could you describe where you live to your classmates? As you try to do so, you would likely access mental pictures, or **images,** from your long-term memory store. How is knowledge in the form of images represented? Allan Paivio proposed the dual-coding model (Clark & Paivio, 1991; Paivio, 1971, 1986) to articulate the difference between images and the other forms of knowledge described earlier. This model describes knowledge as associative networks of verbal and imaginal representations. The verbal system contains word-like codes for objects and events and abstract ideas that are only arbitrarily related to what they represent. For instance, the word *book* has no physical resemblance to an actual book.

The imagery system, in contrast, contains nonverbal representations that resemble the perceptions giving rise to them. It includes visual images (e.g., of a bell), auditory images (the sound of the bell), actions (motion required to ring the bell), sensations related to emotion (your racing heart when you hear the bell ring and you are not in your classroom), and other nonverbal representations. Thus, for the book example, an image of a book shares visual and tactile qualities with the perception of an actual book.

Items in the imagery system are connected to items in the verbal system. For example, the connections between your image and verbal representations permit you to make mental images given words or to generate the names of items depicted in pictures. Connections within both the verbal and the nonverbal systems exist. In the verbal system, words are associated to other words, so that some students associate the word *school* with the words *friends, work,* and *challenge.* Categories and their instances are connected within the verbal system, so that the word *tree* is associated with the words *maple, oak,* and *pine.* In the nonverbal system, images are connected within or across sensory modalities. Thus, an image of your grandmother may be associated with the warm feeling of a hug and the smell of chocolate chip cookies in the oven.

Is there research support for Paivio's dual-coding theory (Paivio, 1986)? Concrete materials, which more readily elicit images, are more memorable than abstract materials, and pictures are learned better than words. Words can be read faster than pictures can be named, suggesting that words access the verbal code directly and pictures access the verbal code only through the image. Mental imagery can have a powerful effect on recall. Material that is easy to image is recalled more easily. For example, readers who construct mental images as they read facilitate their understanding of what they read (Pressley, 1976, 1977; Sadoski, 1983, 1985; Sadoski & Paivio, 2001), with much prior knowledge actually represented as images. For example, think of what you know about bears or skyscrapers—it is almost impossible to think about these concepts without activating images stored in long-term memory (Sadoski, Paivio, & Goetz, 1991).

Stephen Kosslyn and his colleagues (Kosslyn, Thomas, & Ganis, 2006) have summarized research evidence supporting the psychological reality of mental imagery. In a classic study, Shepard and Metzler (1971) presented adults with a complex geometric figure and a second figure, which was either the same figure (but rotated 0 to as much as 180 degrees) or a mirror image (also rotated some number of degrees). The task was to decide whether the original figure and the rotation were the "same" figure or a "different" figure. The amount of time needed to recognize the same figure as "same" was a linear function of the number of degrees of rotation required to make the figure parallel the original figure.

Since the time required for mental rotation corresponds to the physical process of rotation, the participants were likely "flipping" the figures in their heads, using some kind of image. Even 4-year-olds seem to rotate figures in their heads. It takes longer for a 4-year-old to decide that a capital *R* and an upside-down *R* (i.e., an *R* flipped 180 degrees) are the same letter than it takes to decide that the *R* and an *R* on its side (i.e., flipped 90 degrees) are the same letter (Marmor, 1975; see Figure 4.2). With increasing age during childhood and continuing to adulthood, speed and facility in mental imagery rotation increase (Kosslyn, Margolis, Barrett, Goldknopf, & Daley, 1990; Zabalia, 2002). Additional support for the psychological reality of images comes from people's descriptions of having and using mental images. For

FIGURE 4.2. It takes 4-year-olds longer to decide that the figure on the left is an *R* than to decide that the figure on the right is an *R*, thus indicating that children rotate images in their heads. From McCormick and Pressley (1997). Copyright © 1997 Christine B. McCormick and Michael Pressley. Adapted by permission.

instance, people report flipping the cubes in their head in the Shepard and Metzler (1971) task. People report images more often when learning concrete materials than when learning abstract materials (and report relying on their images during recall of the concrete materials).

Schemas

Not all types of knowledge can be captured by the knowledge representations we have already discussed. Sometimes specific units of information commonly co-occur in particular situations, forming larger chunks of knowledge best described as schemas **Schemas** are generalized knowledge about objects, situations, or events. For example, your knowledge of what you might expect to see when you go to a play is represented in a schema. You would expect scenery, costumes, actors, props, separate acts, and an intermission. Schemas are the skeleton structures of commonly encountered events, with the particular ways the skeleton takes on flesh varying from instance to instance.

Consider an example of a schema for an event that unfolds over time, specifically, the schema for a ship christening (Anderson & Pearson, 1984). It includes the purpose, which is the blessing of the ship. It includes information about where it is done (in dry dock), by whom (a celebrity), and when it occurs (just before launching of a new ship). The christening action is also represented (breaking a bottle of California champagne that is suspended from a rope). These parts of a schema are referred to as *variables*, or *slots*. At any particular christening, these slots are instantiated with particular instances (New Haven, Connecticut, with the president of the United States breaking a bottle of California champagne on a new submarine). There are constraints on the instances that can occur in these slots. The celebrity is usually from government and is unlikely to be someone of ill repute (e.g., a politician facing ethics charges or an actor just released from rehab). There are constraints on the champagne as well, with a bottle of California champagne acceptable but a rare bottle of French champagne unlikely. Generalized knowledge, such as a ship christening schema, assists the interpretation of new information. If you see a picture of the First Lady hitting something large with what looks to be a champagne bottle, you will understand that picture more quickly if you have a ship christening schema. Schemas help us process information in a variety of different contexts (e.g., see the reference to gender schema in Chapter 5).

Children's Use of Schemas

Do children store knowledge in schemas, and, if they do, how do schemas affect their processing of new material? Not surprisingly, the schemas that children possess are determined by events that recur in their lives. Thus, children have schemas representing events such as dinner, bedtime, making cookies, and going to a museum (Hudson & Nelson, 1983; Hudson & Shapiro, 1991; McCarthy & Nelson, 1981; Nelson, 1978; Nelson & Gruendel, 1981). If children listen to a brief story pertaining to one of their schemas, they can answer inferential questions about the story. These questions require knowledge about the situation described in the text that is over and above the information specified in the text, knowledge contained in the children's schemas. Consider the following short story (Hudson & Slackman, 1990):

Johnny and his mom and dad were going to McDonald's. Johnny's father told him he could have dessert if he ate all his dinner. They waited in line. They ate their hamburgers. And they had ice cream. (p. 378)

When presented with the question "Why did they stand in line?," the 4- to 7-year-olds had no difficulty responding since the schema for McDonald's contains this information, even though the story did not.

The powerful effect of schemas on children's comprehension and memory is evident when children listen to stories that include information inconsistent with schemas stored by most children. Consider this story that Hudson and Nelson (1983) presented to 4- to 7-year-olds:

One day it was Sally's birthday and Sally had a birthday party.
Sally's friends all came to her house.
Sally opened her presents and found lots of new toys.
Everybody played pin the tail on the donkey.
Then Sally and her friends ate the cake.
They had some chocolate and vanilla ice cream.
Everybody had peppermint candy, too.
Sally blew out all the candles on the cake.
Sally's friends brought presents with them.
Then it was time for Sally's friends to go home.

Is there anything wrong about this story? You probably realized that Sally opened the presents before the friends brought them. In addition, the children ate the cake before the candles were blown out. The children in Hudson and Nelson's (1983) study used a birthday party schema to comprehend and remember this story. Some children repaired the story during recall by not mentioning either one or both of the out-of-order elements. Others reported the out-of-order acts in the schematically correct order rather than as specified in the story. In short, recall of the story was consistent with the schema for the birthday party even though the original presentation of the story was not consistent with this schema.

Text Structure Schemas

Students develop schemas for recurring intellectual tasks. For instance, texts have conventional structures that are familiar to readers (Clariana, Wolfe, & Kim, 2014; Kintsch & Greene, 1978). Both **narrative text structures** (i.e., the structures of fictional stories) and **expository text structures** (i.e., the structures of factual texts) have been identified.

Narratives, that is, stories, have a structure: a grammar. A story has a *setting* and an *event structure*, which is composed of *episodes* (Mandler, 1978, 1987). Each episode has a *beginning*, which is an event initiating a complex reaction; a *complex reaction*, which is composed of an emotional or cognitive response and a state the protagonist wishes to achieve; a *goal path*, which involves a plan of action by the character and the consequence of setting the plan of action in motion; and an *ending*, which is a reaction.

Here is a simple two-episode story adapted from Mandler (1978, p. 22):

Once there were twins, Tom and Jennifer, who had so much trouble their parents called them the unlucky twins [*setting*]. One day, Jennifer's parents gave her a dollar bill to buy a turtle she wanted, but on the way to the pet store she lost it [*beginning* of first episode]. Jennifer was worried that her parents would be angry with her so she decided to search every bit of the sidewalk where she had walked [*reaction*]. She looked in all the cracks and in the grass along the way [plan of action, part of the *goal path*]. She finally found the dollar bill in the grass [consequence, part of the *goal path*]. But when Jennifer got to the store, the pet store man told her that someone else had just bought the last turtle, and he didn't have any more [*ending*]. The same day, Tom fell off a swing and broke his leg [*beginning* of second episode]. He wanted to run and play with the other kids [*reaction*]. So he got the kids to pull him around in his wagon [plan of action, part of the *goal path*]. While they were playing, Tom fell out of his wagon and broke his arm [consequence, part of the *goal path*]. Tom's parents said he was even unluckier than Jennifer and made him sit in bed until he got well [second *ending*].

How does story grammar knowledge influence story recall? First, stories that do not conform to the story grammar structure are difficult to remember (and are processed more slowly) compared to stories that do conform. This is true for both children and adults (Kintsch, Mandel, & Kozminsky, 1977; Mandler & Johnson, 1977; Stein & Nezworski, 1978). Second, when story information is presented in an order inconsistent with conventional story grammar, both children and adults tend to "fix the story up" at recall, remembering the elements of the story in an order consistent with the story grammar (Mandler & DeForest, 1979; Stein & Glenn, 1979). Third, the probability that an element will be recalled from a story depends on the role it plays in the story as defined by story grammar (Mandler, 1984; Mandler & Johnson, 1977; Stein & Glenn, 1979). Fourth, reading times for material at the beginning of episodes are greater than for material in the middle of episodes. Content at the end of episodes is processed especially quickly (Haberlandt, 1980; Mandler & Goodman, 1982).

Just as stories have structures, so do expository texts. Perhaps an English teacher once asked you to write an expository text designed to achieve a specific purpose. Maybe you were asked to write a descriptive text or a text that compared and contrasted two perspectives. These types of text are examples of expository text structures. Meyer (1985) outlined five common expository text structures: *description* (providing information about the attributes of something), *cause/effect* (explaining a causal relationship), *compare/contrast* (highlighting similarities and differences), *sequence* (placing things in order, typically corresponding to the passage of time), and *problem/solution* (showing how a problem can be solved.) Expository text structures typically are associated with words signaling the underlying structure. For example, signal words associated with the cause/effect text structure include "as a result . . . ," "in order to . . . ," "if . . . then," "this is why," "the reason . . . ," and so on (Yeh, Schwarz, & Baule, 2011). Texts consistent with well-known expository structures are easier to understand and remember (Kintsch, 1982; Kintsch & Yarbrough, 1982).

Mathematics Problem Schemas

Most of the mathematics problems presented in elementary and high school textbooks have common underlying structures. Mayer (1981) analyzed high school algebra texts and identified about 100 typical problem types. For example, an algebra textbook may contain a problem like this one:

If a car travels 10 hours at 30 miles per hour, how far will it go?

For many students, this problem activates their mathematical problem schema for "distance = rate × time" problems. Here's another problem example:

How much will be earned if $1,000 is invested at 8% interest for 1 year?

This problem activates the "interest = interest rate × principal" schema.

Students who have completed high school math and science courses have developed schemas for the problem types in these courses and can classify problems into types (Hinsley, Hayes, & Simon, 1977). In addition, students use their problem-solving schemas as they identify the critical information needed to solve the problems (Hayes, Waterman, & Robinson, 1977; Mayer, 1982; Robinson & Hayes, 1978). This may be one reason students who possess greater knowledge of problem schemas—and hence, are more proficient at problem classification—also are better able to solve problems (Silver, 1987). Researchers studying mathematical problem solving at the elementary school have also identified word problem schemas sharing defining features and requiring similar solutions (Fuchs et al., 2010; Powell, 2011). Recognizing the mathematical problem schema provides a framework and a solution plan. The problem types encountered in early elementary school include *total or combine* problems (small groups combined into a larger one), *difference or compare* problems (two quantities compared in terms of magnitude), and *change* problems (an increase or decrease in an initial quantity.)

Educational Implications

What are the implications of schema theory for educators? Schemas have a powerful effect on the comprehension and recall of information in learners of all ages. Schemas focus student attention, influence the inferences students make, and have a bearing on students' recall of information. When teachers introduce new lessons, they need to try to activate schemas that will facilitate students' understanding of the new material. Some students, however, may not have developed the text structure schemas or mathematics schemas they need to succeed. Fortunately, teachers can teach explicitly the appropriate schema to these students. For example, poor readers can be taught story grammar elements and to look for story grammar information as they read. Weak readers in the elementary grades who are taught to look for setting, character, and episodic elements of text remember more of what they read (Nolte & Singer, 1985; Short & Ryan, 1984). Lauren and Allen (1999) included story grammar instruction as part of a package of reading interventions in the elementary grades (in combination with word recognition instruction, silent reading by students, and parents reading with their children).

Awareness of expository text structure increases with age, but students can be taught to better detect underlying text structure, which improves their reading comprehension and recall of text. In a meta-analysis of 45 research studies examining the effectiveness of expository text instruction for students ranging from second graders to twelfth graders, Hebert, Bohaty, Nelson, and Brown (2016) concluded that teaching students about expository text structure improves reading comprehension. Yeh, Schwarz, and Baule (2011) found that instructions that increased recognition of the five main types of expository text and the word signals commonly used in the text structures resulted in better awareness of structure and better recall. Moreover, tracking the eye movements of the students revealed that they looked back at the problem statement and associated signal words as they were reading the texts. Expository text instruction typically includes text analysis, recognizing clue words or signals, or comprehension strategies such as creating a graphic organizer. This instruction can be effective even when provided in a web-based delivery system (Williams et al., 2016).

Schema instruction has also proved beneficial in increasing mathematical problem-solving performance (Fuchs et al., 2010; Powell, 2011). In these instructional approaches, students typically are asked to read mathematics word problems and are explicitly taught to identify the underlying structure (the schema) of the problems and to apply the solution method corresponding to that type of problem. Students are also taught that the superficial features of a problem, such as vocabulary or format, may not be relevant to identifying the underlying problem structure.

Situated, Distributed Knowledge

Some knowledge is not separable from the actions that give rise to it or from the culture in which those actions occur (Brown, Collins, & Duguid, 1989). That is, knowledge and thinking are not just "in-the-head" things. For instance, your knowledge of this course is in your head, but also in the notes you take in class! Consider the 747 pilot. His or her thinking involves juggling information in the head and then combining it in meaningful ways with information on the many digital displays in the cockpit. There are manuals to consult as well, which are sometimes consulted in flight as part of decision making. Thinking involves both in-the-head activity and representations and external representations. It is distributed between the head and the environmental situation. The knowledge and thinking can be described as **situated cognition** (Jenlik, 2013; Moore & Rocklin, 1998).

Thinking and knowledge sometimes are also distributed in another way, across several heads in interaction or across a human head and a computer (Derry, DuRussel, & O'Donnell, 1998; Hewitt & Scardamalia, 1998; Olson & Olson, 2003). This is **distributed cognition** (sometimes referred to as "socially distributed" or "socially shared cognition"; Resnick, Levine, & Teasley, 1991). Think back to the 747 pilot. The pilot is not alone in the cockpit. Co-pilots interact with the pilot, providing key information and additional perspectives. Distributed cognition occurs during conversations. The meaning constructed during the conversation is not a product of one head but a product of several heads in interaction with one another (Bereiter, 1990; Hutchins, 1991). By heads coming together in conversation, more powerful interpretations and understandings sometimes emerge than would have occurred to any one of the participants in the conversation thinking alone. Why? First of all, the different heads have different prior knowledge. Moreover, the different heads have attended to different aspects of the information being considered. As the talk in the group proceeds, connections are made. Something Mariah says connects with knowledge activated in Billy, who in turn responds. In doing so, Billy may combine some of what he knows in common with Mariah and something Mariah said that he did not know previously to produce a new inference. This inference might trigger something in Lukas and so it goes. . . . Consider another example offered by Rogoff (2003): the distributed cognition displayed by girl scouts during cookie sales. The members of a troop put their heads together to come up with a planning strategy and ponder a number of issues. What neighborhoods are appropriate for selling? How can they get permission to sell in front of a grocery store? What varieties of cookies should they preorder and in what number? How can they help themselves make change? Typically, this conversation is guided by the troop leader or that year's "cookie mom," but as the troop gets older, the troop members themselves handle more and more responsibility. The power of socially distributed cognition in classroom conversations will be taken up further in Chapter 6.

Chapter Summary and Evaluation

Cognitive development occurs as a function of increasing short-term memory or working memory capacity, increasing use of strategies, and an increasing and more accessible knowledge base. The increasing functional capacity of working memory can be explained by neurological development, speed of information processing, rehearsal strategies, prior knowledge that enables chunking, and inhibition of irrelevant information.

Whether or not a child uses a memory strategy depends on the child's age and the strategy in question. Preschoolers routinely use some simple strategies, such as looking at a spot where a to-be-remembered item is hidden. Familiarity of setting, materials, and task combine to permit greater strategic competence by preschoolers. Rehearsal strategies develop during the early grade school years and elaboration strategies emerge during the later grade school and high school years. Many complex strategies are not always common even among university-age students. Some cultures encourage use of strategies more than other cultures. Whether parents and educators encourage and teach strategy use in children is an important determinant of whether or not children use strategies.

If given a small amount of instruction, students can often successfully apply strategies they do not use on their own. Unfortunately, even when children receive instructions to carry out strategic processes effectively, there is no guarantee that they will maintain and transfer strategy use. Metacognitive knowledge, such as knowledge about where and when to use a strategy (conditional knowledge) and the gains produced by a strategy (utility knowledge), increases maintenance and transfer of a strategy. Students do not always develop metacognitive knowledge on their own.

A variety of different types of representations function in thinking (see Table 4.5). Knowing how to do something is *procedural knowledge*. Knowing about something is *declarative knowledge*. By adulthood, adults have built up complex networks of procedural and declarative knowledge through experience. Procedures develop from declarative representations through repeated practice.

Features of stimuli are critical to classification in both feature comparison and prototype theories of concept formation. Prototype theories can better explain how nondefinitive features contribute to classification (such as "over 40" for grandmothers) and how people classify instances of fuzzy concepts. Concepts are related to each other in hierarchically organized semantic networks. Although some of children's knowledge probably is in categorical hierarchies like those of adults, many concepts held by children differ from those of adults. Moreover, children are less likely to rely on hierarchical concept knowledge than are adults.

Connections between units of information are best represented in neural networks. Nodes in neural networks are linked by either simultaneous excitation or

TABLE 4.5. Summary of Different Representations of Knowledge

Concepts

Description: Mental representation of a category of items. Concepts may be connected in hierarchical semantic networks.

Classroom example: Animal phyla, types of rocks.

Neural networks

Description: Connected nodes in distributed networks. Knowledge is in the connections.

Classroom example: Features of letters associated with letter names.

Schemas

Description: Generalized knowledge about objects, situations, and events.

Classroom example: What goes into an essay (expository schema)? What kind of math problem is this (mathematics problem schema)?

Images

Description: Nonverbal representations that resemble perceptual experience.

Classroom example: Visualizing follow-through in throwing a baseball. Visualizing a dance performance.

inhibition. Learning is the creation of connections and the strengthening of connections between nodes.

Images are nonverbal representations that resemble perceptual experience. According to Paivio's dual-coding model, items in the imagery system are connected to items in the nonverbal system. Evidence for the psychological reality of images is found in self-reports and studies of mental rotation.

Adults and children have schemas for familiar events, and these schemas determine how new information is processed, interpreted, and retrieved. The availability of this generalized representation from a very young age suggests that schematic representation is a fundamental human competency.

Research derived from the information-processing perspective and cognitive science has informed many of the Big Ideas of developmental psychology introduced in Chapter 1.

Nature and Nurture

Both short-term and long-term memories depend on human biology, with neuropsychology providing insights into the biological mechanisms underlying memory. Psychologists interested in the learning sciences are increasingly allying with neuropsychologists, making the biological foundations of cognition more apparent. The environment plays an important role as well. Institutions, such as school, can have a profound effect on the information-processing abilities of students. For example, some schools are teaching their students strategies that can be applied to academic tasks, such as reading and writing.

Continuity and Discontinuity

The information-processing perspective is that change is more continuous than discontinuous or stage-like. Some theorists (such as neo-Piagetians) have used evidence of increases in short-term memory capacity with development to explain stage-like development (such as Piaget's stages).

Universal and Culture-Specific

It's a safe bet that people everywhere have the kinds of representations described in this chapter. Even so, research on cognitive development makes it obvious that experience really matters. The specific strategies used by a child depend on culture and experience. The specific schemas known by children depend on experience. Children learn the strategies and the knowledge emphasized in the culture, by the schools they attend, and by the family.

Active and Passive Child

Activity, from the information-processing perspective, comprises using strategies and relating current stimulation to prior knowledge. Because strategic competency and knowledge increase with development, the older child can be much more intellectually active than the younger child. How active the child is depends on a number of factors, including the child's goals and motivational beliefs (see Chapter 9). For example, children who believe that their efforts can make a difference are more likely to exert academic effort than those who believe their performance is determined by innate ability.

REVIEW OF KEY TERMS

concept A mental representation of a category of related items.

conditional knowledge Knowledge of when and where strategies are useful.

cumulative rehearsal A strategy for remembering information in which the learner repeats all the items in a series, in order, as each new item is presented.

declarative knowledge Knowledge about things; knowledge that something is the case.

distributed cognition Thinking that is not the product of one student but of several students in interaction with one another.

distributed practice Practice that is spaced out over a period of time, leading to better performance than the performance resulting from massed practice.

elaboration A strategy for remembering information by constructing a meaningful context, either visual or verbal.

encode To create a memory.

executive function Cognition necessary for conscious control of actions and thoughts in pursuit of goal-directed behavior.

expository text structures Schemas for factual texts.

images Information stored in mental pictures.

labeling A strategy used by young children on serial recall tasks in which the name of an item is said as it is presented.

maintain Continue to use a strategy when it is appropriate.

massed practice Practice that is crammed into one long episode, leading to lower performance than the performance resulting from distributed practice.

metacognition Knowledge about and awareness of thinking, including the knowledge of when and where to use acquired strategies.

narrative text structures Schemas for fictional stories.

neural networks Connections linking units of information.

organization Grouping information into categories or patterns on the basis of relationships or connections.

procedural knowledge Knowledge of how to do things.

proceduralization The movement, developed with practice, from a declarative representation of a sequence of actions to a single procedure.

rehearsal A strategy of repeating information to be remembered.

retrieve To access a memory.

schemas Generalized knowledge about objects, situations, and events.

semantic networks The way in which concepts are connected to each other in a pattern of associations.

serial recall task A task in which students are asked to remember items in the order they were presented.

short-term memory A memory store of limited capacity and duration; closely related to the concept of "working memory." Short-term memory typically refers to passive storage of information.

situated cognition Knowledge that cannot be separated from the actions that give rise to it or from the culture in which those actions occur.

spreading activation The way in which concepts connected to each other in a semantic network are activated.

strategies Plans of action that may result in a solution to a problem or achievement of a goal.

transfer Apply strategies to new situations and tasks.

utility knowledge Knowledge of the potential benefits of using a strategy.

working memory A memory store of limited capacity and duration; closely related to the concept of short-term memory. Working memory typically includes updating or manipulation of information.

CHAPTER 5

Social Theories of Development and Learning

This chapter summarizes theories of learning and development that place emphasis on the influence of social variables upon development. The three perspectives featured in this chapter—social learning theory, Freud's theory of psychosexual development, and Erikson's theory of psychosocial development—have all inspired extensive research and are reflected in current thinking about children's relations with others and the effects of others on children's personalities, social behaviors, and cognition.

In recent decades, social learning theory has clearly been the most influential of the three theories presented in this chapter, stimulating a great deal of research and producing widespread applications to educational settings. Thus, we begin with an analysis of social learning theory, a theoretical perspective favored by many contemporary developmental psychologists.

Social Learning Theory

Children learn many things just from watching others. That is, other people serve as **behavioral models.** This is the main principle of **social learning theory,** proposed by Albert Bandura and his colleagues (Bandura, 1969; Bandura & Walters, 1963). Developmental psychologists have studied observational learning of a wide range of behaviors including aggression, altruism, sex-typed behaviors, caregiver–infant attachment, and social dependency. Whatever the behavior, social learning theorists have been able to generate evidence supporting the conclusion that what people see and hear influences their development (e.g., alcohol abuse, Maisto, Carey, & Bradizza, 1999; spirituality, Bandura, 2003; psychopathology, Thyer & Myers, 1998).

Social learning theory began as a *behavioral theory*, meaning a theory that focuses on behavior that can be observed rather than on internal, unobservable explanatory variables (such as Piaget's operations, described in Chapter 3). It quickly became obvious that children's social learning could not be understood through studying behavior alone—cognitive processes clearly influenced behavior. Social learning theory is now very much a cognitive-behavioral approach to explaining social and personality development (Zimmerman & Schunk, 2003), one that can explain development in virtually all cultural contexts (Bandura, 2002a), as well as the effects of contexts that are only experienced at a distance, such as through the media of film and television (Bandura, 2002b).

Observational Learning of Behaviors and Expectancies

In observational learning, people learn through **vicarious experiences.** That is, when they see others experience rewards and punishments, they form expectations about the rewards or punishments they might receive for their own behaviors. For example, in a seminal research study, Albert Bandura (1965) asked young children to view a film in which a child exhibited some very novel physical and verbal aggressive behaviors toward a set of toys. At the completion of the film, the child model was either punished for the aggression (spanked and verbally rebuked), reinforced for it (given soft drinks, candy, and praise), or not given any consequences for the behavior. After watching the film, the children were left alone in the room where the film was made with an opportunity to play with the toys seen in the film. Children who watched the film where the child model was spanked for aggression were much less likely to exhibit the aggressive behaviors when interacting with the toys than if they watched the film depicting reward or no consequences for the aggression. Then, all children in the experiment were offered stickers and fruit juice if they would show the experimenter the aggressive behaviors that the film model had exhibited. The children had little difficulty reproducing the behaviors.

What was going on in this situation? The children had clearly learned the aggressive behaviors in question because they could reproduce those behaviors when given an incentive to do so. However, they were less likely to perform the aggressive behaviors after viewing the film in which the child model had been punished because they also learned to expect punishment for aggressive behaviors from the film. Performance of a behavior depends on knowing a response as well as the expectation of rewards. When punishments are expected, performance often will not occur unless there are offsetting rewards. For many children in the Bandura study, the fun of playing aggressively with the toys was not worth the risk of punishment.

Consider another example. Although you have seen many high-speed car chases on television or at the movies, they are statistically rare. Why? People know that if they speed away from a traffic stop, they may be caught and punished. This *expectancy* has been established through years of observing the villains on television or in the movies being punished for their wicked deeds. Moreover, the punishments are usually very aversive (i.e., they have negative *value*), ranging from personal remorse and guilt to imprisonment. Whether a person executes a given behavior depends on his or her expectations of rewards or punishments for performing the behavior and the value of these rewards and punishments. In other words, the probability of performing a behavior *X* is a function of the *expectancy of reward or punishment* for *X and* the *value of the reward or punishment* (Rotter, 1954).

Try this little test of your understanding if you are not sure whether you understand expectancy–value theory:

1. You expect that studying for a test will make it very likely that you will pass the test. The test does not count in your grades and is on material that is boring. Will you study or not?

2. You expect that studying for a test will not increase the likelihood that you will pass it or earn a better grade. Your entire semester's grade depends on this test. Will you study or not?

3. You expect that studying for a test will increase your grade, you like the content, and the grade in this course is important to you. Will you study or not?

For situation 1, you probably will not study because the value of the reward is low and there is a negative value (boredom) associated with studying. For situation 2, you probably will not study because your expectation of reward following studying behavior is low. For situation 3, however, you likely will study since the expectation of reward is high and there are two sources of positively valued reward: the pleasure of studying this material and an important course grade.

Cognitive Mechanisms of Social Learning

Imitation in its most basic form is apparently innate. Within hours of birth, infants who observe an adult opening his or her mouth or sticking out his or her tongue respond by opening their mouths or sticking out their tongues (Meltzoff, 1985, 2002; Meltzoff & Moore, 1977, 1983). That newborns can do it does not mean that it is simple, however. There is extensive cognitive mediation of most behaviors that children learn through observation. Four cognitive processes, in particular, mediate social learning (Bandura, 1986; Meltzoff & Prinz, 2002; Schunk, 2012): *attentional processes, retention processes, production processes*, and *motivational processes*.

Attentional Processes

What the learner observes or attends to depends on characteristics of the model and characteristics of the observer. Not everyone has equal access to the same types of models. Children who are raised in environments with gentle people have more opportunities to view gentle behaviors than children who are raised in environments filled with aggressive people. To some extent, all of us, with the exception of very young children, have some control over the social models available to us. For example, children who elect to play soccer in a league surround themselves with models of athletic behaviors. Adolescents who elect gang life select themselves into situations where aggression is modeled. In both the soccer and the gang situations, some of the participants will command greater attention than others. Thus, the best player on the soccer team is more likely to be watched and imitated than other players, both with respect to soccer behaviors and other behaviors (such as shoe styles or hair styles). The leader of a gang also is much more likely to be watched and imitated than someone who is not as respected by gang members.

Retention Processes

Once a person attends to a behavior, it must be remembered if it is to affect future behaviors. Thus, processes that enhance memory, such as imagery and rehearsal, are mediators of observational learning (Bandura, Grusec, & Menlove, 1966; Bandura & Jeffery, 1973; Bandura, Jeffery, & Bachicha, 1974; see also Chapter 4). For example, imaging speaking in public may improve public speaking performances and visualizing leaping over hurdles may improve performance in a race.

Production Processes

Not only must learners perceive and remember a behavioral sequence, they must be able to produce it themselves. In some cases, the observed sequence is readily reproducible. In other cases, the observer can carry out components but not the entire action. Sometimes individual components must be acquired before the entire sequence can be executed. For example, a skilled gymnast can watch another gymnast's routine (e.g., on the balance beam) and copy most or all of it immediately. Less skilled gymnasts have to break the routine into segments (such as practicing the mount over and over again, practicing a particular type of handstand over and over, practicing the dismount over and over) before attempting to integrate the segments. For some of us, it would never be possible to execute a routine on a balance beam no matter how frequently we had observed it.

Motivational Processes

A child who really wants to learn how to score goals in soccer pays closer attention to the coach demonstrating kicking at the post than does a child who has little real interest in the game. The interested child sometimes can be observed kicking at the post of a goal jerry-rigged in the backyard, rehearsing what he or she saw the coach do at practice. What is learned through observational mechanisms depends on the particular motivations of the child, which determine what the child attends to, attempts to remember, and rehearses later.

A child's motivation goes far in allowing the child to be a determinant of his or her own social learning. But the child also has a major role in controlling what he or she had opportunity to observe via a process called **reciprocal determinism** (Bandura, 1986). Reciprocal determinism refers to dynamic interactions between a person, a person's behavior, and the environment. A child's reactions to environmental events can affect subsequent events. Thus, the child at soccer practice who attends carefully to the coach and works hard to copy the coach's approach to kicking gets more of the coach's future attention, including additional modeling by the coach of even more advanced skills. The child's cognitive processing of modeled behaviors affects the child's subsequent behaviors, which in turn changes the future environment in ways that affect what the child sees and hears in the future. Observational learning is very complicated, determined by the environment, but also by the child, who in turn affects the environments to come (Bell, 1968; Bell & Harper, 1977; Schneirla, 1957).

Other Mechanisms of Social Learning

Social learning involves more than observational learning. It also depends on other learning processes, classical and operant conditioning, and is shaped by the pattern of reinforcement and punishment in the environment.

Classical Conditioning

Ivan Pavlov first identified **classical conditioning** in the late 19th century (Bower & Hilgard, 1981). Pavlov observed that when meat powder is placed in a dog's mouth, the dog salivates. The food is an **unconditioned stimulus** that elicits an **unconditioned response:** salivation. Pairing a neutral stimulus, such as the sound of a bell, with the food powder results in conditioning dogs to salivate at the sound of the bell. The bell is a **conditioned stimulus** that has acquired the power to elicit what is now the **conditioned response** of salivation. Thus, neutral stimuli that accompany (usually precede) unconditioned stimuli often become conditioned stimuli.

Classical conditioning is not a very prominent part of what we typically think of as school learning, but humans frequently do develop emotional responses through classical conditioning. For example, fearful reactions to stimuli associated with pain are easily learned by humans via classical conditioning (Bandura, 1986; Hoffman, 1969; Watson, 1927). Thus, a student who trips over a hurdle may become classically conditioned to fear gym class. Or a student who was embarrassed by knocking over a podium during a speech may become classically conditioned to fear public speaking.

Classically conditioned emotional responses often are not maintained. They can undergo a process called **extinction** by subsequent experience with the conditioned stimulus that is not followed by the unconditioned response. Thus, if future experiences in gym class or speaking in front of the class are pleasant, after a while the fear subsides.

Operant Conditioning

Operant conditioning applies to more learning situations than classical conditioning. In classical conditioning, the focus of learning is on the stimulus that elicits a response, typically an involuntary emotional response or reflex. In operant conditioning, the focus is on an emitted response, a behavior the learner can control. Although B. F. Skinner is the psychologist most associated with operant conditioning (Skinner, 1953), E. L. Thorndike detailed its most fundamental principle in 1913. Thorndike's Law of Effect describes the following relationship: the likelihood of an operant response being emitted is increased when it is followed by a reinforcer.

Consider an example. Suppose a teen is thirsty. She puts $1.50 in a soda machine and receives a soda. Receiving the soda is reinforcement for depositing the $1.50. When she is thirsty in the future, she will be more likely to put $1.50 in a soda machine as a result of this experience. The operant response of putting money in a soda machine can undergo the process of extinction, however. This process begins when a person makes a response and does not receive the expected reinforcement. If the same teen had put $1.50 in a soda machine and no soda came out, the best guess is that the teen would not put any more money in that machine. One trial of not receiving a soda may be enough to extinguish the response of putting money in the soda machine, at least with this particular soda machine at this particular time. Usually, extinction only occurs after several instances of unreinforced operant responses.

Receiving a soda is an **unconditioned reinforcer** in that it satisfies a biological deprivation, that of thirst. Other unconditioned reinforcers include food, sex, and exposure to aesthetically pleasing stimuli, such as when a child is reinforced for correctly adjusting a telescope by seeing a vivid detailed view of the Moon. Most reinforcers that people receive are not unconditioned reinforcers, however, but **conditioned reinforcers.** Thus, for coming to work and doing your job, your employer gives you a check. No biological need is satiated by the check directly. The check does allow you to purchase food, drinks, and entertainment, all of which do fulfill your basic needs for nourishment and stimulation. Conditioned reinforcers acquire their reinforcement properties by being paired with unconditional reinforcers. That is, money was not always valuable to you but became so because it allowed you to acquire unconditioned reinforcers.

There are two general categories of reinforcers, **positive reinforcers** and **negative reinforcers.** The occurrence of both of these types of reinforcers following a behavior increases the likelihood of that behavior. The difference between the two is in the type of consequence that causes the increase in the behavior. Many high school students are positively reinforced for turning on the family car's stereo system and hearing music that they like. When a student turns off a car stereo that is blaring some type of disliked music, however, that is negative reinforcement. *Positive reinforcement* involves the presentation of a stimulus following a response; *negative reinforcement* involves the cessation of an aversive stimulation following a response. That is, if polka music is aversive to a student, the student would be reinforced for the behavior of turning the car stereo off because cessation of the polka music occurs after the radio is turned off, and it is more likely the student will turn the radio off again next time she or he hears polka music. In other words, the student has been conditioned to escape the stimulus of polka music. Consider another example of negative and positive reinforcement. If a young child whines loudly about wanting a certain kind of sugary cereal while shopping with mom in a grocery store, the mother may give in just to stop the whining. The mother's behavior would be negatively reinforced; the aversive stimulation of the child's whining has been stopped. Unfortunately, the child's whining in the grocery store behavior has also been reinforced!

How can teachers get students to exhibit the behaviors they want by using the principles of operant conditioning? If the students sometime exhibit the desired behavior, then teachers can increase its frequency through positive or negative reinforcement. How can teachers get students to exhibit behaviors they have not yet exhibited? Teachers can do this through a process called **shaping,** that is, by reinforcing behaviors that become closer and closer to the desired behavior. Thus, when students learn to write, teachers first reinforce them for whatever they can do and keep at them to write more. Then the demands of the teachers increase. Initially, students are reinforced for forming letters correctly, but later they are only reinforced if their groups of letters form words, and eventually they are only reinforced for writing complete sentences. Finally, they have to put sentences together in coherent paragraphs. The demands increase as schooling continues. Ultimately, college students only receive reinforcement for an accurate and clearly written 15-page paper. Many patterns of response important in education are learned through shaping.

Teachers can also vary the delivery of reinforcements. Typically, reinforcements occur intermittently rather than after every response. Learning that occurs via **intermittent reinforcement** is more resistant to extinction than learning that occurs under continuous reinforcement. For example, perhaps one in three football games is really exciting. Yet people keep coming back for more despite the high likelihood of a boring game. Although Skinner did not use the word *expectation*, other behaviorists have used that term in their explanations of such behavior (Rotter, 1954). Continuous reinforcement produces an expectation of reinforcement every time, which increases vulnerability to extinction whenever a reinforcement fails to occur. In contrast, intermittent reinforcement creates an expectation that reinforcement is a sometimes occurrence and that if a person persists reinforcement eventually occurs.

Reinforcement can be intermittent in two ways. In a **ratio reinforcement schedule,** reinforcement follows a certain number of responses. Thus, children in a class who receive stickers for completing 10 worksheets are on a ratio schedule of reinforcement. Alternatively, reinforcement can be delivered at certain time intervals or on an **interval reinforcement schedule.** Some teachers reinforce a class on Fridays with extra time to talk to friends if the class has been able to get weekly work in on time. The two types of schedules lead to different patterns of response. The ratio schedule tends to produce high rates of responding that do not vary much, except perhaps for a small reduction in responding immediately after payoff. The interval schedule tends to produce a rapid decline in performance immediately after payoff that only gradually increases until it reaches a maximum just before payoff. Thus, for the teacher with the Friday reinforcement schedule, fewer assignments would be coming in on Monday, Tuesday, and Wednesday, compared to Thursday and Friday.

Punishment

Negative reinforcement is often confused with punishment, a common misconception (see the discussion of how difficult it can be to overcome misconceptions in Chapter 3). One way to avoid this misconception is to focus on the different outcomes of negative reinforcement and punishment. Negative reinforcement *increases* the likelihood of behavior; punishment *decreases* the likelihood of behavior. **Punishment** is the presentation of aversive stimulation following a response. Thus, if a preschooler darts into the parking lot at the day care center, the teacher gives the child a stern reprimand that serves as a punishment. The response of darting away was followed by the aversive stimulation of adult disapproval. So the likelihood of the child running into the parking lot should decrease. Consider this example of negative reinforcement: if the sound of a car's warning buzzer is aversive, a high school student taking behind-the-wheel instruction will buckle up the seatbelt in order to make the sound stop. The behavior of buckling up the seatbelt is negatively reinforced, and the probability of this behavior occurring increases. In the example of negative reinforcement, the response (buckling the seat belt) resulted in the cessation of the aversive stimulus (the car buzzer) and the likelihood of the behavior (buckling the seat belt) increased. In the example of the punishment, the aversive stimulus (the reprimand) was not present until after the response and the likelihood of the behavior (darting in the parking lot) decreased.

In Skinner's view, behaviorism is a very positive approach to student learning and development. The emphasis is on catching the students doing well and reinforcing them for it. If the students cannot do well given their current competencies, then reinforce them for behaviors in the right direction and gradually shape the appropriate response. Skinner (1953) suggested that when teachers use punishment, they should also provide an alternative behavior that will be reinforced. For example, if a student is talking during a quiet study time, the teacher should remind the student firmly that this is the time to study quietly, but should also make sure the student has something interesting to work on. Skinner also argued that reductions in the frequency of undesirable behaviors using punishment were short lived and that punishment led to undesirable by-products, such as emotional responses of anxiety or anger.

Other researchers have found that punishment can have stable effects on elimination of undesirable behaviors without lasting side effects (Walters & Grusec, 1977). A number of variables affect the efficacy of punishment, such as timing, consistency, intensity, the child's relationship to the person handing out the punishment, and whether or not a rationale is also provided (Cheyne & Walters, 1969; Kanfer & Zich, 1974; LaVoie, 1973, 1974; Parke, 1969, 1974, 2012). Rationales can not only make punishment more effective, but also rationales by themselves can be as effective as punishment and may also help students internalize prohibitions, making it more likely they will behave in the future. Rationales presented to young children (e.g., preschoolers) need to be concrete (e.g., "You might break this toy if you play with it because it is fragile"). Abstract rationales that focus on the rights and feelings of others (e.g., "The owner of this toy will feel bad if you play with it"), however, are increasingly effective with advancing age during childhood. Thus, undesirable behaviors often can be suppressed without resorting to punishment.

Nevertheless, punishment still exists in schools. Effective school punishments are those that have a reasonable connection to the infraction. In Blackwood (1970), junior high students who had misbehaved copied essays as punishment. Some students copied an essay emphasizing the negative effects of classroom disobedience, while others copied an essay about steam engines. The students who copied an essay emphasizing why misbehavior was a problem were less likely to misbehave following the punishment than were students who copied the steam engine essay. MacPherson, Candee, and Hohman (1974) conducted a similar study with elementary students who had misbehaved in a cafeteria. Again, behavior after the punishment was better for students who had copied essays providing rationales for obeying school rules. **Time-out** is a punishment procedure widely used in many educational settings (Donaldson, Vollmer, Yakich, & Van Camp, 2013). Time-out involves the physical removal of a student from a reinforcing environment, that is, moving the student away from reinforcers such as other students or activities for a short period of time. The student can be moved to an isolated corner of the classroom or to an empty room. Time-out is punishing because the student no longer has access to reinforcers. For time-out to be effective, the area left must contain reinforcers and the time-out area must not have any reinforcers. Teachers must take care that the amount of time spent in time-out is appropriate. For elementary school children, only a few minutes in time-out may be required.

Despite evidence that corporal punishment, even when used by parents, is largely ineffective and can create negative consequences (for meta-analyses of the research, see Gershoff, 2002; Gershoff & Grogan-Kaylor, 2016), it is a punishment still employed in schools, primarily in the form of "paddling" (Hyman, 1990; Hyman & Wise, 1977). Gershoff, Purtell, and Holas (2015) analyzed current practices of corporal punishment in U.S. public schools. Corporal punishment is legal in 19 states (compared to 49 states in 1971 and 28 states in 1992), although it is not allowed in some school districts in states where it is legal. Gershoff et al. noted differences in the pattern of use of corporal punishment in schools in terms of gender (more often used with boys), race (more often used with blacks than whites or Latinos), and disability status (more often used with students with disabilities). They also pointed out that corporal punishment is not an effective technique to use in schools because it does not teach students why a particular behavior was wrong and what students should be doing instead. It can also create negative side effects such as offering aggressive models, causing physical pain, eliciting feelings of sadness, anger, and fear, and damaging the relationship between the child and the person handing out the punishment.

Skinner (1977) himself was opposed to corporal punishment and believed that it teaches that might makes right: "The punishing teacher who punishes teaches students that punishment is a way of solving problems" (p. 336). Moreover, punishment has other undesirable side effects, including causing children to avoid future interactions with their punishers (Bandura, 1986). Does a disciplinary technique that causes children to learn physical aggression and to avoid their teachers really make sense?

Behavior Modification: Applied Operant Conditioning

One of the most important applications of operant conditioning is behavior modification (Bandura, 1969). The main idea of behavior modification is to reinforce behaviors that are valued. If students are not capable of the desired behaviors at present, teachers should reinforce behaviors they are capable of performing that are in the direction of the desired response. Gradually, teachers increase the criterion for reinforcement until the students can produce the desired behavior. In other words, teachers shape the response. In some classrooms, children are reinforced for completing homework by receiving stickers. The stickers are a form of **token reinforcement.** Other token reinforcements sometimes include chips that can be accumulated and eventually traded in for goodies or privileges.

Teachers typically use reinforcement systems on an intermittent basis, since it is difficult for a classroom teacher to monitor and reinforce every appropriate response by all of the students in a classroom and also so that the student responses are less susceptible to extinction. An important goal of any behavior modification plan is to increase the ratio, or interval, between reinforcements until the desired behaviors are occurring with only typical classroom reinforcements, such as praise. The gradual reduction in reinforcement is known as **fading.**

Good behavior modification environments often have other features as well. Correct and preferred behaviors are consistently modeled by teachers. Adult attention, which is a powerful reinforcement for many children, is provided for appropriate action rather than inappropriate action. Thus, if the teacher wishes to reduce talking out of turn in a student, the student does not get the teacher's attention when talking out of turn. Instead, the teacher responds to the student only when the student raises his or her hand and waits for acknowledgment before speaking.

Behavioral contracting is another behavior modification option. The student makes an agreement with the teacher to attempt to reach a particular goal, such as the following:

> When I, _____, hand in all of my assignments on time, 5 days in a row, I will be able to (read a magazine, play a computer game, or put my head down to rest) for 10 minutes during class time. This contract will be in effect during the month of October. For every month that passes, 2 days are added to the number of days of on-time assignments necessary before I receive my reward (for example, November—7 days, December—9 days, etc.).

Usually, the contract is negotiated, with students helping to decide what the goal will be, what reinforcement might be earned, and how much progress toward the goal is required before they receive any reinforcement.

Often parent training complements classroom behavioral programs. Parents learn how they, too, can use behavioral principles to provide reinforcement consistent with the school's program. Thus, a teacher who is reinforcing a student for bringing homework into school also trains the parent to reinforce the student at home for doing homework.

Some forms of punishments are widely accepted in behavior modification programs. For example, one form of punishment for engaging in inappropriate behavior is **response cost.** With this technique, students are first given a number of tokens. If they engage in the unwanted behavior, they must forfeit some of these tokens. The students refrain from the unwanted behavior in order to keep the tokens. Time-out is also widely used.

Cognitive-Behavior Modification

Consistent with the main tenets of conditioning, classical behavior modification focuses on changing behaviors more than cognitions. Cognitive-behavior modification also attempts to change children's thinking, largely by changing the way children talk to themselves. Arguing that self-speech could be used to organize behavior (see also the discussion of children's private speech in Chapter 6), Donald Meichenbaum (1977, p. 19) cited the following example of child speech that directed the construction of a Tinkertoy car:

> The wheels go here, the wheels go here. Oh, we need to start it all over again. We have to close it up. See it closes up. We're starting it all over again. Do you know why we wanted to do that? Because I needed it to go a different way. Isn't it pretty clever, don't you think? But we have to cover up the motor just like a real car (Kohlberg, Yaeger, & Hjertholm, 1968, p. 695).

Although young children often use such self-instructional speech on their own, they also benefit from explicit instructions about how to self-verbalize. (Review the use of self-instruction to teach writing skills to fifth- and sixth-grade students with learning disabilities as described in Chapter 4.) Cognitive-behavior modification typically combines instruction in self-verbalizations with other techniques, including modeling, reinforcement, and gradual fading of reinforcement. For example, Meichenbaum and Goodman (1971) reduced the impulsive responding of hyperactive second graders by teaching them to instruct themselves to go slowly and reflect before responding. Using teacher modeling, guided practice, and the gradual fading of teacher cuing, they taught students to make self-verbalizations such as the following:

> Okay, what is it I have to do? You want me to copy the picture with the different lines. I have to go slowly and carefully. Okay, draw the line down, down, good; then to the right, that's it; now down some more and to the left. Good, I'm doing fine so far. Remember, go slowly. Now back up again. No, I was supposed to go down. That's okay. Just erase the line carefully. . . . Good. Even if I make an error I can go on slowly and carefully. I have to go down now. Finished. I did it! (Meichenbaum & Goodman, 1971, p. 117)

The teacher first described and modeled positive self-verbalization. Then the teacher provided external support and guidance as students attempted to apply the approach to problems. The teacher encouraged the students to internalize the self-verbalizations by guiding the students to whisper rather than to talk aloud and then eventually only to think about the problem definition, task focusing and guiding directions, and self-reinforcement as they performed the task.

An important component of the self-instructional approach is a teacher who consistently models self-control by explicitly using self-instruction (Manning, 1991). Anyone who has ever taught knows the frustration of trying to figure out why technology isn't working. A self-instructing teacher might cope by first defining the problem verbally, followed by self-verbalizations to direct appropriate actions:

> "Why won't this projector turn on? Let me see. I'll make sure I have the connector in the right place. Let me see, do I use this one or the other one? I will try both. This one first." When frustrated, the teacher models coping via self-instruction: "It's easy to get frustrated. Take a deep breath and relax. There must be a solution." Once a solution is found, the teacher self-reinforces: "Hey! I stuck with it and found that I was using the wrong connector. I'll try this other cord. Yay! It works." If there is no success, the teacher models more coping and adapting: "I've tried all I know. I'll either show you this information by putting it on the board or I will call tech support to troubleshoot the problem. We could even wait to talk about this tomorrow. Which solution makes the most sense?" (Adapted from Manning, 1991, p. 134)

The self-instructing teacher also models for students how to cope with problems and with temptations to behave impulsively or inappropriately. Thus the teacher might model the following sequence for a student who is unprepared for a test and is caught attempting to cheat. Again the teacher starts with a verbalization of the problem and then models self-direction and self-coping until a solution is achieved that can be self-reinforced:

> I forgot to study for my test. Should I look at my friend's test? I can see her paper easily. But, is that right? Just do my best. I'll feel better about myself if I don't look. This is hard. I know my answers are wrong. That's okay. I've done the best I can. Next time I won't leave my book at school. I'm glad I didn't take answers that didn't belong to me. I feel good about that! (Manning, 1991, p. 135)

Cognitive-behavior modification principles, including self-instruction, can be effective in the classroom, particularly in increasing on-task behavior and reducing disruptive behavior (Hoff & Ervin, 2013; Manning, 1990; Robinson, Smith, Miller, & Brownell, 1999). For example, Manning (1988) randomly assigned the most behaviorally inappropriate first- and third-grade children in a school to either a self-instructional treatment group or a control condition that received additional instruction and attention, but no self-instruction. When the students in the experimental condition saw a teacher self-instruct to inhibit inappropriate behaviors, the student in the control condition received additional explicit instruction in the school rules prohibiting the inappropriate behaviors. Both experimental and control students received 8 hours of instruction, and the classroom teachers did not know which condition the children were in. The results were compelling—both immediately following training and 3 months later. The students receiving self-instructional training were perceived as more self-controlled by their teachers, were more often on-task, working when they were supposed to be working, and believed themselves to be more in control of their behaviors. School-based interventions based on principles of cognitive-behavior modification have also been successfully implemented with students, teachers, and parents to treat the mental health disorders exhibited in schools, specifically anger and aggression, anxiety and phobias, depression, and attention-deficit/hyperactivity disorder (see Mayer, VanAcker, Lochman, & Gresham, 2009).

Perhaps the idea developed from social learning theory with widespread application in educational contexts is the concept of self-regulation (see also Chapter 9). Self-regulation emphasizes the role of the individual in modifying behavior rather than the influence of external factors such as reinforcement and punishment imposed upon the individual by others. In its basic form, self-regulation consists of the processes of self-observation, self-judgment, and self-reaction (Schunk, 2012). *Self-observation* refers to paying attention to some aspect of behavior; *self-judgment* refers to comparing current performance to a standard or goal; and *self-reaction* refers to a cognitive and behavioral response to the self-judgment. For example, a student has been given an assignment to write a brief essay for English class but is having difficulty getting past the first paragraph. A self-regulating student would first look at how much of the task is completed: "OK, I have a decent first paragraph" (self-observation). Next, the self-regulating student would make a self-judgment: "One paragraph isn't enough, I know my teacher will want at least three or four paragraphs." The self-reaction of a self-regulating student in this circumstance might be disappointment in progress thus far and an awareness of the need to motivate further work. "I need to work on this more. I bet if I work hard for one more hour, I can get this done. I know I can do it. One thing that has worked for me in the past when I am stuck is to first just write down every idea I have without worrying about putting the ideas in sentences. Once I have done that, I can start putting those ideas together in a paragraph." Self-regulation for academic tasks, called self-regulated learning, involves students setting academic goals, monitoring progress toward those goals, and then reinforcing themselves for meeting goals (Schunk & Zimmerman, 2013). The reinforcement can be intangible, such as allowing themselves to feel a sense of accomplishment, or more tangible, such as rewarding themselves with a fun activity once the task is accomplished.

Classroom Management

Principles of social learning theory are commonly applied in classrooms as techniques for managing student behaviors. Principles of classroom management provide teachers with guidance about how to maintain order in the classroom without creating an aversive environment (Doyle, 1986; Emmer, Evertson, & Worsham, 2006; Evertson, Emmer, & Worsham, 2002; Poole & Evertson, 2013), even with children who can be otherwise disruptive (Mather & Goldstein, 2002). Classroom management starts before the school year begins. One essential step is to *arrange the physical classroom so that the teacher can maintain order and monitor students easily*. In many elementary school classrooms, small reading groups meet with the teacher in one section of the room while the rest of the class does seatwork. The classroom arrangement must allow the teacher to easily look up to scan the rest of the classroom while working with the reading group.

The teacher also needs to *establish early the rules and procedures of the classroom*. The beginning of the school day, including the opening activities and the morning's administrative activities (e.g., taking attendance, collecting lunch tickets), should become routines that are carried out automatically and quickly. The point of establishing routines is not just to promote quiet and order but also to achieve rapid transition. Time spent in transition is time lost: student achievement in school depends on the amount of time students are engaged in instruction.

In addition, the teacher needs to *clarify expectations*. Students must be made aware of what is permitted and what is prohibited. Providing students with positive reinforcement when they comply with classroom rules is a must. Teacher praise, such as "Row 2 has really been working hard this morning—way to go!", is common in well-managed classrooms. Teachers need to monitor the classroom and signal when they are concerned about classroom misconduct well before the misconduct accelerates into a situation requiring sanctions. When sanctions are necessary, the teacher needs to deal with the situation quickly and as unobtrusively as possible. For example, a teacher can dispense mild punishers, such as directive eye contact and gentle touches to move students away from distractions. Persistent misconduct should be dealt with more directly, but efficiently and with little, if any, disruption of the class.

Teachers need to *model self-control and on-task behaviors*. They model their own enthusiasm for academic tasks, make it clear that they find their own academic competencies to be rewarding, and convey the message that students can reap the same types of rewards by learning the lessons offered in school. Students in well-managed

---

Applying Developmental Theory to Educational Contexts

BOX 5.1. Praising Students

Praise is a form of reinforcement that teachers use every day in the classroom. Unfortunately, effective use of praise is complicated (Henderlong & Lepper, 2002). All too often praise provided by teachers does not make clear what the student did well, or teachers may praise behaviors that really are not praiseworthy. For example, teachers frequently offer praise for participation alone ("I'm so glad you are taking part") rather than for participation consistent with what is being taught. In a review of research on rates and types of classroom praise, Jenkins, Floress, and Reinke (2015) found that teachers used more general praise (for example, "good job") rather than behavior-specific praise (for example, "I liked the way you raised your hand to get my attention"). They also reviewed a number of intervention studies indicating that teachers can be trained to increase their rates of praise, both general and behavior-specific, and that when behavior-specific praise increases, off-task and disruptive behavior decreases. In a classic article, Brophy (1981) described how to make praise in classrooms maximally effective. Some of the following may seem obvious, but it is surprising how often teachers fail to follow these simple guidelines:

- Effective praise is delivered *contingent* upon desirable student behaviors.
- Effective praise is *specific*, with the teacher focusing attention on what the student did that was praiseworthy.
- Effective praise is *sincere*, reflecting that the teacher is attentive to the student's accomplishments.
- Effective praise implies that students can be similarly successful in the future if they exert appropriate effort.
- Effective praise conveys the message that students expended the effort that led to praise because they enjoyed the task or wanted to develop the competencies that merited the praise.

classrooms learn a great deal about how to achieve life's long-term rewards as well as how to achieve short-term reinforcements, such as positive teacher attention for carrying out assignments in ways consistent with classroom policies.

Does classroom management work? Gottfredson, Gottfredson, and Hybl (1993) demonstrated how conduct in middle schools improved when school rules were made clearer, consequences for violating them were more certain, classrooms were organized and managed more efficiently, parents were kept informed about the good behavior and misbehaviors of their children, and reinforcement was increased for good conduct. Not surprisingly, high-quality classroom management has also been linked to student achievement. For example, Freiberg, Huzinec, and Templeton (2009) found that elementary students in classrooms implementing a prosocial classroom management program outperformed matched control students on state math and reading assessments. One of the most striking observations in classrooms and schools that produce high engagement and achievement is that classroom management is so good that behavior infractions rarely occur (Bohn, Roehrig, & Pressley, 2004; Dolezal, Welsh, Pressley, & Vincent, 2003; Pressley, Allington, Wharton-McDonald, Block, & Morrow, 2001).

In summary, social learning theory is a developmental theory with tremendous practical implications. That is one of the reasons it has commanded so much attention from developmental and educational researchers. Even so, applying social learning principles well can be difficult. See the Applying Developmental Theory to Educational Contexts special feature (Box 5.1) for a summary of the challenges involved in applying a seemingly simple type of classroom reinforcement, praise, which is anything but simple to use well!

Development According to Freud: The Psychosexual Stage Theory

Social learning theory emphasizes the role of the situation in determining behavior—that the way children develop depends on what they observe as well as what the environment reinforces and punishes. The contrast to a theory that emphasizes the situation would be a theory that emphasized the consistency of the individual across situations, a theory proposing that behavior is determined more by enduring characteristics of the person than by factors that vary with the situation. One of the most influential of these theories is Freud's theory of psychosexual development.

Sigmund Freud was a physician by training, but more importantly he was completely immersed in the scientific thinking of his time (Sulloway, 1992; Wollheim, 1989). Living in Vienna, a center of culture and intellect, permitted Freud to interact with contemporaries who were questioning the prevailing view of the late 1800s—that man's basic nature was rational. Freud proposed that much of the time emotions governed more than reason (Hale, 1995; Tyson & Tyson, 1990). He proposed that much of behavior was determined by unconscious processes, sexual and aggressive instinctual processes, an idea very much in contrast with the prevailing belief that behavior was rationally determined. Most shocking of all during the Victorian era, a time when sexuality was kept out of public sight and attention, Freud contended that sexually energized conflicts during childhood determined much of personality in later life.

Freud referred to the unconscious as the *primary process*; it contrasted with the *secondary process*, which was responsible for more rational and logical processes. As the names for these processes imply, Freud believed that the logical side of thinking was a small part of mental activity compared to the unconscious primary process. Much like an iceberg, the secondary process was the tip of an iceberg, and the majority of the iceberg was primary process, below the surface.

Freud arrived at insights about behavior and development through working with patients who experienced a variety of psychological disorders, such as anxieties and neuroses. During psychoanalysis, the patient talked, freely associating to ideas presented by the therapist, and sometimes relating recurring dreams. Freud believed that free associations and recurring fantasies were very revealing about unconscious conflicts. As the therapist detected troubling conflicts, the therapist and the patient then worked together to replace the conflict with a story that might make the conflict less troubling for the patient.

Freud recognized that the unconscious thoughts revealed during therapy were probably not memories of objective events. One of Freud's most important insights was that when his patients reported sexual relations with parents during their childhood, they likely were reporting fantasies. Freud also realized that in helping the patient bring these fantasies to consciousness, the story that emerged was a co-construction of the patient and the therapist, not just the patient's story. See the Considering Interesting Questions special feature (Box 5.2) for a discussion of memories recovered during therapy.

Freud studied and restudied his cases in his quest to understand the human experience. Freud wrote about many of these cases, which continue to be read and studied by contemporary students of psychoanalysis. Most of the ideas offered in this section were derived from analysis of cases, either by Freud or his followers, including his daughter, Anna Freud.

Psychosexual Stages of Development

Freud contended that the most basic force in life is instinctual energy, **id,** which is present at birth. The id seeks pleasure and immediate gratification (such as food, drink, and contact comfort), an idea Freud summarized as the *pleasure principle*. With maturation during the first few years of life, a new personality structure emerges, the **ego.** The ego is the rational side of personality and operates according to the *reality principle*. Reality demands deferring gratification in order to pursue more long-range goals than the short-term, hedonistic goals of the id. Later still, between age 3 and age 6 or 7, yet a third personality structure emerges, the **superego.** The superego is the conscience and as such directly conflicts with the id. The rationality of the ego balances the demands for gratification by the id with the inhibitions of the superego.

Thus, Freud proposed a biologically determined invariant sequence of development, such that instinctual urgings (id) preceded the development of the rational side of the personality (ego), which began to develop before the moral aspect of personality (superego). The psychological developments paralleled physical development of the mouth, anus, and genital regions, pleasure centers in Freud's view. For example, many of the newborn's pleasures and frustrations are associated with the taking in of nourishment. Hence, the first stage of development according to Freud is the *oral stage*. If the child experiences too much frustration or unchecked pleasure during this period of time, oral fixation can occur. Freud suggested that

BOX 5.2. Are Recovered Memories Likely to Be True?

In a number of well-publicized cases in the early 1990s, people entered therapy for symptoms such as bulimia, depression, or low self-esteem, and exited therapy believing that their problems were caused by sexual abuse in childhood, memories that they had repressed. What must be emphasized here is that when they came into therapy, they had no idea that they had been abused. Memories of abuse had been recovered during therapy, leading sometimes to criminal charges and court proceedings.

How were these memories recovered? The therapist might have used any of a number of techniques to elicit memories, including hypnosis (which is a state that makes the hypnotized person susceptible to suggestions from the hypnotist). When suggestions of abuse were mentioned by patients during these sessions, the therapist pursued them. If the patient objected to an emerging interpretation of abuse, the therapist may have reassured the patient that not remembering violence clearly was to be expected, perhaps reflecting the defense mechanism of denial. Over many sessions, the therapist continued to work with the patient to uncover more details. In the end, the patient and therapist believed that what they had uncovered were actual memories, previously repressed, from the unconscious.

A few of these recovered memories were ultimately disproved through police investigations and legal proceedings. Memory experts provided evidence that certain methods employed by some therapists during memory recovery therapy sessions very likely distorted memory (Lindsay & Read, 2006). Researchers have established that false memories of emotional events in childhood, such as being lost in a store or hospitalized overnight, can be created in some people's memories (Laney & Loftus, 2008). The extensive research on the creation of false memories, however, indicates that false memories are typically familiar events that fit the context of the memory (Bookbinder & Brainerd, 2016).

Casting doubt on recovered memories of childhood sexual abuse in no way suggests that people who have vivid memories of childhood abuse are mistaken. In fact, an important criticism of Freud was that he classified most reports of childhood sex abuse as fantasies. Researchers generally agree that true memories make up a substantial portion of recovered memories, although they also agree that suggestive therapeutic techniques may promote false memories (Belli, 2012). People may be motivated to reduce their awareness of memories tied to negative emotions (Anderson & Huddleston, 2012), and children may not understand sexual abuse when it occurs and may not encode it as a traumatic experience until later when they recall the experience and understand it better (McNally, 2012). Geraerts (2012) suggested that there are two types of recovered memories. One is the result of prolonged attempts to remember in association with suggestive therapy, which are less likely to be corroborated. The other type, spontaneous recovered memories, in which previous instances of remembering sometimes have been forgotten, are more likely to be corroborated. The bottom line is that by ignoring real memories of abuse in the past, in part because of the Freudian assertion that such memories often were fantasies, harm was done; but by having complete confidence in recovered memories as reflections of actual events, harm was done as well.

oral fixation causes long-term problems such as overeating, drinking, smoking, and overdependency on others. It can also be the beginning of a verbally aggressive personality (Agmon & Schneider, 1998).

The ego emerges as the child is weaning and is learning to control elimination, largely because of the frustrations associated with weaning and toilet training. It develops as the mediator between the instinctual demands of the id and the demands being placed on the child during weaning and toilet training by the parent. Because so much of the development of the ego occurs as a function of the conflicts surrounding toilet training, which is enabled by the physical development of the anal region, the second stage is known as the *anal stage*. During this stage, the anal region is associated with pleasure (such as parental approval when the child eliminates at the appropriate place and time) and frustration (such as when the child does not control elimination appropriately). If the child experiences a great deal of frustration during this period, anal fixation is likely. Anal fixation can result in stubborn overattention to punctuality, neatness, and routines. Alternatively, it can play out as overmessiness. Extreme negativism or unwillingness to part with anything (individuals who hoard things) also can be indications of anal fixation.

As the genitals mature, pleasures and frustrations are centered on the reproductive organs. This is the *phallic stage*, which proceeds somewhat differently for boys and girls, a realization that Freud came to as he listened to patients talk about their childhoods. Although Freud at first believed his patients were telling him about events that actually happened, he came to believe that the patients were relating fantasies, ones reflecting unconscious desires and conflicts that occurred during childhood.

Boys experience the *Oedipus complex*. They come to desire their mothers sexually. This unconscious desire is a dangerous desire. The obvious competitor for mother—the father—is much bigger and stronger than the young boy. According to Freud, this unconscious desire (a reflection of the id) conflicts with the ego-mediated recognition of the reality of the father. At the center of the reality is the possibility that the father would retaliate for any sexual advances of the son on the mother. This retaliation would take the form of castration. The resolution of this conflict between id and ego is that the son identifies with the father. In identifying with the father, the boy can vicariously possess the mother. Part of the identification process is the adoption of the father's moral standards, which is the beginning of the third personality structure, the superego. Because the development of the son's superego is mediated by a great fear, the possibility of castration, the superego is very strong in boys.

In contrast, girls experience the *Electra complex*. The preschool girl unconsciously comes to desire her father. Reality for the girl is in the form of the mother, who while threatening is not as threatening as the father is to a son. After all, the mother cannot castrate her daughter. The daughter nonetheless resolves her conflict between id and ego by identifying with the mother, permitting her vicarious possession of the father. The superego that emerges from this resolution is not as strong as the superego of a boy, however, because the threat giving rise to it was not as great. According to classical psychoanalytical theory, this is the explanation for stronger conscience in males than in females. Moreover, according to Freud, young girls experience *penis envy*, when they recognize that boys have a much more prominent sexual organ than they possess. Freud argued that penis envy is the basis for female feelings of inferiority throughout life. Not surprisingly, Freud's conceptions of female development (and his limited interest in female development) have met with more resistance than his conceptions of male development (de Fiorini, 1998). Revised conceptions of psychoanalytic theory have been offered that are not so clearly gender-biased (Horney, 1967), for instance, focusing on how females are much more concerned with interpersonal connections to others than are males (Chodorow, 1989; see also the discussion of Kohlberg's theory of moral development in Chapter 3).

Phallic fixations were possible if the child experienced difficulties in resolving the instinctual demands of this period with external reality—that parents cannot be objects of sexual attention. According to Freud, such fixations could translate into a variety of problems later in life, including sexual identity problems and excessive guilt surrounding sexual interactions.

Once the superego emerges, the emotional turmoil subsides and there is a period of time during which sexual desires are not much in evidence, the *latency stage*. During the latency stage, which corresponds roughly to the elementary school years, boys prefer to interact with boys and girls prefer to interact with girls. Children's attentions during latency are directed toward acquiring intellectual and social skills. There is no latency fixation, largely because so little attention is devoted to satisfying the pleasures of the id, and hence there is less likelihood of frustration during this period than other periods in development.

With the onset of adolescence and puberty, the final stage, the *genital stage*, arises. The id is reenergized as the sexual organs mature and is now expressed as masturbation, sexual experimentation, and strong interest in the opposite sex. Adolescents are concerned with acting like men and women rather than like boys and girls. If the child is orally, anally, or phallically fixated because of failures to resolve instinctual and social demands during early childhood, unconscious conflicts can interfere with sexual relations during the genital stage and more generally with psychological functioning in other areas of life.

In summary, biological development is the basis for psychological development in Freud's psychosexual theory. There are innate sexual and aggressive instincts. As physical structures mature, these instincts seek gratification in new ways. But these instincts meet external demands from parents and others. These demands can be frustrating, such as the frustrations surrounding weaning, toilet training, and regulation of affection with the opposite-sex parent during the preschool years. If the conflicts between instinctual and external demands are unresolved or only resolved with great difficulty, the result can be oral, anal, or phallic fixations, which are the unconscious causes of a variety of personality problems experienced later in life.

Anxiety and Defense Mechanisms

According to Freudian theory, anxiety is an omnipresent danger, capable of overwhelming the individual. There are some very good reasons to be anxious, such as when confronted with an objectively distressing or threatening situation (e.g., an ill parent, a broken favorite toy). A fact of life for Freudians is that humans are always at risk for being instinctually impulsive (e.g., overeating or drinking too much, indulging in prohibited or socially unacceptable sexual activities, or aggressing in unacceptable ways). That is, the risk of the id overwhelming the ego is always present. Anxiety results when the id prevails and individuals engage in objectionable behaviors. Such anxiety could be overwhelming if not managed. The ego manages anxiety through the use of defense mechanisms (A. Freud, 1936).

Although different psychoanalytic theorists have proposed different numbers of defense mechanisms (Plutchik, 1995), the following are commonly included in most listings, presented here roughly in their order of development, from least mature to most mature (Rohwer, Ammon, & Cramer, 1974). In general, the less mature ones are less cognitively complex than the more mature ones:

- *Repression* is the forgetting of painful or threatening events. Thus, memories of Oedipal and Electra conflicts are repressed because it is so anxiety-provoking to remember having sexual feelings for a parent.

- *Denial* is simply to deny an objectionable external reality. Thus, a child may deny that a pet has died by claiming that it will be coming home from the pet hospital next week.

- *Negation* is claiming to desire the exact opposite of actual desires. Thus, the child who wants the teacher's attention may tell her parents that she wishes the teacher would leave her alone.

- *Projection* is attributing to another person what is actually an objectionable characteristic of the self. Thus, a bully is projecting when he or she accuses the victim of being the aggressor.

- *Identification* is taking on the characteristics of a threatening person. Thus, the child who fears another child may begin to imitate the threatening child. The resolution of the anxiety-ridden Oedipal and Electra conflicts is through identification with the threatening parent of the same sex, taking on their behaviors and values as part of resolving the conflict.

- *Displacement* involves venting anger toward individuals who are less threatening than the real object of anger. Thus, a child may displace anger at a teacher or parents by screaming at a classmate.

- *Reaction formation* involves behavioral expressions of interest that conflict directly with actual interests. Thus, the habitual consumer of pornography who publicly calls for censorship is engaging in reaction formation.

- *Sublimation* is channeling objectionable tendencies into acceptable directions. Thus, someone who loves to overeat may expend great energies to be a great cook for others. A highly aggressive individual may sublimate by directing energies into competitive athletics.

- *Rationalization/intellectualization* is the development of elaborate rationales for engaging in anxiety-provoking behaviors. An adolescent girl may break up with a same-age boyfriend because she wants to explore relationships with older boys. She is engaging in rationalization if she tells the old boyfriend that the breakup is for his own good, so that he can get to know other girls.

Anna Freud (1936) viewed defense mechanisms as appropriate during childhood, when the ego is underdeveloped and needs protection from being overwhelmed by anxiety and instinct. Children as young as 2-year-olds evidence simple defense mechanisms like denial; by 8 years of age, a variety of defense mechanisms have been observed, including rationalization/intellectualization (Safyer & Hauser, 1995).

When defense mechanisms persist after childhood, for the most part, the result usually is immature and neurotic thinking. The exceptions are defense mechanisms that translate into behavior that could be considered mature. For example, sublimation may result in a person directing instinctual energies into socially accepted channels, such as the lawyer who redirects sexual energies into a 70-hour-a-week law practice. In mentally healthy adults, most of the defense mechanisms give way to more mature mechanisms of coping.

Defense mechanisms do not eliminate disturbing instincts and conflicts but rather relegate them to the unconscious. Because the unconscious can affect future conscious behaviors, this is problematic. Thus, the sexual conflicts of the phallic stage that are repressed can interfere with mature sexual functioning later. Defensive thinking is not optimal thinking, although defense mechanisms can protect a fragile, developing ego.

Unconscious and Conscious Processing

Freud's belief that both conscious (rational, secondary process) and unconscious (emotional, primary process) thinking occurs is receiving renewed attention. Epstein (1994) reviewed various types of evidence consistent with the idea that thinking is dualistic, that humans sometimes process information holistically rather than analytically, emotionally rather than rationally, and imagistically rather than verbally. In other words, there is evidence supporting the duality of Freud's primary and secondary processes.

Cognitive scientists also are examining relationships between conscious and unconscious processing. For example, researchers interested in memory have been studying differences between conscious, *explicit memory* versus unconscious, *implicit memory* (Graf & Schacter, 1985; Roediger, 1990; Schneider, 2015). Performance on implicit memory tasks is influenced by past experiences, without conscious awareness, whereas explicit memory tasks elicit intentional access of memories.

Perceptual priming is one task used to study implicit memory (Lloyd & Miller, 2014; Lloyd & Newcome, 2009; Schacter, 1987, 1992; Schacter, Chiu, & Ochsner, 1993). Suppose children are shown a fragmented picture of something, perhaps a horse, and are asked to identify what is in the picture as the picture is gradually completed. Later, the children would be presented with another series of fragmented pictures and asked to identify what is depicted as the pictures are gradually completed. The children are likely to recognize the pictures of items they had seen before, the horse, for example, more certainly and more quickly than items they had not seen before. That is, recognition that the fragment depicts a horse would have been primed by the previous exposure to the picture of the horse. The effect of perceptual priming is evident by age 2 or 3 and does not seem to increase after that. This contrasts with clear demonstrations that explicit memory, such as the intentional recall of pictures seen previously, definitely increases with development (Greenbaum & Graf, 1989; Lorsbach & Morris, 1991; Naito, 1990; Parkin & Streete, 1988). Performance on implicit memory tasks that rely on access to prior knowledge rather than perceptual processing, however, does seem to increase with development (Lloyd & Newcome, 2009; Murphy, McKone, & Slee, 2003).

Nonetheless, implicit, unconscious cognition appears to be distinct from explicit, conscious memory. Implicit memory seems to be in place early in life and is more functional in young children than explicit memory (Lloyd & Miller, 2014; Schneider, 2015). In addition, cognitive neuroscience research indicates that different brain structures are responsible for explicit and implicit memories (Adeyemo,

2002; Squire, 1992, 2004). Consistent with Freudian theory, brain structures that are more implicated in implicit memory seem to develop earlier (i.e., in the first year of life) than those implicated in explicit memory, which develop rather slowly during the childhood years (Nelson, 1995). Further research using neurophysiological measures holds great promise for better understanding of the development of implicit and explicit memory (Lloyd & Miller, 2014; Schneider, 2015).

Psychoanalysis and Education

Psychoanalytic theory inspired educational reform in the first half of the 20th century, particularly the mental hygiene movement (Hale, 1995). One purpose of this movement was to apply theories of psychiatry and psychology in schools with the goal of curbing delinquency and improving the mental health of children, thereby bettering society as a whole.

The mental hygiene movement was critical of conventional parenting, regarding it as being too controlling. According to this perspective, homes needed to be more democratic since this would reduce the likelihood of children experiencing too much frustration, thereby reducing the likelihood of fixation. The mental hygiene movement was also extremely critical of conventional schooling, especially its emphasis on orderliness and control, and advocated for a reduced emphasis on academic competition. The mental hygienists were confident that if psychoanalytic ideas were incorporated into the rearing and education of children, the result would be lowered rates of childhood mental illness, behavior problems, and delinquency.

Although proponents of the mental hygiene movement attempted to have their ideas incorporated into public schooling, the most complete translations of psychoanalytic theory into education occurred in private schools specifically designed according to principles derived from psychoanalytical thought. The best known example of these schools, and one still in existence today, is Summerhill School, an independent English boarding school founded in 1921. The school received widespread attention with the publication in 1960 of the book, *Summerhill*, authored by the founder of the school, A. S. Neill.

Neill was completely committed to the idea that children are innately good and schools should do little to interfere with their natural state. He believed a key factor in the development of children's mental health was freedom. He also believed that children should be educated according to their interests and should be trusted to seek out experiences that would allow them to fulfill their potential. Consider this quote from Neill (1960):

> What is Summerhill like? Well, for one thing, lessons are optional. Children can go to them or stay away from them—for years if they want to. There is a timetable—but only for the teachers. The children have classes usually according to their age, but sometimes according to their interests. We have no new methods of teaching, because we do not consider that teaching in itself matters very much. Whether a school has or has not a special method for teaching long division is of no significance, for long division is of no importance except to those who want to learn it. And the child who wants to learn long division will learn it no matter how it is taught. (p. 5)

The Summerhill of today (*www.summerhillschool.co.uk*) refers to itself as the "oldest children's democracy in the world," enrolling around 75 students between the ages of 5 and 17, with the school community totaling around 100 members. Summerhill still rejects compulsory attendance, exams, and report cards (Stronach & Piper, 2008). The community, including the faculty, staff, and students, gathers together in Meeting to decide how the school will be run. It is not that the school doesn't have rules (according to Stronach & Piper, 2008, as many as 174 rules were in place in 2008), but the rules (some individualized for a specific student) can be changed or adapted easily in Meeting. Breaches of the school culture are discussed, and disputes are dealt with informally or by Ombudsmen (of both genders), if required. Privileges can be removed as a result of infractions of rules, but the primary means of maintaining a cohesive community is social. One student interviewed by Stronach and Piper (2008) responded to feedback from the community about his behavior by saying, "Everyone thinks I'm a right twit now and I have to calm down and build relationships" (p. 15). Many of the other students interviewed described Summerhill as a place where you can live your own life, where you do not have to pretend to be someone you are not.

Summerhill has experienced challenges during its long history. In 1999, Her Majesty's Inspectorate tried to close down the school, primarily because of the policy of voluntary attendance. After a legal battle, the school eventually prevailed. And in 2001, as reported in Stronach and Piper (2008), an inspector raised issues of "inappropriate touching" at the school, one example being a teacher giving a student a piggy-back ride. When asked what touching would be appropriate, the inspector apparently replied "no touching." Even in a climate of increasing public accountability for teachers and schools, the ideals underlying Summerhill School, particularly its emphasis on freedom, equality, community, celebration, and play, can be illuminating for educators (Weeda, 2013).

Evaluation of Freudian Theory

Freudian theory was very vague, and it has proven difficult to test definitively. When important Freudian applications were devised and implemented, such as schools based on psychoanalytic ideas about development, formal evaluations were rare. Moreover, when others reviewed Freud's cases, they did not always come to the same conclusion that Freud drew. One example is the case of Little Hans, who was terrified of horses. Freud attributed this fear to castration anxiety. Others suggested, based in part on interviews with the original Little Hans when he was an adult, that the child may have been frightened by a horse in his youth, an event that was especially traumatic because of repeated family warnings about how horses sometimes bite (Goleman, 1990). Freud seemed ready to dismiss reports of what could have been real traumas, in particular childhood sexual abuse, as fantasies. Recall Box 5.2 and the criticisms of Freud's dismissal of reports of childhood sexual abuse.

When researchers were able to devise tests of Freud's theory, it often was not supported. For example, the conflicts during the phallic period require knowledge of the differences between male and female genitalia. Some preschool children lack this knowledge (Bem, 1989; Katcher, 1955; Tavris & Wade, 1984). According to Freudian theory, divorce before or during the preschool years, resulting in a boy growing up in a household lacking a father, should disrupt normal development and result in a variety of behavioral problems. Research evidence indicates that boys from families experiencing divorce exhibit more behavior problems and academic difficulties, but these problems are not confined to families in which divorce occurred during the phallic stage (Hetherington, 1989; Kline, Tschann, Johnston, & Wallerstein, 1989).

Nonetheless, Freud identified ideas that continue to contribute to our understanding of development (Emde, 1992, 1998):

1. The recognition that the unconscious can be important in determining behavior was an insight of enduring significance, with work on the cognitive unconscious continuing a century after Freud's initial writing on the unconscious.

2. Freud also recognized that development largely was a function of biology and environment in interaction. Specifically, during development, children experience conflicts between sexual and aggressive instincts and parental and social demands that clash with these instincts.

3. Freud proposed that development was stage-like, owing largely to biological maturation. The idea of developmental stages would endure throughout the 20th century.

4. Freud recognized that what happens early in life can have implications throughout life. Although conceptions about how early development affects later life have changed considerably since Freud, the idea that a connection exists between experiences across the lifespan was an important one.

5. Specific issues that Freud emphasized became issues that were studied throughout the 20th century, including how babies relate to their mothers, the development of aggression, identification, learning of sex roles, and moral development. Freud's contribution to developmental psychology was enormous.

Freud was uncompromising about his theory. When his belief in the primacy of instinctual processes was not shared by some prominent students of psychoanalysis, who emphasized the importance of rational, conscious, realistic, and problem-oriented thinking—ego processes—these students broke away from Freud. One such ego theorist who began as a Freudian was Erik Erikson.

Development According to Erikson: The Psychosocial Stage Theory

Like Freud, Erik Erikson proposed a theory of personality development (Erikson, 1963, 1968; Erikson & Coles, 2000). Unlike Freud, who felt that the most important determinants of development occurred during early childhood, Erikson proposed that much of the most important development came later, with development continuing across the lifespan. Thus, in Erikson's theory, early experience was important but not as important as Freud's theory suggested. Moreover, Erikson based many of his ideas on analyses of the functioning of healthy people, whereas Freud studied individuals being treated for mental health problems. Over the course of his career, Erikson studied many different types of people and was struck by the adaptability of people to their surroundings.

Psychosocial Stages of Development

Freud's emphasis on instinctual energy as a determining life force resulted in his psycho*sexual* theory of development. In contrast, Erikson proposed a psycho*social* theory of development. For Erikson, what mattered were key social interactions at each stage of development. Yes, development was caused in part by biological unfolding. But the particular social, cultural, and historical environment the child experienced mattered as well, so that the social interactions that were the focus of each stage of development would vary somewhat depending on where and when the child developed. Development also depends on the individual. In particular, if social interactions during previous stages of development had proceeded well, resulting in healthy development, present development was likely to be smoother.

According to Erikson, people pass through eight stages of development. Each stage involves a central conflict, with either a positive or negative resolution of the conflict possible. Thus, Erikson's theory is similar to Freud's in that the stages are defined by conflicts that can be resolved either positively or negatively, with subsequent development dependent, in part, on previous conflict resolutions. Erikson's eight stages of psychosocial development are summarized in Table 5.1.

It should be emphasized that although each of the conflicts was the focus for a particular stage, the eight developmental challenges can occur and be revisited in different forms across the lifespan (Malone, Liu, Vaillant, Rentz, & Waldinger, 2016; Marcia, 2002). An early conflict, such as trust versus mistrust, which is resolved poorly in infancy because of the lack of a loving mother–infant relationship, may be revisited later. Perhaps a particularly supportive and healthy loving relationship later in life will result in greater trust than was present earlier in life. More often than not, challenges related to identity and intimacy persist throughout the lifespan. Unlike Freud, who viewed fixations as insidious and irreversible without a psychoanalytic therapeutic experience, Erikson felt that adaptations across the lifespan are common. Nonetheless, progress through the Eriksonian stages is associated with other positive life outcomes. For example, data from the over 75-year longitudinal Study of Adult Development indicate that the participants in the study (the sample included only white men) who exhibited higher psychosocial development at midlife also displayed higher levels of cognitive functioning and lower levels of depression decades later (Malone et al., 2016).

Identity and Identity Crises

Without a doubt, the most prominent crisis in Erikson's theory is the identity crisis, which receives more research attention than any of the other stages (Schwartz, 2001; Schwartz, Donnellan, Ravert, Luyckx, & Zamboanga, 2013). In part, the salience of the identity crisis in Erikson's thinking reflects how his own life proceeded. Although he was fathered by Danish parents, his stepfather was Jewish, and he was raised in a home that respected Jewish traditions. He did not realize during boyhood that his stepfather was not his biological father. Since his tall, blonde-haired presence contrasted with those of many of his father's Jewish friends and associates, he experienced identity confusion, feeling something of an outsider in his father's circles. As a Dane growing up in southern Germany in the early part of the 20th century during a time of fierce nationalism in Germany, he experienced other tensions regarding

TABLE 5.1. Erikson's Eight Stages of Psychosocial Development

Conflict-defining stage	Approximate age	What happens during stage
Trust versus mistrust	First year	During infancy, children either form a trusting relationship with an adult or they do not. Lack of interaction with an adult who can be trusted to meet the infant's needs results in long-term mistrust.
Autonomy versus shame and doubt	Second year	Children begin to do things independently, such as feeding or dressing themselves, thereby establishing some autonomy from others. Part of autonomy is self-control. During this stage, much of the conflict involving self-control centers around toilet training. If children have difficultly establishing self-control and autonomy, the result may be feelings of shame in not being more independent and doubt about autonomy is possible.
Initiative versus guilt	3–6 years	As the preschool years proceed, the child has many more initiations into the world and tries new roles. If children are overly punished for their initiative, feelings of guilt result.
Industry versus inferiority	6–12 years	During the elementary school years, children are expected to begin to master the skills of the culture. For example, in Western culture, children are expected to develop fundamental literacy and numeracy skills. Success leads to a sense of industry; failure can lead to a sense of inferiority.
Identity versus role confusion	Adolescence	During this period, people begin to establish who they are, what they believe in, and what they want to become, thus developing an identity. Successful identity achievement requires trying out various possible identities and struggling with them before making a commitment. Failure to achieve an identity results in confusion.
Intimacy versus isolation	Early adulthood	A person either achieves intimacy with others, usually a marital partner or the equivalent, or is at risk for feeling psychological isolation.
Generativity versus stagnation	Middle adulthood	Adulthood is either a period of contributing to society and to the development of the next generation, or there is a risk of stagnating.
Integrity versus despair	Late adulthood	The person who resolves all of life's crises in a positive fashion is likely to look back and feel a sense of integrity. Those who fail to resolve positively one or more life crises are at risk for disgust and despair.

ethnic identity. Rather than pursue university studies and a profession, as his family would have liked, Erikson chose to live the life of an artist and distinguished himself among those who knew him as someone who was trying to find himself (Coles, 1970). Erik Erikson definitely experienced complex identity crises during his own youth, and those personal experiences obviously affected the developmental theory he would later envision and write about.

According to Erikson's theory, the main task of adolescence and young adulthood is to develop an identity. A healthy identity can develop if the youth experiences alternative possibilities and reflects on alternative identities. A variety of specific identity-related conflicts occur during adolescence and young adulthood that correspond to the conflicts taken up at other points in the lifespan (as presented in Table 5.1). That is, there are identity subcrises with respect to trust versus mistrust, autonomy versus shame and doubt, initiative versus guilt, industry versus inferiority, intimacy versus isolation, generativity versus stagnation, and integrity versus despair. As part of these subcrises, adolescents and young adults struggle to determine what they believe with respect to sexual orientation, intellectual interests, life philosophy, vocation, religion, and so on.

Identity-related struggles are made possible by the increased intellectual power that comes with adolescence—referred to by Piaget (1983) as formal operations (see Chapter 3). Of special importance is the adolescent's new intellectual ability to think about hypothetical situations and to compare hypothetical outcomes. The ability to reflect on the possible permits adolescents to challenge themselves about what they believe (Boyes & Chandler, 1992).

One noteworthy researcher, James Marcia, advanced Erikson's theory by identifying four different identity statuses, reflecting the degree to which adolescents have experienced and resolved their identity crises (Kroger & Marcia, 2011; Mallory, 1989; Marcia, 1966; Meeus, Iedema, Helsen, & Vollebergh, 1999). Specifically, the four statuses vary in terms of degree of exploration and commitment. In our years of teaching at the university level, we have found that most of our students can readily identify relatives, friends, and acquaintances who fit into each of the following four identity statuses:

People who are **identity achieved** have experienced crises and made choices, having gone through a process of exploration they have committed. They may still exhibit some flexibility in terms of direction, but they are not easily swayed by those around them. Those who are identity achieved are perceived as productive, consistent, and independent. Their "self-sameness and continuity," descriptors used by Erikson, lead them to be described as dependable and to be seen as potential sources of support.

Individuals in **foreclosure** have come to commitments without exploration and have not experienced crises. One example would be young adults who follow the life course devised by their parents without question. The plan may be to go to a prestigious college and then on to law school, to accept a place in the family firm, and to settle down in the same community as their parents. Foreclosed individuals often have conservative values, are moralistic, conventional, sex-appropriate in their behaviors, and are satisfied with themselves. They appear to be well adjusted within the constraints of conformity and may experience their lives as satisfying, albeit with limitations.

People in **diffusion** have not experienced crises in that they have not tried out, nor are they trying out, new roles; and have made no commitments. Youth and adolescents in diffusion are perceived to be living lives without personal meaning. They are viewed as being reluctant to commit themselves to positions, as avoiding close relationships, and as being unpredictable and changeable. At their best, they appear to be flexible and adaptable, shifting in response to external influences. At their worse, they appear isolated, their lives empty and meaningless.

People in **moratorium** are actively exploring potential identities or ruminating about them but have not made a commitment. According to Erikson's theory, this is a healthy and appropriate status for adolescents and youth. Young people who are in moratorium are perceived by others as introspective, anxious, struggling, and valuing independence. Those in moratorium differ from those in diffusion with respect to concern and direction. Those in moratorium may experience anxiety as they consider alternatives, whereas those in diffusion are relatively unconcerned about their lack of commitment.

The healthy progression according to Erikson's theory is into moratorium, with identity eventually achieved. It is considered less healthy to come to an identity without conflict (as in foreclosure) or to never experience conflict or identity (as in diffusion). The danger is that those in foreclosure or diffusion may end up living lives very different from the ones they would have chosen if they had experienced the process of crisis and reflection, with the possibility that later in life they will realize they have been living the wrong life, an unsatisfying one.

Interested in understanding the role played by the college experience in the development of identity, Pascarella and Terenzini (1991) reviewed the research and concluded that college provides an opportunity for students to be in moratorium and eventually to move into identity achievement. The college experience affords students an opportunity to interact with students different from themselves and introduces them to diverse possibilities potentially leading to changes in identity status (Komarovsky, 1985; Madison, 1969; Newman & Newman, 1978). In general, college students exhibit increasing commitments with respect to vocation lifestyle and philosophy from freshman to senior years.

Identity achievement, however, is anything but certain by the end of the college years. For example, Waterman and Goldman (1976) observed that only a little more than half of the college seniors they studied had achieved identity with respect to religious or political philosophies, a result consistent with other data reviewed by Pascarella and Terenzini (1991). In a longitudinal study of identity formation, Carlsson, Wangqvist, and Friesen (2015) interviewed Swedish women at age 25 and again at age 29 and found the four identity statuses equally common at both ages and, with the exception of those in moratorium, the typical pattern was stability across the two ages. Thus, little evidence exists to support the assumption that students will have achieved identity by the end of high school. The Eriksonian perspective is that exploration is a good thing, something to be encouraged, during high school and young adulthood.

Ethnic and Racial Identity

When Erikson (1943, 1945) spent time with two Native American tribes, the Yurok and the Sioux, he recognized that their developmental patterns were different not only from each other but also from those in white America and Europe. In the last few decades, a significant amount of the research on identity development has explored the role of ethnic and racial identity in the developmental process (Santos

& Umaña-Taylor, 2015). Phinney (1989), for example, demonstrated that issues of ethnic identity were much more prominent in the development of U.S. minority adolescents, who are continually confronted with issues of identity related to their ethnicity, than in the development of white Americans. For some time, researchers and theorists had focused on studying and developing theories of ethnic identity and racial identity as separate constructs (Cross & Vandiver, 2001; Sellers, Smith, Shelton, Rowley, & Chavous, 1998; see Hudley & Irving, 2012, for a review). Relatively recently, however, the leading researchers of ethnic and racial identity recommended against distinguishing between racial identity and ethnic identity and instead proposed a construct encompassing both, the construct of ethnic–racial identity (Umaña-Taylor et al., 2014; see also Cross, Grant, & Ventuneac, 2012, and Yip, Douglass, & Sellers, 2014). Although these researchers acknowledge that the constructs of race and ethnicity are distinct, they emphasize that there is substantial overlap between the two constructs. The integrated construct of ethnic–racial identity is multidimensional, reflecting the "beliefs and attitudes that individuals have about their ethnic–racial group memberships, as well as the process by which these beliefs and attitudes develop over time" (Umaña-Taylor et al., 2014).

During middle childhood, children develop the ability to identify and classify themselves and others according to ethnic and racial labels and to recognize the constancy of those labels (an individual isn't white one day and black the next). They also begin to develop a knowledge base about race, ethnicity, and culture. Family ethnic socialization has considerable impact on the ethnic–racial identity process, as do influences outside of the family such as peers and neighbors. The demographic characteristics of schools and community can shape the socialization messages given by parents and therefore the ethnic–racial identity development of their children (Hudley & Irving, 2012). For example, if a child attends a school that is primarily white, ethnicity may be particularly salient. If a child attends a school that is ethnically diverse, parents are more likely to provide more messages of pride and skills in coping with hostility than if a child tends a school that is primarily composed of members of his or her own ethnic or racial group. Parents' perception of school climate affects their socialization messages.

Adolescence, with its increased maturity particularly in terms of cognitive skills, creates more opportunities to explore race and ethnicity. In line with Erikson's theory, exploration leading to eventual resolution is central to ethnic–racial identity formation, and exploration during adolescence results in initial decisions about the meaningfulness of ethnicity and race in identity formation (Douglass & Umaña-Taylor, 2016; Umaña-Taylor et al., 2014). In a longitudinal study of adolescent girls of Mexican origin (65% of them born in the United States) attending school in Phoenix, Arizona, Gonzales-Bracken, Bamaca-Colbert, and Allen (2016) observed that exploration, commitment, and affirmation (positive feelings about ethnic group membership) increased over a 3 ½-year time frame.

Ethnic–racial identity is multidimensional (e.g., Sellers et al., 1998; Umaña-Taylor et al., 2014). The dimension of *salience* refers to the extent to which ethnic–racial identity is relevant to the self-concept in a specific situation, at a particular moment. Salience varies across time and situations. *Centrality* refers to the extent to which an individual considers race or ethnicity to be an important part of self-concept. Centrality is stable across situations. *Regard* refers to the affective dimension of ethnic–racial identity. The degree of affirmation (positive or negative regard) can be either private or public. Private regard refers to a personal affective judgment, that is, how an individual feels. Public regard refers to how an individual feels that others view ethnicity or race—the extent to which an ethnic–racial group is viewed positively or negatively by others.

Similar to identity development in general, the exploration of ethnic–racial identity does not end with adolescence. College students who are exposed to diverse experiences in terms of other students, course readings and discussion, and social activities may be prompted to reflect on ethnic–racial identity in new ways. In emerging adulthood, ethnic–racial identity is not contemplated in isolation but along with other identity themes.

Ethnic–racial identity is associated with identity development in general. In a study of more than 300 13- to 16-year olds representative of the ethnic groups present in five New York City schools, Yip (2014) found that the students who exhibited a more developed identity status, having experienced higher levels of exploration and commitment, also reported that their ethnic identity had more relevance to their daily lives. Ethnic–racial identity is also associated with other developmental outcomes. Research evidence, including a meta-analysis, suggests that positive feelings about belonging to an ethnic or racial group are positively associated with psychosocial adjustment for African American and Latino youth and with positive academic outcomes for African Americans, Latinos, Asian Americans, and Pacific Islanders (Rivas-Drake et al., 2014a, 2014b; Zirkel & Johnson, 2016; see also Chapter 6). The Applying Developmental Theory to Educational Contexts special feature (Box 5.3) describes why supporting identity development is a relevant goal for educators.

Evaluation of Eriksonian Theory

Rooted in Freudian theory, Erikson's outlook about human development was in part biologically determined. In particular, he argued that the biological stage of life contributes to the current internal conflict. Even so, resolution of the eight life crises is determined by social factors. Contextual variables are important in determining whether one's responses to a crisis are developmentally adaptive or result in long-term psychic pain.

Just as cultural anthropologists, such as Malinowski (1927), concluded that processes like Oedipal conflict in Freudian theory vary from culture to culture, those interested in Eriksonian theory have observed cultural variations in development. The difference is that Erikson's theory predicted such differences, whereas Freudian theory did not, positing instead that human biology destined universal development as Freud depicted it.

Marcia (1994) also emphasized the importance of contextual determination of identity development. For example, identity achievement was associated with healthy functioning for both males and females since he began his work in the 1960s. In the early studies, however, foreclosure appeared to be a healthy identity status for females. The times have changed for women, and accordingly, so has women's psychosocial development. It is less likely now that women will simply follow the expectations of parents or boyfriends or husbands than it was decades ago. Nevertheless, the research finding that the identity construct varies with context is consistent with Erikson's theory.

One of the more important tenets of psychoanalytically oriented theories is that what happens during early childhood affects subsequent development. There

---

Applying Developmental Theory to Educational Contexts

BOX 5.3. Identity Development in the Classroom

Schachter and Rich (2011) proposed that educators acknowledge identity development as an explicit instructional goal, a goal that supports the achievement of other instructional goals. The idea is for teachers to become purposefully involved with the identity exploration process of their students, recognizing that through the knowledge and experiences they provide, teachers impact who their students are and who they will become. Cooper (2014) argued that educators should take advantage of the link between adolescent identity exploration and their engagement in classroom activities, outlining what she described as connective teaching practices. Connective teaching practices entail creating an emotional connection to the teacher and to the curriculum by promoting relevance to students' lives, conveying concern and caring for students, demonstrating an understanding of students and the challenges they face, relating to students through humor, providing affirmation of students, and enabling student self-expression.

For example, Cooper (2012) conducted case studies of five Latina 10th graders, collecting both interview and observational data. She followed the students from class to class on two consecutive days, asked them to rank their classes in terms of level of engagement, and interviewed them about each class. Cooper identified five themes influencing the students' perceptions and their classroom engagement: supporting the development of a sense of identity, signaling the value of the course content, nurturing linguistic competence, communicating genuine caring, and creating a psychologically safe environment.

Supporting identity development in schools, particularly ethnic–racial identity in minorities, is likely to lead to other positive outcomes (Ford, 2016; Hudley & Irving, 2012; Nasir, Rowley, & Perez, 2016; Spencer et al., 2012). Teachers can help minority students learn to successfully navigate the dominant culture while retaining the foundation of their home culture, practices, and beliefs. For adolescent students, teachers can emphasize activities to facilitate socialization within and across diverse groups and to encourage identity exploration. Students can be exposed to a wide range of positive adult role models, in the community and in the curriculum. To be effective in supporting identity development, the teachers themselves must examine their own identity and perspectives on diversity. Culturally competent educators exhibit an awareness and respect of cultural differences and acknowledge the effect of differential effects of history on different ethnic and racial minorities.

---

is evidence that infants who experience trusting relationships with their mothers are more socially adept from preschool through adolescence: friendlier, more open to new friendships, and more interpersonally competent in general (e.g., Sroufe, Carlson, & Schulman, 1993). Thus, as Erikson theorized, the result is continuity and connection with the issues of trust and mistrust across development.

Chapter Summary and Evaluation

Social learning is both a behavioral and a cognitive theory. It is biological as well, with Bandura (1986) making the case that humans have evolved to be social learners. The ability to learn from others through observation, classical conditioning, and response to reinforcements and punishments is certainly adaptive. Both parents and teachers can make use of social learning principles to promote desirable behaviors.

Some of the more systematic ways of doing so are behavior modification, cognitive self-instruction, and prominently in education, classroom management.

Social learning researchers have generated a tremendous amount of evidence that situational variables matter. How a child behaves in any given situation depends not only on the interests, abilities, and predilections of the child but also on characteristics of the situation and the child's expectations about the situation. If the child has come to expect punishment for trying in school—for example, in the form of public teacher comments about his or her difficulties in learning—the child may be less willing to try than if the teacher has previously reinforced the student for taking chances (see Chapter 9 for a discussion of other ways teachers influence motivation).

In contrast, the biological bases of development suggested by Freud and Erikson seem rigid—a particular unfolding of stages. A development conflict is experienced at each stage. Freud's stages emphasize psychosexual conflicts; Erikson's stages emphasize psychosocial conflicts. In Freud's theory, the failure to resolve a conflict in the appropriate developmental period leads to issues that can be resolved only through therapy. In Erikson's theory, earlier conflicts can be revisited and resolved later in life. The lifespan approach of Erikson's theory is also evident in the inclusion of stages corresponding to middle adulthood and old age.

One way of understanding the three theories covered in this chapter is to review them in terms of the Big Ideas of development introduced in Chapter 1.

Nature and Nurture

All three theories assign roles to nature and nurture, although the emphasis varies. Social learning theory is the most environmental of the three; Freudian theory is the most biological. Erikson believed in biological unfolding to some degree but emphasized the social and cultural environment much more than Freud.

Continuity and Discontinuity

Social learning theory is the classic example of a theory emphasizing continuous development, with the effects of experience accumulating over time. Both Freud and Erikson proposed stage theories. In both cases, cumulative experiences matter in determining future development, although development is focused on a particular psychosexual conflict or psychosocial crisis. Erikson's theory also allowed for revisiting earlier crises throughout development.

Universal and Culture-Specific

According to social learning theory, the same processes of development (observation, classical and operant conditioning, punishment) operate across the human species. What the child observes and is reinforced and punished for will vary with culture, however. In contrast, Freud believed that his theory was universally applicable. One point of departure for Erikson from Freud was Erikson's understanding that development is affected by culture, although Erikson also believed that the same types of conflicts, from "trust versus mistrust" to "integrity versus despair," occur across cultures. In recent decades, researchers have expanded Erikson's ideas by highlighting the development of ethnic and racial identity.

Active and Passive Child

Although some critics of social learning theory suggest that it is a passive theory of development, in fact, children are very active in determining what they will observe. In contrast, Freudian theory suggests a more passive role of the child, with the mother largely determining the degree of frustration or indulgence the child receives with respect to oral and anal stage conflicts. The inevitability of the Oedipal and Electra conflicts makes it obvious that the child is active in these conflicts only as an actor is active in a play. Yes, there is a different player on the stage, but it is the same story no matter who is playing the part. Erikson certainly plays up the importance of active decision making more than Freud does, especially with respect to the identity crisis. It is healthy to be active in seeking one's own identity and unhealthy to be passive, accepting parentally expected values and desires.

REVIEW OF KEY TERMS

behavioral contracting An agreement between teacher and student that specifies what the student's goal will be, what reinforcement might be earned, and how much progress toward the goal is required for reinforcement.

behavioral models People who display behaviors that are imitated.

classical conditioning The conditioning of a stimulus to elicit a particular response. Classical conditioning occurs when a neutral stimulus is paired with an unconditioned stimulus that elicits a response. The neutral stimulus becomes a conditioned stimulus when the conditioned stimulus presented alone elicits what is now the conditioned response.

conditioned reinforcers Reinforcers, such as money, that acquire their reinforcement properties by being paired with unconditioned reinforcers.

conditioned response The response elicited by a conditioned stimulus.

conditioned stimulus A neutral stimulus that has been paired with an unconditioned stimulus to evoke a conditioned response.

diffusion An identity status in which people have not experienced identity crisis or commitment to an identity.

ego The rational side of personality that operates according to the reality principle.

extinction The process by which classically conditioned responses cease (are extinguished) when subsequent experiences of the stimulus are not followed by the conditioned response.

fading In behavior modification programs, a gradual reduction in the use of reinforcement once the behavioral goals are reached.

foreclosure An identity status in which people have committed to an identity without experiencing an identity crisis.

id The instinctual part of personality, present at birth, which seeks pleasure and immediate gratification (pleasure principle).

identity achieved An identity status in which people have undergone identity crises and have committed to an identity.

intermittent reinforcement Reinforcers that are presented only on occasion rather than continuously, thus making behaviors more resistant to extinction.

interval reinforcement schedule Intermittent reinforcement that is provided at certain time intervals.

moratorium An identity status in which people are in ongoing crisis, actively exploring potential identities.

negative reinforcers The cessation of aversive stimulation following a response, thus increasing the likelihood of the response.

operant conditioning Conditioning that, depending on the consequences (reinforcement or punishment), increases or decreases the likelihood of a response.

positive reinforcers A stimulus that increases the future likelihood of a response when presented following the response.

punishment The presentation of aversive stimulation after a response, thus decreasing the future likelihood of the response.

ratio reinforcement schedule Intermittent reinforcement that is provided after a certain number of desired responses.

reciprocal determinism The process by which individuals through their reactions to environmental events influence future environmental events and their own subsequent development.

response cost A form of punishment used in some behavior modification programs in which unwanted behavior results in the loss of token reinforcers.

shaping Molding behavior by reinforcing closer and closer approximations of the desired response.

social learning theory A theory of learning that emphasizes learning through observation of behavioral models.

superego Conscience, the last personality structure to emerge in Freudian theory.

time-out A form of punishment sometimes used in behavior modification programs in which a student is physically removed from other students or activities (i.e., potential reinforcers) for a short period of time.

token reinforcement Reinforcement that uses symbolic reinforcers, such as chips or marbles, that can be accumulated and traded for other reinforcers.

unconditioned reinforcer Reinforcers that satisfy biological deprivation such as thirst or hunger.

unconditioned response The response elicited by an unconditioned stimulus.

unconditioned stimulus A stimulus that evokes a particular response, the unconditioned response.

vicarious experiences In social learning theory, experiences that are observed in others.

CHAPTER 6

Sociocultural Theories of Development and Education

P eople learn from other people. This is certainly not a new idea. For example, social learning theorists have long argued for the powerful roles of imitation and modeling in learning (see Chapter 5). People not only imitate specific models, they also respond to general influences of behavior in their surrounding culture. In this chapter, we explore the role of the learning context and the mediation of the cultural environment in determining thinking. We begin with the most prominent contemporary theory emphasizing the role of cultural context in determining cognitive development, Vygotsky's theory (1962, 1978).

What will become clear in our discussion of Vygotsky's theory is that the communications children experience are critical in stimulating the development of their thinking skills. According to this perspective, instructional conversations make a big difference in the development of a child's mind. By the end of this chapter, it will also be clear that a child's cultural environment influences success in school.

Vygotsky's Sociocultural Approaches to Mind

Lev Vygotsky lived in the first half of the 20th century in what was then the Soviet Union, but English translations of his works did not appear until the 1960s and 1970s. In the last two decades, no theorist has commanded the attention of psychologists interested in instruction as much as Vygotsky has (Göncü & Gauvain, 2012; Mahn & John-Steiner, 2013; Wertsch, 1985, 1991). The main theme of Vygotsky's theory is that it is impossible to understand development without considering the culture in which development occurs, including the social institutions of a culture, such as its schools. Cultural tools, such as language and technology, also greatly influence the development of cognitive abilities in each new generation.

The Developmental Relationship between Thought and Speech

According to Vygotsky (1978), throughout life, language plays an important role in thought. The relationship of thought to speech is different for adults than for children, however.

Thought and Speech in Adults

Vygotsky (1962) believed that inner speech plays an important role in adult thought. In contrast to outer speech, which should be readily understood by others, **inner speech** is an internal dialogue that is often abbreviated and fragmentary, with the meaning of complex thoughts captured in very few words or even in abbreviated words (Wertsch, 1991).

What is the relationship between thought and inner speech? Consider a complicated task, one that requires some thinking. For example, let's say you want to search for information on the topic of language at the library and you are unfamiliar with the databases available. Your inner speech will guide the search process. Perhaps you begin by saying to yourself something like, "How do I get to the right place? . . . OK, there's the menu . . . What do I need?" Then you may mumble to yourself an abbreviated, "Pick it," as you select the PsycINFO database. As you gain more experience using the database, you learn to access it without any awareness of additional inner speech. Inner speech is no longer necessary, since you are solving a familiar problem.

Thought and Speech in Children

In Vygotsky's theory, much of the development of thinking is the development of inner speech. This process goes through four stages. During the first 2 years of life, in *the first stage*, thought is nonverbal and speech is nonconceptual, with no relationship between thought and speech. Beginning with the development of language at around age 2, thought and speech begin to merge in *the second stage*. During this second stage, the child labels many objects by their names and develops verbal communications with others. Children do not use speech to direct thinking during this second stage, but they will respond to the directive speech of others (Luria, 1982). For example, while 2-year-olds often live up to their "terrible" reputation, frequently they will "come" when you ask them to. Younger children typically require nonverbal cuing about the appropriateness of coming, such as an adult offering outstretched arms.

In *the third stage*, the role of speech in directing thought and behavior begins to emerge as children exhibit **egocentric speech**. That is, preschoolers often talk to themselves about what they are doing. For example, they will say "I'm going to play with the dog" before they go play with the dog, or say "I'm going to ride my tricycle" before they go ride their tricycles. Often these utterances come when children are trying to figure out what to do. Piaget argued that preschoolers talk to themselves because of their immature understanding of communication (see Chapter 3). In contrast, Vygotsky viewed the emergence of egocentric speech or **private speech** that voices what children are thinking or doing as a sign of maturation. Private speech is an overt step to the development of inner speech.

In one study, Vygotsky asked preschoolers to complete tasks that were complicated by some obstacle. For example, the obstacle might be that something needed to complete the task was missing. The amount of egocentric speech uttered by the preschoolers during the completion of these tasks was much greater than when they performed the same tasks without obstacles. Consider this monologue produced by a preschooler faced with a task difficulty: "Where is the pencil? I need a blue pencil now. Nothing. Instead of that I will color it red and put water on it—that will make it darker and more like blue" (Vygotsky, 1987, p. 70). This child is clearly using speech as part of thinking.

During *the fourth stage* of the development of inner speech, the egocentric speech that was overt becomes covert and abbreviated . . . becoming inner speech. For example, the egocentric speech described above would become brief, internalized inner speech, perhaps as follows: "Where's pencil? Need blue. Use red, add water." The actions are much more prominent in the inner speech in Stage 4 compared to Stage 3, when the egocentric speech is more obvious and clearly preceding the actions.

In Vygotsky's view, learning begins in the social world. Speech is originally external to children: they speak to address others, not to talk to themselves. Only after establishing speech for others can children internalize it. Thus, children can have *monologues* with themselves only after they have developed the ability to *dialogue* with others. Internalized speech is not egocentric in the Piagetian sense: it is social speech that has been internalized and used to guide thinking and behavior.

Researchers studying the transition from private speech—speaking out loud to guide thinking and action—to covert inner speech have noted a developmental progression in line with Vygotsky's theory (Winsler, 2009). In a cross-sectional study of a large, diverse sample of 5- to 17-year-olds, Winsler and Naglieri (2003) reported that overt private speech declined linearly with age (observed in 43% of the 5-year-olds, decreasing to 10% of the 17-year-olds). Self-reports of the use of covert, inner speech increased with age (reported by 4% of the 5-year-olds and 30% of the 17-year-olds). Observations of whispering and muttering, partially covert private speech, started at 13% for the youngest group, increased to a peak of 28% for children in the middle of the age range, and decreased to 11% for the oldest group. Across all age levels, the overall percentage of students who used some kind of verbal mediation (overt private speech, partially covert private speech, or covert inner speech) remained at 60% for all age levels. Although private speech is more common in younger children than older children, even adolescents and adults have been observed to use private speech, sometimes without being aware they are talking to themselves, particularly when working on a challenging task. The relationship between use of private speech and performance on a task is complex, varying as a function of task characteristics (familiarity, difficulty) and child characteristics such as age, motivation, and skills relevant to the task at hand (Winsler, 2009).

See the Considering Interesting Questions special feature (Box 6.1) for a description of a study exploring the relationship of children's private speech to classroom performance.

Development of Sophisticated Thought

Adults often assist children in thinking about problems they face. For example, they may help children solve a puzzle or help them figure out how many days there are until their next birthday. What goes on in these interactions is thinking, but thinking involving two heads. Children could not possibly think through many problems without help, but with adult assistance they make progress. After years of participating

Considering Interesting Questions

BOX 6.1. What Is the Relationship between Private Speech and Classroom Performance?

Interested in exploring the relationship between private speech to task performance, Berk (1986) observed first and third graders working on math seatwork in the naturalistic setting of their own classrooms. As predicted by Vygotskian theory, Berk noted developmental differences in the children's use of private speech for self-guidance. Private speech was more common in younger students, whereas older students were more likely to have internalized their private speech in inner speech.

The focus of the private speech also varied with development. The speech changed from task-irrelevant, self-stimulating content to task-relevant content such as describing or guiding their work. Berk found that task-relevant private speech predicted greater attentional focus and fewer extraneous behaviors in the classroom, and that the relationship of private speech to intelligence shifted with age. The total amount of private speech produced by the children was positively related to intelligence for the first graders ($r = .33$), but was negatively related to intelligence for the third graders ($r = -.49$). (See Chapter 1 to review of the meaning of correlation coefficients.) Thus, in the first grade, high levels of private speech were associated with high intelligence test scores. In the third grade, however, high levels of private speech were associated with low intelligence test scores. The more intelligent third graders had internalized their private speech.

in such interactions, children internalize the types of actions they once carried out with adults (Mahn & John-Steiner, 2013; Rogoff, 1998). Vygotsky summarized this developmental progression as follows:

> Any function in the child's cultural development appears twice, or on two planes. First, it appears on the social plane, and then on the psychological plane. . . . Social relations or relations among people genetically underlie all higher functions and their relationships. . . . (1981, pp. 163–164)

According to this perspective, cognitive development moves forward largely because the child is in a world that provides aid when the child needs it and can benefit from it.

Two-year-olds can do some things for themselves. A responsive social world lets children do those things independently. For example, a parent may allow a 2-year-old to pick out a T-shirt to wear, especially when the child insists, "I do it." But there are other things that 2-year-olds could never do, no matter how much help they were given. The responsive social environment does not encourage children to do these sorts of things and, in fact, often discourages their attempts at overly difficult tasks. For example, a parent would try to steer a young child away from trying to put together a 1,000-piece jigsaw puzzle.

Most critically, however, the responsive social world provides assistance on tasks that are within what Vygotsky called the **zone of proximal development**. Tasks in the zone of proximal development are those that children cannot accomplish independently but can accomplish with assistance. Children learn how to perform tasks within their zone through interactions with responsive and more competent others who provide hints, prompts, and assistance to them on an as-needed basis. These hints and prompts encourage children to process a task appropriately, until they eventually can perform the task without assistance. For example, a kindergartner can write a story with help from a parent. This help may include the parent printing the words to the story as the kindergartner dictates and showing the kindergartner where to copy the words onto a page, leaving room for the child to draw an accompanying picture. The task of writing a story is within the kindergartner's zone of proximal development. The zone of proximal development is without a doubt the Vygotskian idea that has received the most attention from educators (Gauvain & Perez, 2015; Göncü & Gauvain, 2012).

The concept of **scaffolding** is based on the principles of Vygotsky's theory (Wood, Bruner, & Ross, 1976). Builders use a scaffold to erect a building, gradually removing it as the building becomes self-supporting. Likewise, adults or older children who are helping younger children with a task should gradually remove their prompts and hints. That is, more capable people assist children but only enough to allow them to get started. Scaffolding means providing just enough support and assistance to ensure that the child does not fail, eventually removing that support as the child is capable of performing independently (Gauvain & Perez, 2015; O'Donnell, 2012; Reiser & Tabak, 2014).

One example of scaffolded instruction is found in Reading Recovery, which is a method for remediating the reading of primary-grade children who are experiencing reading difficulties. A Reading Recovery teacher permits children to do as much as they can independently and intervenes as needed with hints and supports that can lead children to process effectively when they stumble (Clay & Cazden, 1990). Thus, children in Reading Recovery work within their zones of proximal development. The following dialogue illustrates how an adult tutor scaffolded the instruction of a tutee, Larry, during his first reading of a new book (Clay & Cazden, 1990, p. 214):

LARRY: The great big enormous turnip. Once an old man planted a turnip.

TEACHER: Good. (*Ignores the omission of "Once upon a time."*)

LARRY: He said grow, grow little turnip, grow. (*Pauses at the next word.*)

TEACHER: How does that word start? Can I help you start it off? How does it start? S_____. . . . He tells it to grow sw_____ sweet. . . . (*The child doesn't reread the prompted text but moves on.*)

LARRY: Grow little turnip, grow s_____. . . .

TEACHER: How else does he want it to grow? He wants it to grow sweet and he wants it to grow str_____. . . .

LARRY: . . . Strong.

TEACHER: Good boy, that's lovely. Grow strong.

LARRY: And the turnip grew up sweet and strong and. . . .

TEACHER: What's the other word that begins with *e*? Enor_____. . . .

LARRY: Enormous.

TEACHER: Good.

And so it goes. The teacher continues to provide hints and support as needed. In this case, the hints encouraged the student to apply "word attack" skills to decode words. The teacher is scaffolding this instruction by providing input only when the child stumbles, never when the child can proceed on his own. During Reading Recovery, children reread a text until they are 90% successful in decoding, with teacher support decreasing at each rereading. The teacher supports independent functioning in the children by not intervening. Once a child can read a text at the 90% level, another text is selected, one that is within the child's zone of proximal development. The child will not be able to read this text fluently without support but can get through the text if provided with hints and prompts. An evaluation of a widespread implementation of Reading Recovery in multiple schools across the United States provided evidence of its effectiveness as an instructional technique for early readers (see May et al., 2015).

Instructional scaffolding means providing help to students on an as-needed basis, enough that the child can progress, with instructional support reduced as student competence increases (Wood et al., 1976). Sociocultural theorists contend that mature thought processes develop through interaction with others (Feurstein, 1980; Todorov, 1984; Vygotsky, 1962). Thus, when adults explain, model, and scaffold problem solving for children, they prompt children's attention to important dimensions of problems. Eventually, students attend to the same dimensions without prompting, having internalized the problem-solving process initially experienced in interaction with others.

Apprenticeship

Educators who agree with Vygotsky believe that excellent instruction involves social interactions between an apprentice student and a more expert adult. Apprentice carpenters learn to build houses by working with experienced builders. Airline captains learn how to fly planes from years of experience flying as first officers working with captains. Medical residencies are really apprenticeships in many ways: They are opportunities for young physicians to learn through direct contact with senior physicians.

Barbara Rogoff (1990, 1998, 2003) argued that apprenticeship occurs in many cultures and may be a universal part of human life. She believed it is the principal means for adults to pass on knowledge to children about the intellectual tools valuable in the culture, a truly Vygotskian idea. Typically, these tools are complex enough that years of apprenticeship are necessary. In some societies, apprenticeships provide education in a wide range of accomplishments such as agriculture, hunting, fishing, weaving, and healing. Rogoff contended that a number of similarities exist across the various types of apprenticeships.

During an apprenticeship, the master provides bridges from what an apprentice knows to what an apprentice needs to know. The master translates the task into terms the apprentice can understand, and the master makes demands on the apprentice that the apprentice can meet. As the apprentice learns, the master gradually increases the demands. Thus, there is a process of **guided participation** for the apprentice, with the master providing the guidance. Gradually, the master transfers responsibility to the apprentice. Scaffolding is the key process here, with the master providing as much support as the apprentice needs to function until support is entirely withdrawn because the apprentice can do it alone.

What do apprentice learners do during this process (Collins, Brown, & Newman, 1989; Collins & Kapur, 2014; Rogoff, 1990, 1998)? They *observe*, they attend to *coaching* from their mentors, and they *practice* the tasks required in the profession, although always while being coached by their mentors. Good mentors "scaffold" their input, providing assistance as it is needed—not so much that the apprentices become dependent on it and not so little that they falter. Less is provided as the apprentice is able to go it alone.

Is it sensible to think about teaching elementary school-age students within an apprentice relationship? Working one on one with a tutor is a form of apprenticeship. Mark Lepper and his colleagues (Lepper, Aspinwall, Mumme, & Chabey, 1990; Lepper & Woolverton, 2002) observed expert math tutors as they worked with individual elementary students. The expert tutors possessed extensive knowledge bases, not only of the content domain but also of the best ways to teach it. What did the expert tutors do? They gave little direct help and rarely gave students the answers to the problems. When students made errors or had difficulties, the tutors provided hints of three sorts: (1) *questions or remarks* implying that the previous move had been an incorrect one; (2) *suggestions*, often in the form of questions, about a potential direction the student might take with the problem; and (3) *hints*, often in the form of questions, about the part of the problem the student might want to think about. That is, the tutor scaffolded the student's problem solving. For example, when a student added 36 and 36 and came up with 126, the tutor inquired, "Now how did you get that 6?" When this did not work, hints in the forms of questions became increasingly specific: "Which column do we start in?" followed by "Where is the 1's column?" Good tutors know when and where to provide hints, prompts, explanations, and modeling. They realize that this assistance is contingent on the need of the student. Expert tutors also ask students to reflect on what they are doing, to articulate their thinking processes.

The interactions of tutors with their students also include subtleties related to the affective and motivational component of academic performance. They consistently let their students know that the task they were trying was difficult, but also that the students had the ability to accomplish the task. There is a good reason for this approach. If students fail, and they blame the failure on the difficulty of the task, attributing the failure to task difficulty is less likely to discourage their efforts on future tasks as other attributions might (Weiner, 1979; see also Chapter 9). For example, if a student thinks that the current failure reflects her or his low ability, why bother to try harder when confronted with similar tasks in the future? Thus, the tutor tries to foster attributions that will encourage future efforts. For example, after a student successfully completes a problem, a tutor might say, "I guess we'll have to try to find an even harder problem for you. You tried hard and did well with this one." This is a subtle way of making the point that the last problem was hard and yet the student succeeded on it by exerting effort.

By studying excellent tutoring and instruction in detail, researchers have developed a more complete understanding of effective apprenticeship for academic tasks. See the Applying Developmental Theory to Educational Contexts special feature (Box 6.2) for an overview of the components of cognitive apprenticeship.

Realizing that it would be very difficult and costly to secure expert human tutors for all the students who would benefit from tutoring, researchers in a variety of fields, including cognitive science and artificial intelligence, have been collaborating in the development of **intelligent tutoring systems.** Intelligent tutoring systems are computer programs that can model a learner's cognitions in order to deliver individualized instruction and feedback. They are self-paced, interactive, and adaptive,

Applying Developmental Theory to Educational Contexts

BOX 6.2. Components of Cognitive Apprenticeship

Applying apprenticeship techniques to cognitive activities in the classroom can be an effective educational approach but is also complex, consisting of the following components (Collins et al., 1989; Collins & Kapur, 2014).

Modeling

Masters show their apprentices how to do essential tasks, making their actions obvious and ensuring that the apprentice sees the actions and hears a rationale for why the actions were taken. For example, a math teacher would demonstrate how to solve a long division problem as slowly as possible, making sure to explain all of the steps.

Coaching

Masters watch students attempt a task and offer hints, feedback, and guidance. As they coach, they sometimes extend additional modeling or explanation. For example, a science teacher would walk around the room observing students conducting a laboratory exercise, offering additional explanations, encouragement, or feedback as needed.

Scaffolding

Masters provide specific support, guidance, and reminders. The goal is to avoid providing too much support and to withdraw it as apprentices learn to function independently. Scaffolding requires experts to determine both when the apprentice needs help and how to offer appropriate redirection. To scaffold appropriately, masters must understand the many different types of errors apprentices can make and know how to deal with such errors.

Articulation

Articulation is a form of assessment. Masters require their apprentices to explain what they are doing, so that students are required to reflect on their knowledge and to put their thinking into words. For example, an expert math teacher may ask students how they solved a problem and why they picked a particular solution method over alternative methods.

Reflection

Masters encourage apprentices to compare their work to a set of standards or to the work of others, including the master and other apprentices. For example, young teachers often watch videotapes of themselves teaching and reflect on their work, perhaps discussing their teaching actions with their classmates, their supervisors, or more expert teachers.

Exploration

Apprentices cannot be mere copies of their mentors. The apprenticeship relationship permits safe exploration. Good mentors teach their apprentices how to explore, and they encourage them to do so. For example, a good writing teacher assists writers in finding their own writing voice rather than encouraging students to mimic the teacher's own writing style.

able to adjust to learner characteristics. In Vygotsky's terms, the computer becomes the more capable other, providing scaffolding within the learner's zone of proximal development. Intelligent tutoring systems have proved to be effective, particularly as a replacement for homework or seatwork in the typical classroom. Are intelligent tutoring systems more effective than high-quality human tutors? In general, the answer revealed by a meta-analysis of 107 studies is that intelligent tutoring systems are not as effective as human tutors or well-designed small-group work but produce higher achievement than teacher-led large-group instruction, reading textbooks, and completing workbooks for all levels of education and for many different content areas (Ma, Adesope, Nesbit, & Liu, 2014). Two other meta-analyses, one of 35 studies at the college level (Steenbergen-Hu & Cooper, 2014) and another of 26 studies of the mathematical learning of K–12 students (Steenbergen-Hu & Cooper, 2013), also indicated that intelligent tutoring systems were generally effective but not as effective as human tutors. As complicated as it is, it is easier to create and improve intelligent tutoring systems than to develop expert human tutors; once an intelligent tutoring system is developed for a given content domain, it can be widely used reaching students who do not have access to expert human tutors.

Research Validating Sociocultural Positions

Despite the prominence of Vygotsky's ideas in education in recent decades, much of the instruction that goes on in classrooms is inconsistent with Vygotskian theory. See the Considering Interesting Questions special feature (Box 6.3) for a description of the types of conversations characteristically observed in classrooms. A reasonable question is whether instruction in the "zone of proximal development" is common at all. Do adults assume the more demanding roles in such interactions in order to reduce the workload for the child? Do adults eventually cede control of tasks to their students?

Consistent with Vygotsky's ideas, adults regularly provide instruction to children that is supportive, providing scaffolding for children in naturalistic settings (Gardner & Rogoff, 1982; Rogoff, 1998). For example, Wood et al. (2016) observed parents scaffolding their young children's interactions with IPads. Adults also adjust their support in response to children's developmental level. For example, academic tutors provide more support to younger students, such as 7-year-olds, than to older, 11-year-old students (Ludeke & Hartup, 1983). When expert weavers teach weaving, they intervene more with younger and less experienced learners (Greenfield, 1984). In addition, adults reduce their control of an instructional situation as a student becomes more and more capable of doing a task independently (Childs & Greenfield, 1980; Rogoff, 1998; Wertsch, 1979). For example, Mayan girls learn to make tortillas a little bit at a time (Rogoff, 1990, 2003). Toddlers first observe their mothers making tortillas and practice rolling and flattening a small piece of dough. Mothers support the efforts of their children as they get older by giving hints and suggestions and continually demonstrating how to construct a high-quality tortilla. Eventually, the girls can produce acceptable tortillas on their own. Thus, Vygotskian-like instruction seems to occur, at least in observations of naturally occurring adult–child instructional interactions.

Gelman, Massey, and McManus (1991) recognized some limits to adult scaffolding as they studied the types of instruction that parents provide to their children during museum visits. First, the types of interactions between parents and children

BOX 6.3. How Well Do Typical Instructional Conversations Reflect Vygotskyian Ideas?

Conversation is probably the most common form of human interaction both inside and outside classrooms. What is the nature of typical classroom conversations? As it turns out, they often take forms that are not consistent with instructional approaches inspired by Vygotsky's theory. For example, many classroom conversations conform to a pattern called initiation–response–evaluation (IRE) cycles (Cazden, 1988; Mehan, 1979), where the teacher *initiates* an interaction, often with a question; the student *responds*; and the teacher *evaluates* the response before making another initiation. With IRE cycles, teachers are in control of the conversation, can conduct lessons in an orderly fashion, and make certain the points they consider important are "covered" in a whole class activity. Both teachers and students are familiar with this type of classroom interaction and know how to interact with each other in this way.

IRE cycles, however, have strikingly negatives aspects (Bowers & Flinders, 1990; Cazden, 1988)—especially when contrasted with tutoring and teaching in the zone of proximal development described in this chapter. For example, the questions used in IRE cycles are typically literal and factual, focusing on low-level knowledge acquisition. In addition, because only one student can be active at a time, this can be a passive instructional approach for the other students who are not involved in the interaction. If the goal is for students to learn to control their thinking, IRE cycles are particularly unattractive since they are almost completely teacher-controlled. The students generally do little except answer questions they had no part in formulating. IRE cycles can give students the message that education is receiving knowledge from an authority, rather than working with knowledge to understand it in ways that are personally meaningful and that create new knowledge.

Not all the news about classroom interaction patterns resembling IRE cycles is as discouraging. Wells and Mejia Arauz (2006) observed teachers who had been participating in a project to implement inquiry approaches, including creating more real dialogue, in their science classrooms. Analyzing the interactions in the classrooms of three teachers who participated throughout the 6-year project, the researchers noted a shift toward increased dialogue. However, there were still significant amounts of patterns described as IRF: initiation–response–follow-up (rather than evaluation as in IRE cycles). Over the course of the project, the number of classroom conversations initiated by teachers decreased, although they still accounted for half of the conversations, with more conversations initiated by students. The questions teachers asked tended to be open-ended, posing a problem and inviting student interpretations. Generally, the teacher was in control of the process, but at times the teacher-led discussions resulted in lengthy consideration of a topic, explored multiple perspectives, and ultimately ended in agreed upon conclusions. Molinari, Mameli, and Gnisci (2012) also reported IRF cycles as the most pervasive and dominant pattern observed in whole-class activities in primary schools. Some of the classroom interactions they observed, however, were complex and lengthy, with strings of individual IRF cycles chained together involving multiple students. The key variables affecting the quality of the classroom conversations included the type of question posed by the teacher (focused or more authentic, open-ended), the nature of the student's response (minimal or complex), and the quality of the teacher's follow-up (did it encourage further discussion or input from other students).

Although Molinari et al. (2012) observed that sometimes IRF cycles led to open discussion, with students taking control over the path of the discussion; more often teachers control the conversation process, if not the content. Haroutunian-Gordon (1991) warned that conversations in which the teacher tries too hard to control the discussion are "phony conversations." Although it is appropriate for teachers to gently steer conversations so that students stay on topic, interpretive discussions at their best probably involve issues the students value and ideas they find intriguing. Students are more likely to perceive discussions that center on such issues as "genuine" discussions. Often, a real tension develops. Interpretations that the teacher feels are important do not get out on the floor, and others that the teacher might consider to be misinterpretations are embraced by the group.

varied with the type of exhibit. In an interactive grocery store exhibit, parents prompted, requested, and ordered their children to do things. In this setting, the adults provided support for their children, although the parents rarely adjusted the support according to the child's level of competence. In contrast, even though an exhibit intended to develop number skills was designed as a parent–child interactive activity, adults rarely helped their children with this exhibit. Gelman and colleagues speculated that the adults may have felt more competent to help their children in the more familiar grocery setting than in a math exhibit, since math is an area in which many adults do not have readily accessible knowledge of many basic concepts. Finally, even when Gelman and colleagues themselves designed an exhibit intended to stimulate experimentation, they observed little scaffolded interaction between parents and children.

In summary, while many demonstrations of adult–child apprenticeships exist, parent–child and teacher–child scaffolding are anything but universal. Educators, however, continue to develop instructional approaches that are consistent with Vygotskian thinking, emphasizing teacher–student dialoguing and scaffolding in these approaches. There are Vygotskian approaches to early childhood education (Bodrova & Leong, 2003, 2009), special education (Gindis, 2003), second-language education (Johnson, 2015; Lantolf, 2003), as well as Vygotskian educational approaches in the content areas, including mathematics (Lampert, 2001; Schmittau, 2003), history (Haenen, Schrijnemakers, & Stufkens, 2003), science (Driver, Asoko, Leach, Mortimer, & Scott, 1998; Giest & Lompscher, 2003), and literacy (Miller, 2003). Two of the most prominent, effective, and well-researched approaches to instruction consistent with Vygotskian principles, reciprocal teaching and problem-based learning, are described next.

Reciprocal Teaching

Reciprocal teaching is a form of instruction that is often showcased as illustrating Vygotskian principles (Brown & Palincsar, 1989; Palincsar, 1998, 2013; Palincsar & Brown, 1984). It involves instruction of comprehension strategies, namely, summarizing, questioning, clarifying, and predicting, in the context of a reading group. *Summarizing* refers to identifying and paraphrasing important information from the text; *questioning* refers to generating and asking questions about the text; *clarifying* asks students to pay attention to why the text may be difficult to understand and to seek out clarification; and *predicting* asks students to make predictions about what might come up next in the text and to read on to confirm or disprove their predictions. Thus, students learn to make predictions when reading, to question themselves about the text, to seek clarification when confused, and to summarize content. The adult teacher initially explains and models these strategies for students, but very quickly students learn to work with each other in their reading group. One student is assigned the role of group leader. The group leader supervises the group's generation of predictions, questions, and summaries during reading. The group leader also solicits points that need to be clarified and either provides clarifications or elicits them from other group members. The group interactions are cooperative, and the students take turns in the role of leaders. The teacher provides support on an as-needed basis, that is, scaffolded instruction.

During reciprocal teaching, the students experience multiple models of cognitive processing: The teacher models and explains. Peers in the group are continuously modeling reasoning about text as part of group participation. The discussions permit students to air their perspectives and requires them to justify their claims. These discussions also allow students to review and comment about the strategies as well as the content they are learning. The teacher is progressively less involved as the students gain competence. The assumption is that by participating in the group, students will eventually internalize use of the strategies encouraged as part of reciprocal teaching. This is consistent with the Vygotskian perspective that individual cognitive development develops from participation in social groups.

Research evidence supports the benefits of reciprocal teaching. Rosenshine and Meister (1994) conducted a meta-analysis of 16 studies comparing reciprocal teaching to other forms of instruction. In general, the effects of reciprocal teaching were greater when explicit teaching of comprehension strategies occurred before participation in reciprocal teaching. Although the benefits of reciprocal teaching were modest when measured by standardized tests, the effects were quite striking on measures assessing directly the processes stimulated by the strategies. Students of various ages and abilities benefited similarly from reciprocal teaching. More recent studies (Schünemann, Spörer, & Brunstein, 2013; Spörer, Brunstein, & Kieschke, 2009) also provide evidence of the effectiveness of reciprocal teaching. For example, Spörer et al. (2009) taught elementary school students the strategies of summarizing, questioning, clarifying, or predicting in one of three instructional conditions (reciprocal teaching in groups, in pairs, or teacher guided). All three instructional conditions produced better performance in comparison to a control group, but reciprocal teaching was the most effective instructional strategy leading to better performance on a test of reading comprehension and of strategy use. Moreover, only students in the reciprocal teaching group showed evidence of transfer, with better performance on a standardized test.

Problem-Based Learning

Problem-based learning is another active and collaborative approach to instruction that requires appropriate scaffolding by a facilitator to maximize its effectiveness (Belland, Kim, & Hannafin, 2013; Lu, Bridges, & Hmelo-Silver, 2014; see also the discussion of cooperative learning in Chapter 9). In problem-based learning, teachers present students with ill-structured real-world problems, problems without a single, clear-cut solution. The types of problems best suited to this approach include those requiring diagnosis, design, and decision making. Given the types of problems best suited to this approach, it is not surprising that problem-based learning has been extensively studied within the professional fields of nursing education, medical education, and, more recently, teacher preparation. Typically, students work in groups of three to five on problems that require group members to share knowledge, search for more information, construct arguments, and negotiate understandings to reach solutions. Steps in the process normally include presenting the problem scenario, identifying the facts available, generating hypotheses, identifying knowledge gaps, seeking out new information to fill the gaps via individual, self-directed learning, applying new knowledge to the problem, and evaluating possible solutions. The group may need to return to the problem scenario and perhaps reengage some steps in the process. Scaffolding provided by the teacher can include support for structuring or simplifying the problem, facilitating group problem solving through use of open-ended questioning, summarizing, checking for consensus, asking for clarifications, eliciting reflection, and providing motivational support through encouragement, attention focusing, and frustration reduction. White boards can be used as tools for identifying information relevant to the problem, encouraging visual representations of the problem, and listing agreed upon facts, possible ideas, and action plans—basically providing a place to articulate and reflect on the group process. White boards can—and invariably are—erased and revised throughout the process. Why would the problem-based learning approach to instruction be effective? It allows for activation of prior knowledge, recall of information, theory building, active dialogue with teacher and peers, and cognitive conflicts potentially leading to conceptual change.

González and Dejarnette (2015), interested in observing the nature of student–teacher interactions during the initial implementation of problem-based learning, introduced a problem-based lesson in six high school geometry classes, taught by two different teachers. Neither teacher had used a problem-based approach in the classroom before (but both were familiar with the approach from their teacher preparation programs), and the students were unused to working in groups. Examples of the kinds of scaffolding used by teachers included presenting challenging student ideas, asking for clarification, and summing up solution progress. The teachers also provided clues and expansions to ensure that the students accessed the information they needed to solve the problem, and the teachers helped the students maintain focus and motivation through encouragement. Although the researchers noted that the teacher was the "primary knower" in the classrooms, a role more typical of the initiate–response–evaluate patterns of interaction described in Box 6.3, the students in the groups demonstrated agency by initiating engagement with the teacher through requests for demonstrations or information and by controlling the timing and pace of teacher scaffolding.

The instructional goals of problem-based learning are varied but include the development of flexible, organized knowledge, effective problem-solving skills, ability to engage in self-directed learning, and successful collaboration skills (Hmelo-Silver & DeSimone, 2013). Has the problem-based learning approach to instruction proved to be effective? Hmelo-Silver and DeSimone (2013) summarized the research in a number of disciplines and across educational levels. In medical education, problem-based learning produced better performance than traditional instruction on knowledge in problem-solving contexts but not always on multiple-choice assessments. In teacher education, students in problem-based learning courses were better able to diagnose and solve educational problems than those in conventional courses. The use of problem-based learning in undergraduate university courses has generally resulted in learning gains.

Fewer studies have explored the effectiveness of problem-based learning in K–12 education. In one such study, Wirkala and Kuhn (2011) compared problem-based learning to the traditional lecture/discussion teaching method at the middle school level. The problem-based learning approach resulted in better performance on comprehension and application tests than the traditional instructional approach. In an analysis of 10 studies examining the effectiveness of problem-based learning in high school classrooms, Wilder (2015) concluded that problem-based learning does positively influence student achievement, but tempered that conclusion because of the relatively small number of studies available to review and because the studies typically did not randomly assign students to problem-based learning and traditional instruction groups, instead using a quasi-experimental, pretest/posttest design.

Larger effects of problem-based learning were observed in the studies where the teachers were extremely knowledgeable in the content domain and had experience with problem-based learning. Wilder also speculated that the effects of problem-based learning might be larger if implemented over longer periods of time (the typical high school study utilized problem-based learning for one curriculum unit) and if student performance was assessed on measures other than conceptual and factual knowledge. Hmelo-Silver and DeSimone (2013) described some initial indications that students become more self-directed as they proceed in programs utilizing problem-based learning design and that self-direction and the quality of collaboration are greatly influenced by how well the facilitator scaffolds the interactions. Researchers are currently investigating how scaffolding can be technology-based and are developing computer-supported collaborative learning methods (Dennen & Hoadley, 2013).

The Challenges of Scaffolding and Teaching as Apprenticeship

As appealing as Vygotskian-inspired constructivist teaching is, implementing such teaching presents real challenges (Hogan, Nastasi, & Pressley, 2000; Hogan & Pressley, 1997). For example, the apprenticeship model suggests that teachers should be real readers, writers, mathematicians, scientists, and social scientists rather than people who just talk about reading, writing, mathematics, science, and social science. Some teachers are real readers and let their students know how excited they are about reading particular authors. Other teachers bring real writing to the classroom. They teach writing by having everyone write a lot, including the teacher. The best writing teachers identify themselves as writers.

Even when teachers are masters, however, they must be highly motivated to teach using the Vygotskian model. Scaffolding demands much of teachers, and for teachers to work that hard, they must care about their students. According to Noddings (1984, 1996); see also Tappan, 1998), caring is at the center of teacher–student apprenticeships. Emphasizing caring for students can be challenging for teachers, given how many students they have, the limited time available to them, and the numerous objectives they are required to meet. Yet Noddings urges teachers to give up some of their control and to foster trust in their classrooms. She argues that true dialogue promotes deep contact with the ideas presented in the curriculum and stimulates the development of active thinkers who are willing to take intellectual risks.

As educators have attempted to provide instruction in the zone of proximal development, the challenges of this approach to teaching have become increasingly apparent. The following are some of the major challenges facing educators trying to apply the principles of scaffolding and apprenticeship to the classroom.

Knowledge of the Curriculum

In order to provide effective scaffolding, teachers must know the curriculum well, particularly portions of the curriculum that are troubling to students. It is easy to underestimate just how demanding this is, even for elementary-level content. For example, many teachers do not have a deep understanding of elementary mathematics and do not know the strategies that can be used to solve even simple addition and subtraction problems (Carpenter, Fennema, Peterson, & Carey, 1988; Fennema & Franke, 1992). Evidence from a recent study (Lui & Bonner, 2016) indicated low levels of conceptual understanding of mathematics in both preservice elementary teachers (in teacher preparation programs) and in-service teachers (in this case, teachers currently in classrooms, with less than three years of experience). More than knowing how to compute, scaffolding math teachers must also know their students' potential misconceptions about computing and how such misconceptions translate into observable behaviors. It may take years of experience with students to build up such knowledge.

Knowledge of Individual Students

To provide effective scaffolding, the teacher must know what a particular student already knows, what the student's misconceptions are, and what is in the student's current zone of proximal development. That is, the teacher must know what competencies are developing and which ones are far beyond the student's current level of functioning. If it is demanding to have this kind of insight into *one* student in *one* area of the curriculum, think about the enormity of this challenge for a classroom of students across the curriculum and when a class contains students with a variety of learning disabilities. Or think about how demanding it is for a high school teacher who teaches many students.

Communication Challenges in Generating Prompts

Providing hints to students about the academic problems they are experiencing requires great facility in generating hints and comments that provide enough assistance so that the student can make progress in solving academic problems without becoming overly directive. Such prompts invite students to make the inferences a mature thinker would make, and they encourage students to construct understandings of the task at hand. Sometimes the student does not make necessary inferences at the first prompt, requiring generation of another prompt and sometimes another one still . . . and then another, and so on. The scaffolding teacher is constantly required to think of new ways of prompting when initial prompts fail.

   This scenario is challenging, in part, because students' understanding of cognitive processes and the associated vocabulary develops slowly (Flavell, Miller, & Miller, 1993). For example, abstract concepts such as "interpret," "infer," "conclude," and "assume" are often difficult even for high school and college students to understand (Astington & Olsen, 1990; Booth & Hall, 1994), let alone younger students and students with cognitive disabilities. Moreover, English Language Learners become fluent in conversational English some years before becoming facile with academic language, the language used in schools (Salma, 2012). Teachers must talk about cognitive processes with students in concrete ways, in terms students can understand.

   Another challenge is that many students experience difficulties in talking about the problems they are having. If students cannot express precisely what they don't understand, the task of scaffolding their learning is even more demanding. In addition, the children who are most in need of academic help are often less likely to seek it than are other children. Webb (2013b) outlined some of the reasons why students fail to see or obtain help. Students may not be aware they need help, may not wish to be judged as incompetent or dependent, may believe that no one can help them, and may believe that seeking help is not appropriate. Students also sometimes ask for help, but often the help is not useful because they appealed to others as confused as they are or because they made general, vague entreaties such as "I don't get this," rather than asking specific questions.

Maintaining a Positive Tone

Good scaffolders are always positive and patient when they provide prompting and hinting. Sometimes this takes a great deal of patience, especially since the scaffolding teacher provides implicit messages that students do not "have it" yet. If the scaffolding is going well, the student does not construe such feedback as criticism. Unfortunately, it is hard for many adults to be unambiguously and consistently positive with children, especially when confronted with their uncertain progress. As a result, their hints and tones of voice may be perceived as criticisms.

Diverse Causes of Academic Difficulties

A child may have academic difficulties for a number of reasons. How scaffolded instruction should occur and how much of it is necessary depend in part on the reason for underachievement. For some children, the problem lies in their *home environment*. Their homes may be understimulating, that is, places where rich academically related experiences are rare. These children can arrive at school far behind classmates in the basic understandings critical to achievement in literacy and numeracy. These children will require intensive experiences such as one-to-one tutoring that includes much scaffolding for student progress to occur (Slavin, Karweit, & Wasik, 1994; Wasik & Slavin, 1993). Understimulation in the home environment may continue throughout the schooling years (Purcell-Gates, 1995). Thus, years and years of scaffolding are needed for these children.

A variety of *biological/neurological deficiencies* also can cause learning problems (see Chapter 8). Some children experience difficulties with academics because of deficits in their general cognitive abilities. Among these children, some are more responsive to instruction than others—perhaps because they have wider zones of proximal development (Budoff, 1987). In contrast to children with general cognitive handicaps, other children have specific learning disabilities, where they are neurologically different from the norm, in a way that undermines typical academic achievement with respect to some specific competency (e.g., reading, writing, mathematics; Zeffiro & Eden, 2001). The variety of biological differences potentially underlying academic disorders complicates educational intervention.

Finally, as helpful as scaffolding may be with some children, it may not work with all children. In some cases, the zone of proximal development may be so narrow (e.g., in the case of children with profound intellectual disabilities) that a great amount of tutor support and prompting is required even for minimal progress to be made. Vygotsky's (1978) presumption that all students respond to stimulation in their zone of proximal development represented his socialist convictions about the power of environment in developing cognition rather than a conclusion based on research. A scientific challenge for the future is to determine when scaffolding can work, which teachers can do it, and which students can benefit from it.

Cultural Differences and Their Implications for Classroom Practice

Educational anthropologists are particularly interested in the implications of cultural differences for education. Their emphasis on *differences* in students contrasts greatly with those who assume that students who live outside the mainstream culture have *deficits*. This approach has led to significant contributions to the generation of new ways of thinking about multiculturalism and education.

Anthropologists have relied heavily on qualitative methods to conduct their research, particularly ethnography (review the qualitative research methodologies described in Chapter 1). Educational anthropologists distinguish between macro-ethnographic and microethnographic analyses. The *macroethnographic* approach is multilevel, considering particular cultures in relation to other cultures, both at present and historically. In contrast to studying cultures more broadly, the *microethnographic* approach hones in on a specific context, such as interactions in classrooms (see Streeck & Mehus, 2005). Many educational researchers using a microethnographic approach have focused on differences in interpersonal communications as a function of culture, with the view that differences in language between cultures have profound implications for education.

John Ogbu's Macroethnographic Analysis

John Ogbu (1978, 1981, 1997, 2003; Ogbu & Stern, 2001) set out to understand differences in the academic achievement and career trajectories of ethnic and cultural groups in the United States. In so doing, he proposed a distinction between what he termed autonomous minorities, immigrant minorities, and caste-like minorities.

Autonomous minorities, for instance, Mormons and Jewish people in the United States, have some things about them that make them distinct from the majority culture, such as their ethnic or religious background, and they act to preserve that distinction. Although autonomous minorities experience some discrimination, their relationship with the dominant culture is not one of perceived inferiority. Furthermore, autonomous minorities are not economically subordinate to the majority culture and, on average, benefit from obtaining educational credentials at the same socioeconomic levels as the majority culture.

Immigrant minorities are *voluntary* minorities, who have decided to move to their host society. Tending to see the dominant culture as a barrier to overcome, they typically tolerate the discrimination they experience largely because they believe they are better off in the host society than in the place from which they fled. They anticipate upward social and economic movement across generations and view education as the path to that mobility. Voluntary immigrant minorities have generally experienced upward mobility in the United States.

Caste minorities, in contrast, are typically *involuntary* minorities, such as African Americans who were brought to North America against their will and Native Americans who were conquered. According to Ogbu (2003), the majority culture dominates involuntary minorities and views them as inferior. In turn, involuntary minorities see the dominant culture as oppressors and often dislike and oppose the majority culture. For example, Ogbu (1981, 1987, 2004) argued that many African

Americans reject the values of U.S. public education, seeing them as more white than black values. Even when members of caste-like minorities succeed in obtaining an education, their upward mobility is limited owing to their minority status.

Ogbu believed that schools make decisions that result in differential education of caste-like minority children compared to other children, differences in education that undermine their intellectual development. Educational researchers have found evidence consistent with Ogbu's argument. For example, Rist (1970) analyzed the experiences of a classroom of ghetto kindergarten children, demonstrating that the more economically disadvantaged children received less favorable treatment from the very first days of school. Once assigned to lower level reading groups in kindergarten, an assignment that was directly related to their socioeconomic status, no children moved to more capable groups in kindergarten or in first or second grade. Allington and McGill-Franzen (1989; Allington, 1991a, 1991b) studied the educational adaptations made for elementary school students in programs designed for students performing poorly in school, many of whom are members of caste-like minorities. They found that the supplementary instruction provided to these students was likely to be at a lower level than regular education, meaning that the minority students in these programs received less grade-level instruction than other students. Similar patterns are observed at the high school level where minorities are much more likely to be placed in lower tracks, which generally receive inferior instruction (Oakes, 1985). A significant number of minority students attend schools that have fewer resources, spend less on staff and teacher salaries, and employ less experienced teachers with less formal education and lower scores on teacher licensure exams than their majority counterparts (Valent & Newark, 2016). Minority students are also overrepresented in special education, receive more suspensions, and are underrepresented in gifted programs. Not surprisingly, there is still an achievement gap between black–white and Hispanic–white students. However, the SES achievement gap between high-income and low-income groups has widened in the last 40 years and is now twice as large as the black–white achievement gap (Ford, 2016; Valent & Newark, 2016). Finally, caste-like minorities drop out of high school in larger proportions than children from other groups (Snyder & Dillow, 2012; Waggoner, 1991). In 2011, the percentage of 25- to 29-year-olds who completed high school were as follows: Asians (95%), whites (94%), blacks (88%), and Latinos (71%).

Perhaps the most controversial aspect of Ogbu's theoretical perspective, however, is his contention that blacks themselves also contribute to their lack of success in school. Fordham and Ogbu (1986; Fordham, 1988) studied black high school students in Washington, DC, inner-city schools. They found strong resistance in these students to many things that they perceived to be "white," including a number of behaviors that are important to success in U.S. education, such as speaking and writing standard English, visiting museums, reading literature, studying, and getting good grades in school. In his last book before his death, Ogbu (Ogbu & Davis, 2003) analyzed black underachievement in Shaker Heights, Ohio. Even in this very affluent community, Ogbu found that black students distrusted the school and perceived racism in the school, as indicated by the disproportionate representation of blacks in less advanced academic courses and special education. The black students believed that counselors and teachers pushed them less intensely to do well academically than they pushed white students. They also perceived that their parents had lower academic expectations about them than did the parents of white students. Black students anticipated that they would have to work much harder than whites to get ahead economically after high school. Peer groups in Shaker Heights were racially divided, with white peer groups more encouraging of school work and academic pursuits than black peer groups. In short, just as was the case with his observations of inner-city schools in Washington, DC, Ogbu identified ways black academic achievement was undermined in one of America's most economically advantaged communities.

Recent research demonstrating that strong ethnic identity is related to positive outcome (review the discussion of ethnic–racial identity in Chapter 5) has led theorists to reevaluate Ogbu's ideas and, in particular, his description of African American students' rejection of academic activities out of a resistance to "acting white." A positive black racial identity, a consciousness of the historical and social context of what it means to be black, a sense of pride in being black, and an awareness of race and racism are all linked to positive educational outcomes (Ford, 2016; Nasir et al., 2016; Zirkel & Johnson, 2016). Moreover, high school students of *all* races and ethnicities who are serious about their academic endeavors are vulnerable to teasing from peers. High-achieving black students may downplay their academic accomplishments when interacting with friends who are not academically successful, but they also pursue friendships with peers who are also good students (Hudley & Irving, 2012). Resistance to "acting white" may be more about rejecting white style and speech than about rejecting standards of achievement (Zirkel & Johnson, 2016).

For example, in a two-year longitudinal study of racial identity in a primarily African American urban high school, Nasir, McLaughlin, and Jones (2009) collected observational, interview, and survey data. Their data revealed a range of African American racial identities available to the students. One pattern they noted involved students who exhibited a socially conscious African American identity with a strong allegiance to their community, integrated with a commitment to education. These students did not have to "act white" to succeed academically. In fact, the researchers caution that teachers should not assume that a student's style, particularly in terms of speech and clothing, is at all related to the student's academic orientation. Researchers have criticized the small, select samples studied by Ogbu and have noted that the rejection of educational values he described in his study of the affluent Shaker Heights high school is more likely to be observed in schools where African Americans are greatly in the minority, where perhaps there is a more stereotypical idea of what it means to be black and a more restricted range of acceptable behavior (Nasir et al., 2016; Zirkel & Johnson, 2016).

Many students who are members of caste-like minorities, including blacks, *do* succeed in school (Erickson, 1987; Gibson & Ogbu, 1991; Wells & Crain, 1997). In fact, after controlling for socioeconomic and academic characteristics, data from the National Educational Longitudinal Study reveals a "net black advantage" where blacks are more likely to continue their education from 10th grade to postsecondary than their white counterparts (Merolla, 2013). Researchers have also identified an "immigrant advantage" in that first- and second-generation students are more likely to graduate from high school and enroll in college than their third-plus generation peers (Callahan & Humphries, 2016; Urdan, 2012). There is also, however, a "language minority disadvantage" in that the immigrant advantage for college enrollment is found only in students who are not enrolled in English as a Second Language programs.

Consider in more detail a classic study establishing clear linkages between environmental support for educational achievement and actual achievement in African American families. Using qualitative methods, Clark (1983) studied economically disadvantaged high school students, half of whom were much more successful in school than the other half of the students in the sample. There were marked differences in the homes of successful and unsuccessful students.

- The parents of successful students had *higher expectations* than the parents of unsuccessful students. Parents of successful students expected to play a major role in their children's schooling, initiated more contact with the school, expected their children to play a major role in their own schooling, and anticipated that their children would obtain postsecondary education. Parents of unsuccessful students expected much less achievement from their children.

- The parents of successful students had more *explicit achievement-oriented rules* operating in their homes. They exercised more consistent monitoring and more enforcement of rules than the parents of unsuccessful students, and the successful students were more accepting of these rules than less successful students.

- The parents of successful students established *clearer role boundaries* in their homes than the parents of unsuccessful students, which resulted in calmer interactions and less family conflict.

- The parents of successful students more often *engaged in teaching their children* and were more nurturing and supportive than the parents of unsuccessful students.

Clark's findings have been supported by other researchers. For example, Pressley, Raphael, Gallagher, and DiBella (2004) studied Providence–St. Mel School, a K–12 school on the West Side of Chicago, serving African American students. Since 1978, 100% of its graduates have been accepted into four-year colleges—a remarkable record. Using qualitative research methods, Pressley and colleagues identified the many elements that coalesce at the school to produce such success, some of which echo those found by Clark. These include:

Human Commitments
- Strong, dedicated, caring administrators
- Capable, dedicated, caring teachers
- Families of students who work responsively and constructively with the school
- Supportive alumni who have succeeded after completing the school
- Donors who provide ideas and financial backing for the school
- Students willing to meet high behavioral and academic demands

Capital
- A secure building, one adequate to support state-of-the-art instruction
- Sufficient funding
- Extra financial resources (e.g., for scholarships, tutoring, test preparation classes, field trips)

Policies
- High teaching standards, including efficient use of class time
- Frequent monitoring of teaching performance

- Extensive monitoring of student achievement, permitting meaningful feedback to students
- Instruction balancing learning of basic facts and skills, with emphasis on higher-order skills and understanding
- Deliberate use of research-based teaching approaches
- A curriculum that increases students' respect of their own heritage and themselves through integration of African American content

Ambience

- An environment that intensely celebrates academic achievement above all else
- A generally positive and motivating environment, one that expects much from students and offers a variety of rewards to those who do achieve
- An environment that makes clear that a positive future depends on hard academic work during the K–12 years
- A mentoring atmosphere that encourages dreams, builds confidence, stresses the importance of education, and shepherds the student to high goals—especially admission to a good college

A consistent pattern has emerged from studies of successful and unsuccessful minority students: The environments of educationally successful minority students, including the environments that students and their families create for themselves, support educational achievements in ways that the environments of unsuccessful same-minority students do not—with this generalization holding for students from diverse ethnic groups (Abi-Nader, 1990; Delgado-Gaitan, 1990; Lee, 1994; Smith-Hefner, 1993). This strong association has been a powerful stimulus for intensive study of the home and school environments of minority students in microethnographic studies.

Microethnographic Research

In a well-known qualitative study of children's lives at home and school, Snow, Barnes, Chandler, Goodman, and Hemphill (1991) followed three samples of children from low-income homes for 2 years, studying one group of students as they moved through grades 2 and 3, a second group as students traversed grades 4 and 5, and a third as students went through grades 6 and 7. Snow and colleagues found that home and school influences were inextricably intertwined in determining the success of students in school. That is, whether or not the child did well depended on both the school and the family and the ability of the family to support the instruction that went on in school. An especially important finding was that the parents of many students were increasingly at a disadvantage as their children progressed through elementary school. Many well-intentioned parents could help their children with beginning reading but could not help as much with the more demanding reading required in the upper elementary grades. Thus, the parents were in a better position to make up for poor instruction during the primary years than they were at later points in schooling. Consequently, the success of the students, especially after the primary school years, depended more and more on the quality of the schooling they received.

An important question for microethnographers has been whether minorities receive lower quality instruction because of cultural differences in the communication styles of minority students and their teachers, who often come from majority populations. One of the most influential studies addressing this question was conducted between 1968 and 1973 on the Warm Springs Indian Reservation in central Oregon (Philips, 1983). Philips lived on the reservation, observing both Anglo and Native American children in grades 1 and 6. She visited the homes of children and became thoroughly familiar with community life. Consistent with her hypothesis that communications problems were at the heart of the Native American children's difficulties in school, Philips observed that the tribal children often did not understand the teacher, frequently were inattentive, and rarely talked in class. Moreover, she noted that the teachers were not sensitive to the ways by which Native Americans communicate. The tribal children used less body language, tended not to look at others when they spoke, and spoke softly and slowly. Because of these communication attributes, the Native American students did not participate well in teacher-driven **initiate–response–evaluation (IRE) cycles** (review Box 6.3). That is, the Native American students did not react well to being put on the spot when the teacher posed questions (initiation) that students were expected to answer quickly in front of a group (response), with a teacher evaluation following the attempted response (evaluation).

In contrast, when the Native American children were in situations more consistent with their own culture (such as one-on-one discussion with an adult or interactions within a small group of children), communications were much better (see also Lomawaima, 1995). Others have also observed that education does not go well for Native American students when teachers are insensitive to their communication styles and preferences (Erickson & Mohatt, 1982; Van Ness, 1981; Wilson, 1991). See the Considering Interesting Questions special feature (Box 6.4) for a discussion of other differences in communications styles studied by educational researchers.

Au and Mason (1981) demonstrated that the education of minority students can be improved by providing them with instruction sensitive to and consistent with their own culturally defined communication styles and preferences. Au and Mason evaluated individual lessons of two teachers at Kamehameha School, which serves native Hawaiian students. One teacher used conventional teaching—for example, teaching that included many IRE-like cycles. The other teacher used participation structures that were more familiar to Hawaiian children. Rather than individual children responding to the teacher, several children responded by commenting on particular points in a conversational fashion. What went on was much more like naturalistic dialogue than typically occurs during IRE cycles. The teacher was less concerned with right answers than with the children's interpretations, and the students were more likely to participate than in typical IRE structures.

One of the most striking findings in the Au and Mason (1981) study was that academic engagement was much greater when instruction was culturally congruent. The children in the culturally congruent discussions made more reading-related responses and many more appropriate inferences than those in the more traditional reading lessons. In general, culturally congruent interactions have fared quite well in formal comparisons with more conventional teaching, including on measures such as standardized test scores (Tharp, 1982; Tharp & Gallimore, 1988).

BOX 6.4. How Do Cultural Differences in Conversational Style Influence Classroom Interactions?

Educators need to be aware of and sensitive to cultural differences in conversational styles to increase the likelihood of realizing the potential of all students. What kinds of conversational differences have been observed? For example, Heath (1989) studied African American communities in rural southeastern communities and found that older adults do not censor or simplify talk around children. Instead, they expect the young to adapt to changing contexts and speakers. Adults in these communities only ask children *real* questions, not questions the adults already know the answers to. For example, these adults would not ask a child, "What color is your shirt?" since the adult already knows the answer to that question. Also, in some cultures, it is considered inappropriate for students to show off what they know. Thus, the traditional classroom interaction of initiation–response–evaluation cycles (Cazden, 1988; Cazden & Beck, 2003), in which the teacher asks factual-level questions (what everyone should know) would be a particularly poor instructional tactic for students of some cultural backgrounds (Carlsen, 1991).

Consider this example of a first-grade student who had been considered a behavior problem in kindergarten because his way of responding to questions was considered "talking back" to the teacher (Souto-Manning, 2009). His first-grade teacher, inspired by Brice Heath's work, began to listen carefully to him and to consider George's manner of speaking as just another one of the dialects and languages taught in the class.

JORDAN: Would you like to sit down?

GEORGE: You know, you aks [*sic*] me if I want to sit down, right?

JORDAN: Yes, please.

GEORGE: So then, this a question or you tellin' me to sit down?

JORDAN: I am asking you to sit so that I can get on with calendar.

GEORGE: Then just tell me sit down.

JORDAN: Then I'd be rude.

GEORGE: Not in my momma home. You want me to sit. I will. You don't care if I wanna sit. It just a different way of aksin', you know. I get it. In kindergarten I didn't know. But I ain't dissin' you or you momma. (Souto-Manning 2009, p. 1090)

Now that he is in the first grade, George understands that sometimes teachers ask questions that are really directives and not questions at all, something he didn't understand when he was in kindergarten. He is also now aware that the conversation style at home is different than that at school. He is beginning to become bidialectical, more able to switch between the academic language of school and his home dialect.

Perhaps the most prevalent and certainly the most studied nonstandard English dialect is African American Language (AAL). AAL shares common grammatical, phonological, and lexical features with forms of English but also has linguistic rules and features that distinguish it from standard American English (Vetter, 2013; Wyatt, 1995). For example, one of these distinctive features, termed zero copula by linguists, refers to the absence of the verb *be*. Zero copula doesn't happen all the time in AAL. It rarely occurs in the past tense or when first-person singular is used, but it is very likely to be used after a personal pronoun subject, especially before an adjective as in "He a big baby." Another distinctive feature of AAL is using the unconjugated form of the verb *to be*, to signify the habitual be, as in "We

(continued)

be watching TV" meaning "We watch TV regularly." Another feature is the use of the double negative and the verbal s marker as in "So I says to him."

It is important to keep in mind that AAL is not a substandard form of English but rather a coherent language system of its own. AAL is a symbol of identity, conveying cultural and historic meaning, and is observed in the United States within populations of African descent, especially among members of the working class in urban and rural communities (Vetter, 2013). AAL is observed only in some African American communities, and a range of language is used among African Americans living in the communities where AAL is found (Wyatt, 1995).

AAL is not spoken only by African Americans. Paris (2009) observed the use of African American Language at a multiethnic urban high school. The African American students he observed were bidialetical—using AAL in their everyday speech inside and outside of the classroom but shifting to standard American English when a situation demanded it. Moreover, the African American students were also aware that their Latino/a and Pacific Islander peers had also adopted AAL. The African American students considered this use of AAL by other peers acceptable cultural and linguistic sharing, as long as the use was perceived as authentic and not a ploy for attention or acceptance.

Boutte and Johnson (2013) recommend that teachers learn to see AAL as a rule-governed language system and to build upon the communication capacities children possess in the classroom. Teachers can also help children move from one communication system to the other and to learn to recognize when one way of speaking is a better match to a situation than the other. Vetter (2013) suggested that teachers respond to their students' language practices in ways that communicate that their language practices are valued and that allows students to be included in the learning community. If teachers hold a deficit perspective, devaluing their students' home language, the result can be lower achievement expectations and reductions in learning opportunities.

The successes at Kamehameha School and the generally positive associations between culturally congruent communications and school participation stimulated other researchers to think about how schooling can be made more comfortable and effective for minority students. An important part of the approach is construction of curricula that will enable the students to learn concepts that relate to familiar concepts. For example, McCarty, Lynch, Wallace, and Benally (1991) developed social studies curricula for Navajo students in kindergarten through grade 9. In the unit on culture and community, students discuss the ideas with reference to their own culture and local community. In the unit on government, U.S. majority culture conceptions of government are related to Navajo conceptions of government. Stimulating students to talk and think about new information in relation to their prior knowledge is a powerful way of teaching. The Navajo students participate actively in these discussions—indeed, the entire class often joins in. Achievement, as documented by improved test scores, has increased for the Navajo students experiencing this curriculum. The same approach has been adapted for Native Americans in Alaska (Lipka & McCarty, 1994).

An important goal of such teaching is to encourage learning through interaction. Thus, instructional interventions such as these can be conceptualized in terms of Vygotsky's theory of cognitive development through social interactions. According to Vygotsky, people learn how to think as individuals by first experiencing thinking with others. Although research has focused most directly on the achievement of minority students, the power of conversation as a means of learning both content and how to think likely would benefit all students.

Cross-Cultural Differences and the Testing of Minority Students

The anthropological research described in this chapter sensitized educators to the communication and values differences between some minorities and the majority population. This research has led to intense reflection about language and communications factors that can impact performance on standardized tests, potentially creating bias against minority students (Geisinger, 2003, 2015a; Valencia & Suzuki, 2001; see also Chapter 8).

The use of standardized tests for discriminating against minorities has a long history. Two of the earliest intelligence tests (*Army Alpha* and *Beta*) were used by the U.S. Army during World War I. After analyzing the test results of hundreds of thousands of young recruits and conscripts, Carl Brigham (1923) concluded that recent immigrants to the United States were less intelligent than white people born in the United States. He reached this conclusion because recent immigrants had not done as well on the Army tests as whites born in the United States. Imagine the communication difficulties experienced by an immigrant being tested in an unfamiliar language by a strange person who represented his new country's government. Unfair testing has occurred for generations in the United States and has been used to make inequitable decisions about students' education, such as placement in special education or admissions to college (Graves & Aston, 2016; Lopez, 1997).

Steele and Aronson (1995) provided a provocative analysis of why African American students may not perform well on standardized tests. They argued that such testing is threatening because of the possibility that the test will confirm the negative cultural stereotype that African American students are less intellectually able than white students. This phenomenon is known as **stereotype threat**. College students at Stanford University participated in Steele and Aronson's original experiments. The directions given before a verbal ability test emphasized that the test was either diagnostic of ability or was not. When given nondiagnostic instructions, African American students and white students performed equally on the test. When given diagnostic instructions, African American students performed more poorly than whites and more poorly than African American students given the nondiagnostic directions. The power of stereotype threat in testing situations for African American students has been confirmed in follow-up studies (Steele, 2004; Steele & Aronson, 2004; also see Inzlicht & Schmader, 2012).

Mulitple explanations have been offered for why stereotype threat disrupts performance. Situational cues (such as being told a test is diagnostic of ability) activate a physiological stress response that impairs processing and a heightened vigilance to performance monitoring. Knowledge of a negative stereotype also leads to efforts to halt negative thoughts and emotions induced by the negative stereotype. It is possible that the situational cues could motivate efforts to disconfirm the stereotype, but the stress response, vigilant performance monitoring, and efforts to control thoughts and emotions reduce the executive processing space available to perform the task at hand (Levy, Heissel, Richeson, & Adam, 2016; Schmader & Beilock, 2012; Schmader, Johns & Forbes, 2008). Stereotype threat has lowered performance in a variety of situations where knowledge of a negative stereotypes is present, such as in women performing in male-dominated domains, especially math, technology, and engineering; white men performing certain athletic tasks; and white men compared to Asians in math performance (Blake, Smith, & Knight, 2016). Interventions that have successfully reduced stereotype effect include asking students to write self-affirming essays, teaching them that performance on the task at hand is malleable and not fixed, and providing reassuring feedback about performance (Blake et al., 2016; Bowen, Wegmann, & Webber, 2013; Nasir et al., 2016).

Differences in communication styles suggest other explanations for lower performance of minority students on standardized tests. Test-taking behaviors are culturally learned, so some students may have different understandings about what it means to take a test and what the long-term implications of tests are (Rodriguez, 1992; Weiss, Prifitera, & Munoz, 2015). Fluency in the English language and knowledge of the majority culture also influence performance on standardized tests. Limited-English speakers are at a real disadvantage when standardized tests are administered in English (Geisinger, 2015b). The *Standards for Educational and Psychological Measurement* (1999, 2014), created by a joint committee formed by the American Educational Research Association (AERA), the American Psychological Association (APA), and the National Council on Measurement in Education (NCME), recognize that cultural and linguistic factors introduce construct-irrelevant elements to the testing situation, thereby reducing the accuracy of construct measurement. The *Standards* also emphasize fairness as a fundamental characteristic of a high-quality test. All students must have the opportunity to learn what is being assessed, the test content must be appropriate for all, the test format and how the test is scored must be appropriate for all, and finally the testing context must reduce the likelihood of stereotype threat (Worrell & Roberson, 2016)

In some parts of the United States, laws once required that all children be tested in English, with decisions about school placement into special education or giftedness classes based on test performance (Donlon, 1992; Oakland & Gallegos, 2005; Rodriguez, 1992). It is not surprising then that disproportionately high numbers of children who were not native speakers of English ended up in special education and disproportionately low numbers of non-native English speakers were offered accelerated programs. Fortunately, such laws were struck down by courts, litigation, and changing professional standards. For example, the ruling in *Diana v. California State Board of Education* (1970) was that students must be tested in their native language (Geisinger, 1992). In this case, an English-administered IQ test had been used to place children who were non-native speakers of English in special education. The court ruled that all Spanish-speaking and Chinese-speaking children in the state who had been placed in classes intended for children with intellectual disabilities had to be retested using procedures that did not discriminate on the basis of language. The court also ruled that the retesting had to eliminate test items tapping vocabulary and general information that might not be encountered in the minority cultures. The retesting determined that seven of the nine students who had brought the case were much more intellectually capable than originally assessed (Constantino, 1992). The California legislature subsequently passed laws to prevent the abuses that had produced the *Diana* case, and additional court action has been directed to reducing the overrepresentation of minorities in special education classes (Constantino, 1992; Geisinger, 1992).

Even so, when tests are reliable and valid and are not being used intentionally to discriminate, they have been upheld as appropriate, even if disproportionate numbers of minorities perform poorly on them. In *Parents in Action on Special Education v. Hannon et al.* (1980), a federal judge upheld the use of standardized tests to classify minority children in Chicago as having intellectual disabilities (Graves & Aston, 2016; Koocher & Keith-Spiegel, 1990; Oakland & Parmelee, 1985). Tests can be abused with minorities, but they can also be used to make valid decisions about minority students. Research on cultural differences in communication and thinking styles is being translated into better understanding about how to construct and administer culture-fair tests (Geisinger, 2003, 2015a; Graves & Blake, 2016). Best practices include using multiple measures, seeking out technically sound instruments in the child's native language if possible, using an interpreter if necessary, offering extended time when appropriate, providing glossaries defining specific words in multiple languages, simplifying the English language used in an instrument, and working to create rapport between the examiner and test-taker (Faulkner-Bond & Sireci, 2015; Oakland & Gallegos, 2005; Weiss et al., 2015). That testing often has not served minorities well in the past does not mean that testing in the future cannot play a more constructive role in educational decision making for minority students.

Cross-Cultural Insights about the Effects of Schooling on Cognitive Development

Ceci (1991) investigated the impact of schooling on children's development and concluded, based on a variety of analyses, that schooling increases general intelligence. But just what does that mean? A child's IQ could increase because he or she improved on some very specific cognitive competencies tapped by IQ tests or because of generalized improvement on a variety of items covered on IQ assessments (see Chapter 8). In either case, the IQ score would increase.

In trying to unravel the effects of schooling on IQ, Scribner and Cole (1981) reported what has become a classic study. Their study focused on the Vai people of Liberia and their language skills. Many members of this culture learn to write in Vai script, a form of writing indigenous to the culture. The person who knows Vai script can engage in a variety of informal communications, such as writing friendly letters. Typically, Vai script is taught by family, friends, or neighbors. In addition to the informal Vai, some members of the culture learn Arabic as part of Quranic study. Such study involves a great deal of memorization of religious texts. Some members of the culture also learn to read and write English in Western-style schools. Learning to read and write English allows participation in a wide range of formal activities not permitted by the learning of Vai or Arabic, such as participation in government and business beyond the village level.

Scribner and Cole (1981) administered a wide range of tasks to members of the Vai culture who had learned to read and write Vai, Arabic, or English. They also tested individuals who had not acquired any literacy skills. What they found was that *schooling had particular effects*. Performance on tasks varied depending on the type of schooling received. Thus, English schooling positively affected some tasks (e.g., tasks that required giving an explanation) and made little difference on other tasks (e.g., tasks that required classifying objects on the basis of conceptual similarity).

Which group do you think did best on tasks measuring the ability to memorize the order of items? If you thought it was the students who had learned Arabic, you were right. All that practice memorizing religious texts, which requires remembering ideas in order, improved the students' serial learning ability (Wagner & Spratt, 1987).

What skills were stronger as a result of learning Vai, the indigenous language? Those who were Vai-literate were better able to use symbols than Vai-illiterates. Also, Vai-literates knew more Vai grammar than did Vai-illiterates. Still, the positive effects of learning Vai were restricted to a few measures.

So what does this study tell us about schooling? People can do what they are taught to do and what they are asked to do often. Neither literacy nor schooling promotes cognitive development generally (Scribner & Cole, 1981). Rather, educational and cultural experiences have their own specific impacts on cognitive development. For example, the memory and learning strategies of children living in North America are only observed in non-Western countries when people experience Western-style schooling (Cole, Gay, Glick, & Sharp, 1971; Wagner, 1974, 1978). Experience with Western schooling increases facility in analyzing two-dimensional forms and in classifying and categorizing information into taxonomies (Gauvain & Perez, 2015; Rogoff, 2003). It also increases the ability to remember for the sake of remembering—for instance, using memory strategies such as rehearsal and elaboration to learn lists of words (see also Chapter 4). In contrast, non-Westerners who have attended Western-style schools have no advantage when asked to do cognitive tasks that are common in the non-Western culture, tasks familiar also to nonschooled people (Mandler, Scribner, Cole, & DeForest, 1980; Rogoff & Waddell, 1982). In African cultures in which storytelling is an important part of life, the story memory of non-schooled African students can be better than the story memory of schooled U.S. students (Ross & Millson, 1970). Cross-cultural evidence supports the conclusion that cultural-specific experiences enhance cultural-specific competencies, which in turn develop additionally as the person participates in the culture that demands and supports such competencies (Cole, 1998). Moreover, when children in different cultures have comparable educational and environmental experiences, their thinking and learning skills are often comparable. Culture is an inextricable part of development, as conveyed through social interactions and through cultural tools such as language (Gauvin & Perez, 2015).

Chapter Summary and Evaluation

The world in which a child is immersed affects the development of the child's mind. Vygotsky's theory was that a great deal of mature thinking is dialogic, in that the mature thinker can think about a situation much like two people seem to think about a situation as they talk about it. Such dialogical thinking skills are developed through interactions with others.

Anthropologists have also accumulated evidence that the world has a powerful effect on a child's thinking and behavior. Microethnogrophers have particularly focused on how communication processes differ as a function of culture. Such differences in communication style can affect success in conventional schooling as well as performance on tests, which count heavily in the conventional educational accountability system. Macroethnogrophers have substantiated that culture can more broadly affect how minority children relate to school—including how much they value it. School is not a passive player in the shaping of the mind, however. Psychologists who have conducted cross-cultural studies have been able to confirm that Western schooling has particular types of effects on thinking. Other types of schooling have other effects.

Sociocultural theorists and researchers have confirmed that a variety of forces determine behavior and development, which can be reviewed in light of the Big Ideas of development introduced in Chapter 1.

Nature and Nurture

Although sociocultural theories emphasize the power of the environment in determining behavior and development, they also include some strong biological assumptions. For example, Vygotsky's assumption that social interaction is necessary for cognitive development implies that evolution has favored an organism sensitive to environmental input. This is in striking contrast to the position of behavior geneticists, who hold that individual differences in intelligence are genetically determined. Vygotsky's theory reflects no such presumption about biology.

Continuity and Discontinuity

Vygotsky did offer an explicit stage theory for the development of inner speech. Other sociocultural theorists and researchers are less explicit about age-related development, emphasizing more the continuous impact of society and culture throughout the lifespan.

Universal and Culture-Specific

Vygotsky is a universalist, believing that social factors operate in development across the human species. Anthropologists, while believing that humans of all cultures share a biological heritage, focus more on human differences, depending on circumstances, including the cultural pressures the individual experiences. For example, although anthropologists would agree that much development occurs because of interpersonal communications, they point out that the structures of communication differ as a function of culture.

Active and Passive

Although the effects of the sociocultural environment are emphasized in the theories summarized in this chapter, it is important to note that when schooling is congruent with a child's culture, the child is more active. This understanding would ideally stimulate the development of schools congruent with the cultures from which students come.

REVIEW OF KEY TERMS

autonomous minorities Groups of people who act to preserve some of what makes them distinct from the majority culture but who typically do not experience discrimination.

caste minorities Groups of people who are viewed by the majority culture as inferior and who experience widespread discrimination.

egocentric speech Speech of young children, directed to themselves about what they are doing.

guided participation A teaching method in which teachers explicitly direct processing done by students.

immigrant minorities Groups of people who are voluntary recent arrivals to the majority culture who may experience discrimination but have opportunities for upward mobility.

initiate–response–evaluation (IRE) cycles The typical classroom conversation structure where the teacher initiates, usually through questions; the students respond; and then the teacher evaluates the students' responses. Teachers frequently follow-up on a student response rather than evaluate in a pattern called initiate–response–follow-up.

inner speech An abbreviated and often fragmentary internal dialogue that according to Vygotsky plays an important role in thinking.

intelligent tutoring system Self-paced, adaptive computer programs that provide individualized instruction and feedback.

private speech Thoughts spoken out loud by someone working on a task.

scaffolding An instructional technique in which teachers provide help to students on an as-needed basis.

stereotype threat A fear of minority students that a standardized test will confirm the cultural stereotype that minorities are not as intellectually able as whites, resulting in poorer performance on the test than when such threat is not present.

zone of proximal development A range of achievements that includes tasks that learners cannot accomplish independently but can accomplish with assistance.

PART II

Key Topics in Child Development and Education

CHAPTER 7

Language Development and Linguistic Diversity

Language development has been an area of active research for a number of decades. One motivation for this work was Noam Chomsky's (1957, 1959) proposition that humans are biologically predisposed to acquire language. According to Chomsky, each human is born with a **language acquisition device**, which includes a basic understanding of the syntax of language: the rules governing the combining of words and phrases and the rules needed to express and understand the complex meanings encoded in sentences. Because all humans share this biological mechanism, Chomsky believed that language functioning should be similar across languages and cultures.

Given Chomsky's strong biological claims, we begin this chapter with an overview of the evidence that language is greatly determined by biology. The case for biology playing a large role in human language is strong, but so is the case that the language environment surrounding the child matters greatly.

Biological Foundations of Language

Researchers have produced a great deal of data substantiating the critical role biology plays in language development. This section provides an overview of some of the most important work concerning the biological foundations of language.

Left-Hemisphere Involvement in Language

Particular areas of the brain appear to be more important in language than are other areas. One form of evidence in support of this conclusion was that injuries to certain regions of the brain affected language in particular ways. In the 19th century, Carl Wernicke discovered that damage to a particular region in the left hemisphere of the brain (see Figure 7.1) resulted in verbal comprehension problems, often affecting comprehension both of speech that is heard and text that is read. The speech of patients suffering injury to Wernicke's area, however, remains relatively fluent, although some minor problems may exist such as difficulty finding the right word and adding syllables to words. The comprehension difficulties of patients with Wernicke's aphasia translate into difficulties in expressing the ideas that they have in mind (Kandel, Schwartz, & Jessell, 1995).

Damage to another part of the left hemisphere (see Figure 7.1), Broca's area (discovered in the 19th century by Paul Broca), results in a very different set of symptoms. Patients suffering Broca's aphasia comprehend, but have difficulty producing, language, either by speaking or through writing. If they can speak at all, they typically demonstrate a breakdown in syntax (Kandel et al., 1995).

Until relatively recently, the best evidence that the left side of the brain was more responsible for language than the right side was the data on the effects of brain injuries or lesions. In recent decades, however, the development of sophisticated methods for imaging the structures and functioning of the brain has resulted in a revolution in the understanding of brain functioning (Goswami, 2004; Mody, 2004; Papanicolaou, Pugh, Simos, & Mencl, 2004; Shaywitz, 2003; Shaywitz & Shaywitz, 2004; 2008; 2014). Computerized tomography (CT) scanning distinguishes between the gray and the white matter in the brain (see Chapter 2) and shows many structures within the brain. Magnetic resonance imagery (MRI), a further advance in CT scanning, permits exploration of neurological structures with even higher resolution than CT scans. Although left-side structures are still more often implicated than right-side structures in language functioning, language functioning involves complex articulations and interactions between parts of both the left and the right hemispheres of the brain (Mody, 2004; Papanicolaou et al., 2004; Shaywitz, 2003; Shaywitz & Shaywitz, 2004; Zeffiro & Eden, 2001). Language processing in the brain is more about connectivity between brain structures than about specific areas.

Of the imagining procedures, positron emission tomography (PET) scans have been especially revealing about cognitive processing. With PET scanning, the subject either is injected with or inhales a substance that emits radiation. Why? Some substances that emit radiation, such as radioactive fluorine, can bind with one of the

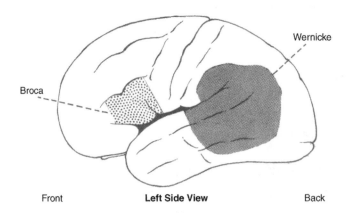

FIGURE 7.1. Side image of the left hemisphere of the brain with Wernicke's and Broca's areas labeled.

products of metabolized glucose. When neurons are active, they metabolize glucose. The PET scan detects the accumulated radioactive glucose product, which is present in the parts of the brain that are active. The result is an image of the brain that literally glows where thinking is occurring.

What is being learned about language from use of this imaging technology? Quite a bit. For example, studies have been conducted determining the regions of the brain activated by complex auditory input, such as a story (Hutton, et al., 2015; Mody, 2004; Risberg, 1986; Vernon, 1991). Consistently, the left side of the brain has been more active than the right side during verbal tasks, at least when verbally normal adults have been studied (Martin, Schurz, Kronblichler, & Richlan, 2015; Papanicolaou et al., 2004; Shaywitz, 2003; Shaywitz & Shaywitz, 2004).

When individuals with verbal impairment have been studied with these imaging techniques, deviations from normality have been detected. For example, differences in structure and function (more in the left hemisphere than in the right hemisphere, but some in the right hemisphere as well) have been found in individuals with dyslexia (those who have great difficulty learning to read even with intensive instruction) as compared to normal readers (Galaburda, Sherman, Rosen, Aboitz, & Geschwind, 1985; Jernigan, Hesselink, Sowell, & Tallal, 1991; Larsen, Hoien, Lundberg, & Ødegaard, 1990; Shaywitz, 2003; Shaywitz & Shaywitz, 2004, 2008, 2014).

Genetic Studies of Language Functioning

A substantial amount of evidence suggests that individual differences in language ability may be due to genetics (Grigorenko, 2007a; Stromswold, 2001). For example, the verbal abilities of identical twins are much more similar than the verbal abilities of fraternal twins (Bakwin, 1973; Gilger & Wise, 2004; Locke & Mather, 1989; Olson, 2006), as expected if individual differences in verbal abilities are largely determined by biology (see Chapter 2). Also, language disabilities tend to run in families (Eley et al., 1999; Pennington, 2001; Stromswold, 1998), consistent with the conclusion that language differences are genetically related.

Because of the great interest in reading disabilities as an educational problem, dyslexia has been studied by behavior geneticists more than other aspects of language functioning (see Chapter 2). Consistent with the hypothesis that language development is determined, at least in part, by genetics, the co-occurrence of dyslexia in identical twins is more likely than its co-occurrence in fraternal twins (Bakwin, 1973; Dale, Dionne, Eley, & Plomin, 2000; DeFries, Fulker, & LaBuda, 1987; Gilger & Wise, 2004; Olson, 2006; Pennington, 1989; Rosenberg, Pennington, Willcutt, & Olson, 2012). Also, consistent with the genetic hypothesis, the reading abilities of adopted children and their biological parents are more highly correlated than the reading abilities of adopted children and their adopting parents (Cardon, DiLalla, Plomin, DeFries, & Fulker, 1990; Gilger & Wise, 2004). Moreover, it has been possible to locate particular genes responsible for dyslexia in some families (DeFries, Olson, Pennington, & Smith, 1991; Grigorenko, 2007b; Gilger & Wise, 2004).

Increased understanding of genetics creates difficulties for some of Chomsky's theory. For example, Chomsky's universal and invariant language acquisition device would have to be transmitted by multiple genes, with the potential for variability enormous given the many potential genetic combinations (Lieberman, 1984, 1989). The enormous variability in human language competencies (i.e., some people are more verbally facile than others) is more consistent with the conclusion that language ability varies like other genetically determined characteristics (Gilger & Wise, 2004) than it is consistent with Chomsky's position that human language capabilities are generally invariant.

Chomsky also believed that language was "uniquely human," a claim that is not well supported. Evolution is gradual, and differences between species with respect to communications and symbolic skills tend to reflect this gradualness (Parker & Gibson, 1990). For example, research has established that the great apes share language and cognitive skills with humans. Great apes other than humans use categories to some extent, can learn to use sign language with some sophistication, may be able to invent grammatical rules, and can communicate flexibly (Greenfield & Savage-Rumbaugh, 1990; Matsuzawa, 1990; Miles, 1990; see also Bohn, Call, & Tomasello, 2016). Moreover, some evidence indicates that human speech and neural speech perception mechanisms continue to evolve (Lieberman, 1984, 1989; 2015). That said, no species approaches human communication competence, as even simple syntax is acquired slowly by nonhuman primates and only by means of great teaching effort by humans (Kako, 1999; Tomasello, 1994). The same holds for the language of other animals (e.g., dolphins) based on what is now known (Herman, 2002, 2010; Herman & Uyeyama, 1999).

Critical Periods for Language Development

Recall from Chapter 2 that some acquisitions, such as some visual capabilities, occur during critical periods, or they do not develop well at all. That is, the human nervous system is programmed to be sensitive to certain types of input at certain points in the life cycle. If the stimulation that is required to develop the competency in question is experienced during the critical period, the acquisition occurs. Otherwise the potential for acquiring the competency is lost or severely compromised.

Lenneberg (1967) proposed that there was a critical period for language, believing that language acquisition needed to occur before adolescence if it was to occur at all. For example, occasionally children are discovered who have been reared without exposure to language. These children, termed **feral children**, are typically the victims of abusive parents who have locked them away. When such children are discovered by age 7, it is more likely that they will develop language than if they were to be discovered later (Skuse, 1984). Consider another example. Some deaf children are exposed to sign language from birth, whereas others experience sign language for the first time sometime during childhood. Complete language functioning using signs is more certain in children who are exposed to signing from birth. Consistent with the critical period hypothesis, for children whose first immersion in sign language occurs during childhood, the earlier the child begins immersion, the more complete the sign language competence in adulthood (Newport, 1990); similarly, earlier cochlear implants lead to better spoken language (Spencer, 2016). The language development of deaf children is described more completely later in this chapter.

The acquisition of a second language also appears to occur more completely during a sensitive period. Johnson and Newport (1989) studied native Korean and Chinese adults who immigrated to the United States and found a strong correlation between the age at which people immigrated and their syntactical competence in English: Those who arrived between 3 and 7 years of age were more competent in English syntax than those who arrived between 8 and 10, who were more competent than those arriving between 11 and 15, who were more competent than those arriving at an older age (see also Hakuta, Bialystok, & Wiley, 2003; Huang, 2014). In general, the research evidence is consistent with Lenneberg's position that language proficiency is more certain if acquisition of a language begins early in life. It is unclear, however, whether the critical period for second-language acquisition is the first 5 or so years of life or the first 12 or so years of life, or even the first 20 years of life (Birdsong, 1999, 2005; Birdsong & Vanhove, 2016). Yes, acquiring a second language is easier and more certain in many ways during childhood than during adolescence (Snow, 2002). Those starting to learn a language earlier are more likely to attain native-speaker competence. But the ability to acquire a second language certainly does not disappear with the arrival of adulthood (Steinhauer, 2014). Adults can learn much more of a second language in the first year or two of exposure than children (McLaughlin, 1978; Snow & Hoefnagel-Hohle, 1978). Bilingualism is discussed more fully later in this chapter.

Speed of Acquisition Relative to the Amount of Input for Language Development

One of the strongest arguments that biology plays a large role in language acquisition is that children acquire language with relatively little intervention. As is discussed in the next section, infants are sensitive to the particular sounds in the language they are hearing and soon begin to produce those sounds. By the end of the first year of life, infants begin to learn some vocabulary words with one exposure. Children start using syntax in the second year of life, making great progress even though they could not have experienced examples of all the subtleties that apply to syntactic constructions. Many who study child language believe that children's ability to learn language given relatively little input is proof that powerful biological mechanisms are responsible for language acquisition (Maratsos, 1989; Meisel, 1995; Pinker, 1994). As we will see, children's language tends to be more competent when they are immersed in rich linguistic worlds, surrounded by adults who talk with them a great deal.

Language Acquisition

Language acquisition is complicated in that children's comprehension and production of language involve a variety of skills, with a large body of research on each of the relevant skills (Hoff, 2001; Wagner & Hoff, 2013). Research on language acquisition can be organized into study of the various language competencies, which are reviewed briefly in this section.

- *Speech perception* refers to the hearing and interpretation of speech that is encountered. Although speech perception is studied across the lifespan, work in infancy has received the most attention.

- *Speech production and phonological development research* focuses on when and how humans can make particular speech sounds. Again, speech production and phonological development during early language development has been of special interest.

- *Lexical development* refers to the learning of words and their meanings.

- *Semantic development* includes lexical development but is also concerned with children's production and understanding of meanings expressed in combinations of words.

- *Grammatical and syntactical development* focus on when and how children can combine individual words into higher-order constructions, such as phrases and sentences.

- *Pragmatic development* refers to the increasing ability to use speech and language in a variety of situations. One example is the study of children's conversational skills.

- *Metalinguistic development* refers to children's increasing awareness and understanding of language. One aspect of metalinguistic awareness that is particularly relevant to educators is phonemic awareness (i.e., the awareness that words are composed of sounds blended together), which is a critical competency for success in beginning reading.

Cutting across many of these areas of inquiry about language is a fundamental distinction between comprehension, imitation, and generative production of language. Although there are exceptions to the general rule, typically comprehension precedes imitation, which precedes generative production (Bates, Bretherton, & Snyder, 1988; Goldstein, 2015; MacWhinney, 2015). For example, infants can discriminate particular sounds in their native language long before they can imitate them or generate them on their own. Many words can be comprehended before a child uses them. Thus, although some 16-month-olds can comprehend more than 300 single words, they generally tend to use far fewer words in their utterances. Children's language production provides an underestimation of what they know about language.

Prelinguistic Development: Speech Perception and Production

A great deal of language development occurs before babies can comprehend meaning from language. Researchers have focused on infants' abilities to recognize the basic sounds in their language and to produce those sounds.

Speech Perception

Babies are hearing speech sounds even before they are born, which probably accounts for their very early discrimination of their mother's voice from other female voices (DeCasper & Fifer, 1980; Gibson & Spelke, 1983; MacWhinney, 2015). Moreover, even as early as a few days of age, babies seem to be able to discriminate between the language they have been immersed in during the first few days of their lives (and during the prenatal period) and other languages. For example, French 4-day-old infants can discriminate French from Russian and prefer French, and 2-day-old infants who were immersed in Spanish could discriminate Spanish from English and prefer Spanish (Mehler et al., 1988; Moon, Panneton-Cooper, & Fifer, 1993).

During the first month of life, babies can discriminate a number of the most basic sounds in their native language from one another. These most basic sounds that combine to form words are called **phonemes**. See Table 7.1 for a list of the 20 phonemic vowel sounds and 24 phonemic consonant sounds found in most English accents. In contrast, there are only 11 phonemes in Hawaiian and as many as 60 in some African languages (Goldstein, 2015). The phonemes in Table 7.1 are particularly relevant to future primary-grade teachers since these sounds are the ones that beginning readers must learn to decode from letters and letter combinations and then blend in order to pronounce printed words.

How do researchers know that babies can make discriminations between sounds? In many studies, children have been given a nipple to suck that is rigged to equipment that records the rate and intensity of the baby's sucking. When a sound is presented to the child, for example, the "pa" sound, sucking at first increases in frequency and amplitude. Then, as the baby gets used to the sound, the sucking gradually decreases. Once sucking is slow and steady, a new sound is presented, perhaps "ba." Babies as young as 1-month-old will increase their rate of sucking when such a change occurs, thus demonstrating that they can discriminate the basic sounds in

TABLE 7.1. Vowel and Consonant Phonemes in English

Consonant phoneme sounds	Vowel phonemes
"p" sound in *pie* and *up*	Vowel sound in *sea, feet*
"b" sound in *by* and *ebb*	Vowel sound in *him, big*
"t" sound in *tie* and *at*	Vowel sound in *get, fetch*
"d" sound in *die* and *odd*	Vowel sound in *sat, hand*
"k" sound in *coo* and *ache*	Vowel sound in *sun, son*
"g" sound in *go* and *egg*	Vowel sound in *calm, are*
"ch" sound in *chew* and *each*	Vowel sound in *dog, cough*
"j/g" sound in *jaw* and *edge*	Vowel sound in *cord, more*
"f" sound in *fee* and *off*	Vowel sound in *put, wolf*
"v/f" sound in *view* and *of*	Vowel sound in *soon, do*
"th" sound in *thigh* and *oath*	Vowel sound in *bird, her*
"th" sound in *they* and *booth*	Vowel sound in *the, sofa*
"s" sound in *so* and *us*	Vowel sound in *ape, waist*
"z" sound in *zoo* and *ooze*	Vowel sound in *time, cry*
"sh" sound in *shoe* and *ash*	Vowel sound in *boy, toy*
"g" sound in *genre* and *rouge*	Vowel sound in *so, road*
"h" sound in *he*	Vowel sound in *out, how*
"m" sound in *me* and *am*	Vowel sound in *deer, here*
"n" sound in *no* and *in*	Vowel sound in *care, air*
"ng" sound in *hang*	Vowel sound in *poor, sure*
"l" sound in *lie* and *eel*	
"r" sound in *row* and *ear*	
"w" sound in *way*	
"y" sound in *you*	

Note. Based on Crystal (1995).

human languages (Eimas, Siqueland, Jusczyk, & Vigorito, 1971; Kent & Miolo, 1995). Between 1 and 4 months, babies' sensitivities to these sounds increase further. They can discriminate between the same vowel said by different voices and can recognize the same phoneme even if spoken at a different speed (Jusczyk, Pisoni, & Mullenix, 1992).

Not only can babies learn much from the speech sound, they pay more attention to speech than other sounds (Vouloumanos & Werker, 2004). Thus, the speech surrounding a baby has a profound effect on the child's ability to perceive sound. Six- to 8-month-old infants can discriminate between phonemes that occur in a foreign language but not their own language, but older infants, 10-month-olds, lose the ability to discriminate phonemic distinctions that occur in foreign languages but not in their own language (Jones, 2004; Werker & Pegg, 1992). Some evidence indicates that the loss of the ability to discriminate foreign phonemes from one another occurs even earlier (Mehler & Christophe, 1995). Thus, babies seem to be born with the ability to discriminate many more phonemes than the ones used in their language. If sounds do not occur in the language surrounding them, they lose their ability to discriminate them (Werker, 1995).

In addition to the sounds themselves, babies are sensitive to the rhythm or tonal structure of language. By 4–6 months of age, babies prefer to listen to speech that conforms to the pause patterns that occur in their native language (Fernald & Kuhl, 1987). In the Fernald and Kuhl (1987) study, babies were trained to turn their heads in order to activate a speaker. The babies were more likely to turn their heads for language rhythmically consistent with the language they were experiencing at home. The babies were also more likely to turn for language offered in a high-pitched tone and musical in its rhythm. That is, they preferred **motherese** (also referred to as parentese to include fathers), the high-pitched, singsong speech mothers often use when interacting with their infants (Fernald, 1991; Zauche, Thul, Mahoney, & Stapel-Wax, 2016). Motherese is simplified syntactically relative to the speech a mother uses when talking to adults. Such simplification makes it easier for children to understand the mother's meaning as well as to attend to the language used by the mother. Just as is the case for discrimination of phonemes, babies seem to lose the ability to discriminate between pausal patterns that do not occur in their native language (Hirsh-Pasek & Golikoff, 1991). Less than a year of immersion in a language community profoundly affects a baby's speech recognition abilities and preferences (Aslin, Jurczyk, & Pisoni, 1998).

Speech perception during infancy plays an important role in subsequent language development. The 6-month-old infant who is more sensitive to speech sounds becomes the 2-year-old who knows more words, speaks more words, and generally understands better what is being said (Tsao, Liu, & Kuhl, 2004). That, of course, makes a great deal of sense because even during the first year of life infants seem to be able to pick out words in sound streams based on pause and stress cues (Aslin et al., 1998). Learning the perpetual characteristics that define a word begins early.

Speech Production: Babbling

Babbling begins a few months into life and continues into toddlerhood (MacWhinney, 2015; Mowrer, 1980; Rothganger, 2003). The earliest babbling, primarily a vowel sound like "uuuu" or "aaaa," is often referred to by mothers as "cooing." In the next few months, the vowel sounds give way to babbling that is filled with consonant and vowel combinations. The first consonants to be combined with vowels often are those that are formed in the back of the mouth, such as the "g" and "k" sounds. Common combinations in the babbling of English-surrounded 6-month-olds are the "da," "ba," "wa," "deh," "ha," and "heh" sounds (Vihman, 1992). These sounds are repeated and repeated, as if the child is practicing them. The content of babbling is affected by the language the child experiences. By the end of the first year, the sounds that are more frequent in the surrounding culture definitely are more frequent in baby babbling (Boysson-Bardies, Halle, Sagart, & Durand, 1989; Boysson-Bardies et al., 1992; Oller & Eilers, 1988). A baby's babbling, however, plays a role in this shaping, since babbling increases parental attention and communication efforts. When the baby babbles, parents talk back, providing the baby with a richer language environment (Locke, 2002).

Semantic Development

Most children begin to talk at about 1 year of age, using single words as their first utterances (Bailey, 2016). At first, children typically use only a few select words, adding a few new ones each month (Barrett, 1989). The rate of word learning during this early phase varies widely. By 2 years of age, some children have as many as 450 words in their vocabulary, and others are using only 10 (MacWhinney, 2015).

Although single-word acquisition seems to be slow at first, toward the end of the second year the pace rapidly increases for many children, especially once a child has acquired 50 words (Bailey, 2016; Goldfield & Reznick, 1990). Throughout much of childhood, acquisition of single vocabulary words is rapid (Anglin, 1993; Beck & McKeown, 1991; Biemiller & Slonim, 2001; Miller, 1977). How rapid? A conservative estimate is that by the end of first grade, children know 6,000 words well enough that they can recognize them; by fifth grade, the figure climbs to 20,000 (Anglin, 1993). During kindergarten and the preschool years, children learn about three or four new words a day. Between first and fifth grades, they are learning 9 or 10 new words a day. An important distinction is between words and *root words*, with root words being those words that expand into whole families of words. So, *child* is a root word for *childhood, children*, and *childish*. The number of root words acquired increases dramatically during the elementary school years, although there are individual differences between children (Biemiller & Slonim, 2001). Interestingly, the acquisition of root words appears to be orderly, with some words reliably acquired by younger children (e.g., *fish, flood*) and others more likely to be acquired only by older children (e.g., *sliver, knoll*).

The rate of vocabulary growth varies widely, often reflecting the actions of the child. One of the best ways to increase vocabulary is to read more (Stanovich & Cunningham, 1993). To appreciate the lexical advantages that active readers create for themselves, consider the following numbers generated by Nagy and Anderson (1984): A middle school student who is not motivated to read may read 100,000 words a year. An average-achieving, average-motivated middle school reader might read 1,000,000 words a year. In contrast, the best and most voracious middle school readers will read between 10,000,000 and 50,000,000 words a year! Some children's vocabularies increase more rapidly than other children's vocabularies because they choose to read more.

A number of explanations have been proposed for how children learn vocabulary. Most vocabulary words are learned incidentally through experiencing them in contexts, both social contexts and text contexts (Sternberg, 1987). This is challenging since children often cannot discern the meaning of novel words from *context clues* (Nagy, Anderson, & Herman, 1987; Nagy, Herman, & Anderson, 1985). For example, when Schatz and Baldwin (1986) had high school students read difficult text, they found little evidence that the students understood the meanings of new vocabulary words encountered in these texts. Contexts that provide more clues about meaning lead to more certain learning of novel vocabulary, and high-ability children are more likely to learn vocabulary from context than low-ability children (Herman, Anderson, Pearson, & Nagy, 1987; McKeown, 1985; Van Daalen-Kapteijns & Elshout-Mohr, 1981). Beyond reading, parental interactions seem to matter a lot, as does learning of vocabulary from television and other media. When children are immersed in vocabulary, they will acquire many words (Biemiller, 2003).

One reason is that sometimes words are learned via *fast mapping* (Carey, 1978; see also Bailey, 2016). That is, with one exposure in context, the child understands the word somewhat, enough to recognize its meaning later in a less explicit context. For example, the child who hears a teacher refer to a "lavender" shirt may be able to select the correct color a few days later from a choice of four colors (Behrend, Scofield, & Kleinknecht, 2001; Waxman & Booth, 2000).

Fast mapping certainly does not lead to complete knowledge of a word. Complete knowledge (*extended mapping* to use Carey's [1978] term) is acquired over exposure in a number of contexts. A number of researchers besides Carey have offered evidence that children can and do refine their understandings of word meanings as they process words in multiple contexts (McGregor, 2004; McKeown, 1985; Werner & Kaplan, 1952). It is not understood exactly how children extract meaning from context, but we do know that multiple exposures to a word are necessary for a rich understanding of the word's meaning. As part of learning words from context, children get better at figuring out what words must mean by attending to meaning clues in sentences and paragraphs as well as by knowing the meanings of more root words, prefixes, and endings as their experiences with words increase (Carlisle, 2004; Sternberg & Powell, 1983). The more children read, the more they are exposed to new vocabulary in a variety of contexts, and the more opportunities they have to infer word meanings.

Since complete understanding is unlikely to occur from exposure to a word in a single context, should vocabulary be directly taught? An argument against direct teaching is that it is like attempting to fill a swimming pool with an eyedropper. Adults know so many vocabulary words, over 100,000, that direct teaching seems impractical (Nagy & Anderson, 1984). Others believe that the number of words known by literate adults has been overestimated and that the number of different words in English that need to be known is not overwhelming, perhaps more like 15,000–20,000 altogether (root words). Based on this root-word estimate, direct instruction of vocabulary over the 12 years of schooling might have quite an impact on semantic development (d'Anna, Zechmeister, & Hall, 1991), with each root word taught providing a foundation for understanding the meaning of multiple additional words. Does teaching vocabulary to children increase their reading comprehension? After reviewing the available research, Beck and McKeown (1991) reported that sometimes teaching vocabulary increased comprehension and sometimes it did not. Comprehension increases are more likely when students not only learn new vocabulary but are also provided opportunities to make deep and extensive connections between vocabulary words and their definitions (see also McKeown & Beck, 2006).

As described in Chapter 4, children do not learn words as isolated bits of knowledge, but rather they develop semantic networks relating the concepts and words that they know. From infancy, children are learning how the vocabulary and concepts they know relate to one another. Children often relate words to one another in ways that are different from the ways favored by adults—for example, by using thematic relations rather than the categories adults use (Bruner et al., 1966; Gelman & Mayer, 2011). Do you recall the example presented in Chapter 4 of how young children sometimes group objects by themes rather than by categories? When given a pile of plastic animals and play fruit, rather than grouping the objects as animals and fruits, they come up with interesting little stories (e.g., monkeys eating bananas; elephants and giraffes going together because they live in the same house at the zoo; a bear eating apples, oranges, and grapes, consistent with the child's observation that the bears at the zoo are fed fruit). Themes and categories are both salient in children's semantic relationships.

Children's incomplete understanding of the words they "know" has been consistently noted (MacWhinney, 2015). In particular, children often *undergeneralize* vocabulary. If they know that the word "dog" refers to the greyhound that lives at their house, they might use the word *dog* when they see other greyhounds but not when they see other breeds of dogs. Similarly, children sometimes *overgeneralize* vocabulary, with some children sometimes referring to a variety of four-legged animals as dogs, perhaps deer, cows, and pigs (Bloom, 1973; Clark, 1973). The presence of underextensions and overextensions in children's language simply reinforces the point that it takes a while for children to acquire complete understanding of the words they are learning. All that said, the evidence is that teaching children vocabulary does, in fact, have a positive impact, including on their reading comprehension (Kamil, 2004).

Syntactic Development

Roger Brown identified five early stages of syntactical development in his influential book, *A First Language: The Early Stages* (1973), inspiring a great deal of research. Before we present these stages, we will define some terms. **Morphemes** are the smallest units of language that convey meaning. There are two types of morphemes: unbound and bound morphemes. *Unbound morphemes* can stand alone; that is, they are words. For example, *dog, fire, tractor,* and *stand* are all single, unbound morphemes (i.e., these are all *root words* in the way Biemiller & Slonim, 2001, defined root words). In contrast, *bound morphemes* cannot stand alone; bound morphemes include prefixes, suffixes, possessives, and plurals. The length of children's utterances is calculated in morphemes, with an important measure being the **mean length of utterance (MLU).**

Roger Brown (1973) portrayed the morphemic development of three children: Adam, Eve, and Sarah. The children's MLUs as a function of age are displayed in Figure 7.2.

First, note the individual differences in the language development of the children. Eve's language development was considerably in advance of Sarah's and Adam's as indicated by examining the MLUs for each child at 28 months of age. Eve's MLU is more than 4; Adam's and Sarah's MLUs are closer to 2. Some 2-year-olds have more complex language than some 3-year-olds, as was the case for Eve compared to Adam and Sarah. The mean length of utterance and the structural and linguistic

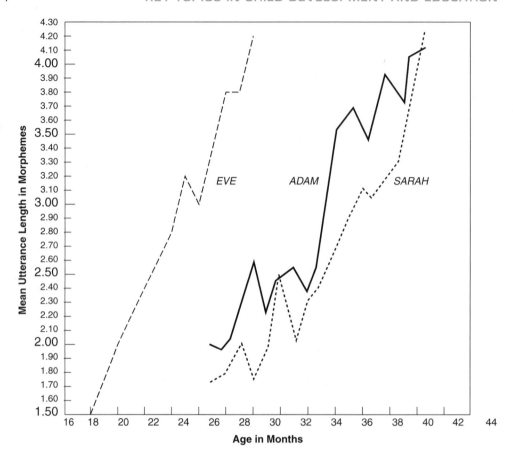

FIGURE 7.2. Children's mean length of utterance (MLU) as a function of age. From Brown (1973). Copyright © 1973 the President and Fellows of Harvard College. Reprinted by permission.

complexity used in utterances increase with each new stage of syntactic development. The stages are described as follows:

Stage 1

Once children have a speaking vocabulary of 50–100 individual words, their language changes dramatically. The first syntactic stage begins, with this stage characterized by two-word utterances, such as "See ball," "Two ball," and "Doggie run." Because Stage-1 speech is like a telegram in that it contains only important words conveying a lot of meaning, Brown (1965; Brown & Bellugi, 1964) referred to it as the period of **telegraphic speech**. Notably, the two words are not in random order, but rather in the order that would be expected in an adult sentence, except that less important morphemes are not present.

Braine (1963) noted that many times the first word in two-word utterances is an action word (i.e., a verb, such as *see* or *go*) or a preposition (e.g., *off*) or a possessive (e.g., *my*). The second word is usually a noun. Braine termed the first words "pivots" because they almost never occur alone and do not occur with other pivots, only with nouns. Many pivot-open constructions, such as "No mama," "Off bib," "More cookie," and "Alldone juice," are possible during the two-word stage (Braine, 1976). The constructions that children use during Stage 1 reflect individual differences. For example, some children use many more pivot-open relationships; some use pronouns and others do not. Yet children in Stage 1 have meanings that they intend to communicate with some elementary rules for translating those meanings into utterances. Those elementary rules are the beginning of syntax.

Stage 2

Many Stage-2 utterances are still two words, but sometimes simple, functional morphemes (e.g., prepositions, such as *in* and *on*) are added. One of the more striking phenomena in this period is the overgeneralization of syntactical rules, sometimes referred to as **overregularization**. For example, even children who have previously used the irregular past tense of go correctly ("went") may begin to say "goed" once they acquire the regular past tense rule (Marcus et al., 1992). For most children, the rate of overregularization is typically quite low, though some children produce many more overregularizations than others (Kuczaj, 1977).

Stage 3

In this stage (which occurs for many children during the third year of life), children begin to use negatives in simple sentences, sometimes with auxiliary verbs missing (e.g., "There no doggies," and "I not eating"). They also begin to form simple questions. Sometimes questions simply involve raising the voice near the end of a statement ("Doggie eat the food?"); sometimes questions involve the *wh*- elements (Who, What, Where, When, and Why). Often, the word order is not quite right in early questions. For example, it is not unusual for the Stage-3 child simply to place a *wh*-element in front of a declarative statement, such as "Why doggie sit in house?" and "Where Mommy sleeping?" During Stage 3, children also begin to utter imperatives ("Go to house doggie!").

Stages 4 and 5

Syntax begins to get much more complex, with the beginning of compound (e.g., sentences connected by *and*) and complex sentences. Passive constructions also begin to enter the child's speech. DeVilliers and deVilliers (1992, pp. 379–380) provided some examples of children's speech in these stages:

> "The teddy and the doll are going to play."
> "I didn't catch it but Teddy did."
> "After I clean my teeth can I have a story?"
> "Where did you say you put my doll?"
> "It was the man that the dog bit."

The typical 4-year-old's syntax is much more complex than that of the typical 2-year-old. Even so, children's syntactic skills are anything but complete by 4 years of age, although their errors always represent the use of syntactic rules. Sentences like the following, which reflect a great deal of understanding about the rules of syntax, are common among 4-year-olds (Crystal, 1987, p. 243). Each of these sentences is correct, except for the application (or lack of it) of one syntactic rule:

"You bettern't do that."

"Are there much toys in the cupboard?"

"It just got brokened."

"Are we going on the bus home?"

In summary, during the first 4 years of life, children utter progressively longer utterances. With increasing length, meaning is more completely expressed in the utterances, as indexed by the number of morphemes in utterances (MLUs). Moreover, sentences become more syntactically complex, with children gradually using the syntactical devices required to form compound and complex utterances, questions, passives, and imperatives. The acquisition of syntactic complexities is orderly, with Stromswald (1995) reporting that children acquire 11 complex syntactic structures in an invariant order. By the start of formal schooling, children understand syntactic rules related to declaratives, questions, and imperatives, but other syntactic knowledge, such as passive construction, continues to develop (Bailey, 2016). All of this implies a natural unfolding in normal language development, but direct instruction can also influence the process. See the Considering Interesting Questions special feature (Box 7.1) for a discussion of the role learning principles can play in language acquisition.

Pragmatics

Anyone who has ever tried to converse with a 2-year-old knows that it is challenging. Why is that so? Conversation requires connecting what you are saying with what the other person is saying. Thus, during conversation, people respond to the comment just directed at them, often offering a response that comments on the last remark. This new remark often implies an opportunity for a response from the partner in the conversation. Although children as young as 18 months old sometimes exhibit rudimentary turn-taking skills by looking at another person when they expect them to talk (Rutter & Durkin, 1987), a typical 2-year-old's response to the remark of another is simply to repeat it (Bloom, Rocissano, & Hood, 1976; Gallagher, 1981). Conversations involving a number of turns are much more likely with 3- and 4-year-olds than with 2-year-olds. The older the preschooler, the more likely the conversation will be rich in requests, elaborative commentary on previous remarks, and clarifications (Goelman, 1986; Shatz, 1983). In short, over the preschool years, children learn how to carry on conversations, how to talk about things, and how to relate their memories and perspectives to others.

The ability to understand the perspective of others contributes to the development of the ability to communicate with others in dialogues. Piaget believed that children communicated poorly because they could not understand the perspectives of others—that is, they were egocentric (Piaget, 1926; see also Chapter 3). For example, Krauss and Glucksberg (1969) asked 4- and 5-year-olds to provide clues to another child about the appearance of strange-looking objects, so that the other

BOX 7.1. Do Learning Principles Apply to Language Acquisition?

Can principles of social learning theory (review Chapter 5), such as observation, imitation, and reinforcement, be used to facilitate language acquisition? The answer appears to be yes. For example, I. Brown (1976) established that nursery-school children could induce the grammatical rules governing the production of passive constructions if they were presented with a sample of passive sentences accompanied by enactments of the actions specified by the sentences. After hearing 50 such sentences with enactments, the children were able to understand passive constructions involving different materials that had been used during the 50-sentence training. In fact, presentation of the sentences with enactments produced about 80% correct comprehension compared to 50% comprehension for controls who did not receive the 50-sentence training. Most impressive were the large gains due to exposure and enactment by children who had very little understanding of passives at the beginning of the study.

Parent–child interactions also can have implications for language learning (Zauche et al., 2016). Parents often simplify speech when they talk with young children (i.e., they use parentese). If they also recast and expand the utterances of their children, they increase the likelihood that their children will induce important language rules (Ochs & Schieffelin, 1995). For example, when a child says, "Mommy sock," Mommy might reply with a recasting or expansion such as, "Yes, Mommy wears socks." The child's exclamation of "Doggie runs" might be expanded by a parent to something like "The dog is running fast." Positively reinforcing children to use language increases their competent use of it (Whitehurst & Valdez-Menchaca, 1988). Challenges and barriers to high-quality parent–child interactions supporting language development in the first 3 years include parental educational level, parental verbal abilities, parental mental health (e.g., depression and anxiety), and other factors limiting interaction, such as television viewing and even the fact that strollers face away from the parent (Topping, Dekhinet, & Zeedy, 2011).

The discovery that learning mechanisms such as reinforcement and imitation can affect language acquisition has had a profound influence on the development of interventions for children whose language is not as advanced as that of their age-mates (Bos & Vaughn, 1991; Brown, 1979; Schiefelbusch & Bricker, 1979; Wiig, 1992). Such interventions typically involve exposing children to many examples of language structures (e.g., syntactical constructions) that the children need to acquire, sometimes explicitly reinforcing children for using these constructions (Fey, Windsor, & Warren, 1995). The theory, supported by a growing database, is that children experiencing language difficulties can extract the rules of language from exposure to multiple models of the targeted language rules, just as social learning theory would suggest.

child could select the object from a group of strange-looking objects. Consistent with Piaget's ideas about children's limitations as communicators, the children were not very good at this task. This task, however, is very unusual and unfamiliar to children, which might account for the children's communications shortcomings in the study.

Researchers who have studied preschoolers' communications with tasks and in settings more familiar to them have provided evidence that children's communication skills are much more adept than Piaget believed. For example, preschoolers can look beyond the words for the meaning of an utterance. They understand that intended meaning can be expressed in a number of ways and that it is not always equivalent to the literal meaning of utterances (Garvey, 1974). Thus, by 4 years of age, children understand that, following a request for a snack, the following responses mean "No": "You've just had one" and "It will be dinner soon" (Crystal, 1995, p. 287).

In addition, preschoolers can make adjustments, reflecting understanding of the cognitive skills and perspectives of others. For example, when 4-year-olds were asked to describe a toy, either for a 2-year-old or for an adult, they spoke differently. When they addressed the 2-year-old, their utterances were shorter and simpler compared to the statements intended for adults (Shatz & Gelman, 1973; see also Tomasello & Mannle, 1985; Weeks, 1971).

In summary, conversations are more complete with increasing age during the preschool years for a number of reasons. Yes, the comments made by children are longer and more complex, both syntactically and semantically. More than that, however, when older preschoolers converse with others, their comments take into account the conversational context and the perspectives of the individual with whom they are talking.

Metalinguistic Awareness

Just as *metacognition* is cognition about thinking (see Chapter 4), *metalinguistics* is thinking about language. It is knowledge about and awareness of language. Metalinguistic theorists (e.g., Gombert, 1991) believe that metalinguistic awareness is critical for the regulated use of language. For example, an accomplished author knows a great deal about how words work, how syntax can be adapted depending on linguistic context, and what is required for a written piece to communicate to various audiences.

Perhaps the most important finding with respect to development of *metasyntax* is that by the end of the preschool years children can discriminate some syntactically correct sentences from incorrect ones, something that is impossible for 2-year-olds to do (deVilliers & deVilliers, 1972; Smith & Tager-Flusberg, 1982). A striking *metalexical/metasemantic* outcome is that children's understanding of the nature of a word increases dramatically between 5 and 7 years of age (Bowey & Tunmer, 1984). For example, by age 6–7, children can segment some simple sentences into component words, although this ability continues to develop throughout the elementary school years. From 4–8 years of age, children are becoming aware of how language must vary with social context. For example, they are beginning to understand contexts that require more polite language versus contexts that permit impolite language (Bates, 1976; Gleason, 1973).

Without a doubt, however, the most educationally important research on metalinguistic development is in the area of *metaphonological* development: Reading researchers have determined that **phonemic awareness**, which is awareness that words are composed of separable sounds (i.e., phonemes) and that phonemes are combined to say words, is a critical competency in learning to read. Think about it. Is the teaching of letter–sound associations going to make any sense if the child does not know that words are composed of such sounds blended together? This is a critical understanding for beginning reading instruction to make any sense at all. A related metalinguistic competency is understanding the *alphabetic principle* that the letters in words represent sounds (Adams, 1990), which goes hand in hand with phonemic awareness.

Phonemic awareness is one of the best predictors of success in early reading in school (Adams, 1990; Bond & Dykstra, 1967; Scarborough, 1989; Troia, 2004).

Children who fail to learn to read during the first several years of schooling often lack phonemic awareness (Pennington, Groisser, & Welsh, 1993; Stanovich, 1986, 1988). Children who lack phonemic awareness have a difficult time learning to spell and developing understanding of letter–sound relationships (Griffith, 1991; Juel, Griffith, & Gough, 1986). Poor phonemic awareness at 4–6 years of age predicts reading difficulties throughout the elementary school years (Juel, 1988; Stuart & Masterson, 1992). Poor readers at all age levels often are less phonemically aware than same-age good readers (Bruck, 1992; Pennington, Van Orden, Smith, Green, & Haith, 1990; Pratt & Brady, 1988). Just as development of phonemic awareness leads to improved reading, reading increases phonemic awareness (Perfetti, 1992; Perfetti, Beck, Bell, & Hughes, 1987; Wimmer, Landerl, Linortner, & Hummer, 1991). As summarized by Goswami and Bryant (1992), the research findings on phonemic awareness reveals "a strong (and consistent) relationship between children's ability to disentangle and to assemble the sounds in words and their progress in learning to read" (p. 49).

In normal readers, for phonemic awareness to develop, formal instruction in reading seems essential in that only a very small proportion of children develop phonemic awareness in the absence of such instruction (Lundberg, 1991). Notably, the one out-of-school literacy experience that predicts phonemic awareness is parental teaching of letters and their sounds (Crain-Thoreson & Dale, 1992). Many parents, however, do not engage in such teaching, so instruction that impacts phonemic awareness typically occurs in school. Phonemic awareness in 5- and 6-year-olds can be increased with instruction that heightens children's attention to the component sounds in words (Adams, 1990; Murray, 2006). See the Applying Development Theory to Educational Contexts special feature (Box 7.2) for a discussion of the importance of providing experiences for children that will develop their phonemic awareness.

Concluding Comment on First-Language Development

The progress in language development during the first few years of life is impressive. During the first 6 months, children are already becoming sensitive to the sounds represented in the language surrounding them, as reflected in their babbling. In the second 6 months, babbling increasingly sounds like speech and begins to take on the rhythm of sentences. By the end of the first year, children are saying their first words, sometimes making two-word utterances. In the second year of life, children acquire many words and two-word sentences become diverse and common. Children are understanding a lot and expressing much more meaning than during the first year. In the third year, sentences get longer and more complex. Morphemes such as plurals, some past-tense markers, and *a* and *the* begin to be used. Children are better able to communicate their intentions. In the fourth year of life, sentence constructions become more complex still, with children asking questions, using negation in sentences, and often using imperatives ("Give that to me!"). They use several sentences together to express meaning, with continued growth in vocabulary. In the fifth year of life, children's communications become more sophisticated still. They adjust their speech depending on the audience and situation and are more aware of whether or not they are communicating well. Of course, language development continues for years beyond the preschool years, with the syntactical competencies of the 11-year-old far exceeding those of the 6-year-old, and many college students

Applying Developmental Theory to Educational Contexts

BOX 7.2. Instruction that Supports the Development of Phonemic Awareness

Lynette Bradley and Peter Bryant (e.g., 1983) hypothesized that providing instruction to children about how to categorize words on the basis of their sounds would increase their phonemic awareness, and hence their long-term reading achievement. An important principle emphasized in the Bradley and Bryant (1983) instruction was that the same word can be categorized in different ways on the basis of sound when it is in different sets of words. Thus, if *hen* is in a group of words that include *hat, hill, hair*, and *hand*, it would make sense to categorize all of these words together as starting with *h*, especially in contrast to other words starting with another letter. If *hen* were on a list with *men* and *sun*, however, these three words could be categorized as ones ending in *n*. If *hen* were on a list of words that included *bed* and *leg*, it would be possible to categorize the words as ones with short *e* in the middle.

The training involved 40 10-minute sessions spread out over 2 years, although another version of the instruction was implemented over a period of 4 months (Bradley, 1988). During the first 20 sessions, 5- and 6-year-olds who initially lacked phonemic awareness were taught to categorize words on the basis of common sounds using pictures of the objects. For example, in one lesson a set of pictures of objects starting with the letter *b* was shown to the child, who named the objects. The child repeated the names, with the teacher urging the child to listen to the sounds. The child then was asked if he or she could hear a sound common to each word. This process continued until the child could identify the common sound, with the adult providing help and hints if the child experienced difficulty.

This sound identification task was repeated a number of times during training, with a number of variations. For example, children were given sets of pictures, asked to group them together on the basis of common sounds, and then asked to provide justifications for their classifications. In another variation, the children were required to eliminate a word starting (or ending or containing) a sound different than the other pictures in a set. Many exercises were given for each sound, with the teacher moving on to a new sound only when children seemed to be proficient with the sound previously introduced.

The 20 sessions with pictures were followed by 20 sessions with words, with children required to determine whether words rhymed or began with the same sound (alliteration). After the children achieved proficiency on this task, they were given tasks on end sounds (such as elimination of the word ending in a sound different from the others). After children could categorize on the basis of final sounds, they learned to categorize on the basis of middle sounds in words.

In this training, pictures yielded to purely aural presentations. Various discrimination exercises eventually gave way to production exercises. In the latter half of the curriculum, children were required to spell words using plastic letters, with the teacher providing help as needed, up to and including spelling the word for the child if that was what was needed to move the lesson along. Spelling exercises included sets of words sharing common features. Thus, for a set involving *hat, cat*, and *rat*, an efficient strategy was simply to change the first plastic letter as each new word was requested.

This training produced substantial gains in standardized reading performance—about a year advantage—relative to a control condition in which children were trained to categorize pictures and words conceptually (e.g., *cat, bat*, and *rat* are all animals). The sound-categorization-trained students were even further ahead of control participants who had received no categorization training. Even more striking, however, were the results of a 5-year follow-up. Although many of the students in the control condition had received substantial remediation during the 5-year interval following the study, students who had experienced the

(continued)

sound categorization training when they were in the primary grades still held striking reading advantages (Bradley, 1989; Bradley & Bryant, 1991).

Since Bradley and Bryant's classic research, there have been many demonstrations showing that instruction designed to improve phonemic awareness impacts beginning reading success (Ehri et al., 2001; Murray, 2006; National Reading Panel, 2000; Tunmer & Arrow, 2013). Because this instruction is consistently effective, it is one of the reading practices favored in the No Child Left Behind Act (107th Congress) as worthy of federal support in schools receiving funds to improve their programs. Teaching children that words are composed of sounds blended together, and helping them to practice analyzing words into their sound components and blending sounds to produce words are important aspects of language development that contribute to beginning reading competence (Ehri, 2004; Troia, 2004).

still learning how to wordsmith as they write, including learning how to combine sentences so they efficiently convey intended messages. Vocabulary acquisition is a lifespan process, with increases in vocabulary possible even for the 90-year-old whose mind remains active. Indeed, language continues to develop in the adult years (Foley & Thompson, 2003).

None of this happens unless children are exposed to language—a lot of language. Sadly, many children do not experience frequent, high-quality language during their preschool years. Their parents do not engage them in frequent conversations, and they attend preschools or day care where conversations with adults are rare. On average, the language development of such children is impaired relative to children who experience rich conversations in their families (Dickinson, McCabe, & Clark-Chiarelli, 2004; Hart & Risley, 1995, 1999; Hoff & Naigles, 2002; Huttenlocher, Haight, Bryk, Seltzer, & Lyons, 1991; Huttenlocher, Vasilyeva, Cymerman, & Levine, 2001; Huttenlocher, Waterfall, Vasileya, Vevea, & Hedges, 2010). Many subtleties of language cannot develop unless children experience high-quality language and have the opportunities to see how language maps to the objects and events of the world (Tomasello, 2000). A parent who converses responsively with a child promotes the child's language development (Akhtar, Dunham, & Dunham, 1991; Benigno, Clark & Farrar, 2007; Tamis-LeMonda, Bornstein, Kahana-Kalman, Baumwell, & Cyphers, 1998; Tamis-LeMonda & Song, 2013; Tomasello & Farrar, 1986; Tomasello & Todd, 1983). Such parents talk about topics that interest the child but also talk so the child can understand them, using simplified speech ("parentese"), which is often accompanied by gestures, facial expressions, and other hints that make it easier for the child to understand (Chong, Werker, Russell, & Carroll, 2003; Jones, 2004; Zauche et al., 2016). Children also play an active role in this interaction. By getting their parents to talk about the toys and objects in the world that interest them and with which they interact most, children learn the names of things in the world that matter most to them (Bloom, Margulis, Tinker, & Fujita, 1996; Bloom & Tinker, 2001).

One aspect of preschool language interaction that has received substantial attention from scholars is picture-book reading. The more that parents interact with children over books, the better developed is children's language (Farrant & Zubrick, 2012; Ninio, 1980; Payne, Whitehurst, & Angell, 1994; for reviews, see Bus, van IJzendoorn, & Pelligrini, 1995; Saracho, 2017). Moreover, parents and teachers of low-income preschool and primary-grade children can be taught to interact with children over picture books in ways that increase emergent language skills, including vocabulary development (Arnold, Lonigan, Whitehurst, & Epstein, 1994; Lonigan & Whitehurst, 1998; Valdez-Menchaca & Whitehurst, 1992; Whitehurst et al., 1988; 1999; Whitehurst, Arnold, et al., 1994; Whitehurst, Epstein, et al., 1994; Zevenbergen, Whitehurst, & Zevenbergen, 2003). These studies demonstrated that teaching parents and teachers to interact more responsively during storybook reading increased children's language abilities.

Does acquiring language competence during the preschool years make a difference to later success in school? Absolutely. For example, learning to read depends on phonemic awareness (Adams, 1990), semantic (vocabulary) development (Kamil, 2004; McGregor, 2004), and understanding of the subtleties of syntax (Scott, 2004). Just about every aspect of language that can be measured in the preschool years is associated with later reading competence, with preschoolers who have better developed language becoming better readers during the elementary years (Scarborough, 2001). If readers of this text remember nothing else from this chapter, they should keep in mind that preschoolers being seen and not heard (or talked with) is a disastrous prescription, one that is played out too often by children spending hours with the television or in overcrowded day care settings where little language interaction takes place between adults and children. Communicating with children is at the heart of their language development.

Bilingualism

People who are bilingual, or even multilingual, comprise a significant portion of the human population worldwide (Garcia, 1993; Nicoladis & Montanari, 2016). Increasingly, the United States is a multilingual nation, with the percentage of young adults who speak a language other than English at home increasing from 11% in 1980 to 25% in 2013 (U.S. Census Bureau, 2014). Educators need to know about bilingualism if they are to fully understand the children in their midst.

Bilinguals are a diverse group, varying in the languages they speak, the number of different languages spoken in their homes, their immigration status, and their socioeconomic levels, just to mention a few dimensions of difference (Cohen & Horotwitz, 2002). One way to study bilingualism is to conduct in-depth, typically longitudinal case studies, and to document extensively the language development of a child and the contexts in which language development occurred. Sometimes these studies are referred to as "diary studies" since those conducting them invariably construct diaries about the child's language development. Such investigations are resource-demanding, requiring years of a researcher's life to collect the data, followed by years to sort through the data, and perhaps years to write up the study. Thus, not many diary studies have been conducted (Hoffmann, 1991).

For example, Werner Leopold documented the first 2 years of his daughters' language development, particularly the development of his older daughter, Hildegard. The girls were raised in the United States in a home in which their father spoke German to them and their mother spoke English. Leopold kept detailed diaries of his daughters' language. The result was four books: the first dedicated to phonological development, the second to vocabulary, the third to word formation and syntax, and the fourth to other observations (Leopold, 1939, 1947, 1949a, 1949b).

Were there difficulties for Leopold's daughters in language acquisition? Not really. Leopold reported that Hildegard acquired and used both English and German words. She seemed to have few difficulties with the sound differences between the two languages. For a while she used some German words in particular situations and their corresponding English words in other situations (e.g., she used *bitte* in formal situations and *please* in less formal situations), but in general Hildegard acquired both German and English. Between 2 and 3 years of age, she was very much aware that German and English were separate languages, and she readily translated between the two languages. She learned the syntax of both German and English and did not seem to confuse them.

It was clear that community mattered. For example, Hildegard did not continue to use German words she acquired during a 3-month visit to Germany at age 1 once the family returned to the United States. As Hildegard continued to live in the United States, English became her dominant language. Karla, the younger daughter, never was as fully bilingual as her sister. However, when Karla had a chance to live in Germany during her late teen years, she rapidly acquired the German language.

One of the most important conclusions coming out of the Leopold study, and other diary studies, was that there is little evidence that learning and using two languages interfered with the development of either language. Subsequent research has confirmed that Hildegard was a typical bilingual, whose speech included a small amount of code switching, which decreased in frequency with increasing age (Lindholm & Padilla, 1978; Redlinger & Park, 1980; Swain & Wesche, 1973). Code switching, however, can persist in the language of adult bilinguals, often as an identity marker in bilingual communities, and may indicate sophistication rather than deficiency in the acquisition of either language (MacSwan, 2016).

Review of the diary studies makes it clear that language exposure dramatically affects language acquisition. For example, when two bilingual parents in the midst of a bilingual community raise children, their children tend to mix the languages more than do children raised in situations in which languages are more clearly separated (Romaine, 1995). If the context demands, children can learn several languages at once. For example, Oksaar (1977) reported on a child who lived in Stockholm, in a home in which Swedish and Estonian were spoken. The child moved to Germany at age 3. The child spoke Swedish and Estonian like a monolingual and acquired German easily, with clear German pronunciation. Although the child's German syntactical development reflected the influence of Estonian and Swedish, in general the child experienced little difficulty in acquiring German.

In short, the diary studies provide a substantial amount of information about how bilingual development proceeds. When the diary study data are combined with information gathered using other research methods, a picture of bilingual language development emerges.

Bilingual Language Development

One of the best ways to understand bilingual language development is to understand first-language development, as detailed earlier in this chapter. As it turns out, the development of a particular language by a child who is also acquiring another language is not much different from the development of the same language by a child in a monolingual environment (de Houwer, 1995). Because bilingual development is not much different from monolingual development, one way to organize the research on bilingual development is to use the categories of language development described earlier.

Prelinguistic Development: Speech Perception and Production

As described earlier, children quickly develop sensitivity to phonemes that occur in the language community in which they are immersed, so that by the end of the first year of life they have difficulty hearing the differences between phonemes that occur in another language. By adulthood, people really cannot hear phoneme distinctions that are not represented in a language they know. One of the most commonly cited examples of this perceptual phenomenon is Japanese adults' inability to discriminate between /ra/ and /la/, because these two sounds, which are distinct phonemes in English, are variations of a single phoneme sound in Japanese (Strange & Jenkins, 1978).

As described earlier, the content of a baby's babbling is affected by the language the child experiences. By the end of the first year, the sounds that are more frequent in the surrounding language definitely are more frequent in baby babbling (Boysson-Bardies et al., 1989, 1992). What happens with bilingual development? Analyses of the diary studies led to the general conclusion that young bilinguals develop the sound systems for the languages they are learning in parallel. Yes, there is a little blending and the occasional mixing of sounds, but, for the most part, when a child learning German and English speaks in German, the sounds are German. When the child speaks in English, the sounds are English (Hoffmann, 1991). Whereas monolinguals tune in to the phonemes of their language sometime between 6 and 12 months, the bilingual child may require just a little more time to discriminate the phonemes for two languages and to set up what seem to be two separate phonological systems (Hammer et al., 2014). A delay in phoneme production may be observed in the less dominant language.

One of the most important issues with respect to phonological production is whether a critical period exists for the acquisition of a language so that it is spoken without an accent. In general, the available evidence is consistent with the conclusion that the younger children are when they learn a second language, the greater the likelihood that they will not have an accent (McLaughlin, 1984). Study of immigrant populations is revealing on this issue. In general, the younger an immigrant came to the United States, the less pronounced the accent (Asher & Garcia, 1969; Birdsong & Vanhove, 2016; Oyama, 1976). Notably, the diary studies are filled with examples of children learning several languages without accents, consistent with the conclusion that learning several different sound systems is not formidable for young children.

Semantic Development

During the one-word stage, the bilingual child uses words from both languages. Sometimes words from the two languages are blended together, so that a French–English bilingual child might say "pinichon" for "pickle," blending the English word *pickle* and the French word *cornichon* (Grosjean, 1982). Bilingual children seem to develop two separate vocabularies, and as a result they may start school knowing fewer English words than monolingual children but may acquire new words more quickly and eventually they do catch up (Bailey, 2016; Hammer et al., 2014).

Semantic (vocabulary) development correlates with academic achievement (especially in reading) for English-second-language students just as it does for English-first-language students (Anderson & Nagy, 1991). From fourth grade on, English-second-language students' knowledge of English vocabulary is strongly correlated to their reading achievement in English, at least as defined by standardized tests (Fitzgerald, 1995). The more vocabulary people know in a language, the more capable they are at reading. Not surprisingly, when students who are English-second-language learners are taught English vocabulary, their reading comprehension improves (Carlo et al., 2004; Lesaux, Kieffer, Kelley, & Harris, 2014).

Syntactic Development

A number of researchers interested in bilingualism have examined the syntactic development of bilingual compared to monolingual children (de Houwer, 1995). In general, syntactic development is the same whether a child is acquiring only one language or is an emergent bilingual (Hoffmann, 1991). The differences that do occur are subtle compared to the similarities. For example, Meisel (1984; reported in Hoffmann, 1991) studied German and French bilingual children. He noticed that the bilingual children tended to be more rigid in their adherence to German word-order conventions than monolingual German children. Even so, both the bilinguals and the monolingual German students acquired the German word-order conventions, with little difference in the rate of acquisition.

Bilingual children appear to develop separate syntactical systems, acquiring synaptic conventions in independent parallel paths (de Houwer, 1995; Hammer et al., 2014). For example, children do not attempt to transfer syntactic rules and conventions that occur in only one of the languages they are learning to the other language. Thus, when the two languages have different ways of expressing tense, children do not use the tense conventions of one language with the other language (Schlyter, 1990). When the languages differ in how gender is marked, children do not confuse the markings in their speech (de Houwer, 1987). When one language has particular rules for expressing questions, children do not extend those rules to the other language when trying to form questions (de Houwer, 1990). As with sounds and vocabulary, children tend to keep the languages they use separated.

Metalinguistic Awareness

Bilingual children are more aware of language than monolingual children (Bialystok, 1997; Bialystok, Shenfield, & Codd, 2000; Hammer et al., 2014; Levy, 1985; Romaine, 1995). They are more aware than monolinguals of the arbitrary relationship between words and things (Genesee, 1981). Bilingual children are also more knowledgeable about the properties of words, as reflected in their abilities to perform tasks requiring understanding the nature of words. For example, bilingual preschoolers are more facile at identifying single words in contexts (such as sentences) than are monolinguals (Bialystok, 1997). Bilingual children know more about syntax than monolinguals (Swain & Lapkin, 1982). Bilingual children can translate from one language to another early in life (Malakoff & Hakuta, 1991). Another competency requiring a high degree of language awareness is using languages appropriately as a function of speaker and context (e.g., using Spanish when speaking to a

Spanish speaker at the bus stop, using English to speak to the bus driver who is an English speaker), which bilingual preschoolers do well (Hoffmann, 1991).

What about the development of phonemic awareness, a metalinguistic skill critical to learning to read, as described earlier in the chapter? There appear to be high cross-language correlations in phonological awareness, although the size of the relationship varies across languages (Branum-Marin, Tao, & Garnaat, 2015). Dual-language learners may perform below monolingual children in preschool on tasks of phonological awareness, but they later catch up (Hammer et al., 2014). The more vocabulary a bilingual child has, the better the phonological awareness tends to be and phonological instruction should improve performance in both languages.

It is important to realize that the development of language is a long-term process. We emphasize this point because many believe that young children acquire a second language more easily than adults. McLaughlin (1984) considered the evidence pertaining to this question and offered the following comparison. In the first 6 years of life, a child experiences 9,000 or more hours of language exposure and experience, and yet the child's vocabulary and syntax are far from that of a mature adult. In contrast, during the Vietnam War, the Army Language School could develop a soldier into a native-level speaker of Vietnamese in about 1,300 hours of immersion in Vietnamese (i.e., the soldier lived and worked in a community that spoke Vietnamese). As we pointed out earlier, at least at first, adults can learn a second language faster than children. The individual who begins learning a second language as a child, however, has a much better chance of eventually attaining native language competence, including a native accent.

Bilingualism and Cognitive Development

Researchers are extremely interested in the question of whether or not bilingualism affects cognitive development. Often the question has been posed with respect to general intelligence as measured by intelligence tests. It is difficult to draw sound conclusions on this issue, however, for bilingual experience often is correlated with development outside of the mainstream community, and IQ tests contain many items that depend on knowledge of the majority community (Hakuta, 1986; see also Chapter 8).

In a classic study relevant to this issue, Peal and Lambert (1962) studied 10-year-old children in Montreal. They carefully assessed the language competencies of their participants and made sure that the bilingual and monolingual participants were comparable socioeconomically. The bilingual children outperformed the monolingual children on intelligence tests, on items tapping both verbal and nonverbal intelligence. The superiority of the bilinguals was particularly noticeable on items requiring cognitive flexibility. Moreover, the bilinguals had a better understanding of a number of concepts. Perhaps knowing two names for a concept stimulates more reflection on it than knowing only one name (Carringer, 1974)?

Research since Peal and Lambert (1962) has supported their general conclusion that bilingualism is associated with cognitive flexibility (Hakuta, 1986). Beginning with infancy and early childhood, bilingual children exhibit more advanced monitoring skills as they flexibly switch from one language to another (Kovacs, 2016). Bilingual children also have an advantage in terms of developing theory of mind and executive function (see Chapters 3 and 4), demonstrating greater cognitive flexibility and attentional control (Nicoladis, 2016). Hsin and Snow (2017) found that fourth- to sixth-grade bilingual students displayed better social-perspective taking in their academic writing than their monolingual peers. The cognitive processing of skilled bilingual adults as they read entails cross-language lexical activation, requiring the development of high-level executive function skills to ignore irrelevant information and switch between the two languages (Kroll, Gullifer, & Zirnstein, 2016). Finally, there is some initial evidence that bilingualism may delay the onset of some forms of dementia (Duncan & Phillips, 2016). See the Considering Interesting Questions special feature (Box 7.3) for a discussion of how bilingualism affects private speech.

Education and Bilingual Students

It is not surprising that children who start kindergarten speaking a language other than English tend to have lower math and reading scores (Han, 2012). Schooling can help close the gap. English ability in kindergarten, however, does predict the developmental trajectory. For example, Han (2012) found that children who entered school as mixed bilinguals (that is, neither language was dominant at home) closed the gap in their math scores compared to English monolinguals by the fifth grade. On the other hand, non-English dominant bilingual children and non-English monolingual children improved in math and reading but did not close the gap. Home language factors are also important in the academic achievement of bilingual children. For example, Branum-Martin, Mehta, Carlson, Francis, and Goldenberg (2014) found that Spanish-English bilingual families that used more English at home increased their kindergartner's English listening and vocabulary; whereas families that use more Spanish at home increased their kindergartner's Spanish listening and vocabulary. Cha and Goldenberg (2015) studied home language in more than 1,400 Spanish-English bilingual kindergarten children in Texas and California and found that learning English quickly was associated with high-quality English spoken at home, with the cost of potentially losing proficiency in Spanish. Speaking Spanish at home did not appear to interfere with acquisition of English and was associated with continued proficiency in Spanish. Cha and Goldenberg (2015), however, warned that if parents are not competent English speakers, progress in both languages may be hampered.

Educators are exploring many different ways of educating bilingual students (Genesee, Lindholm-Leary, Saunders, & Christian, 2006). These programs can be fit into two major categories (Lambert, 1974, 1977; see also Cha & Goldenberg, 2015). The first category of approaches, *additive programs*, has the goal of adding a second language, without eliminating the first language. In contrast to additive programs, the other major category of approaches, *subtractive programs*, have the explicit goal of replacing the students' native language with the majority language, with the overarching goal of assimilating minority children to the mainstream culture (Lambert, 1974, 1977). Typically, students in subtractive programs do not receive instruction in their native language. Hence, such programs are often referred to as "submersion programs," analogous to throwing a child into a body of water that is very much over the child's head! Although the most extreme subtractive approaches involve language-minority students receiving instruction entirely in the majority language, in some cases "sheltered English" instruction occurs. That is, the teachers use simplified English and consciously teach English to the students.

The number of dual-language immersion programs in the United States that use an additive approach to bilingual education has been growing (Steele et al.,

Considering Interesting Questions

BOX 7.3. How Does Bilingualism Affect Private Speech?

Recall from Chapter 6 that young children often talk to themselves as they work on tasks ("Let's look at everything first. That's the biggest piece of the puzzle, so I use it first. . . . There's green on one side. . . . Where's another green one?"). This private speech helps children organize their behavior, assists their problem solving, and increases self-control (Meichenbaum, 1977). Private speech is absent in the early preschool years, gradually increases with age, and then decreases as children enter the elementary school years (Kohlberg et al., 1968). According to Vygotsky, the decrease in audible private speech reflects the internalization of thinking. Private speech sometimes is discernible, however, when children encounter challenging problems (Kohlberg et al., 1968).

Diaz, Padilla, and Weathersby (1991) examined whether bilingualism affects children's private speech. They studied 34 Mexican American preschoolers between the ages of 3 and 6 who were enrolled in an additive bilingual preschool program. The children performed three tasks. One was a block design task, which involved creating a block pattern shown in a picture. The second task was a classification task, requiring children to search a set of picture cards to find pairs of pictures that relate to one another (e.g., hammer and nails, toothbrush and toothpaste, lock and key). The third task required the children to order sets of pictures that depicted the act of baking a cake, with the task to put the pictures in the correct order of events. As children performed the tasks, they were videotaped. The videotapes were then transcribed, and the private speech was coded as to whether or not it was task-relevant. Task-relevant remarks were further broken down into the following categories: labels and descriptions of materials, directives ("I am putting the purple one here"), planning statements ("I'll put the one with the bowl first"), transitional statements ("OK, I'm done with this one"), questions and answers ("What goes here? . . . Oh, the cow goes here"), and self-praise/self-reinforcement ("I did them all!").

The private speech of these bilingual students was very similar to the private speech of other children who have been studied. For example, they used more task-relevant private speech than task-irrelevant speech. As children's mental age increased, task-relevant private speech first increased, followed by a decline. As audible private speech declined, inaudible whispers and mutterings increased, suggesting that private speech was being internalized. When the task was more difficult, more audible private speech increased. Children who were more skilled in both languages tended to emit more task-relevant private speech than the less bilingual children. This is consistent with other research suggesting that, if anything, bilingualism facilitates cognition.

In a review of the available research on private speech and bilingualism, Sawyer (2016) concluded that the private speech of bilingual children follows a similar developmental trajectory as monolinguals and bilinguals use it for the same purpose. Bilinguals who are about equally proficient in both languages—balanced bilinguals—commonly exhibit code switching in their private speech. The evidence as to whether bilinguals have a cognitive advantage in private speech is mixed. More balanced bilinguals, in comparison to less balanced bilinguals, tend to apply private speech more broadly and flexibly, are more developmentally advanced in their use of private speech, and are capable of reasoning in both languages in private speech.

2017). In dual-language immersion programs, both native English speakers and English-language learners receive instruction in two languages starting in kindergarten. With the goal of promoting both English and the partner language, these programs have increased in popularity because the evidence is that children are more likely to become bilingual, performing at or above grade level in English and the partner language, compared to those in other programs (Lindholm-Leary, 2016; Perez, 2004). This is attractive not only to parents of children who enter school looking to learn English but also to the parents of English-speaking children who are looking for an opportunity to enhance their children's language skills in an increasingly global society.

Conducting high-quality evaluations of bilingual education programs has proven challenging (Fitzgerald & Releyea-Kim, 2013), primarily because of variability across programs but also because the data tend to be correlational owing to a lack of random assignment. Steele et al. (2017), however, were able to study seven cohorts of dual-language immersion programs where the students were selected by lottery and hence randomly assigned to programs in kindergarten. Students who participated in the dual-language programs performed better than control students in the fifth and eighth grade on measures of reading performance. There was little benefit, but also no negative effect, on math performance.

Dual-language programs may be popular with parents but are not necessarily valued in some communities in the United States. One complicating factor in the policy debate in the United States is that a variety of political forces are opposed to conducting any instruction in U.S. schools in a language other than English. Another complication is that, increasingly, U.S. schools are dealing with many different first-language minorities. It is not unusual at all for more than 50 first languages to be represented in school districts. The presence of so many different languages almost mandates that many language minorities will experience education only in English.

Deafness

About one child in a thousand is born deaf. For a small percentage of these children, the problem definitely is genetic. Others are the victims of teratogenic diseases, such as maternal German measles (see Chapter 2). Still more children become deaf during their first 2 years of life due to middle-ear infections or as a result of meningitis, with profound childhood hearing loss relatively rare after the first 2 years of life (Crystal, 1987).

It is difficult to study deafness (Marschark, 1993; Marschark & Spencer, 2016), especially since only rarely will a researcher have a large sample of deaf children to study. Thus, many studies of childhood deafness are based on just a few children. This is problematic because the childhood deaf are a diverse lot. Some children are born profoundly deaf, whereas others have significant residual hearing. Some are diagnosed early, and some are diagnosed only several years after birth. Some are the children of deaf parents, some are born to hearing parents. Of those born to hearing parents, some parents are more committed to and skillful at signing for their infant than others. Moreover, deaf children differ systematically in a variety of ways from hearing children (Marschark, 1993). For example, lack of appropriate prenatal care increases the odds of birth defects in the infants of economically disadvantaged mothers, with deaf children often having co-occurring disabilities (Knoors & Verv-loed, 2003).

Consider, for example, that even the deaf child in an economically and other-wise advantaged situation will have very different social relationships and interac-tions than a hearing child. Lederberg and Mobley (1990) studied the interactions of hearing-impaired and hearing-normal toddlers (1½–2 years of age) with their mothers. They observed less interaction between hearing-impaired infants and their mothers than between hearing-normal infants and their mothers. When interactions did occur, the hearing impairment affected the exchanges negatively. For example, hearing-impaired children often would cut off an interaction because they did not hear some input from the mother. Mother–child relations are different for deaf ver-sus hearing-normal infants, which makes it very difficult to conclude that develop-mental differences between deaf and hearing-normal children are due to hearing loss itself rather than to the effects of hearing loss on social interaction opportuni-ties.

Oral Communication versus Sign Language Debate

An essential difference between deaf children is the means of communication that parents use with their children, whether oral communication or sign language. This decision affects both the quality and the quantity of the input the child receives and the communications the child can make. Debates about whether deaf children should experience oral language only or be taught to use sign language are longstanding (Crystal, 1987). The creation of new technology has reinvigorated the debate.

The problem with sign language is that it only allows limited social interactions, mainly, with others who know how to sign (Antia & Kriemeyer, 2003), although this is a situation favored by many who support a separate deaf culture (Woll & Ladd, 2003). The problem with the oral approach is that it typically results in a person who speaks poorly and hence also ends up being isolated (Conrad, 1979). From the point of view of language development and school achievement, oral communicators do not do as well as sign language users (Marschark, 1993). One point argued by those favoring the oral approach is that learning to use sign language somehow will inter-fere with subsequent learning of oral language. A related point is that a child who begins in an oral communication setting will stop using oral language if sign lan-guage instruction begins. Essentially, there is no evidence to support either of these suppositions (Conrad, 1979; Marschark, 1993; Quigley & Paul, 1984).

A third alternative to the exclusive oral or sign language approaches is the total, or simultaneous communication, approach in which the communicating child uses both oral communications and sign language. The research to date is supportive of this approach. The child reaps the cognitive benefits that use of sign language permits (Marschark, 1993), but also enjoys social benefits. For example, Cornelius and Hornett (1990) observed preschoolers in a total communication setting enjoying better social relations with peers than preschoolers in an oral-only setting. Given the advantages of this approach, it is not surprising that it is common relative to pure oral or manual approaches.

Technology, as we have pointed out, reinvigorated this debate and in many ways has transformed it. A device known as a "cochlear implant" can be surgically implanted into children and adults with deafness, with the result that after a few years many recipients can understand much more oral language than they would have understood without the implant (Harkins & Bakke, 2003; Niparko & Blanken-horn, 2003; Spencer & Marschark, 2003). How much this improves the language, academic achievements, and quality of life for recipients is an area of active research, which occurs as part of research on a number of technologies intended to improve the functioning of deaf populations, ranging from captioned television to a variety of assistive hearing devices (Harkins & Bakke, 2003; Spencer & Marschark, 2003). Research indicates that if cochlear implantation occurs before 18 months of age (lit-tle data is available on implants before the first birthday), better oral language skills result (Spencer, 2016). The benefits of early implantation is aligned with the idea of critical periods for phonological and syntactic development. The suggestion is that without a cochlear implant or the use of other hearing aids, a deaf or very hard of hearing child receives little to no auditory stimulation. As a result, the auditory system is likely to be used for other sensory systems such as visual and tactile infor-mation, a result termed cross-modal plasticity (Knoors, 2016). Cochlear implants and other assistive technology continue to be improved and hold great promise for changing the lives of future generations of individuals with deafness.

That deaf children do experience different communication systems, of course, complicates the study of the development of deaf children. Despite the many chal-lenges, a great deal of progress has been made in understanding the development of these children. In the following, we summarize briefly some of the most important findings of this research.

Language Development

Although the language development of deaf children has not been studied as exten-sively as the language development of hearing-normal children, our understanding of the language of deaf children has advanced. There are both similarities and dif-ferences between the language development of deaf and hearing-normal children.

Babbling

Although deaf children babble, their babbling tends to be much less extensive than that of hearing-normal children, with hearing-impaired infants emitting fewer sounds resembling native language syllables than hearing-normal infants (Oller & Eilers, 1988). Indeed, one indication to parents and physicians that an infant may be deaf is that the child does not babble as hearing-normal children babble.

An intriguing observation is that deaf infants who have deaf parents who use sign language exhibit manual babbling (Lederberg, 2003; Schick, 2003). The deaf signing parent communicates extensively with the infant, using a form of "signing motherese," with the signs presented slowly and in a somewhat simplified fashion (Bloom, 1998; Erting, Prezioso, & O'Grady Hynes, 1990). Just as the syllable, which occurs in vocal babbling, is part of a word, signs can be decomposed into parts. Deaf infants have been observed producing such part signs (Petitto & Marantette, 1991). The first years of life are a time when children practice the basic elements of com-munication that they will eventually employ to construct words and more complex messages, whether those elements are syllables, as they are for hearing children, or parts of signs, as they are for deaf children in signing families. The power of expo-sure to signs to elicit infant manual babbling comes through when hearing infants are exposed to signing during their first year of life: Their hands babble (Petitto,

Holowka, Sergio, Levy, & Ostry, 2004; Petitto, Holowka, Sergio, & Ostry, 2001). From the first months of life, all children, regardless of hearing status, attend to and respond to communications they encounter repeatedly.

Around 95% of deaf children have hearing parents who may not have had much interaction with a deaf person before their child was diagnosed (Knoors, 2016). Deaf parents sign to their child right away at birth, but it is difficult for hearing parents to be fluent in a language they are just learning themselves. So, initially, deaf infants and hearing parents tend to rely on gestures.

Gestures

All children gesture, including deaf children (Lederberg, 2003; Schick, 2003). The most common gesture is pointing, but other gestures have some physical resemblance to their referents (e.g., a child making a spiral upward motion to draw attention to a bear spiraling up a tree on television; Marschark, 1993). Some deaf children, whose parents do not sign to them, come to use gesturing extensively. By 2 years of age, these children can be combining several gestures to express their meaning, somewhat parallel to hearing 2-year-olds who are beginning to combine words to form sentences. Such gestural systems do not seem to develop further, however (Goldin-Meadow, 1985; Goldin-Meadow & Mylander, 1984).

First Signs and the Development of Vocabulary

Early vocabulary development can be quite advanced for the deaf child relative to hearing children (Lederberg, 2003; Marschark, 1993). The first signs of deaf children with deaf parents often are acquired several months earlier than the first words of hearing-normal infants (Bailey, 2016; Goodwyn & Acredolo, 1993). At a minimum, deaf children with deaf-signing parents produce their first signs no later than hearing-normal children produce their first spoken words (Meier & Newport, 1990).

The advantage of deaf signers over hearing-normal children continues into the second year of life (Lederberg, 2003). During the second year, deaf signers acquire vocabulary at a much faster pace than hearing-normal children, with some evaluations suggesting as much as a 4:1 advantage in the number of vocabulary words used for deaf signers over hearing-normal children by the end of the second year (McIntire, 1974, cited in Marschark, 1993). Within deaf children, one of the biggest differences in favor of sign language over oral communication approaches is in the development of vocabulary. The vocabulary development of deaf 2- and 3-year-old oral communicators lags far behind that of deaf signing and hearing-normal 2- and 3-year-olds (Meadow-Orlans, 1987).

Unfortunately, the vocabulary advantage of the deaf toddler eventually gives way to a long-term vocabulary disadvantage for deaf children compared to hearing-normal children (Blarney, 2003; Lederberg, 2003). During the schooling years, deaf children have less extensive vocabularies. Moreover, they have less knowledge of the relationships between words. Undoubtedly, an important factor accounting for the less extensive vocabularies of deaf compared to hearing-normal schoolage children is that hearing-normal children de facto are exposed to much more content than deaf children (Marschark, 1993). A lot of information communicated aurally—over television, radio, and around the dinner table—is missed by the child who cannot hear.

In summary, language development in deaf children depends largely on the input they receive. The healthiest situation seems to be when deaf parents begin early to sign to their infants, which results in early use of sign and rapid vocabulary development during the first 2 years (Gallaway & Woll, 1994). Only a small proportion of deaf children, however, are in this category since most deaf children have hearing parents who either cannot sign, cannot do so fluently, or simply do not sign at all. Moreover, deafness often is diagnosed late (Marschark, 1993). In addition, little is known about the language development of deaf children relative to what is known about normal language acquisition. For example, little systematic work has been done on the syntactic, metalinguistic, or pragmatic development of deaf children, although what literature does exist suggests strong parallels between normal language acquisition and the language acquisition of both deaf who communicate orally and those who use sign language (Blarney, 2003; Marshark & Spencer, 2016; Schick, 2003). What should be emphasized, however, is that like language acquisition in hearing children, acquisition of language by deaf children depends on social interactions that are filled with high-quality language that, in the case of deaf children, they can see (Lederberg, 2003). As noted earlier, however, technological advances are changing the landscape of language development in deaf children.

Cognitive Differences in Deaf and Hearing-Normal Individuals

Although there are some inconsistencies in the evidence, in general, deaf children perform below hearing-normal children on a variety of conventional assessments of general intelligence, including nonverbal measures (Marschark, 1993). Moreover, when tested on some theoretically derived measures of intellectual development, such as Piagetian measures of conservation, deaf children do less well than hearing-normal children (Furth, 1964, 1966; Watts, 1979).

The acquisition of theory of mind in deaf children (see Chapters 3 and 10) is dependent on their surrounding communication context (Wellman, 2014). Deaf children growing up in hearing families do not have anyone to talk with about psychological states until entering school since their parents typically do not possess the necessary fluency in sign language for such complex communications. The small minority of deaf children who grow up in a household headed by deaf parents (5%) demonstrate false belief understanding and other theory-of-mind concepts on the same timetable as hearing children. The key is having the ability and opportunity to engage in conversation. However, there does not appear to be a critical period for the acquisition of theory of mind, and it does develop once communication opportunities have improved. That is, deaf children with hearing families experience delay on theory-of-mind tasks, the same developmental sequence but slower rate of acquisition.

The development and use of private speech by deaf children is similarly affected by the communication context (Winsler, 2009). Deaf children use private signing much like hearing children use private speech, and the private signing of deaf children with deaf parents is more extensive than the private signing of deaf children with hearing parents. Again, this is because deaf children with hearing parents have less opportunity to engage in extended conversations unless their parents become quickly fluent in sign language. Deaf adults visualize signing sentences activating the language areas of the brain much like what is seen when hearing adults talk to themselves using inner speech. Deaf parents interact with their deaf children during problem-solving tasks, much as hearing parents interact with hearing children by providing scaffolding and other supports, and eventually releasing responsibility of completing the task to the child. Hearing parents of deaf children talk to their deaf children as they attempt to solve problems (which is not much help to the child) and are less likely to gradually release the responsibility of completing the task to their children.

Deaf children typically experience difficulties in school, as reflected by achievement test data (Karchmer & Mitchell, 2003). A number of studies suggest that deaf children's lack of knowledge of vocabulary and English-language syntax, relative to hearing-normal students, contributes to their difficulties in learning to read and write, in particular, but also to achieve more generally in school (Conrad, 1979; Marschark, 1993; Paul, 2003; Power & Leigh, 2003; Quigley & Paul, 1984). An important advance in understanding in the past quarter century is that many of the instructional techniques that work with regular education populations can be adapted to increase the reading and writing skills of deaf students. For example, deaf students can be taught to use reading and writing strategies and their prior knowledge as they read and write (Albertini & Schley, 2003; Schirmer & Williams, 2003; see Chapter 4).

Chapter Summary and Evaluation

Researchers identifying with a number of different disciplines and perspectives study children's language. Chomsky's theory inspired many biologically oriented researchers to evaluate the neurological and genetic determinants of language. Much is now understood about which brain structures support particular language competencies. Language functioning depends greatly on an intact left hemisphere, and individual differences in language ability are associated with individual differences in left-hemisphere structure and function. Such work is being carried out at an accelerated pace today because of technological advances in brain-imaging techniques, particularly techniques that permit localization of cognitive processing. Advances in behavior genetics methodologies have led to increased understanding that some individual differences in language functioning can be traced to genetic differences, with language acquisition more certain during childhood than during later life. Despite the support for Chomsky's conviction that language is biologically determined, genetic and evolutionary analyses have not supported Chomsky's formulation of an invariant language acquisition device unique to humans. The symbolic capacities of the great apes are greater than Chomsky imagined. The individual differences between people in their language competencies are also greater than Chomsky originally supposed. Even when genes determine biology, there is always variation in biology!

The effects of immersion in a language are apparent from the earliest days of life, with babies a few days old clearly differentially sensitive to sounds from the language surrounding them. Children's earliest babbles reflect the sound structure of the language they have been hearing. Their awareness of that sound system will take years to develop and depends on particular types of experiences. Six months of experience in school playing games that require analysis of the sounds of words increases phonemic awareness, which increases the likelihood that the child will learn to decode well. Children also learn vocabulary from contextual experiences, including explicit teaching of vocabulary.

Bilingual language development is not all that much different from monolingual language development. The differences that do occur are small compared to the similarities. Most critically, acquisition of a language does not appear to be negatively affected by acquiring a second language at the same time. Indeed, bilingual children have some language capabilities not possessed by monolingual children, including greater awareness of language.

Deafness significantly impacts language development, although much of the language development of deaf children parallels normal language development. With the advent of technologies such as cochlear implants, there is new thinking about how deaf children can communicate to maximize their language development. Improvements in the new technologies offer great promise for much better language outcomes for individuals with deafness than have occurred in the past.

The work on language development has proven fundamentally important to understanding many issues regarding development, including some of the Big Ideas described in the first chapter.

Nature and Nurture

Language depends on and is determined by biology. But experience matters too. At the extreme, children do not develop language unless they are exposed to it. Beyond exposure, however, rich language experiences in the home and explicit educational experiences do promote important aspects of language development, including developing phonemic awareness, learning new syntactic structures, experiencing lexical development, and learning to decode. Both nature and nurture affect language development.

The similarities in language development across a range of language competencies—babbling, first words, gradual development of syntactic competence—suggest that biology plays a significant role. Even so, language development also depends greatly on experience. The sounds that children can hear and produce depend in part on the languages they experience during their first year of life. For some language-impaired children, production of certain sounds depends on intensive therapeutic experience. Whether a deaf child becomes an adult with some degree of oral language depends on his or her oral experience during childhood.

Continuity and Discontinuity

Childhood probably is a critical period for language development. The stage-like progression for the development of syntax proposed by Roger Brown decades ago still seems sensible. The data on accent in bilinguals strongly suggest that there is a sensitive period for acquiring the ability to produce the sounds of a given language.

Extreme language deprivation during childhood has lasting effects. So can less extreme forms of deprivation, however. For example, an impoverished language environment during the preschool years can devastate future academic achievement. Failing to have the educational experiences that promote phonemic awareness leaves a child at risk for long-term reading failure. The lack of exposure to sign language or oral language during the first 2 years of life, generally because of late detection of deafness, can negatively impact development. With respect to language, early experience very much matters.

feral children Children who have been reared in isolation, without exposure to language.

language acquisition device According to Chomsky, an innate biological mechanism that allows us to understand the syntax of language.

mean length of utterance (MLU) A measure of the length of children's utterances used to track language acquisition.

morphemes The smallest units of language that convey meaning.

motherese The high-pitched, singsong speech often used by mothers to interact with their infants.

overregularization The tendency of children to overgeneralize syntactic rules, thereby making grammatical errors that they had not made previously.

phonemes The most basic sounds of a language that combine to form words.

phonemic awareness Awareness that separate sounds (phonemes) are combined to make words.

telegraphic speech Speech in which only the most important words are expressed.

CHAPTER 8

Intelligence and Individual Differences in Academic Competence

P eople differ in ways that influence their academic competence. Traditionally, psychologists and educators have measured such individual differences using standardized instruments, including intelligence tests and achievement tests. Thus, this chapter begins with a discussion of standardized tests and consideration of two important characteristics of tests: their reliability and their validity. This section is followed by an extended discussion of the assessment of intelligence, including potential biases in intelligence assessment. Since intelligence tests often figure prominently in the intellectual classification of students, this sets the stage for discussion of learner diversity.

Standardized Tests

Standardized tests are given under controlled conditions so that every person taking the test has approximately the same examination experience. Developers of standardized tests also provide test norms. A **norm** is the typical level of performance for a clearly defined reference group. For example, norms might be provided for students of various ages or for students in different grades. An individual score can then be interpreted by comparing it to the norm, the typical performance, for the group to which the individual belongs. It is important for norms to be up to date and truly representative of the reference group. For example, a norm obtained in 1975 from a white, middle-class suburban population is not appropriate for interpreting scores obtained in 2018 in a culturally diverse urban school.

It is very likely you have taken a standardized test. Perhaps your performance on that test influenced decisions about your future. For example, admission to college or graduate school often involves standardized testing of academic achievement.

Many readers of this book have taken the SAT (originally named the Scholastic Aptitude Test, but only the three-letter acronym is now being used), which was revised in 1994 and in 2005, when an essay test portion was added. In 2016, a new version of the SAT was introduced. The 2016 SAT includes significant format changes from previous versions, such as offering four multiple-choice options instead of five, no scoring penalties for guessing, and scoring ranges of 200–800 for the two content domains (Mathematics, Reading and Writing). The Reading and Writing portions of the revised test shift away from testing general reasoning ability and knowledge of isolated vocabulary to assessing knowledge of words used in context and critical reasoning skills, such as evaluating evidence, analyzing arguments, and editing prose passages. The Mathematics sections focus on applying mathematical reasoning to real-world contexts, and 22% of the math items are not multiple choice, requiring test-takers to fill in their responses. The essay portion of the test, now optional rather than required, assesses comprehension, analytical, and writing skills by asking test-takers to read a passage and explain how the author creates an argument, supporting their case with evidence from the passage. Other readers may have taken the ACT (originally the American College Test but now only the initials are used), which measures readiness for college in four content domains: English, mathematics, reading, and science. Like the SAT, the ACT also offers an optional writing section, but the four main portions of the test are in multiple-choice format with a composite score (averaged across the content domains) ranging from 1 to 36. Most colleges and universities accept either the ACT or SAT, and some do not require the submission of any standardized test results for admission consideration.

In addition, states use standardized tests to assess student progress—and may use the student test results as a measure of teacher performance or school accountability. In fact, No Child Left Behind (NCLB) legislation, passed by Congress in 2002, required more testing in schools than had occurred previously (Public Law 107-110). The Every Student Succeeds Act (ESSA), signed into law in late 2015, shifts some aspects of accountability from the federal government to the individual states but still mandates testing of student achievement (Hess & Eden, 2017). At one point, more than half of the U.S. states required students to pass standardized exit exams in order to graduate from high school (Center on Education Policy, 2012). However, in recent years a number of states have placed a moratorium on exit exams, are considering alternative routes to graduation, or have discontinued the exams altogether. The Common Core State Standards, adopted by many states but not federally mandated, were developed in an attempt to establish consistent educational standards across states about what K–12 students should be learning in English language arts and mathematics. Two consortiums of states have developed assessment systems based on these standards. Policies about testing and accountability in schools are politically sensitive and often driven by political agendas. As a result, it is difficult to predict what the emphasis on testing and accountability might be in the years to come. Nonetheless, standardized tests are part of the educational landscape, and it is essential that educators and parents be informed about the features of high-quality standardized tests.

Two important characteristics of tests are reliability and validity. **Reliability** is a first requirement of a test, which means that it must measure consistently. Without reliability, a test cannot possibly have **validity**, that is, measure what it is presumed to measure (Anastasi & Urbina, 1997; Cronbach, 1990; Miller, Linn, & Grunlund, 2013; Popham, 2017).

Reliability

The first step in understanding reliability is to grasp that any *observed score* on a test is actually composed of two scores: the *true score* and *error*. Thus, *observed score = true score + error*. Error represents the part of the score that is due to irrelevant and chance factors. On some occasions, performance is higher than it typically would be, such as when the tester is lucky guessing between two responses, and on other occasions it is lower than it typically would be. Some typical sources of testing error that may lower the scores of students taking any test are lack of sleep, illness, and an unusual level of anxiety. The greater the error, the lower the reliability.

One way to reduce error and to increase the reliability of a test is to make testing conditions as consistent as possible for all people taking the test. In other words, follow the standardization procedures. For instance, reported SAT reliability scores were established with group administration of the test items, under explicit time constraints and under conditions where students were not permitted to interact with one another or to consult notes or textbooks. If a student took the SAT with notes and open books, the reported reliability and validity would not hold true under these circumstances. Reliability is also increased if the directions for the test are easy to understand, the test questions are clearly worded, and scoring is as objective as possible.

How is reliability estimated? One method of establishing a test's reliability, **test–retest reliability**, is simply to administer the same test twice to a group of test-takers. The correlation between the two scores earned on each testing occasion indicates whether or not the test is measuring consistently (see the discussion of correlation in Chapter 1). If the students' relative performance on one test occasion is highly correlated with his or her relative performance on another testing occasion, the test is reliable.

Another form of reliability, **alternate-forms reliability**, measures the consistency of performance between two, supposedly equivalent, forms of the test. In this method of estimating reliability, students take two forms of the measurement. The correlation between performances on one form of the test and on the other form is the reliability of the test. The more similar the alternative forms of a test, the higher the reliability. Similar alternative forms cover the same content with the same number of roughly equally difficult items for each topic. Standardized tests often have multiple forms.

It is possible to estimate the reliability of a test even if the test is administered only once. This type of reliability measures the internal consistency of the items on the test. To calculate **split-half reliability**, a test is literally split in half. For example, scores for the odd and even items on the test are computed, and the correlation between the score on the odd items with the score on the even items is the "estimate of reliability." The problem with this approach is that the reliability estimate will vary depending on how the items are split. In most cases, the correlation between odd–even halves would differ from a correlation based on halves produced by randomly assigning items to half-test scores. One solution to this problem is **coefficient alpha**, which is the average of all possible split-half reliabilities (Cronbach, 1951).

Validity

The reliability of a measurement is not enough; the measurement must also be valid for its purpose. Thus, although we can measure the circumferences of children's heads with high reliability, head circumference is not a valid measure of intelligence (an example from Gould, 1981). A measurement can be no more valid than it is reliable, however, so test developers must consider issues of validity and reliability simultaneously.

Does this test measure what it is supposed to measure? That is the main validity question. More specific validity questions depend somewhat on what is being assessed. Three common types of validity are *construct, content*, and *criterion* validity.

Construct Validity

The question addressed by **construct validity** is, "Does this test measure the construct it is intended to measure?" To understand this question, it is first necessary to define *construct*. Many psychological variables are abstract rather than concrete. For example, "ability" cannot be directly observed, nor can "intelligence." Such constructs must be inferred from behavioral observations. Thus, "mathematical ability" is inferred from consistent, exceptional performance in mathematics. "Anxious personality" is inferred when an individual exhibits anxiety in situations that do not provoke anxiety in others. "Intelligence" is inferred from performances on academic tasks.

If test developers are attempting to create a new test for a construct measured by existing instruments, construct validation requires demonstrating that the new test correlates with the accepted tests measuring the construct. For example, if test developers are trying to create a short intelligence test that can be given in groups, they must demonstrate high correlations between their new measure and accepted measures of intelligence.

Content Validity

The question addressed by **content validity** is, "Does this test include the content it is supposed to cover?" Suppose a national testing agency wishes to devise a test of high school mathematics achievement. What should the test include? A content-valid assessment would include items from general mathematics, algebra, geometry, trigonometry, and calculus. Depending on the test's purpose, the proportions of these items might vary. If the purpose is to determine whether students have obtained basic numerical competencies, the test might consist primarily of general math items. If the purpose is to decide who should be selected as a finalist for a scholarship in mathematics, the test would include a much greater proportion of items testing advanced mathematics than general math items.

Content validity is an important concern for an educational achievement test. When test developers are devising a test to assess knowledge in some undergraduate major area, they first must decide what should be covered and in what proportions. For example, developers of the Graduate Record Examination (GRE) in psychology might lay out all of the subfields of psychology that they wish to assess, such as developmental, social, clinical, behavioral neuroscience, and experimental. Then they must decide on the proportions of test items for each subfield, based on their conception about which areas deserve emphasis relative to others. For example, core content that all psychology majors would have studied would receive more emphasis than completely elective areas. The 2016–2017 version of the GRE offers two subscores, experimental and social, in addition to the total score.

Criterion Validity

The questions addressed by **criterion validity** are, "Does this test make the distinctions it is supposed to make?" "Does it predict performance on some criterion measure?" For example, does the SAT predict which students will be successful in college? It does in that SAT performance is positively correlated with college grades (Lawlor, Richman, & Richman, 1997; Pearson, 1993) The correlation of SAT or ACT scores with college performance is approximately .50, explaining about 25% of the variance (Popham, 2017). When the criterion is in the future, as it is when the SAT or ACT is used to predict college grades, the criterion-related validity is referred to as *predictive validity*. When both a measure and its criterion can be collected close in time, criterion-related validity is sometimes referred to as *concurrent validity*. For example, when the extent of brain damage evident from using medical technology such as a CAT (computerized axial tomography) scan correlates highly with a behavioral measure of neurological damage, this would be evidence of concurrent validity for the two measures.

Questions Educators Should Ask about Tests

Educators should ask themselves some important questions about measurements and tests that they encounter:

- *Is this test reliable?*
  - Does it measure consistently, and how was this consistency determined?
  - Test–retest? Alternate forms? Split-half?
  - Does the test have enough questions?
  - Is the scoring relatively objective?
  - Are the test-takers prepared?
- *Is this test valid?*
  - Does it measure what the test developers indicate?
  - How are the test results being used?
  - What is the evidence of test validity?
  - Construct validity? Content validity? Criterion validity?
- *Are the norms appropriate?*
  - Is the norming group representative?
  - Is the norming up to date?
- *Are standardized testing procedures followed?*

These questions can be answered by seeking out information provided in testing manuals for the tests in question. In addition, test consumers can consult publications found in reference libraries, such as the *Mental Measurements Yearbook* (Carlson, Geisinger, & Jonson, 2014) and *Tests in Print* (Anderson, Schlueter, Carlson, & Geisinger, 2016), which review published tests and discuss how well they perform their purposes. A test should only be given great weight in decision making if it is reliable, valid for the intended purpose, appropriately normed, and has been administered as it was intended to be administered.

The Nature of Intelligence

The origin of scientific theories of intelligence can be traced back to Francis Galton's *Hereditary Genius: An Inquiry into Its Laws and Consequences* (1869). Galton's contributions to the scientific analysis of intelligence were enormous. For example, he devised a rudimentary individual-differences test based on reaction time, strength, eyesight, and motor abilities. He also devised rudimentary correlation coefficients to analyze the data he collected. Galton performed the first twin studies in an attempt to separate the contributions of heredity and environment in determination of individual differences (see also Chapter 2). Galton's thinking was a source of stimulation for both European and U.S. researchers who were interested in individual differences in intellectual abilities.

A significant advance in the study of intelligence was Spearman's (1904) conceptualization of intelligence as consisting of multiple factors, one general factor (*g*) and the others more specific (*s*), such as mathematical abilities or verbal competence. Every item on an intelligence test was assumed somehow to be related to general intelligence, with the degree of correlation to *g* varying among individual items. Every measure of intelligence also tapped specific functions, *s*, independent of *g*. Spearman definitely understood that intelligence was a construct, something that had to be inferred. He also understood that powerful inferences could be made based on correlations between measurements, and he developed the statistical methods that permitted the identification of patterns of correlations that indicated *g*. See the Considering Interesting Questions special feature (Box 8.1) for a discussion of the process used to identify patterns of correlation indicating *g*.

Considering Interesting Questions

BOX 8.1. How Do We Know There Is a *g* Factor in Intelligence?

Sometimes tests assess more than one process or knowledge domain. How do test-makers determine which items on the test are assessing the same construct? When items test the same construct, performances on these items correlate more highly with one another than performances on other items (see the discussion of *correlation* in Chapter 1). **Factor analysis** is a way of making sense of the correlations between items (Gorsuch, 1983). The starting point for factor analysis is identifying how performance on each item of a test correlates with performance on each other item on the test. For example, if every time a student is correct on item 12, he or she is correct on item 16, and every time a student is wrong on 12, he or she is wrong on 16, the correlation between 12 and 16 would be 1. If this is the case, performance on 16 can be predicted perfectly from performance on 12. If there is a 50/50 chance that a person who gets 12 correct will get 16 correct and a 50/50 chance that a person who gets 12 wrong will get 16 right, the correlation between 12 and 16 would be 0. If this is the case, it is impossible to predict performance on 16 from knowing the performance on 12. If there are 50 items on a test, there will be 1,225 (50 × 50) correlations to review, a difficult task made easier through factor analysis.

Factor analysis identifies clusters of items, or "factors," that correlate with one another. Then the investigator examines items in each factor to identify what might be causing the correlations. When intelligence test data are factor-analyzed, most or all of the items or subtests frequently cluster in one common factor, which has become known as *g* for general intelligence.

Fluid and Crystallized Intelligence

Many intelligence tests used today are organized around items that can be thought of as tapping either knowledge or the ability to process information quickly and flexibly (Cucina & Howardson, 2016; Kyllonen, 2016). Knowledge and the ability to process correspond to Cattell and Horn's two factors of intelligence: crystallized and fluid ability (Cattell, 1987; Cattell & Horn, 1978; Horn, 1985; Horn & Cattell, 1967; Horn & Hofer, 1992; Horn & Stankov, 1982). **Crystallized intelligence** refers to the accumulated knowledge acquired through experience and education and is assessed by test items indicating the breadth and depth of that knowledge, such as vocabulary knowledge or verbal comprehension. **Fluid intelligence** is measured by items requiring abstract reasoning, detecting and understanding the relations among stimuli, comprehending implications, and drawing inferences. Crystallized intelligence is accumulated through the utilization of fluid intelligence.

During the childhood and adolescent years, both fluid and crystallized abilities increase (Sattler, 2002). During adulthood, however, there are important differences in the course of fluid and crystallized intelligence (see Figure 8.1). Why? The nervous system naturally deteriorates with advancing age during adulthood. For example, adults lose something like 50,000 neurons a day during adulthood due to normal cell death. Unlike other cells that die, neurons do not regenerate. Thus, fluid intelligence, which is strongly dependent on biological wholeness, declines with advancing age (Brody, 1992; Kaufman, 1990). This means that older adults exhibit reductions in their ability to quickly execute steps in problem solving (Salthouse, 1982, 1985, 1988, 1992, 2009). On the positive side, life experiences accumulate with advancing age. Thus, knowledge continues to grow through most of the adult lifespan. Not surprisingly, crystallized intelligence, which is determined by knowledge, can increase with advancing years (Hertzog, 1989; Kaufman, 1990; Kaufman, Reynolds, & McLean, 1989; Roberts & Lipnevich, 2012; Schaie & Labouvie-Vief, 1974).

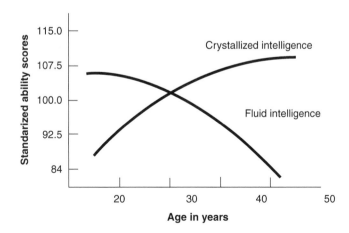

FIGURE 8.1. Fluid and crystallized intelligence across the lifespan. From "Major Abilities and Development in the Adult Period" by J. L. Horn and S. M. Hofer, 1992. In R. J. Sternberg and C. A. Berg (Eds.), *Intellectual Development*, New York: Cambridge University Press. Copyright © 1992 by Cambridge University Press. Reprinted with permission of Cambridge University Press.

Cattell–Horn–Carroll Model of Intelligence

Arguably the most influential perspective on intelligence today is what is referred to as the Cattell–Horn–Carroll (CHC) model (McGrew, 2009). Carroll (1993) reanalyzed over 460 data sets of performances on various tests collected between 1927 and 1981 (including data on more than 130,000 people). Using factor analytical techniques to identify distinctive aspects of intelligence (review the description of factor analysis in Box 8.1), Carroll constructed a model with one general factor, eight broad abilities, and a large number (at least 69) of narrow abilities. The general factor, *g*, was similar to that originally proposed by Spearman. The eight broad abilities of intelligence are crystallized intelligence, fluid intelligence, general learning and memory, broad visual perception, broad auditory perception, broad retrieval ability, broad cognitive speediness, and processing speed (reaction time decision speed). Narrow abilities include such things as spelling and speech sound discrimination. A consensus model, combining the perspectives of Cattell and Horn (fluid and crystallized intelligence) with Carroll's, the CHC model has become a unifying force in the field since it includes *g* but also provides substantial evidence and support for a range of more specific abilities (Kamphaus, Reynolds, & Vogel, 2009). Given the influence of this combined model, it is interesting to note that although Cattell, Horn, and Carroll discussed the commonalities between their perspectives, they never produced a collaborative publication and disagreed on one major issue—the prominence and nature of *g*. Cattell and Horn downplayed the significance of *g*, considering it mainly an artifact of measurement. Carroll, however, theorized that *g* exerted more influence than any other ability, having a direct impact on test scores independent of the influence of the broad and narrow abilities (Cucina & Howardson, 2016). Kyllonen (2016) suggests that evidence for the *g* factor, outside the realm of intelligence testing, can be found in the high correlations between performance on the different content domains (math, science, and reading) of the Program for International Student Assessment (PISA) taken by 15-year-olds in 70 different countries.

Alternative Perspectives about the Nature of Intelligence

Traditional approaches to intelligence tend to emphasize academic skills relevant to education. Some theorists have offered alternatives to the traditional approach, broadening the perspective on the nature of intelligence. For example, in two sets of essays on *What Is Intelligence?* (Khalfa, 1994; Sternberg & Detterman, 1986), intelligence was variously defined as acting appropriately and responsibly, being skilled in problem solving, having and being able to apply a great deal of knowledge, knowing and being able to do what is valued in one's culture, possessing the ability to learn, possessing the ability to make inferences, and having the ability to make and use tools. The *Encyclopedia of Intelligence* (Sternberg, 1994) included 250 articles about intelligence, showcasing a vast array of alternative conceptions of the construct. Two of the most cited alternative conceptions to the traditional view—the triarchic theory of successful intelligence and the theory of multiple intelligences—are described in the next sections.

Triarchic Theory of Successful Intelligence

Arguing that traditional approaches to studying intelligence do not adequately consider practical and creative abilities, Robert Sternberg (1985, 2013) has chosen to study what he has called "practical" or "successful" intelligence, proposing the *triarchic theory* of successful intelligence. The triarchic theory is composed of three subtheories: contextual, experiential, and componential. The *contextual* subtheory highlights the sociocultural context of an individual's life. Intelligent individuals adapt in order to maximize the fit between themselves and their environment. They may also shape their environment to increase the fit or, if a satisfactory fit is not possible, they select an alternative environment. According to this perspective, what is intelligent behavior depends on the cultural context.

The second subtheory, the *experiential* subtheory, emphasizes the role of experience in intelligent behavior. Sternberg argues that intelligent behavior sometimes reflects the ability to deal with novel experiences by drawing upon past experiences but also refers to the ability to deal with familiar situations quickly and efficiently. Thus, intelligent behavior involves accessing prior knowledge and developing automaticity (these concepts were introduced in Chapter 4).

The third subtheory, the *componential* subtheory, specifies the mental structures that underlie intelligent behavior. These components correspond well to the characteristics of information processing described in Chapter 4. *Metacomponents* are higher-order executive processes, such as planning and monitoring. These include processes such as deciding what the problem is, selecting a strategy, and monitoring progress toward a solution. *Performance components* are processes used to execute the plans to complete a task. Examples include recalling information, integrating and comparing pieces of information, and outputting solutions once they are determined. *Knowledge-acquisition components* are the processes used to acquire knowledge or solve problems. These include distinguishing relevant from irrelevant information, combining encoded information into a coherent whole, and comparing new information with information acquired in the past. Sternberg (2013; Sternberg et al., 2014) also highlights three broad abilities: analytical, creative, and practical. *Analytical* refers to the ability to analyze and evaluate, *creative* refers to the ability to generate options for solving a task, and *practical* refers to the ability to successfully implement options in the real world.

Theory of Multiple Intelligences

In his *theory of multiple intelligences*, Howard Gardner (1983, 1993, 1999) argues that people have a set of specific intelligences that are biologically determined. These include linguistic intelligence, musical intelligence, logic–mathematical intelligence, spatial intelligence, body–kinesthetic intelligence, interpersonal intelligence (i.e., the ability to notice and make distinctions among other individuals), and intrapersonal intelligence (i.e., access to one's own feelings). People with high linguistic abilities may excel in fields requiring verbal skills, such as journalism. People with high musical intelligence may excel as musicians or composers. High logic–mathematical intelligence would predict success as a mathematician or engineer. Those high in spatial intelligence may excel in fields such as sculpting or architecture. Body–kinesthetic intelligence is necessary for athletes. Interpersonal intelligence is a key characteristic of salesmen and therapists, and intrapersonal intelligence is important for successful actors. Almost every human endeavor, of course, requires more than one type of intelligence. For instance, dancers would need to be high in musical as well as in body–kinesthetic intelligence. Trial attorneys would need to be high in linguistic and in interpersonal intelligence. Engineers would need spatial intelligence as well as logic–mathematical intelligence.

One of the most critical features of this theory is that people vary in the strength of their particular faculties. Gardner argues that it makes no sense to think of someone as smart or not-so-smart in general, as is implied in traditional views of intelligence. Rather, people with musical intelligence would be expected to excel in music given appropriate stimulation; while those who have superior capacity in mathematics would be expected to do well given appropriate exposure to mathematics.

Gardner believes that one of the problems with contemporary schooling is that linguistic and logic–mathematical intelligences are emphasized to the exclusion of others. Schools do little to gauge the strengths and weaknesses of students in terms of the various intelligences. He argues that educators should realize the multiple nature of abilities. This awareness would lead them to help students discover their own patterns of strengths and weaknesses. Then teachers could encourage students to accentuate their strengths as well as help their students learn to compensate for their weaknesses or even teach them ways of remediating their weaknesses.

Commentary on the Alternatives Proposed by Sternberg and Gardner

The theory of multiple intelligences has captured the attention of many, particularly educators, but a number of criticisms of the theory have been voiced. Chief among these is the argument that other capabilities meet the criteria for inclusion (e.g., spirituality), and it is not clear how decisions for inclusion were made (Roberts & Lipnevich, 2012). In fact, Gardner has added an eighth intelligence, naturalistic intelligence, which is the ability to recognize and classify components of nature. In addition, few published research studies support the tenets of the theory, and little evaluation has been done of the effectiveness of the educational interventions it inspired (Sternberg, 2013). The alternative perspective proposed by Sternberg, the triarchic theory of successful intelligence, has also been criticized for limited empirical support (Roberts & Lipnevich, 2012), although Sternberg and his colleagues have published a number of research studies supporting their perspective (Sternberg, 2013). Others have suggested that many of the components found in Sternberg's model can be found in other, more widely accepted models (Kyllonen, 2016). An ambitious evaluation of instructional interventions based on the three broad abilities described by Sternberg (analytical thinking, creative thinking, and practical thinking) in fourth-grade language arts, science, and math classrooms led to rather disappointing results (Sternberg et al., 2014). Perhaps the greatest drawback to the alternative approaches is the lack of accepted and widely used measures of their underlying constructs. The traditional approaches to intelligence, in contrast, have inspired a veritable testing industry.

Intelligence Testing

For well over a century, theorists and researchers who were interested in exploring the nature of intelligence not only focused on the conceptualization of what intelligence might be, but also investigated techniques for measuring it. This history is a rich one, although it has been charged with controversy from its beginning. In his book *The Mismeasure of Man* (1981), anthropologist Stephen Jay Gould provides an exceptionally interesting history of intelligence testing.

Why were the first intelligence tests developed? Early in the 20th century, Alfred Binet was charged by the Minister of Public Instruction in Paris to find a way to discriminate between normal children and those with intellectual disabilities. The result, developed in collaboration with Theodore Simon, was the Binet–Simon intelligence scale for children (1905a, 1905b, 1905c). Lewis Terman shared Binet's vision that useful discriminations could be made between normal and low intelligent children, but he also felt that the tests could be useful in identifying unintelligent adults. Terman's revision of the Binet–Simon scale, the Stanford–Binet scale, was carefully normed on U.S. children (Terman & Childs, 1912). In the United States, Yoakum and Yerkes (1920) designed tests for the U.S. Army to help it to discriminate between the mentally unfit and those who attempted to fake stupidity to avoid World War I. These U.S. Army tests were able to make discriminations in ability in that higher ranking troops generally performed better than lower ranking troops (Yoakum & Yerkes, 1920).

It is impressive that these early tests resemble contemporary intelligence assessments, although a number of other tests of intelligence were proposed and dismissed or discontinued after a short period of use. An analysis of intelligence tests used today (Kamphaus, Reynolds, & Vogel, 2009) reveals that all of the major tests include measures of general intelligence, crystallized intelligence, spatial abilities, and memory abilities. Nearly all of the major tests also measure fluid intelligence. True to their origin, intelligence tests remain one of the best predictors of academic achievement. Following is a description of the most influential contemporary measures of intelligence (Kranzler & Floyd, 2013; Reynolds & Kamphaus, 2003; Roberts & Lipnevich, 2012).

Stanford–Binet

The *Stanford–Binet, Fifth Edition* (Roid, 2003; Youngstrom, Glutting, & Watkins, 2003), represents the continuation of a long tradition begun with Terman's completion of the American version of the Binet–Simon scale. The Stanford–Binet can be used for a wide age range (Bain & Allin, 2005). The normative sample, composed of 4,800 participants ages 2–85 plus, closely matches the 2001 U.S. Census in terms of factors such as age, sex, race/ethnicity, geographic area, and socioeconomic status. Drawing upon the CHC consensus model of intelligence, the Stanford–Binet provides a general score, Full Scale IQ (FSIQ), which is a weighted composite of five factors: Fluid Reasoning, Knowledge, Quantitative Reasoning, Visual–Spatial Processing, and Working Memory. The subscale of Fluid Reasoning is assessed through inductive or deductive reasoning tasks. The Knowledge subscale assesses acquired information, or in other words, crystallized intelligence. Quantitative Reasoning is assessed by the ability to work with numbers, with an emphasis on applied problem solving. Visual–Spatial Processing is the ability to identify patterns and visual relationships. The subscale of Working Memory is the ability to hold and use information. The composite score and subscale scores have means of 100 and standard deviations of 15. See the Applying Developmental Theory to Educational Contexts special feature (Box 8.2) for more information on how to interpret standardized test scores.

Internal consistency for the Stanford–Binet is established by high split-half reliabilities that range from .91 to .98 for the composite score across age groups. Test–retest reliability for the composite score is also high, ranging from .93 to .95 across the age groups. Content validity is established through the judgment of experts in the CHC model, coverage of constructs, and empirical item analysis. Construct and concurrent validity is established through strong correlations to other accepted

Applying Developmental Theory to Educational Contexts

BOX 8.2. Interpreting Standardized Test Scores

Many different standardized tests, such as intelligence tests or achievement tests, are used routinely in today's classrooms. It is important that future educators (and future parents and taxpayers) understand better what a standardized test score means. Simply reporting the number of items a student got correct on a standardized test gives little information about the student. In contrast, comparing a student's raw score to a measure of central tendency for the distribution of scores provides more information about the student's performance in relationship to the performance of others. The most commonly used measure of central tendency in reporting standardized test results is the mean.

The **mean** of a distribution of scores is the average score. The mean is computed by adding up the scores and dividing the sum of scores by the number of scores. For example:

If there are raw scores of 2, 4, 5, 7, 1, 3, 8, 9, 1, 10
The sum of scores = 50; number of scores = 10
Therefore, the mean is 5.

In this set of scores, six of the students (those scoring 2, 4, 5, 1, 3, and 1) scored at or below the mean. The other students (those scoring 7, 8, 9, and 10) scored above the mean.

Measures of variation, such as the **standard deviation**, provide still more information. The standard deviation is a measure of how widely scores vary from the mean. The larger the standard deviation is, the more spread out from the mean the scores are. The smaller the standard deviation, the more the scores are clustered around the mean.

The norms for standardized tests are typically normally distributed. In a **normal distribution**, most of the scores fall near the mean; that is, fewer scores are further away from the mean (see Box Figure 8.1). Using the mean and the standard deviation, we can divide the

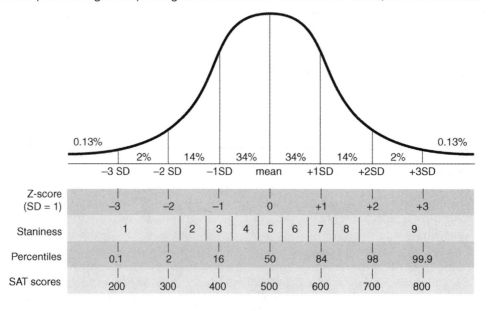

BOX FIGURE 8.1. Normal distribution, with percentiles, z-scores, stanines, and SAT scores clearly indicated.

(continued)

normal distribution into parts. Approximately two-thirds of the scores (68%) fall within 1 standard deviation of the mean. Fewer scores (28%) fall between 1 and 2 standard deviations from the mean, and very few scores (4%) are over 2 standard deviations from the mean. For example, scores on the SAT are normally distributed with a mean of 500 and a standard deviation of 100. In all the Wechsler intelligence scales, the mean performance is 100 with a standard deviation of 15.

Scores on standardized tests are often expressed in **standard scores**. A very common standard score, the **z-score**, tells how many standard deviations above or below the mean a raw score is (see Box Figure 8.1):

$$z\text{-score} = (X - M)/SD$$

where X is any raw score, M is the mean of the raw scores, and SD is the standard deviation of the raw scores.

Scores on standardized tests are also often expressed in terms of stanines. **Stanines** are standard scores with only nine possible categories corresponding to ordered regions of the normal distribution. The mean is 5, and the standard deviation is 2. As you can see from Box Figure 8.1, each stanine corresponds to a band of raw scores with the width of half a standard deviation except for stanines 1 and 9, which include the ends of the distribution. Although stanines are less precise measures for the extreme scores, one advantage of this method of scoring is that performance can be expressed in only one digit, from a low of 1 to a high of 9.

Finally, perhaps the most easily communicated method of expressing standardized test scores is in terms of percentile ranks. **Percentile ranks** are expressed in terms of relative position within a norm group. The percentile rank shows the percentage of students in the norming sample who scored at or below a particular raw score. For example, a percentile rank of 75 means the student scored the same or better than 75% of the other students in the norm group. Parents and teachers often more easily understand percentile ranks than the other methods of reporting standardized test scores.

measures of intelligence. The Stanford–Binet is particularly strong in childhood assessment for special education placement, including diagnosing developmental or cognitive delays, intellectual disabilities, and giftedness (Roberts & Lipnevich, 2012).

Wechsler Intelligence Scales

In the 1930s, David Wechsler began work on the test that would become the standard for assessment of adult intelligence, the *Wechsler Adult Intelligence Scale* (WAIS). The test has been revised four times, most recently in 2008 as the Wechsler Adult Intelligence Scale–IV (WAIS-IV), and is arguably the most widely used assessment of intelligence in adults. The norming sample of the WAIS-IV consists of 2,200 individuals, ages 16 years, 0 months, to 90 years, 11 months, representative of the 2005 U.S. Census in terms of age, sex, and race/ethnicity and sampling 49 states of the United States (excluding Alaska). Drawing heavily from theories of fluid reasoning, the WAIS-IV yields a Full Scale IQ, a composite of the Verbal Comprehension, Perceptual Reasoning, Working Memory and Processing Speed index scores (Climie & Rostad, 2011; Hartman, 2009). The WAIS-IV has a high internal consistency reliability with split-half reliability of .98 for the composite score. The test–retest reliability is also high, .96 for the composite score. The validity of the WAIS-IV is supported by high correlations of WAIS-IV scores with scores obtained from measures assessing similar constructs and low correlations with instruments measuring different constructs (Climie & Rostad, 2011).

The WAIS has been adapted for use with children. The *Wechsler Intelligence Scale for Children* (WISC-IV), published in 2003, is well respected and widely used (Baron, 2005). It can be administered to children ages 6 through 16 years, 11 months (Kranzler & Floyd, 2013; Roberts & Lipnevich, 2012; Weiss, Saklofske, & Prifitera, 2003). The norming sample consists of 2,200 individuals in 49 of the United States (excluding Hawaii), with equal number of males and females in each age group and ethnic–racial composition matching the 2000 U.S. Census. Similar to the adult test (the WAIS-IV), the WISC-IV yields four index scores and a Full Scale IQ, a composite of the Verbal Comprehension, Perceptual Reasoning, Working Memory, and Processing Speed scale scores. Verbal Comprehension is assessed by vocabulary, similarities, and comprehension subtests; Perceptual Reasoning by block design, picture concepts, matrix reasoning; Working memory by digit span and letter number sequencing; and Processing Speed by coding and symbol search subtests. See Figure 8.2 for a description of the subscales used in the index scores. The composite score and index scores have means of 100 and standard deviations of 15, with a high internal consistency reliability (.98). Concurrent validity is supported by correlations with other

---

Verbal Comprehension

- *Vocabulary:* shown a picture or a word is spoken, child asked to name the object or define the word
- *Similarities:* presented pairs of words, child asked to describe how the pairs are similar
- *Comprehension:* asked questions dealing with everyday problems requiring understanding of social rules and concepts

Perceptual Reasoning

- *Block Design:* shown pictures of designs in two colors, child asked to construct a matching design with plastic blocks (timed)
- *Picture Concepts:* shown rows of pictured objects, child asked to indicate the picture from each row that shares a characteristic in common with a single picture from the other rows
- *Matrix Reasoning:* shown matrices or visual patterns with something missing, child asked to select missing part from a set of options

Working Memory

- *Digit Span:* lists of digits, child asked to recall either in order of presentation (forward span) or reverse order of presentation (backward span)
- *Letter–Number Sequencing:* presented with mixed series of digits and letters, child asked to recall by first repeating the numbers in order (low to high), followed by the letters in alphabetical order

Processing Speed

- *Coding:* shown key with common shapes or numbers paired with symbols, child asked to put correct symbol under a grid made up of shapes and letters (timed)
- *Symbol Search:* shown a target geometric symbol, child asked whether the target appears in a group of presented geometric symbols (timed)

FIGURE 8.2. Scales of the WISC-IV.

standardized measures of intelligence. Because sometimes information is needed about preschool children, the *Wechsler Preschool and Primary Scale of Intelligence–Fourth Edition* (WPPSI-IV; Wechsler, 2012) was developed for use with children 2 years, 6 months, through 7 years, 7 months (Kranzler & Floyd, 2013).

Other Intelligence Tests for Children

Although the Weschler scales are the most commonly used measures of intelligence and the Stanford–Binet has the longest history, other intelligence tests are available and also used to assess children's intellectual abilities. One example is the *Kaufman Assessment Battery for Children, Second Revision* (KABC-II; Kaufman & Kaufman, 1983, 2004), which is based on multiple perspectives of intelligence, particularly CHC, and standardized to be used with children ages 3 years to 18 years, 11 months (Bain & Gray, 2008; Cucina & Howardson, 2016). One strength of the KABC-II is assessing the intelligence of diverse populations and children with limited language skills (Roberts & Lipnevich, 2012). Another measure that like the Stanford–Binet can be used with a wide age group is the *Woodcock–Johnson III Test of Cognitive Skills*. Standardized for ages 2 to 90 plus years, the WJ-III also has wide applicability across diverse populations (Roberts & Lipnevich, 2012). All of the intelligence tests described in this section are individually administered, entail a substantial investment of time (45–90 minutes), and most require trained administrators. Brief intelligence tests, ones that take 15–30 minutes to administer, are also available and can be used for screening purposes. These include the *Kaufman Brief Intelligence Test, Second Edition* and the *Wechsler Abbreviated Scale of Intelligence–Second Edition* (Bain & Jaspers, 2010; Kranzler & Floyd, 2013).

All intelligence tests with excellent reliability and validity are individually administered, including the ones described thus far, although some tests of mental ability that can be administered to groups of children have acceptable reliability and validity. Since group measures are not as reliable as individual measures of intelligence, they are not used for placing children in special programs. Group-administered tests such as the *Otis–Lennon School Ability Test, Eighth Edition* (OLSAT), or the *Cognitive Abilities Test* (CogAT) can provide helpful information to researchers and educators (Sattler, 2002; Braden, 2003; Miller et al., 2013). As with all standardized tests, users should take care to read the manuals and supporting materials carefully before administering the tests or attempting to interpret the scores.

Bias in Mental Testing

As introduced in Chapter 6, there has been a historic tendency in the United States to denigrate the intelligence of minorities and to conclude that their minds are biologically inferior. For example, intelligence data collected during World War I was interpreted to mean that recent immigrants (e.g., Irish, Italian, and Swiss) were not as intelligent as people born in the United States. Group differences in scores on intelligence and achievement tests continue to be observed (for example, between Asians and whites, whites and blacks, males and females). Some have pointed to such differences as being due to genetic or biological factors (Herrnstein & Murray, 1994; Lynn, 2006), a perspective that has led to controversy and extensive debate (Hunt

& Carlson, 2007; Sternberg, Grigorenko, & Kidd, 2005). Others have emphasized the impact of sociocultural factors, such as socioeconomic status, to explain some of the group differences observed on intelligence and achievement tests (Sattler, 2002). As noted in Chapter 6, although the achievement gap between black–white and Hispanic–white students has narrowed (Yeung, 2012), the SES achievement gap between high-income and low-income groups has widened in the last 40 years and is now twice as large as the black–white achievement gap (Ford, 2016; Valent & Newark, 2016). Another source of group differences may be stereotype threat. As discussed in Chapter 6, Steele and Aronson (1995) argued that standardized testing can be threatening because of the possibility that the test will confirm a negative stereotype. Knowledge of a stereotype about performance in the domain being tested and situational cues that invoke the stereotype activate a physiological stress response and heightened performance monitoring, which impair performance on the test.

What else might explain group differences on standardized intelligence tests or achievement tests? Are there potential systematic biases in intellectual testing that put some groups at a disadvantage relative to others (Geisinger, 2015a; Graves & Blake, 2016; Reynolds & Kaiser, 2003; Reynolds & Ramsay, 2003)? If so, how can these sources of test bias be addressed?

Potential Sources of Test Bias

Bias can be introduced in tests in a number of ways (Kranzler & Floyd, 2013; Worrell & Roberson, 2016). First, the *content of items* can tap concepts and experiences that are more familiar to some groups than to others. For example, the vocabulary used to test a concept may be unfamiliar to some people taking the test. Although test constructors attempt to eliminate "content bias," even experts in a culture cannot reliably identify items that will pose difficulty for children in their culture (Jensen, 1976; Sandoval & Mille, 1980). Fortunately, in well-constructed standardized tests, high correlations in the difficulty level of items across populations are found (Reynolds & Kaiser, 2003), thereby reducing the likelihood that some items are particularly difficult for minority groups.

A second possible bias concerns the *predictive validity of the tests*. Some tests may predict educational or other types of successes better for some groups than for others. Well-constructed tests, however, predict equally well across racial and cultural groups. For example, if the purpose of the test, such as the SAT and ACT, is to predict "Will this person do well in this college?," it is unbiased if the answer it generates is "correct" about the *same* proportion of times for *all* groups.

A third potential source of bias is in the *samples* (i.e., predominantly white, English-speaking) used to norm standardized tests. In particular, there may be sociocultural differences in understanding what it means to take a test and what the long-term implications of tests are (Rodriguez, 1992; Weiss, Prifitera, & Munoz, 2015). Producers of well-constructed tests are aware of the need for representative national norming samples, however, and they make the effort to generate such samples (Reynolds & Kaiser, 2003; Sattler, 2002).

A fourth potential source of bias is *mismatch between the test language and the primary language of the test-taker* (Geisinger, 2003, 2015b; Ochoa, 2003). As discussed in Chapter 6, laws in some parts of the United States required that all children be tested in English and decisions about school placement into special education or giftedness classes were based on these tests (Donlon, 1992; Rodriguez, 1992).

When that was the case, disproportionately high numbers of Spanish-speaking children ended up in special education classes. and disproportionately low numbers of Spanish-speaking children experienced accelerated offerings (Pennock-Román, 1992; Schmeiser, 1992). Ability tests administered in English to Spanish-speaking students sometimes do not correlate at all with ability tests administered in Spanish and may grossly underestimate intelligence.

A fifth potential source of bias is *mismatch between the race and/or culture of the examiner and the test-taker* (Geisinger, 2003; Ochoa, 2003). The race of an examiner, however, apparently does not make a difference in the test score earned by a person being examined (Graziano, Varca, & Levy, 1982). What does seem to matter is "familiarity" between the examiner and the person being tested, with personal familiarity between them boosting the performance of the examinee slightly. The "familiarity effect" seems to be especially large for lower socioeconomic populations (Fuchs & Fuchs, 1986).

In conclusion, we are more sensitive now than ever before about potential sources of bias in intelligence tests and other standardized measures. Fortunately, test constructors are committed to producing reliable, valid, and fair tests (see also the discussion about testing minority students in Chapter 6), not only because it is the right thing to do but also because those who use tests have become increasingly knowledgeable about potential test bias. Educators should be on guard with respect to these sources of bias when selecting tests for use in assessing people and in interpreting test data already collected.

Learner Diversity

Children can differ in many ways as learners. First, we introduce three common classifications of exceptional learners: (1) gifted students, (2) students with learning disabilities, and (3) individuals with intellectual disability. Then we provide an overview of students who exhibit general characteristics that make them at risk for school difficulties. These include students living in poverty, students with a serious disease or medical condition, students who have been victims of environmental assaults, and substance abusers. Another very large group of students at risk for school failure, students who are non-native English speakers, are considered in detail in Chapter 7. Practices for including these diverse learners in schools are described in the Applying Developmental Theory to Educational Contexts special feature (see Box 8.3).

Giftedness

The intellectually gifted are a great societal resource, with some of the gifted becoming great writers, physicians, statesmen, and business, academic, and industrial leaders. The gifted are a diverse group. One distinction is between **prodigies**, those who are very talented in one particular domain, and those who are generally highly intelligent but not exceptionally talented in any one area. Thus, the gifted include both specialists and generalists (Feldman, 1986).

What defines a gifted student? Federal regulations, outlined in the No Child Left Behind Act of 2002 and based on the Jacob Javits Act of 1988, describes giftedness as high-performance capability in intellectual, creative, and/or artistic areas.

Applying Developmental Theory to Educational Contexts

BOX 8.3. Inclusion of Diverse Learners in U.S. Classrooms

In the past, some students with disabilities were placed in regular classrooms where they received few, if any, special services. More students with disabilities, however, were placed in **self-contained classrooms** where they were taught by special education specialists and had little contact with regular instructional programs, or they attended separate schools designed for students with particular special needs (such as schools for the visually or hearing impaired, or schools for students with intellectual disabilities). Today, students with disabilities often take their place next to nondisabled students in regular education classrooms. Educational practices for students with disabilities have changed greatly in response to criticisms of the failure to maximize the educational opportunities for all students and the passage of a series of laws beginning with Public Law 94-142 in 1975.

Public Law 94-142 stipulates that students with disabilities be provided a free, appropriate education in the **least restrictive environment**. The term "least restrictive environment" is interpreted as meaning that students with disabilities must be educated with their nondisabled peers to the maximum extent appropriate. This provision has led to **mainstreaming**, or the practice of placing students with disabilities as often as possible in regular classrooms with their nondisabled peers, rather than in separate classrooms or schools. Implementation of the principle of least restrictive environment can range from **inclusion,** in which all instruction is received in the regular classroom (often including consultation or collaboration with special education teachers or other specialists), through temporary removal to a **resource room** for special services, to placement in a self-contained special education classroom.

One of the most important provisions of Public Law 94-142, elaborated and revised by subsequent legislation, was to require the development of an **individualized education program (IEP).** The IEP describes a particular student's disability and outlines an educational plan to address the student's learning difficulties. The team that draws up the IEP is typically comprised of the special education teacher, the regular education teacher, school administrators, special services provider(s), and the parent(s) or guardians. Other advocates for the child may also participate in the meeting. An IEP has the following components:

- A summary of the student's present level of educational performance, both academic and nonacademic, based on sources such as standardized tests and classroom observations.

- A listing of long-term goals for the students (typically annual goals) and a plan for support services the student needs to reach the goals.

- A method for evaluating whether or not the student attains the goals and a plan for distributing reports of evaluations.

- A plan for participation in statewide assessments, including possible individual accommodations for testing or a rationale for alternative assessments.

Thus, many educators work in teams to provide appropriate instruction for students who have a wide range of special needs. The three common classifications of learning differences—giftedness, learning disabilities, and intellectual disability—are discussed more fully in this chapter. Other needs include physical and sensory disabilities, such as visual and hearing impairments; speech and communication disorders, such as articulation difficulties and stuttering; and emotional and behavioral problems, such as conduct disorders, including aggressiveness and withdrawal.

There is no current federal mandate to provide special services to the gifted, and there's considerable range in how the various states define giftedness (Kranzler & Floyd, 2013). One criterion is IQ score, and although many different IQ cutoff points have been used as the starting point for giftedness, typically scores of 130 are considered the lower part of the gifted range. Of course, a high IQ score alone does not define giftedness. For example, there are underachievers who perform well below how they are capable of performing based on their IQ scores. Some students are much stronger on some subscales of intelligence tests than on other subscales, so their overall IQ score does not adequately represent their giftedness. And using intelligence test scores only may lead to the underrepresentation of minority groups in those identified as gifted (Ford, 2012). Not surprisingly, some have argued in favor of expanding the definition of giftedness beyond being a label for the upper end of the IQ distribution (Richert, 1991). Consider, for example, the discussion of Gardner's multiple intelligences earlier in this chapter. A person can have much greater intelligence in music, or math, or for physical activities than for other competencies.

Prodigies

Who is a prodigy? John Radford offers one definition (1990, p. 200): "Statistically, a prodigy comes at the extreme end of a distribution of achievement in a particular activity." Examples of well-known prodigies include Wolfgang Amadeus Mozart in classical music, Stevie Wonder in popular music, Bobby Fischer in chess, Marie Curie in science, Tiger Woods in golf, and Wayne Gretsky in hockey.

How can the giftedness of talented individuals be fostered? What variables influence whether a person with a great talent becomes a leading figure in a field of specialization? If the talent is there, how can we increase the odds of producing a great mathematician, scientist, athlete, or musician? The following factors are often mentioned as important to the development of prodigious genius (Bloom, 1985; Feldhusen, 1986; Feldman, 1988; Nandagopal & Ericsson, 2012; Pleiss & Feldhusen, 1995; Radford, 1990; Tannenbaum, 1986):

- Instruction related to exceptional abilities. Prodigies benefit from a series of teachers of increasing sophistication who coach the student in the area of his or her giftedness.
- Opportunities and willingness to engage in extensive goal-directed practice with instructive feedback, practice that is initially designed by a teacher or coach and later self-designed.
- Sustained motivation to develop his or her ability, often to the point of obsession where it is as much play as work.
- Parents who are generally nurturing but who are also supportive of the development of their child's particular talent.

This list makes it clear that the development of prodigious talent is the happy coincidence of many factors. A talented child is raised by a supportive family; the child is excited by his or her special competency and dedicated to developing it; and the talent is something valued by society at that moment in time.

For the child who does not have parents who are committed to developing his or her talent, school usually is society's best shot at directing the talent appropriately.

Emerging genius requires some creative linking of resources to educate well. For example, conventional educational options may not serve well the brilliant fifth-grade computer programmer. Perhaps a solution for this child would be to match him or her with community members who are skilled programmers. Such individuals may be able to introduce an exceptional student to a much larger world of computer technology than anyone in the school could offer.

People Who Are Generally Highly Intelligent

Suppose we accept an IQ score of 130 as the cutoff for high general ability. Since that figure represents roughly only 2% of the population (Kranzler & Floyd, 2013), it is obvious that general high intelligence is a scarce resource; yet many educators encounter it on a regular basis. For example, if a high school teacher interacts with approximately 125 students each day, it is likely that two or three of those students would have IQ scores exceeding 130. Thus, all educators should have a working understanding of highly intelligent students. One of the most influential sources of information for those interested in learning more about the development of highly intelligent individuals was Terman's longitudinal study of the gifted.

Terman's Study of the Gifted

Genius fascinated Lewis Terman, a professor at Stanford University. During the years when he was developing the Stanford–Binet test, Terman encountered a number of children who scored in the 140 range or higher. He was absorbed by the tales the parents of these children told of their sons and daughters reading and writing early. Terman knew of the stereotypes: Geniuses were quirky, eccentric, and even unhealthy. He also realized, however, that most of the geniuses he was meeting were well adjusted and happy (Shurkin, 1992; Terman, 1925; Terman & Oden, 1947, 1959).

In the early 1920s, he began a longitudinal study of very bright children. He administered intelligence tests and other assessments to a large number of children throughout California. A sample of 643 children was identified as gifted, with a criterion of IQ scores of 135 or higher. Eventually, other children from outside the geographical areas searched were added to the sample, as was a group of children with special talents, so that the final sample was over 1,500 children.

Contrary to the stereotypes, Terman's gifted children were healthier and slightly superior physically to the population as a whole. They excelled in school and often moved ahead in the curriculum. Half of the sample was able to read before they began school. They tended to graduate from high school early and entered college at a young age, where they typically performed extremely well. In addition to being academically successful, these gifted people were also socially adept and accepted by their peers.

As adults, the participants in Terman's study were more likely to earn doctorates and professional degrees than members of the general population, with the majority eventually earning some kind of graduate degree. Quite a few excelled in their fields, and their incomes were also well above population averages. Not surprisingly, given the historical era of the study's time frame, a significant portion of the women in Terman's study became non-income-producing homemakers.

The majority of Terman's adults reported being very satisfied with their life and life's work. In general, they reported that personal satisfaction was more important than occupational satisfaction. In addition, alcoholism was low for the group; so was criminality. Terman's adults married other bright people and gave birth to children with IQ scores that were well above average. In the twilight of their lives, the surviving Terman men and women appeared happy and mentally active. Terman's study is one of the most visible pieces of evidence that gifted people tend to be happy and to be socioemotionally healthy (Kern, Hampson, Goldberg, & Friedman, 2012; Reis & Renzulli, 2004).

One interesting comparison is between the very successful children in the Terman study and the minority who were less successful. The successes had parents who encouraged them to achieve in school and to go to college. Thus, as with prodigies, parents seemed to play a guiding, shaping role in the lives of successful people with high intelligence. Ability alone does not guarantee great success.

Terman's study is sometimes criticized on the basis of how the children were selected to participate. Many of the children had been nominated by their teachers as exceptionally bright. These teachers may have been biased toward the nomination of well-adjusted children, those children doing well in a conventional school. Some very intelligent children may not have been nominated because they did not do well in school. Other children were identified in a haphazard fashion by those familiar with the study, such as the brothers and sisters of nominated children. Although some precautions were supposedly taken to reduce bias due to language and cultural differences, the total sample included much lower proportions of minorities than were present in California in the 1920s. The initial sample was also biased toward the inclusion of boys and children from middle-class and upper-middle-class families.

Terman's study is not the only longitudinal research on the development of gifted children. For example, in the 1970s, researchers began to study 13-year-olds who performed in the top 1% on measures of mathematical reasoning. For both the males and females who participated in the study, nearly twice as many males as females, mathematical talent predicted success as measured by creative accomplishments and leadership in chosen occupations nearly 40 years later (Lubinski, Benbow, & Kell, 2014). Although there were differences in occupational and income patterns, both males and females were satisfied with their lives and their careers.

The evidence of longitudinal studies belies the stereotypes about the maladjustment of the gifted. A meta-analysis of studies of mental disorders observed in the gifted also indicates no differences between the gifted and nongifted in terms of depression or suicidal ideation and suggests lower levels of anxiety in the gifted (Martin, Burns, & Schonlau, 2010). Yet, stereotypes prevail. In a recent study, preservice teachers associated maladjustment problems more strongly with gifted males than with males of average ability (Preckel, Baudson, Krolak-Schwerdt, & Glock, 2015).

Other researchers have added to our understanding of the gifted by analyzing specific aspects of the information processing of gifted individuals compared to the population at large (see also Chapter 4). This research has illuminated ways in which the intellectually gifted differ from other children.

Strategies and Metacognition

The gifted use more advanced strategies than peers of average intelligence on memory and problem-solving tasks (Jackson & Butterfield, 1986; Robinson & Kingsley, 1977; Steiner & Carr, 2003). They also have superior metacognition (Hannah &

Shore, 1995; Snyder, Nietfeld, & Linnenbrink-Garcia, 2011; Sternberg, 1981). Gifted children are more likely to continue to use effective strategies and to transfer them from one task to another task where the strategies might be useful (Chan, 1996; Cho & Ahn, 2003; Coyle, Read, Gaultney, & Bjorklund, 1998). Some gifted underachievers, students whose classroom performance does not match what would be predicted based on their scores on intelligence tests, have not acquired effective study strategies (Ford, 2012). Underachieving gifted children, however, can benefit from instruction in strategies for accomplishing academic tasks (Jausovec, 1994; Manning, Glasner, & Smith, 1996; Muir-Broaddus, 1995).

Processing Efficiency: Interactions between Working Memory, Speed of Processing, and Knowledge

Gifted people process information more efficiently than do other people (Jausovec, 1998; Kanevsky, 1995; Saccuzzo, Johnson, & Guertin, 1994). For example, they can scan a set of items being held in memory more rapidly than people of average intelligence (Keating & Bobbitt, 1978; McCauley, Kellas, Dugas, & DeVillis, 1976). They also can retrieve information more rapidly than can people of average intelligence (Hunt, Lunneborg, & Lewis, 1975; Jackson & Myers, 1982). Gifted students process information more efficiently than do less talented people, with their superior efficiency freeing up more of their working memory capacity for consideration and manipulation of strategies and other knowledge.

The gifted also have great facility in combining information and working with knowledge to produce new ideas and solve problems (Feldman, 1982; Geary & Brown, 1991; Nandagopal & Ericsson, 2012; Sternberg & Davidson, 1983). They acquire early mastery of knowledge in the field in which they are gifted. and their knowledge is deeper and broader than that of people of average intelligence (Feldhusen, 1986; Gagné & Dick, 1983; Tannenbaum, 1983).

Motivation

It is critical for the gifted to maintain their motivation to achieve. This is especially true for prodigies whose performances at early ages are remarkable but, as they mature, they must be committed to continue to excel in order to sustain their superior levels of performance (Nandagopal & Ericsson, 2012). The gifted typically exhibit a strong commitment to excellent performance in one or more fields (Clinkenbeard, 2012; Terman & Oden, 1959) and display high positive self-concepts (Feldhusen, 1986; Feldhusen & Kolloff, 1981; Ringness, 1961). Some research indicates that gifted boys express higher self-confidence and are more motivated than gifted girls in academic settings, although this pattern appears relevant for only some academic domains, such as math, and depends on how academic tasks are presented (Dai, 2002; Preckel, Goetz, Pekrun, & Kleine, 2008). Behavioral signs of motivation in classroom contexts include reading ahead, studying even when a test is not anticipated, and seeking out information from a wide variety of sources. Underachieving gifted students sometimes don't apply themselves to academic tasks for a variety of reasons, perhaps in response to negative peer pressure, because they no longer believe in the value of academic tasks, or as a way of saving face in response to academic challenges (Ford, 2012; Snyder & Linnenbrink-Garcia, 2013).

Researchers have identified instructional practices that support continued superior academic performance in the gifted (Callahan, Moon, Oh, Azano, & Hailey, 2015; Ford, 2012). These include incorporating choices and options in classroom activities, providing opportunities for independent work, providing less basic detail in presentations, and moving at an accelerated pace. Effective curricular materials for the gifted are more numerous, more in depth and complex, and present diverse perspectives about a given topic. Technology can be a tool used to meet the motivational needs of the gifted in classroom contexts (Housand & Housand, 2012).

Learning Disabilities

Students identified as having learning disabilities exhibit "unexpected academic underachievement" (language from the Individuals with Disabilities Education Improvement Act (IDEIA), Public Law 108-446, passed in 2004) in specific academic domains such as reading, writing or math but otherwise perform within expected levels of achievement for age and grade (Kranzler & Floyd, 2013; Lewanski & Lovett, 2014). The students are of average or above-average intelligence, have intact hearing and vision, and the discrepancy between intelligence and achievement is not due the absence of adequate educational support or emotional disturbance.

Approximately 5% of students are classified as having learning disabilities and account for approximately 30–40% of the students receiving special education in schools (Kranzler & Floyd, 2013; McFarland et al., 2017). Eighty percent of the students identified with learning disabilities are classified as having reading disabilities, although the nature of the reading disability varies (Lewanski & Lovett, 2014). For example, some students exhibit deficits in word recognition, either in decoding or sight reading. The inability to decode words despite intensive educational efforts is called **dyslexia.** Other students with reading disabilities are able to recognize words but are not able to do so fluently and/or experience difficulty in comprehending once decoding is accomplished. Disabilities in writing vary, including difficulties with handwriting, spelling, and grammar as well as disorders in written expression, such as difficulty producing organized pieces of writing containing sufficient detail to achieve an intended purpose. Writing disability often, but not always, co-occurs with reading disability. Still other students are identified as having a math disability, specifically deficits in calculation skills and/or mathematical reasoning.

Despite advances in brain-imaging techniques and an accompanying expansion in research data about brain function, the analysis of neurological deficits underlying learning disabilities is only just beginning (Byrnes, 2012; Kranzler & Floyd, 2013; Lewanski & Lovett, 2014; Shaywitz & Shaywitz, 2014). Skilled reading is a complex activity involving phonological processing (sound), orthographic processing (visual), and making connections to semantic memory. Specific brain areas are activated for each of these activities, and understanding of how these activities interact is rudimentary at best. Phonological deficits are clearly related to decoding difficulties, and differences in the brain functioning of students with reading disability have been noted. Still, many more studies are needed to identify the regions of the brain associated with normal processing of academic tasks, to study how increases in expertise in typically developing children is reflected in brain functioning, and then to look for consistent differences in children with disabilities. It is also important to keep in mind that experience impacts brain development, so observed differences in the brain functioning of skilled readers may be the result of experiences these students had as they developed the expertise rather than a difference that produced the expertise. Brain plasticity (see Chapter 2) also means that early interventions—for example, to support emergent phonological processing in the case of reading—can be effective (Byrnes, 2012; Kranzler & Floyd, 2013).

Although learning disabilities were not first defined in terms of information processing (see also Chapter 4), analyzing the information-processing characteristics of students with learning disabilities compared to typical learners has enhanced our understanding of learning disabilities. The results of this research have influenced the design of instructional interventions that increase the academic performance of students with learning disabilities.

Strategies and Metacognition

Students with learning disabilities are less likely than normally achieving students to use strategies for performing academic tasks (Bauer, 1977a; Torgesen & Goldman, 1977). Fortunately, students with learning disabilities are able to carry out effective strategies when instructed to do so (Bauer, 1977b; Mastropieri, Sweda, & Scruggs, 2000; Tarver, Hallahan, Kauffman, & Ball, 1976; Torgesen, 1977). For example, students with reading disabilities benefit from instruction in reading comprehension strategies (Anderson, 1992; Berkeley, Mastropieri & Scruggs, 2010; Gersten, Fuchs, Williams, & Baker, 2001; Klingner, Vaughn, & Schumm, 1998). Students who have writing difficulties can learn to use strategic interventions such as the plan–write–revise approach to composition (Gersten & Baker, 2001; Graham & Harris, 2003; Harris et al., 2010; see also Chapter 4). Students who struggle to learn mathematics benefit from instruction in problem-solving strategies (Fuchs & Fuchs, 2003; Montague, Enders, & Dietz, 2011; Montague, Krawec, Enders, & Dietz, 2014). Effective strategy instruction for students with learning disabilities includes extensive attention to metacognition, including efforts to increase student awareness of when and where the strategies can be used, and many prompts encouraging students to monitor their own performance (Berkeley et al., 2010; Swanson & Sáez, 2003; Wong, Harris, Graham, & Butler, 2003).

Processing Efficiency: Interactions between Working Memory, Speed of Processing, and Knowledge

Students with learning disabilities make less efficient use of their limited-capacity working memory than normally achieving students (Hulme & Mackenzie, 1992; Swanson, 2003, 2016). In a meta-analysis of 50 years of research, Peng and Fuchs (2016) found that children with reading disabilities, mathematical disabilities, and disabilities in both reading and writing all exhibited deficits in working memory compared to typically developing children. Many students with learning disabilities have difficulty strategically allocating attention and inhibiting inappropriate responses, and so much of their attention may be diverted that little of their capacity is available for the task at hand (Cutting & Denckla, 2003; Lewanski & Lovett, 2014; Swanson & Alloway, 2012). These problems are compounded by lacking prior knowledge possessed by many others, which reduces the likelihood of forming meaningful "chunks," which are easier to hold in working memory.

Motivation

Students with learning disabilities are more passive than other students (Torgesen, 1975, 1977). They can become caught in a terrible cycle. Because they have done poorly in school, they think of themselves as academic failures—they begin to believe they are stupid. Such a belief does nothing to motivate academic effort, which results in additional failure, which in turn strengthens the perception of low ability (Borkowski, Carr, Rellinger, & Pressley, 1990; Licht, 1983, 1992; see also Chapter 9). Consequently, compared to normally achieving children, students with learning disabilities lack academic self-esteem, and they expect to do poorly in school (Butkowski & Willows, 1980; Rogers & Saklofske, 1985; Winne, Woodlands, & Wong, 1982).

This situation is not hopeless. Students with learning disabilities can learn to attribute their successes and failures to effort rather than to factors that are out of their control, such as ability or luck. When they do make "effort attributions," their motivation improves (Dev, 1998). As students are taught strategies that improve their task-related performances, they can also learn to attribute their task performances to use of the strategies (Berkeley, Mastropieri & Scruggs, 2011; Borkowski et al., 1990; Licht, 1992). The long-term commitment of students with learning disabilities to the use of new strategies increases when they understand that using these strategies is improving their performance (see also Chapter 4).

Other instructional procedures also increase the sense of competence and control in students with learning disabilities (Licht, 1992). Focusing students' attention on successful attainment of concrete and immediate goals, such as getting today's problems correct, increases student self-efficacy. **Self-efficacy** refers to students' beliefs that their performances are under their own control (Bandura & Schunk, 1981; see also Chapter 9). In contrast, focusing on progress toward long-term goals, such as on how many more days it will take to cover the entire unit of material, has much less of an impact on sense of self-efficacy. In addition, modeling can increase the sense of self-efficacy. When students see another student like themselves struggling with a task, but finally accomplishing it, their self-efficacy is likely to improve (Schunk, Hanson, & Cox, 1987).

Intellectual Disability

Intellectual disability (ID) is the term used for students who display deficits in intellectual functioning and in adaptive behaviors identified in infancy, childhood, or adolescence (Kranzler & Floyd, 2013). Thus, individuals with intellectual disability exhibit both limitations in intelligence and problems adapting to the environment beginning when they are young. Federal laws such as the IDEIA, passed in 2004, and Rosa's Law, passed in 2010, eliminated the terms *mental retardation* and *mentally retarded* from the federal legal code, but those terms still may exist in regulations at the state level. Individuals with IQs below 70 and those who exhibit deficits in at least two of three areas of adaptive functioning (conceptual, social, and practical) would be considered to have ID. There are levels of severity of ID, *mild* (IQ 50–55 to 70), *moderate* (IQ 35–40 to 50–55); *severe* (IQ 20–25 to 35–40), and *profound* (IQ below 20–25), but the majority are classified as mild (Witwer, Lawton, & Aman, 2014). The best intelligence tests for identifying intellectual disability are those that include individuals with disabilities in their norming groups and have techniques for considering the impact of sensory and motor disabilities, which may occur with ID, upon test performance. Adaptive behaviors are typically assessed by behavior scales, used by multiple observers in a variety of settings.

Approximately two-thirds of ID cases are traced to causes such as genetic disorders, abnormal prenatal development, birth difficulties, perinatal or childhood illness, or trauma as described below (Witwer et al., 2014):

- Genetic causes include chromosomal abnormalities and abnormal genes, for example, as in Down syndrome, fragile X syndrome, and Williams syndrome (Batshaw & Tuchman, 2002; Evans & Hamerton, 1985; Roizen, 2002).

- Prenatal causes include disease and infection, such as syphilis, rubella, and zika, exposure to radiation; malnutrition; and exposure to lead, alcohol, and other drugs (Beker, Farber, & Yanni, 2002; Berg, 1985; Spiegel & Bonwit, 2002; Stern, 1985; Wunsch, Conlon, & Scheidt, 2002).

- Perinatal factors, such as injury at birth, including oxygen deprivation (Berg, 1985; Ward & McCune, 2002), low birthweight, and premature birth, which results in greater susceptibility to injury such as brain hemorrhage (Berg, 1985; Rais-Bahramai, Short, & Batshaw, 2002).

- Neonatal hazards, including head injury, disease (e.g., meningitis), chemical assault (e.g., lead exposure), and malnutrition

- Postnatal (childhood onset), due to a devastating illness (e.g., meningitis), severe traumatic brain injury, chemical assault (e.g., lead), and malnutrition (Berg, 1985; Stern, 1985).

Approximately 1% of the population is identified as having intellectually disability, with males more often identified than females (Witwer et al., 2014). Some of the causes of ID such as disorders related to the X chromosome are more likely to be observed in males and males are more affected by prenatal factors. Socioeconomic status is also related to incidence of intellectual disability, with low-SES individuals more likely to be exposed to a variety of toxins, to experience malnutrition, receive poor health care, and live in less intellectually stimulating and more stressful home environments.

In general, the long-term prospects for independent functioning vary with the degree of intellectual disability. Most individuals with severe and profound intellectual disability require substantial social services and support for their entire lives. But many individuals with mild intellectual disability manage to live reasonably independent lives as adults (Batshaw & Shapiro, 2002). Intervention in the first 5 years of life that involves intensive, direct engagement of multiple types of support with long-term follow-up can have lasting positive effects (Witwer et al., 2014; see also Chapter 2).

There is nothing magical about establishing an IQ of 70 as the cutoff for considering an individual to have intellectual disability (Burns, 2003). In fact, there is a long history of considering people who have IQ scores between 70 and 85 as borderline for intellectual disability, with these students at greater risk for failure in school than students with average intelligence (IQ scores around 100). Four times as many people are in this borderline group, with IQ scores between 70 and 85, as people in the group with IQ scores of 70 or less (Zetlin & Murtaugh, 1990).

Although intellectual disability continues to be defined in terms of performance on intelligence tests, it is useful to analyze intellectual disability in terms of the components of information processing. Thus, we describe briefly the information-processing characteristics of children with intellectual disability.

Strategies and Metacognition

Individuals with intellectual disability are less likely to develop learning strategies than are normally intelligent individuals (Ellis, 1979). When given strategy instruction, however, students with intellectual disability can learn to use a variety of techniques, including rehearsal, categorization, organization, and elaboration (Bray, Fletcher, & Turner, 1997; Hua, Morgan, Kaldenbergy, & Goo, 2012; Hua, Woods-Groves, Ford, & Nobles, 2014; Joseph & Konrad, 2009), Students with intellectual disability, however, do not regulate their use of the strategies that they know, at least not as well as children with normal intelligence (Bebko & Luhaorg, 1998; Brown, 1974). Moreover, students with intellectual ability exhibit less self-regulation and metacognition than younger, typically developing children of the same mental age (Nader-Grosbois, 2014). Successful strategy instruction for students with intellectual disability includes metacognitive instruction, such as explicitly describing why the strategy is effective and when to use it. Self-regulation during strategy use is more likely to be observed in students with intellectual disability who have higher verbal competence (Nader-Grosbois, 2014).

Processing Efficiency: Interactions between Working Memory, Speed of Processing, and Knowledge

Working memory capacity is more limited in students with intellectual disability than in students with normal intelligence (Alloway, 2010; Rosenquist, Conners, & Roskos-Ewoldsen, 2003; Schuchardt, Gebhardt, & Maehler, 2010). It is uncertain whether students with intellectual disability actually have less neurological capacity or if it only seems so because they use their capacity inefficiently (Brewer, 1987; Henry & MacLean, 2002; Numminen, Service, & Ruoppila, 2002). Although students with intellectual disability can learn to do many tasks faster with practice, they remain far slower than normally intelligent students who are given equivalent practice (Brewer, 1987; Nettlebeck & Wilson, 1997). In addition, students with intellectual disability do not possess as much knowledge of the world and academic content areas as normally intelligent students. This means that they are less able than normally intelligent students to "chunk" information into larger units that are more easily held in working memory, such as recoding the sequence of numbers 7–4–7 as "747 jet" or 4–1–1 as "directory assistance." In summary, a variety of factors, such as working memory capacity, knowledge, motivation, and strategies, combine to reduce the efficiency of processing by students with intellectual disability compared to students with normal intelligence (Bray et al., 1997).

Motivation

Students with intellectual disability often undermine their own learning by making attributions that reduce future effort (see also Chapter 9; Merighi, Edison, & Zigler, 1990; Zigler & Hodapp, 1986). When students with intellectual disability fail at tasks, they tend to blame themselves more than do normally intelligent students (MacMillan & Knopf, 1971). Their failures lead them to doubt whether they could possibly solve problems presented to them and increase their dependency on others to provide solutions to them (Achenbach & Zigler, 1968; Zigler & Balla, 1982). Ironically, this dependency is particularly a problem for students with intellectual disability since they tend to be more wary of helpful adults than other students (Merighi et al., 1990).

The observation that students with intellectual disability have little confidence in themselves as learners or problem solvers may depend on the comparison group and on the learning environment. The competence perceptions of students with intellectual disability are lower than those of typically developing peers matched on the basis of chronological age but are no different than the perceptions of competence of younger, typically developing peers matched on the basis of mental age (Gilmore, Cuskelly, & Browning, 2015; Nader-Grosbois, 2014). Students with intellectual disabilities who attend specialized schools with other students with intellectual disabilities tend to have positive self-perceptions of competence, sometimes overestimating their competence.

Behavior modification, which involves the provision of reinforcement for appropriate behaviors (see also Chapter 5), is often successful and motivating for students with intellectual disabilities (Kiernan, 1985). Behavior modification can improve communication skills, increase attention span, decrease hyperactivity, decrease aggression, and increase social interaction. A variety of reinforcers, ranging from opportunities to interact with others to earning money, are powerful motivators for behavior changes in individuals with intellectual disability.

Ultimately, however, the goal is for individuals with intellectual disability to live independent lives. Self-instruction and self-management techniques, especially if they are generalized to different tasks, can be helpful in learning and maintaining life skills (Smith, Shepley, Alexander, & Ayres, 2015; see also Chapter 5). A wide range of assistive technologies improve self-management and self-instruction in students with disabilities using picture prompts, tactile prompts (e.g., vibration), and auditory prompts to improve performance on everyday tasks (Ayres, Mechling, & Sansosti, 2013; Mechling, 2007). Even first graders with intellectual disability can be taught to use a paper chart and stickers to self-monitor and reduce off-task behavior when working independently (Coughlin, McCoy, Kenzer, Mathur, & Zucker, 2012).

Other Students at Risk for School Difficulties and Failure

Students other than those with identified learning disabilities or intellectual disability are also at risk for school failure. Many different classifications of students who are at risk for school difficulties exist, and within every one of these categories individual differences can be found, with some students functioning much better than others. At-risk students also are more likely to have language problems, to experience difficulties in social relations, and to be slow to acquire problem-solving and decision-making skills (Stevens & Price, 1992). Fortunately, the functioning of at-risk students can often be improved through environmental interventions. A broad generalization is that the earlier the interventions are introduced, the better the results.

For example, *children living in poverty* are at risk for school failure. In 2014, 21% of children in the United States lived in poverty (DeNavas-Walt & Proctor, 2015). Children living in poverty are less likely than age-mates to master basic skills and less likely to be orderly in the classroom—and much more likely to be classified with intellectual disability (Birenbaum, 2002). Moreover, children living in poverty are more likely to be exposed to dangerous levels of lead in their environment (Centers for Disease Control and Prevention, 2000). Lead exposure can reduce IQ scores, impair language, and decrease self-regulation and attention (Canfield, Kreher, Cornwell, & Henderson, 2003; Coscia, Ris, Succop, & Dietrich, 2003; Needleman, 1992; Needleman & Bellinger, 1991; Wasserman et al., 2003). Fortunately, interventions, particularly early interventions, can reduce the impact of living in poverty. For example, early intervention in preschool programs can be successful. Unfortunately, however, only some children living in poverty receive such services (Gilliam & Zigler, 2000; Reynolds, 2000; Ripple & Zigler, 2003). As noted earlier, the achievement gap between low- and high-SES groups has increased over the last 40 years.

Children with medical conditions are also at risk for school failure. Some students who attend school are seriously ill. For some of these students, their illness will be terminal; others will experience complete recovery; and some will live with lifelong disabilities caused by their childhood sickness or injury. Some diseases and injuries cause mental impairment, and some treatments produce side effects that affect participation and progress in school. For example, children who have recovered from cancer are at risk for school failure (Langeveld et al., 2003). The illness and treatment dramatically disrupt normal life and school attendance (Vance & Eiser, 2002). Often, the treatment produces side effects, such as fatigue, that hamper normal academic activities (Zebrack & Chesler, 2002). The treatments also can affect long-term cognitive development negatively (Espy et al., 2001). For example, radiation to the brain because of a brain tumor is likely to impair long-term functioning. How much impairment occurs depends on a number of factors, including the age of the child when the cancer occurs and how much radiation therapy is given (Kieffer-Renaux et al., 2000; Palmer et al., 2003). Chronic diseases can also impact cognitive functioning. Diabetes, for example, can disrupt attentional and memory processes, lowering school achievement (Ryan, van Duinkerken, & Rosano, 2016).

Children who have been exposed prenatally to alcohol or other drugs are at risk for school failure (Wunsch, Conlon, & Scheidt, 2002). More people have intellectual disabilities because of prenatal exposure to alcohol than for any other reason (Burgess & Streissguth, 1992). The child experiencing the full effects of **fetal alcohol syndrome (FAS)** is subject to low birthweight (itself a risk factor), facial disfiguration, and central nervous system damage that can translate into behavioral disorders ranging from retardation to learning disabilities (Lockhart, 2001). The mean IQ score for individuals with fetal alcohol syndrome is about 65–70, with a range of 30 to a little more than 100, which is significantly lower than the distribution of IQ scores in the normal population. Children with FAS often have limited communication abilities, which impact their school performance and their social relationships.

Children and adolescents who are substance abusers are also at risk for school failure. Substance abuse negatively impacts cognition, learning, and memory and also undermines motivation to learn (Bryant, Schulenberg, O'Malley, Bachman, & Johnston, 2003; Chassin, Bountress, Haller, & Wang, 2014; see also Chapter 12).

Chapter Summary and Evaluation

It is difficult to grow up in the United States without experiencing standardized achievement tests, such as the SAT or ACT, or tests used by public school systems to assess student progress. Consumers of information generated by tests must always verify whether the test measures what it claims to measure (*validity*) and whether the test does what it claims to do consistently (*reliability*).

Intelligent functioning is described in a variety of ways, with a great deal of debate about the nature of intelligence. Initial theories differed in the degree to which they emphasized general and specific factors in intelligence, which informed the development of measures of intelligence. Shifts in the nature of thinking abilities across the lifespan are illuminated from analyses of intelligence test data. The quick and somewhat content-less reasoning skills that are the endowment of the young (fluid intelligence) give way with advancing age to content-filled knowledge acquired throughout the lifespan (crystallized intelligence).

Minorities often perform at lower levels than members of the majority population on intelligence tests. Much of this lower performance, however, can be traced to a number of factors, including socioeconomic status and potential sources of test bias.

Although it is something of an oversimplification, in general, evidence of strategy use increases, going from students with intellectual disability to students with learning disabilities, to normally achieving students, to gifted students, as does evidence of metacognition, extensive world knowledge, and motivation supporting academic behaviors. In addition, the speed and efficiency of information processing increases moving from students with intellectual disability to gifted students. Although it is not possible to know if the amount of neurological capacity allocated for short-term processing differs between these classifications, functional short-term capacity certainly does, with performance on short-term memory tasks improving steadily, going from intellectual disability to learning disability, to normally achieving, to gifted classifications.

We know less about the many types of learners who are at risk for school failure. For the most part, we have been better at documenting the existence of learning problems for economically disadvantaged students, students with serious illnesses, and students exposed to environmental hazards than we have been at understanding their cognitive problems in ways that might lead to more effective education of these children.

Theory and research on intelligence and intellectual diversity contribute to understanding many of the larger issues in developmental psychology, including the Big Ideas of development introduced in Chapter 1.

Nature and Nurture

The nature versus nurture debate has been played out most fiercely with respect to intelligence. In general, most psychologists agree that individual differences in intelligence are largely heritable, although what is inherited is a reaction range of intellectual outcomes rather than a specific intelligence quotient (see Chapter 2). Where a person falls in the reaction range depends on the quality of environment that the person experiences. Of course, extreme environmental experiences, such as serious injury or disease, can result in great intellectual decrement.

Active and Passive Child

People do play a role in determining their own intelligence. Children and adolescents can choose to spend their free time with more capable and academically oriented peers who may reinforce an emphasis on academic activities (see also Chapter

10). Children who are already doing well in school, for example in reading, are the ones most likely to read more, which increases their academic competence further. In general, smarter people make choices leading to experiences that make them more knowledgeable, thereby increasing their ability to learn more, so that the intellectually rich get richer (Nandagopal & Ericsson, 2012; Stanovich, 1986).

REVIEW OF KEY TERMS

alternative-forms reliability A measure of a test's reliability established by administering two forms of the test to test-takers. The correlation between performance on one form of the test and performance on the other form measures the test's reliability.

coefficient alpha The average of all possible split-half reliabilities for a given test.

construct validity The standard of a test that establishes how well the test measures the construct it is intended to measure.

content validity The standard of a test that establishes how well the test measures the content it is purported to cover.

criterion validity The standard of a test that establishes whether or not the test makes the distinctions it is supposed to make, such as whether or not the test predicts scores on some criterion measure.

crystallized intelligence The knowledge acquired through the processes of intelligence.

dyslexia The inability to decode words despite substantial reading instruction.

factor analysis A statistical technique that identifies clusters of items, or "factors," that correlate with one another.

fetal alcohol syndrome (FAS) Birth defects, such as learning difficulties and intellectual disability, caused by damage to the central nervous system as a result of maternal alcoholism.

fluid intelligence The reasoning ability that allows the acquisition of knowledge.

inclusion An implementation of the principle of least restrictive environment in which students with disabilities receive all instruction in the regular classroom, often in collaboration with special education teachers or other specialists.

individualized education program (IEP) A program that describes a student's disability and outlines an educational plan to address the student's learning difficulties.

least restrictive environment A term interpreted as meaning that students with disabilities must be educated with their nondisabled peers to the maximum extent appropriate.

mainstreaming The practice of placing students with disabilities as often as possible in regular classrooms with their nondisabled peers.

mean An arithmetic average.

norm A typical level of performance for a clearly defined reference group.

normal distribution A frequency distribution of scores on a test that resembles a bell-shaped curve, with most scores falling near the mean and fewer scores falling further away from the mean.

percentile ranks An expression of scores in terms of relative position within a norm group.

prodigies Those who display extremely high aptitude for a particular activity.

reliability Consistency, as in a test that obtains the same results consistently.

resource room A place where a student with disabilities can go to receive special services.

self-contained classrooms Classrooms where students with disabilities are taught by special education specialists and where these students have little contact with regular instructional programs.

self-efficacy A learner's perception of his or her capability of reaching a desired goal or a certain level of performance.

split-half reliability A measure of a test's reliability established by correlating the scores for half the items on the test with the scores on the other half of the test items.

standard deviation An index of how much individual scores on a test differ from the mean.

standard scores An expression of scores on standardized tests that can be compared across contexts.

standardized tests Tests that are given under controlled conditions so that every student taking the test has the same examination experience.

stanines Standard scores with only nine possible categories, corresponding to ordered regions of the normal distribution.

test–retest reliability A test's reliability that is established by administering the same test twice to a group of test-takers. The correlation between the two scores earned by test-takers on each testing occasion indicates whether the test is measuring consistently.

validity Relevance and meaningfulness, as a test that measures what it is purported to measure.

z-score A type of standard score that tells how many standard deviations above or below the mean a raw score is.

CHAPTER 9

The Development of Academic Motivation

An important goal of many educators is to keep students motivated. You have already read about some important ideas concerning motivation in the other chapters in this textbook. For example, as described in Chapter 5, behaviorists such as Skinner emphasized the effects of reinforcements and punishments on behavior. Recall also from Chapter 5 that the expectancy of reinforcement influences motivation in that people are more likely to be motivated to do something if they expect that the activity will be reward*ing* and reward*ed*. Contemporary developmental and educational psychologists focus much more on cognitive factors affecting motivation, such as children's beliefs and perceptions, including how competent they feel about performing a task, what they think as a consequence of being reinforced or punished, and how much they value participation in an activity. An important theme in this chapter is that cognitions about performance vary somewhat depending on the developmental level of the child and the context in which the child is functioning. In addition, we discuss many other factors that influence children's motivational beliefs, motivation, and achievement.

One of the most troubling findings of researchers interested in motivation is the trend of declining academic motivation with increasing age during the school years. In general, students like and value school less, and are less interested in school and what is studied in school, the more that they experience school (e.g., Eccles et al., 1989; Linnenbrink-Garcia & Patall, 2016; Lepper, Corpus, & Iyengar, 2005; Usher, 2016; Wigfield, 1994; Wigfield & Eccles, 1992; Wigfield, Eccles, Mac Iver, Reuman, & Midgley, 1991). We begin this chapter with a discussion of explanations for the developmental decline in academic motivation as students advance in school. Then we introduce general ideas and specific methods for promoting motivation in schools. Finally, we discuss the influence of contextual variables upon motivation.

Why Might Academic Motivation Decline with Increasing Grade in School?

We consider two important factors in explaining the observed general pattern of *declining* motivation with *increasing* grade in school. First, children's perspectives and beliefs about their competencies change with increasing age during the elementary school years. Thus, we examine a number of different theoretical perspectives on children's cognitions about their own performance. Second, reinforcement contingencies change with advancing grade level, such that competition for grades and other rewards becomes keener and more obvious. Thus, we also examine changes in classroom context that influence motivation.

Self-Efficacy

One of the best predictors of student academic achievement is student perceptions of their own academic abilities (Bandura, Barbaranelli, Caprara, & Pastorelli, 1996; Graham & Weiner, 2012; Wigfield, 1994; Wigfield & Eccles, 1992; Zimmerman & Bandura, 1994). Even though, in general, academic motivation declines with advancing grade level in school, some students do remain interested in school and do stay motivated to do their best in school. Such students approach the academic demands placed on them with confidence and resourcefulness. They are very diligent, sticking with a task until they complete it. One of the most important characteristics of motivated students is that they have high academic self-efficacy (Bandura, 1977, 1993, 1997; Schunk, 1990, 1991; Zimmerman, 1989; Zimmerman, Bandura, & Martinez-Pons, 1992). **Self-efficacy** refers to beliefs about competence or ability to perform a task. High self-efficacy in a subject area is important because it motivates students to attempt tasks in the same and related subjects in the future, and thus has a major impact on future academic achievement (Bong, 2013; Lee, Lee, & Bong, 2014; Marsh, 1990a; Marsh & Yeung, 1997b; Schunk & Pajares, 2004). What children and adolescents believe they can do goes far in shaping their academic aspirations, persistence, and even their career aspirations (Bandura, Barbaranelli, Vittorio-Caprara, & Pastorelli, 2001; Parker et al., 2012).

For example, one motivation for a high school student to enroll in Algebra 2 is his or her previous success in Algebra 1. Suppose that the student does well in Algebra 2: Now his or her self-efficacy with respect to mathematics is increased even more, which in turn can motivate his or her future choice of mathematics courses and even thinking about an engineering career. What if the student did poorly in Algebra 2? His or her sense of self-efficacy with respect to mathematics will likely decline, reducing the probability that he or she will enroll in mathematics courses in the future and pursue careers that require mathematics. Self-efficacy is determined in part by present attempts at learning and performance, which in turn affect future attempts at learning and performance and life pursuits as well as actual achievement. That is, believing that you can do well in math based on your past performance contributes to your future successes in mathematics performance (Butz & Usher, 2015; Chen, 2002; Guay, Marsh, & Boiven, 2003; Marsh & Yeung, 1997a).

Mastery experience, the previous experience in a domain, is a major source of information factored into a sense of self-efficacy. What else shapes self-efficacy in addition to previous success or failure in the domain? A second influence on the development of self-efficacy is vicarious learning through *social models* (see Chapter 5). When people who are similar to us can do something, we are more likely to believe that we could do it too and are willing to try (Schunk, 1991; Usher, 2016). Observing or learning about coping models who at first struggle and then find a way to succeed has a particularly strong impact on the development of self-efficacy (Lin-Siegler, Ahn, Chen, Fang, & Luna-Lucero, 2016; Usher & Pajares, 2008).

Another source of information for the development of self-efficacy is social persuasion or the *opinions of others* (Butz & Usher, 2015). So teachers who want to encourage their female students to be confident in their math abilities convey the message that women can do well in math; teachers who want to encourage their female students to think about occupations requiring math communicate the fact that women become engineers, accountants, and math teachers. The social persuasion of teachers may or may not be supported by messages given by parents or peers. Unfortunately, it is probably easier to undermine self-efficacy through social persuasion than to support it (Usher & Pajares, 2008).

Although modeling and the opinions of others have an impact on self-efficacy, *feedback* resulting from mastery experience has an even greater impact (Butz & Usher, 2015; Schunk, 1990, 1991; Usher, & Pajares, 2008). For example, nothing will convince an adolescent female that she can do math as much as doing well in math classes, which happens a lot since gender differences in mathematics achievement are small when they occur at all, as revealed by two meta-analyses published 30 years apart (Hyde, Fennema, & Lamon, 1990; Lindberg, Hyde, Petersen, & Linn, 2010; see Chapter 11). Cues derived from e*motional and physiological states* also provide information that shapes self-efficacy. If the thought of speaking in front of the class or taking a math test elicits sweaty palms, a thumping heart, and panicky thoughts, inferences can be made about feelings of competence for those activities. *Context* can also affect the level of self-efficacy. When students attend a selective school with many high-performing classmates (or a gifted and talented program within a school), a student's self-efficacy is likely to be lower than if the same student attends a less-selective school or program with generally weaker students, a phenomenon known as the "*big fish in the little pond*" effect (Marsh et al., 2008, 2015; Marsh, Chessor, Craven, & Roche, 1995; Marsh & Hau, 2003; Seaton, Marsh, & Craven, 2010). There is some evidence, however, that by the end of the school year, placement with high-achieving students can have a positive effect on academic performance (Stabler, Dumont, Becker, & Baumert, 2017).

Chen and Usher (2013) studied the sources of self-efficacy in middle and high school science students and found that adolescents who used multiple sources of information about competencies, for example, models and social persuasion in addition to mastery experience, exhibited the highest self-efficacy and achievement in science. Bernacki, Nokes-Malach, and Aleven (2015) found that levels of self-efficacy varied during algebra learning and that students weighed aspects of their performance, such as accuracy and fluency, differently in their judgments of self-efficacy at various points throughout the learning process.

Self-efficacy is subject-specific. For example, students can have high self-efficacy with respect to math and low self-efficacy with respect to composition—and this self-knowledge is generally accurate. People know their own academic strengths and weaknesses (Marsh, 1990b, 1992). Although mastery experience is the most important source of information for self-efficacy judgments over all, upper elementary and middle school students do report using different primary sources of information for judging self-efficacy across domains (Butz & Usher, 2015). Although students improve their understanding of their own strengths and weaknesses with age, even elementary-grade students can articulate differences in their competencies in various subjects (Marsh & Ayotte, 2003; Marsh & Craven, 1991; Marsh, Cravens, & Debus, 1991; Stipek & MacIver, 1989).

Differences in self-efficacy can exist within specific domains. For example, in gymnastics, some students have high self-efficacy with respect to tumbling and low self-efficacy with respect to the parallel bars. Ask a track team member who consistently wins the 440-yard dash about the 440, and that runner will have great confidence in his or her ability in the 440. Ask that same athlete about the 100-yard dash, and the answer may be surprising—No confidence! In fact, many runners move up to the 440 because they have the stamina for the longer dash but not the incredible short-term speed required for the 100—and they know it, so that their self-efficacies for the 440 and 100 are very different. All of us possess detailed knowledge about what we can do well, with specific perceptions of self-efficacy playing a large role in determining our future efforts in a given domain. With respect to athletics, skilled athletes know what they can do and cannot do, and they are very strategic—planning their moves, attributing their successes to selecting and using the right strategies, and consigning their failures to using the wrong strategies. They know they can do well by using the right approaches (i.e., their self-efficacy beliefs mix with their strategy beliefs; see Cleary & Zimmerman, 2001). The next time you see a skilled volleyball player make an unbelievable serve or a darts player get a bull's eye recognize that there was much going through their heads as they performed, including knowing that they could make the serve or hit the bull's eye (Kitsantas & Zimmerman, 2002).

So far we have made it sound as if every attempt at doing something has great consequences for self-efficacy, but this is not the case when a person already has a very strong sense of self-efficacy built up over years. Consider a high school senior who has made straight A's in mathematics throughout high school, including up to this point in calculus. Then this student gets a C on one test. Is there an effect on the student's sense of self-efficacy with respect to mathematics? Probably not, or if there is, it is likely to be a very specific shift, such as "I have a lot of trouble with Simpson's rule—which was what was covered on this test." Thus, performing below par on one occasion in a subject area in which one enjoys a long record of accomplishment does not significantly impact one's sense of self-efficacy with respect to that subject (Bandura, 1986; Schunk, 1991).

Development of Self-Efficacy Beliefs

If academic self-efficacy is important in determining academic motivation and academic motivation declines with advancing grade level, then it would make sense that academic self-efficacy declines with advancing grade level. In fact, students' expectancies for academic success do decline with advancing grade level. Particularly striking are the declines with the transition from elementary school to middle or junior high school (Anderman, 2013; Seidman, Allen, Aber, Mitchell, & Feinman, 1994; Stipek & MacIver, 1989). Compared to elementary school, middle school or junior high school life entails less support and increased emphasis on performance which can translate into decreased academic self-efficacy, less effort spent preparing for school, and lower grades.

For example, Wigfield and colleagues (1991) asked sixth graders to rate how good they were at English, math, and sports just before they entered junior high school. The same students completed a similar questionnaire during the first year of junior high school. Although the declines in perceived competence were not great, perceived competence did decline for each of the three domains. These longitudinal findings support cross-sectional evidence that as students proceed through school, they come to believe less in themselves. By the middle and upper elementary grades, students are more aware of their failures than their successes (Kloosterman, 1988). Students, especially poorer students, often perceive that they are doing worse academically than they actually are doing (Juvonen, 1988; Renick & Harter, 1989). During early adolescence, feelings of **learned helplessness** in reaction to failures also increase (Roeser, Eccles, & Sameroff, 2000). Learned helplessness is the belief that there is nothing you can do to perform better or to achieve success. Once a student comes to believe that success is unlikely, it is hard to change that belief (Fincham, Hokoda, & Sanders, 1989). The "can't-do attitudes" that are so well known by high school teachers have been developing for years. Such attitudes are disastrous since "can't-do" perceptions translate into "won't-try" students. The general pattern of decreases in self-efficacy over time is not observed in all students for all domains (Usher, 2016). For example, Archambault, Eccles, and Vida (2010) observed a general pattern of decreasing self-concept in literacy in students from grade 1 to grade 12, but the decrease was much more evident in some students than in others.

Self-Efficacy and Expectancy–Value Theory

The concept of self-efficacy is appropriately considered in relationship to another theoretical perspective, expectancy–value theory, introduced in Chapter 5. Expectancy–value theory describes when people will perform behaviors that they are capable of performing (Wigfield, Eccles, Fredriks, Roeser, & Schiefele, 2015). If self-efficacy is high in a subject area, the expectancy of reinforcement contingent on performing in the subject area is also high. If, in addition, the potential reinforcements for performing in the subject area are also valued, then the likelihood of a student working hard in the subject is high. If the student works hard in the subject and experiences success, then expectancy of reinforcement remains high. In contrast, if the student experiences failure in the subject, expectancy of reinforcement for the subject area declines, as does the likelihood of working hard in the subject in the future.

A critical assumption of expectancy–value theory is that successful students *both expect and value* academic success. Berndt and Miller (1990) observed that the success of seventh-grade students in English and math was linked strongly both to expectations of success in these subjects and to valuation of potential rewards for success in English and math. That is, successful students both expected and valued academic success. In a longitudinal study, Durik, Vida, and Eccles (2006) found that competence beliefs and perceived value of reading in elementary school predicted leisure reading, number of language arts courses taken, and career aspirations in high school. The perceived value of succeeding on an academic task is something to consider in analyzing school motivation. Even very good teachers sometimes do not make clear to students that the tasks being assigned are valuable (Green, 2002). Moreover, even if students can do the homework they are assigned, they often do not understand the value of it (Trautwein & Köller, 2003). As students advance through the grades, they are given more and more assignments that they perceive as repetitive and boring (Anderman, 2013; Gentry, Gable, & Rizza, 2002). From the perspective of expectancy–value theory, should we be surprised that sometimes students do not do assignments (or do them haphazardly) if the value of doing the assignment is not made clear? Also, one possible explanation why some groups have historically under-achieved in schools is that the value of doing schoolwork is not as apparent to them as to other more mainstream groups who have historically achieved highly in school (Graham & Taylor, 2002; Van Laar, 2000).

Attributions for Success and Failure

Another factor to consider in analyzing school motivation is the explanations students make for their successes and failures. These explanations for performances are called **attributions**. Weiner (1979, 2001; Graham & Weiner, 1996) specified four types of attributions, with each of them having different motivational consequences. Students can explain outcomes by referring to their *efforts*—success was due to their hard work and working effectively, and failure was due to their lack of effort; *abilities*—success was due to their high ability and failure to their low ability; *task factors*—success occurred because the task was easy, but failure occurred because the task was difficult; or *luck*—success reflected good luck, while failure reflected bad luck.

Only the first of these attributions—effort—is likely to promote adaptive motivational tendencies. If students believe that their successes and failures are due to effort, then they believe that their fate is personally controllable. Learners who attribute their successes and failures to high and low efforts, respectively, *expect* that reinforcement will occur if they work hard. The other explanatory possibilities—ability, task difficulty, and luck—are all out of personal control, owing to genes and brain development, teacher task selection, or the whimsical nature of supernatural forces.

Attributions, Learning Difficulties, and Learning Disabilities

Researchers have studied the role of attributions in motivating the academic efforts of students who experience difficulties in school. For example, Jacobsen, Lowery, and DuCette (1986; see also Palladino, Poli, Masi, & Marcheschi, 2000; and Chapter 8) determined that on the one hand children with learning disabilities were much more likely than their normally achieving classmates to believe that their achievements reflected low ability. On the other hand, normally achieving children were more likely to believe that with effort they would be able to succeed in school. Within a group of low achievers, those who believe that they can control their academic progress through effort, *in fact*, do achieve at higher levels than those who believe that their low achievement reflects low ability (Kistner, Osborne, & LeVerrier, 1988). What is going on here? A history of failure following effort led to negative affect and decreasing expectancies for future success (Covington & Omelich, 1979a, 1979b). Observing other students experiencing success following their efforts does not help, and, in fact, probably intensifies feelings of personal incapacity (Covington, 1987). This is a situation that leads to learned helplessness. Doing nothing can become a preferred choice for these children (Covington & Omelich, 1981, 1984). Is it any surprise that children with learning disabilities often seem passive in school (Fulk, 1996a, 1996b)? Trying gets them nowhere; not trying permits them to offer themselves an explanation of failure that is not as damaging to their self-esteem as failure following effort.

Can a teacher make a difference in this situation? *Yes.* Students with learning disabilities often receive more assistance with their classroom work than other students. On the one hand, if teachers give a great deal of support, these students may not attribute any success they have to their own efforts but instead will attribute it to the help they received. On the other hand, just enough help that gets the student moving in the right direction—the amount of help that provides just enough "scaffolding" (a concept first introduced in Chapter 6 and revisited later in this chapter) can result in students attributing success to their own efforts and presumably increase their long-term motivation (Ring & Reetz, 2000).

Developmental Differences in Attributions

How do children's attributions explain the increasing tendency with advancing grade in school to be less motivated for academic work? Why is it that with increasing age during the elementary and middle school years, feelings of learning helplessness in response to failures increase?

Nicholls (1978, 1990) offered an explanation, one that suggests that young elementary students think very differently than do older students. Preschool, kindergarten, and first-grade students do not differentiate between *effort* and *ability.* Thus, a positive academic outcome is viewed as reflecting their effort, and young children believe that success following high effort is an indication of high ability. What does failure after effort imply? The young child may believe that she or he simply did not try hard enough. With increasing age during the elementary years, children more clearly differentiate effort and ability. For example, they begin to believe that if students who experience equal outcomes differ in their efforts, the one expending less effort probably has the higher ability. As they grow older, children increasingly begin to explain accomplishments in terms of ability, with poor outcomes reflecting low ability and positive outcomes reflecting high ability. That is, with increasing age, students are less likely to think that they can improve their performance by trying hard (Freedman-Doan et al., 2000; Stipek & MacIver, 1989).

Another factor explaining developmental differences in response to academic difficulties is that, as children progress through school, they become more accurate in their self-appraisals. Elementary school-age children are often optimistic and may overestimate their competencies, but as they mature they are better able to understand evaluative feedback and become more realistic in their appraisals (Nicholls, 1984; Wigfield et al., 2015). These changes in self-assessments are corroborated by children's increasing reliance on social information to understand their own performance—that is, they rely more on what teachers, parents, and peers say to them about their own achievement (Altermatt, Pomerantz, Ruble, & Greulich, 2002). Also, with increasing age, the importance of parents' perceptions and feedback decreases as the importance of teachers' perceptions and feedback increases.

Similar developments occur with respect to children's understanding of task difficulty (Nicholls & Miller, 1983, 1985). If a young child can do a task, it is considered easy and the child believes that she or he is smart. If a child at this age performs poorly on a task, the task is difficult, and the child concludes that she or he lacks ability. With increasing age during the elementary years, children become more sophisticated in their thinking about the relationships between task difficulty and ability. For example, they come to recognize that good performance on very difficult tasks is indicative of high ability, but that good performance on a task that is performed competently by most people provides little information about ability.

Children also come to understand the difference between *luck* and *skill* with increasing age during the elementary years (Nicholls, 1990; Nicholls & Miller, 1985). Very young children believe that task performance is due to effort and/or ability, even when the task outcome truly depends on chance (such as winning a coin toss). With development, children come to understand that performance on tasks involving chance has nothing to do with effort or ability.

In summary, with increasing age, students are increasingly at risk for a sense of low self-efficacy, due in part to the attributions they make about their own successes and failures. Thus, early in the grade school years, thinking about task outcomes in terms of effort, ability, task difficulty, and luck is fuzzy. As children begin to differentiate these alternative explanations of task performance, they are increasingly likely to explain outcomes, including academic performances, in ways that undermine motivation. For example, they may interpret failures as indicative of low ability. Even success can be taken as an indication of low ability, if such success comes after much greater effort than that expended by others to achieve at the same level. These perceptions can undermine children's academic self-esteem, encouraging the conclusion that if ability is low, there really is not much reason to try hard, for ultimately failure is inevitable. With so many converging developmental factors that increase the likelihood of students being more doubtful about their performances and abilities, is it any wonder that older children are less confident about their competencies and have lower expectancies for success than younger children (Covington, 2000; Nicholls, 1984, 1989)? *No*, especially when differences in the nature of school with advancing grades are also considered.

Classroom Competition

Competition is a way of life in many classrooms. Grading practices may reflect absolute performance without consideration of individual progress. Sometimes grades are made public and salient in the classroom, as when students look through all the papers in the "graded bin" before finding their own. Other forces outside of the school also support competitiveness. Some parents respond to their children's report card by asking how "So-and-So" did, perhaps followed by remarks about how it would be nice if their son or daughter were more like "So-and-So." Local papers carry news about the academic achievements in schools, for example, by publishing honor rolls. Bumper stickers on family cars proclaim the academic success of a child on the honor roll.

What is the result of this focus on identifying publicly the highest academic performers? Nicholls (1989) argued that this practice probably undermines the academic motivation of many children. He contended that such classroom competition and evaluation fosters what he called **ego involvement**. This means that students interpret success in the classroom (especially relative to peers) as indicating high intellectual ability and failure as indicating low intellectual ability. Since most students will not end up doing "best" in the class, feelings of failure, self-criticism, and negative self-esteem often occur. Emphasizing competition has high potential for undermining effort when success is not certain (e.g., attempting a new task), for trying and failing leads to feelings of low ability. The research indicates that competitive classroom environments can undermine student motivation and achievement (e.g.,

Anderman et al., 2001; Anderman, Maehr, & Midgley, 1999; Anderman & Midgley, 1997; Maehr & Anderman, 1993; Midgley, Anderman, & Hicks, 1995; Turner et al., 2002; Urdan & Midgley, 2003).

Students will often go to great lengths to avoid trying something that is academically risky in order to avoid feelings of failure relative to other students who succeed at the task. See the Considering Interesting Questions special feature (Box 9.1) for a discussion of how students maintain their feelings of academic self-worth.

Grade-Level Differences in Classroom Reward Structures

One reason for the decline in perceptions of academic self-efficacy and academic motivation from kindergarten to the middle grades is that comparative evaluations, for example tests, are more frequent in the later elementary and middle grades than in the early elementary grades (Anderman, 2013; Harter, Whitesell, & Kowalski, 1992; Stipek & Daniels, 1988). With increasing age, children also become more aware of the competitiveness in their classrooms (see Harter et al., 1992; see also Schmidt, Ollendick, & Stanowicz, 1988) and of the implications of not succeeding. Academic standing is also made more salient by the transition from elementary school to a multiple classroom environment in middle school where different tracks in academic preparation become more evident. For example, some students transitioning to middle school from the same elementary school might be enrolled in general math classes, whereas others are enrolled in pre-Algebra math classes. Even those in the college-preparatory track may experience detriments in academic self-esteem due to social comparison (remember the big-fish-in-the-little pond effect). Paying attention to how one does compared to others affects perceptions of one's own competency, with these perceptions affecting expectancies about future success and having the potential to affect school performance. Shifts with increasing grade level in the saliency of competition are accompanied by developmental shifts in making comparisons between self and other, which contributes to the impact of classroom competitiveness.

Developmental Differences in the Making of Social Comparisons

The cognitive egocentrism of young children (see Chapter 3) has some advantages. Young children tend not to compare themselves much with others, especially with respect to psychological characteristics—such as intelligence or reading ability or extent of prior knowledge. Yes, preschool children can and do compare the tangible "goodies" they have with the tangible "goodies" another child has (Ruble, Boggiano, Feldman, & Loebl, 1980): "I have more orange juice than you" "Do not!"–"Do too!" But they do not make much of differences or similarities in performance on academic tasks. Thus, a first grader who feels badly because she or he is having difficulty with two-column addition is unlikely to feel better if the teacher mentions that the other children in the class are experiencing the same difficulty. With increasing age during the elementary-grade years, students become more concerned with how they are doing academically relative to others (Eccles, 1999; Eccles & Roeser, 2011; Ruble, 1983). The increasing focus on comparing one's own achievement with that of others has the potential for leading to negative conclusions about one's own ability. Such conclusions can then translate into reduced motivation to achieve.

Considering Interesting Questions

BOX 9.1. How Do Students Preserve Feelings of Academic Self-Worth?

Martin Covington (1992, 2004; Covington & Roberts, 1994; De Castella, Byrne, & Covington, 2013) proposed that academic motivations can be broken down into motives to try for success and motives to avoid failure. In order to understand students' academic behaviors and motivations, both of these motives need to be considered. Other relevant characteristics include the presence or absence of defensive pessimism and self-handicapping strategies. Defensive pessimism refers to changing the meaning of failure by holding unrealistically low expectations for performance. Self-handicapping also changes the meaning of failure but through lining up ready excuses for low performance. Using this framework, Covington and colleagues identified four types of students:

- *Overstrivers:* These students are highly motivated to strive for success, but they are also very highly motivated to avoid failure and may engage in defensive pessimism. They put in a great deal of effort and avoid self-handicapping, often preparing extensively—indeed, much more than is necessary to achieve success. The anxiety produced by their numerous thoughts of failure and their dread of failure are so motivating that they keep on studying and studying.

- *Success-Oriented Optimists:* These students value academic achievement but are not particularly worried about failing. These students work hard, but, unlike the overstrivers, their efforts are not motivated by anxiety. They exhibit little self-handicapping and defensive pessimism.

- *Failure avoiders:* These students are not motivated to work hard since academic success means little to them. However, they do want to preserve their sense of academic self-worth—their feelings that they are intelligent and capable. If a failure avoider does fail, it must be in a way that the failure cannot be attributed to low ability. How is that managed? Don't study!! A failure avoider can then attribute failure to low effort. Failure avoiders employ a number of self-handicapping strategies (such as procrastination or staying up all night) so they are exhausted (see Urdan & Midgley, 2001). In this way, the failure-avoiding student is actually increasing the likelihood of failure but is avoiding having to conclude that failure was due to low ability. Students who focus on avoiding failure also engage in defensive pessimism.

- *Failure acceptors:* These students seem to care little about either academic success or failure. They are students who have become learned helpless or have rejected the academic system and do not see the value of succeeding in school. Some minority studies reject majority academic values (review the discussion of Ogbu's work in Chapter 6) and can be thought of as failure acceptors (Covington, 1992). Failure acceptors tend not to engage in self-handicapping or defensive pessimism.

An important idea emerging from Covington's work is that effort is a double-edged sword. If a student must expend a great deal of effort to achieve success that comes easier to others, the student is at risk of coming to the conclusion that he or she is low in ability. Which of the four types of students face this type of risk? The other edge of the sword is that not expending effort also is a self-worth-preserving strategy, with failure following low effort not attributable to low ability. Which of the four student types is on this edge of the sword? From a self-worth perspective, which two of the four types of students are in the best position for academic success?

Other Characteristics of Schools and Classrooms That Undermine Achievement

In addition to increased competitiveness, school changes in other ways with advancing grade, most of which probably do more to undermine student motivation than support it (Anderman, 2013; Eccles & Roeser, 2011; Wigfield et al., 2015). As children get older during the elementary years, they can feel less accepted by their teachers, possibly because the teachers are less accepting than their primary-grade teachers, which can undermine academic motivation and engagement (Furrer & Skinner, 2003). Middle schools are larger and less personal than schools serving primary-level students and students in the middle elementary grades. Rather than spending the day with the same teacher and the same group of 20–25 students, middle school students move from teacher to teacher and classroom to classroom over the course of the day, encountering many more people for less time than was the case in elementary school. This provides fewer opportunities to form meaningful relationships with teachers and peers, at a time in child development when a child's needs for belongingness are especially important (Eccles & Roeser, 2011; Osterman, 2000). Compared to elementary school teachers, secondary school teachers tend to exert more control (e.g., discipline is more certain and firmer) and permit less student decision making, with these changes occurring at a time in development when students desire more autonomy (Brophy & Evertson, 1976; Deci & Ryan, 1985; Eccles et al., 1993).

An Alternative to Competition

Rather than rewarding students for *being better than one another*, it is possible to reward students for *doing better than they did previously*, that is, to reward personal improvement on academic tasks. Nicholls refers to such classrooms as fostering **task involvement**. Nicholls and Thorkildsen (1987) found that work avoidance is much more commonly reported in ego-involved (competitive) classrooms than in task-involved (noncompetitive) classrooms. The students in the task-oriented classrooms believed that success in school depended on interest, effort, and attempting to learn, whereas the students in the ego-involved classrooms believed that success depended on being smarter than other kids and trying to beat out other students.

Nicholls and Thorkildsen (1987) also found that students in the task-oriented classrooms were much more satisfied with school and learning in school than students in the ego-oriented classrooms (see also Duda & Nicholls, 1992; Weinstein, 2002). Task-oriented classrooms are much more likely to keep students interested in and committed to school than are ego-oriented classrooms (Nicholls, 1989). The problem is that many more classrooms are ego-involved than task-involved. In far too many classrooms, the goal is to get better grades than the ones earned by peers rather than to actually learn (Ames, 1992; Blumenfeld, 1992). This has big consequences for students.

For example, Nolen (1988) provided evidence that classroom competition can undermine the quality of thinking that occurs in the classroom. She assessed whether eighth-grade students were task- or ego-oriented. In addition, Nolen asked the students to indicate whether they would use particular strategies for reading and understanding textbook material. Students' reported strategy use was then compared to their actual strategy use as observed when they studied some text material. Although both task- and ego-oriented students endorsed and used surface-level strategies for processing text (such as "Read the whole thing over and over"), the task-oriented students were much more likely than the ego-oriented students to endorse and use strategies that involved deeper processing of text (such as "Try to see how this fits with what I've learned in class"). Thus, task orientation, academic effort, and use of sophisticated strategies are linked (Covington, 1998).

Transition and Competition: Group Differences

The transition from elementary school to middle school or high school may be even more challenging for ethnic minority students (Wigfield et al., 2015). Middle schools and high schools tend to be larger, more performance-oriented, and more stratified into racial and ethnic groups than elementary schools. Members of minority groups also perceive increasing discrimination and differential treatment as they move through school, but a strong ethnic identity (see Chapter 6) can ameliorate negative effects (Eccles & Roeser, 2011).

In a longitudinal study, Benner and Graham (2009) followed students from seventh to tenth grade, collecting data twice a year on their psychological functioning, perceived school climate, and academic behaviors. The students in this study had been doing well when located in smaller middle schools, and they transitioned to large urban high schools during the course of the study. During the transition, the students reported disruptions in psychological function and lower grades. The negative effect of transition was particularly evident in African American and Latino students when they moved to a high school with a different ethnic composition (fewer members of their ethnic group) than their middle school

Consistent with the multicultural differences in classroom participation styles described in Chapter 6, classroom competition is more compatible with the styles of students from some cultures than others. For example, Farkas, Sheehan, and Grobe (1990) analyzed the grades given in grades 7 and 8 of one urban school district, taking into account whether the students knew the material as reflected on course mastery tests and their rate of absenteeism. Even with mastery and absenteeism controlled, some students still earned better grades than others: In particular, Asian students were graded higher than Anglos, and more affluent students received better marks than students living in poverty. Farkas and colleagues speculated that perhaps the behaviors of Asian and more affluent children suggested to their teachers that they were working harder or that their behaviors were somehow more pleasing to their teachers. Because students from Asian cultures believe more strongly than members of many other cultures that effort largely determines achievement, Asian students are more likely to work hard and achieve at high levels in school (Salili, Chiu, & Lai, 2001). Working hard does more than promote achievement; it also brings positive attention to the student. If the teacher perceives that a student is working hard, the teacher is more likely to provide rewards and support than if the teacher feels the student is not trying (Weiner, 2003).

Grades are a salient characteristic of more competitive schooling environments found in secondary school. Poorthuis et al. (2015) assessed emotional and behavioral engagement in school before and after students received their first secondary school report card. After controlling for prior level of engagement, they found that grades were associated with school engagement, with lower grades predicting lower emotional and behavioral engagement later in the year (and higher grades predicting higher engagement over time). Emotional responses to the grades mediated this effect, with students who perceived themselves as receiving lower grades than others in their class being particularly affected. Male students were also more vulnerable to declining engagement as a result of lower grades, given that they tended to receive lower grades than female students and had more intense responses to the grades. Thus, the first grades received after transition to secondary school play a role in declining motivation, particularly for males and low achievers.

Views of Intelligence: Fixed or Growth Mind Set

Dweck and Leggett (1988; Dweck, 2002a, 2002b; Henderson & Dweck, 1990) have proposed that a critical determinant of achievement motivation is whether a person believes that intelligence is *fixed* biologically, and hence not affected by environmental variables, or believes that intelligence is malleable and capable of *growth*. People who believe intelligence is fixed are said to possess a **fixed mindset.** That is, they believe that intelligence is an asset that one either has in great quantity or does not. Those who believe intelligence is modifiable subscribe to a **growth mindset**.

The particular view of intelligence held by an individual has a powerful impact on his or her achievement behaviors (Elliott & Dweck, 1988; Jones, Slate, Blake, & Sloas, 1995; Meece, Blumenfeld, & Hoyle, 1988; Wood & Bandura, 1989; Yeager & Dweck, 2012). First, consider academic goals. Students with fixed mindsets are oriented to seeking positive evaluations of their abilities and to avoiding negative evaluations. This perspective can be damaging when negative feedback occurs, as it inevitably does in school. Such students are likely to interpret failures as indications of low intelligence, and hence they will be discouraged by failures. In contrast, students with growth mindsets are much more oriented to increasing their abilities, believing that daily efforts lead to small gains. Such students keep trying when obstacles occur because they see obstacles as a natural part of the learning process.

In short, students who have fixed mindsets are more likely to experience negative emotion when confronted with failure, believing that failure signals low ability, with that belief undermining future attempts at the academic task in question. Indeed, those with fixed mindsets may be motivated not to engage in the task in the future to avoid additional evidence of low ability. (Recall the idea of effort as a double-edged sword as described in Box 9.1.) In contrast, students with growth mindsets experience much less negative affect in response to failure, interpreting the failure as part of the improvement process, which motivates high persistence. As long as there is success, little difference exists in the behaviors of those with fixed or growth mindsets. It is when failure occurs that the differences in their outlooks become apparent, with a fixed mindset leading students to be more at risk for believing that they are helpless when they experience difficulties during challenging tasks, with low persistence and task avoidance the likely outcomes. Students with growth mindsets are much more likely to keep plugging away following a failure. In a longitudinal study, Blackwell, Trzesniewski, and Dweck (2007) found that students who held growth mindsets at the beginning of junior high displayed more learning goals, more effort attributions, and higher levels of achievement two years later. Adolescents who believed that intellectual capabilities can be developed (growth mindset) exhibited higher achievement throughout a challenging school transition (Yeager & Dweck, 2012). Instructional practices used in first and second grade can influence the development of mindset even in the early elementary school years (Park, Gunderson, Tsukayama, Levine, & Beilock, 2016).

Students' views of intelligence can be shaped through interventions. For example, an intervention designed to encourage a growth mindset, which included research on how brains develop and information that brains can grow through persistence during challenges and by using appropriate learning strategies, produced higher academic performance (Blackwell et al., 2007). Yeager et al. (2016) examined the effectiveness of a two-session growth mindset program delivered via the Internet to over 3,000 ninth-grade students in nine schools throughout the United States. The intervention asked students to read a scientific article about brain research supporting the idea that brains can be developed through learning, to generate a personal example of learning and getting smarter, and to write a letter encouraging a future student who is struggling in school and feeling "dumb." Students who participated in the intervention improved their core GPA, and low-achieving students reduced the number of low grades (D's and F's) received.

To the extent that classrooms foster competition rather than improvement, students are discouraged from trying hard, using potentially effective learning procedures, or being optimistic in the face of academic difficulties. That is, to the extent that classrooms are "ego-oriented," to use Nicholls's term (1989), or foster "entity views of mind," to use Dweck's vernacular, motivation is undermined. Students are better off in classrooms in which the mentally healthy messages associated with noncompetitive classrooms are prominent. These include the following:

- Trying hard fosters achievement and intelligence.
- Failure is a natural part of learning.
- Being best is not what school is about; getting better is.

Goal Orientation

Those interested in achievement goal orientation and its impact on motivation study the reasons underlying behaviors associated with pursing achievement goals. A distinction is made between mastery goals and performance goals (e.g., Dweck & Leggett, 1988). **Mastery goals** are concerned with learning and improvement, and **performance goals** with demonstrating ability and competence (Anderman, Gray, & Chang, 2013). Thus, mastery goals are more focused on *developing* competence; performance goals are focused more on *demonstrating* competence (Linnenbrink-Garcia & Patall, 2016).

The initial assumption was that mastery goals would be associated with higher achievement, greater effort, and more persistence on a task than performance goals. Instead research indicated that sometimes performance goals, particularly goals to outperform others, were more strongly correlated with achievement than mastery goals. It also became clear that someone could possess both performance and mastery goals in a given learning situation. In fact, meta-analysis indicated that the correlation between mastery and performance goals is low but positive (Hulleman, Schrager, Bodmann, & Harackiewicz, 2010). The original model of performance and mastery goal orientation was expanded to include approach versus avoidance orientations (Anderman et al., 2013; Elliot, 1999). That is, a performance approach orientation would be to demonstrate greater competence than others; a performance avoidance orientation would be to avoid the demonstration of incompetence. Thus, for performance goals, success is determined in comparison to others. A mastery approach goal would be to increase competence or knowledge; a mastery avoidance goal would be to avoid a misunderstanding or failing to learn. Thus, for mastery goals, success is defined by task-based or self-referential standards. Mastery avoidance orientations are the least common and the least studied of the goal orientations (Huang, 2012; Linnenbrink-Garcia & Patall, 2016).

Both mastery approach and performance approach goals have small but significant positive correlations with achievement (Linnenbrink-Garcia & Patall, 2016), although there is some evidence that performance approach goals (performing better than others) may be more strongly correlated with achievement than mastery learning goals (Senko et al., 2011). Performance goals, however, also may be more associated with fear of failure, fixed mindsets, test anxiety, procrastination, and cheating and may interfere with successful collaborative learning (Linnenbrink-Garcia et al., 2012; Senko, Hulleman, & Harackiewicz, 2011). Mastery goals, in contrast, are associated with an emphasis on understanding and learning from mistakes, deeper processing when working in collaboration, and more interest and engagement when allowed opportunity for choice (Benita, Roth, & Deci, 2014; Lam, Ruzek, Schenke, Conley, & Karabenick, 2015; Sims, van Joolingen, Savelsbergh & van Hout-Walters, 2008).

Classroom practices differ in terms of their propensity to encourage mastery and performance goal orientations (Anderman et al., 2013; Butler, 2014). Performance-oriented classrooms emphasize correct answers, frequent examinations, grades, class standing, and competition; mastery-oriented classrooms focus on meaningful learning, learning from mistakes, and progress in evaluations of performance. In performance-oriented classrooms, cheating, self-handicapping, and ability attributions for failure are more likely. In mastery-oriented classrooms, help-seeking, effective use of strategies, and persistence when challenged are more likely. It is difficult, however, to assess classroom goal orientation with consistency, given individuality in student perceptions, potential disconnects between what teachers say versus the instructional practices they employ, and possible differential treatment of students by teachers (Lam et al., 2015)

In a meta-analysis of 151 studies, 172 independent samples, Huang (2012) found that approach motivations (both mastery and performance) were associated with higher achievement and both avoidance motivations with lower achievement, but goal orientations were not strong predictors of achievement. In another meta-analysis of 77 studies, 93 independent samples, Huang (2011) examined the relationship between goal orientations and emotions. Huang found that mastery approach goals were strongly related to more intense positive emotions such as interest, enjoyment, pride, and hope and that performance avoidance goals were related to strong negative emotions such as anxiety, worry, shame, and anger.

Patterns of goal orientations, however, are complex, with multiple goals operating in specific contexts. Luo, Paris, Hogan, and Luo (2011) identified four patterns of goal orientation in Singapore high school students—(1) Diffuse (moderate levels of the three major goal orientations—mastery, performance approach, and performance avoidance); (2) Moderate Mastery (moderate-mastery, low-performance approach, and low-performance avoidance); (3) Success-oriented (moderate-mastery, high-performance approach and high-performance avoidance); and (4) Approach (high-mastery approach, high-performance approach, and low-performance avoidance). Students in the Success-oriented and Approach groups were higher in self-efficacy and metacognition, exhibited greater engagement with class activities and homework, and were more skilled at time management than the other groups. Students in the Approach and Moderate Mastery groups exhibited lower test anxiety, were more likely to persist after encountering difficulties, and had higher grades than the other groups. The conclusion reached was that, in this context, secondary mathematics learning in Singapore, combining moderate-mastery approach goals with high-performance approach goals and low-performance avoidance goals (the Approach group) may be the most adaptive! Clearly, goal orientation is a complicated motivational construct.

Rewards and Intrinsic Motivation: Overjustification Effects

According to White (1959), people have an inherent need to feel competent and to interact effectively with their environment. Thus, we can have **intrinsic motivation** to engage in some activities for their own sake. Not all school tasks are intrinsically motivating, and as a result, often rewards are used to get children to complete tasks that are not intrinsically motivating. Rewards, however, have the potential for undermining performance of behaviors that children would adopt in the absence of reward, tasks that are intrinsically motivating to them. That is, even though a task was previously done for its own sake, once it is rewarded, there is less likelihood that it will be done for its own sake in the future.

Lepper, Greene, and Nisbett (1973) provided the classic demonstration of this effect. They asked preschoolers to do an art activity, one that was very interesting to preschoolers when they did it as part of class activities. Some children were rewarded for completing the activity and others received no reward. When given an opportunity to do the art activity in class later, the nonrewarded children were more interested in the activity than the rewarded children. The goal of the research following this initial demonstration was to determine when and why rewards undermine performance. Rewards can undermine motivation when initial interest in the rewarded activity is high and when the reward to perform the behavior is so salient that it could be construed as controlling (Deci & Ryan, 1985; Lepper, 1995; Lepper, Keaveney, & Drake, 1996). When students can justify their willingness to do something in terms of an extrinsic reward, it is harder in the long term to justify doing the same activity in the absence of reward—an outcome that Lepper and colleagues (1973) dubbed the **overjustification effect**. Rewards can be effective even when intrinsic motivation is high, however, if the situation is arranged so that the rewards come after the performance occurs as an unanticipated bonus (Lepper, 1983; Lepper & Hodell, 1989). In that case, the reward cannot be interpreted as controlling or as coercing the student to perform the task.

Even so, teachers give many rewards, including grades, in a coercive fashion. Students know that positive outcomes depend on doing tasks that the teacher wants them to do. Students become more oriented to the extrinsic rewards that are increasingly emphasized with advancing grade, and so intrinsic motivation to perform academic tasks decreases. Hence, with increasing grade level, students increasingly believe that what should be done in school are those activities that are explicitly rewarded (Bacon, 1993; Harter, 1992). A corollary of this belief is that in the absence of rewards, there is no reason to perform, and hence intrinsic motivation to do things academic declines.

Given this pattern of outcomes, why would anyone ever use rewards to motivate performance? One reason is that students often are not intrinsically motivated to perform tasks that are good for them! When initial interest in a task is low, rewards can increase the likelihood of academic engagement and performance of important academic tasks (Bandura & Schunk, 1981; Lepper & Hodell, 1989; Loveland & Olley, 1979; McLoyd, 1979). Behavior modification theorists have understood this principle for many years (see Chapter 5). The general finding is that unexpected rewards and information rewards like specific, contingent praise (review Chapter 5) are likely to increase motivation; evidence from neuroscience research on the reward circuitry in the brain suggests that the overjustification effect can be traced to the loss of the reward rather than the perception that the reward was controlling (Hidi, 2016).

In conclusion, the observed decline in academic motivation with advancing grade has been analyzed through the lens of many different theoretical perspectives (see summary in Table 9.1). One conclusion is that competition undermines student motivation because many students end up feeling they can never make the grade. Those who coast to high grades have no incentive to do better, so it is hard to make the case that classroom competition for grades is good for anyone. We do not know how much of the developmental decline in academic motivation could be eliminated by replacing competition with an approach that emphasizes improvement. Other classroom characteristics—such as perceived control and choice for students and caring, supportive teachers—are associated with greater classroom motivation. Educators can do much more to foster motivation and promote achievement.

How Can Motivation Be Supported and Encouraged in School?

Ideas for how to promote academic motivation have been generated from the theoretical constructs described above, and a number have been successfully applied in educational contexts (Hulleman & Barron, 2016; see Lazowksi & Hulleman, 2016, for a meta-analysis). One group of interventions focuses on changing students' beliefs.

TABLE 9.1. Different Perspectives on Motivation

Self-efficacy	Am I able to do the task?
Expectancy–value	How will I do on the task?
	Do I want to do the task? Is it worthwhile doing?
Goal orientation	Why am I doing the task?
Mastery approach	Do I want to learn the material?
Performance approach	Do I want to get a high grade? Do better than others?
Performance avoidance	Do I want to avoid failing, or doing poorly?
Attributions	Why did I succeed (or fail) at the task?
View of intelligence	Can my capabilities grow as a result of working on this task?

Based on Graham and Weiner (2012) and Wigfield et al. (2015).

Interventions to promote growth mindset have already been described. Another technique, described in the next section, focuses on encouraging students to think differently about the causes of successes and failures, followed by a technique that supports the development of positive future visions of the self. Other approaches include focusing on classroom tasks, classroom processes, and relationships within the classroom.

Retraining Attributions for Success and Failure

Attribution retraining involves teaching students to think differently about the causes of their success and failures. If students learn to attribute their performances to factors that can be controlled, their motivation and achievement will likely increase. Given that many low-achieving children attribute their failures to uncontrollable ability factors, and hence are not motivated to exert academic effort, some researchers, especially John Borkowski and his colleagues, have developed interventions aimed at shifting the attributions of low achievers in order to promote their academic performances (Borkowski, Weyhing, & Carr, 1988; Carr, Borkowski, & Maxwell, 1991; Reid & Borkowski, 1987). Since skilled academic performance depends on a variety of factors—at a minimum, strategies, metacognition, and conceptual knowledge (see Chapter 4)—Borkowski recognized that merely getting students to attribute success to effort would probably do little for low-functioning students. Thus, Borkowski and his colleagues persuaded students that as they learned strategies, they were acquiring tools that would permit them to improve their academic performances, which was a powerful motivation for them to use the strategies (Chapman, Skinner, & Baltes, 1990).

For example, in one study (Carr & Borkowski, 1989), underachieving elementary students were assigned to one of three conditions: (1) In the Strategies + Attribution Training condition, students were taught comprehension strategies. They were instructed to read paragraphs and to self-test whether they understood the content. The students were also taught summarization, topic sentence, and questioning strategies as means of understanding text. The attributional part of the training consisted of emphasizing to students that they could understand text by applying the comprehension strategies. They learned that their comprehension of text was a function of how they approached text rather than of any inherent comprehension abilities. (2) Students in the Strategies-Only condition were taught the same strategies, but without the benefit of attributional training. (3) Students in the Control condition were provided neither strategies instruction nor attributional training. Children in all conditions participated in six half-hour sessions.

What a difference in the Strategies + Attributional Training condition! When tested 3 weeks following the conclusion of the training sessions, the students in the Strategies + Attribution condition were more likely to use the strategies than other participants in the study, and they also recalled more text information than students in the other conditions of the study. In addition, the Strategies + Attributions students were using the training strategies in the classroom much more than the students in the other conditions of the study. Using a similar approach with a similar result, Berkeley et al. (2011) taught seventh, eighth, and ninth graders reading comprehension strategy instruction alone or combined with attribution retraining. Students in both strategy conditions performed better on the summarization test of comprehension than control students, but those in strategy instruction with

attribution retraining better maintained their performance on a delayed comprehension measure.

Attribution retraining has been demonstrated to be effective with a wide variety of students, ranging from young elementary school students to college students,
including both normally achieving students and those with learning disabilities
(Foersterling, 1985). For example, Horner and Gaither (2004) found that second
graders who received attribution retraining, shifting to controllable factors, in their
math class increased their math scores and were less likely to make attributions about
their math performance to uncontrollable factors. Perry, Stupnisky, Hall, Chippefield, and Weiner (2010) explored attribution retraining for students making the
transition from high school to university. Transition to university includes a number
of adjustments, such as increased autonomy and the need to adopt better study strategies and time management techniques. These changes may also lead some students
to underestimate the factors under their control and to make attributions to uncontrollable factors, such as ability and task difficulty, resulting in reduced effort and
persistence. The attribution retraining intervention used in the Perry et al. study,
given to students at the beginning of a year-long, two-semester course, consisted of
a videotape of students discussing attributions and how poor performance can be
changed through controllable facts. This presentation was followed by commentary
from the course professor supporting the main points made in the video. Students
then took an aptitude test and discussed potential attributions that could be made
for performance using the main ideas in the video as a resource. At the end of the
year, students who received the attribution retraining were more likely to endorse
controllable attributions (such as amount and quality of study) than uncontrollable
factors (such as the quality of professor's teaching). For students who were initially
low or medium achievers in the course, the changes in attributions were also accompanied by better performance at the end of the semester

Nurturing Possible Selves

Ask yourself the following question: What am I going to be in 10 years? This question is tapping your conception of the **possible selves** that you might become, which
is another way to conceptualize your perceptions and expectations about yourself (Erikson, 2007; Markus & Nurius, 1986). Students reading this book who are
enrolled in teacher preparation programs may anticipate that they will be teachers,
administrators, or curriculum developers. Students in music programs may envision
themselves as concert soloists, conductors, or teachers. Functional possible selves are
not frivolous fantasies but realistic goals. Possible selves provide direction and the
energy for behaviors that reduce the distance between the current true self and the
possible self that one aspires to become.

It is important to have a realistic possible self. Many students believe that they
have a high probability of becoming professional athletes when, in fact the odds of
attaining such a possible self are extremely low. This unrealistic possible self motivates effort directed toward athletic accomplishment, effort that could have been
expended in pursuit of a self that is a more realistic possibility. Attainable "dreams,"
however, can be powerful motivators. For example, Gooden (1989) reported the case
of a dishwasher whose dream was to become a chef, a dream that motivated him to
make it through cooking school. Gooden also described cases of young black males
whose lofty goals, such as becoming a famous scientist or physician, kept them on

track academically so that they did eventually become professionals, although they did not attain their specific dreams. Even students identified as gifted exhibited increased motivation and interest in a science career after receiving social support in visualizing their future selves working in science (Buday, Stake, & Peterson, 2012).

The motivational impact of possible selves lies in the fit between the context and the future *hoped-for* or *feared* possible selves (Oyserman, Destin, & Novin, 2016). In a success-likely context, the hoped-for self is more motivating, whereas in a failure-likely context, the feared self is more motivating. In a context requiring self-regulation of health-related behaviors, a feared self was found to be generally more motivating than a desired self (van Dellen & Hoyle, 2008). In a community college setting, the balance between hoped-for and feared self was related to lower levels of self-handicapping behaviors in academic pursuits (Seli, Dembo, & Crocker, 2009).

Given the potential of possible selves for motivating interest in and commitment to academic attainment, Day, Borkowski, Dietmeyer, Howsepian, and Saenz (1994) designed an intervention to encourage possible selves that are more likely to keep students in grades 3 through 7 on track. Most of the Mexican American students participating in this study came from neighborhoods with few, if any, professionals. Thus, these children did not see neighborhood models who could inspire them to believe that they themselves could become professionals. Even so, these children highly valued success in school and had ambitious possible selves: 92% expected to graduate from high school, 75% expected to graduate from college, and 17% expected to graduate from a postcollege professional school. But they also feared that these dreams might not come true. Half of the children feared that they would end up in jobs that required less than a high school education.

The intervention was designed to help the children maintain their dreams through the many, potentially frustrating, steps of the educational process. This training package was aimed at increasing awareness of the many types of jobs these students might attain in their lives and to make it clear that completion of high school is essential for many vocations. In addition, the training package focused on how to cope with negative feedback and failure, including the unjustified reactions of others. Consistent with the principles of attribution theory described earlier in this chapter, the training was designed to increase student understanding that their successes were under their control—that is, that their own academic efforts would pay off.

The results of this intervention were promising. In comparison to control students who were not receiving the intervention, students participating in the possible-selves training had greater expectations of success in the future. They were more likely to believe they might attain especially high-status occupations, such as judge or physician, and showed modest improvements in grades.

In another invention study, Oyserman, Bybee, and Terry (2006) designed a multisession program to enhance the academic possible selves of low-income, and primarily minority, eighth-grade students. The intervention supported the development of academic possible selves by making academic possible selves salient, providing instruction in how to interpret failure, to understand that obstacles are a normal part of school life, and how to recover from typical setbacks encountered in school. The intervention also helped the students make connections between their academic possible selves and their social identity. The intervention resulted in a change in academic possible selves, accompanied with behavioral outcomes such as increased school attendance, more positive classroom behaviors, increased time spent on homework, higher achievement, and less depression in comparison to students in a control group. The positive effects were maintained over a 2-year follow-up. The intervention was also found to moderate the effect of low parental involvement in school, in that low parental involvement negatively affected the achievement of control students but not students in the intervention condition (Oyserman, Brickman, & Rhodes, 2007).

Hock, Schumaker, and Deshler (2003) developed a set of materials that teachers could use to promote healthy possible selves in their classrooms. These include exercises for thinking about *hoped-for* possible selves, *expected* possible selves, and *feared* possible selves. The approach is also filled with suggestions for encouraging students to set healthy goals for the short and long term.

Matching Academic Tasks to Student Competencies

Do you recall from Chapter 3 the Piagetian idea that students should be provided tasks just a bit beyond their current competence, as well as the related Vygotskian (Chapter 6) idea that teaching should be in the zone of proximal development and scaffolded? This idea of providing students with tasks that are just a bit beyond them is also supported by motivational theory. If students attempt an easy goal, they make progress rapidly, but they do not acquire information about their abilities to tackle more ambitious tasks. If students attempt too difficult a task, they experience little progress toward meeting the goal, resulting in diminished self-efficacy and motivation to continue with the task. Only tasks that are challenging for the learner, but not so challenging as to prevent progress, are capable of providing information to students that increases their sense of self-efficacy and promote their future attempts to meet challenging tasks (Wigfield et al., 2015). Teachers need to encourage students to select appropriate goals, ones that are not too easy and not too hard, and to provide the scaffolding, perhaps instruction in strategies appropriate for the task, needed for students to be successful.

Teachers need to encourage students to challenge themselves appropriately because some students do not do so, and there are big differences between students who seek challenge and those who avoid it. There are also consequences for seeking challenge versus avoiding it (Meyer, Turner, & Spencer, 1997). Students who seek challenge generally are more confident in their ability to do a task, and, if they struggle, they do not get upset but instead rebound, confident that they'll make progress and learn something with additional effort. Any initial frustration might prompt deeper thinking in such students. Those students who avoid challenge often lack confidence that they can make progress, and, if they experience a little failure, react negatively to it, perhaps giving up. They tend not to expend the effort to use strategies that get below the surface of a problem, and hence they do not learn as much as those who challenge themselves. One of the best ways to encourage those students who avoid challenges to accept one is to scaffold their attempts to learn.

Does teacher scaffolding of learning, consistent with Vygotskian theory, impact self-efficacy? The answer is a definite yes. For example, if students are learning how to use an electronic search engine, learning goes better and is more satisfactory when a teacher scaffolds the instruction rather than requiring students to discover how to search on their own. Most important here, students' self-efficacy with respect to their search skills is greater when such learning is scaffolded rather than when it is left to discovery and chance (Debowski, Wood, & Bandura, 2001).

Making Academic Tasks More Interesting: Increasing Choice and Perceived Value

John Dewey (1913) was the first educational philosopher to emphasize the critical role of interest in learning. Unfortunately, many students find that what they are asked to learn in school is boring (e.g., Farrell, Peguero, Lindsey, & White, 1988). Of course, this is a problem, since students pay more attention to content that is interesting and remember interesting material better (Hidi, 1990; Renniger & Hidi, 2011; Renninger & Wozniak, 1985).

Richard Anderson and his colleagues conducted studies to determine the mechanisms underlying the "interest effect." Students spent more time reading interesting texts as compared to less interesting texts. In addition, interesting texts were so absorbing that readers failed to respond to an external signal as quickly as they did when reading uninteresting texts (e.g., by pressing a button in response to a sound heard while reading). Even so, greater attention alone did not account for the greater learning of the interesting materials, for when differences in attention and effort were factored out of learning data (i.e., amount of time spent reading sentences was controlled statistically), there were still large differences due to interest (e.g., Shirey & Reynolds, 1988). Thus, interest can directly affect both attention and learning, with only some of the increases in learning due to the effects of interest on attention to academic content.

When Anderson, Shirey, Wilson, and Fielding (1987) analyzed school textbooks, they found that one of the most frequent approaches to making texts interesting is to add interesting anecdotes. Unfortunately, however, texts filled with anecdotes may lack coherence (e.g., Sadoski, 2001). In addition, often the personal anecdotes or interesting bits of information, **seductive details**, are recalled, but memory of the more important, abstract, and general points is unaffected (Garner, 1992; Garner, Alexander, Gillingham, Kulikowich, & Brown, 1991; Garner, Gillingham, & White, 1989; Hidi & Baird, 1988; Wade & Adams, 1990). That is, students might remember well that John F. Kennedy played touch football on the White House lawn with his family, but this interesting but unimportant detail does not help them remember key facts about the Kennedy administration. Care should be taken when adding interesting, but unimportant, pieces of information to textual material. Seductive details capture students' attention but may also disrupt students' processing of text, although the disruption may be less for narrative texts than less well-structured expository texts (Abercrombie, 2013; McCrudden & Corkill, 2010). Yet, seductive details do engage the learner and increase interest levels and may be useful in certain contexts such as narrated multimedia learning, when the learner has prior knowledge of the topic, or when the material is not difficult to process (Korbach, Brunken, & Park, 2016; Park, Flowerday, & Brunken, 2015; Wang, 2016).

Trying to make classroom texts more interesting and to increase student interest in school materials has generated a great deal of research (Hidi, 2001; Renniger & Hidi, 2011; Schraw, Flowerday, & Lehman, 2001; Schraw & Lehman, 2001; Wade, 2001). Teachers can increase student interest in several ways (Schraw et al., 2001), including the following: (1) offer meaningful choices to students by allowing them to select some texts themselves; (2) select well-organized, vivid, and relevant texts to use in the classroom—a text can't be interesting if it isn't coherent; (3) consider student prior knowledge—use classroom materials on topics that students already know about, or, if the topic is completely novel, provide some background before the materials are introduced; and (4) encourage students to be active learners. When students read texts that interest them, they like to read more, and they persist in reading longer (Ainley, Hidi, & Berndorff, 2002).

The positive effects of allowing more choice extends beyond text selection. For example, Patall, Cooper, and Wynn (2010) studied the effects of giving students choice in homework assignments in 14 classrooms ranging from grade 9 to grade 12. Students given choice assignments displayed greater motivation to do homework, higher feelings of competency about doing the homework, and better performance on a unit test. Allowing choices increases student perceptions of autonomy and control. If anything, promoting the feeling that they themselves are in control is more important in motivating students as they grow older (Chapman et al., 1990). Motivation and engagement increase if students believe they are exerting effort because *they want to do so*, not because *they are being forced to do so* (Anderman et al., 2013; Patrick, Skinner, & Connell, 1993; Skinner & Belmont, 1993).

Academic tasks also become more motivating if students understand their value and why they are part of the curriculum. Often the value of the curriculum is not explicitly addressed in classrooms, and as we have learned from expectancy–value theory, perceived value is a key motivator. Fortunately, students are responsive to interventions promoting the value of academic tasks. For example, Hulleman and Harackiewicz (2009) demonstrated that increasing the relevance of science curriculum by asking high school students to write about how the knowledge they gleaned from their science class was meaningful and relevant to their lives resulted in higher levels of interest and better grades in science. In a follow-up study, college students randomly assigned to a condition where they made frequent connections of course material to their lives led to greater confidence about learning the material and higher performance in a psychology course compared to students in a control condition (Hulleman, Kosovich, Barron, & Daniel, 2017). The effect was largest for low-achieving students. Gaspard et al. (2015) developed a 90-minute intervention highlighting the relevance of mathematics for ninth-grade students. The intervention included a presentation on the utility of mathematics for future education plans and careers and activities designed to increase personal relevance, such as asking students to write evaluations of quotations from young adults talking about how mathematics made a difference for them. The students' perceived value for mathematics increased, and the increase was maintained 5 months later. Not all components of an academic curriculum, however, can be made interesting for most students. In those instances, Yeager et al. (2014) suggest calling on a "higher purpose," beyond the self, for learning the material. For example, students might be asked to write testimonials to future students about reasons for learning, even uninteresting materials, in pursuit of higher-order goals. This kind of intervention resulted in more persistence, higher grade point averages, and deeper learning of "tedious material."

Promoting Cooperative Learning

As discussed earlier in this chapter, classroom environments can be structured so that they have devastating effects on the motivation of many students. Researchers interested in cooperative learning believe that much can be done to improve student motivation in classrooms, even if the classroom has competitive grading.

Johnson and Johnson (1985, 2013) describe three types of social structures found in classrooms. (1) A *cooperative* social situation exists when the goals of the separate individuals are linked together, so that an individual can obtain his or her goal only if the other participants can achieve their goals. (2) A *competitive* social situation exists when the goals of the separate individuals are in opposition, so that an individual can obtain his or her goal only if the other participants cannot obtain their goals. (3) Finally, an *individualistic* social situation exists when there is no relationship among the goal attainments of the participants—that is, whether an individual accomplishes his or her goal has no influence on whether other individuals achieve their goals. For example, when students work together to put on a play, they are participating in a cooperative situation: The play is a success only if all students do their part. A spelling bee is an example of a competitive situation: Only one student can win; the others must lose. Finally, a student working to master the multiplication tables is an example of an individualistic situation—whether or not the student accomplishes this task has no bearing on the other students in the class.

Cooperative learning is more likely to produce better learning and more motivated learners than competitive learning and individualistic learning (Johnson, Maruyama, Johnson, Nelson, & Skon, 1981; Marr, 1997; O'Donnell & King, 1999). Moreover, the approach has been demonstrated to facilitate learning at *all* grade levels, for *all* subjects, and for *all* achievement levels (Qin, Johnson, & Johnson, 1995; Slavin, 1995, 2013). Cooperative learning also produces many positive social effects, including increases in self-esteem, attitudes toward school, and acceptance of differences. Slavin (e.g., 1995, 2013) emphasizes that cooperative learning is most likely to be effective if there are both *group rewards and individual accountability*.

Cooperative Learning Groups

Cooperative learning typically takes place in the context of small groups. Key elements of effective cooperative learning in groups include the following (Johnson & Johnson, 1985, 2013):

* Learning should be *interdependent*. Task completion should require everyone's help, and group members should perceive that their individual success depends on everyone in the group succeeding. Members of cooperative learning groups share resources and support each other's efforts.

* *Individual and group accountability* is essential. The group must be accountable for completing the task, and each member is responsible for contributing to the group work. One reason individual accountability is so crucial is that some students are tempted to coast when they are in small learning groups, leaving the majority of the work to one or two group members (Hogan et al., 2000; Lindauer & Petrie, 1997).

* Students need to be taught *interpersonal and small-group skills*. Students need to learn not only the academic subject matter but also how to work effectively in a team. They need to learn the social skills that permit more productive interactions.

* Effective cooperative learning groups also engage in *group processing* in order to assess progress toward goal completion and to evaluate interactions among the group members. When difficulties are encountered, the group needs to regroup and refocus their efforts.

One cooperative learning approach, Student Teams Achievement Divisions (STAD), is adaptable to most subjects and grade levels (Slavin, 1991). Students are assigned to four-member teams, mixed in performance level, sex, and ethnicity. The teacher presents the lesson, and the teams work together to make sure all students master the lesson. The students take individual quizzes, without the assistance of team members, to assess what they have learned. The teacher compares the students' quiz scores to their own past averages and computes a team average based on student improvement. Perfect performances always receive a maximum score no matter what the previous performance.

In this approach, every student must know the material. Thus, there is *individual accountability*. The teams can also earn *team rewards* if they achieve at or above a designated criterion. The teams are not in competition with each other in that all teams could earn a team reward. Since team averages are computed in consideration of students' past averages, all students have *equal opportunity for success* and can contribute to the team performance by improving on their past performances.

Why Is Cooperative Learning Effective?

A number of theoretical explanations for the effectiveness of the cooperative learning approach have been given (Webb, 2013a, 2013b). According to a Piagetian perspective (see Chapter 3), cooperative learning is effective because group discussions induce cognitive conflict. An analysis based on Vygotskian ideas would invoke the concept of the zone of proximal development and scaffolding provided by a more capable peer (see also the discussion of problem-based learning in Chapter 6). An information-processing approach would emphasize the construction of knowledge through the connections made as group members share knowledge and provide explanations. Social learning theorists would stress learning through modeling and the effect of the reward structures.

Nonetheless, organizing and implementing successful collaborative learning can be challenging (Rogat, Linnebrink-Garcia, & DiDonato, 2013; Webb, 2013b). For example, difficulties may be encountered in the interpersonal dynamics of cooperative groups in that some students engage in off-task socializing behavior and rely on the others to do the work. Some students may find it difficult to engage with the group work due to shyness or discomfort sharing ideas with others; others may dominate the group processes. Group work can be more effortful than working alone, requiring more time and social negotiation. Sometime, the group interaction can create too much conflict and can become too adversarial if students do not listen to the perspectives of others. Acknowledging that collaborative learning generally facilitates learning, Nokes-Malach, Richey, and Gadgil, (2015) analyzed why it works and why it sometimes does not work in a review of the research. Failures may be due to the cognitive costs associated with coordinating and collaborating with others that may impact memory and attention and disrupt individual processing. The researchers also identified social factors related to failure such as loafing or lack of participation out of fear of others' evaluations. Explanations for success included cognitive factors such as the cueing effect of collective knowledge and associated memory consolidation. Another plus was the potential for error correction in that group members can check on each other's developing knowledge. There are also cognitive benefits associated with reexposure to material through discussion and through negotiation of multiple perspectives. Group members can possess complementary knowledge and contribute to different aspects of a solution, explaining ideas to each other, which benefits all. Social processes associated with success include observational learning and increased engagement as the group works together to stay on task. There are also the social benefits of identifying common ground and shared perspectives.

Teachers can structure cooperative learning situations in their classrooms and support their students in the process in order to maximize the benefits for learners (O'Donnell & King, 1999). Specifically they can prepare students by teaching them how to take turns, listen actively, ask clear questions, create high-level questions, summarize what has been accomplished, and monitor understanding (Slavin, 2014; Webb, 2013a). Some suggestions for creating cooperative learning groups are provided in the Applying Developmental Theory to Educational Contexts special feature (Box 9.2).

Fostering Positive Teacher–Student Relationships

Positive teacher–student relationships are significantly related to student engagement and achievement (Davis, 2013). What do positive relationships between teachers and students look like? The teacher behaviors identified include treating students fairly

---

Applying Development Theory to Educational Contexts

BOX 9.2. Creating Cooperative Learning Groups

Research on cooperative learning has been enlightening about how to structure cooperative learning groups so as to maximize student achievement (Slavin, 2014; Webb, 1984, 1989, 2013a). Here are some of the best teaching tips emerging from this work.

• Be sure to use both *group rewards and individual accountability*. Individual accountability helps to eliminate freeloading, and a group reward provides incentive for the students to work together.

• Students who do the explaining often learn the most, so it is important to structure groups so that a high percentage of students participate.

• Make sure the students in each cooperative group represent a *range of ability*, although cooperative learning seems to work better if groups do not include the full range of ability. For example, place high-ability and medium-ability students together. Similarly, place medium-ability and low-ability students together.

• Make sure the groups are *gender-balanced* as well. Girls are more likely to be interactive and have higher achievement in cooperative learning groups if there are equal numbers of boys and girls. If there's a majority of boys, girls are more likely to be ignored. If there's a majority of girls, proportionately more interactions are directed at the few boys.

• If at all possible, try to make the groups racially or ethnically balanced as well.

• As much as possible, *monitor* group interactions. Make sure groups stay on task and that all students have equal opportunities for learning.

• Teach students appropriate social skills for academic interactions, such as how it often makes sense to compromise and that disagreements are all right as long as students who disagree are respectful in their disagreements. Recall the discussions in Chapter 3 about how Piagetian-oriented theorists interested in education consistently encourage cognitive conflict as a means of cognitive growth. An important point here is that engaging in such conflict can be highly motivating. Respectful discussions involving students arguing for their perspectives do much to promote cognitive growth. Such discussion is often engaging.

and with respect, providing academic help and encouragement, and using positive approaches to classroom management (Cooper & Miness, 2014). Teacher–student relationships are bi-directional. The students who perceive their relationships with their teachers as positive exhibit increased school attendance, increased participation in class activities, and less oppositional or disruptive behavior in the classroom (Cornelius-White, 2007).

In a meta-analysis of 99 studies in settings ranging from preschool to high school, Roorda et al. (2011) examined how teacher–student relationships influence student achievement and engagement. Positive relationships were characterized by empathy and warmth, whereas negative relationships were marked by conflict. A moderate to large effect size was found for the association of relationships to engagement, and a small to moderate effect size was found for the association of relationships to achievement. The effects were stronger in the higher grades of high school, with the exception that the effects of negative relationships were stronger in elementary school than in high school. An analysis of a large longitudinal data set of students from first through fifth grade revealed that higher levels of conflict between students and teachers were associated with lower levels of reading achievement in elementary school (McCormick & O'Connor, 2015). Elementary school girls who experienced more conflict in their relationships with teachers had lower levels of math achievement and less growth in their math achievement across the time frame than boys who had similarly conflictual relationships.

Sabol and Pianta (2013) described a developmental pattern where children's perceptions of closeness (perceived support, sense of belongingness and acceptance, and willingness to rely on the teacher) with their teachers declined after the transition to elementary school from early childhood school experiences, but positive relationships still significantly affected student outcomes. As noted earlier in this chapter, the transition to middle and high school is difficult for many students. Unfortunately, student perceptions of teacher support typically decline in middle school and is associated with increased depression and decreased self-esteem. Adolescents, particularly urban youth of color, are much more engaged in academic tasks if their developmental needs are met—notably, if they feel they are being heard, perceive they are being taken seriously, and believe their teachers truly know them (Wallace & Chhuon, 2014). An emotionally supportive environment in the classroom creates positive effects for students of all ages and can moderate the negative effects of early experiences (McCormick & O'Connor, 2015; Sabol & Pianta, 2013). Fortunately, teachers can learn how to improve their relationships with students through professional development (Sabol & Pianta, 2013).

How Do Really Motivating Teachers Motivate Their Students?

Despite the fact that motivation declines during the elementary school years and beyond for many students, many other students stay motivated. What do teachers do to increase the likelihood that their students will be motivated?

Michael Pressley and his colleagues observed the differences in the practices of teachers who produce consistently high engagement in their students and those who fail to do so. From first grade through middle school grades, they found a consistent pattern (Bogner, Raphael, & Pressley, 2002; Dolezal et al., 2003; Pressley et al., 2003). Engaging teachers *flood* their classrooms with motivating instruction, doing something to motivate students *every* minute of *every* hour of *every* day, using all of the positive motivational mechanisms covered in this chapter. That is, these teachers communicate high expectations about today's work and students' long-term futures, praise specific accomplishments, use cooperative learning, permit choices for students, and much, much more. From the very first days of school, motivating teachers send the message that students need to self-regulate, making certain the students know what they are supposed to do and are doing it without the teacher reminding them constantly. If a student is foundering, the most effective teachers provide just enough scaffolding on an as-needed basis to ensure that all students are progressing (Bohn et al., 2004).

Brophy (1987) suggested that many teachers do not understand all that they *could* do and *need* to do to maximize motivation in their classrooms. So he provided seventh- and eighth-grade social studies teachers with brief training in the various ways of making instruction more motivating. The teachers in the study used the motivational tactics they had learned in one of their classes and continued to teach another section in their customary fashion. Although the positive effects of the intervention were not large, and the effects were obscured somewhat by teachers carrying over what they had learned about motivation into their "control" classes, the outcomes were in the right direction. Thus, teachers can develop more motivating classrooms when provided with the right kinds of information about motivation. Turner, Christensen, Kackar-Cam, Trucano, and Fulner (2014) found that some, but not all, middle school teachers who received professional development combining four principles of motivation (autonomy, competence, relatedness/belongingness, and meaningfulness) and related instructional strategies were able to successfully implement the practices in their classroom and increase student engagement over a 3-year period. See the Applying Developmental Theory to Educational Contexts special feature (Box 9.3) for a list of classroom practices that foster motivation derived from the research described in this chapter.

Contextual Determination of Academic Motivation

Recall Bronfenbrenner's (1979, 1989, 1992) *ecological systems theory*, introduced in Chapter 1. Bronfenbrenner contends that children's proximal environments (i.e., the **microsystem:** community, school, church, immediate family) have great impact on children, but so do more distant environmental factors and cultural forces (i.e., the **macrosystem**). These forces operate simultaneously and interactively.

Research evidence indicates that academic achievement is associated with students' social environments (Wigfield et al., 2015). Virtually all of this research is correlational, and thus determining cause and effect is often very difficult. Of course, if Bronfenbrenner is correct, it should be impossible to determine whether the environment causes a child's academic achievement or if the child's achievement affects the environment. Children and the social context reciprocally interact. For example, parents affect children, who in turn affect their parents.

Microsystem

There are probably few simple effects of the environment. For example, *parents* can affect cognitive development and achievement in complex ways (Fan & Chen, 2001; Grolnick, Raftery-Helmer, & Flamm, 2013; Steinberg, 1997, 2001). Parents who are accepting of their children, who supervise them appropriately, and who grant them

Applying Developmental Theory to Educational Contexts

BOX 9.3. Classroom Practices That Foster Motivation

The following list of qualities displayed by teachers and features found in classrooms where student engagement is high incorporates suggestions made by Brophy (1987, 1998) along with the other various ideas discussed in this chapter.

Classrooms should be:

- Orderly and well managed but not rigid environments
- Low-anxiety places
- More improvement-oriented than competitive

Academic curriculum should be:

- Meaningful, relevant, interesting, and worth learning.
- At an appropriate level of difficulty, not too easy but not so difficult that most students will not be able to meet task demands with reasonable effort.

Teachers should have an extensive repertoire of motivational practices including the following:

- Modeling interest in learning, letting students know that they like learning and find academic activities rewarding and generally satisfying.
- Communicating why the upcoming content is valuable.
- Encouraging student autonomy and choice.
- Modeling thinking and problem solving as they occur, conveying how to approach tasks and showing that academic tasks are engaging and meaningful.
- Inducing curiosity and suspense by asking students to make predictions or by inducing cognitive conflict.
- Including novelty, humor, fun, and games as part of learning.
- Using evaluation procedures that encourage a focus on learning rather than performance.
- Communicating expectations that students can be successful.
- Promoting visions of positive future academic selves.
- Promoting student attributions that success and failure is under their control.
- Maintaining positive relationships with students, conveying caring and understanding.

autonomy as their children can handle it (i.e., authoritative parents; see also Chapter 10) are more likely to have academically motivated and successful adolescents. Parents influence their children's academic motivation by being role models, by providing appropriate levels of support, and by communicating academic values and expectations (Wigfield et al., 2015). They also impact their children through their more direct involvement with schools, including ensuring attendance, appearing at school events, and supporting and monitoring homework. Level of parental involvement is associated with academic achievement in terms of both grades and standardized test scores (Cheung & Pomerantz, 2015; Grolnick, Raftery-Helmer, & Flamm, 2013). Potential barriers to parent involvement include language differences, long working hours, limited educational experience, and lack of transportation (Martin, 2013).

Peers are also prominent in the microsystem of children—again using Bronfenbrenner's term for factors that affect a child's life through direct contact (see also Chapter 10). Peers become increasingly important as children grow older (Choukas-Bradley & Prinstein, 2014; Levitt, Guacci-Franco, & Levitt, 1993; Parker, Rubin, Erath, Wojslawowicz, & Buskirk, 2006). Better peer relations are associated with better academic motivation and performance, and good students are more likely to have supportive peers than weaker students (Levitt et al., 1994; Wentzel, 1998, 2003; Wentzel, Russell, & Baker, 2016).

School and the various elements of instruction encountered there are salient in the child's microsystem, with the motivational effects of what happens at school very much depending on a variety of contextual variables. As described earlier in this chapter, the quality of the relationship between teachers and students has a significant effect on motivation and engagement. In the larger context, the perceived quality of the school climate as a whole influences students' feelings of support, autonomy, and competence (Hoigaard, Kovac, Overby, & Haugen, 2015; Wigfield et al., 2015). School and district-level policies such as physical space and size of the school building, grade configuration, start and end time, discipline policies, and tracking policies also impact student engagement and achievement (Eccles & Roeser, 2011; McNeely, 2013). For example, some gifted students' academic motivations are much better maintained when they remain in regular classrooms, where they can be "big academic fish" in the regular classroom pond, than if they were to be put in gifted classes filled with "big fish" (Marsh et al., 2008, 2015; Marsh & Hau, 2003).

Macrosystem

Culture exerts an impact on students, influencing their motivations by affecting elements of the microsystem. Japanese culture's emphasis on effort translates rather directly into familial and schooling support of student effort, with the role of uncontrollable factors that might determine achievement downplayed (Heine et al., 2001; Holloway, 1988; Tuss, Zimmer, & Ho, 1995). German parents and teachers emphasize the teaching of strategies, consistent with German cultural norms about the determinants of achievement (Kurtz et al., 1990; see also Chapter 4). Self-efficacy tends to be lower in non-Western cultures even when performances are equivalent or higher (Klassen, 2004; Schunk & Mullein, 2013). For some cultures, collective self-efficacy—a group's shared belief to take actions to achieve collective goals—is more of an influence on motivation and achievement than individual goals (Klassen, 2004). Culture influences what is considered success and failure and how students participate in classroom activities (Wigfield et al., 2015). Cultural variations in academic motivation have been identified, as have some commonalities such as the finding that mastery goals are adaptive across cultures (King & McInerney, 2014). In Bronfenbrenner's terms, there are striking effects of the macrosystem.

Role of the Individual Child

The individual child is part of the context and as such is a determiner of his or her own motivation and achievement, although always in interaction with other factors.

For example, researchers have documented how the naturally shy kindergarten student or first grader, or the 5- or 6-year-old who is afraid of taking academic risks, succeeds in isolating her- or himself in the classroom, setting off a cycle of increasing isolation that undermines participation, which is so critical to high achievement in school (Evans, 2010; Finn & Cox, 1992; Jones & Gerig, 1994). Teachers often do not push shy children to participate, perhaps believing that participation may be too stressful for the child. Thus, the child's nonparticipation can shape the teacher's perceptions and behavior in ways that support the continued nonparticipation of the child. Teachers can, however, learn ways to support increased classroom participation of shy children (Coplan, Hughes, Bosacki, & Rose-Krasnor, 2011; Evans, 2001; O'Connor, Capella, McCormick, & McClowry, 2014).

Chapter Summary and Evaluation

The research conducted in the past few decades to map out the development of academic motivation and identify the causes of developmental shifts in motivation and achievement has been impressive. The work links well with the experiences of educators and parents. Every high school teacher knows that many secondary students are not motivated. Every kindergarten teacher senses enthusiasm for learning in most of her students. Teachers' perceptions are not illusions but rather correspond with developmental declines in academic motivation. These declines can be explained in part by declines in self-efficacy, shifts in attributional tendencies, perceptions of relationships with teachers, increasing competitiveness, and other changes in schooling practices as students move from the primary to the middle grades and into high school.

Understanding of motivation occurred in the last two decades because researchers focused largely on students' thinking about themselves as learners (i.e., self-efficacy) and their thinking about the causes of achievement (i.e., a function of effort, ability, task difficulty, or luck) and about their achievement goals (i.e., mastery and performance) as a function of various types of experiences (e.g., participation in competitive vs. cooperative classrooms, elementary vs. secondary schools). What the child thinks often affects what the child does . . . and what the child is motivated to do.

Understanding of developmental declines in motivation also occurred because researchers mapped out how schooling changed with increasing age in ways that affect motivation. Most critically, school becomes more competitive with "winners" and "losers" more apparent. Since most children do not consistently come out on top, their self-efficacy and related motivational beliefs can be affected negatively. Secondary school formats, with multiple subject-based classes and increased demands, also lessen the likelihood that close relationships will be formed with the multiple teachers encountered throughout the day.

More positively, much has also been learned about increasing motivation in school. Cooperative learning methods have been developed and have been linked to greater achievement by students. As students are taught new intellectual skills, instruction can be engineered to make it clear that effort pays off. Thus, students can be encouraged to attribute their academic performances to the controllable factor of *effort*, rather than to factors that are out of the student's control, such as *ability*, *task difficulty*, or *luck*. Academic tasks can be made more interesting. Teachers can be taught about student motivation and how to apply insights from research on motivation to their classrooms. With respect to long-term motivation, teachers can foster healthy "possible selves" as part of encouraging students to try hard in school. By doing so, they are developing a set of expectations about how academic effort today can translate into lifelong success.

The importance of success expectations has been discussed in detail in this chapter. Without expectations of success through expenditure of effort, there is no reason to expend effort. In classrooms where there is high academic engagement, teachers flood the classroom with motivating instruction, using all of the positively motivating mechanisms reviewed in this chapter and doing nothing that could undermine academic achievement.

Research on academic motivation highlights the contextual determination of motivation and achievement. A student's academic motivation is greatly determined by the interaction of family, peer, and school factors, all of which are embedded in a complex larger society and world. The downside of the contextualist perspective is that prediction of motivation and achievement will always be iffy, for motivation depends on so many forces in interaction. The positive side of contextualist approaches is that there are many ways to intervene in order to affect student motivation positively: through the family, the peer system, the school, and/or through attending to the biological health and individual needs of the child.

Research on motivation has produced much evidence relevant to the Big Ideas about development introduced in Chapter 1.

Nature and Nurture

A perspective supported by a great deal of data is that humans are born with an intrinsic motivation to be more competent, to try hard to improve. Whether such intrinsic motivation translates into high academic motivation, however, depends a great deal on experience. As frustrations accumulate in school, intrinsic motivation to do school-like things seems to decline in general. Intrinsic motivation is more likely to be fostered in cooperative than in competitive academic environments and depends in part on how interesting and valued the new material is. In short, environmental variables are extremely important in determining academic motivation, with recent evidence making it clear that the most effective and engaging classrooms are those in which the teacher creates a classroom environment that incorporates many practices that support motivation. As we have concluded again and again in this text, nature and nurture interact to determine development and behavior.

Continuity and Discontinuity

Theorists and researchers interested in academic motivation do not identify much with discontinuous stage models. Developmental regularities are more often attributed to shifts in the environment experienced by all children with advancing age or to gradually changing biological factors (e.g., mental capacity) than to any biologically mediated, stage-like progression.

Universal and Culture-Specific

The universal most often referred to in discussions of student motivation is that children are born with an intrinsic interest in improving themselves (White, 1959). Whether that motivation is maintained and how that motivation translates into behavior depends largely on the child's culture, which affects the behaviors of families and peers and goes far in determining the nature of important institutions making contact with the child, such as school.

Active and Passive Child

Although children seem to be born to be naturally active and motivated, the developmental declines in motivation suggest increasing passivity with advancing age and grade. Alternatively, with increasing age there is increasing motivation for other things besides school, including motivation to be with friends and to make money. It is not that high school students are not motivated or that they are passive; rather, it is that they are not motivated to do school things!

REVIEW OF KEY TERMS

attributions Explanations for behavior, often for successes or failures.

ego involvement A determination of success whereby students compare their performances to those of others.

fixed mindset The belief that intelligence is fixed, not malleable.

growth mindset The belief that intelligence is modifiable by experience.

intrinsic motivation Motivation generated within the learner.

learned helplessness The belief that there is nothing one can do that will lead to success.

macrosystem In ecological systems theory, the cultural influences affecting a child.

mastery goal orientation Motivation to learn, to develop knowledge.

microsytem In ecological systems theory, the direct experiences of the child in various settings such as home and school.

overjustification effect The effect of extrinsic rewards perceived as controlling upon intrinsic motivation.

performance goal orientation Motivation to perform well, to demonstrate knowledge.

possible selves Envisioning of what one might become; learners are motivated to reduce the difference between their current selves and their possible selves.

seductive details Interesting bits of information that may distract attention from the main idea.

self-efficacy A learner's perception of his or her capability of reaching a desired goal or a certain level of performance.

task involvement A determination of success whereby students evaluate their own improvement.

CHAPTER 10

Family and Peer Relationships

At first, an education student may wonder how a child's family and peer relationships are relevant to teaching. As it turns out, scholars have identified a number of key issues related to how a child relates to others and that child's learning potential. It is these issues that we intend to explore in this chapter. Typically, a child's earliest social relationships are in the context of a family, with his or her primary adult caregiver, other family adult caregivers, and siblings. These relationships set the tone for the future relationships a child forms. To better understand a child's capacity for relating to others, we need to begin by examining how children and parents establish attachments to one another. We follow this discussion with an examination of how parent–child and sibling relationships transform as a student matures. Contemporary families cope with a number of needs and demands, and we consider how some of these stressors—in particular, having children in day care/after-school care, economic duress, and family transitions like divorce and remarriage—affect family relationships and a student's adjustment and capacity for learning.

As a child ages, and especially as a child nears and enters adolescence, his or her peer relationships play an increasingly important role in his or her development, so this chapter also explores the role of peer relationships in a child's development and how they can facilitate or derail a student's attitude toward school and learning. We conclude by summarizing how social relationships affect academic achievement, noting that social development and cognitive development are strongly related.

The Child's First Relationship: Adult–Infant Attachment

Babies are wholly dependent on the adults who care for them. Consequently, forming a bond with a primary adult caregiver is the first and foremost psychological competency required of infants. Babies that master this skill acquire the capacity to trust others, experience how to appropriately depend on others, and learn to discriminate between healthy positive others and those who may do harm to them. Only by developing this **"secure base"** do infants acquire the confidence needed to explore their world and to seek interpersonal contact for help or affiliation. Of course, as in all relationships, forming an intimate bond with an adult caregiver depends not only on the capacities of an infant but also on the capacities and availability of a caring adult, which we consider in this chapter.

How infants and parents go about this process has been the subject of intense research for decades. This research begins with René Spitz's post-World War II studies of children raised in relative isolation in orphanages who failed to thrive, and with Harry Harlow's pioneering studies of primates deprived of maternal contact, who sought "contact comfort" and preferred to cling to inanimate surrogates covered in cloth rather than wire surrogates, even when the latter were the source of food. John Bowlby and Mary Ainsworth were among the first to extensively study human infant–caregiver attachment and develop a comprehensive theory about the course of attachment and the biological and social mechanisms that might account for attachment. Bowlby, a British psychiatrist, was particularly interested in child–parent attachment and child–parent separation following attachment and studied children separated from their parents because of hospitalization. Ainsworth, a Canadian-American psychologist, developed a research method called the "Strange Situation" that provided empirical evidence of the nature of parent–child attachment.

Bowlby was influenced by *ethological theory*, one important tenet of which is that humans have evolved to be sensitive to signals that elicit attachment responses from adult caregivers (Cassidy, 2016). For example, the large eyes and round face of infants elicits affectionate responses from adults (Alley, 1981; Glocker et al., 2009) that cues attachment behavior. In addition, adult humans are innately sensitive to the signals that babies emit and react instinctively to babies' smiles, vocalizations, and cries, attending to and interacting with infants appropriately when they signal adults with a grin, by babbling, or with a wail of distress (Bowlby, 1969; Keller & Scholmerich, 1987; Laurent & Ablow, 2012; Lin, Manuel, McFatter, & Cech, 2016).

Moreover, infants are innately disposed to signal adults, to act in ways that elicit adult attention, and to pay attention to adults. During the first months of life, infants emit signals that lead adults to respond. Infant cries are a means by which babies communicate their needs to adults (Laurent & Ablow, 2012; Lin, Manuel, McFatter, & Cech, 2016). The presence of other people elicits smiles from 2-month-olds, and even hearing human voices can evoke a smile during the first month of life. From very early in infancy, babies prefer voices over other auditory stimulation, and they are especially sensitive to high-pitched voices, sound frequencies more characteristic of female than male voices. In addition, babies come into this world ready to attend to perceptual displays like the human face, preferring faces to displays that have similar visual qualities (Bremmer, 2011; Kwon et al., 2016; Turati et al., 2005).

Although infants signal adults somewhat indiscriminately at first, over time infants come to prefer adults who have been responsive in the past. When the primary caregiver's attention is sensitive and consistent, an infant begins to develop confidence that the caregiver will be present for him or her, and a bond and secure attachment form. The security afforded by this type of attachment gives the child the assurance he or she needs to explore the world (Cassidy, 2016; Marvin, Britner, & Russell, 2016).

In short, both babies and adults have a biological predisposition to respond to one another (Laurent & Ablow, 2012; Polan & Hofer, 2016). Theoretically, this capacity has been selected by evolutionary processes because it confers a survival benefit to the human species. Parents sensitive to infant signals that caused them to stay in contact with the infant would be more likely to have babies that survive and mature into adulthood. Similarly, babies who signaled their parents when they needed parental attention would be more likely to mature to reproductive age and give birth to children of their own, passing along their genes to the next generation. In contrast, parents who lacked sensitivity to infant cues and infants who inadequately cued adults would lead to circumstances that minimized survival; hence, their genes would not be as likely to enter future generations. Over the course of human evolution, traits that led to parental sensitivity and infant attentiveness to adults were selected and passed on to future generations (Simpson & Belsky, 2016).

Infant Cognition and Attachment

Ordinarily, babies will experience parental attempts to bond with them dozens of times each day, hundreds perhaps thousands of times each week, tens of thousands of times a year. Over time, infants begin to develop expectations and "beliefs' about the availability and reliability of a primary attachment figure, which are the rudiments of an attachment system. The development of an infant's attachment to an adult depends somewhat on the level of cognitive development of the infant (Marvin, Britner, & Russell, 2016; Thompson, 2016). Before the age of 6 months, infants have a limited awareness that objects (including attachment figures) continue to exist when they are out of sight or not in the infant's proximity (Bremmer, 2011; Bremmer, Slater, & Johnson, 2015; Cacchione, 2013). But both Bowlby and Piaget believed, and studies have confirmed, that infants begin to acquire object permanence and the ability to discriminate between familiar people and strangers by 6 months of age (Marvin, Britner, & Russell, 2016; Pallini & Barcaccia, 2014; see Chapter 3). This facilitates the development of a more mature attachment system.

Bowlby (1973, 1980) recognized that attachment requires more than simply recognizing the continuing existence of other people. It also involves the development of mental representations of the self and the attachment object. As discussed in Chapter 4, young children form schematic representations of the world. During the first years of life, infants form schemas about how their primary caretakers respond in various situations. These representations of recurring events in their world serve as the basis for future expectations about what will happen in similar situations. Bowlby and subsequent attachment theorists refer to these expectations and schemas as an **internal working model** (Bretherton & Munholland, 2016; Sherman, Rice & Cassidy, 2015). This model, and the schemas that make it up, becomes the basis on which infants and children understand their interpersonal experiences. It becomes a template that children use to interpret and understand the social world and ultimately their own self-perceptions (Bretherton & Munholland, 2016; Thompson, 2016).

When infants and children experience primary caretakers that are dependable, consistent, and sensitive, they develop secure attachment schemas. Moreover, they are more likely to establish a representation of their self as valuable and self-reliant.

When infants experience less optimal caregiving, particularly parent bonding that is inconsistent and unresponsive to an infant's needs, they are more likely to develop an insecure attachment as an internal working model and a more anxiety-ridden and less worthy sense of self. As a child's internal working model of attachment matures, it becomes a major contributor to that child's capacities for initiating and maintaining positive and productive close relationships, with parents, peers, and even *teachers* (Berlin, Cassidy, & Appleyard, 2008; Kerns & Brumariu, 2016; Maldonado-Carreño & Votruba-Drzal, 2011; Thompson, 2016). But it is also important to note that secure attachment in infancy has an effect on cognitive development (Ding, Xu, Wang, Li, & Wang, 2014). More securely attached infants have more confidence that adult caregivers are present and attentive, which enables them to explore their immediate environment. Infants and children who have experienced less adequate parental bonding and lack this attachment security are more psychologically preoccupied with anxiety and are less likely to engage with their environment in a manner that promotes cognitive development. We explore this idea in more detail later, but first it is important to understand what researchers have found about the nature of attachment and how it contributes to a child's development.

Researching Attachment and Identifying Types of Attachment

Consider for a minute, if you can, being less than 2 years old. You can walk, but you like to be carried. You are not yet fully potty trained, and you don't talk yet, although you can use a few words. One day, your mother takes you to a place you've never been before; it's an office in a building kind of like the doctor's office, and for a moment you are a little worried you are going to see a doctor and get another shot. But that doesn't happen; instead the people there put you in a room with some toys and a couch and a lot of mirrors on the walls. They tell you that you can play with the toys, and you look at your Mom to see if it is okay. She nods, so you sit down and look through the toys to find one you like. But then a stranger walks in, and before long your mother walks out leaving you alone with this person. This is a little disconcerting for you, but your Mom comes back, and you start to feel better. Then everyone leaves the room, which is bewildering. The stranger then comes back, and this is really weird. Thankfully, your Mom comes back after a few minutes that seem like ages. What you have just experienced was a research protocol called the "Strange Situation," which is used to study attachment between infants and parent caregivers.

Individual differences in the quality of infant–mother attachment have been documented, with general agreement among researchers as to the types of attachment relations that occur between parents and infants (Feeney & Woodhouse, 2016; Simpson & Belsky, 2016). These individual differences have been studied most extensively in what Ainsworth and her colleagues (Ainsworth, Blehar, Waters, & Wall, 1978) dubbed the "Strange Situation." This research protocol involves eight episodes, each 3 minutes long except for the first one, which only lasts 30 seconds or so. The episodes are as follows (Solomon & George, 2016):

1. A researcher introduces the mother and infant to the experimental room and then leaves.
2. The infant is free to explore the room with the mother present. The mother is inactive, unless the infant does not begin to explore in the first 2 minutes.

At that point, she encourages the infant to play with the toys that are in the room.

3. A second researcher (a stranger) enters the room, remaining silent for about a minute. Then the stranger talks to the mother. In the third minute, the stranger approaches the infant. At the end of the third minute, the mother slips out of the room.

4. The second researcher and the infant are left alone in the room for the entire 3-minute episode.

5. The mother returns, greeting and comforting the infant. The second researcher leaves. Then the mother encourages the infant to play some more with the toys. At the end of this 3-minute reunion between the mother and infant, the mother leaves again.

6. The infant is alone for 3 minutes.

7. The separation from the mother continues for 3 more minutes, as the second researcher enters the room for 3 minutes with the infant.

8. The mother reunites with the infant as the second researcher slips out of the room. Mother greets and picks up the baby.

The critical data in Strange Situation research are the infant's responses to the various episodes, especially the behaviors during the reunion with the mother. Researchers have observed several different types of reactions, which are summarized in Table 10.1. Children with a secure attachment (Type B) tended to get upset when separated from their mothers but were easily consoled at reunion and greeted their mother with pleasure. Children with insecure attachment—there are two types A (anxious-avoidant) and C (anxious-ambivalent/resistant)—had a much different response to the Strange Situation. Children with anxious-avoidant attachment (Type A) seemed on the surface to be unruffled by their mother's and strangers' comings and goings and tended to ignore their mother and her efforts to connect when she returned. Children with an anxious-ambivalent/resistant attachment (Type C) were more often clingy and afraid to explore the room and became obviously agitated upon separation from their mother. When their mother returned, these children sought contact with their mother but also angrily resisted efforts to be soothed. Some children were difficult to classify in one of these preceding categories; they did not seem to have a sense of security, but neither did they express the kinds of behaviors that infants with insecure attachment exhibited. Infants with disorganized attachment (Type D) seemed to exhibit both approach and avoidance of their caregiver and subtle signs of fear.

The association between responsiveness and security of attachment is not always large, but a great deal of evidence indicates that maternal sensitivity is an important factor in the development of mother–infant attachment and maternal responsiveness is clearly associated with attachment security (Braungart-Rieker, Garwood, Powers, & Wang, 2001; Fearon & Belsky, 2016; Feeney & Woodhouse, 2016; NICHD Early Child Care Research Network, 2005a). Mothers of securely attached infants tend to encourage their children to explore and are sensitive to their children's needs; they respond promptly to their children's distress and sooth them appropriately. Secure attachment is considered the optimal or most positive of the attachment statuses. Mothers of anxious-avoidant infants (Type A infants) tended to be less available

TABLE 10.1. Patterns of Attachment

Secure (Type B)

- Prevalence in population: 55–65%
- Uses caregiver as a "secure base," explores freely when the caregiver is available, may or may not be distressed at separation but greets positively on reunion, seeks contact if distressed, settles down, returns to exploration.

Avoidant (Type A)

- Prevalence in population: 20–25%
- Appears minimally interested in caregiver, explores busily, minimal distress at separation, ignores or avoids caregiver on reunion.

Resistant/ambivalent (Type C)

- Prevalence in population: 10–15%
- Minimal exploration, preoccupied with caregiver, has difficulty settling down, both seeks and resists contact on reunion, may be angry or very passive.

Disorganized/disoriented (Type D)

- Prevalence in population: 15–20%
- Disorganized and/or disoriented behavior in the caregiver's presence, approaches with head averted, trance-like freezing, anomalous postures

Other

- Although rare, some children do not fit any of the other patterns.

Note. Based on Goldberg (1995).

to their children and intruded on their children's exploration more than mothers of secure infants. Mothers of infants with an anxious-ambivalent/resistant attachment style (Type C) seem to be unpredictable and inconsistent in their response to their infants' needs more than mothers of securely attached infants (Feeney & Woodhouse, 2016; Solomon & George, 2016). The Type D profile of disorganized attachment in infants and children tends to occur when temperamentally vulnerable children are exposed to multiple risk factors like maltreatment or parental psychopathology (Lyons-Ruth & Jacobvitz, 2016). Their behaviors in the Strange Situation tend to be confused and disorganized. The attachment system these children have internalized is easily disrupted and overwhelmed. They want to seek comfort from an attachment figure, but they are guarded and cautious. The freezing responses and uncertainties exhibited by Type D children may represent fear, a natural reaction of a child when interacting with an abusive adult in a Strange Situation.

Measuring Attachment with Older Children, Adolescents, and Adults

The Strange Situation was originally designed to assess attachment in infants age 2 and younger, and the scoring was based on infant behaviors such as seeking proximity to the caregiver, seeking caregiver contact, avoiding the caregiver, or resisting the caregiver's efforts to make contact. The Strange Situation is a labor- and time-intensive way to measure attachment and is most useful for classifying attachment in infants. As attachment research matured, it became necessary to develop measures of attachment that could be used with older children. This made it necessary to take into account older children's more developmentally advanced capacities, especially language and the fact that the parent–child relationship transforms as children age (Madigan, Brumariu, Villani, Atkinson, & Ruth-Lyons, 2016; Warmuth & Cummings, 2015). Fortunately, other measures of attachment have been developed that can be used more efficiently and are appropriate for other parts of the lifespan (Solomon & George, 2016). There have been several adaptations to the Strange Situation that can be used with preschoolers. Other procedures have been developed that use codes based on children's narratives in response to pictures showing various separation scenarios, doll play, and family drawings, but it is not clear how reliable and valid these measures are, and they are less frequently used in attachment research.

Perhaps the most widely used alternative to the Strange Situation has been the Attachment Q-Sort (AQS) measure. In the Q-sort procedure (Solomon & George, 2016; Waters, 1995), a trained observer, or a person who knows a child well (even sometimes a parent), is asked to sort 90 statements into one of nine piles. The "9" pile includes statements describing the child well; the '1' pile is for statements that do not describe the child. Each of the statements refers to a behavior that is characteristic of either secure, avoidant, or resistant attachment. Thus, for a securely attached child, the following items would be placed in the high-end piles (Waters, 1995, pp. 236–237):

- Child clearly shows a pattern of using mother as a base from which to explore. Moves out to play; returns or plays near her; moves out to play again, and so on.
- Child will approach or play with things that initially made him or her cautious or afraid if receives reassurance from mother.
- Child keeps track of mother's location when playing at home. Calls to her now and then; notices when she changes activities.
- When frightened, or upset, the child stops crying and quickly recovers when held.
- Child recognizes when mother is upset. Tries to comfort her; asks what is wrong.

Conversely, for a securely attached child, the following items would be placed in the low-end pile, for they represent insecurity of attachment (Waters, 1995, pp. 244–246):

- Child easily becomes angry at mother.
- When upset, the child stays put and cries, rarely asks mother for help.
- At home, child gets upset or cries when mother walks out of the room.
- Child sometimes signals that she or he wants to be put down and then fusses or wants to be picked right back up.

The advantage of the Q-sort procedure is that it can be used in a home or other environment; it doesn't require a laboratory setting like the Strange Situation, and the measure is designed to be used with infants or preschoolers (Solomon & George, 2016). The AQS seems to work well across cultural groups; when mothers and child development experts in seven different countries (China, Colombia, Germany, Israel, Japan, Norway, and the United States) were asked to sort the 90 Q-sort items so as to describe the ideal child, they tended to sort them in a similar way (Posada et al., 1995). The AQS does a reasonably good job distinguishing securely attached children from those with insecure attachment but may not be as reliable for distinguishing between the different types of insecure attachment (Solomon & George, 2016). It seems to have better reliability and validity when used with younger infants than with older children (Groh et al., 2014; Solomon & George, 2016; Symons, Clark, Isaksen, & Marshall, 1998).

As the construct of attachment gained more attention, researchers became interested in relating a person's attachment style to various mental health and interpersonal outcomes, particularly romantic relationships. To do this, it was necessary to develop measures of attachment that could be used with adolescents and adults. The primary method of doing this has been the Adult Attachment Interview (AAI) pioneered by Mary Main and her colleagues (Hesse, 2016). The AAI is a semistructured interview with about 20 primary questions each of which can lead to a number of additional probes that usually takes an hour or two (sometimes much more) to complete. The purpose of the questions is to have interviewees reveal memories and attitudes relevant to their early experiences that formed their internal working model of attachment and ultimately their attachment style. For example, during the interview, participants are asked to select adjectives to describe their childhood relationships with their parents, their recollections of what their parents did when they were upset in childhood, whether they felt rejected by parents during childhood, and whether their parents had ever threatened separation from them. The interviewee's responses are rated in terms of security themes. Some adults clearly value secure attachment relationships, believing that secure attachments are important in the development of a healthy personality. They see their own parents as warm, responsive, available, and sensitive. In contrast, some adults do not believe that attachment relationships are valuable or influential. Sometimes adults express extreme dependency themes during the interview, including the desire to continue to please their parents. Sometimes they lost a parent early in life and continue to mourn. In short, adults with beliefs reflecting insecure attachments also tend to believe that they had less than optimal rearing.

The AAI has been used extensively in research on attachment with adolescents using a very similar format with modifications in vocabulary to better match adolescents' verbal abilities. However, this practice has been criticized as developmentally inappropriate and yielding suspect results (Warmuth & Cummings, 2015). More recently, researchers have turned to using the Child Attachment Interview (CAI) (Kerns & Brumariu, 2016; Venta, Schmueli-Goetz, & Sharp, 2014) for use with older children and adolescents. The CAI is quite similar to the AAI. The CAI is somewhat shorter and asks questions that are developmentally appropriate, and instead of asking respondents to provide retrospective details about attachment relationships, the CAI focuses on current relationships and experiences (Venta et al., 2014).

Lastly, several self-report questionnaires have been developed to assess attachment. Many of these measures are used in research with adults, although some are used primarily to measure attachment constructs in adolescents (Crowell, Fraley, & Roisman, 2016; Venta et al., 2014). These measures and this method of determining attachment status have been criticized because the adolescents responding to them may give socially desirable responses or the responses they think the researcher wants to see, and they are unlikely to measure an adolescent's internal working model of attachment since that is typically not something people are conscious of (Warmuth & Cummings, 2015).

Knowing something about how attachment is measured is important for determining the veracity of attachment research and how generalizable it is. Using the measures discussed above, researchers have determined there is modest stability between the attachment status a person has as an infant and the attachment style he or she has throughout childhood and adolescence and into adulthood (Boldt, Kochanska, Yoon, & Nordling, 2014; Chiu & Yip, 2012; Madigan et al., 2016; Solomon & George, 2016; Warmuth & Cummings, 2015). Finding continuity in a person's attachment status over a long period of time is challenging because of the many changes that occur as people mature psychologically and physically, but also because of changes in a person's social environment, each of which makes attachment a difficult construct to measure across developmental stages. Nonetheless, attachment researchers have associated early attachment patterns with a wide variety of psychological, social, and educational outcomes

Attachment, Psychological Adjustment, and Academic Achievement

The relationship between early attachment and subsequent social relationships, early attachment and subsequent behavioral problems, and early attachment and cognitive development are three themes that have particular relevance to educators. In general, children with optimal attachment experiences tend to do better socially with adults and peers; they tend to have fewer behavioral problems, and they tend to do better academically. But these are complicated relationships, and so we consider each in detail below.

Attachment and Subsequent Social Relations

Bowlby (1969) contended that secure attachment was a precursor of mental health and believed that securely attached infants are more likely to be well adjusted and sociable when they are older. Often preschoolers who were securely attached infants have more advanced social competence; they tend to be more outgoing, more sensitive to the needs of other children, and more popular than preschoolers who were insecurely attached during infancy (Berlin et al., 2008; Bernier, Beauchamp, Carlson, & Lalonde, 2015; Drake, Belsky, & Fearon, 2014; Williford, Carter, & Pianta, 2016). Throughout childhood, security of child–mother attachment is associated with better social and emotional functioning with peers (Allen & Tan, 2016; Kerns & Brumariu, 2016; Sroufe, 2016). In contrast, insecurity of child–parent attachments is associated with dysfunctional peer relationships, including aggression, withdrawal from peer relations, and acting out inappropriately (DeKlyen & Greenberg, 2016; Dozier & Rutter, 2016; Fearon, Bakermans-Kranenburg, van IJzendoorn, Lapsley, & Roisman, 2010; Kehle, Bray, & Grigerick, 2007; Lyons-Ruth & Jacobvitz, 2016). Similarly, adolescents who were securely attached as infants also seem to have better social skills than those who were insecurely attached as children. They appear to be more comfortable with intimacy and developing and maintaining close personal relationships, and they may be more adept at developing age-appropriate autonomy in adolescence (Allen, Porter, McFarland, McElhaney, & Marsh, 2007; Allen & Tan, 2016; Chiu & Yip, 2012; Fearon et al., 2010; Venta et al., 2014).

The improved social competence that children with secure attachment have also extends to relationships with adults. So, for example, the relationships that children form with their teachers often have the emotional and motivational components of attachment, leading some to speculate that teachers of young children may serve as a secondary attachment figure (Cassidy, 2016; Howes & Spieker, 2016; Maldonado-Carreño & Votruba-Drzal, 2011; Ramsdal, Bergvik, & Wynn, 2015; Sabol & Pianta, 2012; Verschueren & Koomen, 2012). Securely attached children seem to have better quality relationships with teachers, while children with less secure attachment may be less likely to see teachers as a source of support (Kehle et al., 2007; Ramsdal et al., 2015). Although the relationships between parent–infant attachment and later social functioning tend to be small to moderate, they are striking in their consistency (Ramsdal et al., 2015; Pallini, Biaocco, Schneider, Madigan, & Atkinson, 2014; Thompson, 2016).

Attachment and Behavior

Early attachment experiences seem to have a strong influence on psychological adjustment throughout childhood and adolescence. In general, children with secure attachment histories seem to have better self-regulatory and executive functioning skills than their peers with insecure attachment (Bernier et al., 2015; Drake et al., 2014). Children with secure attachment histories tend to have fewer behavioral problems and are better able to cope with emotionally and/or academically challenging situations (Bernier et al., 2015; Drake et al., 2014; Fearon et al., 2010). However, children with poor or insecure attachment as infants are at greater risk of developing behavioral problems later in childhood. They tend to express more hostility and aggression, experience more anxiety, and withdraw from social situations (Kehle et al., 2007; NICHD Early Child Care Research Network, 2005b). As a consequence, teachers often experience these insecurely attached children as difficult, and they acquire a reputation for having behavior problems (Ramsdal et al., 2015).

Attachment, Cognition, and Academic Achievement

Recall from Chapter 6 the sociocultural perspective that social interactions, particularly between caregivers and children, are critical to mature cognitive development. Accordingly, high-quality parenting and secure attachment in children are associated with better cognitive development and academic outcomes (Bergin & Bergin, 2009; Chiu & Yip, 2012; Ding et al., 2014; Drake et al., 2014). Because children with secure attachment tend to have better executive function skills, they are better prepared to seek social support when they encounter socially and cognitively challenging circumstances and sustain positive relationships with parents and teachers (Bernier et al., 2015; Drake et al., 2014; Ramsdal et al., 2015). But children with insecure attachment styles tend to have problems sustaining attention, they participate less in classroom environments, and consequently earn lower grades and have poorer school adjustment (Kehle et al., 2007).

The cognitive advantages of secure attachment begin early in a child's life. Two-year-olds with secure attachment styles demonstrate enhanced problem-solving skills working together with their mothers (Colman & Thompson, 2002). Studies of mother–child problem solving indicate that mothers of securely attached children offer higher quality support to their children during problem-solving tasks. The problem-solving process is more pleasant for securely attached children compared to the less securely attached children, who more often rejected their mothers' suggestions, even responding aggressively when suggestions were offered. In general, when there is a secure attachment, parental directions and support are more likely to be at an appropriate level, neither too little nor too much (Colman & Thompson, 2002).

The quality of mother–child attachment also has an influence on literacy and math skills (Bergin & Bergin, 2009; Deckner, Adamson, & Bakeman, 2006; Dexter & Stacks, 2014; Han & Neuharth-Pritchett, 2015; Karrass & Braungart-Rieker, 2005; McCormick, O'Connor, & Barnes, 2016). Parent–child interactions during emergent literacy tasks are more positive for securely attached than for less securely attached children. Securely attached children are more attentive and less distractible during emergent literacy interactions, and they do more reading together than less securely attached child–mother dyads. Mothers of the securely attached children expect more of their children, and the children met these expectations. Insecure dyads exhibit less engagement during reading than securely attached children and mothers. The less secure the attachment, the more the children are inattentive, the more the discussion digresses from the story, and the harder it seems for the children to get the message of the text.

In short, security in attachment predicts healthy interactions as parents and children tackle intellectual challenges together, including reading with one another. Much of what secure attachment is about is responsive interaction between mother and infant. These responsive interactions continue into early childhood and extend to interactions in problem-solving situations. Recall that, according to Vygotsky, much of thinking is the internalization of social interactions by the child. Thus, the better the interactions, the better should be the internalizations that form the basis of thought (Topping, Dekhinet, & Zeedyk, 2013). Because secure attachment relates to long-term cognitive development and academic achievement, those wishing to optimize intellectual development should target children's social interactions, beginning with parent–child interactions during the first year of life.

Attachment Interventions

Some children are at substantially greater risk than others for not developing secure relationships with parents during infancy, sometimes because their parents are less responsive, sometimes because of the child's difficult temperament (Chess & Thomas, 1987; Thomas & Chess, 1977). (See the Considering Interesting Questions special feature in Box 10.1.) This raises the question: To what extent can intervention increase the likelihood of secure attachment and cognitively productive interactions? One interesting possibility is that if child–parent attachment is not as secure as it could be, relationships with educators might provide some compensation for the cognitive disadvantages that accompany less than optimal parent–child attachment.

BOX 10.1. How Does Infant Temperament Affect Attachment Security and Academic Performance?

Early studies defined child temperament by the child's activity level, emotional reactivity, sociability, and attentiveness (Rothbart, 2012). Chess and Thomas used qualities like this to identify three different temperamental patterns in infancy: children with *easy* temperaments, those with *difficult* temperaments, and children who were *slow to warm up* (Chess & Thomas, 1987; Thomas & Chess, 1977). Easy infants seem to be curious about novelty, typically have a pleasant mood, are fairly regular in their eating and sleep cycles, and are readily adaptable to changing circumstances. In contrast, infants with a difficult temperament tend to be irregular in their feeding and sleeping, react fearfully to novelty, and are often colicky and irritable. Slow-to-warm-up infants often initially have somewhat negative reactions to novelty and require some time to adjust to new situations. Sometimes they are described as shy. More contemporary theories of temperament emphasize factors such as extraversion, which is characterized by a positive mood and curiosity; negative emotionality, primarily fear and irritability; and effortful control, which is the ability to focus and sustain attention (Rothbart, 2012).

There have been ongoing debates for several decades about the relationship between attachment and temperament (Groh et al., 2016; Vaughn & Bost, 2016). Temperament is believed to be a consequence of genetic inheritance, while attachment is associated with a child's caregiving environment. But a child who is difficult or has an abundance of negative emotionality may challenge a parent's capacities to provide consistent nurturance and a secure base. Parents may be more sensitive to an easy or extraverted child. This raises a key question. Is it the mother's sensitivity that results in a secure attachment or the effect of the child's temperament on maternal sensitivity, which in turn affects the security of attachment? Debate continues on just how much security of attachment is determined by maternal sensitivity, infant temperament, and the goodness of fit between a mother and an infant (Vaughn & Bost, 2016). The latest studies seem to indicate some limited interaction between attachment and temperament (Groh et al., 2016; Planalp & Braungart-Rieker, 2013).

Nonetheless, there are associations between temperament and school performance (Gartstein, Putnam, & Kliewer, 2016; Karrass & Braungart-Rieker, 2004; Rispoli, McGoey, Koziol, & Schreiber, 2013). Children with positive emotional moods and effortful control tend to have better cognitive abilities and higher academic achievement than children with negative emotional temperaments, although effective parenting and secure attachment may moderate these effects. In other words, an infant with a difficult temperament may do better when he or she experiences sensitive and patient parenting. The same seems to be true of the teacher–student relationship. Teacher sensitivity to children's temperamental styles is associated with better school engagement and peer relationships. Teachers who develop supportive and responsive relationships with young students and make reasonable adaptations to their teaching style to match their students' temperaments help ease them into a positive school experience and better academic achievement (Buhs, Rudasill, Kalutskaya, & Griese, 2015; Oakland & Joyce, 2004; Rudasill, Gallagher, & White, 2010).

Teacher–child relationships can and do have attachment aspects to them, and teachers can become a secondary attachment figure (Cassidy, 2016; Howes & Spieker, 2016; Maldonado-Carreño & Votruba-Drzal, 2011; Ramsdal et al., 2015; Sabol & Pianta, 2012; Verschueren & Koomen, 2012). For example, when preschoolers who have insecure parental attachments experience a secure, trusting attachment relationship with a preschool teacher, their social interactions in preschool go better than when they have not experienced such a compensatory relationship with an educator (Copeland-Mitchell, Denham, & DeMulder, 1997). Still, the consequences of poor parent–child attachment can be overwhelming. Recent intervention studies have focused on improving parent responsiveness (Berlin, Zeanah, & Lieberman, 2016) to improve child attachment styles, but the technicalities of this work exceed what most educators can offer.

In summary, we emphasize that considerable evidence indicates that early attachment status predicts later attachment status for many individuals. That is, parent–child socioemotional relationships tend to be stable from early childhood to later childhood, adolescence, and even adulthood (Magai, Frias, & Shaver, 2016). That said, under some circumstances child–parent attachment is not stable. Parents sometimes change so that the mother and father who were always there and responsive to their children when infants, become parents who are less attentive later in their children's lives, sometimes because of work stressors and mental health issues, other times because of family strife and parental divorce (Feeney & Monin, 2016; Kobak, Zajac, & Madsen, 2016).

How Does Day Care Affect Child Development?

In the United States, the majority of children experience nonparental day care; for many, day care begins in infancy (Huston, Bobbitt, & Bentley, 2015; Vandell, Burchinal, & Pierce, 2016). As the prevalence of day care has increased, so have concerns about the effects day care may have on children. In particular, some researchers worry that day care might result in poor infant–parent attachment and/or create neuroendocrine stress responses in children, which in turn would have effects on their psychological and neurological development (Belsky, 2006; Bowlby, 2007; Brandtjen & Verny, 2001; Brooks-Gunn, Han, & Waldfogel, 2010; Huston et al., 2015; Shpancer, 2006). For several decades, social scientists have been studying day care in an attempt to ascertain what its respective risks or detrimental effects and its benefits are for child development. It turns out to be quite difficult to draw firm and simple conclusions about the effects of day care. Some studies have found positive short-term effects of day care on children's cognitive development, while others concluded there are some detrimental effects on behavior. Some have concluded there are positive long-term effects, while others have not. Some studies have found that day care has both risks and benefits. Shpancer (2006) concluded: "Different types of children incur different types of effects in different types of settings at different times in different contexts" (p. 235).

These inconsistent results are a consequence of the complexity of this topic and the limitations of the research methodology (Belsky, 2006; Keys et al., 2013; Schpanzer, 2006). A large number of important variables have to be taken into account to optimally understand the effects of day care. Different results come about depending on the participating families' socioeconomic status and ethnicity, parent education, home environment, and child gender and temperament, to name just a few variables (Brooks-Gunn et al., 2010; Shpancer, 2006). To truly draw causal conclusions about the effects of day care would require experimental research designs. However, it is not ethically feasible or practical to conduct experimental studies on the effects of day care that would randomly assign children to different day care conditions and then observe what happens over the course of years.

Instead, researchers have been analyzing data from several large longitudinal U.S. and international studies on early child care, and some researchers have combined studies to do meta-analytic analyses or draw conclusions from comprehensive reviews of the empirical literature. One of the more prominent studies is the U.S. National Institute of Child Health and Human Development Study of Early Child Care and Youth Development (NICHD SECCYD) study. This study did not find evidence of any general deleterious attachment as a result of day care use during a child's infancy and preschool years, although some children with vulnerable temperaments may have more difficulty (Brooks-Gunn et al., 2010). However, the NICHD SECCYD study was designed to respond to other important research questions, in particular, the effects of the quality, quantity, or type of day care on child development (Belsky et al., 2007). The study began in the 1990s and included over 1,300 participating families from 10 different communities in the United States who entered the study at the time of the birth of a child. More than 70% of these children had some nonparental child care during their first year, beginning, on average, at 3 months of age for 27 hours per week (Huston et al., 2015). Rather than attempting to cite all the studies that have been produced by this NICHD Early Child Care Research Network, we cite only some of the more recent studies here, along with other similar studies. A complete bibliography of research from this project is available at *www.icpsr.umich.edu/icpsrweb/ICPSR/series/00233*.

Quality of Day Care

Arguably, the most consistent finding that has emerged from the NICHD SECCYD data and other studies has been the importance of the quality of day care provided (Belsky et al., 2007; Brooks-Gunn et al., 2010; Burger, 2010; Dearing, McCartney, & Taylor, 2009; Keys et al., 2013; MacKenzie, Liu, & Sameroff, 2013; Sosinsky & Kim, 2013; Vandell et al., 2010, 2016; Wen, Bulotsky-Shearer, Hahs-Vaughn, & Korfmacher, 2012). There are different facets of day care quality; some are *structural* components, and others have more to do with the *process* of providing day care. High quality in the structure of the day care setting includes the following:

- Furnishings that support routine care (e.g., a changing table for infants).

- Furnishings that permit the children to relax and be comfortable (e.g., beanbag chairs, large pillows).

- Materials to support learning activities (e.g., books, games, art supplies, musical toys, sand and water, dress-up clothes).

- Materials that support both fine (e.g., drawing) and gross (e.g., playground equipment) motor activities.

- Space for free play and group activities (e.g., a rug for whole-group meetings).

- A sufficient number of adults to care for the children in the setting. The number of adults needed depends on the ages of the children and the type of setting. They range from one adult for every two to four infants 2 years old or less, one adult for every 3-year-old, one adult for every eight 4- and 5-year-olds, and one adult for every 10–12 elementary school-age child (American Academy of Pediatrics, American Public Health Association, National Resource Center for Health and Safety in Child Care and Early Education, 2011).

- Caregivers educated in early childhood development and education.

- A space where adults can meet (e.g., an office where teachers can interact with parents).

Beyond having adequate personnel and supplies, the furnishings, equipment, and materials at a good child care facility are clean and safe. Moreover, the available supplies and space comfortably accommodate all children who are present in the setting. In addition, the space is arranged so that children can self-regulate their activities to a large degree (e.g., all toys and books are within reach).

A high-quality process requires caregiving staff to be nurturing, positive, and responsive to the children under their care (Keys et al., 2013; Landry et al., 2014), notably:

- The adult caregiver greets children on arrival and says good-bye when the children depart.

- A regular snack and meal are scheduled, with food served in a positive atmosphere.

- Activities are on a regular schedule.

- Nap or rest periods are part of the routine.

- Diapering and toileting are uneventful.

- The children keep themselves clean (e.g., they wash up before meals).

- The adults talk with the children a great deal and provide ample opportunities for the children to talk with them. The caregiver's language is at a child-appropriate level.

- The adults reason with the children, for example, explaining to a child the reason for a rule when a rule violation occurs.

- The caregivers provide adult supervision of motor activities (e.g., playing on playground equipment) and creative activities (e.g., art, music, building blocks).

- The tone of the interaction between children and adults is positive. The caregivers clearly like children and are enthusiastic when they are around children. They initiate interactions with the children rather than simply responding when children seek them out.

- When children want to speak to an adult, there are adults who listen.

- The center activities reflect the cultural diversity of the children in attendance, with all of the cultures treated with respect.

- The caregivers encourage the children to try new experiences.

- The caregivers encourage prosocial behavior by the children.

- The caregivers are aware of individual differences between children and make accommodations to such differences and to special needs when planning activities.

- Regular conferences with parents are scheduled.

In general, higher quality day care tends to result in more positive developmental outcomes. Unfortunately, in the United States, high-quality day care is not the norm; some estimates suggest that the majority of day care in the United States is mediocre at best. The day care industry suffers from high turnover in child care providers, low wages, poor training, insufficient supervision, and inappropriate child-to-caregiver ratios (Belsky et al., 2007; Landry et al., 2014; MacKenzie et al., 2013; Sosinsky, Lord, & Zigler, 2007; Vandell et al., 2010). These circumstances lead to low morale for caregivers, resulting in less than optimal interactions with children. In these situations, caregivers tend to adopt overcontrolling methods, to the point that they are critical of, irritated by, or detached from the children. They also tend to become punitive and restrictive, emphasizing what the children should not be doing rather than what the children should be doing.

Quantity of Day Care

Considerable attention has been paid to the question of what effect day care and the amount of time spent in day care has on child development. Some initial results from the NICHD SECCYD study and others suggested that the more time children spent in day care, the more subsequent school teachers rated them as having behavioral problems, principally, externalizing behavioral issues (e.g., excessive assertiveness, disobedience, and aggression; Belsky et al., 2007; Huston et al., 2015; McCartney et al., 2010). For most children, this effect is small, but it raises some concern. Will children who have behavior problems in the early grades experience a cascading series of negative teacher interactions that will ultimately lead to disaffection from school and more serious conduct problems later in life (Huston et al., 2015; Vandell et al., 2016)? Fortunately, Vandell et al. (2016) did not detect this effect in their study of high school graduates from the NICHD SECCYD study. It appears that the behavioral problems that are related to time spent in day care depend a great deal on the quality of the day care. Children who experience high-quality day care with smaller group sizes may in fact have better social skills, especially if they come from higher risk groups, chiefly, low-income, single-parent, ethnic minority families (Huston et al., 2015; MacKenzie et al., 2013; McCartney et al., 2010).

Type of Day Care

Different varieties of day care options have been researched. Some families have access to relatives (other than a parent) who care for their children. Some employ nonrelative caregivers to provide in-home care (e.g., nannies, babysitters, or au pairs). Some children are in "family" day care provided in someone else's home for a fee. Much of day care in the United States, however, is center-based care (e.g., day care centers, nursery schools, and preschools) provided for groups of children in a non-residential for-profit setting and sometimes in a nonprofit community setting (e.g., church; Sosinsky & Kim, 2013; Sosinsky et al., 2007). In general, the more formal the day care setting is, the more likely it is to have a higher quality and an educational structure, in contrast to family-type settings that tend to involve primarily free play (Côté, Doyle, Petitclerc, & Timmins, 2013; Vandell et al., 2016). However, not all center-based day care facilities are equal. Some for-profit businesses tend to engage in cost cutting that results in larger group sizes, lower wages, and less educated care-givers, all of which reduces overall quality (Sosinsky et al., 2007). In short, the type of day care is probably less important than the quality of care provided.

The Overall Effects of Day Care on Cognitive and Social Development

Studies conducted over decades show that *high*-quality day care can provide some developmental benefits for some children. Specifically, high-quality day care can be a positive public investment that can improve cognitive and social skills and school readiness and overall academic achievement, both in the short term and over the course of a child's maturation into emerging adulthood (Belsky, 2006; Belsky et al., 2007; Brooks-Gunn et al., 2010; Burger, 2010; Côté et al., 2013; Dearing et al., 2009; Keys et al., 2013; MacKenzie et al., 2013; Sosinsky et al., 2007; Vandell et al., 2010, 2016; Wen et al., 2012). The overall effects are generally somewhat small for any individual child, although they are potentially quite significant when considering the entire population of children who experience day care. These positive outcomes are most consistent and reliable for cognitive development. They also seem to be more important for children from underprivileged backgrounds because the posi-tive aspects of high-quality day care may compensate for some of the disadvantages they encounter (Burger, 2010; Burchinal et al., 2011; Côté et al., 2013; Keys et al., 2013; Vandell et al., 2010).

Care for Children after School

In recent years, it has become almost the norm for parents to be working during after-school hours. As a result, many children are self-care or "latchkey" children, who are unsupervised after school. There are few recent studies on self-care chil-dren and adolescents. In the past, some social scientists concluded that unsupervised self-care children were at no greater risk than children who were supervised after school. The prevailing contemporary opinion is that unsupervised self-care children are at greater risk for behavior problems and reduced academic achievement; this is especially the case for underprivileged children who live in high-risk neighborhoods (Atherton, Schofield, Sitka, Conger, & Robins, 2016; Lord & Mahoney, 2007).

Various forms of after-school care are utilized, including school-based after-school programs, center-based care, supervision in another family's home, and home-based babysitters. The types of structural and process features that distinguish good from not-so-good preschool day care also distinguish good from not-so-good after-school care (Baldwin, Stromwall, & Wilder, 2015; Leos-Urbel, 2015). However, the little research that exists on after-school care suggests that after-school care has few developmental or academic benefits (Kremer, Maynard, Polanin, Vaughn, & Sar-teschi, 2015; Roth, Malone, & Brooks-Gunn, 2010). Given the concerns families, edu-cators, and policymakers have about children and adolescents who are unsupervised after school, much more work is needed to develop effective after-school program-ming that will both benefit children and adolescents and protect them from the risks inherent to self-care.

Family Factors That Influence Child Development

Few, if any, other relationships in life have more impact on a child than family relationships. Healthy families perform a variety of roles and responsibilities that promote optimal development, including providing essential resources, nurturance, structure, discipline, education, and skill acquisition. Moreover, cultural and social norms are transmitted and filtered through families. Not surprisingly, then, families and family relationships have been the focus of an enormous amount of research on children and adolescents. In this section, we review just a sliver of that empirical literature; namely, how parents and their parenting habits affect children, what effect siblings have on a child's development, and how the stresses of contemporary life affect families and children.

Parenting Style

Parents get an overabundance of advice from health care providers, religious leaders, mass media, family, friends, and neighbors on how best to raise children. So, understandably, in recent decades social scientists have begun to hone in on this issue in an attempt to derive empirically based recommendations for parents. One of the more influential approaches has been the study of parenting styles. This work began with Diana Baumrind (1972), who conducted a longitudinal study of parent–child relationships, beginning in the preschool years and continuing into the middle elementary years. She observed children in school settings and at home with their parents, taking special note of how parents interacted with their children. This observational data was complemented by interviews with the parents. Based on these observations and interviews, Baumrind identified two dimensions that characterized parenting style. One dimension was the *degree of parental responsiveness*, which varied from highly responsive and child-centered to rejecting and parent-centered. The second dimension was the *degree of demand* on the child by the parent, which ranged from challenging to easygoing. Baumrind and others (Crockett & Hayes, 2011; Maccoby & Martin, 1983) combined these two constructs and defined four different types of parenting styles: (1) highly responsive, highly demanding, **authoritative** parenting; (2) highly responsive, low-demanding, **permissive** parenting; (3) low-responsive, high-demanding, **authoritarian** parenting; and (4) low-responsive, low-demanding, **uninvolved** parenting.

Authoritative parents set high expectations for their children and they provide nurturing support to assist their children in meeting these expectations. In general, authoritative parents engage their children in a more reciprocal and bidirectional style; they tend to rely less on dominating a child and instead work to strike a balance between control and age-appropriate autonomy. Authoritative parents are generally good communicators with their children about what they expect, and they explain the reasons for their standards in the context of dialogues in which the children's voices and perspectives are heard and taken seriously. This parenting strategy tends to foster and exercise cognitive skills and prosocial engagement in their children (Padilla-Walker, Carlo, Christensen, & Yorgason, 2012). As a consequence, authoritative parents and their children tend to have more affectionate and understanding relationships.

In contrast, permissive parents have very few expectations or standards they require their children to meet. They favor being indulgent and giving their children the freedom to behave however they want and to make their own decisions. They are generally positive to neutral in the emotional expressions they direct toward their children, but they are passive about providing guidance or structure for their children.

Authoritarian parents demand strict obedience. Their parenting features more dominance and control tactics. Compared to authoritative parents, authoritarian parents do not engage in empathic parental–child dialogue, and they are more inclined to rely on punishment and threat to gain compliance.

Uninvolved parents are indifferent to their children. They prefer to not invest much time and effort into parenting either by establishing standards or by providing support. In some cases, uninvolved parents are negligent; they may have little or no interest in knowing where their children are or what they are doing. They tend to be more absorbed in their own needs.

Authoritative parenting is associated with more positive developmental outcomes than the other parenting styles (Crockett & Hayes, 2011; Larzelere, Cox, & Mandara, 2013; Mattanah, 2005; Panetta, Somers, Ceresnie, Hillman, & Partridge, 2014). Children raised by authoritative parents tend to be responsibly independent, mature in their social interactions, and cooperative with adults and other children, and to have high self-esteem (Darling & Steinberg, 1993). The authoritative style is generally associated with better academic achievement as well (Areepattamannil, 2010; Mattanah, 2005; Pinquart, 2016; Spera, 2005). Authoritative parenting leads to better child outcomes compared to authoritarian parenting in most ethnic–racial groups. Originally, researchers thought the advantages of authoritative parenting on achievement were greater for some groups than for others (Chao, 2001; Leung, Lau, & Lam, 1998; Spera, 2005). Recent studies have taken a more nuanced approach to this topic and suggest that the extent to which authoritative parenting is beneficial for ethnic minority populations in the United States depends on a variety of factors, including acculturation and racial socialization (Pezzella, Thornberry, & Smith, 2016; Spera, 2005; Yu, Cheah, & Calvin, 2016).

In contrast to the positive benefits associated with authoritative parenting, children raised by authoritarian parents are more likely to exhibit poor peer relations, social anxiety, and antisocial behaviors (Maccoby & Martin, 1983; Mattanah, 2005; Tang & Davis-Kean, 2015). Difficulty in social adjustments (e.g., to the social constraints and demands in school) tend to characterize the children of permissive parents as well (Lamborn, Mounts, Steinberg, & Dornbusch, 1991). Children of uninvolved parents suffer socioemotionally as well as with respect to cognitive development and academic achievement (Panetta et al., 2014).

Parental Discipline and the Promotion of Self-Control

Parents and families are the primary instrument for socializing children and fostering the development of self-control. One method for accomplishing this is through parents' choice of discipline tactics. Many parents rely on the use of **corporal punishment** (inflicting pain) to gain control over their children. Although common, this practice elicits considerable controversy. The United Nations Convention on the Rights of the Child considers corporal punishment a human rights violation, and several countries have outlawed the practice (Gershoff, 2002; Lansford et al., 2014; Larzelere, 2000; United Nations Office of the High Commissioner for Human Rights, 1989). Corporal punishment is practiced less in North America than it once was, although many parents still endorse the practice, especially for use with young children (Choe, Olson, & Sameroff, 2013; Frechette & Romano, 2015; Larzelere, 2000). Whether or not judicious use of corporal punishment is a useful discipline tactic has been the subject of considerable debate (Gershoff, 2002; Gershoff & Grogan-Kaylor, 2016). Most studies suggest that corporal punishment has a negative effect on children's behavior and psychological adjustment (Altschul, Lee, & Gershoff, 2016; Choe et al., 2013; Gershoff, 2016; Lansford et al., 2014). Others have questioned the methodology of these studies, noting that the effects of corporal punishment likely vary depending on the intensity and frequency of punishment, the cultural context in which the parent and child abide, and the presence of parental warmth (Choe et al., 2013; Lansford et al., 2014; Larzelere, 2000).

Corporal punishment does tend to achieve immediate child compliance with parental instruction (Choe et al., 2013; Lansford et al., 2014), but there are a number of reasons why corporal punishment is not an effective tactic for promoting optimal child development (Gershoff, 2002; Gershoff & Grogan-Kaylor, 2016). One potential side effect of punishment stems from the operant conditioning principles of stimulus generalization and the "spread of effects." When a person is punished (or rewarded) for a behavior, behaviors that occur in temporal proximity to the punishment (or reward) can also be inhibited (or encouraged). In other words, when a child is punished, the punishment may result in inhibiting other, perhaps prosocial or adaptive behaviors the parent did not intend to inhibit.

Punishment also tends to create resentment in children toward the parent who is punishing them, which can lead to children distancing themselves from their parents. This has the potential to establish a behavioral cycle or bi-directional effect (Newton, Laible, Carlo, Steele, & McGinley, 2014; Sheehan & Watson, 2008). The child, frustrated by the punishment, retaliates against the parent or misbehaves with more intensity, and as a result the parent is even harsher with the child (Choe et al., 2013; Wang & Kenny, 2014). This cycle of aggression can escalate out of control and lead to child maltreatment (Gershoff, 2016). Cycles of aggression can lead to habits of aggression extending beyond the home. Recall from Chapter 5 the power of social models and how children often imitate what they see. When a parent asserts control by hitting a child, the parent is modeling physical aggression. Social modeling of aggression increases children's aggression, especially in the case of boys (Maguire-Jack, Gromoske, & Berger, 2012; McDonald, Baden, & Lochman, 2013). The child who is spanked at home is more likely to be an aggressive child at school than the child who is not spanked, with aggression accompanied by poorer peer relations in general (Gershoff & Grogan-Kaylor, 2016; McDonald et al., 2013). Moreover, punishment-oriented homes often are cold and rejecting and in the absence of parental warmth that may mitigate the effects of punishment, children become more aggressive than prosocial in their interactions with others (Davidov & Grusec, 2006; Deater-Deckard, Ivy, & Petrill, 2006; Lansford et al., 2014; Lee, Altschul, & Gershoff, 2013; McDonald et al., 2013; Wang & Kenny, 2014).

Lastly, and perhaps most importantly, punishment does not provide children with information about what to do; it only provides feedback on what not to do. Providing children and adolescents with corrective feedback requires a different disciplinary tactic. This is more likely to happen when parental discipline is characterized by the use of a method known as induction than if parents rely mostly on punishment. **Inductive discipline** involves reasoning with a child about the potential harm of the misdeed, the consequences of making another person feel bad, as well as helping a child understand what is socially appropriate conduct (Choe et al., 2013; Patrick & Gibbs, 2012). For example, a parent might say, "Don't push your brother. Think about how he'll feel if he gets hurt. It is better to use your words if you are frustrated with him." An inductive approach encourages children to be empathetic, to think about other people and their feelings. Providing children with explanations about why they should behave a particular way helps assure children's long-term compliance with sanctions and is associated with more prosocial behavior (Padilla-Walker et al., 2012).

The Challenges of Contemporary Family Life

Families encounter a variety of challenges that have a formative influence on the development of children and adolescents. Some of these challenges are relatively routine and the consequence of normative transitions in families. Others are more problematic and create tension and stress in families that are detrimental to children and adolescents.

The Family Life Cycle

Under ordinary circumstances, families go through stages of development much like individuals do (McGoldrick & Shibusawa, 2012). Family development comprises at least five notable transitions coupling, raising young children, parenting adolescents, launching, and contending with later life. The coupling stage occurs when individuals create an attachment to one another and commit to creating a family. On the other end of family development is contending with later life, which is a time when parents age and often become reliant on their offspring to assist them with the activities of living. The three other stages of family life are the ones most relevant to child and adolescent development.

After establishing a committed attachment relationship, many couples decide to raise children. This transition into parenthood establishes a generational boundary and requires individuals to create an identity as parents. Young parents face a number of complicated issues. They have to determine what kind of parenting they want to adopt, who will assume what parenting responsibilities, how to create a work and family life balance, and decide on effective parenting skills. Just about the time that parents feel they have mastered the skills needed to raise young children, some of their children mature into adolescents, which requires a whole new set of parenting skills and changes in family life.

Raising adolescents requires families to develop flexible boundaries that enable normal adolescent autonomy and recognize the increasing importance of peer groups and peer relationships for the adolescent. The close ties adolescents forge with their peers may compete with the bonds that parents want to maintain in the family and reduce family cohesion. At the same time, parents of adolescents need to provide clear expectations and limits. This requires altogether different discipline tactics that emphasize supervision and monitoring, joint decision making, and negotiation. And then, at just about the time parents get the hang of raising adolescents, their children are ready to leave home and start their own families.

The launching phase is a bittersweet time in family life; while it is exciting and rewarding to see children mature and become productive adults, it is also a time when parents are coping with the loss of their children and their identity as parents that gave their life so much meaning for decades. Sometimes parents have an adverse reaction to this transition. While their sons and daughters are entering into the fullness of their youth, some parents are grieving the loss of their youth and depending on how parents handle this "midlife crisis," this can be problematic for family and marital relationships.

These transitions can affect families and child and adolescent development in other ways as well. Families are generally stable when they are in the midst of a stage. But they are placed under more stress during the transitional times; the period of time when the families are moving from one stage into another. Furthermore, families frequently find themselves coping with more than one stage of family life at the same time. For example, parents may be raising adolescents or launching children from the family at the same time they are coping with the aging and loss of their own parents. This phenomenon happens quite regularly in stepfamilies. Stepfamilies often engage in coupling while also raising young children and adolescents. Times like these test a family's mettle and can create tensions that destabilize families and distract them from attending to their children and raising them effectively.

Sibling Birth and Sibling Relationships

Approximately 80% of children in the United States have a sibling, so the birth of a sibling and being a brother or sister is a fairly normative experience for most American children (Volling, 2012). In the past, the conventional wisdom was that the presence of many siblings strained family resources and that the birth of siblings disrupted family life and caused distress for previously born siblings. However, more nuanced contemporary research has cast some doubt on both of these assumptions (Volling, 2012; Workman, 2016). Nonetheless, siblings have a profound effect on each other's development (Kramer & Conger, 2009). Sibling relationships are the only interpersonal relationships that can last a lifetime, and siblings share experiences that are significant life events. Moreover, for many of them, this is their first "peer" relationship and the first opportunity to learn about competition and cooperation.

How does life change for a child when a new member of the family arrives? Although the popular assumption is that the birth of a sibling is a disruptive transition for children, the research on this topic is equivocal. Many children show no negative effects from the introduction of a sibling into the family. However, some children do tend to regress behaviorally, and some resent the introduction of a new child into the family. The arrival of a second child can decrease the quality of parent–first child interaction. After the birth of a new baby, mothers and their firstborn children interact less often and less positively (Volling, 2012). In general, though, children display widely varying reactions to the birth of a sibling.

How do siblings' relationships affect development? Siblings do tend to spend a lot of time together and often share emotionally intense relationships, affecting one another's social and emotional development. Often, siblings have a positive influence on one another through the development of prosocial skills like the recognition of emotions and empathy for others' feelings, social-perspective taking, negotiation, and compromising (Kramer & Conger, 2009; Lam, Solmeyer, & McHale, 2012; Pike & Oliver, 2016; Stormshak, Bullock, & Falkenstein, 2009; Tucker & Updegraf, 2009; Whiteman, Becerra, & Killoren, 2009). But siblings can also have a negative influence on one another. Conflict and intimidation between siblings can lead to behavioral problems, academic difficulties, and poor peer relationships (Pike & Oliver, 2016; Whiteman et al., 2009). Also, sometimes siblings model and encourage their brothers and sisters to engage in antisocial behavior (Tucker & Updegraf, 2009).

Do parents treat their children equally? Siblings do engage in social comparisons and often express the feeling that a brother or sister gets preferential treatment. In recent years, there has been a growing recognition and interest in differential parental treatment. It is relatively common for parents to treat their children differently; after all, children behave differently and often have different temperaments. But there is a difference between parenting children differently yet fairly and favoring one child over others. In general, parents favoring one sibling over another has a deleterious effect on sibling relationships and on the psychological adjustment of the less favored child (Feinberg, Solmeyer, & McHale, 2012; Jeannin & Leeuwin, 2015). To some extent, this is dependent on perceptions. Siblings and parents often do not agree on this issue of whether or not they are treated fairly. The effect of differential treatment may well depend then on the extent to which family members concur on its occurrence and meaning (Kowal, Krull, & Kramer, 2006)

Lastly, are "only" children spoiled or disadvantaged relative to other children? Although there is a common and pejorative assumption that only children are indulged, overprotected, and prone to social maladjustment, there is no scientific evidence to support this view (Faldo, 2012; Mancillas, 2006). Actually, studies of only children have found very few differences between only children and children with siblings (Faldo, 2012). If anything, they tend to be a little smarter (Faldo, 2012) perhaps because the intensive involvement with parents they receive provides more experience with mature social and intellectual stimulation (Faldo, 2012). But even this difference is small, especially in comparison to children raised in a small, two-child family (Faldo, 2012).

In summary, family dynamics and parental style vary with family composition. In general, in smaller families each child receives more parental attention (and the associated cognitive and social benefits) than in big families. The addition of a new child to a family can affect the relationship between the parent and the older child. The long-term prognosis is more favorable, however, with comparable treatment of children more likely than differential treatment as children mature, and more evidence of friendly sibling relations than negative ones. Siblings model behaviors for one another and explicitly teach each other new things; they also provide emotional support for one another (Howe, Della Porta, Recchia, & Ross, 2016).

Divorce and Family Dissolution

Another altogether too common family issue that can have a deleterious effect on children, their development, and their academic performance is parents divorcing. It turns out that it is rather difficult to quantify the prevalence of divorce or how many children in the United States experience divorce. Some estimates suggest that as many as 40% of children will witness their parents' divorce (Sun & Li, 2009). Regardless of the actual number, it's quite likely that educators will work with children whose parents are getting or have been divorced.

The dissolution of a family causes a variety of behavioral and academic problems for children. In general, children whose parents have divorced have poorer psychological adjustment than children whose parents have not divorced (Amato & Anthony, 2014; Lansford, 2009; Lucas, Nicholson, & Erbas, 2013; Potter, 2010;

Sentse, Ormel, Veenstra, Verhulst, & Oldehinkel, 2015; Weaver & Schofield, 2015) In the short term, it is quite common for children to express shock and disbelief, followed by anger and grief, although over the long term most children make an adequate adjustment to their parents' divorce and only a few have enduring problems with psychological adjustment. How a child will cope with his or her parents' divorce depends on a wide variety of factors, including the child's age at the time of the divorce, the child's temperament and adjustment prior to the divorce, the family's financial resources, parental adjustment and social support, the degree of parental conflict both before and after the divorce, and the extent to which the parents can effectively co-parent (Lansford, 2009; Lucas et al., 2013; Sentse et al., 2015; Weaver & Schofield, 2015). Not surprisingly, children who have experienced divorce tend to have compromised academic performance (Anthony, DiPerna, & Amato, 2014; Potter, 2010; Sun & Li, 2009).

Poverty and Economic Stress

Economics factors have significant direct and indirect effects on family life and child development (Engle & Black, 2008; Evans, Li, & Whipple, 2013; Heberle & Carter, 2015; McLoyd, Mistry, & Hardaway, 2014; Parke et al., 2004; Yoshikawa, Aber, & Beardslee, 2012; Wagmiller, 2015). Economic hardship is associated with food insecurity and poorer nutrition, less effective health care, more negative life events, residential instability, family conflict and disorganization, and neighborhood risks such as substandard housing, greater exposure to environmental toxins, noise, crowding, and community violence (Lengua, 2012). Moreover, economic hardship increases parental stress, which affects parenting behaviors, thereby affecting children's functioning and development. When families are under stress, positive parent–child interactions often decrease and more punitive and authoritarian tactics increase (McLoyd et al., 2014; Neppl, Senia, & Donnellson, 2016; Nievar, Moske, Johnson, & Chen, 2014; Parke et al., 2004).

Statistics from 2012 reveal that in the United States one in six children face hunger, more than 20% of children live in poverty, and another 20% live in near poverty (Yoshikawa et al., 2012). It is therefore safe to assume that almost all educators will have contact with impoverished children and families. Moreover, in the United States, the effects of poverty disproportionately affect children from ethnic minority groups (Heberle & Carter, 2015; McLoyd et al., 2014; Parke et al., 2004). As a consequence of both the direct and indirect effects of poverty, children who grow up in impoverished families are often less prepared to start school, more likely to experience learning and academic problems, and often have more emotional and behavioral problems than peers from families with more financial resources (Anderson, Leventhal, & Dupéré, 2014; George, Koss, McCoy, Cummings, & Davies, 2010; Heberle & Carter, 2015; Lengua, 2012; Nievar et al., 2014; Neppl et al., 2016). These consequences are due in part to how chronic stress alters brain development and hormone regulation, which in turn impairs the development of executive functions, in addition to affecting how children think, their self-perceptions, and the effects of self and other expectations (George et al., 2010; Heberle & Carter, 2015; Lengua, 2012; Lepina & Evers, 2017; Luby et al., 2013; Yoshikawa et al., 2012).

When parents are employed, families can experience considerable stress from the pressures associated with work demands. Having to work when one does not want to work, not being able to work when one would like to work (e.g., during layoffs), having to work at a job one does not like, and working alternating shifts are all sources of stress that can negatively affect parenting (Bass, Butler, Grzywacz, & Linney, 2009; Bianci & Milkie, 2010; Gassman-Pines, 2013; Lee et al., 2015; Li et al., 2014; Nomaguchi & Johnson, 2016; Perry-Jenkins, Goldberg, Pierce, & Sayer, 2007; Perry-Jenkins, Smith, Goldberg, & Logan, 2011; Vieira, Matias, Ferriera, Lopez, & Matos, 2016). These stresses related to work do seem to have some adverse effects on children's development, their psychological adjustment, and their academic competence (Li et al., 2014; Strazdins, Obrien, Lucas, & Rodgers, 2013; Vieira et al., 2016).

In summary, both stress and social support can impact on parents so as to affect their parenting behaviors in ways that affect their children. Whether a child experiences a positive, authoritative environment or a negative, authoritarian (or neglectful) environment depends on a variety of contextual factors—biological, economic, and social.

Beyond the Family: Peer Relationships

Social relationships are essential to healthy child and adolescent development and psychological well-being across the lifespan. The evolution of social skills and peer relationships is quite complex and is linked to many of the other aspects of development that we are exploring in this text, including the neurological growth of the central nervous system, a child's cognitive development, the attachment opportunities available to a child and his or her internal working model of attachment, and the quality of family life a child experiences. Moreover, a child's peer relationships and social competence has a significant effect on his or her academic performance. So, let's review the steps involved in healthy social development, the theories that guide our studies of peer relationships, and the implications of peer relationships for the education of children

Developmental Milestones of Peer Relations

Evolutionary psychologists posit that social behaviors in humans are a consequence of natural selection. Moreover, there is a burgeoning literature on how brain development and various structures of the brain contribute to sociality (Grossman, 2015). As a consequence of this innate ability, the rudiments of social behavior can be observed early in infancy. Initially, these social interactions are necessarily nonverbal in nature and consist of establishing reciprocal attention and responsiveness to the cries of other infants (Hay, Caplan, & Nash, 2009). By the second half of a child's first year, he or she is smiling at peers, gesturing toward them, and making physical contact, and by the age of 1, children are able to engage in shared activities with others (Choukas-Bradley & Prinstein, 2014; Hay et al., 2009; Parker et al., 2006). Still the social interactions infants have with one another are rather infrequent and brief; year-old infants can be together and completely ignore one another, or at most interact only a little (Rubin, Chen, Coplan, Buskirk, & Wojslawowicz, 2011).

During the second year of life, children's peer interactions increase in both frequency and quality as their abilities to ambulate and use speech increases (Rubin et al., 2011). Two-year-olds begin to show a preference for specific peers; they play together, coordinate their efforts, take turns, and imitate one another (Brownell, 2016). Over the remaining toddler years, prosocial behaviors such as sharing and expressions of empathy become increasingly common (Imuta, Henry, Slaughter, Selcuk, & Ruffman, 2016; Parker et al., 2006). As children's language abilities improve and their self-regulation skills develop, they become better able to resolve conflicts without resorting to **instrumental aggression**, which is aggression directed at others to achieve a goal, commonly seen in younger children (Choukas-Bradley & Prinstein, 2014; Hay et al., 2009; Parker et al., 2006; Rubin et al., 2011). These prosocial skills result in children acquiring more positive peer experiences and friendships that promote a smoother transition into elementary school (Parker et al., 2006).

During the elementary school years, peer interactions become even more complex, and the games children play with peers are more sophisticated. The spontaneous and unstructured fantasy play common among preschoolers becomes much less frequent during the middle childhood years. Instead, children become more involved in extracurricular activities and youth sports that provide a wide variety of peer relationship opportunities (Choukas-Bradley & Prinstein, 2014; Parker et al., 2006). The tendency to associate with same-sex peers that begins during the preschool years intensifies, so that by middle childhood, most friendships are exclusively same sex (Parker et al., 2006). Increasingly during the grade school years, children spend time with the children they want to be with, rather than with the children who happen to live next door; friendships become quite stable during this period (Lansford, Yu, Pettit, Bates, & Dodge 2014; Poulin & Chan, 2010; Rubin et al., 2011).

Peers are increasingly important as children enter puberty and emerge as adolescents. They spend more time with peers than they do with their parents or other adults; their friendships become more intimate and self-disclosing; and social comparison and peer feedback have a significant effect on self-concept and identity formation (Choukas-Bradley & Prinstein, 2014; Parker et al., 2006). Friendship is a vital part of healthy adolescent development, although some teenagers are lonely, which is a risk factor for maladjustment and potential psychopathology (Woodhouse, Dykus, & Cassidy, 2012). Adolescents often join small peer groups called a **clique** that organizes without adult direction or supervision (Brown & Dietz, 2009; Henrich, Kuperminc, Sack, Blatt, & Leadbeater, 2000). Clique members are the people teenagers spend the most time with and trust the most. Often, adolescents have one or two very special friends in a clique, people with whom they feel they can be especially honest. Many, if not most, adolescents have a **crowd affiliation**. Crowd affiliation is determined by reputation and stereotype rather than by friends or social interactions and includes identities such as the jocks, the brains, the druggies, or the nerds (Brown & Dietz, 2009; Sussman, Pokhrel, Ashmore, & Brown, 2007). Crowds serve as a reference group for adolescents, enabling them to do social comparison and evaluate their social standing; they can also be a basis on which adolescents explore identity and self-concept. However, there are some kids who are not distinguishable as members of the aforementioned categories—they're just regular teens. Crowds vary in social status, and some crowds are more associated with antisocial behavior and activities. So, the potential arises for falling into a bad crowd, which can lead to participation in delinquent behaviors, although this is not inevitable. Children of nurturing and involved parents are less likely to fall into such a crowd, even in community situations where the risk of encountering wrong-crowd peers is great (Cook, Buehler, & Henson, 2009; Walters, 2016).

Understanding People and Social Situations

The thoughts and attitudes that guide our interpersonal interactions and our under-standing of other people and the nature of the social world are referred to as **social cognition** (Carpendale & Lewis, 2015). Social cognition, which is highly correlated with social competence, develops in tandem with cognitive development and is inex-tricably linked with social interaction with others (Brink, Lane, & Wellman, 2015; Caputi, Lecce, Pagnin, & Banerjee, 2011).

Just as infants engage in rudimentary social interactions, researchers have deter-mined that infants also possess some basic understanding of their social context. Studies that track infants' gaze and looking-time suggest that within the first year of life children are acquiring an appreciation that the actions and expressions of others are intentional and goal directed (Brink et al., 2015; Hughes & Devine, 2015). During the grade school years, children begin to understand that other people have stable characteristics—they have traits such as friendliness, shyness, or aggressiveness—and they begin to understand that males and females exhibit some differences in their social interactions (Chalik, Rivera, & Rhodes, 2014; Liu, Gelman, & Wellman, 2007; Markovits, Benenson, & Dolenszky, 2001). As they experience the preschool and elementary years, children acquire an understanding of many social rules (Smetana, 1993). They learn who to address politely and when, how dress varies with occasions (e.g., clothes for "dress up" vs. clothes for play), and how to negotiate the world safely (e.g., waiting for the walk light). Children also learn about status differences and how these translate into differences in human interaction and power (Nobes & Paw-son, 2003). With increasing age, children understand that other people are better defined by their internal characteristics (i.e., feelings, knowledge, thought) than by their external characteristics (i.e., possessions, dress). In short, as children develop, they acquire a great deal of information about how to act, when, and with whom—knowledge required for effective social interactions with others.

Development of Social-Cognitive Abilities

Since a strong relationship exists between general cognitive abilities and social cog-nition, it is no surprise that the initial theories and research about social-cognitive development mirrored theories of cognitive development, particularly Piagetian concepts. Robert Selman (Elfers, Martin, & Sokol, 2008; Selman, 1976) proposed a complex developmental sequence for social-perspective taking that was influenced by Piaget and Kohlberg. Like Kohlberg, Selman asked children to reason about dilemmas. One was about Holly, who was good at climbing trees but had promised her father, who feared for her safety, that she would not climb them. One day, when confronted with a kitten stuck in a tree, Holly faced a dilemma: whether to climb the tree in defiance of her father's direction and save the kitten, or obey her father and leave the kitten in the tree. Selman asked children to make the choice for Holly and explain the choice.

Selman concluded that preschool-age children begin in an egocentric stage, during which they have difficulty understanding other perspectives and recognizing that others may interpret situations differently than they do. A child in this stage might defend Holly's decision to climb the tree and save the cat by arguing that Holly's father would agree with Holly's decision, seeing the situation precisely as Holly saw it. Children around the ages of 6 to 8 transition into a social-informational role-taking stage, during which they recognize that others have different perspectives but experience difficulties thinking about several perspectives at once. Thus, when talking about Holly, they may mention her father's concern as well as the welfare of the kitten, but not recognize the conflict between these perspectives. Selman's studies indicated that by the age of 10 children enter a self-reflection stage during which they are more attuned to their own perspectives and those of others, but they still experience difficulties thinking about both their own perspectives and those of others at the same time. During early adolescence, children acquire the capacity to consider two viewpoints at once and recognize that other people can do so as well, in a stage Selman called mutual role taking. Children in this stage might argue that the father could be concerned with Holly's safety, but might also be pleased that Holly succeeded in saving the kitten. The highest stage in Selman's theory is social and conventional system role taking, which develops during adolescence, enabling adolescents to think about the situation from a third party's (as well as society's) perspective. In reasoning about Holly's dilemma, the young teen can weigh the perspectives of the different characters in the dilemma, but also can think about what makes sense from the larger perspective of the society. Thus, after detailing Holly's thinking, her father's concern and directive, an adolescent might decide to leave the cat in the tree, recognizing that the risks of injury and the societal costs of injury to a child far outweigh the risks of losing the kitten. Alternatively, the Stage-4 thinker might factor in the animal rights perspective, which could result in the decision that Holly should rescue the kitten.

In general, Selman's theory of the development of perspective taking has been confirmed in the sense that, as children mature, their thinking about social dilemmas shifts much as Selman proposed (Elfers et al., 2008). That is, children do develop an ability to reflect on alternative perspectives, considering both their own ideas, those of other people, and those of the larger society. Such increasing ability to think about and interact with others about social dilemmas should contribute to improved interactions with others. However, Selman's ideas have largely been supplanted by a more contemporary idea, theory of mind.

Theory-of-Mind Research

Much work on social cognition has focused on children's developing *theory of mind*, which refers to children's increasing understanding about how minds function (Hughes & Devine, 2015; see also Chapter 3). Knowing how other people's minds work is essential knowledge for dealing with other people. It is rather amazing that young children acquire an appreciation that internal and unobservable thoughts and emotions drive other's behavior and that this understanding becomes increasingly sophisticated over the preschool and early childhood years (Imuta et al., 2016; Lagattuta, 2005; Lillard & Kavanaugh, 2014).

Since children can pretend, they must understand the distinction between the real world and the imaginary, mental-only world. Theory-of-mind researchers have established that children younger than age 3 sometimes pretend, but they do not understand the properties of imaginary objects compared to real objects as well as do older preschoolers. For example, 3-year-olds know that it is impossible to touch an imaginary cup and they understand that they can flip such a cup over in their head. Yet, preschoolers' understanding of the distinction between real and imagined objects is not complete, especially in response to frightening fantasies (Sayfan &

Lagattuta, 2008, 2009; Zisenwine, Kaplan, Kushnir, & Sadeh, 2013). For example, 4- to 6-year-olds asked to imagine a monster recognized that no one else could see the monster and reported that it was not real, but they were still apprehensive that it might become real (Harris, Brown, Marriott, Whittall, & Harmer, 1991)!

During the preschool years, the understanding that people have desires, beliefs, and intentions also increases (Behne, Carpenter, Call, & Thomasello, 2005; Colonnesi, Koops, & Terwogt, 2008; Schult, 2002; Shiverick & Moore, 2013). Moreover, the ability to differentiate these states of mind substantially improves. Thus, with increasing age during the preschool years, children understand that people can wish for one thing and believe that a different outcome will occur. In contrast, younger children focus on wishes, believing that a person's wishes reflect the individual's belief about what is going to happen (Schult, 2002; Shiverick & Moore, 2013).

Developing a theory of mind has been associated with a number of positive psychological outcomes. Having a mature theory of mind facilitates children's interactions with others. There is some evidence to suggest that children with a more developed theory of mind are more socially competent, tend to be more popular, and may be more sensitive and responsive to others (Caputi et al., 2011; Hughes & Devine, 2015; Imuta et al., 2016; Slaughter, Imuta, Peterson, & Henry 2015). Children increasingly understand that emotions such as happiness and surprise depend in part on a person's desires and beliefs. That is, people cannot be happy about something unless they desired it, and people cannot be surprised unless they expected something else to happen (Hadwin & Perner, 1991; Lagattuta, 2005). Such knowledge is essential for a child who is trying to make another person happy, perhaps by planning a pleasant surprise. Children increasingly recognize they can affect the emotions of another person by acting one way or another. For example, preschoolers learn how to comfort others in distress, which requires clear understanding of the perspective of others (Imuta et al., 2016). It is not until the early grade school years, however, before children have an understanding of the wide range of emotions and how the many human emotions vary depending on the situation (Castro, Halberstadt, & Garrett-Peters, 2016; Lagattuta, 2005).

Theory-of-mind perspectives may offer an important window on one group of children who have puzzled researchers for a long time. One of the most defining characteristics of children with autism is that they do not relate to other people. There is growing evidence that such children lack a theory of mind or at least have much less complete understanding than normal children about the existence of others' thoughts, feelings, and desires, as well as a less complete understanding of themselves as thinkers and doers (Hughes & Devine, 2015). See Chapter 12 for a more complete discussion of autism.

Friendship and Social Status

As children age, their peer interactions become increasingly complex and important to their development. During childhood, peer relationships are an opportunity to develop social skills such as sharing, cooperation, and initiating friendships. This provides a foundation for the friendships that emerge during adolescence, which tend to become more intimate and take on even greater salience. Some members of adolescents' peer network become closer than others, and these especially close friends become confidants, sources of social support, and a means for self-exploration and identity development.

Selman (1981) proposed a theory of friendship based on his perspective-taking ideas. According to Selman, during early childhood, children's friendships are based on proximity and typically are considered transitory playmates. As children progress through the middle childhood years, they begin to understand that others may have a different perspective than their own, and they also recognize that feelings and motivations sustain or deter friendships (Parker et al., 2006). Still, children at this age remain fairly self-centered and less concerned about the experience of others. Gradually, children begin to recognize that friendships require some mutuality; friends become more interactive and attentive to equity rules. By the conclusion of the middle childhood years, children have an appreciation that friendships are based on an emotional connection that has an enduring quality (Parker et al., 2006). Consequently, as children enter into adolescence they consider their friends a source of social support and seek a more intimate connection with them.

Childhood friendships are typically arranged and supported by parents and other adults through school or extracurricular activities and youth sports. These friendships are almost always with same-sex peers. However, as children reach adolescence, the time they spend with their family begins to decline, so that during the high school years adolescents are spending nearly a third of their time with peers and less than half of that time with parents and family (Goede, Branje, & Meeus, 2009; Parker et al., 2006). Consequently, friendships take on a more significant role for healthy adolescent development. As adolescents' competence at social-perspective taking improves, they engage in more social comparison and rely on friends for companionship, validation, corrective feedback, and emotional support (Bornstein et al., 2013; Erdley & Day, 2017; Hiatt, Laursen, Mooney, & Rubin 2015). Adolescent friendships assume a much greater level of intimacy and self-disclosure. Adolescents' friendships drift away from a focus on sharing activities to sharing thoughts, secrets, and ambitions with an implicit expectation of reciprocity, mutual respect, equality, and especially trust (Choukas-Bradley & Prinstein, 2014; Goede et al., 2009; Prinstein & Giletta, 2016). Conflicts between adolescent friends are generally low intensity and easily disengaged from. Adolescent friends tend to seek cooperative, mutually pleasing solutions to conflicts and will defer if an equitable solution is impossible, although this can have a deleterious effect on the friendship (Bornstein et al., 2013; Erdley & Day, 2017).

The Potential Risks of Friendship

The capacity to make and sustain friendships is a key element of psychological well-being for children and adolescents (Vitaro, Boivan, & Bukowski, 2009). Still, some potential hazards accompany friendship, especially for adolescents. One of these hazards is generally known as peer pressure. Peers can and do have positive influences on one another through normative regulation (exerting influence on others to bring their behavior within acceptable norms) and through peer modeling. However, when educators, clinicians, social scientists, and parents allude to peer pressure, they are typically referring to peer influence that leads an adolescent to take impulsive risks or engage in deviant or delinquent behavior. Adolescents do seem to be most influenced by their most intimate friends, and risky behavior does occur more frequently while in the company of friends (Bornstein et al., 2013; Erdley & Day, 2017). Moreover, forming a friendship with a peer that embodies socially undesirable qualities does tend to lead to deleterious outcomes (Shi & Xie, 2012; Vitaro et al., 2009).

Adolescents who engage in delinquency talk to each other and tend to encourage and escalate antisocial behavior in one another (Erdley & Day, 2017; Vitaro et al., 2009). Typically, this vulnerability to negative peer pressure peaks around age 14, after which peer conformity declines, reflecting the fact that older adolescents have a much better sense of themselves than do young teens (Bornstein et al., 2013).

Two related constructs that can prove perilous for adolescents are depression contagion and co-rumination (Choukas-Bradley & Prinstein 2014; Prinstein & Giletta, 2016; Vitaro et al., 2009). Because adolescents tend to seek out others who are like them, peers who experience mood dysregulation and depression tend to flock together. As adolescents with depressed mood commiserate with one another, they can induce more intense mood disruption in one another. Similarly, co-rumination occurs when adolescents, in their efforts to create greater intimacy through self-disclosure, engage in escalating discussions about their distress. These phenomena are particularly evident in female friendships and can lead to more significant mood disorders.

Popular and Unpopular Children

Researchers studying social status among children and adolescents draw a distinction between popularity and social acceptance. Popularity refers to a person's reputation or prestige within his or her peer group; it is an indicator of social power and is often based on a person's appearance, scholarship, wealth, athletic abilities, or use of direct or indirect aggression to secure and maintain social position (Dawes & Xie, 2014; Dijkstra, Cillessen, & Borch, 2013; Gorman, Schwartz, Nakamoto, & Mayeux, 2011). Social acceptance, in contrast, is a measure of likability that typically depends on a person's social competence (Dijkstra et al., 2013; Gorman et al., 2011). A few adolescents achieve both popularity and social preference. When researchers conduct sociometric studies that ask children or adolescents to nominate peers who are most or least liked, these *popular* kids receive a lot of "like" votes and few or no "dislike" nominations. Most children and adolescents are socially successful, but not particularly popular and receive a mix of "like" and "dislike" nominations. Some receive a lot of "like" and "dislike" votes. These *controversial* children and adolescents are popular but broadly disliked primarily because of their use of aversive or manipulative relationship tactics. Some children and adolescents receive no votes in either direction and are characterized as "neglected." Lastly, some unfortunate *rejected* children and adolescents receive a lot of "dislike" votes and few or no "like" nominations (Cillessen & Bukowski, 2000; Gorman et al., 2011; Hymel, Closson, Caravita, & Vaillancourt, 2010; McElhaney, Antonishak, & Allen, 2008; Rubin et al., 2011).

Children and adolescents who have high-quality peer relationships tend to have better psychological and educational outcomes, and conversely, unpopular children tend to experience more educational, socioemotional, and legal problems throughout their lifespan (Choukas-Bradley & Prinstein 2014; Hiatt et al., 2015; Parker et al., 2006; Prinstein & Giletta, 2016). The question many social scientists and educators are asking is "What is happening with these unpopular children and adolescents," and the answer to this question depends to a large extent on what kind of unpopularity they have. Neglected children and adolescents are generally not acknowledged by their peers. They are typically shy kids who rarely behave aggressively (Gorman et al., 2011). Rejected children and adolescents show up in one of two ways. Some are aggressive, while others are immature, withdrawn, and socially inept (Choukas-Bradley & Prinstein, 2014; Gorman et al., 2011; Prinstein & Giletta, 2016; Rubin et al., 2011).

Adolescents are highly motivated to seek both popularity and social acceptance, although peer acceptance and peer rejection statuses are quite stable over time and situations, so it can be very challenging for a neglected or rejected adolescent to improve his or her social status (Choukas-Bradley & Prinstein, 2014; Li & Wright, 2014; Prinstein & Giletta, 2016). Sometimes lower-status adolescents try to improve their social standing by befriending higher-status adolescents. However, higher-status adolescents will often keep lower-status peers at bay out of concern that associating with a neglected or rejected status peer will reduce their social status. Sometimes higher-status adolescents abuse lower-status adolescents as a way to improve or maintain their social status distance (Dijkstra et al., 2013; Gorman et al., 2011; Li & Wright, 2014). These issues with neglected children and adolescents can be addressed to some extent by providing them with friendship initiation skills and facilitating friendship relationships. Having at least one friend tends to minimize the potential of peer victimization, reduces loneliness, and builds social confidence and increases the potential of seeking future friendships (Choukas-Bradley & Prinstein 2014; McElhaney et al., 2008; Prinstein & Giletta, 2016; Woodhouse et al., 2012). The situation is somewhat direr for rejected children and adolescents. In addition to the likelihood of peer victimization, rejected children and adolescents typically have more significant deficits in their social-cognitive capacities. They either don't receive or fail to comprehend corrective feedback from peers; they often misinterpret social cues and infer hostile intent where none existed; and they tend to congregate into maladaptive peer groups that only increases their social rejection and maladaptive social skills (Choukas-Bradley & Prinstein, 2014; Prinstein & Giletta, 2016).

Researchers have studied a number of ways to successfully intervene with children who lack social skills, although more for the treatment of aggressive behaviors than for withdrawal. Some of these efforts are designed for working with families to teach parents how to interact with their children to promote social skills and to reduce other stressors in the family's life. Other interventions are school-based (Menting, Koot, & van Lier, 2015). (See the Applying Developmental Theory to Educational Contexts special feature in Box 10.2.) These interventions target children's and adolescents' social skills and tend to be more successful when implemented over a number of years. Some programs are carried out in recreational centers and other community-based facilities, and also involve direct teaching of social skills and reinforcement for using the skills. Recently, a variety of computer games and online applications have been developed to enhance children's social skills (Craig, Brown, Upright, & DeRosier, 2016; Ramdoss et al., 2012).

Teaching children how to act skillfully with other people makes a great deal of conceptual sense. Popular children know how to begin, sustain, and end social interactions, and children who cannot do these things are much more likely to be rejected by peers. Intervention programs simply teach socially unskilled children to do what works for popular children. In general, these approaches utilize cognitive-behavioral tactics to improve a child or adolescent's social problem-solving skills. Students are taught to recognize when they are in a situation in which they might behave inappropriately. They are taught to think before acting and to generate alternative ways that they might deal with the situation and to reflect on the consequences for behaving appropriately and inappropriately. The children are typically taught to approach situations in a step-by-step fashion, and to verbally self-instruct along the way to size up the situation, think of appropriate ways to act and the benefits of doing so, and then carry out the action.

Applying Developmental Theory to Educational Contexts

BOX 10.2. Social-Emotional Learning (SEL) Interventions in Schools

Educators and social scientists have increasingly recognized the importance of social and emotional skills for learning. Children who have effective self-regulatory skills like the ability to set goals, a positive attitude, the capacity to manage their emotions and to cope with emotionally unsettling events, and interpersonal skills such as being a good listener and communicator, and having the ability to engage in social problem-solving and negotiation tend to be more motivated and engaged learners and achieve more academically (Domitrovich, Durlak, Staley, & Weissberg, 2017; Durlak, Weissberg, Dymnicki, Taylor, & Schellinger, 2011; Kendziora & Osher, 2016). As a consequence, some schools have begun to implement social and emotional learning programs.

Social–emotional learning (SEL) programs are typically preventive in nature and applied to all students regardless of their psychological adjustment or needs. There are a variety of SEL programs. Some of these programs involve direct instruction to students that target social skills like anger management, social skills training, or empathy building. These defined interventions usually begin with some explanation of the skill, provide an observable example of the desired behavior, and then require students to practice the actual skill. Other SEL interventions focus on improving school climate and include features such as demonstrating respect between students and between teachers and students, creating a psychologically trusting and physically safe environment, and developing quality collaborations between students and school staff as well as enhancing parental involvement in school. Often SEL programs have elements of both types of interventions (Domitrovich et al., 2017; Kendziora & Osher, 2016).

The empirical evidence on the effectiveness of SEL programs is convincing. Studies consistently demonstrate that SEL programs in schools improve students' academic achievement as well as their long-term psychological adjustment (Domitrovich et al., 2017; Durlak et al., 2011; Kendziora & Osher, 2016). However, implementing SEL programs in schools can be challenging. Sometimes an inspired teacher finds ways to infuse SEL into his or her instruction. However, this piecemeal method is not nearly as effective as when a school or school district makes SEL a key aspect of its mission, engaging all school staff in the endeavor, and integrating it into the academic curriculum. Convincing a school or school district to take on this responsibility can be very difficult. Schools must meet a wide variety of local, state, and federal education mandates that often are not aligned with SEL goals. Moreover, although SEL has been demonstrated to be quite cost effective in the long run (Domitrovich et al., 2017), it may take quite some time before a school or school district begins to realize any cost savings. It will take a concerted effort to educate the public about the benefits of SEL for children, parents, schools, and our society.

Bullying

Bullying behavior has received considerable attention in recent years and rightly so. Bullying has a deleterious effect on the children and adolescents who are bullied, on the children and adolescents who perpetrate the bullying behavior, but also on the teachers and students who witness the bullying. Determining how prevalent bullying is depends on how bullying is defined, what research methodology is used to gather the data, and how the question is asked (National Academy of Sciences, Engineering, and Medicine, 2016; Salmivalli & Peets, 2009; Salmivalli, Peets, & Hodges, 2011). However, it appears that bullying is a quite common phenomenon (as many as 20–30% report being bullied at school) that can be seen as early as preschool, but peaks during the middle school years (National Academy of Sciences, Engineering, and Medicine, 2016). Bullying can be physical, verbal, or relational, or involve the destruction of property, and it occurs in a variety of settings, though primarily at school and increasingly via Internet social media sites.

Educators can be very influential in preventing bullying and intervening when they see it happening; indeed, teachers are perhaps the one group of adults more than any other that see peer group behavior and how individual children are faring with their peers (Audley-Piotrowski, Singer, & Patterson, 2015; National Academy of Sciences, Engineering, and Medicine, 2016). One important consideration is optimizing the school climate. By using a variety of approaches, schools can reduce the incidence of bullying and its negative effects on the school environment (Olweus, 2003; Salmivalli et al., 2011; Wentzel, 2014). Positive school climates with fair, clearly delineated, discipline practices and sufficient adult monitoring that are coupled with empathic and supportive adult guidance tend to minimize bullying among child and adolescent peers. Teachers are more likely to intervene in bullying situations when they have received training about peer bullying that enhances their sense of efficacy. Also, teachers need to use some discretion when employing small-group activities. These types of instruction can be used to develop children's and adolescents' social skills, but they can also put vulnerable students in a precarious situation (Audley-Piotrowski et al., 2015; National Academy of Sciences, 2016; Wentzel, 2014). Lastly, transition times, both within the school day and across the school year, are times when bullying tends to peak (Farmer, Hamm, Leung, Lambert, & Gravelle, 2011). Conscientious educators make concerted efforts to monitor children and adolescents during these times and to intervene quickly if necessary.

Online Social Networking

The use of the Internet for social networking is ubiquitous in the lives of children and adolescents today. Most adolescents possess a cell phone and/or computer, and most are adept digital visitors and increasingly digital residents who connect socially via texting, accessing social media, video gaming, and a variety of messaging applications (Boyd, 2014; Lenhart, 2015; White & Le Cornu, 2011). Parents, educators, and social scientists have been questioning how this pervasive use of digital technology may be affecting children's and adolescents' development, neurologically, cognitively, and psychosocially. Some have questioned whether digital technology use may be altering normal neurological and cognitive development, particularly the prevalent habit of multitasking, which may be detrimental to developing the capacity for sustained attention (Giedd, 2012; Mills, 2014; Sneider & Silveri, 2015). Others have suggested there is little empirical support to suggest that digital technology is dramatically altering brain development and functioning and that Internet use may impart cognitive benefits (Mills, 2014).

The question of how digital technology is changing children's and adolescents' social lives is more complicated. Early studies of Internet use tended to emphasize the risks of digital social networking, raising concern that in the absence of the nuances and extensive nonverbal social cues inherent to face-to-face communications, digital social relationships would be shallow and that children and adolescents obsessed with the Internet would fail to master requisite social skills. However, more recent studies have found that adolescents' use of social media and other digital communications technology can be either positive or negative (Underwood & Ehrenreich, 2017). In general, adolescents' use of digital communications tends to improve their sense of social connectivity and may actually be a necessary skill for contemporary youth (Tsitsika et al., 2014). They use digital technologies to enhance their existing relationships, and they are better able to regulate how they present themselves and how much they self-disclose using digital communications (Blais, Craig, Pepler, & Connolly, 2008; Boyd, 2014; Spies Shapiro & Margolin, 2014; Valkenburg & Peter, 2011). In fact, digital communications may be beneficial to adolescents who are less socially skilled and who have fewer friends because the use of technology filters out some of the social awkwardness they may experience in face-to-face interactions.

Nonetheless, there are risks associated with online social networking. The effect of digital social networking likely depends on the type and frequency of online social networking. Texting and social media sharing tend to augment existing relationships, while chat-rooms and gaming tend to involve engagement with strangers and lower quality friendships and to detract from proximal social opportunities and existing relationships (Blais et al., 2008). There is some evidence that heavy use of the Internet is associated with poorer academic performance (Tsitsika et al., 2014), and there is speculation that social media posts may intensify the already heightened self-consciousness that accompanies the social comparison adolescents engage in (Spies Shapiro & Margolin, 2014). Some of the most significant unease about youth digital social networking involves cyberbullying. Cyberbullying seems to be on the rise, with estimates that upwards of 25% of students experience cyberbullying (Hamm et al., 2015). Cyberbullying takes on a variety of forms (e.g., online fighting or "flaming," harassment, outing, exclusion, impersonating, stalking and sexting) and occurs on a number of different digital formats (Kowalski, Giumetti, Schroeder, & Lattanner, 2014). The anonymity of digital communications may foster abusive communications since cyberbullies are less concerned about getting caught and are more likely to be impulsively offensive than they might be in a face-to-face confrontation (Kowalski et al., 2014; Valkenburg & Peter, 2011). Unfortunately, there is emerging evidence that cyberbullying can have a very negative effect on children and adolescent psychological health (Hamm et al., 2015; Underwood & Ehrenreich, 2017).

Figuring out the effects of digital technology on today's youth and finding effective means of channeling the positive aspects and deterring the negative ones will be a challenging task. Technological changes are occurring rapidly, and so are the ways that young people are using them. The research on digital social networking is hampered by this moving target and, so far, is primarily descriptive, cross-sectional, and based on self-report, making it very difficult to determine what is cause and what is effect. In the meantime, educators can work with children and adolescents to effectively use digital technology by critically evaluating the information they glean from the Internet, consider how their online communications affect them and others, and promote cyberbullying prevention messages (Giedd, 2012; Rice et al., 2015).

How Do Social Relationships Affect Academic Achievement?

Educators, families, and youth are involved in complex dynamic interactions that have significant consequences for how children and adolescents perform academically. In general, the more children and adolescents feel a sense of relatedness, the better they do in school (King, 2015; Moses & Villodas, 2017; Wentzel, Russell, & Baker, 2016). Children with secure attachment with parents tend to exhibit more social competence and hence are more successful in positively connecting with peers and teachers, which leads to better behavioral adjustment and more academic motivation and school engagement. The more parents are positively involved with their children and adolescents, supporting appropriate autonomy, providing guidance and supervision, and offering affection and warmth, the better kids do in school, the more they value education, and the more likely they are to seek additional education beyond high school (Hill & Wang, 2015; Wentzel et al., 2016).

Peers also have a significant effect on each other's academic achievement. When students are friends with high-achieving peers, they are more academically motivated, they are more involved in school, and their in-class behavior is conducive to learning. The opposite is also true; students who befriend low-achieving peers tend to be truant more often and perform poorly academically (King, 2015; Perdue, Manzeske, & Estell, 2009; Rambaran et al., 2017; Schwartz, Gorman, Nakamoto, & McKay, 2006; Wentzel, 2009). There is also evidence to suggest that positive relationships in one or two of the domains of parents, peers, and teachers can help to compensate for poor relationships in one of the others (Moses & Villodas, 2017; Wentzel et al., 2016). For example, children and adolescents with strong peer relationships with prosocial peers and positive relationships with teachers may be better able to cope with the detrimental effects associated with family troubles. Similarly, children and adolescents with good teacher and family relationships may be better able to withstand the stresses associated with negative peer interactions. Lastly, children and adolescents with strong peer and family connections often have more resilience facing academic problems or teachers who undervalue them.

There are a variety of ways in which educators can facilitate their students' social development. First, it is important to keep in mind that teachers have a significant impact on the social lives of the children and adolescents they work with (Wentzel, 2009, 2014). Some of that impact derives from the interpersonal relationships teachers develop with their students. When students have supportive, empathic, and emotionally secure relationships with their teachers, they tend to prosper academically (King, 2015; Wentzel et al., 2016). Conversely, children and adolescents are observant and recognize when a teacher is critical, dismissive, or has negative expectations, verbally or nonverbally, of a peer, and they tend to model that and respond to that student with more rejection (Audley-Piotrowski et al., 2015; Wentzel, 2014). So, it is vitally important for educators to recognize their own expectations and biases and to work to treat each child equally (Audley-Piotrowski et al., 2015).

It is also quite useful for teachers to be aware of the peer relationships that develop among their students. With this knowledge, a teacher can be more intentional about how he or she arranges seating and how he or she pairs children up for group activities; to foster peer interactions between some children and adolescents, and to avoid putting together children and adolescents who are likely to have negative peer interactions (Audley-Piotrowski et al., 2015; Wentzel, 2009). Also, educators can adopt institutional rules and create schoolwide norms that promote positive peer interactions by advocating for the adoption of prosocial values and empathy. To this end, educators need to consider carefully how performance-oriented competitive academics can often influence peer interactions in adverse ways by increasing social comparison and decreasing community integrity (Wentzel, 2014). Lastly, while most educators will not be in a position to affect family relationships, educators can create an inviting atmosphere that encourages parents to be involved with their children's education.

Chapter Summary and Evaluation

Family relationships, particularly those occurring in infancy and early childhood, set a tone for future relationships with peers and other adults. A secure attachment between children and their caretakers is not guaranteed. Differences in maternal responsiveness may explain security of attachment, although a baby's temperament also may play a role. Children who have secure attachment internal working models tend to be more able to cope with the transition into school and succeed in making adaptive relationships with fellow students and teachers. A secure attachment during infancy also tends to contribute to later cognitive development.

Similarly, authoritative parenting, particularly during adolescence, tends to lead to better social and cognitive outcomes than other parenting styles. The most effective socialization mechanisms are consistent with authoritative parenting. Authoritative parenting demands much of parents, however, so that when parents are under stress, parenting often becomes less authoritative. Contemporary families face a number of challenges in raising socially and emotionally healthy children. Working parents with children in day care, family transitions like divorce and remarriage, and economic stressors all affect the capacity of families to provide optimal developmental circumstances for their children and adolescents.

The majority of U.S. children experience some kind of day care at some point during their childhood. The impact of such care depends greatly on the quality of the care received, as defined by the structural resources that are available and the processes occurring during care. When resources are good and the process includes many educationally oriented activities, the outcomes are typically good. The benefits of high-quality, educationally oriented day care especially have been demonstrated with at-risk populations. Creating such high-quality settings requires know-how, especially knowledge about child development.

As children mature, their understanding and appreciation for peer relationships increases. Peer interactions begin in infancy, probably the first time a child encounters another child. They increase in frequency, diversity, and complexity with increasing age until adolescence, when peer relationships begin to take priority over family relationships. Developing effective social skills and maintaining friendships are vital skills for healthy development, and educators recognize the implications of this for academic achievement. As with most of development, peer relations depend in part on cognitive development; they also probably determine cognitive development to some extent.

Much of the scholarship on family and peer effects on development and education involve the enduring issues in developmental psychology.

Nature and Nurture

Attachment theorists have strong assumptions about the biological foundations of mother–infant relationships, believing that human attachment evolved because of its adaptive significance to the human organism. That is, humans who attached to their infants were more likely to have infants who would mature and reproduce. That said, environment matters greatly to the attachment theorists, for the mother's responsiveness to the infant goes far in determining the security of infant–mother attachment. Infant temperament, most likely determined by biology, also affects infant–parent attachment.

Continuity and Discontinuity

Clearly, social interactions evolve through the qualitatively different periods of development: infancy, childhood, and adolescence. The newborn is social only in a rudimentary fashion compared to the securely attached 1-year-old, whose social relations are limited relative to the preschooler and the elementary-age youngster. With the passage from childhood to adolescence, the peer group becomes more salient. But is any of this really discontinuous, really stage-like?

Well, to some extent yes. The developments during infancy seem to follow a developmental timetable that is governed by maturation: perceptual, cognitive, and physical maturation. Also, some social relations during childhood seem to depend on cognitive development in a stage-like fashion. For example, increases in perspective-taking skills are often used to explain children's increasing social interactions between 4 and 8 years of age. The adolescent's formal operational competence is sometimes offered as an explanation for the increased intensity of friendships at adolescence, especially with respect to increased attention to psychological characteristics of friends.

Even so, most changes in social relationships seem gradual rather than sudden. The qualitative differences between adolescents and preschoolers can be traced to gradual changes in number of friends and types of interactions with friends. In short, the developments described in this chapter have both stage-like and non-stage-like properties.

Universal and Culture-Specific

How families operate, the socioeconomic circumstances they have to work with, and the customs and values they hold vary considerably from one culture group to another. Although attachment occurs in all cultural groups, how it is done and variations in attachment are evident across culture. Parenting styles and their relative effectiveness for prompting healthy development varies across cultures. Cultural norms and values are also an important factor in the development and maintenance of peer relationships, and culture plays a role in the context and groups in which peer relationships occur.

Active and Passive Child

Children's behaviors affect social relations and thus development more generally. The temperamental infant may contribute to the development of an insecure attachment to mother. The socially unskilled child is excluded from many social relations that contribute to the positive development of children who experience them. By selecting membership in one crowd or another (e.g., "brains" vs. "druggies"), adolescents greatly alter much in their everyday lives.

authoritarian parenting A parenting style where the parents are highly responsive to their children and highly demanding of their children.

authoritative parenting A parenting style where the parents are highly demanding of their children but not responsive to their children.

clique For adolescents, a peer group of intimate friends, ranging in size from 5 to 10 people.

corporal punishment Inflicting painful punishment to gain behavioral compliance.

crowd affiliation A large group of adolescent friends defined by salient characteristics (e.g., jocks, brains).

inductive discipline A type of parental discipline in which parents provide reasons to a child on why certain behaviors are not desired, with a focus on developing empathy in the child.

instrumental aggression Aggression directed at others with the primary purpose of achieving a goal, commonly seen in younger children.

internal working model An internalized schema of what to expect from interpersonal relationships.

permissive parenting A parenting style where parents are responsive to their children but not demanding of them.

secure base Developing a sense of attachment security through the intimate and consistent attention of a primary caregiver.

social cognition The understanding of other people and the nature of the social world.

uninvolved parenting A parenting style where parents are neither responsive to their children nor demanding of them.

CHAPTER 11

Gender Role Development

The first question most people ask when they learn a baby has been born is about the infant's sex: "Is it a boy or a girl?" Typically, one of the first things people notice when they are meeting someone for the first time is whether the person is male or female. And the foremost way people identify themselves is, commonly, in terms of being female or male. A person's sex is determined at birth based on the anatomical phenotype (observed genitalia) of the infant, which in most cases corresponds to the child's genotype (chromosomes). Exceptions to this rule will be discussed later in this chapter. Gender, in contrast, is socially and culturally constructed. Our biological sex and our gender identity affect much of what happens in our lives, including our experiences in educational institutions. People hold many misconceptions about gender, what it means to identify as male or female, and which attributes are characteristic of males and females.

This chapter begins with a discussion of the concept of gender itself. We then discuss the various ways psychologists have attempted to account for gender role development, followed by a discussion of verified differences between males and females. We note at the outset that the number and size of differences between the sexes have decreased over the last few decades. Next we examine gender differences in academic motivation and achievement, with a particular emphasis on performance in the STEM (science, technology, engineering, and mathematics) disciplines. Finally, we review interventions designed to encourage gender equity in participation in STEM fields.

Gender Identity

Many people think of sex and gender as binary categories—someone is either male or female. A person's chromosomes match their hormones, which produce genitalia corresponding to their gender identity and how they present themselves in terms of physical appearance and interact with the world in terms of preferences. In the next section, we discuss sex development and the ways in which variation can occur in what may seem to be a relatively straightforward process, the determination of biological sex. Societal changes, along with growth in understanding of biological and social influences on gender, have led many to look at gender as more of a spectrum or continuum than a binary category.

Gender identity is not always consistent with sex assignment. People whose gender identity matches the sex assigned at birth are referred to as **cisgender,** whereas those whose gender identity differs from the sex assigned at birth are referred to as **transgender**. Gender identity is different from sexual orientation in that cisgender and transgender people can have any sexual orientation. Still others identify outside of the gender binary completely, embracing gender fluidity, seeing themselves as neither entirely male nor female. In many countries, increasing numbers are identifying as gender nonconforming (Rosenthal, 2016). It is not clear if the numbers are increasing in actuality or if people feel more comfortable acknowledging gender nonconforming identities (i.e., any gender identity other than cisgender) now than in the past. Just to complicate matters further, behaviors can be gender nonconforming without gender identity being nonconforming. As we shall see, gender identity and gender role development are complex and even more so when we consider that advances in scientific understanding of how chromosomes and hormones operate to determine biological sex during prenatal development reveal that for some individuals biological sex itself can be ambiguous. This topic is taken up in the next section.

Theoretical Explanations of Gender Development

Psychologists have been long interested in understanding gender development and have produced a great deal of psychological theory about influences on gender development. None of the individual theories can completely account for gender development and gender differences, since gender differences reflect the interaction of biological, social, and cognitive mechanisms. Each of these theories attempts to explain some aspect of gender development, rather than provide a comprehensive explanation. A fuller understanding of gender development requires integrating across these theoretical perspectives (Maccoby, 2002).

Biological Theories

The biology of sex development is complex and multiple biological mechanisms, such as chromosomes and hormones, contribute significantly to the process (Eid & Biason-Lauber, 2016; Vilain, 2006; Zucker, 2001). Geneticists may focus on the impact of chromosomes; endocrinologists on the hormones produced by testes or ovaries; neurobiologists on how the brain develops in response to genes and hormones; and psychologists on how biology interacts with social factors in the formation of gender identity.

Typical Sex Development

Males and females differ from the moment of conception in terms of chromosomes. Both males and females have 46 chromosomes; two of these are sex chromosomes, with females having two X chromosomes (46, XX) and males having an X and a Y chromosome (46, XY).

Embryos start with the potential to form either male or female gonads (internal) or external genitalia (Eid & Biason-Lauber, 2016; Vilain, 2006). If someone is XY, at around 8–10 weeks of gestation, a gene on the Y chromosome, called *SRY*, signals tissue to develop into testes. The developing testes begin to produce **androgen** hormones. One of the androgen hormones (**testosterone**) prompts the continued development of testes. Another leads to the degeneration of tissues that would have developed into female gonads. If someone is not XY, or if something has gone awry in terms of androgen production due to issues with the *SRY* gene or for other reasons, female gonads (ovaries) are developed at around 12 weeks. The gonads, in turn, produce more hormones to continue the development of gonads and external genitalia.

Prenatal hormones have a significant impact on development, with prenatal androgen levels affecting gender-related behaviors (Henderson, 2013; Lee et al., 2016). Then again at puberty hormones, in interaction with environmental variables and social experiences, produce diverse developmental trajectories. Thus, one explanation for differences in the behaviors of males and females from infancy through old age is that the differences are caused at least in part by hormonal differences between males and females (Maccoby, 1998). This is supported by increasing evidence that females who receive high levels of prenatal exposure to the male hormones exhibit more masculine social behaviors (Hines et al., 2002). For example, exposure to androgens appears to increase interest and participation in activities typically associated with males (e.g., play behaviors, toys, and careers) and is also associated with better spatial abilities (Berenbaum & Beltz, 2016).

Brain Differences

Differences in the brains of male and females have also been detected. The brains of males are 9–12% larger than the brains of females, a large enough disparity that cannot be explained simply by variation in average body sizes (Burgaleta et al., 2012; Lenroot & Giedd, 2010). The size of the brain is not related to general intelligence but does have a relationship to processing of spatial information (Burgaleta et al., 2012). There is some evidence that the brains of females have a larger proportion of gray matter and male brains have a higher proportion of white matter (Eliot, 2011; review the discussion of myelination and white matter in Chapter 2), but the difference typically is not found until adolescence and sometimes is not found at all (Burgaleta et al., 2012). One assumption is that prenatal exposure to sex hormones causes structural and functional differences in the brain. For example, differences between males and females have been observed in the hippocampus and the amygdala, although the extent and potential significance of the observed variation are currently being investigated. Differences in the connectivity of the hemispheres have also been noted. Females are more likely to use the left and right side of their brains for a variety of tasks than males, who tend to use more left hemispheric processing as they perform verbal tasks and more right hemispheric processing as they perform tasks with a visual–spatial component (Halpern, 2000). A number of studies suggest that males and females may exhibit dissimilar patterns of brain activity without performance disparities, suggesting that they use distinct strategies to reach the same goal (Lenroot & Giedd, 2010).

Most of the research, however, has been conducted with adult brains, and little is known about sex differences in the developing brains of children. Variations in maturation rates triggered by pubertal hormones, with females reaching peak brain volume two years earlier than males, make comparisons difficult. Neural plasticity also has a significant impact in that experiences change the developing brain (Eliot, 2011; Hines, 2015). Finally, it is important to remember that studies report group averages with substantial overlap between males and females. The similarities far outweigh the differences.

Intersexuality: Differences/Disorders of Sex Development

The sex of a newborn is not always unambiguous. The process described above can be disrupted by a number of factors, including the expression of a number of different genes that are still being identified (Eid & Biason-Lauber, 2016). **Intersexuality** is an umbrella term used for DSD (disorders/differences of sexual development). Advocacy groups argue for the use of the less stigmatizing language of difference rather than disorder. A diagnosis of DSD indicates that chromosomal, gonadal, and/ or anatomic sex development is atypical. Sometimes the differences are identified at birth because of noticeable ambiguity in an infant's genitalia. Other times differences are not detected until puberty or when puberty is delayed. And, in some cases, a diagnosis is not made until adulthood when fertility problems become evident. It is estimated that DSD, where sex assignment at birth is challenging due to ambiguity of genitalia, occurs in 1 in 4,500 births, although if relatively minor variations in genitalia are included, the estimate increases to 1% of the population (Lee et al., 2016; Roen, 2015; Vilain, 2006). There are more than a dozen possible medical diagnoses for the same appearance of genitalia and in 50 to 75% of the cases of DSD, a cause cannot be determined based on current knowledge.

So how does sex development go awry? Sometimes there is an issue with the sex chromosomes. Recall that typical females have two X chromosomes (46, XX) and typical males have an X and a Y chromosome (46, XY). Not all people have the standard complement of sex chromosomes. The most common sex chromosome abnormality in females, 1 in 2,500 births, is **Turner syndrome** (45, X) signifying that the individual has only one X chromosome, or only a small portion of a second X, and 45 chromosomes altogether (Culen, Ertl, Schubert, Bartha-Doering & Haeusler, 2017; Lee et al., 2016; Vilain, 2006). Females with Turner syndrome are short in stature, infertile with underdeveloped ovaries, and at risk for heart and kidney problems. They tend to exhibit weak performance on math and spatial ability tasks but perform within the normal range on verbal tasks. Twenty to 30% are diagnosed at birth, especially those who also have an associated physical characteristic of a webbed neck, but others are not diagnosed until their short stature during childhood raises concerns or until a delay in puberty is evident. The most common sex chromosome abnormality in males (1 in 100–500 births) is **Klinefelter syndrome** (47, XXY), indicating an extra X chromosome, for a total of 47 (Lee et al., 2016; Vilain, 2006). Males with Klinefelter syndrome are tall, infertile with smaller than normal testes, and puberty is often delayed. Many individuals with Klinefelter syndrome are not diagnosed until problems, such as delayed puberty and fertility issues, emerge. The *SRY* gene has also been identified as a source for DSD. For example, some individuals, with XX chromosomes, develop testes and other masculine characteristics because they have *SRY* on an X chromosome. Other individuals with XY chromosomes are missing the *SRY* gene on their Y chromosome and develop ovaries rather than testes.

Issues associated with the production and reception of androgens are also responsible for DSD (Lee et al., 2016; Reiner & Reiner, 2011). For example, females with congenital adrenal hyperplasia (XX, with CAH) were exposed to high levels of androgens and as a result developed more masculine-appearing genitals (the clitoris is larger than usual resembling a penis and labia are fused). The range of masculinization depends on timing and duration of the exposure. They do, however, have female internal sex organs (uterus and ovaries) and are fertile. Females with CAH, are typically raised as girls and identify as females. XY individuals with androgen insensitivity syndrome (AIS), meaning the androgens responsible for masculinization of gonads and genitalia have had little to no effect, have female genitalia and are often not diagnosed as having a DSD until puberty. The majority of the XY people with AIS identify as female. XY individuals with partial AIS, however, have a range of physical manifestations in terms of feminization and gender identity. A number of additional disruptions of typical development leading to DSD have also been identified.

How do parents and physicians respond when they encounter an infant who is intersex (or who has been diagnosed with DSD)? This is a complicated and controversial topic, and there isn't a clear answer for what the best and most ethical response might be. In the past, the goal was for the individual to have as normal as possible physical appearance, sexual functioning, and fertility. Interventions included surgery and hormone treatment, typically begun as soon as possible after diagnosis. Many individuals with ambiguous genitalia were assigned to be females since it was surgically possible to create a vagina. For example, Money and Ehrhardt (1972) argued that if the irregularity of the external genitalia was detected in the first year of life and corrected surgically, few problems would emerge. They believed that after the first couple of years of life, however, surgical corrections would be more challenging and psychological adjustment would be much more uncertain. They also argued that the child should not be fully informed about the surgery and the issues it was trying to correct, so that the child could be raised unambiguously as the assigned gender.

Serious doubts were raised, however, about Money and Ehrhardt's (1972) conclusion that the first few years were a critical period for development of gender identity. For example, surgical gender corrections at adolescence have been accompanied by successful gender identity shifts (Herdt & Davidson, 1988; Imperato-McGinley, Peterson, Gautier, & Sturla, 1979). In addition, some cases of surgical and psychological gender changes during the first two years of life have created extreme difficulties later in life. One well-known example is a boy whose penis was accidentally severed, whose sex was then changed surgically. Although raised as a girl and psychologically a girl during childhood (Money & Tucker, 1975), this individual developed identity confusion and unhappiness about being a girl in adolescence and later transitioned back to being male (Colapinto, 2001; Diamond & Sigmundson, 1999). Other similar gender reassignments have been successful (Hines, 2015).

Given the increased awareness about DSD worldwide, international groups have been meeting to discuss how the medical profession should respond (Lee et al., 2016). The factors to consider include anticipated quality of sexual functioning, potential for fertility, risk of surgical procedures, predictions for future gender identity, and the social ecology of family and culture. The emphasis is on fully educating the parents and the individual and on the evaluation of ethical, legal, and cultural factors. Some have called for any surgery to be delayed until the individual can participate in the decision making. Given the need for hormone therapy and, in some cases, hormone suppression at various ages, consideration must also be given to global availability of the relevant pharmaceuticals. The movement toward adopting more of a "wait-and-see" attitude in place of the early sex assignment standard of care of the 1970s to 1990s is supported by data suggesting that the most important factor in long-term adjustment appears to be future gender identity, more so than chromosomes, gonads, hormones, or external genitalia (Henderson, 2013). Previously, it was thought that nurture would override nature. Nonetheless, culture and legal standards of practice expect identification of gender at birth.

Consensus has been reached on a recommendation for assignment to female for the most common XX DSD (46, XX with CAH—females exposed to high levels of androgens prenatally) in that 95% develop female gender identity (Henderson, 2013; Lee et al., 2016; Reiner & Reiner, 2011; Rosenthal, 2016). Females with CAH do, however, tend to exhibit interests that are considered more masculine and often end up in male-dominated occupations. Recall also that females with CAH have normal internal gonads and are fertile. Surgery to feminize external genitalia (which would perhaps improve body image but might also reduce sensitivity) is something that could be postponed until the individual could participate fully in the decision making. Assignments aren't as clear for many of the XY DSD, due to a variety of causes, some of which are not yet understood. In the past, the assignment would most likely have been female, with early surgery to feminize genitalia.

In closing, gender role identification is clearly very complex, with children varying in their response to biological and socialization factors. Typical biological development entails a complicated process of gene regulation and hormonal influence, with many avenues to the range of outcomes considered DSD. We are still identifying genes critical to the process and have even more to learn about how genes, hormones, physical appearance, brain development, and environmental influences intermingle in the formation of gender identity. It is difficult to estimate accurately, and estimates have doubled in recent years, but as many as 1 in 200 adults identify as transgender (Rosenthal, 2016). See the Applying Developmental Theory to Educational Contexts special feature (Box 11.1) for an examination of the experiences of gender-nonconforming, transgender, and sexual minority youth in schools.

Social Learning Theories of Gender Role Development

The role of social forces in gender role development has been recognized since the earliest theory of gender role development, Freud's psychosexual theory. As you might recall, Freud portrayed the preschool years as key in this development, with the development, of castration anxiety in boys—and the lack of it in girls (see Chapter 5). Freud believed that children identify with the same-sex parent, adopting many of that parent's behaviors, after recognizing the impossibility of sexually possessing the opposite-sex parent. Thus, according to Freud, gender role socialization occurs within the family structure.

Although Freud's recognition that gender role development had a social component and could not be explained by biology alone was an enormous contribution, the specific mechanisms of development he proposed do not explain gender role

Applying Developmental Theory to Educational Contexts

BOX 11.1. School Experiences of LGBT Students

Students who are in the sexual minority and/or gender variant experience a range of difficulties in schools (Poteat, Scheer, & Mereish, 2014). Students who identify as lesbian, gay, bisexual, or transgender (LGBT) report higher levels of victimization (name calling, teasing, harassment, and assault) than heterosexual and cisgender youth. This hostile school climate disrupts attention processes, challenges mental health, and decreases motivation to attend school. Mental health concerns, in particular depression, can also hamper cognitive processes. Decreased motivation to attend school can ultimately lead to school dropout. The victimization tends to occur throughout the years of schooling, and the sustained nature of the harassment lowers academic achievement. LGBT young adults report that the experience of victimization during their years of schooling has had long-term effects, reporting increased depression and lower life satisfaction in young adulthood (Toomey, Ryan, Diaz, Card, & Russell, 2010). School climate is particularly hostile for transgender students, with transgender students reporting pervasive hostility and lower levels of safety than LGB students (McGuire, Anderson, Toomey, & Russell, 2010). Transgender students also face some unique challenges such as name changes, pronoun uses, and access to physical spaces (bathrooms and locker rooms). It is difficult to estimate accurately, but perhaps as many as 1 in 200 people identify as transgender (Rosenthal, 2016). Transgender youth and young adults tend to experience more anxiety, more suicidal ideation, more suicide attempts and higher rates of self-harm than other students. LGBT students, however, also indicate that the impact of victimization can be ameliorated if they feel connected to teachers and peers, a sense of belongingness, rather than feeling isolated and unsafe.

Schools can act to improve the school climate for LGBT students (McGuire et al., 2010; Poteat et al., 2014; Sadowski, 2016). They can establish nondiscrimination policies, with language that explicitly includes sexual minority and gender-variant students, which can be controversial in some communities but does lead to increased feelings of safety and belongingness in LGBT students. Schools can also support the establishment of Gay-Straight Alliance (GSA) organizations (Poteat, Heck, Yoshikawa, & Calzo, 2017). GSAs are student-led organizations, supported by an adult advisor, that help create a more open and respectful school climate by providing a sense of community and advocacy. LGBT students in schools with GSAs report feeling safer, have better mental health, and experience lower levels of truancy. Antibullying programs, in general, can also improve school climate. Teachers and other school personnel play a primary role in establishing school climate for LGBT youth. Often, teachers witness harassment of LGBT students, and even if they haven't witnessed it directly, they are certainly aware of climate issues. Many teachers, however, know little about their LGBT students and would benefit from professional training. Even school personnel such as school counselors and psychologists receive too little training. Graybill and Proctor (2016) analyzed eight journals for education professionals, such as school counselors, school psychologists, and school nurses, published between 2000 and 2014 for content about LGBT issues. LGBT issues were barely present in the professional literature, ranging from a low of 0.3% to a high of 3% of the content. Yet, LGBT youth report that the explicit support of even one adult in the school can make a difference in their feelings of safety and belongingness. They believe that if teachers and other school professionals intervened more often, the school climate for all would improve. LGBT youth are now more visible in schools and at earlier ages. Thus, more than ever before, educators need the professional training required to promote a positive school climate for all students (Espelage, 2016).

development adequately. For Freud's theory to be credible, preschoolers would have to have a clear understanding of how males and females differ physically. They do not (Bem, 1989). Moreover, children do not seem to identify with parents who are seen as aggressors but rather with parents who are nurturing and responsive (Hetherington & Frankie, 1967).

In contrast to the failure of Freudian theory to account for gender role development, social learning theory has been more successful. Recall that the three main mechanisms of social learning theory are reinforcement, punishment, and observational learning (review Chapter 5). All three of these mechanisms operate to promote the development of gender-related behaviors.

Reinforcement and Punishment

In many ways, parents treat daughters and sons similarly (Lytton & Romney, 1991; Maccoby & Jacklin, 1974). Even so, they influence gender role development by reinforcing appropriate and punishing inappropriate gender role behaviors (Brody, 1999; Hines, 2015; Meece & Askew, 2012; Turner & Gervai, 1995). For example, parents in traditional gender roles raise children who behave in ways consistent with traditional gender roles (Turner & Gervai, 1995; Leaper, 2015). Parents with traditional views endorse gender-stereotyped beliefs ("Boys need to be tough"; "Girls are sensitive"). Even parents with more egalitarian views socialize gender roles by using generalizations in their speech ("Girls like . . ."; "Boys do . . ."), by not challenging gender-stereotyped comments made by children, and by encouraging gendered activities (boys playing with toy trucks; girls playing with dolls). A variety of differential reinforcements and punishments for gender-appropriate behavior are apparent from early in life:

• Parents, especially fathers, play more roughly with their sons beginning in infancy than they do with their daughters and encourage gross motor activity more in males than in females (Parke, 2002; Smith & Lloyd, 1978; Stern & Karraker, 1989). Parents provide children with gender-appropriate toys and encourage their children to play with gender-appropriate toys and in gender-appropriate ways (Eisenberg, Wolchick, Hernandez, & Pasternack, 1985; Fagot, 1978; Fagot & Hagan, 1991; Fagot & Leinbach, 1989; Frisch, 1977; Schau, Kahn, Diepold, & Cherry, 1980; Snow, Jacklin, & Maccoby, 1983; Weisner & Wilson-Mitchell, 1990). Before 2 years of age, children understand which toys are appropriate for their gender (Levy, 1999). Toy preferences emerge early, and the differences are large (Hines, 2015).

• Children's peers send clear messages about the appropriateness of play behaviors. For example, boys are quick to criticize, tease, and ostracize other boys who don't conform to gender norms (Langlois & Downs, 1980; Leaper & Brown, 2014). Peers are powerful socializers of gender-conforming play and express disapproval of gender atypical or cross-gender play (Hines, 2015; Leaper, 2015; Lee & Troop-Gordon, 2011). When boys and girls play in mixed groups, a wider range of play behavior is tolerated.

• One point that comes through clearly in reviewing the research on reinforcement and punishment of gender-appropriate behaviors is that the pressure is higher on boys to conform to the male gender role than for girls to conform to the female gender stereotype (Leaper, 2015; Sandnabba & Ahlberg, 1999). For example, fathers react especially strongly and negatively to inappropriate gender role play in sons (Langlois & Downs, 1980). In general, males are discouraged much more strongly not to do things feminine than girls are discouraged from doing things masculine (Fagot, 1978; Langlois & Downs, 1980; Maccoby & Jacklin, 1974). Children vary in how much they engage in gender-typed activities, but they understand that it is more difficult for boys to challenge gender stereotypes than girls and that challenging gender stereotypes can result in negative consequences such as isolation and victimization (Leaper, 2015; Mulvey & Killen, 2015).

Observational Learning

The world is filled with models of women and men behaving as women and men do, all of which provide observational learning opportunities for the child. Yes, there is considerable variability in the way women behave, with some more stereotypically feminine than others, and there is variability within men, with some more stereotypically masculine than others. Children seem to be able to keep track of the behaviors most often associated with women and those most often associated with men, learning both female and male behaviors and roles in the process (Bussey & Bandura, 1984; Bussey & Perry, 1982; Perry & Bussey, 1979).

Parents are gender role models for their children, particularly in the areas of division of labor, child care responsibility, and occupational choice. If parents model traditional roles at home, children are more likely to exhibit gendered behavior (Hines, 2015). The ideal division of household labor advocated by young adults (18-year-olds) is influenced by maternal gender attitudes when they were young and the degree of division of labor in the household during their adolescence (Cunningham, 2001). Children who lived in homes where parents divide the labor (both home and outside the home) unequally have more gender traditional occupational expectations (Fulcher, Sutfin, & Patterson, 2008)—even if the parents themselves are nontraditional (gay or lesbian). The children of mothers who espouse nontraditional attitudes have more nontraditional occupational aspirations (Fulcher, 2011), but parental behaviors have more of an effect on them than their attitudes. In a longitudinal study, Halpern and Perry-Jenkins (2016) examined the gendered attitudes and gendered behaviors of working-class parents. The gendered behaviors of the parents were better predictors of their 6-year-old children's gender-role attitudes than their ideology.

Peers are a powerful source of role models. Children play more with same-sex peers and accept feedback from same-sex peers, which assures that boys will pick up more from other boys and girls from girls (Benenson, Apostoleris, & Parnass, 1997; Fagot, 1985; Maccoby, 1998; Underwood, Schockner, & Hurley, 2001). Children begin to segregate, preferring to play with same-gender peers, during preschool; sex segregation occurs across cultures (Martin et al., 2013; Martin, Fabes, & Hanis, 2014). Sex segregation is facilitated by similar interests (e.g., toy preferences) and styles of play.

What do children learn in sex-segregated play groups? Different styles of play develop different skills and styles of interactions (Hines, 2015; Leaper; 2015). Boys' play tends to be more action-oriented, rough and tumble; girls are more likely to play dress up, play house and play with dolls. On one hand, play with construction toys and videogames (observed more in boys) facilitates the development of spatial skills and mechanical reasoning. Playing house and play with dolls, on the other hand, encourage the development of verbal skills. The more children play with same-sex peers, the more they are exposed to gender-appropriate behavior (Martin, Fabes, & Hanish, 2014). Martin et al. (2013) conducted a longitudinal study of children in preschool classrooms, observing children during free time when they could do what they wanted and play with whomever they wanted. The predominant pattern was for children to play with same-sex peers and to select peers with similar levels of gender-typed activities. The children then influenced each other's choice of activities, thereby increasing sex segregation. In choosing same-sex playmates, children play a major role in their own gender role development by immersing themselves in same-sex peer groups who model and reinforce boys being boys and girls being girls (Martin et al., 2014)

Observational Learning from Symbolic Models

Beyond the family, culture provides many symbolic models to children, with most symbolic models that children experience being gender-stereotyped. Television is gender-stereotyped (Coltrane, 1998; Gerding & Signorielli, 2014; Huston & Wright, 1998), with male characters frequently portrayed as aggressive and powerful and female characters as hypersexualized (Leaper, 2015). Television commercials also are filled with gender-stereotyped figures (Bretl & Cantor, 1988; Coltrane, 1998; Leaper, 2015; Singer & Singer, 2001), with female characters extolling the virtues of cleaning products and toy commercials making clear distinctions (e.g., girls with dolls; boys with machines). Videogames also frequently portray males as aggressive and females as sexual objects (Leaper & Brown, 2014). The symbolic models that children encounter in the textbooks and literature they read can also be gender-stereotyped (Leaper & Brown, 2014; McDonald, 1989; Sadker & Sadker, 1994; Tepper & Cassidy, 1999; Turner-Bowker, 1996), although efforts are being made to reduce gender stereotyping in textbooks and children's trade books.

Not surprisingly, children who experience high levels of exposure to gender-stereotyped media are more gender-stereotyped in their thinking and behaviors (Berry, 2000; Morgan, 1987; Signorielli & Lears, 1992). For example, Davidson, Yasuna, and Tower (1979) exposed 5- to 6-year-old children to gender-stereotyped cartoons or more neutral cartoons. Following this exposure, the children who saw the gender-stereotyped cartoons were more gender-stereotyped in answers they provided to specific questions about male and female roles. Certain well-known media characters can have significant effects on gender-stereotyped behaviors. For example, Coyne, Linder, Rasmussen, Nelson, and Birkbeck (2016) measured 4- to 5-year-olds' level of engagement with Disney Princess media and products. Controlling for initial level of gender-stereotyped behavior, Coyne et al. found that the level of Disney Princess engagement was associated with more gender-stereotyped behavior in girls one year later.

Cognitive Theories

Recent formulations of social learning theory have emphasized how much cognition is involved in observational learning. Observational learning of gender roles requires a great deal of memory, the classification of behaviors as female or male, and the comparison of one's own characteristics and behaviors with those of social models (Bandura, 1986). Two cognitive theories have been prominent in debates concerning the development of gender role. One was part of the Piagetian revolution that swept developmental psychology in the 1960s; the other reflects the information-processing perspective that prevails today.

Kohlberg's Theory

Lawrence Kohlberg (1966), whose work on the development of moral thinking was described in Chapter 3, proposed what was for some time the most influential of the cognitive developmental conceptions of gender development. Kohlberg's theory of moral judgment was an extension of Piaget's theory. Not surprisingly, his theory of gender role development also was informed by Piaget's thinking.

Infants during the first year of life can discriminate females from males, on the basis of what males and females sound and look like (Fagot & Leinbach, 1993). The first couple of years of life provide a baby with a great deal of information about maleness and femaleness, about how she or he should behave, and about how males and females in the world behave (Fagot & Leinbach, 1993). At about 2–3 years of age, however, according to Kohlberg, a child comes to an important insight. That insight for girls is, "I am a girl." For boys, it is, "I am a boy." Understanding of gender is anything but complete at that point, however. Femaleness and maleness are defined by physical features—such as length of hair or wearing of gender-appropriate clothing—that correlate with biological sex but do not define it in a biological sense (Emmerich, Goldman, Kirsh, & Sharabany, 1977; McConaghy, 1979; Thompson & Bentler, 1971). Thus, a 2- to 3-year-old child sometimes believes that if a lady gets a buzzcut, she becomes a he! With advancing age during the grade school years, children understand that an individual's gender is stable. That is, the person who is a boy today was a boy yesterday and will be a man someday. The child comes to understand that gender is consistent, that it does not change with appearances. Progressing from labeling gender to understanding its stability and consistency across situations takes 3–5 years, with a mature understanding of gender consistency often not present until the early elementary grade years (Slaby & Frey, 1975).

Kohlberg argued that once a child understood that she or he was a girl or a boy and that was not going to change, this understanding motivated the child to learn how to be a girl or a boy, resulting in differential attention to information pertaining to one's own gender rather than to the opposite gender. Kohlberg believed that the development of the understanding of gender consistency was related to the development of the understanding of conservation as Piaget defined it (see Chapter 3). Recall that conservation is the understanding that the amount of something remains constant, despite superficial changes in appearance, unless material is added to or subtracted from it. Analogously, **gender consistency** is the understanding that gender does not change with superficial changes in appearance. In fact, understanding of gender consistency does correlate with development of conservation abilities (Marcus & Overton, 1978).

There are problems with Kohlberg's theory, however. First, other cognitive understandings besides conservation, such as knowledge of female and male genitalia, are strongly related to understanding of gender consistency. Bem (1989) showed preschool children pictures of nude male and female children and asked them to identify the gender of each photographed child and to explain their answers. Some preschoolers did better than others, labeling females as females and males as males and doing so with reference to possession of sex-defining genitals. The children who were so knowledgeable also continued to label the male as male and the female as female, even when the same children were depicted as cross-dressed! Children who did not classify the nude photos correctly, using sex organs in their justifications, were more likely to believe that clothing defined gender. Thus, even if they recognized the boy was a boy when he was pictured nude, they would claim that the boy was a girl when he was pictured wearing a dress. Bem (1989) demonstrated that understanding gender consistency was tied to understanding the biological basis of gender.

Second, children make much progress in their gender role development before they are 5–7 years of age (Bussey & Bandura, 1992). That is, it does not seem to be necessary for children to understand that gender is stable and consistent for them to acquire a great deal of knowledge about gender and to be motivated to learn behaviors appropriate to their own gender. For example, the behaviors of children who can label themselves as boy or girl during the early preschool years are more gender-stereotypical than are the behaviors of children who are not yet referring to themselves as boy or girl (Fagot, 1985; Fagot & Leinbach, 1989, 1993; Hort, Leinbach, & Fagot, 1991). The implication is that once children label themselves, they are motivated to learn gender-appropriate behaviors and behave in more gender-appropriate ways (Fagot & Leinbach, 1989). Not surprisingly, by 5–7 years of age, children know a great deal about maleness and femaleness and generally pay more attention to and know more about behaviors associated with their own gender than with the other gender (Boston & Levy, 1991; Bradford & Endsley, 1983; Levy & Fivush, 1993). A specific information-processing theory, *gender schema theory*, provides a basis for understanding the development of knowledge about gender and gender-appropriate behaviors well before children can conserve or understand the consistency of gender.

Gender Schema Theory

Recall from Chapter 4 that even 1- to 2-year-old children are capable of acquiring schemas pertaining to situations that they encounter often. Thus, 2-year-olds know about birthday parties and going to McDonald's. Particularly pertinent here, they also have schemas for "boyness" and "girlness," schemas that continue to develop over the preschool years, but schemas that are present from the time when children first learn to label boys and girls, men and women (i.e., between 1 and 2 years of age). Organized knowledge of gender is referred to as **gender schemas** (Bem, 1981; Martin & Halverson, 1981, 1987).

Like Kohlberg, the proponents of gender schema theory believe that thinking and knowledge about gender play a major role in children's perceptions and in their motivation to learn about gender-appropriate behavior (Leaper, 2015; Martin, Ruble, & Szjrybalo, 2002; Starr & Zurbriggen, 2016). Unlike Kohlberg's theory, gender schema theory does not suggest that children's thinking evolves in stages. Gender schema theorists believe that labeling is the critical knowledge that motivates children to learn about and act like members of one sex versus the other. That is, once a boy begins to label himself as a boy, the boy is motivated to acquire knowledge about "boy things." There is so much to learn that is part of gender schematic knowledge (Halim et al., 2014; Martin, 1993; Signorella, Bigler, & Liben, 1993), such as which toys are considered girl toys and which ones are considered boy toys, how boys and girls should dress, which specific behaviors are considered female versus male behaviors, which roles and occupations are more typically feminine versus masculine, and which traits are more often feminine traits and which more masculine

For the young preschooler, the gender schema is powerful. Once children know that someone is a male, they begin to make inferences that the person acts and thinks like males do. Once they know someone is female, they believe that the individual is female in everything she does. Also, if all they know is that a person did something stereotypically associated with males (e.g., fixed a car or a leaky faucet), young preschoolers are firm in their belief that the person is a male. If an activity is labeled as consistent with one's own gender, young children like the activity more and are more interested in it (Martin, Eisenbud, & Rose, 1995). Gender schemas are a major force in children's thinking about gender-related issues (Halim et al., 2014; Martin, 1989; Martin, Wood, & Little, 1990), with children making many inferences about other children on the basis of whether the other child behaves in gender-appropriate or gender-inappropriate ways (Lobel, Bempechat, Gewirtz, Shoken-Topaz, & Bashe, 1993).

Gender schemas affect children's learning as well. When preschoolers are presented information consistent with gender-stereotyped knowledge (e.g., a picture of a male firefighter, a female nurse), they remember it better than information not consistent with gender conventions (e.g., a picture of a female firefighter, a male nurse; Liben & Signorella, 1993; Martin & Halverson, 1983; Signorella & Liben, 1984). Gender schemas probably affect children's memory beginning at about 2–3 years of age (Bauer, 1993; Cherney & Ryalls, 1999). Coyle and Liben (2016) demonstrated that gender schema affects learning and intensifies interest in activities. They invited preschool girls to play a game where they learned about occupations through a feminized character (Barbie) or a more natural female character (based on a playmobil figure). The occupations were either traditionally feminine (e.g., nurse, librarian), traditionally masculine (e.g., firefighter, explorer), or novel occupations. Girls preferred the more feminine occupations, but the girls who scored high on a measure of the degree to which they use gender to interpret the world (gender salience) displayed extreme levels of interest in feminine activity only when Barbie described the occupations.

The perspective of gender as a cognitive structure that guides perception, learning, and memory led Sandra Bem to explore the impact of gender in policy and practice. Liben and Bigler (2017) summarized some of Bem's major contributions such as advocating for reductions in gendered language, highlighting how gendered organized classrooms can enhance gender stereotypes, and the emphasis on the child's active role in gender socialization.

Gender Differences

There are many folk beliefs about gender differences (Ruble & Martin, 1998), with many stereotypes favoring "masculine" qualities over "feminine" qualities. Males are strong, tough, aggressive, and competitive, whereas females are weak, passive, nurturing, caring, and sympathetic. Little boys are adventurous in their play, whereas little girls are quiet. Sports are for boys, and the arts are for girls. Boys are boisterous, girls are chatty. Boys are good at math and science, girls excel in reading and language arts. Males respond to reason, and females are more easily influenced by opinion. There are differences in gender stereotypes across cultures, but generally the submissive, supportive "feminine" is contrasted with the aggressive, independent "masculine." Is there any truth to these stereotypes, which have persisted for centuries and continue today (Lueptow, Garovich, & Lueptow, 2001; Powlishta, Sen, Serbin, Poulin-Dubois, & Eichstedt, 2001; Spence, 2011)?

Social and Personality Differences

Few verifiable social and personality differences between females and males exist. That is, female and male personalities are more similar than different; females and males are more similar than different in their social interactions. What are the differences supported by research evidence?

One is that males are more physically aggressive than females on average (Maccoby & Jacklin, 1974). Even so, when it comes to indirect aggression and verbal aggression, girls and boys, women and men, are more equivalent (Maccoby & Jacklin, 1974; Underwood, 2002). What must be kept in mind is that a group difference in physical aggression does not predict aggression in individual children. Why? Observe all the males on an elementary school playground and give each a score for physical aggression on a 1 (never aggressive) to 10 (frequently physically aggressive) scale. Chart the result. Visit enough playgrounds and you will get a bell-shaped distribution, centered on an average value. Score all the females on the same playgrounds on the same scale and graph the data. Again, you will obtain a bell-shaped distribution, centered on an average value. Yes, the male average will be greater than the female average (that is the group difference), but plenty of females will have higher scores than many of the males! Graphing physical aggression observed in boys and girls on the playground would produce overlapping distributions, as shown in Figure 11.1. It is important to realize that the female and male distributions for any characteristic will always overlap. Moreover, average female versus average male differences are typically small. What this means is that it is impossible to know, based on knowing an individual person's gender, whether they are more or less aggressive (or more verbal or mathematical) than a person of the opposite gender. Finally, within-gender differences can be much larger than average differences between genders.

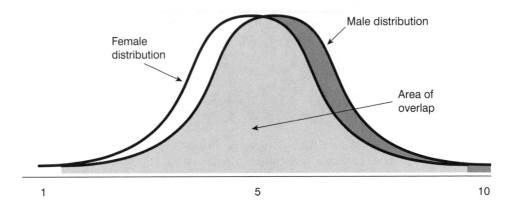

FIGURE 11.1. Hypothetical distributions showing overlap.

The following gender differences in social and personality characteristics have been demonstrated:

- Aggression—boys are slightly more physically aggressive than girls (Hines, 2015; Leaper, 2015). Girls are more likely to use persuasion rather than force to get their way with peers, a tactic that is more effective with other little girls than with little boys (Borja-Alvarez, Zarbatany, & Pepper, 1991; Leaper, Tenenbaum, & Shaffer, 1999). Both boys and girls are verbally aggressive. If there is a difference between the sexes, boys tend to be overt, more direct, and openly insulting, whereas girls tend to be more covert, talking behind someone's back and engaging in exclusionary tactics (Crick & Werner, 1998).

- Altruism—Both males and females exhibit helping behaviors, but the contexts in which they are likely to help differ (Petersen & Hyde, 2014). Males are more likely to help with action-oriented tasks, particularly those requiring strength; females are more likely to help with care-oriented tasks requiring relational skills such as aiding a lost child.

- Communication style—Tannen (1990) described gender differences in communication style as being based on two different views of the world. Males engage in a hierarchical world where they are constantly jockeying for position. To them, conversations are negotiations in which they try to achieve and maintain the upper hand if they can. Their goal is to attain status and preserve independence. Women, in contrast, engage the world as individuals in a network of connections. To them, conversations are negotiations for closeness and intimacy. Females are more likely to add tag-on questions to engage their listeners, such as "Don't you think?" or "Isn't it?" As a result, they sound less decisive and certain of themselves than males. Who interrupts more? Females are more likely to display cooperative overlappings, where they show support and anticipate where the speaker is heading. Males are more likely to interrupt to change the course of the conversation. A meta-analysis of 29 research studies (35 samples) investigating gender differences in tentative speech (tag-on questions; qualifiers) indicated that this difference in conversational style was small (Leaper & Robnett, 2011).

- Anxiety and confidence—Females tend to be more anxious and more cautious than males (Christopherson, 1989; Ginsburg & Miller, 1982; Last, 1989; Miller, Boyer, & Rodoletz, 1990). Males tend to have slightly higher self-concepts than females (Petersen & Hyde, 2014) and are more often overconfident about their abilities (Butler, 2014).

Remember that these average differences between males and females are fairly small and there is great deal of overlap in the distributions (as displayed in Figure 11.1), so that many boys are not physically aggressive; many females are not anxious; and so on.

Cognitive Differences

A great deal of research evidence supports the conclusion of no overall difference in the intelligence of males and females as measured by psychometric tests of intelligence. That is, the mean IQ scores for males and females are both about 100; intelligence is normally distributed for both males and females, with the standard deviation for IQs equal to 15 for both sexes (see Chapter 8). When cognitive processing and abilities are examined more closely, however, some differences have been noted (Halpern, 2000; Leaper, 2015; Shea, Lubinski, & Benbow, 2001).

Verbal ability, including word fluency, grammatical competence, spelling skills, reading, vocabulary, and oral comprehension, is greater in females than in males. Dysfunctions in verbal abilities are more common in males than females, with most stutterers and dyslexics being male. Verbal differences favoring females are apparent from early childhood, with girls exhibiting more proficiency in language earlier than boys. Differences are apparent throughout the schooling years as well, although not as pronounced as during preschool or as they will be in adulthood. Consistent with the effect size for most gender differences, gender differences in verbal abilities are small on average (see also Hyde & Linn, 1988; Hyde & Plant, 1995; Meece & Askew, 2012; Pargulski & Reynolds, 2017; Peterson & Hyde, 2014). It is certainly not inconsequential, however, that clinically significant verbal impairments, including acquisition of the critical skill of reading, are much more likely in males than females (Campbell, Hombo, & Mazzeo, 2000; Halpern, 2000; Liderman, Kantrowitz, & Flannery, 2005). In addition, even after accounting for reading, attention, spelling, and handwriting, second- and third-grade boys score lower than girls on assessments of written comprehension (Kim, Otaiba, Wanzek, & Gatlin, 2015).

Quantitative skills as measured by the mathematical portions of standardized tests (e.g., SAT, NAEP) indicate small differences favoring males over females when gender differences are detected (Meece & Askew, 2012; Pargulski & Reynolds, 2017; Petersen & Hyde, 2014). Males are more likely to score in the right tails of the distributions of scores, with males outnumbering females 7 to 1 in the high end of the distribution (Ceci, Williams, & Barnett, 2009). In a meta-analysis of 242 studies from 1990 to 2007, Lindberg et al. (2010) reported only small gender difference favoring high school males in complex mathematical problem solving. Yet the differences in the ratios of males to females in the upper and lower ends of the distribution of scores in quantitative reasoning are still present, with some evidence that they might even be increasing (Lakin, 2012).

One explanation for the differences in performance on standardized math tests is the effect of stereotype threat on the performance of females (review the discussion of stereotype threat in Chapters 6 and 8). In a meta-analysis of 86 studies, Doyle and Voyer (2016) reported that stereotype threat manipulations produced small, but significant, math performance decreases for females. Ganley and Vasilyeya (2014) found that higher levels of anxiety reported by female college students taking a challenging math test reduced available working memory resources and decreased performance. Mrazek et al. (2011) found that females in stereotype threat conditions (informed that a math problem solving task was diagnostic of differences in male and female math abilities) exhibited greater distractibility and mind wandering than females who were told that the task was just an exercise. Smelding, Dumas, Loose, and Regner (2013) hypothesized that they could reduce stereotype threat effects for girls by giving verbal tests before math tests. In line with their hypothesis, administering the verbal test first resulted in higher performance of girls on the math test. Neither girls' verbal performance nor boys' performance on either test was affected by the order manipulation. Finally, Galdi, Cadinu, and Tomasetto (2014) found that the math performance of girls as young as 6 years old could be decreased under stereotype threat conditions.

Visual–spatial ability, which involves the ability to imagine figures, including moving them around "in the head" in order to envision relationships between various objects, is predictably found to be greater in males. Differences in visual–spatial ability can be detected during childhood (Levine, Huttenlocher, Taylor, & Langrock, 1999). Although the effect size varies with the task, small to moderate differences in spatial abilities are usually reported (Maeda & Yoon, 2016; Petersen & Hyde, 2014). Large differences are often found in tasks requiring the mental rotation of 3-D figures. In a meta-analysis of 40 studies examining gender differences in mental rotation ability measured by the Purdue Spatial Visualization Test (PSVT), males outperformed females (Maeda & Yoon, 2013). The gender differences, however, were larger when time limits to complete the test were imposed. A sample item from the PSVT, developed to measure 3-D mental rotation in STEM fields, is found in Figure 11.2. Mental rotation ability is related to performance in STEM fields, even for students as young as eighth grade (Ganley, Vasilyeva, & Dulaney, 2014).

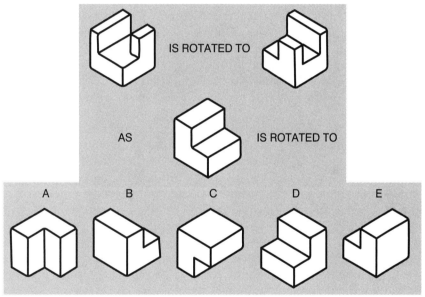

You are to:

1. study how the object in the top line of the question is rotated;
2. picture in your mind what the object shown in the middle line or the question looks like when rotated in exactly the same manner;
3. select from among the five drawings (A, B, C, D, or E) given in the bottom line of the question the one that looks like the object rotated in the correct position.
   What is the correct answer to the example shown above?

   Answers A, B, C, and E are wrong. Only drawing D looks like the object rotated according to the given rotation. Remember that each question has only one correct answer.

FIGURE 11.2. An example of an item from the Purdue Spatial Visualization Test (PVST). Copyright © 1977 by the Purdue Research Foundation. Reprinted by permission.

Prenatal hormonal exposure may partially account for the gender difference in visual–spatial abilities. What is the evidence for this conclusion? Females with congenital adrenal hyperplasia (CAH) who experienced higher levels of androgen prenatally than normal females do better on spatial tests than females in general (Collaer & Hines, 1995; Perlman, 1973; Resnick, Berenbaum, Gottesman, & Bouchard, 1986; Berenbaum, Bryk, & Beltz, 2012). Individuals with Turner syndrome (45, X—only one X chromosome) have low levels of both androgen and **estrogen** prenatally and, as described earlier, tend to perform poorly on tests of spatial cognition (Alexander, Walker, & Money, 1964; Rovet & Netley, 1982).

Gender differences in mental rotation task performance may also reflect distinctive strategies employed by males and females to solve the task (Boone & Hegarty, 2017). The ratio of available visual–spatial working memory to verbal working memory affects strategy selection and implementation, which in turn impacts performance (Wang & Carr, 2014). A meta-analysis of visual–spatial working memory development indicates that there is a small but significant advantage for males, initially appearing during adolescence (Voyer, Voyer, & Saint-Aubin, 2017).

Can girls and women be trained to increase their spatial ability? A meta-analysis of 217 studies concluded that training can improve the spatial abilities of men and women, girls and boys, and training in one task can transfer to other spatial ability tasks (Uttal et al., 2013). Gender differences, however, still existed after training. A promising approach to eliminating gender differences focuses on the different strategies males and females use to approach spatial tasks. Strategic instruction combining an analytical strategy with a more holistic imagery strategy eliminated gender differences in the performance of college students on chemistry problems requiring spatial problem solving (Stieff, Dixon, Ryu, Kumi, & Hegarty, 2014). This work is particularly important in addressing the gender differences in interest in and pursuit of careers in STEM disciplines—a topic taken up at the end of the chapter.

In closing, one striking aspect of this list of gender differences is that it is so short! Many aspects of performance produce no gender differences. Gender differences in academic achievement have narrowed, and the performance of average-achieving students is approximately equal, with gender gaps evident primarily at the lowest and highest ends of achievement (Meece & Askew, 2012). Cognitive similarities between the sexes are greater than differences (Halpern, 2000), and individual differences in virtually all skills and attributes are much greater *within* each gender than *between* genders (again review Figure 11.1).

Gender Differences in Educational Contexts

A variety of explanations can be offered for gender-related differences in academic performance. In this section, we will examine gender differences in motivation (see also Chapter 9), evaluate the impact of the classroom context, and analyze gender differences in performance in STEM disciplines.

Gender Differences in Academic Motivation

Butler (2014) argued that the differences in academic motivation observed in boys and girls could be described as a pattern of "to prove" versus "trying to improve."

That is, males tend to focus on demonstrating and defending their proficiencies, a pattern of competition and self-promotion; females focus on addressing deficiencies by working hard and often emphasize cooperation. Both patterns have costs and benefits. The pattern exhibited by girls is better matched to schooling contexts. Whether or not the pattern exhibited by boys is beneficial depends on achievement level. High-achieving boys can excel as a result of their self-confidence and desire to prove themselves, but the same motivational pattern in low-achieving boys is not likely to result in success.

Expectancies, Values, and Interest

Generally, males score higher on measures assessing perceptions of competence. The size of the gender difference varies with country and degree of gender-role stereotyping as well as with the academic domain (Butler, 2014; Lee et al., 2014; Usher, 2016; Wigfield et al., 2015). Boys tend to base their evaluation of their competence on past successes, perceptions of ability, and social comparisons, and are more likely to discount negative feedback from teachers. In contrast, in the competence evaluations they make, girls place great weight on the feedback they receive from teachers and others. There is a developmental progression in that perceptions of competency for academic tasks decrease throughout the years of schooling for both boys and girls (Meece & Askew, 2012; see also Chapter 9). Children begin school with gender differences in perceptions of competencies, with boys expressing higher competences in math, girls in language arts. These gender differences in perceived competencies decrease for math (but do not go away) and increase for language arts.

Even when boys and girls perform equivalently—or when girls outperform boys—boys tend to believe that they did much better than they actually did and girls tend to be less confident about their performances (Butler, 2014; Entwisle & Hayduk, 1978; Frey & Ruble, 1987; Parsons & Ruble, 1977; Pressley & Ghatala, 1989; Stipek & Hoffman, 1980). Boys are more certain they do well than girls (even when it is not true) and hence are more confident (even when there is no justification for the confidence). Noticeable gender differences in interest in and perceived value of various academic domains emerges early and predicts choices made, such as courses selected, later in the schooling years (Butler, 2014). Males are more likely to overestimate their competence in fields they value (math, science) but are less likely to do so in areas they perceive as more feminine (e.g., verbal tasks.) Nonetheless, the confidence of boys and girls is more comparable in high school than earlier in their lives (Jacobs, Lanza, Osgood, Eccles, & Wigfield, 2002).

Reactions to Success and Failures

Males and females react differently to failure. Dweck (1986) reported a study in which otherwise high-achieving boys and girls reacted differently to a failure experience on a concept formation task. The high-ability girls tended to be devastated by the failure much more than the high-ability boys, and this reaction affected subsequent performances: the high-ability boys outperformed the high-ability girls on subsequent trials of the same task. High-ability girls seemed to be especially disadvantaged, with initial failures and difficulties disrupting their subsequent performances more than the performances of less able girls (Licht & Dweck, 1984).

The attributions girls and boys make for their success or failure (see Chapter 9) depend on the academic domain. Girls, encountering difficulties in academic domains in which they believe boys excel (e.g., mathematics), are more likely than boys to attribute the difficulties they are having to unchanging abilities (rather than to low-effort, high-task difficulty, or bad luck). Girls are also more likely to attribute success in math to effort than to ability (Meece &Askew, 2012). Boys tend to shrug off initial failures, attributing them to something other than their own ability, which allows them to maintain a high level of confidence (Butler, 2014). Believing that one is able can be extremely motivating even when it is not true! Believing one is not able can undermine motivation to try new and challenging tasks even when ability is high.

Effects of Schooling

Sexism maintains different levels of status and power and is present in schools in the forms of prejudice and discrimination (Leaper & Brown, 2014). Prejudice refers to beliefs or stereotypes about what is appropriate and what is not. Discrimination refers to actions taken against those striving to succeed in areas outside of traditional norms. Thus, sexism is present not only when females try to succeed in prestigious, male-dominated areas of accomplishment but also when boys are pressured to conform to traditional standards of masculinity.

Teacher Beliefs and Stereotypes

Teacher beliefs about gender differences and stereotypes are quite apparent in some classrooms, with some teachers clearly signaling that there are boy things and girl things (Koch, 2003; Ruble & Martin, 1998). These beliefs may be explicit and conscious but more often are implicit and unconscious. This is a concern because when powerful adults, such as teachers, model and reinforce such thinking, it does cause some children to become more gender-stereotyped in their own thinking (Bigler, 1995). Teachers' implicit and explicit biases can impact expectations they hold for students. Fortunately, teacher gender bias is observed less now than in past (Leaper & Brown, 2014; Meece & Askew, 2012) since most teachers strive for equity in their interactions with students. Often, however, teacher bias is implicit, and teachers may unintentionally model stereotypes. For example, a female elementary teacher may model anxiety and lack of confidence in her own math skills. Parents, for that matter, also hold stereotypes about children's abilities and interests that can impact performance. For example, a parent may intend to comfort a child experiencing failure by saying "Oh that's OK; I wasn't good at (academic domain) either" when instead the message conveyed is "failing at (academic domain) runs in the family and can't be helped."

Gender differences in STEM fields favoring males will be discussed in the next section, but it is important to note here that boys, with a gender gap in reading, writing, and the arts, also experience bias in schools (Leaper & Brown, 2014). In a longitudinal study of teachers' gender stereotypes, Retelsdorf, Schwartz, and Asbrock (2015) found a negative relationship between teachers' gender stereotypes assessed at the beginning of fifth grade and boys' reading self-concept in the second half of sixth grade. The greater the stereotypical belief of the teachers, the lower the reading self-concept in boys.

Classroom Practices and Interactions

Some classroom practices make gender more salient and increase the likelihood of gender stereotyping. For example, Hilliard and Liben (2010) found that gender segregation in preschool led children to express greater gender stereotyping and exhibit lower likelihood of playing with children of the opposite sex. Another study found that although the behaviors of preschool teachers indicated a preference for gender-neutral activities, they also tended to facilitate gender-typed activities for boys-only and girls-only groups (Granger, Hanish, Kornienko, & Bradley, 2017). Other practices, such as lining up boys and girls separately and using gender-specific language, also increase the salience of gender in the classroom (Martin et al., 2014).

Boys receive more attention in the classroom from teachers—both encouragement when they are doing well academically and negative attention to reduce disruption and increase compliance—than do girls (Butler, 2014; Meece & Askew, 2012). Teachers call on boys more to answer high-level, complex questions. For low-achieving boys, the greater attention, primarily negative, may be discouraging. A higher proportion of the feedback given to girls relative to that given to boys focuses on academic problems the girls are experiencing, while boys receive a higher proportion of comments about their misbehavior (Dweck, Davidson, Nelson, & Enna, 1978; Meece, 1987; Sadker & Sadker, 1995). The differential patterns of interaction are seen more often in stereotyped male academic domains such as math.

Teachers encourage characteristics considered more feminine, such as being compliant with teachers' requests, than male characteristics (Brophy & Good, 1974; Fagot, 1981). Indeed, teachers generally expect girls to be more successful on academic tasks (except for perhaps math) and expect boys to be more disruptive in class (Leaper, 2015). As a result, school, particularly early elementary school, can seem especially unwelcoming to boys, with the potential of undermining boys' commitments to do things valued by school (McCall, Beach, & Lan, 2000; Ruble & Martin, 1998). Since boys are pressured to conform to traditional views of masculinity, complying with the teacher and putting forth effort in traditionally feminine areas of endeavor such as reading and art are not valued (Leaper & Brown, 2014). High-achieving girls also may feel pressure to not excel in competitive classroom contexts, to avoid standing out and making others feel bad (Butler, 2014). Boys, however, tend to be more comfortable navigating a competitive environment (see the discussion on competitive classrooms in Chapter 9).

In the end, girls are more successful in school in terms of grades earned and completion. In a meta-analysis of more than 500 effect sizes from more than 350 samples culled from published articles (in English and other languages), unpublished reports, and dissertations, Voyer and Voyer (2014) found that the grade advantage for girls was largest for language arts and smallest for math. Girls also are more likely than boys to complete high school (Meece & Askew, 2012). Undergraduate college admissions tests, however, underestimate females' academic performance in college and overestimate the college performance of males (Fischer, Schult, & Hell, 2013).

Peers in School

Peer influence and impact are most salient during middle school. Peers can promote sexism and intolerance in schools by teasing and ostracizing those who don't conform to gender norms, particularly nonconforming boys, and by sexual harassment, typically boys to girls, with the implicit support of observing peers (Leaper & Brown, 2014; see also Box 11.1). Eder, Evans, and Parker (1995) spent 3 years conducting a qualitative study of life in middle school, focusing on gender role development and gender inequalities. They found that the middle school students they studied were under great pressure to conform to traditional gender roles and that the penalties for deviation were great. Sexual harassment (sexual comments, unwanted interest and touch, physical and verbal coercion), either face to face or via social media, is also common in schools (Leaper & Brown, 2014). In a 2011 survey of grade 7 to grade 11 students, the American Association of University Women found that 56% of girls and 40% of boys reported having had experiences with sexual harassment. A gender gap was more evident in older students, with 62% of the girls and 32% of the boys in 12th grade reporting instances of sexual harassment. Girls are also more likely to report being affected by sexual harassment, experiencing anxiety, depression, and school avoidance. Educators can successfully intervene by implementing schoolwide programs focused on improving school climate (Leaper & Brown, 2014). Teachers and students can be encouraged to confront and counter sexism in schools and to decrease the complicit acceptance of bystanders. Some have even argued for single-sex schools or for single-sex programs within schools—a topic taken up in the Considering Interesting Questions special feature in Box 11.2.

Gender Differences in STEM Performance and Careers

Women in the United States are underrepresented in the pool of undergraduate bachelor degrees in certain STEM disciplines, particularly in computer science and physics. In 2014, females accounted for 57.2% of the bachelor's degrees awarded but only 18.1% of the degrees in computer science and 19.8% of the degrees in engineering (National Science Foundation, National Center for Science and Engineering Statistics, 2017). Not all the news is dismal in that the percentage of bachelor's degrees awarded in mathematics and statistics was higher (40%), but it still indicated a substantial gender gap given that females accounted for a higher percentage of college degrees awarded (e.g., 57.2). This is a real dilemma since occupations requiring degrees in STEM fields are among the more prestigious and financial rewarding of vocational possibilities. In 2016, 44% of the U.S. workforce was female, but women comprised only 25% of computer and mathematical occupations and accounted for just 14% of architects and engineers (U.S. Department of Labor, 2017).

How do we account for the gender gap in STEM occupations? Differences begin to appear in adolescence and persist into college (Ganley & Vasilyeva, 2014; Leaper & Brown, 2014). Boys and girls express similar confidence in their math abilities in early elementary school and exhibit similar performance in math in elementary school, but differences emerge after transition to middle school (Leaper & Brown, 2014; Usher & Pajares, 2008). As mentioned earlier, girls earn higher grades than boys in all school subjects, but the smallest advantage is in mathematics (Voyer & Voyer, 2014). Males and females take advanced math courses at the same rate in high school, but this was not true in the past (Lindberg et al., 2010). Yet, boys take more AP exams in STEM disciplines, with the exception of biology (Liben & Coyle, 2014). As discussed earlier in the chapter, males score slightly higher on standardized math (and also science) tests, with more males than females in the extreme high end of the distribution (Ganley & Vasilyeva, 2014; Reilly, Neumann, & Andrews, 2015). In

BOX 11.2. Are Single-Sex Schools More Effective than Mixed-Sex Schools?

In 2000, there were only a handful of public single-sex schools in the United States, but the No Child Left Behind Act eased the restrictions originally established by Title IX in 1972, so that in 2010, the number of public single-sex schools had increased to around 600 (Bigler, Hayes, & Liben, 2014). Some of the rationales for single-sex schooling include arguments about innate brain differences between boys and girls, different learning styles, and interests of boys and girls, and the contention that boys do not thrive in the typical school culture. What have we learned from comparisons of single-sex and mixed-sex, co-educational schools? Is there evidence that single-sex schools are more effective?

The answer seems to be probably not: single-sex schools are not more effective than mixed-sex schools in terms of increasing academic achievement or improving attitudes toward school (Martin et al., 2014; Pahlke & Hyde, 2016). Some studies and evaluations initially touted as demonstrating the greater effectiveness of single-sex schooling were found to have failed to control for potentially confounding variables (Bigler et al., 2014). These variables include selectivity of the school, in terms of both the achievement level of the students and the educational level of the parents. In many cases, students choose to apply to a single-sex school, which may indicate higher levels of academic motivation. Some studies also failed to consider the extended school day and longer school year adopted by some single-sex schools, two variables that are closely linked to achievement. Pahlke et al. (2014) conducted a meta-analysis separating controlled studies from uncontrolled studies (primarily because of the use of selection criteria for admission) and found that single-sex schooling was not more effective than mixed-sex schooling. For example, Pahlke, Shibley Hale, and Mertz (2013) investigated the effects of single-sex compared with mixed-sex schooling on the mathematics and science achievement of Korean students. The middle school students were randomly assigned to schools, eliminating potential confounding due to selectivity, and no differences in academic performance were detected.

Proponents of single-sex schooling also claim that single-sex schooling reduces sexism, harassment, and attention paid to gender. Unfortunately, sexism, both from teachers and students, continues to exist in single-sex schools, and single-sex schooling may even heighten awareness of gender (Martin et al., 2014). For example, Fabes, Pahlke, Martin, and Hanish (2013) studied a middle school with both gender-segregated and coeducational classes. Controlling for initial gender-stereotyped beliefs, these researchers found that seventh-grade students who took more gender-segregated classes in the fall exhibited more gender-stereotyped beliefs in the spring.

Some studies do, however, indicate positive effects of single-sex schooling—at least for some students. For example, Else-Quest and Peterca (2015) compared the standardized test performance of eleventh-grade low-income students enrolled in single-sex public schools without a selective admissions process to similar students enrolled in mixed-sex schools. Different patterns of achievement for boys and girls were observed, with girls in single-sex schools performing *higher* than girls in mixed-sexed schools in math, science, reading, and writing but boys in single-sex schools performing *lower* than boys in mixed-sex schools in reading and math. Rather than making large investments of time, money, and effort in creating single-sex schools for mixed results, at best, Else-Quest and Peterca (2015) proposed focusing on improving the academic engagement and climate of mixed-sex schools. Suggested improvements include revising the curriculum to make it more engaging for both boys and girls; providing professional development for teachers to reduce gender salience in the classroom, including gender bias in terms of teacher expectations, interactions, and attention; and implementing programming for students to reduce gender stereotyping and harassment.

addition, recall that males also tend to outperform females on tasks measuring spatial skills, particularly mental rotation, and spatial skills are related to performance on some STEM tasks (Liben & Coyle, 2014; Tosto et al., 2014; Voyer, 2011).

Riegle-Crumb, King, Grodsky, and Muller (2012) examined the data from three national cohorts collected across three decades and observed that prior achievement does not explain the gendered pattern in college majors, with many highly qualified females not choosing to major in physical sciences and engineering. In a review based on over 400 studies, including 20 meta-analyses, Ceci et al. (2009) concluded that differences in motivation, interests, and beliefs substantially contributed to gender differences in STEM performance and careers. Females proficient in math prefer non-math-intensive fields at a higher rate than math-proficient males, and they are more likely to also have high verbal skills than their male counterparts, which opens ups other career avenues (Ceci et al., 2009; Lubinski & Benbow, 1994; Lubinski, Benbow, & Kell, 2014).

A meta-analysis of interest inventory data including half a million respondents revealed that women greatly preferred working with people and that men preferred working with things (Su, Rounds, & Armstrong, 2009). Women tend to seek more social contact than they perceive would be available to them in STEM careers, supported by the large effect size favoring males for interest in engineering careers and a medium effect size for interest in science careers also favoring males. There are also gender differences in perceived value of STEM disciplines. For example, Gaspard et al. (2015) found that ninth-grade girls expressed lower intrinsic motivation for math than boys, described math as being less personally important and less useful for their personal and professional goals than boys, and reported that math required more effort and entailed more emotional cost than boys. As noted earlier in the chapter, even mathematically skilled girls are less likely to attribute their successes in mathematics to ability and their failures to bad luck than do same-age boys; elementary-age girls are less likely to be confident that mathematics success can be achieved through effort than elementary-age boys; girls take less pride in their math successes than do male classmates; and girls are more disrupted by math failures than are boys (Hyde et al., 1990; Meece & Askew, 2012; Stipek & Gralinski, 1991).

International comparisons indicate that culture plays a role in gender differences in STEM performance and stereotypes. In a meta-analysis of national data sets, Else-Quest, Hyde and Linn (2010) observed substantial variability in gender gaps on math assessments reflecting the level of gender equality in each nation. Nations with more gender equality produced smaller or no gender differences in math performance. In general, girls and boys achieved similarly on the math assessments, but the boys expressed more positive attitudes toward math. Analyzing data from approximately 350,000 participants in more than 66 nations, Miller, Eagly, and Linn (2015) found that women's representation in science fields predicted national gender stereotypes for science. Although participants strongly associated science with men when women were represented equally or less, greater representation of women was associated with reduced gender-science stereotypes.

As described earlier in the chapter, socialization processes influence the development of gender roles. Males and females are treated differently from the moment the delivery room nurse reaches for a blue blanket for a boy or a pink one for a girl. Girls might have less interest in math and in careers requiring mathematics because they have internalized societal, stereotypical beliefs such as "Math is for boys," "Engineers and scientists are men," and "Science requires cold objectivity"—a male stereotypic trait—rather than interpersonal warmth and human contact, female stereotypic traits. Western society does much to discourage female interest in mathematics and science (see Halpern, 2000, for a review). Fortunately cultures do evolve. Chambers (1983) asked children in the United States and Canada to draw a picture of a scientist and less than 1% drew a woman. More than four decades later, Farland-Smith (2009) asked the same question of children in the United States and this time 35% drew a woman.

Yet children develop implicit, if not explicit, gender stereotypes at young ages. For example, Baron, Schmader, Cvencek, and Meltzoff (2014) reported that by 8 years of age both boys and girls associate mathematics more with males than females and boys more strongly relate their self-concept with mathematics than girls do. Cvencek, Meltzoff, and Greenwald (2011) examined gender stereotypes for math in around 250 children ranging between 6 and 10 years of age and found that as early as second grade, children exhibited stereotypic beliefs that math is for boys and boys expressed greater identification with math than girls. In a study of adults, Nosek and Smyth (2011) observed that females with strong implicit "math is male" stereotypes had more negative attitudes toward math, lower self-described ability in math, participated less in math-related activities, and had lower math achievement. Survey and interview data indicate that the culture of science is still characterized as masculine and that science curriculum is not aligned with the values of girls but the most pervasive issue to address is fostering identities in girls as future scientists and engineers (Archer, Moore, Francis, DeWitt, & Yeomans, 2017).

Perhaps not surprisingly, parents also tend to have gender-stereotypic expectations about math and science achievement and valuation (Butler, 2014). That is, they do not expect their daughters to do as well in mathematics and science as their sons. Parents also are much more concerned that sons do well in mathematics and science than daughters. Moreover, parents communicate their beliefs to their sons and daughters (Eccles & Jacobs, 1986; Eccles-Parson, Adler, & Kaczala, 1982; Meece & Askew, 2012). In Tomasetto, Mirisola, Galdi, and Cadinu (2015), the math gender stereotypes of the mothers of 6-year-olds predicted their daughters' self-perceptions of their math ability. Unfortunately, parents do their share to undermine their daughters' confidence in their mathematical and science abilities, probably impacting short- and long-term motivation and achievement (Eccles, Freedman-Doan, Frome, Jacobs, & Yoon, 2000).

As discussed earlier in the chapter, teacher expectations and beliefs affect their behavior in the classroom. Thomas (2017) assessed teachers' implicit gender stereotypes about science and gender by comparing reaction times to associated pairs of humanities/female and science/male. Faster reaction times to pairs such as art/mother, English/sister, engineering/father, physics/brother compared to art/father, English/brother, engineering/mother, physics/sister would indicate an implicit stereotype. Implicit stereotypes of the teachers were positively related to their male students' self-concept and negatively related to their female students' motivational beliefs.

Classrooms that are supportive of developing high math self-efficacy in females tend to be noncompetitive and to play down ability comparisons (Butler, 2014). The focus is on meaningful learning and seeing errors as opportunities to learn rather than on performance. The teachers emphasize the value of mathematics, sending the message that math is important for males and females alike. Classrooms that foster high self-efficacy with respect to math and science achievement also tend to involve a great deal of hands-on, cooperative activity between students over math and science problems (see Eccles, 1989, for a review; see also Campbell, 1995; Koch, 2003; Wilkinson & Marrett, 1985). Teachers who foster high self-efficacy in females make certain that all students are involved in class discussion, interacting productively with one another and with the teacher, and distribute their attention to the males and females in their class as equitably as possible.

Interventions to Increase Female Participation in STEM

Recall the discussion of expectancy–value theory in Chapters 5 and 9. In order for people to be motivated to do something, they must expect that they can succeed at doing that something and that the reward they will receive will be one they value. Young women are less confident in their mathematics and scientific abilities than young men, which translates to lower expectations with respect to success in mathematics. In addition, females are less likely than males to value careers involving mathematics and sciences. With lower expectancies of reward for taking math and science and lower interest in the potential rewards associated with mathematics and scientific achievement, both components of the expectancy × value product are lower for females than for males. Hence, the probabilities of pursuing careers in STEM fields are lower for females than for males.

The material presented in this section might lead us to conclude that the forces converging to shape gender differences in science and mathematics achievement and interest are overwhelming. Another way to look at it, however, is to recognize that these multiple determinants permit multiple opportunities for intervention (Liben & Coyle, 2014). Educational decision makers at all levels can elect options that decrease gender discrimination (Jacobs & Wigfield, 1989). For example, Jones and Wheatley (1988) catalogued many ways that teachers can make their teaching less gender-biased (see also Koch, 2003). These techniques include projecting clear expectations for science achievement by both girls and boys, doing all possible to assure comparable interactions with girls and boys (e.g., making certain both girls and boys play active roles in science laboratory activities), and referring to scientific contributions by both females and males.

Particularly encouraging is the fact that interventions seem to work. For example, Mason and Kahle (1988) studied the effects of teaching science teachers how to create a more gender-free learning environment, largely as described in the last paragraph. The treatment did boost the interest of female students in science, with self-reported increases in participation in science activities outside of school. Martinez (1992) provided evidence that modifying science materials and activities to enhance the interestingness of the activity and its social appeal promotes the interest of girls in the activities. The modifications included posing questions as part of the activity that elicit discussion, requiring sharing and joint answers, and using personal references in the materials. Burbules and Linn (1988) observed that providing junior high girls with additional experiences during laboratory exercises (e.g., enriched opportunities to examine the laboratory equipment and to generate hypotheses based on these examinations) improved their learning of scientific ideas that clashed with their misconceptions. Master, Cheryan, and Meltzoff (2016) found that creating a physical class environment that is welcoming, invoking a sense of belonging rather than isolation, increased the interest of girls, but not boys, in taking an introductory computer science course. Walton, Logel, Peach, Spencer, and Zanna (2015) explored interventions designed to increase the social integration of women admitted into engineering programs. The interventions designed to reduce a "chilly climate" resulted in higher grade point averages and improved attitudes toward engineering.

In summary, gender stereotypes about capabilities in STEM disciplines influence beliefs about competency, which in turn influences choice of activities. Gender stereotypes also affect the expectations of teachers and parents, which are communicated through words and actions. Students may adopt the gender stereotypes of the adults in their lives, which in turn affects the choice they make. Stereotypes held by an individual may result in stereotype threat, which has an effect on actual performance. Finally, stereotypes can have an effect on policy decisions impacting the equality of opportunities (review Box 11.2).

Chapter Summary and Evaluation

Gender differences do exist. However, the differences between the sexes are much smaller than one might think, and there is a great deal of overlap in the male and female distributions on almost any characteristic measured. Gender differences are the result of genetic, hormonal, social, cultural, and cognitive influences interacting over time.

Chromosomes alone do not tell much of the story with respect to gender identity and gender-related behaviors, except to the extent that they determine prenatal hormonal exposure and levels. Hormones certainly affect genital development and probably affect development of the central nervous system to some extent. But biology does not operate alone in determining gender identity, for when biology and socialization forces conflict, socialization forces can have a powerful impact.

The world reinforces the tendency for boys to be boys and girls to be girls! Moreover, many live and symbolic models surround the developing child. All of the observational learning opportunities provide plenty of information about what boys are like and what girls are like. There is consistency in the world with respect to the pressures on children to develop in gender-stereotypical ways. Cognition plays a large role in that the learning of gender roles requires a great deal of memory, classification of behaviors as female or male, and comparison of one's own characteristics and behaviors with those of social models.

With schooling, the social world changes. A great deal of effort has been expended in the past two decades to understand how school affects females and males differently. Much of this work has focused on striking differences in the eventual math and science achievement of females and males. To a large extent, gender difference in achievement seems to be due to gender differences in motivation, some of which is determined by the characteristics of conventional schooling.

The work summarized in this chapter is exceptionally informative with respect to the Big Ideas in human development introduced in Chapter 1:

Nature and Nurture

Although claims have been made about gender role development based on nature and others based on nurture, it is clear that both biology and environment play a role. Sex chromosomes and hormones profoundly influence development; yet socialization processes such as reinforcement and observational learning, as well as the child's own cognitions about what it means to be a boy or a girl, also play major roles.

Continuity and Discontinuity

Traditional thinking about gender role development has been stage-like, with Kohlberg's theory being one example (e.g., gender role development depends on the stage of cognitive development). More recent thinking indicates that early on, children have powerful schematic representational abilities that permit them to organize their thinking about gender, which in turn leads to more continuous gender role development.

Universal and Culture-Specific

Some similarities across cultures have been observed, such as the prevalence of sex segregation. There is also evidence that culture has a powerful influence on gender role development, such as differences in achievement patterns and gender stereotypes as a result of cultural influences.

Active and Passive Child

As soon as a child gets the idea that he or she is a boy or a girl, the child begins to pay more attention to male or female things and to develop knowledge and beliefs about gender stereotypes. The child's own gender identity plays a major role in the display of gendered behavior. Even so, there is a great deal of environmental influence, so that some gender role development probably occurs passively.

REVIEW OF KEY TERMS

androgens Hormones that influence sex development, related to masculinization and secreted by testes.

cisgender Individuals whose gender identity matches sex assigned at birth.

estrogen A hormone secreted by the ovaries.

gender consistency The understanding that gender does not change with superficial changes in appearance.

gender schemas Organized knowledge about gender.

intersexuality An umbrella term for disorders/differences of sex development (DSD).

Klinefelter syndrome Males with two X chromosome, one Y chromosome.

quantitative skills Mathematical skills and reasoning.

testosterone A hormone secreted by the testes that is particularly important in the development of masculine characteristics.

transgender Individuals whose gender identity differs from sex assigned at birth.

Turner syndrome Females with only one X chromosome.

verbal ability Skills such as word fluency, grammatical competence, spelling, reading, and oral comprehension.

visual–spatial tasks Tasks requiring the ability to imagine figures, including figure manipulation "in the head."

CHAPTER 12

Recognizing and Understanding Student Mental Health Problems

A broad spectrum of mental health problems is present in school-age children. Estimates indicate that as many as one in four or five children and particularly adolescents suffer from a diagnosable psychological disorder (Hayden & Mash, 2014; Merikangas et al., 2010; Merikangas & He, 2014). Because anxiety, depression, and conduct problems are so common in children and adolescents, it is inevitable that teachers will work with children who have mental health problems that can be challenging to cope with in the classroom and quite debilitating to a child's overall development (Reinke, Stormont, Herman, Puri, & Goel, 2011). Some of these children will have been identified already as having psychological problems, although many others will not. Teachers and other education professionals, because of their experience with applied developmental psychology and their extensive contact with and insight about children, are in a unique position to detect and report mental health problems that need immediate attention before they worsen (Ekornes, 2015; Loades & Mastroyannopoulou, 2010).

This chapter introduces some of the developmental psychopathologies educators may encounter among their students. The chapter begins with descriptions of psychological and developmental disorders that are first evident in preschoolers, followed by explanations of mental health problems most noted in elementary school-age children, and concludes with a brief rendering of some of the mental health issues that are prevalent among teenagers. Some of these problems are rare, and teachers may never observe a child with some of these diagnoses unless they are engaged in educating children with special needs. Unfortunately, other mental health problems are quite common, and a teacher will almost certainly encounter them at some point in his or her career. We hope this chapter will help you recognize when a child is suffering from a serious mental health problem and to understand that child and his or her behavior a little better.

Themes to Keep in Mind

Before we delve into the particulars of developmental psychopathologies found in children, a few key concepts and ideas need to be covered. In particular, it is important to discuss some introductory, but vitally important, themes that mental health professional use to distinguish healthy and acceptable behavior from behavioral patterns that are maladaptive. Sometimes there is a fine line between "normal" and "dysfunctional" behaviors. Teachers and educators need to remember and use these themes when deciding how to respond to the unusual behaviors they may observe in the children with whom they work.

The Quantity and Quality of the Problem Behavior

All children, at some time or another, exhibit behaviors and emotions that are symptoms of mental health problems, notably, temper tantrums or outbursts of anger; impulsive behavior; difficulty sustaining attention; and overwhelming fears and feelings of helplessness and unhappiness. Most adults exhibit these behaviors and feelings now and then too. One characteristic that distinguishes healthy children from those who are suffering from a mental health problem, however, is the *quantity or frequency* of the symptomatic behavior (Campbell, 2002). Healthy individuals experience and express these emotions and behaviors periodically. The behavior or mood occurs and may even endure for a couple of days, but soon enough the feeling or behavior subsides and the person returns to normal (Hayden & Mash, 2014). Actually, children frequently cycle in and out of phases in which they are naughty or excited or worried or unhappy. Children with psychological problems, however, experience negative moods and express problematic behaviors frequently, often multiple times a day. Children with serious psychological problems never really bounce back to their "normal" selves. In fact, their usual demeanor is troubled, and the times when they act and feel fine is the exception, not the rule.

Another factor that separates healthy individuals from those who are struggling with the vicissitudes of life is the *quality* of the symptomatic behavior. When healthy children experience negative moods or exhibit problematic behavior, it is usually in a milder and more manageable form. Healthy children will try to respond to encouragement and limit-settings from adults and seem to learn the boundaries of acceptable behavior. Psychologically troubled children experience more extreme manifestations of problematic moods and behaviors. Their tantrums may be horrific and destructive; they may be exceedingly defiant, not just naughty; their worries are extreme, even bizarre; and when they are unhappy they are morose and inconsolable. They don't seem to respond to the directives from adults to control their behavior, and they often assert they just can't control their feelings and behavior.

In short, two things that often distinguish healthy children from psychologically troubled children are the quantity and quality of their problematic moods and behavior. Healthy children exhibit problem behaviors episodically and generally at a more manageable level. Symptomatic emotions and behaviors in troubled children are persistent. They occur frequently and with a surprising level of intensity. The troubling feelings and behaviors last longer and are seemingly uncontrollable. As a rule of thumb, teachers should expect that all children will exhibit problematic moods and behaviors. Avoid "jumping the gun" and assuming the worst at the first sight of problem behavior. The risk is that you will begin to develop a confirmation bias and "see what you believe." If that happens, then every behavior the child exhibits could be interpreted as part of the child's "pathology." Even worse, you might create a "self-fulfilling prophecy" in which a child lives up to your expectation: if you expect him or her to be a problem child, he or she will become a problem. It's better to begin with the assumption that children are trying hard to be on their best behavior and that sometimes they lapse or struggle with their feelings and behavior. Instead of jumping to premature conclusions about a child's psychological condition, look for enduring patterns of moods and behavior that far exceed what you ordinarily encounter because this is what will confirm or refute the presence of a more serious psychological problem.

The Context in Which the Problem Behavior Occurs

People live within and move between social environments. Each of these environments has different rules or expectations for what is appropriate behavior. The demand characteristics of an environment and the circumstances that lead to the creation of these environments provide the setting or context for interpreting emotional expressions and behavior. We generally think of many emotions and behaviors, like humor and laughing, as prosocial and enhancing of our lives. However, laughing during a solemn occasion, like a funeral, or joking around when you are supposed to be concentrating on a school assignment, is not appropriate and may be indicative of a more serious emotional or behavioral problem. Alternatively, we often consider anger, aggression, and fighting as negative emotions and behaviors, but if they are expressed in reaction to unprovoked aggression from others or in self-defense, these behaviors might be deemed appropriate for the circumstances. The point is, whether or not an emotion or a behavior is symptomatic of a serious psychological problem depends a great deal on the context in which the behavior occurs (Hayden & Mash, 2014).

Ordinarily, when children and adults shift from one social setting to another, they alter their behavior and emotional expressions accordingly. Children with serious psychological problems may have a difficult time adjusting their behavior and emotions to match the social context. The symptoms of a serious emotional or behavioral disorder are not easily turned on and off. Consequently, as a general rule of thumb, when a child has a serious mental health problem, the symptoms of that disorder will be expressed regardless of the context or social environment. So, for example, an adolescent suffering from a serious depression will act and feel depressed at home, at school, and while hanging out with friends. Similarly, a child who has **attention-deficit/hyperactivity disorder (ADHD)** is likely to manifest those symptoms across contexts. When a child expresses psychological problems in one context but not others, however, there may be something about that particular context that accounts for the child's behavior, rather than something endemic to the child (Eccles, Midgley, & Wigfield, 1993). Sometimes teachers take advantage of these environmental and contextual effects. For example, a teacher may make a small change in a social environment—like moving a child's seat from the back to the front of a classroom—to make a difference in how a child behaves.

One mistake people frequently make is the fundamental attribution error of dismissing the effects of context and environment and assuming that a child is behaving inappropriately because there is something wrong with the child. It is really important that teachers not make this error and that they take note of the circumstances in which a child's problem mood or behavior is expressed. Not knowing the context of the problem, a mental health professional may find it very difficult to make an accurate diagnosis When reporting on a child's psychological adjustment, it is useful to note the physical, social, and demand characteristics of the environment. For example, how stimulating is the environment? Is it noisy and overstimulating, or is it bland and boring? Is the child comfortable with the people in his or her midst, or is he or she being teased or tormented? Does the problem emerge during particular times, for instance, during lessons that are really challenging or difficult for the child and not during lessons the child enjoys and feels competent doing? It is also very useful to observe whether the child is exhibiting symptoms of a psychological disorder in more than one setting. Do symptoms of a serious psychological disorder show up in the classroom, during recess, and on the bus to and from school? Is more than one adult observing these problems in different contexts? Finding answers to these questions will make a big difference when a professional diagnoses the child's problems and decides on the best treatment for these issues.

The "It's Probably Not a Zebra!" Issue

One wonderful aspect of human nature is our perpetual curiosity about why something is happening, what's going on, and cause-and-effect relationships. As just noted, this curiosity often leads us to make mistakes. Another of the more common mistakes is assuming that something rare and exotic is causing a phenomenon, when in fact the cause is common and mundane. For example, a person might feel some nausea and a slight pain in his or her side and think, "Oh my god, I have appendicitis!" (a low-frequency event) when it's much more likely that he or she has a touch of food poisoning because he or she ate old leftovers (a high-frequency event). Well, the same is true in child and adolescent clinical psychology. People are apt to attribute a child's problematic behavior to some relatively low-prevalence psychopathology when much more common and frequent factors in a child's life may be causing his or her difficulties.

Many of the developmental psychopathologies we discuss in this chapter occur in a small percentage of children (often less than 1%; usually less than 2–3%; sometimes as many as 5–10%, but rarely more). At the same time, there are some very-high-frequency events in children's lives that are quite disruptive and can cause psychological symptoms. For example, over one in five children (a high-frequency event) in the United States lives in poverty (Heberle & Carter, 2015; McLoyd et al., 2014). Consequently, they are often malnourished and are exposed to more environmental toxins, have less access to medical care and less social support, receive less cognitive stimulation, and are subject to more social and familial turmoil (Evans et al., 2013; Heberle & Carter, 2015; McLoyd et al., 2014; see also Chapter 10). Moreover, some evidence suggests that when poverty is alleviated, psychopathology diminishes (Costello, Compton, Keeler, & Angold, 2003). Similarly, a substantial number of children in the United States experience dramatic family upheaval and transition (e.g., marital separation, parental divorce, remarriage), and as many as one-third live in stepfamilies (Doyle, Wolchik, Dawson-McClure, & Sandler, 2003; see also Chapter 10).

While some controversy surrounds the issue of how traumatic and long lasting the effects of family disturbance may be on children, without doubt family upheaval is stressful and emotionally destabilizing for children both before and following the transition and causes disruptions in their behavior (Weaver & Schofield, 2015). More than a quarter of children are exposed to or witness family violence (Renner & Boel-Studt, 2017), and many of these children are also the victims of domestic violence. Over 9 in every 1,000 children in the United States are confirmed victims of child abuse, and many more than that are suspected victims of abuse (U.S. Department of Health and Human Services, Administration for Children and Families, 2013).

Perhaps even more common and insidious are the effects of sleep deprivation. Recent reports have suggested that perhaps most children and adolescents (and maybe lots of adults too) are getting too little sleep. This has dramatic effects on their behavior, including mimicking psychopathology or exacerbating already existing emotional and behavioral problems (James & Hale, 2017; Meltzer, 2017).

These examples highlight the fact that symptomatic behavior can be caused by many factors. Consequently, when a teacher is trying to understand a child's problematic behavior, he or she should consider the more common causes of problematic behavior before assuming that a child has developed a psychological pathology. Unless educators have received advanced training in abnormal child psychology, it might be better for them to avoid making any diagnosis of a child's behavior.

What's an Educator to Do?

As we have suggested, making psychological diagnoses is complicated, there are many ways to make mistakes, and sometimes having just a little knowledge can cause a lot of trouble. So, as you read through the following pages about the kinds of psychological problems that plague some children, keep the preceding cautions in mind. Remember that all children exhibit problematic behaviors some of the time. Think first about how a child's social and physical environment may be contributing to his or her problems. Consider whether his or her troubled emotions and problem behavior may be a response to common and frequent events in the lives of children and families and avoid jumping to diagnostic conclusions about a child.

All the same, your observations about a child are invaluable to psychodiagnosticians and other mental health professionals. The more precise and specific your observations are, the more useful they will be. For example, reporting that a child gets out of his seat, on average, five times an hour regardless of what subject is being taught, is much more useful than complaining that a child is "hyperactive." Similarly, stating that the child "acts weird" will communicate less than if you observe that a child rarely makes eye contact, has peculiar repetitive movements, or laughs or giggles at inappropriate times. Look for enduring patterns of disturbing behavior, try to avoid allowing any single or brief episode of emotional or behavioral problems to bias your perception of a child, and, above all, look for times when the child behaves competently, which might disconfirm your suspicions of a more serious problem.

Psychological Problems Often First Detected in Early Childhood

Neurodevelopmental Disorders

Neurodevelopmental disorders have a pervasive effect on children and their development. They are debilitating illnesses that impact a child's social, emotional, cognitive, educational, and behavioral development—in other words, all aspects of a child's psychological development. There are several different types of neurodevelopmental disorders, and they range in the types, severity, and manner in which the symptoms develop. At one time, neurodevelopmental disorders were thought to be exceedingly rare, but more recent studies have detected higher rates in the general population: between 60 and 70 per 10,000 children (Fombonne, 2009). It's not clear whether the population of children with neurodevelopmental disorders is increasing or whether people are getting better at detecting them (Constantino & Charman, 2016; Frances & Widiger, 2012; Klinger, Dawson, Barnes, & Crissler, 2014). Either way, educators are finding they are having increasing contact with children plagued by these serious disorders, especially the types that are less debilitating.

Autism and Autism Spectrum Disorders

Autism is a devastating mental disorder characterized by a variety of symptoms. including dramatic deficits in social interaction, severe impairments in communications, and a markedly limited repertoire of activity and interests. Children with autism seem to cope with social situations in ways that are quite different than the way other children cope. Either they seem not to attend to social stimuli (e.g., responding to faces) or they attend to social stimuli in unusual ways from an early age (Constantino & Charman, 2016; Fakhoury, 2015; Klinger et al., 2014; Vargo, 2015). As babies, they seem aloof and passive. They decline to reach out for their caretakers, sometimes stiffen when held, and often fail to smile or make eye contact like healthy babies do. This hinders their ability to imitate and learn social behavior and to respond emotionally. As a consequence, children with autism may seem oblivious to the presence or feelings of others and are unlikely to seek comfort from others. Many children with autism are mute, and those who aren't frequently use language in peculiar ways. They often use *echolalia* (repeating words or phrases they previously heard), *pronoun reversals* (e.g., saying "you" instead of "I" when talking about themselves), *unusual rhythms and intonations*, and *odd nonverbal communications*. Children with autism typically engage in repetitive and stereotypic movements (e.g., rocking or flapping of hands or arms), may become preoccupied and inordinately attached to inanimate objects, and experience extreme distress even to the slightest changes in their environment. Some children with autism adopt self-injurious behaviors like head banging or finger biting. In the 1988 movie *Rain Man*, Dustin Hoffman portrayed an autistic man who had unique mathematical skills. On rare occasions, children with autism will demonstrate extraordinary memory skills or savant behavior in math, drawing, or music. However, the reality for most children with autism is much grimmer; the disorder is so crippling that their overall intellectual abilities are severely impaired.

The cause of autism is still unknown. We know it is *not* caused by poor parenting. Concerns that childhood immunizations may be responsible for some types of autism have been refuted by recent research. Most explanations of the cause of autism are physiological in nature. Advances in genetic and neuroanatomical research have identified potential genes that may contribute to the development of autism and variations in neuroanatomy and how the brain develops in people with autism (Fakhoury, 2015; Johnson, Jones, & Gliga; 2015; Klinger et al., 2014).

There also may be different types of autism: some appear to begin very early in infancy, while others seem to begin after a period of one to two years of seemingly normal development. As we have gained more knowledge about autism, researchers and clinicians have begun to speculate there is a spectrum of autism-like disorders in which individuals have all or only some of the symptoms of autism, depending perhaps on their genetic makeup and the gene by environment interaction they experience. This has led to the concept of "high-functioning autism." The big difference between children with severe autism and those with high-functioning autism seems to be the acquisition of language skills—although the language skill development of high-functioning autistic children is still delayed, and they often still have notable expressive and receptive language deficits. Because of the rarity of autism and the severely debilitating nature of its symptoms, most teachers will not be called on to educate autistic children unless they seek out that opportunity. However, teachers are having more contact with children with high-functioning autism and the related disorder of Asperger syndrome.

Asperger Syndrome and Nonverbal Learning Disorder

It can be quite difficult to distinguish between a child with high-functioning autism and one with **Asperger syndrome**. In turn, it can be challenging to distinguish a child with Asperger syndrome from one with nonverbal learning disorder (NLD). Developmental psychopathologists continue to debate whether these are separate and distinct diagnoses (Semrud-Clikeman, Walkowiak, Wilkinson, & Christopher, 2010a; Stewart, 2007). Many of the symptoms that characterize Asperger syndrome, particularly the social deficits, are similar to the symptoms found in children with autism. Recently, the pendulum seems to be swinging toward the idea that Asperger syndrome is really a form of nonverbal learning disorder (NLD), although some children with NLD have the same kinds of cognitive impairments found in children with Asperger syndrome, but without the serious social interaction difficulties (Semrud-Clikeman et al., 2010a; Semrud-Clikeman Walkowiak, Wilkinson, & Minnie, 2010b). The important issue for educators is to realize they are apt to have contact with children who have complex and serious difficulties with learning and social interaction, but who do not have deficits severe enough to warrant a diagnosis of autism.

In general, children with NLD syndrome disorders will have problems with tactile perception, visual perception, and motor coordination, and they will also have difficulty processing and retrieving information, particularly tactile and visual memory, which makes it hard for them to use past experiences to cope with unique or novel situations. These problems, in turn, lead to deficits in attention and exploration, which lead to deficits in organization, higher-order reasoning, abstract thinking, emotional regulation, and social interaction (Mammarella & Cornoldi, 2014; Stewart, 2007).

More specifically, children with Asperger syndrome usually do not have the kinds of substantial impairments of language and intellectual functioning found in children with autism—in fact, they are often above average in some intellectual abilities. Children with Asperger syndrome are usually proficient in the technical aspects of language (e.g., word recognition, spelling, grammar, articulation), often have excellent auditory or rote memory recall, and frequently have a superior fund of knowledge in some idiosyncratic topic. Still, their perception and expression of nonverbal communications may be odd and uncomfortable. Also, they use language in fairly concrete ways; metaphor, analogy, and humorous plays on words may confuse them, and their comprehension of written language and ability to problem-solve are often impaired.

Although their intellectual abilities may be better than those found in children with autism, children with Asperger syndrome are awkward in social interactions in ways that are reminiscent of the kinds of social deficits found in children with autism (Semrud-Clikeman et al., 2010a). Similar to children with autism, children with Asperger syndrome tend to develop a fixation or obsessive interest in some activity. However, in children with Asperger syndrome, unlike their autistic counterparts, this activity is usually socially acceptable (e.g., playing with Legos). Conversations with children with Asperger syndrome tend to be one-sided; they are often verbose and don't seem to grasp the reciprocal and social nature of conversing. Sometimes children with Asperger syndrome lack physical coordination. Because of these unusual and socially awkward behaviors, children with Asperger syndrome often are socially isolated, and their peers may refer to them as "geeky" or "nerds." Unlike children with autism, though, children with Asperger syndrome seem to be aware of being social outcasts and it bothers them, but they have difficulty adjusting their social behavior enough to remedy their isolation.

NLD and Asperger syndrome may be caused by irregularities in the "white matter" of the brain (Fakhoury, 2015; Semrud-Clikeman et al., 2010a; see also Chapter 2). *White matter* is the myelinated axons that make connections across various brain structures (*gray matter* is the granular appearance of the neuronal cell bodies). Theoretically, the white matter or neuronal connections in the brains of children with Asperger syndrome or NLD either didn't develop correctly, doesn't function correctly, or were damaged in some way. These problems could occur for genetic reasons, as a consequence of prenatal conditions, or because of postnatal illness or trauma.

What Can Teachers Do When Working with Children with Neurodevelopmental Disorders?

Teachers not involved in special education or in teaching young children may not be inclined to work with children with neurodevelopmental disorders and nonverbal learning disorder. The reality is that children with high-functioning autism, Asperger syndrome, and other NLDs are increasingly being found in mainstream classrooms. Nor do children grow out of these disorders. Elementary school, middle school, and high school teachers are therefore finding they need to understand these disorders and how they can best contribute to these children's education.

Teachers can follow some general strategies when faced with children who have an autism spectrum disorder, Asperger syndrome, or an NLD (Stewart, 2007). Because children with these conditions have difficulty responding to novelty and unique situations, they do best when they have consistent and predictable routines. Children with these conditions need more time to accomplish tasks, so it is important to schedule fewer activities and "do more of less" for them rather than try to expose them to a "little bit of a lot." Keep directions simple and short and provide children with autism spectrum disorder, Asperger syndrome, or NLD places to work that are free from distraction. Teach these children how to focus attention on the main idea and how to organize their work by pre-briefing them on how to distinguish between important ideas and superfluous details and how to organize using color codes, notebooks, schedules, and time awareness. Then debrief them at the end of a task about what worked and what didn't work in helping them get their assignment done. These children are, in general, better at auditory learning; they do better with scaffolding and when things are divided into steps; and they work well with facts and logical explanations. They usually don't do well with teaching strategies that emphasize visual learning, learning the gestalt (or whole), and working backward to discover the parts, problem solving, and self-discovery. Furthermore, because children with autism spectrum disorder, Asperger syndrome, or NLDs have difficulty understanding and responding to social stimuli, teachers may need to adapt their lessons accordingly. For example, children with neurodevelopmental disorders and NLDs may have difficulty working in groups, so the group activities they are asked to do should be highly structured and well supervised. Also, teachers can look for opportunities to teach about the intricacies and nuances of social interaction, and to model and practice effective social and communication skills (e.g., making eye contact, making appropriate greetings, reading facial expressions, using polite words, developing listening skills).

Lastly, because children with neurodevelopmental disorders and NLD find it difficult to process feelings, it's best to mute emotional expressions, especially strong negative feelings; otherwise these children will focus on the emotion and not the message and will quickly become overstimulated and frustrated. An excellent resource for information about Asperger syndrome and NLDs, written for parents, though teachers may find it very useful, is Stewart (2007).

Psychological Problems Present during the Elementary School Years

Children's Anxieties

As adults, we have a tendency to idealize childhood, and we generally view the life of a child as carefree and full of fun. The reality, however, is that children experience a great deal of stress. In fact, feeling stressed and anxious is a normative experience and a necessary part of our development (Caes, Fisher, Clinch, Tobias, & Eccleston, 2015; Higa-McMillan, Francis, & Chorpita, 2014). Each time children or adolescents strike out on their own and assume more autonomy or engage in new and challenging activities, they experience and learn to cope with the unpleasant physiological arousal we label "anxiety" and "dread." That arousal, assuming that it's not overwhelming, serves to focus attention and concentration and to facilitate learning. Moreover, anxiety levels in children, adolescents, and young adults in the United States may have been increasing over the past 50 years (Twenge, 2011). Some of this rise in anxiety has to do with the genetic transmission of the predisposition for worry and anxiety. However, a substantial portion also has to do with social trends such as the increasing instability of family life and changes in our social environment. In particular, our perception of greater danger in the world follows from our increased access to media coverage of worldwide crime, war, terrorism, and disease. Another source of this anxiety is the erosion of social connectedness that stems from the increasing mobility of people in our society, and peoples' relative isolation and lack of involvement in developing a sense of community.

Unfortunately, many children lack the experience, insight, and adult guidance they need to cope with the tensions of life and the strong emotional conditions that accompany them. They become confused by their feelings, have difficulty explaining why they feel the way they do, and feel their emotions are in control of them rather than the other way around. Sometimes, as a consequence, their anxieties and fears become overwhelming, and instead of being transitory experiences that focus attention and facilitate learning, they become chronic, encompassing, and debilitating conditions. This is a very serious problem because chronic anxiety in children interferes with healthy development and learning, and may lead to a proclivity for even more serious anxiety disorders, depression, substance use, and suicide in adulthood (Beesdo-Baum & Knappe, 2012; Higa-McMillan et al., 2014; Letcher, Sanson, Smart, & Toumbourou, 2012).

The first step in addressing anxiety problems in children is to determine whether the problem is a normal fear or anxiety, a transitory state-related anxiety, or a more debilitating psychological condition. Children express a variety of very common fears in the course of normal development: for example, stranger anxiety, fear of loud noises, fear of falling, fear of the dark, and even some specific phobia-like fears such as fear of snakes, spiders, or storms (Caes et al., 2015). Although these fears are practically universal, there are considerable individual differences in how much or in what way any particular child may express them. Children with a more robust temperament will be able to tolerate anxiety better; other children, being more timid, may ruminate over anxieties. Generally, the more control a child has over the situation, the less intense the fears.

Although there is a wide range of estimates, depending on the population used in the research, the type of measurement used, and the type of anxiety disorder being considered, between 9 and 20% of children manifest a degree of anxiety that qualifies as a diagnosable anxiety disorder (Beesdo-Baum & Knappe, 2012; Copeland, Angold, Shanahan, & Costello, 2014; Franz et al., 2013; Higa-McMillan et al., 2014; Mian, Carter, Pine, Wakschlag, & Briggs-Gowan, 2015). In fact, anxiety disorders are the most common mental health problem in children and adolescents. When children experience debilitating anxiety, their symptoms may look quite different from symptoms in adults who express anxiety. Anxious children tend to get fidgety and restless. They may become impulsive, distracted, and preoccupied (which may look a lot like ADHD). They may become irritable, moody, and look and act depressed (indeed, they may be depressed, in addition to having an anxiety disorder; see Cummings, Caporino, & Kendall, 2014). The most prevalent symptoms are withdrawal, dependency, somatic complaints, and developmental regression. For example, younger children may become clingy, may become enuretic after years of bladder control, or may start sucking their thumb again; adolescents may withdraw from the family and revert to more childish behaviors; and children of all ages may complain about stomachaches, fatigue, or headaches as their anxiety increases (Crawley et al., 2014). Both children and adolescents develop different kinds of anxiety disorders (e.g., separation anxiety, generalized anxiety, social anxiety, specific phobias, obsessive–compulsive disorder, posttraumatic stress disorder). The following describes the most commonly diagnosed anxiety disorders in children and adolescents.

Separation Anxiety Disorder

The main symptom of **separation anxiety disorder (SAD)** is the expression of extreme anxiety and agitation when separated, or even anticipating separation, from home or from the people to whom a child is most attached (e.g., parents, other important caregivers; American Psychiatric Association, 2013). Children with SAD worry excessively that something cataclysmic or harmful will happen to those they love and depend on; alternatively, they worry they themselves will be kidnapped or lost and in that way, lose their loved ones.

These fears are so overwhelming to the child that he or she begins to avoid being alone or to engage in any activity that would require him or her to be away from the caretakers to whom they are attached. This avoidance behavior often begins with small, reasonable requests for parental comforting, but gradually these requests escalate in frequency and intensity until the child is unwilling to sleep alone, go to school, or allow a parent out of his or her sight even for a moment. Children with SAD often have recurrent nightmares and frequently complain they feel physically ill. As these symptoms intensify, children with SAD encounter greater limitations in where they can go and what they can do. Over time children with SAD lose friends and the opportunity for enriching social interaction, they begin to lag behind their peers in academic achievement because of missed school, and they encounter more family discord as their parents struggle with how to comfort their child, but also set limits on their anxious child's desperate attempts to be omnipresent in their lives. It is important to note that separation anxiety is one cause of school refusal behavior. In the past people erroneously referred to this as "school phobia," but it is neither a "fear of school" nor a "phobia." Also, sometimes kids engage in school refusal for reasons unrelated to anxiety, because refusing to go to school provides gratification (e.g., it's a way to get attention, it's a way to be passively resistant to parents, it results in being able to watch TV and play videogames at home).

Social Anxiety Disorder

Social anxiety, formerly called social phobia, in children and adolescents generally is expressed as excessive shyness and overwhelming anxiety in social circumstances where the child has to interact with or perform for children and/or adults that he or she doesn't know. Children and adolescents with social anxieties tend to be quite self-deprecating and anticipate that they will humiliate themselves and be rejected in social circumstances. Consequently, children with social anxiety will do anything to avoid social situations. In school, they tend to be reclusive at recess and at mealtimes in the cafeteria, and when forced into social engagement, such as during group activities or when asked to read or talk in front of the class, they may experience panic (Detweiler, Cromer, & Albano 2014; Higa-McMillan et al., 2014).

The fears characteristic of social anxiety are pervasive. In other words, they are not occasional or temporary, nor do they just show up in some situations and not in others. Moreover, these fears are quite debilitating and impair healthy social, psychological, and educational development. Children with social anxiety become isolated; they lack friends, won't join social groups or sports teams, and feel very lonely. Even at home or while with their family, children with social anxiety tend to avoid any activity that might require social discourse, like picking up a ringing phone, responding to the doorbell, or visiting with extended family members (Detweiler et al., 2014). Similar to children with separation anxiety, children and adolescents with social anxiety frequently develop school refusal. Even when they force themselves to attend school, their anxiety hinders their ability to learn and achieve academically.

Generalized Anxiety Disorder

Unlike separation anxiety and social anxiety, **generalized anxiety disorder (GAD)** doesn't occur in response to any particular situation. As the name implies, it is a more global and indiscriminant type of anxiety. Children and adolescents with GAD worry *a lot*, in ways that are disproportionate and unrealistic, and they have a very hard time controlling or limiting their worries. In particular, children with GAD view life and the world as capricious and expect catastrophic consequences if they don't perform flawlessly. They lack security, are excessively concerned about the future and future events, and fear that their academic, athletic, and/or social accomplishments will be inadequate. These worries are accompanied by physical distress including headaches, stomachaches, fatigue, restlessness, muscle tension and cramps, and disturbed sleep; and by psychological discomforts such as difficulty concentrating and irritability.

In school, children and adolescents with GAD are perfectionists—so much so that they drive themselves and those who care about them crazy with their obsessive need to be faultless. Nothing seems to console or reassure them, not even their own history of superb accomplishment. In spite of receiving frequent excellent grades, they continue to fear failure and are exceedingly self-punitive should they slip below their own standards (Higa-McMillan et al., 2014). Eventually, the worry, the physical ailments, and the perfectionism intensify and handicap the child's ability to perform academically, socially, and psychologically.

What Can Teachers Do to Attend to Children's Anxiety?

Treating child anxieties can be quite complicated and frequently involves attending to maladaptive family dynamics. Many interventions employ behavioral or cognitive-behavioral strategies. As a teacher, you may be asked to cooperate with mental health professionals and parents by helping a child to monitor his or her anxious thoughts and feelings, to dispute his or her irrational beliefs, to accurately evaluate his or her performance, and to reinforce thoughts and behaviors that counter the child's anxiety and help to build adaptive social, psychological, and academic functioning. Also, as a teacher, you might be called upon to examine your own behavior to guard against unwittingly doing things that might be reinforcing the child's anxiety and the maladaptive behaviors that stem from it.

Teachers also find themselves having to contend with the realistic worries and concerns that children and adolescents have when traumatic events strike a community. Schools and educators are invaluable resources in these times. There are strategies that teachers can adopt, and recommend to parents, to help children and adolescents cope with their realistic concerns about the risks and dangers of today's world. First, restoring children's and adolescents' usual school routines following a disaster or crisis can help to reestablish a sense of regularity and predictability. Moreover, it is useful to encourage children and adolescents to reengage in recreational activities (e.g., playing, art, music, sports) because these are natural ways that children and adolescents use to "blow off steam" and cope with their anxieties.

Second, teachers need to assess to what extent they intend to address dramatic current events in their classrooms. Depending on the developmental maturity of a teacher's students, it may be useful to limit students' exposure in the classroom to repetitive news coverage and gory details. When it is appropriate and necessary to discuss anxiety-provoking events in the classroom, teachers need to remember that children and adolescents look to them (and other respected adults) for cues on how to respond to crises, and will respond more positively when their teachers are composed and reassuring. Validate children's and adolescents' feelings (don't dismiss or discount them) and above all respond with empathy. Answer questions simply and honestly, and address concerns in fairly concrete words and examples. But also express a positive and hopeful perspective: when talking about bad times, balance the bad by also talking about the good times you expect in the future and how things can get better. Remind children and adolescents of ways and times in the past when they mastered challenges and worries, and encourage them to think of ways they can help improve the situation.

Lastly, teachers should look for opportunities to reassure children and adolescents during times of crisis. Sometimes it's useful to review and discuss safety plans and contingencies for what a child can do if he or she is at school or home alone when an emergency occurs (e.g., responding to fire drills, knowing a safe place to go to, making sure kids have proper identity and phone numbers of people they can call in an emergency). Happily, most children have instinctive capacities for coping with stress; a little help will foster their natural buoyancy in the face of adversity.

Disruptive Behavior Disorders

Child and adolescent mental health problems are often classified as either internalizing or externalizing (Hayden & Mash, 2014). **Internalizing disorders** are disorders in which symptomatic thoughts, feelings, behaviors, and physical complaints are experienced primarily by the individual and include anxiety disorders and mood disorders. Because they are more privately experienced, other people often do not realize that a child with an internalizing disorder is having troubles until the problems become severe. Disruptive behavior disorders are **externalizing disorders**. Their primary symptoms are expressed in the social environment. Consequently, disruptive behavior disorders are quite public and relatively quickly detected. They are unique in that the symptoms of disruptive behavior disorders are generally more troubling to other people than to the child who has the disorder. The three types of disruptive behavior disorders are attention-deficit/hyperactivity disorder (ADHD), oppositional defiant disorder (ODD), and conduct disorder (CD).

Attention-Deficit/Hyperactivity Disorder

Perhaps no other child and adolescent mental health issue elicits more controversy than the diagnosis of attention-deficit/hyperactivity disorder (ADHD). Debates rage about whether the condition actually exists or whether it's a bias held by a society that is intolerant of people who are different; whether the condition is over- or underdiagnosed and treated (see the Considering Interesting Questions special feature in Box 12.1 for a discussion of this issue); and whether it is appropriate to use medications to control children's activity levels and other behaviors that are more troublesome to others than to the children diagnosed with ADHD. These and other controversies have become complicated and even muddled over the past 50 years as the diagnostic criteria for the condition have changed, as the theories of what causes ADHD have evolved, and as the agent who is being asked to supply the information needed to confirm and validate the diagnosis is chosen.

BOX 12.1. Are Stimulant Medications for Attention-Deficit/Hyperactivity Disorder Overprescribed?

For over a decade, health care professionals and social scientists have been debating the question of whether or not children are overprescribed medications for attention-deficit/hyperactivity disorder (ADHD). On one side of the debate are those who argue that ADHD is underdiagnosed, that too many children who need psychiatric intervention are not getting it, and that stimulant medications for ADHD are safe and effective (Walkup, Stossel, & Rendleman, 2014). In contrast, there are those who argue that health care professionals are too quick to diagnose ADHD (Posner, 2014), that there are many other types of issues that kids suffer from, sometimes temporarily, that have similar symptoms as ADHD, and that easy-to-administer medications are too often prescribed over other types of behavioral and parent training options that are often just as effective.

Some aspects of each position may be correct. On one hand, in some communities in the United States, particularly affluent communities with abundant health care, significant percentages of children are taking stimulant medication as a treatment for ADHD—sometimes far more than even the highest proposed incidence of ADHD (King, Jennings, & Fletcher, 2014). On the other hand, some communities in the United States, most notably poor, rural, and ethnic communities, lack adequate health care for children and families. Frequently, in these communities, stimulant medication to treat ADHD is not available to the children who could benefit from it. The rates of medication use as a treatment for ADHD are affected by a wide range of factors including advertising by drug manufacturers, regional standards of physician practice, and parents' and teachers' values and expectations (Fulton, Scheffler, & Hinshaw, 2015; King et al., 2014). There does not seem to be any question, however, that in recent times, ADHD is being diagnosed at higher rates than historically has been the case and that there has been a dramatic increase in prescriptions of stimulant medications in the United States (Safer, 2016; Visser et al., 2014). Correspondingly, there has been a rapid increase in the nonmedical use of prescribed stimulants by high school and college students (Hamilton, 2009; McCabe & West, 2013; Setlik, Bond, & Ho, 2009; Wang, Cottler, & Striley, 2015)

What is the role of teachers in this important and controversial issue? Clearly, teachers play a vital role in the diagnosis of ADHD. Medical professionals rely on detailed information about children's behavior in the classroom to help them make accurate diagnoses. Teachers are the best source for this information. It is important, however, for teachers to leave the decision to medicate to medical professionals (King et al., 2014). It is also important for educators to advocate for children and to help them receive the health care they need. Moreover, once a child is on medication, teachers need to carefully monitor and observe the child's behavior and possible side effects, provide appropriate instructional support, and be in close communication with parents.

ADHD-like conditions have been documented for over 100 years. There is little doubt that some children manifest considerable difficulties with attention and impulsivity that significantly detract from their ability to learn and develop optimal psychological functioning (Nigg & Barkley, 2014). ADHD has two main classes of symptoms: developmentally inappropriate and sustained inattentiveness and developmentally inappropriate and sustained disinhibition in the form of impulsivity and hyperactivity (American Psychiatric Association, 2013). Inattentiveness may manifest itself in difficulty listening to and following through on instructions, carelessly done and/or incomplete work assignments, forgetfulness, distractibility, and disorganization. Hyperactivity and impulsivity are evident in the ADHD child's fidgeting, difficulty remaining seated, impulsive speech (talking excessively and frequently interrupting others), and inability to wait for his (or more rarely, her) turn. According to the current diagnostic standards (American Psychiatric Association, 2013), these symptoms must be present for at least 6 months to be relatively certain that the symptoms are an enduring pattern of behavior and not the consequence of some transitory developmental or environmental factor. The symptoms must also exist before the age of 12, since the developmental pathology is theoretically present by then and so the ADHD diagnosis does not get confused with other conditions that may occur later in life.

It's important to consider that most children are not as attentive and are more active and impulsive than most adults. The ADHD diagnosis is based on whether the child's inattentiveness and activity level exceed the norm of similarly aged children, not on whether adults feel the child's behavior is more than they can tolerate. The diagnosis can be complicated because children with ADHD don't display their symptoms in some situations. For example, on one hand, during free play or at times when an adult is intensely monitoring or structuring behavior, many children with ADHD will be indistinguishable from non-ADHD children. On the other hand, the symptoms of a child with ADHD may be very noticeable in settings that require people to behave within restricted limits (e.g., while at fine arts performances, at church, or dining in restaurants). Complicating the diagnosis are indications that some symptoms, principally those that have to do with disinhibition, may develop earlier or be noticed sooner than symptoms related to inattentiveness (Nigg & Barkley, 2014). Consequently, some children who have ADHD may be mistaken for children who are oppositional or who have conduct disorder, and then, of course, some children with ADHD do qualify for these diagnoses.

Estimates of the prevalence rate for ADHD vary dramatically because different researchers use different diagnostic criteria and different sampling techniques, sample different populations and age groups, and use reports from different observers. The best guess is that ADHD occurs in about 4% of the population, although recent research suggests the incidence may be as low as 2% and is probably two times more common in boys (Nigg & Barkley, 2014). ADHD has been found across socioeconomic status (SES) populations and cultural groups, although people of different cultures and nationalities are probably more or less tolerant of some ADHD symptoms and interpret the symptom criteria differently (Nigg & Barkley, 2014).

Barkley (Nigg & Barkley, 2014) has advanced a reconceptualization of what ADHD entails that theoretically explains the disparate symptoms seen in children with ADHD. Barkley's theory deemphasizes the role previously assigned to attention in describing the disorder and instead focuses on deficits in metacognitive and neurological executive functions that regulate self-control (see also Chapter 4). Briefly, Barkley hypothesizes that deficits in behavioral inhibition hinder the development of nonverbal working memory and the ability to use past experience to inform current behavior, the internalization of speech and hence verbal working memory, the use of language to self-regulate emotion and motivation, and the ability to mentally manipulate concepts that aid in organization and planning. These impairments, in turn, result in reduced motor control and reduced ability to sustain goal-directed activity.

As our theoretical and empirical understanding of ADHD advances, research on the etiology or cause of ADHD is also improving. The evidence to date suggests that ADHD develops as a consequence of neurological dysfunction that comes about largely hereditarily, but may also occur because of prenatal complications, exposure to environmental toxins, or some other disease process (Nigg & Barkley, 2014). At one time, people thought that children would outgrow or compensate for these neurological failings, but current research suggests that the majority of children with ADHD continue to be symptomatic in adolescence and a substantial proportion continue to manifest symptoms into adulthood (Nigg & Barkley, 2014). Even when specific ADHD symptoms abate as a child develops, many of the sequelae of ADHD persist, including poorer academic and vocational achievement, social difficulties, parental conflict, and poorer physical health.

Early-Onset Conduct Disorder and Oppositional Defiant Disorder

Conduct disorder (CD) is defined as a persistent pattern of unacceptable social behavior that violates the rights of others and basic societal norms and rules. Children with conduct disorder are not simply naughty or troublesome; they are children who consistently commit delinquent acts. In many respects, they are incorrigible and often a menace to other children and adults. The symptoms that characterize CD vary depending on the age of the child. Elementary school-age children with CD are constantly disobedient and defiant; they may lie and steal, and they may be especially aggressive, bullying other children and tormenting animals. Older children and adolescents with conduct disorder will exhibit these behaviors in addition to engaging in truancy, running away from home, destruction of property, substance abuse, and inappropriate sexual behavior. Many children may engage in some of these behaviors from time to time, but they will only warrant a diagnosis of CD if they *repeatedly* engage in these behaviors for longer than 6 months.

There are subtypes of CD; for example, one type begins in adolescence, and the second type begins prior to age 10. Developmental psychopathologists suspect that the two types of CD often have different etiologies and outcomes (Kimonis, Frick, & McMahon, 2014). It is hard to pin down exactly how many children have CD, in part because researchers from different disciplines use different definitions and interpret the criteria for CD differently. However, prior to puberty, 2 to 16% of children and adolescents have significant conduct problems (Kimonis et al., 2014). More boys than girls are diagnosed with CD, although we are only beginning to learn about CD in girls (Klostermann, Connell, & Stormshak, 2014).

The symptoms of **oppositional defiant disorder (ODD)** are less severe than those of CD, though just as pervasive. The disobedience that characterizes ODD is exhibited in the form of uncooperativeness, argumentativeness, disrespect, and/or insolence toward authority, and a generally negative mood (e.g., frequently angry, easily annoyed). Children with ODD have difficulty controlling their temper, frequently become enraged, and sometimes tantrum wildly. Other children sometimes avoid children with ODD because they perceive them as difficult to get along with, stubborn, and mean. Once again, these symptoms must be consistently present for more than 6 months to warrant this diagnosis. Because it is quite common for *some* children to have *some* of these symptoms *some* of the time, the symptoms must be far in excess of what similarly aged children exhibit, and not just attributable to a normal developmental phase like the "terrible twos" or adolescent "rebellion" and autonomy seeking.

Some developmental psychopathologists suspect that ODD is a mild variant or an incipient form of CD since many children with CD previously qualified for a diagnosis of ODD (Kimonis et al., 2014). However, not all children with ODD develop CD. Also, keep in mind that many children with ODD and CD also have other mental health conditions and qualify for ADHD, learning disability, mood disorder, anxiety disorder, and substance abuse disorder diagnoses (Kimonis et al., 2014).

A child can acquire or develop ODD or CD in a variety of ways. Some children, particularly those with early onset of these disorders, may be genetically or temperamentally inclined toward behavioral problems. For others, it's the consequence of exposure to familial or community risk factors like poverty; parental inadequacies due to criminality or parental mental illness; abusive, critical, hostile, and/or inconsistent parenting; and/or antisocial gang or peer influence. Regardless of the cause, untreated ODD and CD can have serious negative lifetime consequences, including poor academic and vocational achievement, rejection by peers, addictions, depression, and suicide (Kimonis et al., 2014).

What Can Teachers Do to Assess and Intervene for Disruptive Behavior Disorders?

A proper assessment and intervention plan for disruptive behavior disorders will be multimodal in nature. Thus, the evaluator will use a variety of assessment tools and seek input from several sources familiar with the child, including the child, his or her parent, and his or her teacher(s). Teachers are typically interviewed by evaluators and asked to complete some rating scales. The evaluator may ask to come to the classroom to observe the targeted child and may ask to see examples of the child's work. The evaluator typically asks teachers to provide examples of the child's problem behavior and the context in which it occurs, what precedes the problem behavior, how often it happens, and what the teacher has done in response to the child's behavior.

When a child is diagnosed with a disruptive behavior disorder, teachers have an important role in implementing the treatment plan. One effective means of treating the symptoms of ADHD is the use of stimulant medications. Still, some children do not respond favorably to stimulant medications, and for some children with ADHD, medications are not enough to change some of the academic and social consequences of the syndrome. For children who have just ODD/CD, there are few, if any, pharmacological options. Consequently, teachers are called upon to cooperate with the child's parents and other treatment team members in implementing a behavioral intervention. A good behavioral intervention will take a positive approach that emphasizes building the child's academic and social competence by recognizing and praising the child when target behaviors are generated. A number of techniques may be employed, such as a token reinforcement system that prescribes how to monitor and respond to targeted competencies as well as maladaptive behaviors (see also Chapter 5), frequent teaching and review of classroom rules and expectations, and strategy training, in addition to developing individualized instructional strategies (Christopherson & Mortweet, 2001; DuPaul & Stoner, 2015; Fonagy, Target, Cottrell, Phillips, & Kurtz, 2002). Two books written for parents of children with ADHD and ODD that teachers may find useful themselves or may want to recommend to parents are Barkley (2013) and Barkley and Benton (2013), respectively.

Finally, as outlined in Chapter 9, teachers can employ instructional practices that are supportive of students with behavior disorders such as ADHD (McConnell, Ryser, & Higgins, 2000; Rief, 2003) that are also effective with all students. These practices include providing clear, simple directions, limiting distractions, providing frequent breaks (particularly breaks allowing physical outlets), minimizing transition time, and providing structure for presented content (graphic organizers, visual information, etc.). Educators looking for in-depth discussion of assessment and intervention with students with disruptive behavior disorders should consult Barkley (2013) and/or Barkley and Robin (2013) regarding ODD/CD and DuPaul and Stoner (2015).

Psychological Problems That Are Prevalent during Adolescence

Adolescence has been characterized as a period of storm and stress. Adolescents frequently are depicted as addled by hormones, fickle, difficult to get along with, and rebellious. This portrayal is more of a reflection of the ambivalence and intimidation adults feel about youth than a reality. If we stop to think about it (or just pay attention to the news), adults frequently do the very same things they complain about in regard to adolescents (e.g., risk taking, substance use, moodiness). However, most adolescents do not experience tumultuous psychological upheaval, disruptive identity crisis, or alienation and detachment from their parents and family (see Chapters 5 and 10). Most adolescents actually find considerable identity and security through their involvements with their families. It does appear that adolescents spend less time engaged in daily family routines, but not because they are repelled by processes internal to the family or adolescent, but because of pulls or incentives from the external social environment (e.g., sports, jobs). As a rule of thumb, conflict with parents reaches its height in early adolescence and typically involves struggles around minor autonomy issues and not about core substantive values. Most older adolescents and young adults report feeling warmth and mutual respect for their parents and recognize they bear some responsibility for family interactions.

Still, it is obvious that adolescents go through fairly major developmental transitions, including physiological, neurological, cognitive, and social changes. These changes, along with less than optimal social environmental conditions, create risks for adolescent mental health problems. For example, early sexual maturation for girls is sometimes linked with poorer body image, dieting, ridicule from less mature peers, and associating with older adolescents and age-inappropriate activities that they are not mentally or emotionally mature enough to handle, such as experimenting with drugs or sexual encounters (see also Chapter 2). Adolescents may suffer from the psychological problems already discussed in this chapter, or they may qualify for any number of other psychological diagnoses that are used in identifying adult psychopathology. It is beyond the scope of this chapter to describe all the possible psychological maladies that can befall adolescents; instead, the focus here will be on two common and critical concerns: adolescent substance abuse and depression.

Adolescent Substance Misuse

Adolescents with substance misuse problems are diagnosed using the same criteria that are used for adults. Some manifestations of substance use lead to addiction and physiological dependence characterized by maladaptive substance use despite experiencing physiological symptoms (e.g., developing tolerance, taking larger amounts, or withdrawal symptoms) and psychological problems (e.g., drug use interfering with obligations at home, work, or school; using the substance when it is hazardous or dangerous to do so) during the previous year (American Psychiatric Association, 2013). Milder forms of substance use disorder are diagnosed when an individual's drug use causes social and psychological consequences during the previous year—notably, failing to meet work, school, or family obligations; using drugs when it is physically hazardous to do so; encountering legal problems related to substance use; and continuing to use the substance despite its deleterious impact on interpersonal relationships. Substance use is exceedingly common in adolescents, and the statistics regarding adolescent substance misuse are (or at least should be) incredibly alarming. Estimates from national surveys (Johnston, O'Malley, Miech, Bachman, & Schulenberg, 2017; Kann et al., 2016), suggest that more than half of high school seniors have used an illegal drug during their lifetime and over 70% of high school seniors have drunk alcohol. Many of these youths are experiencing significant problems with substance use, with as many as 20% admitting to having been drunk or high at school. Nearly half of high school seniors and almost 10% of eighth graders admit they have been drunk at least once in their lifetime, and 10% at least once in the 30-days prior to being surveyed. The statistics from these surveys regarding illicit drug use (i.e., marijuana, amphetamines and methamphetamines, tranquilizers, hallucinogens, narcotics, cocaine and crack, and club drugs like Rohypnol, GHB, and ketamine) are similarly grim (Chassin et al., 2014; Johnston et al., 2017; Kann et al., 2016; National Center on Addiction and Substance Abuse, 2012).

The good news is that use of illicit drugs by youth in the United States in the past 30–40 years has declined somewhat. However, if only a fraction of adolescents and young adults continue their substance use and abuse into adulthood, our society could be facing a serious public health problem. Underage drinking costs society tens of billions of dollars, including substance abuse treatment, prevention, other health care costs, and the costs of crime.

What leads adolescents to engage in substance misuse? There are no simple answers to this question. Undoubtedly, many different paths may lead an adolescent to substance abuse, depending on the adolescent's age at onset, gender, family environment, and cultural and socioeconomic background (Chassin et al., 2014). Family factors seem to play a large role, through both genetic inheritance and socialization. Prenatal and childhood exposure to drugs, particularly alcohol and nicotine, may predispose an individual to their use. Children with difficult temperaments, who are inclined to behavioral undercontrol, especially when coupled with inadequate parenting, are at greater risk for developing substance use disorders. Poor academic achievement and estrangement from the positive socializing influences of school can exacerbate an inclination toward substance misuse. Regardless of the cause, the effects of adolescent substance abuse are potentially profound. Adolescent substance abusers generally achieve less academically and vocationally. They tend to be more alienated from family and prosocial peers, which leads to greater family conflict, more associations with deviant peers, and a tendency to engage in delinquency. Lastly, and perhaps obviously, adolescents who engage in substance misuse are at greater risk for developing substance addictions.

Mood Disorders

Adolescent Depression

Some mood disorders have serious and unpleasant symptoms that come on quickly, whereas others have less serious symptoms that develop gradually but endure for a long time. Some types of mood disorders are "bipolar," which means that the depressed persons have had some variation in their mood; sometimes they feel depressed, and at least once, and maybe repeatedly, they experienced an episode of mania in which they became uncontrollably excited. In recent years, there has been a flurry of interest in bipolar disorders, and controversy has arisen regarding the extent to which children and adolescents suffer from them. Bipolar disorders probably begin during childhood and adolescence, but it can be very difficult to confirm the diagnosis and distinguish it from other more common juvenile disorders, and it is probably relatively uncommon (perhaps a 1% prevalence rate; Youngstrom & Algorta, 2014). Consequently, this discussion focuses on the more common "unipolar" depressions, of which there are two types: the more severe major depressive disorder and the more chronic persistent depressive disorder (formerly called dysthmic disorder).

The symptoms of depression may be emotional, behavioral/physiological, or cognitive. The emotional symptoms of depression comprise feeling sad or dysphoric, anhedonia (loss of interest or pleasure in usual activities), apathy, a sense of hopelessness, and feelings of worthlessness. Behavioral/physiological symptoms include sleep disturbance (i.e., insomnia or sleeping too much), anxiety, and agitation or alternatively lethargy and fatigue, appetite changes that result in rapid weight gain or weight loss, and neglect of hygiene and appearance. In addition, depression also affects people's cognitive abilities. People with depression may experience diminished ability to think or concentrate; they may be overly pessimistic, excessively guilty, and self-denigrating; they may ruminate over negative events and consider suicide or actually attempt suicide; and when depression is exceedingly severe, they may experience delusions and hallucinations. A diagnosis of major depression is considered when a person feels deep and constant dysphoria in addition to experiencing intense distress from several of the more serious symptoms (especially the behavioral/physiological) for more than two weeks. Persistent depressive disorder is the more appropriate diagnosis when a child or adolescent experiences only one or two of these symptoms and they don't cause quite as much distress, although they are chronic and never diminish much over the course of one year. The kinds of symptoms of depression that children and adolescents have tend to be different, or are at least expressed differently, than the symptoms adults complain about (Fonagy et al., 2002; Hammen, Rudolph, & Abaied, 2014). Children tend to experience fewer behavioral/physiological symptoms of depression; they are unlikely to say they feel hopeless or melancholy and are more inclined to be irritable and to express somatic complaints (e.g., stomachache, headache). Adolescents, particularly older adolescents, are likely to have symptoms that are more like those of adults, although they, too, are more likely to be irritable and aggressive, and to complain about boredom.

Full-blown diagnosable depression is relatively infrequent in children—perhaps less than a 3% prevalence rate. However, the prevalence of depression in adolescents is similar to what is found in adults; about 8 to 13% (depending on the survey and the severity of the symptoms asked about) of adolescents have had a diagnosable depression, and these rates seem to be increasing (Hammen et al., 2014). Moreover, large proportions of adolescents (more than 20%, maybe as many as 35–40%) have experienced a troublesome depressed mood that is "subclinical" or, in other words, a mood that doesn't last long enough or that's not quite serious enough to be formally diagnosable as depression (Hammen et al., 2014).

Depression in children and adolescents is an internalizing disorder; the symptoms are somewhat self-contained, particularly compared to the disruptive behavior disorders. As a result, child and adolescent depression is not always recognized and treated. To complicate matters even more, between 40 and 70% of children and adolescents with depression also have some other diagnosable psychological problem, especially anxiety, and lots of times ADHD, substance use disorders, or eating disorders (Hammen et al., 2014). Sometimes these other disorders get attention, but the underlying depression is missed.

Depression can have very negative consequences for child and adolescent development. Untreated depression can last for years, and even milder manifestations of depression can result in considerable deterioration in adolescent, academic achievement, social development, and psychological adjustment. For example, over 40% of high school students consider engaging in nonsuicidal self-harm, and as many as 12% have seriously considered suicide (some estimates are as high as 38%; Cha & Nock, 2014). Children and adolescents who develop depression are much more likely to experience mood disorders in adulthood, and as many as 7% of adolescents who develop major depression commit suicide in adulthood. Children and adolescents who receive proper treatment often recover from depression, but unfortunately many relapse and have repeated bouts of the disorder.

Many things can cause depression in children and adolescents. Evidence exists that a predisposition for mood disorders can be genetically inherited, particularly the bipolar disorders. Moreover, exposure to unremitting anxiety and/or chronic subclinical depression can ultimately lead to physiological and neurological changes that result in mood disorders. Many, perhaps most, adolescents fall victim to depression through exposure to social and psychological stressors such as traumatic events; poor family relationships (e.g., parental unavailability, disturbed parent–child interactions, family and marital violence); poor, sometimes abusive, peer relationships; and self- or other-imposed pressures to achieve in academics, athletics, or some other activity.

Adolescent Suicide

Suicide is rather rare among children under age 12, but it is the third leading cause of death among adolescents and young adults. Estimates suggest that between 8 and 12 of every 100,000 adolescents (depending on the age range used) commits suicide (American Association of Suicidology, 2015; Cha & Nock, 2014). Many believe that this is probably an underestimate; that perhaps three times as many adolescent deaths are a consequence of self-destructive behavior. Suicide is more common in adolescent boys than girls and more prevalent, or increasing in prevalence, among some populations, particularly gay, lesbian, and bisexual youth, black males, and some American Indian tribes.

What Can Teachers Do to Support and Assist Troubled Adolescents?

The important message for educators who work with adolescents is that a sizeable proportion of the students they interact with have serious psychological problems. As many as 20–30% are using drugs and/or alcohol on a fairly regular basis. For many of these students, their substance use is not just "normative" drug exploration; it is debilitating abuse that is hindering their development and their capacity to learn and be fully engaged in the academic process. As many as 20% of middle and high school students are clinically depressed, and many middle and high school students are contemplating suicide.

Treatment for these conditions is quite complicated and beyond the scope of this chapter. Many of these adolescents need medical attention (e.g., detox, medication) and therapy delivered by skilled specialists in adolescent psychology, family dynamics, and substance abuse. Still, it is a giant misconception for teachers to assume there is nothing they can do to address the mental health concerns of adolescents. The worst thing teachers (and other adults for that matter) can do is try to ignore these problems.

To begin with, teachers need to be caring observers of adolescents and know the warning signs of substance abuse, mood disorder, and possible suicidal risk. See the Applying Developmental Theory to Educational Contexts special feature (Box 12.2). Second, teachers should take action when they observe these warning signs. Many adolescents are quite naïve about mental health issues and may not recognize their troubles as mental health concerns. Moreover, adolescents often associate a great stigma with talking to a counselor; it suggests they might be crazy or weak. So, troubled adolescents frequently don't initiate help-seeking behavior. If a teacher or counselor approaches them privately, however, they are more apt to talk about their problems and concerns. If you don't feel comfortable or qualified to talk with a troubled student, alert another teacher, counselor, or school administrator about the problem. Lastly, be bold and be active in the lives of adolescents. Encourage adolescents to develop strong bonds to their school, to be polite and caring to one another, and to develop prosocial and wholesome friendships. Talk with them about drug abuse and encourage abstinence from alcohol and other substance use. Teach them how to be assertive in declining drug use should their peers offer it. Help adolescents develop healthy habits, especially regular exercise, good nutrition, and getting sufficient sleep.

Teachers play an important role in the lives of the children and adolescents they educate. Their access to children and adolescents and their knowledge about human development put them in an excellent position to spot troubled children and adolescents and to refer them to the mental health services they need. The more teachers know, the more they can get involved; so study children and the troubles they can encounter, stay alert, and get involved. Sure you may make mistakes, but you might also make a significant difference in the life of a student.

BOX 12.2. The Role of Teachers Working with Students at Risk for Suicide and Nonsuicidal Self-Injury

Death by suicide is tragic no matter what the age of the victim, but it seems even more heart-breaking when the victim is lost in the full bloom of youth. While the statistics vary from year to year, we know that suicide is one of the leading causes of death for adolescents (some sources say the second leading cause, others the third), that suicide rates among children and adolescents are increasing, and that we may be underestimating the rate of suicide among youth as some deaths are registered as accidental rather than self-inflicted (Miller & Eckert, 2009). Statistics gathered over the past several years indicate that about 15% of adolescents have seriously considered death by suicide, a substantial portion of these youth make an actual plan for how they would carry out the act of suicide, and about 7 or 8% of youth actually make a suicide attempt.

Even more prevalent is the phenomenon of nonsuicidal self-injury (NSSI). NSSI is the act of inflicting serious bodily harm to oneself without the intention of committing suicide. As many as 15–25% of adolescents have engaged in NSSI (Barrocas, Giletta, Hankin, Prinstein, & Abela, 2015; Klonsky, Glenn, Styer, Olino, & Washburn, 2015). It tends to begin in early adolescence and continues into the middle adolescent years, and sometimes into adult-hood. Although adolescents engaging in NSSI deny their self-harming behavior is suicidal, it often leads to or is associated with suicidal thoughts and behaviors. Most adolescents who engage in NSSI say they are doing it because it helps them regulate negative emo-tions or gain some relief from psychological distress. Sometimes they do it as a form of self-punishment, sometimes they do it at the urging of peers or to fit in with their friends, and sometimes they do it as a way to let others know how bad they feel.

Given the prevalence of suicidal thoughts and behavior and NSSI, the vast majority of educators will have contact with a student who is actively suicidal and/or self-harming. Because educators have so much contact with children and adolescents, they may be in the best position to observe the warning signs of suicidal risk and self-harm. However, although some states require educators to have some training about suicide, most do not, and most teachers feel unprepared for detecting and intervening with a suicidal or self-harming stu-dent (Groschwitz, Munz, Straub, Bohnacker, & Plener, 2017; Martin, Richardson, Bergen, Roeger, & Allison, 2005). In fact, it can be difficult to distinguish more normative adolescent angst from NSSI and true suicidal risk. However, most adolescents give some sort of warn-ing signs that they are considering suicide. The following are some general guidelines for educators:

- Teachers should take all suicide-related comments seriously, whether they are direct statements about suicide or indirect allusions to being dead or perceiving no purpose in life and living. Sometimes students' writing or artwork will have references to death or suicide.

- Teachers should be particularly alert to the possibility of suicide and self-harm with students who have a known psychopathology or who have made previous suicide attempts.

- Students who are expressing intense negative emotions such as rage, depression, and/or intense uncontrollable anxiety, particularly when they feel they cannot get any relief from these feeling or escape the source of what is causing them, are often at greater risk.

- An adolescent who is withdrawing from friends, family, and school or who is making "final arrangements" by giving away prized possessions, making a last testament, or saying goodbyes to people are cause for immediate concern.

(continued)

- Teachers should be alert to any obvious changes in an adolescent's engagement in high-risk activities or substance abuse, which can be an indirect means of suicide.

- Teachers should be concerned about students who have suffered a recent loss or parental divorce, or who have gotten in serious trouble.

One terrible myth about suicide is that asking a person to talk about his or her suicidal feelings might cause that person to do it. Nothing could be further from the truth. Adolescents who are contemplating death by suicide need to talk about their feelings and receive empathy. Adolescents are often very sensitive about revealing their feelings of despair and feel ashamed and humiliated by these feelings, so it is very important for a teacher to respond with acceptance and kindness should a student express suicidal or self-harming thoughts. Lastly, although students who confide in you about their self-harming thoughts and behaviors may ask you to keep this information private, you should never do so. It is vitally important to make sure the student gets the professional help he or she needs. Therefore, even though it may momentarily irritate the student, it is imperative to bring the student's problems to the attention of school counselors, administrators, and probably the student's parents.

Chapter Summary and Evaluation

When trying to assess student behavior, teachers and educators need to be aware of both the quantity and quality of the behavior as well as the context in which the behavior occurs. Nonetheless, educators will likely have contact with students suffering from a variety of mental health problems. Some of these problems, neurodevelopmental disorders, in particular, typically are detected in early childhood. Children with autism exhibit severe deficits in social interaction, greatly impaired communication, and generally poor intellectual functioning. Similar to children with autism, children with Asperger syndrome display social deficits but do not exhibit the same level of impairment in language and intellectual functioning.

Other mental health issues often do not emerge until the elementary school years. Some children experience great difficulties with anxiety disorders such as separation anxiety disorder, social anxiety, and generalized anxiety disorder. Children with attention-deficit/hyperactivity disorder exhibit difficulty paying attention as well as hyperactivity and impulsivity. Children with oppositional defiant or conduct disorders repeatedly engage in unacceptable social behavior.

Still other mental health problems, such as substance abuse, depression, and suicide, are more typically encountered in adolescents than in younger children. These problems are by no means rare, with substantial percentages of high school students reporting substance abuse, depression, and consideration of suicide.

Nature and Nurture

Some of the mental disorders described in this chapter have a genetic or biologically based etiology. For example, autism, Asperger syndrome, and nonverbal learning disorders have some biological underpinnings, most likely due to differences in brain development. Mood disorders have been linked with maladaptive concentrations of neurotransmitters, and bipolar disorder seems to have a strong hereditability quotient. Moreover, children with robust temperaments, which is also most likely biologically determined, are less vulnerable to developing some of the mental health problems described in this chapter.

However, educators should always consider the context in which the problem behavior occurs. It is important to remember that many situations are unsettling for children and adolescents, often more so than for adults. Factors beyond the control of children and adolescents can place situational stress on children and adolescents which, in turn, profoundly affects their mental health. These include family disruption and divorce, child abuse, and alcoholism or mental health problems within the family.

REVIEW OF KEY TERMS

Asperger syndrome Children with Asperger syndrome, who are often average or above average in intellectual abilities, exhibit a variety of symptoms, including awkwardness in social interactions and complex and serious difficulties in learning.

attention-deficit/hyperactivity disorder (ADHD) Students with ADHD exhibit a variety of symptoms including inattentiveness, distractibility, hyperactivity, and impulsivity.

autism A mental disorder characterized by a variety of symptoms including deficits in social interaction, impairments in communications, and a limited repertoire of activity and interests.

conduct disorder (CD) A persistent pattern of unacceptable behavior that violates basic social norms.

externalizing disorders Childhood disorders such as ADHD or Oppositional Defiant disorder in which the symptoms of the disorder are disruptive to other people, often more so than to the person with the disorder.

generalized anxiety disorder (GAD) Children with GAD express a global and indiscriminant type of anxiety.

internalizing disorders Childhood disorders in which the symptoms are primarily experienced by the person with the disorder.

oppositional defiant disorder (ODD) Children with ODD are argumentative, disrespectful, and express generally negative moods, including tantrums. These patterns of behavior, although less extreme than those exhibited by children with conduct disorder, persist for more than 6 months.

separation anxiety disorder (SAD) Children with SAD express extreme anxiety and agitation when separated or anticipating separation from attachment figures.

CHAPTER 13

Integrative Review of Major Concepts

Anyone who writes a textbook on human development faces a dilemma from the outset. Development can be written about from either a chronological or a topical perspective. In a chronological approach, each chapter would focus on a specific period of development (e.g., infancy, early childhood, middle childhood, and adolescence). This text used a more topical approach in that each chapter focused on some important aspect of development, such as biological development, cognitive development, language development, motivation, and so on. Because of the sheer amount of information and the complexity of the ideas represented, we believed it was best to take the topical approach to address each important aspect of development in turn. A chronological overview, however, does have merits. So, in this review chapter, we put some of the Big Ideas together in a brief chronological overview of development. After this chronological review of many of the concepts covered in this book, we review the mechanisms of development, especially as they determine individual differences within developmental levels. If you do not understand any of the points made in this review chapter, you may find it helpful to reread relevant portions of the earlier chapters.

The Major Periods of Development

Because this text focused on the developmental ideas that would be most important to future educators, developmental concepts particularly significant in childhood and adolescence were emphasized in comparison to those key to infancy and adulthood.

Prenatal Development

When an egg and sperm unite, a unique combination of DNA is created, with half of the DNA coming from the egg and half from the sperm. In a very real sense, this combination of DNA goes far in determining development. Most critically, it specifies that the organism that is beginning with this single cell is decidedly human. The billions and billions of developments that occur for all humans are specified by this DNA. Typically, however, educators are not interested in DNA's contribution to the *common* developments that define humans as much as they are interested in the role of DNA in determining *differences* between humans. Certainly one of the major differences between humans is determined by the sex chromosomes. Differences between humans are determined by both biology and environment.

The single cell that is the merger of egg and sperm quickly divides and becomes multiple cells, with the cellular origins of all major organ systems occurring in the first 3 months of the prenatal period. Because so many systems begin during this first trimester, this is a period of time that is especially susceptible to the potential negative effects of teratogens. That is, various environmental agents (e.g., chemicals, radiation) and disease can affect development at the cellular level at this stage in ways that may have profound negative effects.

The cellular beginnings of organ systems are followed by rapid development of the organs themselves through cell division and then organ growth. Normal growth during the prenatal period is affected by factors such as the nutrition and health of the mother. Normal growth and development is a fragile commodity. It is for this reason that there is so much emphasis on prenatal care and on the education of adolescent girls about responsible lifestyles during pregnancy. For example, as harmful as drug intake, smoking, or alcohol abuse is to any female teenager, such abuses have much greater potential for negative impact on her developing fetus.

Much has been learned about prenatal development, and especially about brain development, in recent decades. Since we suspect that educators will eventually make stronger connections to this expanding literature on prenatal development than they do currently, textbooks on development specialized for educators will eventually include even more information about development before birth.

Infancy

The physical development of the brain continues following birth, although no new brain cells are formed after birth. Indeed, much of brain growth is accomplished by brain cell loss, that is, by elimination of excess capacity.

The concept of "critical or sensitive period" has become better understood in recent decades. It is now clear that there are experience-expectant brain cells that require stimulation of a particular type at a particular point in development if they are to function normally for the rest of life. Perceptual development, in particular, has been shown to depend very much on appropriate sensory stimulation during infancy. If the needed stimulation does not occur, the capacity is lost forever.

Major areas of the brain become functional as the brain increases in weight and size, with discernible changes in behavior as a function of such brain maturation. For example, the frontal lobe develops a great deal in the first year of life, which is associated with increases in self-regulation skills as well as the development of understandings such as object permanence.

During infancy and throughout life, brain growth tends to occur in spurts, which translates into discontinuous growth of thinking abilities and emotions. Brain growth is especially rapid during infancy, although the brain will continue to increase in size and weight into adolescence. The efficiency of the central nervous system increases because of development of myelin sheathing, the fatty tissue that insulates nerve cells, and thereby allows faster and more certain transmission of nerve impulses.

Piaget felt that thinking as an internal activity hardly existed during early infancy. That is, he described infants' reactions to their environment as much more *reflexive* than *reflective*. The beginnings of cognition, however, develop during the first 2 years of life, during what Piaget termed the "sensorimotor stage." Infants gradually develop the understanding that objects continue to exist even when they are out of sight (i.e., object permanence). Moreover, symbolic functioning emerges (i.e., the beginnings of language) by the end of the sensorimotor period.

Nonetheless, babies communicate long before they have language. From their earliest days, babies cry differently depending on their need. For example, sudden fright elicits a different cry than slight physical discomfort. Babies also smile differentially, often smiling in reaction to the presence of another human. Babies are biased to attend to social stimuli—for example, to look at perceptual displays that resemble faces and to listen to high-pitched voices, such as mother's voice.

Cognitive scientists have focused on several specific communicative developments that underpin language development. Thus, it is now known that during the first year of life infants come to discriminate speech sounds in the surrounding sound environment from other sounds. In particular, they learn to discriminate the phonemes in their family's and community's language from other sounds. Infants also learn to discriminate the rhythm of language from other rhythms. As speech perception increases, the production of sounds consistent with the surrounding language also increases. Thus, babbling during the first year is increasingly filled with sounds that are characteristic of the language the child hears daily. During the second year of life, most children will have entered the single-word stage, with their single-word utterances serving a variety of functions. For example, the utterance "Mommy" can mean "Mommy come here," "Don't do that, Mommy," or "I prefer Mommy." The exact meaning sometimes must be inferred from context clues and voice intonation.

That infant utterances can express complicated meanings is consistent with the conclusion that by the end of infancy thought is complex. One important discovery is that infant thinking is schematic. Thus, the 2-year-old has substantial understanding about the events and settings she or he has experienced frequently, with these schematic representations providing a basis for expectations about the present. For example, many 2-year-olds in the United States and elsewhere know exactly what to expect from a visit to McDonald's. That children's schematic knowledge is so much more complex than their language is consistent with one of Vygotsky's key points: thought and language emerge separately. While in adulthood thought very much depends on language, thought and language are not so intimately connected during infancy.

Schematic knowledge develops largely because of social interactions, and, as it does, it affects future social interactions. Thus, a mother who is consistently responsive to her child affects the child's representation of the mother–infant relationship and the infant's expectations about how his or her mother will react in the future. An infant who has experienced a responsive mother feels secure in her presence, with this security permitting the child to explore the world beyond mom, as long as mother is there as a secure base to which the child can look for assistance if needed. Such secure relations with a parent (i.e., a secure attachment) permit the child to explore comfortably, promoting the development of a healthy self-concept. The development of a secure attachment during the first year of life fosters feelings in the child that she or he is valuable and self-reliant. In contrast, the lack of a secure relationship with an adult can translate into an emerging self-concept that is negative, one filled with perceptions of being unworthy and incompetent.

The first attachment relationship emerges in the first year and continues to develop during the second year, with parents making increasing self-control demands on children. In the early 20th century, Freud characterized the conflicts surrounding initial attachments and the development of self-control as the oral and anal conflict stages. At midcentury, Erikson reconceived these developments, respectively, as conflicts between trust versus mistrust and autonomy versus shame and doubt. At the end of the 20th century, researchers were digging deeper, attempting to establish the neural and cognitive underpinnings of social relationships between parents and children, as well as between children and children. Although attention to parent–child interactions traditionally have dominated work on the development of social competence, increasing attention is being paid to infant relationships with other children, since responsiveness to other infants increases substantially during the first 2 years of life.

In summary, by the end of infancy, if all has gone well, the child has a larger and more capable brain than she or he possessed at birth. Perceptual, linguistic, conceptual, and social skills have developed substantially. These various systems do not develop in isolation but rather in relation to one another. For example, the development of some types of perceptual skills (e.g., phoneme perception) affects language development, and the development of particular conceptual understandings (e.g., object permanence) affects social relations (e.g., attachment). Moreover, although biological development is certainly salient during this period of life, biological development very much depends on appropriate environmental stimulation during the first 2 years of life. Thus, an essential topic of research is the exploration of effective ways to intervene during the early years of life to ensure optimal development.

Early Childhood

Brain growth continues during the preschool years. Myelination of the nervous system also increases, accounting in part for the increases in speed of information processing between 2 and 5 years of age. It is not easy to separate out the contributions of neural development versus experience in cognitive development, however. For example, traditionally, the increases in short-term or working memory that occur during early childhood and continue until adolescence have been conceived as reflecting neurological development. We have come to realize, however, that there are alternative explanations of such developments. For example, the child's developing knowledge base permits the young thinker to create bigger and bigger chunks of information, so that both 3-year-olds and 15-year-olds might have 5 ± 2 short-term memory slots, but each slot holds more in the case of the older compared to the younger child. Thus, it may be easy for someone to remember the number sequence 23056735481629876521546378 because the sequence can be coded as a familiar identification number (230567354), a relative's phone number (8162987652), and a library account number (15463785). Those of you who do not have these chunks in long-term memory might have more trouble with the sequence since it should involve many more than the 5 ± 2 chunks of information that you can hold in short-term memory. The point to emphasize is that even though it is known that the central nervous system continues to develop during the preschool years, researchers are continuing their efforts to sort out acquisitions that reflect neurological development versus other developments.

The thinking of preschoolers has received a great deal of attention from child development researchers, largely because of the strong claims made by Jean Piaget that early childhood is a different stage of development than middle childhood as defined by differences in the quality of thought possible. Although researchers have confirmed that, consistent with Piaget's concept of the preoperational stage, preschoolers perform less well than older children on conservation and classification tasks, they have also discovered that preschoolers sometimes do conserve and classify. Evidence that preschoolers can learn to conserve and classify greatly challenged Piaget's characterization of the preschool years as a period of time when thinking is completely different from thinking later in childhood.

Piaget's characterization of preschooler thought as egocentric (i.e., intuitive, strongly influenced by perception) also has given way to more complex conceptions of children's thinking. For example, preschoolers can exhibit considerable understanding of other people—their perceptions, desires, beliefs, and emotions; that is, they are developing a theory of mind. During the 1960s, when Piagetian theory about children's thinking prevailed, a conception of preschoolers as nonstrategic relative to older children was given as one more example of preschoolers' cognitive inadequacies. In contrast, it is now understood that preschoolers can be strategic, especially when they are in familiar situations doing familiar tasks. Thus, developmental shifts in thinking can be understood better as *expansion of abilities* rather than as *qualitatively different abilities* at different times in life. Preschoolers' thinking involves strategies, declarative knowledge, metacognition, and motivational beliefs, just as the thinking of elementary-grade children is an articulation of strategies, knowledge, metacognition, and motivations. For example, gender schemas (i.e., knowledge of the complex strategies, knowledge, and motivations that define femaleness and maleness) have their origins in the preschool years. These schemas play a powerful role in organizing and motivating gender-consistent behaviors during middle childhood and adolescence.

Language competencies grow greatly during early childhood, although language development is critically dependent on immersion in language. Syntactic development during the preschool years has commanded a great deal of attention, with documentation of substantial regularity in the acquisition of the various morphemes. The two-word stage is the beginning of syntactical development, with much longer and complex utterances possible by the end of the preschool period. As language production skills improve, so do metalinguistic competencies, such as recognition of syntactical versus nonsyntactical constructions.

Expanding language skills as well as increased understanding of the perspectives of others leads to substantial increases in communication skills during early childhood. Social-communication skills and cognition are intertwined as indicated by the ability to predict cognitive competence in early childhood from attachment status during infancy. What mediates this continuity are more productive parent–child interactions in both infancy and early childhood when parents are responsive to their children. Parental responsivity results in secure attachment during infancy and better parent–child problem solving and intellectual interaction during early childhood. Thus, when parents and children are securely attached, they have more productive emergent literacy experiences (e.g., interactions during storybook read-ings), which help prepare children for more formal literacy instruction in kindergar-ten and first grade.

Although educational television programming, such as *Sesame Street*, can do much to convey knowledge of some fundamental literacy concepts, such as letters and numbers, much important knowledge about reading is better acquired in inter-action with responsive adults. According to Vygotsky, as language develops, it can play a greater role in thought, but for that to happen children must learn how to use language to direct thought. They learn this as they interact with adults who use language to direct the children's thinking and attention as they interact with them. With many such experiences, children internalize the directive role of adults, using self-speech to direct their own thinking and attention. Whereas Piaget viewed chil-dren's talk to themselves as a symptom of egocentricity, Vygotsky saw it as an intel-lectual advance, an early step in the development of directive speech-for-self, which is a prominent part of mature thinking.

Early conceptions of development during the early childhood years focused more exclusively on the parent–child relationship than do more recent conceptions. Thus, in describing the phallic stage, Freud placed relationships with parents at the center of moral development. In contrast, Kohlberg borrowed from Piaget's theory to explain development of moral judgment in terms of cognitive develop-ment, but also acknowledged the large role that peers play in stimulating think-ing about morality. With increasing peer relationships during the preschool years and increasing complexity of children's play, there are increasing opportunities for the types of cognitive conflicts that Kohlberg believed stimulate increases in moral understanding.

In summary, by the end of the preschool years, thinking, language, and social skills have many of the characteristics of adult thinking, language, and social interac-tions. Throughout the preschool years, thinking, language, and social interactions are increasingly linked. Development during the preschool years depends greatly on experiences with supportive adults. Thus, it is important to provide the types of educational experiences most likely to foster development during early childhood.

Middle Childhood

Neurological growth and development continue throughout middle childhood; as does myelination. Potential indicators of increases in brain functioning, such as speed of processing and capacity of working memory, continue to improve. Increased working memory capacity, along with improvements in inhibitory control and atten-tional flexibility, contribute to enhanced executive function.

For Piaget, the hallmark of middle childhood was the ability to conserve, pre-sumably indicative of the development of concrete operational thinking. Conserva-tion, however, did not prove to be an all-or-nothing acquisition, as suggested by Piag-et's theory. Instead, some conservations were acquired before others during middle childhood, and some were not acquired until well into adolescence.

Although Piaget's theory was important in stimulating research on cognitive development in the 1960s and 1970s, information-processing perspectives and cogni-tive science have predominated in discussions of cognitive development in the more recent past. For example, considerable research has documented that strategy use expands during the middle childhood years (e.g., rehearsal of word lists that are to be remembered). Information-processing theorists studying middle childhood have also demonstrated developmental improvements in inhibition of irrelevant thought, increases in resistance to interference, increased cognitive monitoring and self-regulation, and expanding metacognitive understandings. There are concomitant increases in children's theory of mind, their understanding of how other people's minds work, what others are thinking and feeling.

Increasingly, information-processing researchers have been interested in demonstrating the positive effects of strategies instruction on academic competence, with a large body of evidence now pointing to substantial improvements in academic performance, such as in reading comprehension and composition of texts. When students are first taught strategies, their performance of them is anything but automatic. Often strategies use is at first accompanied by overt verbalization, with verbalization increasingly covert as skill in strategies use increases. That is, consistent with Vygotskian theory, during middle childhood, children are capable of self-directive inner speech, and thus thought and language are increasingly intertwined.

Indeed, in general, language development continues to be salient during the middle childhood years. Syntactic skills, vocabulary, and metalinguistic awareness all increase. One form of metalinguistic awareness, phonemic awareness, has proven to be particularly important in early reading. Phonemic awareness is the understanding that words are composed of sounds blended together, sounds that "map to" the constituent letters in words. Phonemic awareness must develop no later than kindergarten or early first grade, if learning to read is to proceed well during the early elementary years. Phonemic awareness can be stimulated by language experiences emphasizing the component sounds of words. This experience can be provided, for example, in games requiring children to say what words would sound like with a different initial, middle, or final letter, such as asking "What would *bam* sound like if it started with *s?*"

Much of reading instruction during the primary years focuses on teaching children how to read words—although the making of meaning is prominent in contemporary reading instruction from the beginning of literacy instruction. Researchers interested in basic reading have documented that learning to read words is most likely if students are explicitly taught decoding skills and given practice using those skills during actual reading and writing. When children are taught to read in school, they are provided a powerful means for increasing their intelligence: Much can be learned by reading. Moreover, good readers often elect not only to read but to reduce other behaviors that are not consistent with maximizing cognitive development (e.g., excessive television viewing).

Provision of strategies instruction and teaching children to read are only two of the ways that schooling can affect the cognitive development of students positively. In general, intelligent performance is affected positively by schooling. That is, at least in Western cultures, middle childhood marks the beginning of an important factor in cognitive development: formal schooling. Interestingly, even psychoanalytic theorists recognized that middle childhood is largely a period devoted to the development of the competencies valued in the child's culture. For Freud, middle childhood corresponded to latency, which he characterized as a period of relative calm with respect to psychosocial development, a calm that permits attention to other matters, such as the intellectual development that occurs in school. According to Erikson, this is a period in which the child develops a sense of industry (i.e., if he or she is successful in accomplishing the demands of the period, such as the development of elementary literacy and numeracy skills) or inferiority (i.e., if he or she is unsuccessful in meeting demands such as learning to read, write, and solve elementary mathematical problems).

A number of other middle childhood developments might be affected in part by the onset of schooling or the concomitants of schooling, such as increased interactions with other children. Thus, Kohlberg noted increases in the conventionality of children's moral judgments during the elementary school years. Understanding of appropriate and inappropriate social behaviors (i.e., how, when, and where to behave in particular ways) also increases. Play increases in diversity and complexity.

More negatively, the academic self-concept does not fare so well with the onset of schooling. The typical kindergarten or first-grade child believes that he or she can do anything, that learning to read, write, and do math will go well. With every passing year, such perceptions decline, as do the motivations to do things academic. How much decline occurs, however, depends on a child's academic successes and failures and is domain-specific. Thus, by the late elementary school years, children know whether they are good at math, reading, or writing, with these self-efficacy perceptions affecting their subsequent motivations to read, write, and take mathematics. The declining motivation during middle childhood reflects the operation of several factors: (1) With increasing age, children believe less in personal effort as the determinant of academic performance and believe more in the role of natural ability, which is not under their own control. (2) With increasing grade level during the elementary school years, school becomes increasingly competitive, with far fewer academic winners than losers.

In summary, during middle childhood, thinking, language, and social skills continue to develop. A significant difference between this period of development and earlier periods is that schooling plays an important role in the cognitive life of the child, mostly for better, but also for worse (e.g., negatively affecting academic motivation). What has been learned about development during middle childhood has permitted many innovations in education.

Adolescence

Neurological development has continued to progress, with the brain reaching its adult weight and size by midadolescence (around age 16). Even so, many cognitive functions continue to expand throughout adolescence. For example, the diversity of memory strategies increases as the teen years proceed. Inhibition of irrelevant cognitions also continues to increase, as do other components of executive function such as resistance to cognitive interference, monitoring of cognitive functions, and flexible allocation of attention. Thought of in another way, both fluid and crystallized intelligence increase as adolescence continues.

Piaget, in particular, portrayed adolescence as the time when cognitive development culminates. With the acquisition of formal operations, more elaborate and flexible thinking is possible. More hypothetical thinking also becomes possible, so that adolescents are able to think about things that have never occurred and to think about abstract concepts. Other theorists, inspired by Piaget, also proposed that formal operations would permit functioning that is not possible during early and middle childhood. For example, Kohlberg proposed that postconventional moral judgment became a possibility during adolescence, in part because of the onset of formal operations during that period.

By the end of his life, Piaget came to realize that formal operations was anything but a universal attainment, with many adolescents not becoming formal operational. In addition, Piaget eventually concluded that formal operational competence was most likely in domains that are very familiar to the thinker. For example, teenage computer "geeks" are much more likely to be flexible and hypothetical in their own thinking about computer programming than in their thinking about other matters. Similarly, Kohlberg eventually came to realize that postconventional moral judgment often did not develop during adolescence. Postconventional thinking is much more likely to develop during early adulthood, that is, after people have had opportunities to experience some complex moral interactions requiring serious reflection.

Just as the nervous system becomes more fully mature during adolescence, so do the sexual organs and functioning. Psychoanalytically oriented theorists (e.g., Freud, Erikson) and others (e.g., G. Stanley Hall) believed that both sexual and intellectual maturity contributed to the conflicts of adolescence. Freud characterized adolescence as the genital stage, a period characterized by great volatility, owing, in part, to the surge in sexual energy experienced with hormonal maturity. G. Stanley Hall termed this volatility "storm and stress." Erikson was one theorist who elaborated on this idea of conflict during adolescence, making the case that adolescence is a period of identity crisis, with conflicts about potential career directions and personal philosophies. Erikson's original concept of identity has been expanded to include the powerful forces of ethnic–racial identity.

How does maturing thinking play a role in development, according to psychoanalytically oriented theorists? With adolescence, the full range of defense mechanisms becomes possible. More positively, with the ability to think about unexperienced possibilities, it is possible to imagine oneself in a variety of occupations, to envision alternative sexual identities, and to contemplate alternative life philosophies. Adolescent thinking differs from childhood thinking in many ways.

One of the most striking differences between life in childhood and life in adolescence is that by the end of adolescence peer interactions become very important. These peer relations are critical to development, including intellectual development. For example, Kohlberg emphasized how peer relations permit cognitive conflicts that promote increases in the development of moral thinking. Lawrence Steinberg and his associates documented how peer relations go far in affecting academic achievement in high school in that successful students naturally tend to associate with other successful students.

In summary, during adolescence, biological maturation occurs. Thinking and social relations expand, with cognitive skills and social interactions reciprocally affecting one another. That is, increasing cognitive abilities permits more sophisticated social functioning, with social functioning positively affecting thinking skills.

See the Applying Developmental Theory to Educational Contexts special feature (Box 13.1) for a description of empirically validated psychological principles particularly relevant to educational contexts.

Summary and Concluding Comment

Whenever you look at a 19-year-old, it is a marvel to realize that that person began as a single cell almost two decades ago. Almost as marvelous is that it is possible now to articulate in some detail the many different ways the individual has grown

BOX 13.1. Top 20 Principles from Psychology for PreK–12 Teaching and Learning

The American Psychological Association brought together a group of psychologists, known as the Coalition for Psychology in Schools and Education, to identify and summarize the principles derived from psychological research that are most relevant to classroom contexts. The list of Top 20 principles considered to be the most useful for PreK–12 teaching and learning can be found on the website of the American Psychological Association (*www.apa. org/ed/schools/cpse/top-twenty-principles*). Information on this website provides a complete description of each principle, an argument outlining the relevance of the principle for the classroom, and a list of supporting research references. The list includes principles generated from a range of psychological disciplines, not just developmental psychology, however, many of the principles have featured prominently in the chapters of this text. A list of the Top 20 principles follows:

How Do Students Think and Learn?

- Principle 1: Students' beliefs or perceptions about intelligence and ability affect their cognitive functioning and learning.
- Principle 2: What students already know affects their learning.
- Principle 3: Students' cognitive development and learning are not limited by general stages of development.
- Principle 4: Learning is based on context, so generalizing learning to new contexts is not spontaneous but instead needs to be facilitated.
- Principle 5: Acquiring long term knowledge and skills is largely dependent on practice.
- Principle 6: Clear, explanatory, and timely feedback to students is important for learning.
- Principle 7: Students' self-regulation assists learning and self-regulatory skills can be taught.
- Principle 8: Student creativity can be fostered.

What Motivates Students?

- Principle 9: Students' tend to enjoy learning and perform better when they are more intrinsically than extrinsically motivated to achieve.
- Principle 10: Students persist in the face of challenging tasks and process information more deeply when they adopt mastery goals rather than performance goals.
- Principle 11: Teachers' expectations about their students affect students' opportunities to learn, their motivation, and their learning outcomes.
- Principle 12: Setting goals that are short term (proximal), specific, and moderately challenging enhances motivation more than establishing goals that are long term (distal), general, and overly challenging.

Why Are Social Context, Interpersonal Relationships, and Emotional Well-Being Important to Student Learning?

- Principle 13: Learning is situated within multiple social contexts.

(continued)

- Principle 14: Interpersonal relationships and communications are critical to both the teaching-learning process and the social-emotional development of students.

- Principle 15: Emotional well-being influences educational performance, learning, and development.

How Can the Classroom Best Be Managed?

- Principle 16: Expectations for classroom conduct and social interaction are learned and can be taught using proven principles of behavior and effective classroom instruction.

- Principle 17: Effective classroom management is based on (a) setting and communicating high expectations, (b) consistently nurturing positive relationships, and (c) providing a high level of student support.

How to Assess Student Progress?

- Principle 18: Formative and summative assessments are both important and useful but require different approaches and interpretations.

- Principle 19: Students' skills, knowledge and abilities are best measured with assessment processes grounded in psychological science with well-defined standards for quality and fairness.

- Principle 20: Making sense of assessment data depends on clear, appropriate, and fair interpretation.

and changed. The portrait of development summarized in Figure 13.1 represents the cumulative efforts of thousands of scientists, with almost all of the conclusions offered here the product of research during the last 60 years. Beyond mere description of how development occurs, understanding is growing as to how biological development relates to psychological development, and, within psychological development, how shifts in thinking skills affect social behaviors and personality. Great progress has been made in understanding the complexities of development.

What processes account for developmental change? These processes are taken up in the next section, where we argue that the same mechanisms that account for developmental shifts also account for individual differences at any given developmental level.

Mechanisms of Development and the Determinants of Individual Differences

The mechanisms of growth and development and the determinants of individual differences can be classified in a number of different ways. One way that has endured, and one that has been used throughout this textbook, is to frame the mechanisms/determinants as principally part of "nature" or "nurture." As we have learned, however, there are always interactions between biological and environmental factors.

Prenatal Period
- Conception.
- Cell differentiation, cell proliferation, and eventual development of organ systems.
- Intrauterine growth and development until birth.
- Sex chromosomes and hormones lead to development of gonads and external genitalia.

Infancy (0–2 years of age)
- Rapid growth of brain and nervous system.
  - Increasing size and weight of brain, with some growth spurts.
  - A number of areas of the brain (e.g., frontal lobes) become functional.
  - Programmed brain cell loss.
  - Experience-expectant synaptic connections made if appropriate experience occurs during critical period.
- Myelination of nervous system with increased efficiency of neural transmission.
- Reflexive reactions gradually give way to reflective reactions.
- Object permanence develops.
- Attachment develops during the first year and continues to develop in the second year.
  - Freud's oral and anal conflicts.
  - Erikson's crises of trust versus mistrust, autonomy versus shame and doubt.
- Emergence of symbolic functioning and language.
  - Increased speech perception during the first year.
  - Babbling becomes more consistent with sounds in the surrounding language.
  - One-word stage by the end of the second year, with single words associated with complex meanings.

Early Childhood (2–6 years of age)
- Brain growth and myelination continue, with speed of information processing and functional short-term memory increasing.
- Piagetian preoperational period, with thought intuitive and influenced by perception.
- Use of elementary strategies in familiar situations.
- Schematic knowledge continues to grow, including gender schematic knowledge.
- Great growth in language skills.
  - Syntax.
  - Vocabulary.
  - Metalinguistic linguistic understanding.
  - Increasing articulation of language and thought as proposed by Vygotsky.
  - Emergent literacy experiences and productive parent–child language interactions.
- Increasing peer relationships, with cognitive conflicts that stimulate cognitive growth.
- Development of theory of mind, knowledge about own and others' mental states and beliefs.
- Development of moral thinking and conscience.
- Freudian phallic stage, the beginning of internalization of conscience.
- Preconventional moral reasoning as defined by Kohlberg.

Middle Childhood (6–11 or 12 years of age)
- Brain growth and myelination continues.
- Piagetian concrete operational period.

(continued)

FIGURE 13.1. A chronological summary of human development.

- Improvements in information processing and executive function.
  - Speed of information processing and growth of functional short-term memory capacity increase.
  - Strategy use expands, with children responsive to strategy instruction.
  - Improved inhibition of irrelevant thinking.
  - Increased resistance to cognitive interference.
  - Increased cognitive monitoring and self-regulation.
  - Expanding metacognitive understandings.
  - Increased social-cognitive understandings.
- Language development continues.
  - Syntax.
  - Vocabulary.
  - Metalinguistic awareness (e.g., phonemic awareness, which can be stimulated with language manipulation games if it does not develop on its own).
- Academic learning is preeminent (e.g., reading).
  - Freud's latency period.
  - Erikson's crisis of competence versus incompetence.
  - Academic self-concept becomes more differentiated and generally declines with increasing age.
  - Academic motivation generally declines with increasing age.
- Social relationships become more complex.
  - Continued development of theory of mind.
  - Play increases in diversity.
  - Increasing understanding of appropriateness in social behaviors.
  - Increases in social-cognitive abilities allow more productive cognitive conflicts, which, in turn, positively affect cognitive development.
- Preconventional moral judgments as defined by Kohlberg.

Adolescence (11 or 12 years of age to the late teen years)
- Biological maturation.
  - Brain attains adult size and weight.
  - Sexual maturity.
- Piagetian formal operational stage, with formal operations most evident when operating in familiar domains.
  - Increased abstract and hypothetical reasoning.
  - Increased cognitive flexibility permits more complex thinking—for example, many ego defense mechanisms as defined by Freudians.
- Improvements in information processing and executive function.
  - Speed of information processing increases.
  - Functional short-term memory capacity increases.
  - Strategy diversity expands.
  - Cognitive inhibition increases.
  - Resistance to interference increases.
  - Cognitive monitoring increases.
- Potential storm and stress.
  - Freud's genital stage.
  - Erikson's identity crisis conflict.
  - Ethnic–racial identity development.
- Peer interactions now are more prominent.

FIGURE 13.1. *(continued)*

The Nature of Nature

Much of development is determined at the moment of conception. At a minimum, the genes all humans inherit do much to ensure that the biological development of any child will be much like the biological development of other humans. Barring some environmental disruption, such as malnutrition or physical injury, the central nervous system develops in orderly and predictable ways following birth. Developments that are universal include the following:

Critical and sensitive periods for the development of some perceptual and language skills occur at about the same time for most humans. Indeed, biology biases humans to orient to and process particular types of sensory and linguistic information. These biases go far in assuring that the developing human will experience needed sensation at critical points in his or her development.

Biology also biases humans to construct meaning and understanding from sensory and linguistic input. Thus, when perceptual arrays are incomplete (e.g., there is a faint image of a ball that is visible) or when linguistic input is sparse (e.g., a person picks up only part of a sentence, "The ball is _____ing on the f_____"), humans often fill in the missing pieces based on their prior knowledge in order to see a ball or to know that the speaker must have said, "The ball is rolling on the floor."

Because the central nervous system develops as it does, most humans will have the conscious capacity to actively manipulate symbols. That is, they will have working memory capacity. They will also have the capacity to form enduring memories.

In general, humans have evolved to be sensitive to information in the environment. That is, the environment makes a difference because of human biology. All humans attend to and learn from social models, can understand explanations, and respond to reinforcements and feedback because their biology equips them—and indeed *biases* them—to do so.

Because of the prominence of behavior genetics research, however, biological determination is typically thought about in terms of the role genes play in determining individual differences in people. Genes specify *reaction ranges* with respect to a number of human characteristics. For example, a person's genes specify neurological development that will permit the individual to be above average, average, or below average in intelligence. In the case of a person whose genes permit above-average intellectual functioning, however, exactly how much above average will depend on the environment. That is, the reaction range for someone who has inherited above-average intelligence might be 115–130, with exact placement in the range depending on the quantity and quality of intellectual stimulation experienced. Similarly, there are genetically specified reaction ranges for more specific intellectual acquisitions (e.g., the ability to read), as well as for personality characteristics and, of course, physical characteristics.

One salient biologically determined characteristic is biological sex. Social and cultural influences, along with biological sex, influence the development of gender identity. Biological sex and/or gender identity can affect some mental functions (e.g., competence to perform tasks with a spatial component) as well as social interaction patterns. Despite these differences, there is much greater variability *among* girls and *among* boys than *between* girls and boys on average.

Nature matters, with human biology going far in explaining aspects of development that are universal as well as how and why developments occur differently when they do. Human biology, however, always unfolds in an environment, so nothing in human development reflects purely genetic or purely biological mechanisms. Like the fish in the sea that fails to understand it is swimming in water, humans sometimes fail to appreciate that physical attributes, intelligence, personality, and gender-related behaviors are often affected dramatically by a number of environmental factors. One of the great contributions of psychology as a science has been its role in heightening awareness of the many ways that nurture can affect development and behavior.

The Nature of Nurture

There are many ways of conceptualizing how experience matters. One traditional approach is to think about mechanisms of development or change, with each of these mechanisms summarizing how environmental input translates into shifts in behavior and knowledge.

Mechanisms of Change

Psychologists who are interesting in learning, in particular, have been active in characterizing development in terms of the mechanisms that cause change. The typical means of learning are as follows:

OBSERVATIONAL LEARNING

Humans have evolved to learn a great deal from what they observe. They are attuned to the behaviors they see modeled by other people. Sometimes, for example, teachers model strategic behaviors, urging their students to attend to these behaviors and intentionally learn them. More often, however, people do not intend to learn from others, but they nonetheless incidentally learn from them. For example, a young child attending a football game for the first time may not intend to learn to stand up and sit down in concert with others, but once the first "wave" passes through the stadium, that child is ready, willing, and able to participate fully in the next round.

Following the cognitive revolution in psychology in the 1960s and 1970s, conceptions of modeling broadened. For example, part of modeling can be verbal explanations, which also have a powerful effect on children's learning. Indeed, the scaffolding of instruction, as conceived by Vygotskian-oriented educators, begins with extensive modeling and explaining, followed by additional modeling and explaining as needed. In addition, cognitive psychologists presented evidence that observational learning very much depends on the learner attending to the model. Social learning researchers, in particular, have devoted a great deal of effort to determine what factors account for learner attention. People attend to others who are well respected, but they also attend to people like themselves who are confronting tasks that they themselves must confront soon.

REINFORCEMENT

Any event that follows another event and increases the probability of the first event reoccurring in the future is a reinforcement. Again, with the cognitive revolution, reinforcements came to be thought of in different ways, in particular, with greater emphasis on their informational value. Reinforcements often signal that the individual performed appropriately at a particular time, providing information about where and when to do something. Such feedback can have an effect on the metacognition of learners, increasing what they know about the occasions when particular tactics make sense.

With the cognitive revolution, understanding has also increased about when reinforcement does not work as it is intended and why. In particular, reinforcements can be construed as controlling, so that a reinforced student begins to think "I am doing this activity to get the reward." Once the reward stops, so does the behavior, even if it is a behavior that the child used to perform for no reward at all.

PUNISHMENT

Punishments have the opposite effect of reinforcements. Any event that follows another event and decreases the probability of the first event in the future is a punishment. Cognitive psychologists have also thought about punishment and made the case that punishment is more effective if the child understands the reason for the punishment and even more effective if punished children are made to understand how their misdeed negatively affected others. These explanations, referred to as "inductions," go far toward decreasing the incidence of punished behaviors in the future.

CLASSICAL CONDITIONING

Humans are born with a variety of reflexes and emotions, which can be elicited by particular forms of stimulation. For example, in school settings, failure often elicits anxiety and even fear. Because the failure and accompanying emotion occur in the context of school, school itself can come to be anxiety arousing. Avoiding school then reduces anxiety.

COGNITIVE CONFLICT

Although it is possible to account for much of development through analyses of the learning mechanisms of observation, reinforcement, punishment, and conditioning, some researchers have favored explaining developmental change with respect to the child's level of development. A key mechanism in promoting developmental change is *cognitive conflict*. Specifically, if a situation is a little bit different than the learner expects based on her or his knowledge and understanding of the world, the learner is motivated to try to understand what is going on. A classic example of this occurs when a nonconserving child is presented with a conservation task such as determining how pouring water from a short, fat beaker into a tall, thin beaker affects the amount of liquid. The nonconserver believes that there is a different amount of liquid when the water is in one of the beakers than when it is in the other. There comes a time, however, when it is very puzzling that water originally in beaker A looks different in beaker B, but when poured back into A once again appears to be the same as before the pouring from A to B. This confusion motivates reflection on the situation and the eventual construction of the understanding that pouring liquid from one beaker to another has no effect on the amount of liquid. Amount of liquid can only be affected by adding or subtracting liquid from the total.

A general principle of instruction that emerges is that cognitive conflict is most likely to stimulate reflection and learning when the task is just a little bit beyond the child's current understanding. This general principle was summarized by Vygotsky as "teaching within the *zone of proximal development.*" According to this approach, find out what the child knows already and what she or he can do, then present tasks to him or her that are just a bit beyond the child's current level of functioning. Many motivational frameworks also include the idea that motivation is maximized by presenting students with tasks that are a little bit challenging for them: not so easy that they can be done immediately, nor so difficult that the tasks become frustrating. Piagetian educators, such as those who were inspired by Lawrence Kohlberg's theory of moral judgment and its development, often refer to this as the "plus-one approach." Being exposed to thinking that is a stage beyond the child's current level of functioning has a fascination for the child that increases attention and his or her attempts to understand the thinking.

Some have labeled teaching and learning within the zone of proximal development as "constructivist," rather than involving cultural transmission of information. The constructivist label emphasizes the theme that the child is active in coming to understand the situation. Educators advocating constructivism as an approach to teaching and learning often believe that modeling and explaining to-be-learned principles for students do not cause the same type of reflection that plus-one approaches stimulate. In this view, modeling, explaining, and reinforcing use of principles that have been explicitly taught does not result in as complete understanding as when learning involves cognitive conflict. The problem is that there is not much evidence for this position that learning via cognitive conflict is better than learning from observation or explanations. Modeling often is the beginning of a constructivist process for the learner. The learner does not fully understand a process simply from watching another person carry out the process, but probably does understand it well enough to try the process. Trying a process results in mistakes, which prompt reflection and gradual construction of understanding.

When students are working in the zone of proximal development, often they are not going to "get it" immediately. They may need support in the form of hints, prompts, and reminders. Such support is at the heart of scaffolding, with the excellent scaffolder providing enough support for the student to make progress but not more than the student actually needs. Discovery in the absence of such support often is uncertain or even unlikely. Constructivist discovery always involves active student thinking, although sometimes the learner requires some prompting in order to begin thinking about a problem in a way that will lead to a solution.

How can individual differences in learners be explained in terms of the learning mechanisms and cognitive conflict? Students are likely to be better informed and more skillful to the extent that they have experienced appropriate models and explanations of information that is important to know. It helps if their efforts to respond to models are reinforced and that appropriate help is provided when it is needed (i.e., when learning is scaffolded). Families differ with respect to the provision of such input, as do schooling environments. Some children experience worlds filled with appropriate modeling and explaining, reinforcing, and scaffolding. Other things being equal, those living in such worlds are far ahead of children coming from less stimulating and responsive environments. Thus, the context in which development occurs is key.

Contexts of Development

In the first chapter of this book, we introduced Urie Bronfenbrenner's (1979, 1989) *ecological systems theory*. Bronfenbrenner divided the environment into the microsystem (i.e., contexts making immediate contact with the developing child, such as home or day care center), the mesosystem (i.e., the linkages between microsystems, such as the family accessing services offered by the school or local community), the exosystem (i.e., elements affecting the child removed from direct experience, such as media and government), and the macrosystem (i.e., the larger culture). In fact, over the course of this textbook, evidence has been reviewed supporting the impact of all levels of the ecological system as Bronfenbrenner described it.

At the microsystem level, a great deal of evidence was summarized about how family and friends affect development. The microsystem shifts somewhat with development, being defined mostly by the family early in life and increasingly by peers as development proceeds. That said, the elements of the microsystem somewhat codetermine each other. Thus, when parent–child interactions during infancy result in a secure attachment, healthy peer relations during the preschool years are more likely. Parents also affect their children's peers by their choice of neighborhood and educational options. In turn, peers can affect a teen's interactions with parents, although more often than not the perspectives and values held by a teen's family are consistent with the perspectives and values held by a teen's peers. The family and friendship relationships that define a child's microsystem of development are strongly interrelated.

With respect to individual differences in children, the microsystem can go far in affecting such differences. How parents react to their children affects them in many ways. Thus, securely attached children develop differently than insecurely attached children, enjoying better social relationships that impact favorably on their intellectual development due to their better academic interactions with adults during the preschool years. Authoritative parents provide a healthier context for development than do permissive or authoritarian parents. Peers can support an academic outlook or an anti-intellectual perspective. How family and peers act toward a child and what families and peers believe go a long way in determining how a child develops.

The microsystem element that has received the greatest consideration in this textbook is school. Schools can be places where instruction is well informed by contemporary research or bastions of tradition, with such curricular decisions having an important impact on what the child learns. Some schools are organized on cooperative principles and emphasize improvement, but others tend to emphasize competition, rewarding those who do better than others. Competitive schooling certainly undermines the motivation of many students.

Schooling can be more or less constructivist. That is, the teacher simply can present information and expect students to learn it, or the teacher can make presentations that are the start of a constructivist process, during which students work with the ideas and attempt to apply them to meaningful tasks with the aid of teacher scaffolding. In some schools that are decidedly constructivist in their orientation, students are apprentice readers, writers, and problem solvers, taking on meaningful academic tasks (e.g., writing a letter to the author of a book just read by the class) in a cooperative, supportive community. In contrast, in the bastions of tradition, they are merely the doers of tasks that do not make much sense to them, tasks that are defined by drills and workbook pages that the teacher specifies as the assignments for the day.

The microsystem of schooling can go far in determining individual differences between children. Whether a child is a motivated learner or lacks academic motivation often depends on school. Whether a child knows how to comprehend and interpret texts or only knows how to answer literal questions about a text will vary with the type of schooling the child experiences. Whether a child understands what it means to live in a just community and the role of individuals in constructing just communities can vary depending on the social organization of the school.

Media is an exosystem variable that was encountered at different points in this text. Character portrayals of men and women, boys and girls, on television and other media outlets do much to shape gender stereotypes. Social media can be used to augment social relationships as well as a vehicle for bullying. Heavy doses of televised aggression are associated with inappropriate aggressive behavior in children. More positively, educational programming that is well informed by research on learning and development can be effective in stimulating academic development. In short, television and other media affect development and individual differences in cognitive outcomes.

The study of macrosystem effects (i.e., culture) on development has been extensive in the past 50 years in particular. Often comparisons have been made between different cultures (e.g., Asian vs. American) or within cultures that vary in the degree to which they conform to Western traditions (e.g., cultures in which some children are Western-schooled and other children are not). Even within the United States, academic development has been analyzed as a function of subcultural membership (e.g., ethnicity/race; socioeconomic status). Time and again, culture has proved to be telling in defining psychologically important differences. For example, Asians are more likely to explain their accomplishments as reflecting ability than are Western students. Africans experiencing Western-style schooling think differently than Africans not so educated.

Culture is determined not only by place and group membership, but also by when development occurs. The culture that today's grandparents experienced during childhood is dramatically different from the culture in which today's children are raised. Such cohort differences in experience translate into a variety of differences in development, including in fundamental knowledge and capacities tapped by intelligence tests.

In summary, Bronfenbrenner's model was well supported by the evidence presented in this textbook. Context consistently makes a difference in development and goes far in explaining individual differences in development. A variety of differences in this textbook have been explained as a function of family and peer relationships, schooling variables, media exposure, and culture. Something else that became apparent, however, was that with increasing age, students became creators and determiners of their own contexts of development. They decide on how much they will interact with family and friends, whether they will be committed to school, which media will engage them, and the subculture they choose to inhabit. For example, what difference will it make to a middle school girl if she makes choices designed to make her more popular and attractive to boys instead of choosing a more academic orientation? With a little thought, it will be clear that the environment such a girl elects to be in will dramatically affect her development. Thus, next we take up how children are determiners of their own contexts and development—that is, how self-regulation determines environment and development.

The Self-Regulating Child as a Determiner of Development

Self-regulation increases with development. For example, Vygotsky highlighted how internalized speech comes to self-regulate behavior and thought. Advancing age, at least in Western societies, brings with it increased strategy use and increased self-monitoring of behavior. With advancing age, children inhibit irrelevant and potentially interfering cognitions. They also acquire a variety of values and beliefs that affect their self-determination. If they come to believe that their accomplishments are due to their personal efforts, this can motivate great effort. If they come to believe that ability mediates academic success—an ability they believe they lack—motivation can very much be undermined. Students can either come to value school or believe it is not valuable in their lives, with these beliefs affecting their willingness to engage in academic tasks.

As children mature, they choose their friends and develop their interests. What friends do largely determines what an individual child does. Interests go far in explaining where a child will direct her or his energies, with interests directly affecting the developing knowledge base of the child. As children mature, their knowledge deepens as a function of experience. A child's state of knowledge becomes an important contextual variable, a context that is developed largely through the child's own choices. Thus, the child who has been interested in computers since the preschool years and has done things with computers through the elementary and middle school years enters high school with a much more elaborated knowledge base about computers than his or her classmates. Such a child is in a better position than his or her peers to understand new information about computers and technology. The prior knowledge provides a basis for expectations that the child may have with respect to a new possibility (e.g., taking the introductory computer course that so many of his classmates take during freshman year of high school), expectations that affect behaviors and decisions (e.g., deciding not to take the class). The knowledge base also provides the basis for interpretations of the world that are not possible for those who do not have the knowledge base (e.g., the course will have to be low level since it is taught in a computer lab with machines that cannot run state-of-the-technology programs).

This developing knowledge base in no way guarantees clarity of understanding. Indeed, to the extent that the child has acquired prior knowledge that is inconsistent with new knowledge, there is reason to expect misinterpretations and interference in learning the new content.

As this knowledge base is expanding, however, so are communication skills and the ability to understand the perspectives of others, with these also part of the context that is the child's own mind. Expanding interpersonal competencies permit the opportunities to cooperate with others in academic endeavors and to work on problems together. It has been known for some time that peers and peer interactions can affect cognitive development. We now are coming to understand how thinking can be distributed between minds and how interacting with others can lead to understandings that would not have been reached by any of the thinkers confronting a situation alone—that is, how the context of people thinking together can affect the development of the individual thinkers.

In short, the state of a child's own mind is an important contextual variable helping to determine the experiences the child will have and what the child will gain from those experiences. To the extent that the child has acquired academic interests, attitudes, and beliefs that support trying hard, and has prior knowledge that permits understanding the new content, the child is more likely to profit from educational opportunities. Thus, an important source of individual differences between children tomorrow is individual differences in their minds today, with the intellectually rich in a better position to become richer, increasing the distance between the academically well prepared and the not so well prepared as development proceeds. Another way to say it is that a child's own mind is an important contextual variable, with some minds better able to profit from experience than others.

Summary and Concluding Comments

Nature and nurture continuously interact to determine development. The child's biology as determined in part by genes goes far in explaining some aspects of development. More can be understood, however, by thinking about the experiential mechanisms that promote change, including observational learning, reinforcement, punishment, conditioning, and cognitive conflict. Such mechanisms always operate in contexts, however, with the contexts coming to have causal properties, or at least becoming part of a causal chain. Hence, experiencing a responsive mother during infancy is part of the cause of secure attachment. Attendance at a school that rewards students for improvement is part of the cause of high motivation in the school. Watching *Sesame Street* can cause children to learn basic literacy and numeracy facts. Experiencing Western culture and schooling can cause children to develop Western-style thinking.

Children are not passive in all of this, however. As children mature, they increasingly self-regulate, including making choices to embed themselves in particular situations versus others. Thus the child who decides to read a great deal becomes a causal force in her or his own literacy development. More negatively, characteristics over which children have little control also affect development, including health status. Many other child characteristics can affect the contexts that a child experiences as part of development. Thus, the athletic child will be admitted to different contexts that affect development than will the clumsy youngster. The easygoing child will have different experiences than the impulsive–aggressive child.

Do we understand nature and nurture completely? Hardly. The findings summarized in this textbook are only the stones in a pathway to additional research on development and education. Every one of the topics covered in this volume will be studied additionally in the near future. This edition of this book is different than the first and other editions will reflect the continual expansion of knowledge about development and education. See the Considering Interesting Questions special feature in Box 13.2 for predictions of topics we anticipate will be most transformed by future research. Educators who wish to know child development must work hard to stay current, for this is a field in which change is a constant. We plan to keep busy doing research on education and development and keeping abreast of the research of others, for it has proven to be an exciting and stimulating life adventure for us. We hope that at least a few of the readers of this textbook will choose to do research and that many more will make a point of becoming consumers and users of research pertaining to development and education.

BOX 13.2. What Does the Future Hold for the Study of Child and Adolescent Development?

Since the first edition of *Child and Adolescent Development for Educators* was published, we have seen shifts in focus and significant advances in the knowledge base in a number of different areas. Looking to the future, where do we predict we will see the most transformation in knowledge of child and adolescent development?

Contributions from Brain and Cognitive Science

- Improved understanding of brain development, both typical development and development gone awry.
- Better understanding of how memory works and how knowledge is stored.
- Increased understanding of the development of executive function, attention, and working memory.

Advances in Technology

- Even more integration of technology into everyday life and in educational environments which will, in turn, have a major effect on the course of development, particularly cognitive development.
- Technological innovations designed to reduce the impact of disabilities, particularly for the deaf and hard of hearing and those who are visually impaired.
- Creation of innovative technologies with instructional implications and greater use of such technologies in classrooms. Researchers are already testing how best to use social media, virtual reality, digital game-based learning environments, intelligent tutoring systems, adaptive learning technologies designed to personalize instruction, and computer-supported collaborations to enhance student performance in a wide range of learning domains.

Changes in Schools

- Comprehensive mental health and social services will become more commonplace in public schools.
- More emphasis will be placed on individualized instruction, which will be made possible by technological innovation. Something like an individualized education program (IEP) will be developed for each and every child.
- More awareness of social stressors, including those mediated through technology, and their effects on learning and development.

If you are interested in keeping abreast of advances like these, keep your eye on the following websites for descriptions of groundbreaking research: National Science Foundation (*www.nsf.gov*), National Institutes of Health (*www.nih.gov*), and Institute of Education Sciences (*https://ies.ed.gov*).

References

Abercrombie, S. (2013). Transfer effects of adding seductive details to case-based instruction. *Contemporary Educational Psychology, 38*(2), 149–157.

Abi-Nader, J. (1990). "A house for my mother": Motivating Hispanic high school students. *Anthropology and Education Quarterly, 21*, 41–58.

Achenbach, T., & Zigler, E. (1968). Cue-learning and problem-learning strategies in normal and retarded children. *Child Development, 3*, 827–848.

Adams, M. J. (1990). *Beginning to read*. Cambridge, MA: Harvard University Press.

Adeyemo, S. A. (2002). A review of the role of the hippocampus in memory. *Psychology and Education: An Interdisciplinary Journal, 39*, 46–63.

Adolph, K. E., & Berger, S. E. (2005). Physical and motor development. In M. H. Bornstein & M. E. Lamb (Eds.), *Developmental science: An advanced textbook* (5th ed., pp. 223–281). Mahwah, NJ: Erlbaum.

Adolph, K. E., & Robinson, S. R. (2015). Motor development. In R. M. Lerner (Series Eds.), L. Liben & U. Müller (Vol. Eds.), *Handbook of child psychology and developmental science: Vol. 2. Cognitive processes* (7th ed., pp. 114–157). New York: Wiley.

Agmon, S., & Schneider, S. (1998). The first stages in the development of the small group: A psychoanalytic understanding. *Group Analysis, 31*, 131–156.

Ahnert, J., Schneider, W., & Bös, K. (2009). Developmental changes and individual stability of motor abilities from the preschool period to young adulthood. In W. Schneider & M. Bullock (Eds.), *Human development from early childhood to early adulthood: Evidence from the Munich Longitudinal Study on the Genesis of Individual Competencies* (pp. 35–62). New York: Psychology Press.

Ainley, M., Hidi, S., & Berndorff, D. (2002). Interest, learning, and the psychological processes that mediate their relationship. *Journal of Educational Psychology, 94*, 545–561.

Ainsworth, M. D. S., Blehar, M. C., Waters, E., & Wall, S. (1978). *Patterns of attachment: A psychological study of the Strange Situation*. Hillsdale, NJ: Erlbaum.

Akhtar, N., Dunham, F., & Dunham, P. J. (1991). Directive interactions and early vocabulary development: The role of joint attentional focus. *Journal of Child Language, 18*, 41–50.

Albertini, J. A., & Schley, S. (2003). Writing: Characteristics, instruction, and assessment. In M. Marschark & P. E. Spencer (Eds.), *Oxford handbook of deaf studies, language, and education* (pp. 123–135). New York: Oxford University Press.

Alexander, D. H. T., Walker, H. T., & Money, J. (1964). Studies in the directional sense. *Archives of General Psychiatry, 10*, 337–339.

Alexander, R., Boehme, R., & Cupps, B. (1993). *Normal development of functional motor skills: The first year of life*. San Antonio, TX: Psychological Corp.

Allen, J. P., Porter, M., McFarland, C., McElhaney, K., & Marsh, P. (2007). The relation of attachment security to adolescents' paternal and peer relationships, depression, and externalizing behavior. *Child Development, 78*(4), 1222–1239.

Allen, J. P., & Tan, J. S. (2016). The multiple faces of attachment in adolescence. In J. Cassidy & P. R. Shaver (Eds.), *Handbook of attachment: Theory, research, and clinical applications* (3rd ed., 399–415). New York: Guilford Press.

Alley, T. R. (1981). Head shape and the perception of cuteness. *Developmental Psychology, 17*, 650–654.

Allington, R. L. (1991a). Effective literacy instruction for at-risk children. In M. S. Knapp & P. M. Shields (Eds.), *Better schooling for the children of poverty: Alternatives to conventional wisdom* (pp. 9–30). Berkeley, CA: McCutchan.

Allington, R. L. (1991b). The legacy of "slow it down and make it more concrete." In J. Zutell & S. McCormick (Eds.), *Learner factors/teacher factors: Issues in literacy research and instruction: Fortieth yearbook of the National Reading Conference* (pp. 19–29). Chicago: National Reading Conference.

Allington, R. L., & McGill-Franzen, A. (1989). School response to reading failure: Chapter 1 and special education students in grades 2, 4, and 8. *Elementary School Journal, 89*, 529–542.

Alloway, T. P. (2010). Working memory and executive function profiles of individuals with borderline intellectual functioning. *Journal of Intellectual Disability Research, 54*, 448–456.

Alloway, T. P., & Alloway, R. G. (2010). Investigating the predictive roles of working memory and IQ in academic attainment. *Journal of Experimental Child Psychology, 106*(1), 20–29.

Alsaker, F. D. (1992). Being overweight and psychological adjustment. *Journal of Early Adolescence, 12*, 396–419.

Altermatt, E. R., Pomerantz, E. M., Ruble, D. N., & Greulich, F. K. (2002). Predicting changes in children's self-perceptions of academic competence: A naturalistic examination of evaluative discourse among classmates. *Developmental Psychology, 38*, 903–917.

Altschul, I., Lee, S. J., & Gershoff, E. T. (2016). Hugs, not hits: Warmth and spanking as predictors of child social competence. *Journal of Marriage and Family, 78*, 695–714.

Alvarado, M. C., & Bachevalier, J. (2000). Revisiting the maturation of medial temporal lobe memory functions in primates. *Learning and Memory, 7*(5), 244–256.

Amato, P. R., & Anthony, C. J. (2014). Estimating the effects of parental divorce and death with fixed effective models. *Journal of Marriage and Family, 76*, 370–386.

American Academy of Pediatrics, American Public Health Association, & National Resource Center for Health and Safety in Child Care and Early Education. (2011). *Caring for our children: National health and safety performance standards; Guidelines for early care and education programs* (3rd ed.). Elk Grove Village, IL: American Academy of Pediatrics; Washington, DC: American Public Health Association. Available from *http://nrckids.org.*

American Association of Suicidology. (2015). U.S. state suicide rates and rankings for the nation, elderly, and young, 2015. Available from *www.suicidology.org/Portals/14/docs/Resources/FactSheets/2015/2015StatesTOY-corrected.pdf?ver=2017-01-09-215406-197.*

American Educational Research Association, American Psychological Association, National Council of Measurement and Evaluation, & Joint Committee on Standards for Educational and Psychological Testing. (1999). *Standards for educational and psychological testing.* Washington, DC: AERA.

American Educational Research Association, American Psychological Association, National Council of Measurement and Evaluation, & Joint Committee on Standards for Educational and Psychological Testing. (2014). *Standards for educational and psychological testing* (2014 ed.). Washington, DC: AERA.

American Psychiatric Association. (2013). *Diagnostic and statistical manual of mental disorders* (5th ed.). Arlington, VA: Author.

American Psychological Association. (1985). *Standards for educational and psychological testing.* Washington, DC: Author.

American Psychological Association, Coalition for Psychology in Schools and Education. (2015). Top 20 principles from psychology for PreK–12 teaching and learning. Available from *www.apa.org/ed/schools/cpse/top-twenty-principles.pdf.*

Ames, C. (1992). Classrooms: Goals, structures, and student motivation. *Journal of Educational Psychology, 84*, 261–271.

Anastasi, A., & Irbina, S. (1997). *Psychological testing* (7th ed.). Saddle River, NJ: Prentice-Hall.

Anastasiow, N. J. (1990). Implications of the neurobiological model for early intervention. In S. J. Meisels & J. P. Shonkoff (Eds.), *Handbook of early childhood interventions* (pp. 196–216). Cambridge, UK: Cambridge University Press.

Anderman, E. M. (2013). Middle school transition. In J. Hattie & E. M. Anderman (Eds.), *International guide to student achievement* (pp. 176–178). New York: Routledge.

Anderman, E. M., Eccles, J. S., Yoon, K. S., Roeser, R., Wigfield, A., & Blumenfeld, P. (2001). Learning to value mathematics and reading: Relations to mastery and performance-oriented instructional practices. *Contemporary Educational Psychology, 26*, 76–95.

Anderman, E. M., Gray, D. L., & Chang, Y. (2013). Motivation and classroom learning. In W. M. Reynolds & G. E. Miller (Eds.), *Handbook of educational psychology* (2nd ed., pp. 99–116). New York: Wiley.

Anderman, E. M., & Maehr, M. L. (1994). Motivation and schooling in the middle grades. *Review of Educational Research, 64*, 287–309.

Anderman, E. M., Maehr, M. L., & Midgley, C. (1999). Declining motivation after the transition to middle school: Schools can make a difference. *Journal of Research and Development in Education, 32*, 131–147.

Anderman, E. M., & Midgley, C. (1997). Changes in achievement goal orientations, perceived academic competence, and grades across the transition to middle-level schools. *Contemporary Educational Psychology, 22*, 269–298.

Anderson, J. R. (1984). Spreading activation. In J. R. Anderson & S. M. Kosslyn (Eds.), *Tutorials in learning and memory: Essays in honor of Gordon Bower* (pp. 61–90). San Francisco: Freeman.

Anderson, M. C., & Huddleston, E. (2012). Towards and cognitive and neurobiological model of motivated forgetting. In R. F. Belli (Ed.), *True and false recovered memories: Toward a reconciliation of the debate* (pp. 53–120). New York: Springer.

Anderson, N., Schlueter, J. E., Carlson, J. F., & Geisinger, K. F. (Eds.). (2016). *Tests in print IX*. Lincoln, NE: Buros Center for Testing.

Anderson, P., Doyle, L. W., Callanan, C., Carse, E., Casalaz, D., Charlton, M., et al. (2003). Neurobehavioral outcomes of school-age children born extremely low birth weight or very preterm in the 1990s. *Journal of the American Medical Association, 289*, 3264–3272.

Anderson, R. C., & Nagy, W. E. (1991). Word meanings. In R. Barr, M. L. Kamil, P. Mosenthal, & P. D. Pearson (Eds.), *Handbook of reading research* (Vol. 2, pp. 690–724). New York: Longman.

Anderson, R. C., & Pearson, P. D. (1984). A schema-theoretic view of basic processes in reading. In P. D. Pearson (Ed.), *Handbook of reading research* (pp. 255–292). New York: Longman.

Anderson, R. C., Shirey, L. L., Wilson, P. T., & Fielding, L. G. (1987). Interestingness of children's reading material. In R. E. Snow & M. J. Farr (Eds.), *Aptitude, learning, and instruction: Vol. 3. Conative and affective process analyses* (pp. 287–299). Hillsdale, NJ: Erlbaum.

Anderson, S., Leventhal, T., & Dupéré, V. (2014). Exposure to neighborhood affluence and poverty in childhood and adolescence and academic achievement and behavior. *Applied Developmental Science, 18*(3), 123–138.

Anderson, V. (1992). A teacher development project in transactional strategy instruction for teachers of severely reading-disabled adolescents. *Teaching and Teacher Education, 8*, 391–403.

Anderson, V., Spencer-Smith, M., & Wood, A. (2011). Do children really recover better?: Neurobehavioural plasticity after early brain insult. *Brain, 134*, 2197–2221.

Anglin, J. M. (1977). *Word, object, and concept development*. New York: Norton.

Anglin, J. M. (1993). Vocabulary development: A morphological analysis. *Monographs of the Society for Research in Child Development, 58*(Serial No. 238).

Annett, J. (1989). Training skilled performance. In A. M. Colley & J. R. Beech (Eds.), *Acquisition and performance of cognitive skills* (pp. 61–84). Chichester, UK: Wiley.

Ansari, D. (2010). Neurocognitive approaches to developmental disorders of numerical and mathematical cognition: The perils of neglecting the role of development. *Learning and Individual Differences, 20*, 123–129.

Anthony, C. J., DiPerna, J. C., & Amato, P. R. (2014). Divorce, approaches to learning, and children's academic achievement: A longitudinal analysis of mediated and moderated effects. *Journal of School Psychology, 52*, 249–261.

Antia, S. D., & Kriemeyer, K. H. (2003). Peer interactions of deaf and hard-of-hearing children. In M. Marschark & P. E. Spencer (Eds.), *Oxford handbook of deaf studies, language, and education* (pp. 164–176). New York: Oxford University Press.

Archambault, I., Eccles, J. S., & Vida, M. N. (2010). Ability self-concepts and subjective value in literacy: Joint trajectories from grades 1 through 12. *Journal of Educational Psychology, 102*(4), 804–816.

Archer, L., Moore, J., Francis, B., DeWitt, J., & Yeomans, L. (2017). The "exceptional" physics girl: A sociological analysis of multimethod data from young women aged 10 to 16 to explore gendered patterns of post-at participation. *American Educational Research Journal, 54*(1), 88–126.

Areepattamannil, S. (2010). Parenting practices, parenting style, and children's school achievement. *Psychological Studies, 55*(4), 283–289.

Arnold, D. H., Lonigan, C. J., Whitrhurst, G. J., & Epstein, J. N. (1994). Accelerating language development through picture book reading: Replication and extension to a videotape training format. *Journal of Educational Psychology, 86*, 235–243.

Arslan, S., Ktena, S. I., Makropoulos, A., Robinson, E. C., Rueckert, D., & Parisot, S. (2017, April 13). Human brain mapping: A systematic comparison of parcellation methods for the human cerebral cortex. *NeuroImage*. [Epub ahead of print]

Asbury, K., & Plomin, R. (2014). *G is for genes: The impact of genetics on education and achievement*. New York: Wiley.

Asher, J., & Garcia, G. (1969). The optimal age to learn a foreign language. *Modern Language Journal, 38*, 334–341.

Aslin, R. N. (1981). Experimental influence and sensitive period in perceptual development: A unified model. In R. N. Aslin & F. Peterson (Eds.), *The development of perception* (Vol. 2, pp. 45–93). Orlando, FL: Academic Press.

Aslin, R. N., Jurczyk, P. W., & Pisoni, D. B. (1998). Speech and auditory processing during infancy: Constraints on and precursors to language. In W. Damon (Gen. Ed.), D. Kuhn & R. S. Siegler (Vol. Eds.), *Handbook of child psychology: Vol. 2. Cognition, perception, and language* (5th ed., pp. 147–198). New York: Wiley.

Astington, J. W., & Olsen, D. R. (1990). Metacognitive and metalinguistic language: Learning to talk about thought. *Applied Psychology: An International Review, 39*, 77–87.

Atherton, O. E. Schofield, Sitka, T. J. Conger R. D., & Robins, R. W. (2016). Unsupervised self-care predicts conduct problems: The moderating roles of hostile aggression and gender. *Journal of Adolescence, 48*, 1–10

Atkinson, R. C., & Shiffrin, R. M. (1968). Human memory: A proposed system and its control processes. In K. W. Spence & J. T. Spence (Eds.), *The psychology of learning and motivation* (Vol. 2, pp. 90–197). New York: Academic Press.

Au, K., & Mason, J. M. (1981). Social organizational factors in learning to read: The balance of rights hypothesis. *Reading Research Quarterly, 27*, 115–152.

Audley-Piotrowski, S., Singer, A., & Patterson, M. (2015). The role of teacher in children's peer relations: Making the invisible hand intentional. *Transitional Issues in Psychological Sciences, 1*(2), 192–200.

Aukett, A., & Wharton, B. (1995). Suboptimal nutrition. In B. Lindström & N. Spencer (Eds.), *Social pediatrics* (pp. 270–296). Oxford, UK: Oxford University Press.

Ayres, K. M., Mechling, L., & Sansosti, F. J. (2013). The use of mobile technologies to assist with life skills/independence of students with moderate/severe intellectual disability and/or autism spectrum disorders: Considerations for the future of school psychology. *Psychology in the Schools, 50*(3), 259–271.

Ayres, P., & Sweller, J. (2013). Worked examples. In J. Hattie & E. M. Anderman (Eds.), *International guide to student achievement* (pp. 408–410). New York: Routledge.

Bacon, C. S. (1993). Student responsibility for learning. *Adolescence, 28*, 199–212.

Baddeley, A. (1981). The concept of working memory: A view of its current state and probable future development. *Cognition, 10*, 17–23.

Baddeley, A. (1986). *Working memory.* New York: Oxford University Press.

Baibazarova, E., van de Beek, C., Cohen-Kettenis, P. T., Buitelaar, J., Shelton, K. H., & van Goozen, S. H. (2013). Influence of prenatal maternal stress, maternal plasma cortisol and cortisol in the amniotic fluid on birth outcomes and child temperament at 3 months. *Psychoneuroendocrinology, 38*, 907–915.

Bailey, A. L. (2016). Language development. In L. Corno & E. M. Anderman (Eds.), *Handbook of educational psychology* (3rd ed., pp. 199–212). New York: Routledge.

Bain, S. K., & Allin, J. D. (2005). Test review. *Journal of Psychoeducational Assessment, 23*, 87–95.

Bain, S. K., & Gray, R. (2008). Test reviews: *Kaufman Assessment Battery for Children. Journal of Psychoeducational Assessment, 26*(1), 92–101.

Bain, S. K., & Jaspers, K. E. (2010). Review of *Kaufman Brief Intelligence Test, Second Edition. Journal of Psychoeducational Assessment, 28*(2), 167–174.

Baker-Ward, L., Ornstein, P. A., & Holden, D. J. (1984). The expression of memorization in early childhood. *Journal of Experimental Child Psychology, 37*, 555–575.

Bakwin, H. (1973). Reading disability in twins. *Developmental Medicine and Child Neurology, 15*, 184–187.

Baldwin, C. K., Stromwall, K., & Wilder, Q. (2015). Afterschool youth program design and structural quality: Implications for quality improvement. *Child and Youth Services, 36*(3), 226–247.

Baltes, P. B., Reese, H. W., & Nesselroade, J. R. (1988). *Life-span developmental psychology: Introduction to research methods.* Monterey, CA: Brooks/Cole.

Bandura, A. (1965). Vicarious processes: A case of no-trial learning. In L. Berkowitz (Ed.), *Advances in experimental social psychology* (Vol. 2, pp. 1–55). New York: Academic Press.

Bandura, A. (1969). *Principles of behavior modification.* New York: Holt.

Bandura, A. (1977). *Social learning theory.* Englewood Cliffs, NJ: Prentice-Hall.

Bandura, A. (1986). *Social foundations of thought and action: A social cognitive theory.* Englewood Cliffs, NJ: Prentice-Hall.

Bandura, A. (1993). Perceived self-efficacy in cognitive development and functioning. *Educational Psychologist, 28*, 117–148.

Bandura, A. (1997). *Self-efficacy: The exercise of control.* New York: Freeman.

Bandura, A. (2002a). Social cognitive theory in cultural context. *Applied Psychology: An International Review, 51*, 269–290.

Bandura, A. (2002b). Social cognitive theory of mass communication. In J. Bryant & D. Zillmann (Eds.), *Media effects: Advances in theory and research* (2nd ed., pp. 121–153). Mahwah, NJ: Erlbaum.

Bandura, A. (2003). On the psychosocial impact and mechanisms of spiritual modeling: Comment. *International Journal for the Psychology of Religion, 13*, 167–173.

Bandura, A., Barbaranelli, C., Caprara, G. V., & Pastorelli, C. (1996). Multifaceted impact of self-efficacy beliefs on academic functioning. *Child Development, 67*, 1206–1222.

Bandura, A., Barbaranelli, C., Vittorio-Caprara, G. V., & Pastorelli, C. (2001). Self-efficacy beliefs as shapers of children's aspirations and career trajectories. *Child Development, 72*, 187–206.

Bandura, A., Grusec, J. E., & Menlove, F. L. (1966). Observational learning as a function of symbolization and incentive set. *Child Development, 37*, 499–506.

Bandura, A., & Jeffrey, R. W. (1973). Role of symbolic coding and rehearsal processes in observational learning. *Journal of Personality and Social Psychology, 26*, 122–130.

Bandura, A., Jeffrey, R. W., & Bachicha, D. L. (1974). Analysis of memory codes and cumulative rehearsal in observational learning. *Journal of Research in Personality, 7*, 295–305.

Bandura, A., & Schunk, D. H. (1981). Cultivating competence, self-efficacy, and intrinsic interest through proximal self-instruction. *Journal of Personality and Social Psychology, 41*, 586–598.

Bandura, A., & Walters, R. H. (1963). *Social learning and personality development.* New York: Holt, Rinehart & Winston.

Barclay, C. R. (1979). The executive control of mnemonic activity. *Journal of Experimental Child Psychology, 27*, 262–276.

Barkley, R. A. (2013). *Taking charge of ADHD: The complete, authoritative guide for parents.* New York: Guilford Press.

Barkley, R. A., & Benton, C. M. (2013). *Your defiant child: Eight steps to better behavior* (2nd ed.). New York: Guilford Press.

Barkley, R. A., & Robin, A. L. (2013). *Your eefiant teen: 10 steps to resolve conflict and rebuild your relationship* (2nd ed.). New York: Guilford Press.

Barnett, W. S. (2011). Effectiveness of early educational intervention. *Science, 333*, 975–978.

Baron, A. S., Schmader, T. Cvencek, D., & Meltzoff, A. N. (2014). The gendered self-concept: How implicit gender stereotypes and attitudes shape self-definition. In P. J. Leman & H. R. Tenenbaum (Eds.), *Gender and development* (pp. 109–132). New York: Psychology Press.

Baron, I. S. (2005). Test review: Wechsler Intelligence Scale for Children–Fourth Edition (WISC-IV). *Child Neuropsychology, 11*, 471–475.

Barrett, M. D. (1989). Early language development. In A. Slater & C. Bremner (Eds.), *Infant development* (pp. 211–241). London: Erlbaum.

Barrocas, A. L., Giletta, M., Hankin, B. L., Prinstein, M. J., & Abela, J. R. Z. (2015). Nonsuicidal self-injury in adolescence: Longitudinal course, trajectories, and intrapersonal predictors. *Journal of Abnormal Child Psychology, 43*, 369–380.

Bass, B. L., Butler, A. B., Grzywacz, J. G., & Linney, K. D. (2009). Do job demands undermine parenting?: A daily analysis of spillover and crossover effects. *Family Relations, 58*, 201–215.

Bates, E. (1976). *Language and context.* New York: Academic Press.

Bates, E., Bretherton, L., & Snyder, L. (Eds.). (1988). *From first words to grammar: Individual differences and dissociable mechanisms.* Cambridge, UK: Cambridge University Press.

Bates, E., & Roe, K. (2001). Language development in children with unilateral brain injury. In C. A. Nelson & M. Luciana (Eds.), *Handbook of developmental cognitive neuroscience* (pp. 281–307). Cambridge, MA: MIT Press.

Batshaw, M. L., & Tuchman, M. (2002). PKU and other inborn errors of metabolism. In M. L. Batshaw (Ed.), *Children with disabilities* (5th ed., pp. 333–346). Baltimore: Brookes.

Bauer, P. J. (1993). Memory for gender-consistent and gender-inconsistent event sequences by twenty-five-month-old children. *Child Development, 64*, 285–297.

Bauer, P. J., & Fivush, R. (2014). *The Wiley handbook on the development of children's memory.* New York: Wiley.

Bauer, R. H. (1977a). Memory processes in children with learning disabilities. *Journal of Experimental Child Psychology, 24*, 415–430.

Bauer, R. H. (1977b). Short-term memory in learning disabled and nondisabled children. *Bulletin of the Psychonomic Society, 10*, 128–130.

Baumgartner, S. E., Weeda, W. D., van der Heijden, L. L., & Huizinga, M. (2014). The relationship between media multitasking and executive function in early adolescents. *Journal of Early Adolescence, 34*, 1120–1144.

Baumrind, D. (1972). From each according to her ability. *School Review, 80*, 161–197.

Bayley, N. (1969). *Manual for the Bayley Scales of Infant Development.* New York: Psychological Corporation.

Bearer, C. F. (1995). Environmental health hazards: How children are different from adults. *The Future of Children, 5*(1), 11–26.

Bebko, J. M., & Luhaorg, H. (1998). The development of strategy use and metacognitive processing in mental retardation: Some sources of difficulty. In J. A. Burack, R. M. Hodapp, & E. Zigler (Eds.), *Handbook of mental retardation and development* (pp. 382–407). Cambridge, UK: Cambridge University Press.

Bechtel, W., & Abrahamsen, A. (1991). *Connectionism and the mind.* Cambridge, MA: Basil Blackwell.

Beck, I. L., & McKeown, M. (1991). Conditions of vocabulary acquisition. In R. Barr, M. L. Kamil, P. Mosenthal, & P. D. Pearson (Eds.), *Handbook of reading research* (Vol. 2, pp. 789–814). New York: Longman.

Beesdo-Baum, K., & Knappe, S. (2012). Developmental epidemiology of anxiety disorders. *Child and Adolescent Psychiatric Clinics, 21*(3), 457–478.

Behne, T., Carpenter, M., Call, J., & Thomasello, M. (2005). Unwilling versus unable infants' understanding of intentional action. *Developmental Psychology, 41*(2), 328–337.

Behrend, D. A., Scofield, J., & Kleinknecht, E. E. (2001). Beyond fast mapping: Young children's extensions of novel words and novel facts. *Developmental Psychology, 37*(5), 698–705.

Beker L. T., Farber, A. F., & Yanni, C. (2002). Nutrition and children with disabilities. In M. L. Batshaw (Ed.), *Children with disabilities* (5th ed., pp. 141–164). Baltimore: Brookes.

Bell, M. A., & Fox, N. A. (1992). The relations between frontal brain electrical activity and cognitive development during infancy. *Child Development, 63*, 1142–1163.

Bell, M. A., & Fox, N. A. (1994). Brain development over the first year of life: Relations between electroencephalographic frequency and coherence and cognitive and affective behaviors. In G. Dawson & K. W. Fischer (Eds.), *Human behavior and the developing brain* (pp. 314–345). New York: Guilford Press.

Bell, M. A., & Fox, N. A. (1997). Individual differences in object permanence performance at 8 months: Locomotor experience and brain electrical activity. *Developmental Psychobiology, 31*, 287–297.

Bell, M. A., Wolfe, C. D., & Adkins, D. R. (2007). Frontal lobe development during infancy and childhood: Contributions of brain electrical activity, temperament, and language to individual differences in working memory and inhibitory control. In D. Coch, G. Watson, & K. W. Fischer (Eds.), *Human behavior, learning, and the developing brain: Typical development*, (pp. 247–276). New York: Guilford Press.

Bell, R. Q. (1968). A reinterpretation of the direction of effects in studies of socialization. *Psychological Review, 75*, 81–95.

Bell, R. Q., & Harper, L. V. (1977). *Child effects on adults*. Hillsdale, NJ: Erlbaum.

Belland, B. R., Kim, C., & Hannafin, M. (2013). A framework for designing scaffolds that improve motivation and cognition. *Educational Psychologist, 48*(4), 243–270.

Belli, R. F. (2012). Introduction: In the aftermath of the so-called memory wars. In R. F. Belli (Ed.), *True and false recovered memories: Toward a reconciliation of the debate* (pp. 11–13). New York: Springer.

Belsky, J. (2006). Early child care child development: Major findings of the NICHD study of early child care. *European Journal of Developmental Psychology, 3*(1), 95–110.

Belsky, J., Burchinal, M., McCartney, K., Vandell, D. L., Clarke-Stewart, K. A., Owen, M. T., et al. (2007). Are there long term effects of early child care? *Child Development, 78*(2), 681–701.

Bem, S. L. (1981). Gender schema theory: A cognitive account of sex typing, *Psychological Review, 58*, 354–364.

Bem, S. L. (1989). Genital knowledge and gender constancy in preschool children. *Child Development, 60*, 649–662.

Benenson, J. F., Apostoleris, N. H., & Parnass, J. (1997). Age and sex differences in dyadic and group interaction. *Developmental Psychology, 33*, 538–543.

Benigno, J., Clark, L., & Farrar, M. J. (2007). Three is not always a crowd: Contexts of joint attention and language. *Journal of Child Language, 34*(1), 175–187.

Benita, M., Roth, G., & Deci, E. J. (2014). When are mastery goals more adaptive?: It depends on experiences of autonomy support and autonomy. *Journal of Educational Psychology, 106*(1), 258–267.

Benjamin, A. S., & Tullis, J. (2010). What makes distributed practice effective? *Cognitive Psychology, 61*, 228–247.

Benner, A., & Graham, S. (2009). The transition to high school as a developmental process among multiethnic urban youth. *Child Development, 80*(2), 356–376.

Bercury, K. K., & Macklin, W. B. (2015). Dynamics and mechanisms of CNS myelination. *Developmental Cell, 32*, 447–458.

Bereiter, C. (1990). Aspects of an educational learning theory. *Review of Educational Research, 60*, 603–624.

Bereiter, C., & Scardamalia, M. (1982). From conversation to composition. The role of instruction in a developmental process. In R. Glaser (Ed.), *Advances in instructional psychology* (Vol. 2, pp. 1–64). Hillsdale, NJ: Erlbaum.

Berenbaum, S. A., & Beltz, A. M. (2016). How early hormones shape gender development. *Current Opinion in Behavioral Sciences, 7*, 53–60.

Berenbaum, S. A., Bryk, K. L. K., & Beltz, A. M. (2012). Early androgen effects on spatial and mechanical abilities: Evidence from congenital adrenal hyperplasia. *Behavioral Neuroscience, 126*(1), 86–96.

Berg, J. M. (1985). Physical determinants of environmental origin. In A. M. Clarke, A. D. B. Clarke,

& J. M. Berg (Eds.), *Mental deficiency: The changing outlook* (4th ed., pp. 99–134). New York: Free Press.

Bergin, C., & Bergin, D. (2009). Attachment in the classroom. *Educational Psychology Review, 21*, 141–170.

Berk, L. E. (1986). Relationship of elementary school children's private speech to behavioral accompaniment to task, attention, and task performance. *Developmental Psychology, 22*(5), 671–680.

Berkeley, S., Mastropieri, M. A., & Scruggs, T. E. (2010). Reading comprehension instruction for students with learning disabilities, 1995–2006. *Remedial and Special Education, 31*(6), 423–436.

Berkeley, S., Mastropieri, M. A., & Scruggs, T. E. (2011). Reading comprehension strategy instruction and attribution retraining for secondary students with learning and other mild disabilities. *Journal of Learning Disabilities, 44*(1), 18–32.

Berkowitz, M. (2012). Moral and character education. In K. Harris, S. Graham, & T. Urdan (Eds.), *APA educational psychology handbook: Vol. 2. Individual differences and cultural and contextual factors* (pp. 247–264). Washington, DC: American Psychological Association.

Berlin, L. J., Cassidy, J., & Appleyard, K. (2008). The influence of early attachment on other relationships. In J. Cassidy & P. R. Shaver (Eds.), *Handbook of attachment: Theory, research, and clinical applications* (2nd ed., pp. 333–347). New York: Guilford Press.

Berlin, L. J., Zeanah, C. H., & Lieberman, A. F. (2016). Prevention and intervention programs to support early attachment security: A move to the level of the community. In J. Cassidy & P. R. Shaver (Eds.), *Handbook of attachment: Theory, research, and clinical applications* (3rd ed., pp. 739–758). New York: Guilford Press.

Bernacki, M. L., Nokes-Malach, T. J., & Aleven, V. (2015). Examining self-efficacy during learning: Variability and relations to behavior, performance, and learning. *Metacognition and Learning, 10*(1), 99–117.

Berndt, T. J., & Miller, K. E. (1990). Expectancies, values, and achievement in junior high school. *Journal of Educational Psychology, 82*, 319–326.

Bernier, A., Beauchamp, M. H., Carlson, S. M., & Lalonde, G. (2015). A secure base from which to regulate: Attachment security in toddlerhood as a predictor of executive functioning at school entry. *Developmental Psychology, 51*(9), 1177–1189.

Berry, G. (2000). Multicultural media portrayals and the changing demographic landscape: The psychological impact of television representations on the adolescent of color. *Journal of Adolescent Health, 275*, 57–60.

Best, J. R., Miller, P. H., & Naglieri, J. A. (2011). Relations between executive function and academic achievement from ages 5 to 17 in a large, representative national sample. *Learning and Individual Differences, 21*, 327–336.

Bialystok, E. (1987). Words as things: Development of word concept by bilingual children. *Studies in Second Language Acquisition, 9*, 133–140.

Bialystok, E. (1997). Effects of bilingualism and biliteracy on children's emerging concepts of print. *Developmental Psychology, 33*, 429–440.

Bialystok, E., Shenfield, T., & Codd, J. (2000). Languages, scripts, and the environment: Factors in developing concepts of print. *Developmental Psychology, 36*, 66–76.

Bianci, S. M., & Milkie, M. A. (2010). Work and family research in the first decade of the 21st century. *Journal of Marriage and Family, 72*, 705–725.

Bidell, T. R., & Fischer, K. W. (1992). Cognitive development in educational contexts: Implications for skill theory. In A. Demetriou, M. Shayner, & A. Efklides (Eds.), *Neo-Piagetian theories of cognitive development* (pp. 11–30). New York: Routledge.

Bidell, T. R., & Fischer, K. W. (2000). The role of cognitive structure in the development of behavioral control: A dynamic skills approach. In W. J. Perrig & A. Grob (Eds.), *Control of human behavior, mental processes, and consciousness: Essays in honor of the 60th birthday of August Flammer* (pp. 183–201). Mahwah, NJ: Erlbaum.

Biemiller, A. (2003). Vocabulary: Needed if more children are to read well. *Reading Psychology, 24*, 323–335.

Biemiller, A., & Slonim, N. (2001). Estimating root word vocabulary growth in normative and advantaged populations: Evidence for a common sequence of vocabulary acquisition. *Journal of Educational Psychology, 93*, 498–520.

Bigler, R. S. (1995). The role of classification skill in moderating environmental influences on children's gender stereotyping: A study of the functional use of gender in the classroom. *Child Development, 66*, 1072–1087.

Bigler, R. S., Hayes, A. R., & Liben, L. S. (2014). Analysis and evaluation of the rationales for single-sex schooling. In L. S. Liben & R. S. Bigler (Eds.), *Advances in child development and behavior: Vol. 47. The role of gender in educational contexts and outcomes* (pp. 325–360). New York: Academic Press.

Binet, A., & Simon, T. (1905a). Application des méthodes nouvelles au diagnostic du niveau intellectuel chez des enfants normaux et anormaux d'hospice et d'école primaire. *L'Année Psychologique, 11*, 245–336.

Binet, A., & Simon, T. (1905b). Methodes nouvelles

pour le disagnostic du niveau intellectual des anormaux. *L'Annee Psychologique, 11*, 191–244.

Binet, A., & Simon, T. (1905c). Sur la necessité d'établir un diagnostic scientifique des états inférieurs de l'intelligence. *L'Année Psychologique, 11*, 163–190.

Birdsong, D. (1999). *Second language acquisition and the critical period hypothesis.* Mahwah, NJ: Erlbaum.

Birdsong, D. (2005). Interpreting age effects in second language acquisition. In J. F. Kroll & A. M. B. de Groot (Eds.), *Handbook of bilingualism: Psycholinguistic approaches* (pp. 109–127). New York: Oxford University Press.

Birdsong, D., & Vanhove, J. (2016). Age of second-language acquisition: Critical periods and social concerns. In E. Nicoladis & S. Montanari (Eds.), *Bilingualism across the lifespan: Factors moderating language proficiency* (pp. 163–181). Washington, DC: American Psychological Association.

Birenbaum, A. (2002). Poverty, welfare reform, and disproportionate rates of disability among children. *Mental Retardation, 40*, 212–218.

Bjorklund, D. F. (1989). *Cognitive development.* Monterey, CA: Brooks/Cole.

Bjorklund, D. F. (2000). *Children's thinking: Developmental function and individual differences* (3rd ed.). Belmont, CA: Wadsworth Thomson Learning.

Bjorklund, D. F., Dukes, C., & Brown, R. D. (2009). The development of memory strategies. In M. L. Courage & N. Cowan (Eds.), *The development of memory in infancy and childhood* (2nd ed., pp. 145–175). New York: Psychology Press.

Bjorklund, D. F., & Harnishfeger, K. K. (1990). The resources construct in cognitive development: Diverse resources of evidence and a theory of inefficient inhibition. *Developmental Review, 10*, 48–71.

Blackwell, L. S., Trzesniewski, K. H., & Dweck, C. S. (2007). Implicit theories of intelligence predict achievement across an adolescent transition: A longitudinal study and an intervention. *Child Development, 78*(1), 246–263.

Blackwood, R. (1970). The operant conditioning of verbally mediated self-control in the classroom. *Journal of School Psychology, 8*, 251–258.

Blair, C., & Raver, C. C. (2012). Child development in the context of adversity: Experiential canalization of brain and behavior. *American Psychologist, 67*, 309–318.

Blais, J. J., Craig, W. M., Pepler, D., & Connolly, J. (2008). Adolescents online: The importance of Internet activity choices to salient relationships. *Journal of Youth and Adolescence, 37*, 522–536.

Blake, J. J., Smith, L. V., & Knight, A. D. (2016). Theoretical frameworks for ethnic minority youth achievement. In S. L. Graves & J. J. Blake (Eds.), *Psychoeducational assessment and intervention for ethnic minority children: Evidence-based approaches* (pp. 23–39). Washington, DC: American Psychological Association.

Blakemore, S. J., & Choudhury, S. (2006). Development of the adolescent brain: Implications for executive function and social cognition. *Journal of Child Psychology and Psychiatry, 47*, 296–312.

Blakey, E., Visser, I., & Carroll, D. J. (2016). Different executive functions support different kinds of cognitive flexibility: Evidence from 2-, 3-, and 4-year-olds. *Child Development, 87*(2), 513–526.

Blarney, P. J. (2003). Development of spoken language by deaf children. In M. Marschark & P. E. Spencer (Eds.), *Oxford handbook of deaf studies, language, and education* (pp. 232–246). New York: Oxford University Press.

Bloom, B. S. (1985). *Developing talent in young people.* New York: Ballantine Books.

Bloom, L. (1973). *One word at a time.* The Hague, The Netherlands: Mouton.

Bloom, L. (1998). Language acquisition in its developmental context. In W. Damon (Gen. Ed.), D. Kuhn & R. S. Siegler (Vol. Eds.), *Handbook of child psychology: Vol. 2. Cognition, perception, and language* (5th ed., pp. 309–370). New York: Wiley.

Bloom, L., Margulis, C., Tinker, E., & Fujita, N. (1996). Early conversations and word learning: Contributions from child and adult. *Child Development, 67*, 3154–3175.

Bloom, L., Rocissano, L., & Hood, L. (1976). Adult–child discourse: Developmental interaction between linguistic processing and linguistic knowledge. *Cognitive Psychology, 8*, 521–552.

Bloom, L., & Tinker, E. (2001). The intentionality model and language acquisition. *Monographs of the Society for Research in Child Development, 66*(Serial No. 267), i–viii, 1–91.

Blumenfeld, P. C. (1992). Classroom learning and motivation: Clarifying and expanding goal theory. *Journal of Educational Psychology, 84*, 272–281.

Bodrova, E., & Leong, D. J. (2003). Learning and development of preschool children from the Vygotskian perspective. In A. Kozulin, B. Gindia, V. S. Ageyev, & S. M. Miller (Eds.), *Vygotsky's educational theory in cultural context* (pp. 156–176). Cambridge, UK: Cambridge University Press.

Bodrova, E., & Leong, D. J. (2009). Tools of the mind: A Vygotskian-based early childhood curriculum. *Early Childhood Services: An Interdisciplinary Journal of Effectiveness, 3*(3), 245–262.

Bogner, K., Raphael, L. M., & Pressley, M. (2002). How grade-1 teachers motivate literate activity by their students. *Scientific Studies of Reading, 6*, 135–165.

Bohn, C. M., Roehrig, A. D., & Pressley, M. (2004). The first days of school in effective and less effective primary-grades classrooms. *Elementary School Journal, 104*, 269–278.

Bohn, M., Call, J., & Tomasello, M. (2016). The role of past interactions in great apes' communication about absent entities. *Journal of Comparative Psychology, 130*(4), 351–357.

Boldt, L. J. Kochanska, G., Yoon, J. E., & Nordling, J. K. (2014). Children's attachment to both parents from toddler age to middle childhood: Links to adaptive and maladaptive outcomes. *Attachment and Human Development, 16*(3), 211–229.

Bolten, M., Nast, I., Skrundz, M., Stadler, C., Hellhammer, D. H., & Meinlschmidt, G. (2013). Prenatal programming of emotion regulation: Neonatal reactivity as a differential susceptibility factor moderating the outcome of prenatal cortisol levels. *Journal of Psychosomatic Research, 75*, 351–357.

Bomba, P. C., & Siqueland, E. R. (1983). The nature and structure of infant form categories. *Journal of Experimental Child Psychology, 35*, 294–328.

Bond, G. L., & Dykstra, R. (1967). The cooperative research program in first-grade reading instruction. *Reading Research Quarterly, 2*, 5–142.

Bong, M. (2013). Self-efficacy. In J. Hattie & E. M. Anderman (Eds.), *International guide to student achievement* (pp. 64–66). New York: Routledge.

Bookbinder, S. H., & Brainerd, C. J. (2016). Emotion and false memory: The context-content paradox. *Psychological Bulletin, 142*(12), 1315–1351.

Boone, A. P., & Hegarty, M. (2017). Sex differences in mental rotation tasks: Not just in the mental rotation process! *Journal of Experimental Psychology: Learning, Memory, and Cognition, 93*(7), 1005–1019.

Booth, J. R., & Hall, W. S. (1994). Role of the cognitive internal state lexicon in reading comprehension. *Journal of Educational Psychology, 86*, 413–422.

Borja-Alvarez, T., Zarbatany, L., & Pepper, S. (1991). Contributions of male and female guests and hosts to peer group entry. *Child Development, 62*, 1079–1090.

Borkowski, J. G., Carr, M., Rellinger, E. A., & Pressley, M. (1990). Self-regulated strategy use: Interdependence of metacognition, attributions, and self-esteem. In B. F. Jones (Ed.), *Dimensions of thinking: Review of research* (pp. 53–92). Hillsdale, NJ: Erlbaum.

Borkowski, J. G., Weyhing, R. S., & Carr, M. (1988). Effects of attributional retraining on strategy-based reading comprehension in learning-disabled students. *Journal of Educational Psychology, 80*, 46–53.

Bornstein, M. H., Hahn, C. S., & Suwalsky, J. T. (2013). Physically developed and exploratory young infants contribute to their own long-term academic achievement. *Psychological Science, 24*, 1906–1917.

Bornstein, M. H., Jager, J., & Steinberg, L. G. (2013). Adolescents, parents, friends/peers. In R. M. Lerner, M. A. Easterbrooks, & J. Mistry (Eds.), *Handbook of developmental psychology* (2nd ed., pp. 393–433). New York: Wiley.

Bos, C. S., & Vaughn, S. (1991). *Strategies for teaching students with learning and behavior problems*. Boston: Allyn & Bacon.

Boston, M. B., & Levy, G. D. (1991). Changes and differences in preschoolers' understanding of gender scripts. *Cognitive Development, 6*, 417–432.

Bouchard, T. J., Jr., & Loehlin, J. C. (2001). Genes, evolution, and personality. *Behavior Genetics, 31*, 243–273.

Bourgeois, J. P. (2001). Synaptogenesis in the neocortex of the newborn: The ultimate frontier for individuation. In C. A. Nelson & M. Luciana (Eds.), *Handbook of developmental cognitive neuroscience* (pp. 23–34). Cambridge, MA: MIT Press.

Boutte, G. S., & Johnson, G. L. (2013). Do educators see and honor biliteracy and bidialecticalism in African American language speakers?: Apprehensions and reflections of two grandparents/professional educators. *Early Childhood Education, 41*, 133–141.

Bowen, N. K., Wegmann, K. M., & Webber, K. C. (2013). Enhancing a brief writing intervention to combat stereotype threat among middle-school students. *Journal of Educational Psychology, 105*(2), 427–435.

Bower, G. H. (1972). Mental imagery and associative learning. In L. Gregg (Ed.), *Cognition in learning and memory* (pp. 51–87). New York: Wiley.

Bower, G. H., & Hilgard, E. R. (1981). *Theories of learning* (5th ed.). Englewood Cliffs, NJ: Prentice-Hall.

Bowers, C. A., & Flinders, D. J. (1990). *Responsive teaching: An ecological approach to classroom patterns of language, culture, and thought*. New York: Teachers College Press.

Bowey, J. A., & Tunmer, W. E. (1984). Word awareness in children. In W. E. Tunmer, C. Pratt, & M. L. Herriman (Eds.), *Metalinguistic awareness in children* (pp. 73–91). Berlin: Springer-Verlag.

Bowlby, J. (1969). *Attachment and loss: Vol. 1. Attachment*. New York: Basic Books.

Bowlby, J. (1973). *Attachment and loss: Vol. 2. Separation*. New York: Basic Books.

Bowlby, J. (1980). *Attachment and loss: Vol. 3. Loss*. New York: Basic Books.

Bowlby, R. (2007). Babies and toddlers in nonparental daycare can avoid stress and anxiety if they develop a lasting secondary attachment bond with one carer who is consistently accessible to them. *Attachment and Human Development, 9*(4), 307–319.

Boyd, D. (2014). *It's complicated: The social lives of networked teens*. New Haven, CT: Yale University Press.

Boyes, M. C., & Chandler, M. (1992). Cognitive development, epistemic doubt, and identity formation in adolesence. *Journal of Youth and Adolescence, 21*, 277–304.

Boysson-Bardies, B. de, Halle, P., Sagart, L., & Durand, C. (1989). A cross-linguistic investigation of vowel formants in babbling. *Journal of Child Language, 16*, 1–17.

Boysson-Bardies, B. de, Vihman, M. M., Roug-Hellichius, L., Durand, C., Landberg, I., & Arao, F. (1992). Material evidence of infant selection from target language: A cross-linguistic study. In C. A. Ferguson, L. Menn, & C. Stoel-Gammon (Eds.), *Phonological development: Models, research, and implications* (pp. 369–91). Timonium, MD: York Press.

Braasch, J. L. G., Goldman, S. R., & Wiley, J. (2013). The influence of text and reader characteristics on learning from refutations in science texts. *Journal of Educational Psychology, 105*(3), 561–578.

Bracht, G. H., & Glass, G. V. (1968). The external validity of experiments. *American Educational Research Journal, 5*, 437–474.

Braden, J. P. (2003). Psychological assessment in school settings. In J. R. Graham & J. A. Naglieri (Vol. Eds.), & I. B. Weiner (Ed.-in-Chief), *Handbook of psychology: Vol. 10. Assessment psychology* (pp. 261–290). New York: Wiley.

Bradford, M. R., & Ensley, R. C. (1983). The effects of sex-typed labeling on preschool children's information-seeking and retention. *Sex Roles, 9*, 247–260.

Bradley, L. (1988). Making connections in learning to read and to spell. *Applied Cognitive Psychology, 2*, 3–18.

Bradley, L. (1989). Predicting learning disabilities. In J. Dumont & H. Nakken (Eds.), *Learning disabilities: Vol. 2. Cognitive, social, and remedial aspects* (pp. 1–18). Amsterdam, The Netherlands: Swets.

Bradley, L., & Bryant, P. E. (1983). Categorizing sounds and learning to read—a causal connection. *Nature, 301*, 419–421.

Bradley, L., & Bryant, P. (1991). Phonological skills before and after learning to read. In S. A. Brady & D. P. Shankweiler (Eds.), *Phonological processes in literacy: A tribute to Isabelle Y. Liberman* (pp. 37–45). Hillsdale, NJ: Erlbaum.

Braine, M. D. (1963). The ontogeny of English phrase structure: The first phase. *Language, 39*, 3–13.

Braine, M. D. (1976). Children's first-word combinations. *Monographs of the Society for Research in Child Development, 41*(164), 1–104.

Brainerd, C. J. (1978a). Learning research and Piagetian theory. In L. S. Siegel & C. J. Brainerd (Eds.), *Alternatives to Piaget: Critical essays on the theory* (pp. 69–109). New York: Academic Press.

Brainerd, C. J. (1978b). *Piaget's theory of intelligence.* Englewood Cliffs, NJ: Prentice-Hall.

Brainerd, C. J., & Reyna, V. F. (1989). Output-interference theory of dual-task deficits in memory development. *Journal of Experimental Child Psychology, 47*, 1–18.

Brainerd, C. J., & Reyna, V. F. (1993). "Memory independence and memory interference in cognitive development": Correction. *Psychological Review, 100*(2), 319.

Brainerd, C. J., & Reyna, V. F. (1995). Autosuggestibility and memory development. *Cognitive Psychology, 28*, 65–101.

Braithwaite, D. W., & Goldstone, R. L. (2015). Effects of variation and prior knowledge on abstract concept learning. *Cognition and Instruction, 33*(3), 226–256.

Brandtjen, H., & Verny, T. (2001). Short and long term effects on infants and toddlers in full time daycare centers. *Journal of Prenatal Psychology and Health, 15*(4), 239–286.

Branum-Martin, L., Mehta, P. D., Carlson, C. D., Francis, D. J., & Goldenberg, C. (2014). The nature of Spanish versus English language use at home. *Journal of Educational Psychology, 106*(1), 181–199.

Branum-Martin, L., Tao, S., & Garnaat, S. (2015). Bilingual phonological awareness: Re-examining the evidence for relations within and across languages. *Journal of Educational Psychology, 107*(1), 111–125.

Braten, I., & Anmarkrud, O. (2013). Does naturally occurring comprehension strategies instruction make a difference when students read expository text? *Journal of Research in Reading, 36*(1), 42–57.

Braungart-Rieker, J. M., Garwood, M. M., Powers, B. P., & Wang, X. (2001). Parental sensitivity, infant affect, and affect regulation: Predictors of later attachment. *Child Development, 72*, 252–270.

Bray, N. W., Fletcher, K. L., & Turner, L. A. (1997). Cognitive competencies and strategy use in individuals with mental retardation. In W. E. MacLean Jr. (Ed.), *Ellis' handbook of mental deficiency, psychological theory and research* (pp. 197–217). Mahwah, NJ: Erlbaum.

Bremmer, J. G., Slater, A. M., & Johnson, S. P. (2015). Perception of object persistence: The origins of object permanence in infancy. *Child Development Perspectives, 9*(1), 7–13.

Bremner, J. G. (2011). Four themes from 20 years of research on infant perception and cognition. *Infant and Child Development, 20*, 137–147.

Bretherton, I., & Munholland, K. A. (2016). The internal working model construct in light of contemporary neuroimaging research. In J. Cassidy & P. R. Shaver (Eds.), *Handbook of attachment: Theory, research, and clinical applications* (3rd ed., pp. 63–90). New York: Guilford Press.

Bretl, D. J., & Cantor, J. (1988). The portrayal of men and women in U.S. television commercials:

A recent content analysis and trends over 15 years. *Sex Roles, 18*(9–10), 595–609.

Brewer, N. (1987). Processing speed, efficiency, and intelligence. In J. G. Borkowski & J. D. Day (Eds.), *Cognition in special children: Comparative approaches to retardation, learning disabilities, and giftedness* (pp. 15–48). Norwood, NJ: Ablex.

Brigham, C. C. (1923). *A study of American intelligence.* Princeton, NJ: Princeton University Press.

Brink, K. A., Lane, J. D., & Wellman, H. M. (2015). Developmental pathways for social understandings: Linking social cognition to social contexts. *Frontiers in Psychology, 6*(719), 1–11.

Brody, L. (1999). *Gender, emotion, and the family.* Cambridge, MA: Harvard University Press.

Brody, N. (1992). *Intelligence.* San Diego, CA: Academic Press.

Bronfenbrenner, U. (1979). *The ecology of human development.* Cambridge, MA: Harvard University Press.

Bronfenbrenner, U. (1989). Ecological systems theory. In R. Vasta (Ed.), *Annals of child development* (Vol. 6, pp. 187–251). Greenwich, CT: JAI Press.

Bronfenbrenner, U. (1992). Ecological systems theory. In R. Vasta (Ed.), *Six theories of child development: Revised formulations and current issues* (pp. 187–249). London: Jessica Kingsley.

Brooks, R., & Meltzoff, A. N. (2015). Connecting the dots from infancy to childhood: A longitudinal study connecting gaze following, language, and explicit theory of mind. *Journal of Experimental Child Psychology, 130*, 67–78.

Brooks-Gunn, J., Han, W., & Waldfogel, J. (2010). First-year maternal employment and child development in the first seven years. *Monographs of the Society for Research in Child Development, 75*(2), 7–9.

Brophy, J. (1981). Teacher praise: A functional analysis. *Review of Educational Research, 51*, 5–32.

Brophy, J. (1987). Socializing students' motivation to learning. In M. L. Maehr & D. A. Kleiber (Eds.), *Advances in motivation and achievement: Enhancing motivation* (Vol. 5, pp. 181–210). Greenwich, CT: JAI Press.

Brophy, J. E. (1998). *Motivating students to learn.* Boston: McGraw-Hill.

Brophy, J. E., & Evertson, C. M. (1976). *Learning from teaching: A developmental perspective.* Boston: Allyn & Bacon.

Brophy, J., & Good, T. (1974). *Teacher–student relationships: Causes and consequences.* New York: Holt, Rinehart & Winston.

Brown, A. L. (1974). The role of strategic behavior in retardate memory. In N. R. Ellis (Ed.), *International review of research in mental retardation* (Vol. 7, pp. 55–111). New York: Academic Press.

Brown, A. L., & Palincsar, A. S. (1989). Guided, cooperative learning and individual knowledge acquisition. In L. B. Resnick (Ed.), *Knowing, learning, and instruction: Essays in honor of Robert Glaser* (pp. 393–451). Hillsdale, NJ: Erlbaum.

Brown, B. B., & Dietz, E. (2009). Informal peer groups in middle childhood and adolescence. In K. H. Rubin, W. M. Bukowski, & B. Laursen (Eds.), *Handbook of peer interactions, relationships, and groups* (pp. 361–376). New York: Guilford Press.

Brown, I. (1976). Role of referent concreteness in the acquisition of passive sentence comprehension through abstract modeling. *Journal of Experimental Child Psychology, 22*, 185–189.

Brown, I. (1979). Language acquisition: Linguistic structure and rule-governed behavior. In G. J. Whitehurst & B. J. Zimmerman (Eds.), *The functions of language and cognition* (pp. 141–173). New York: Academic Press.

Brown, J. S., Collins, A., & Duguid, P. (1989). Situated cognition and the culture of learning. *Educational Researcher, 18*(1), 32–42.

Brown, Ra. (2008). The road not taken: A transactional strategies approach to comprehension instruction. *The Reading Teacher, 61*(7), 538–547.

Brown, Ra., Pressley, M., & Van Meter, P. (1996). A quasi-experimental validation of transactional strategies instruction with low-achieving grade-2 readers. *Journal of Educational Psychology, 88*, 18–37.

Brown, Ro. (1965). *Social psychology.* New York: Free Press.

Brown, Ro. (1973). *A first language: The early stages.* Cambridge, MA: Harvard University Press.

Brown, Ro., & Bellugi, U. (1964). Three processes in the child's acquisition of syntax. *Harvard Educational Review, 34*, 133–151.

Brown, T. T., & Jernigan, T. L. (2012). Brain development during the preschool years. *Neuropsychology Review, 22*, 313–333.

Brownell, C. A. (2016). Prosocial behavior in infancy: The role of socialization. *Child Development Perspectives, 10*(4), 222–227.

Bruck, M. (1990). Word-recognition skills of adults with childhood diagnoses of dyslexia. *Developmental Psychology, 26*, 439–454.

Bruck, M. (1992). Persistence of dyslexics' phonological awareness deficits. *Developmental Psychology, 28*, 874–886.

Bruner, J. S., Olver, R. R., & Greenfield, P. M. (1966). *Studies in cognitive growth.* New York: Wiley.

Bryant, A. L., Schulenberg, J. E., O'Malley, P. M., Bachman, J. G., & Johnston, L. D. (2003). How academic achievement, attitudes, and behaviors relate to the course of substance abuse during adolescence. *Journal of Research on Adolescence, 13*, 361–397.

Buday, S. K., Stake, J. E., & Peterson, Z. (2012). Gender and the choice of a science career: The impact of social support and possible selves. *Sex Roles, 66*(3–4), 197–209.

Budoff, M. (1987). Measures for assessing learning potential. In C. S. Lidz (Ed.), *Dynamic assessment: An interactional approach to evaluating learning potential* (pp. 173–195). New York: Guilford Press.

Buhs, E. S. Rudasill, K. M., Kalutskaya, I. N., & Griese, E. R. (2015). Shyness and engagement: Contributions of peer rejection and teacher sensitivity. *Early Childhood Research Quarterly, 30*, 12–19.

Bui, D. C., Myerson, J., & Hale, S. (2013). Note-taking with computers: Exploring alternative strategies for improved recall. *Journal of Educational Psychology, 105*(2), 299–309.

Burbules, N. C., & Linn, M. C. (1988). Response to contradiction: Scientific reasoning during adolescence. *Journal of Educational Psychology, 80*, 67–75.

Burchinal, M., Steinberg, L., Friedman, S. L., Pianta, R., McCartney, K., Crosnoe, R., et al. (2011). Examining the Black–White achievement gap among low-income children using the NICHD study of early child care and youth development. *Child Development, 82*, 1404–1420.

Burgaleta, M., Head, K., Álvarez-Linera, J., Martinez, K., Escorial, S., Haier, R., et al.(2012). Sex differences in brain volume are related to specific skills not to general intelligence. *Intelligence, 40*, 60–68.

Burger, K. (2010). How does early childhood care and education affect cognitive development?: An international review of the effects of early interventions for children from different social backgrounds. *Early Childhood Research Quarterly, 25*, 140–165.

Burgess, D. M., & Streissguth, A. P. (1992). Fetal alcohol syndrome and fetal alcohol effects: Principles for educators. *Phi Delta Kappan, 74*, 24–30.

Burns, C. W. (2003). Assessing the psychological and educational needs of children with moderate and severe mental retardation. In C. R. Reynolds & R. W. Kamphaus (Eds.), *Handbook of psychological and educational assessment of children: Intelligence, aptitude, and achievement* (2nd ed., pp. 671–684). New York: Guilford Press.

Bus, A. G., van IJzendoorn, M. H., & Pellegrini, A. D. (1995). Joint book reading makes for success in learning to read: A meta-analysis on intergenerational transmission of literacy. *Review of Educational Research, 65*, 1–21.

Buschman, T. J., Siegel, M., Roy, J. E., & Miller, E. K. (2011). Neural substrates of cognitive capacity limitations. *Proceedings of the National Academy of Sciences of the USA, 108*, 11252–11255.

Bussey, K., & Bandura, A. (1984). Influence of gender constancy and social power on sex-linked modeling. *Journal of Personality and Social Psychology, 47*, 1292–1302.

Bussey, K., & Bandura, A. (1992). Self-regulatory mechanisms governing gender development. *Child Development, 63*, 1236–1250.

Bussey, K., & Perry, D. G. (1982). Same-sex imitation. *Sex Roles, 8*, 773–784.

Butkowski, I. S., & Willows, D. M. (1980). Cognitive-motivational characteristics of children varying in reading ability: Evidence for learned helplessness in poor readers. *Journal of Educational Psychology, 72*, 408–422.

Butler, A. C., & Roediger, H. L. (2008). Feedback enhances the positive effects and reduces the negative effects of multiple-choice testing. *Memory and Cognition, 36*, 604–616.

Butler, R. (2014). Motivation in educational contexts: Does gender matter? In L. S. Liben & R. S. Bigler (Eds.), *Advances in child development and behavior: Vol. 47. The role of gender in educational contexts and outcomes* (pp. 2–41). New York: Academic Press.

Butterfield, E. C., & Belmont, J. M. (1977). Assessing and improving the executive cognitive functions of mentally retarded people. In I. Bialar & M. Sternlicht (Eds.), *Psychological issues in mental retardation* (pp. 277–318). New York: Psychological Dimensions.

Butz, A. R., & Usher, E. L. (2015). Salient sources of early adolescents' self-efficacy in two domains. *Contemporary Educational Psychology, 42*, 49–61.

Byrnes, J. P. (2012). How neuroscience contributes to our understanding of learning and development in typically developing and special-needs students. In K. R. Harris, S. Graham, & T. Urdan (Eds.), *Educational psychology handbook: Vol. 1. Theories, constructs and critical issues* (pp. 561–595). Washington, DC: American Psychological Association.

Cacchione, T. (2013). The foundations of object permanence: Does perceived cohesion determine infants' appreciation of the continuous existence of material objects. *Cognition, 128*, 397–406.

Caes, L., Fisher, E., Clinch, J., Tobias, J. H., & Eccleston, C. (2015). The development of worry throughout childhood: Avon longitudinal study of parents and children data. *British Journal of Health Psychology, 21*, 389–406.

Cain, M. S., Leonard, J. A., Gabrieli, J. D., & Finn, A. S. (2016). Media multitasking in adolescence. *Psychonomic Bulletin and Review, 23*, 1932–1941.

Caine, D., & Watson J. D. G. (2000). Neuropsychological and neuropathological sequelae of cerebral anoxia: A critical review. *Journal of the International Neuropsychological Society, 6*, 86–99.

Callahan, C. M., Moon, T. R., Oh, S., Azano, A. P., & Hailey, E. P. (2015). What works in gifted education: Documenting the effects of an integrated curricular/instructional model for gifted students. *American Educational Research Journal, 51*(1), 137–167.

Callahan, R. M., & Humphries, M. H. (2016).

Undermatched?: School-based linguistic status, college going and the immigrant advantage. *American Educational Research Journal, 53*(2), 263–295.

Campbell, D. T., & Fiske, D. W. (1959). Convergent and discriminant validation by the multitrait–multimethod matrix. *Psychological Bulletin, 56,* 81–105.

Campbell, D. T., & Stanley, J. C. (1966). *Experimental and quasi-experimental designs for research.* Chicago: Rand-McNally.

Campbell, F. A., Pungello, E. P., Burchinal, M., Kainz, K., Pan, Y., Wasik, B. H., et al. (2012). Adult outcomes as a function of an early childhood educational program: An Abecedarian Project follow-up. *Developmental Psychology, 48,* 1033–1043.

Campbell, F. A., Pungello, E. P., Miller-Johnson, S., Burchinal, M., & Ramey, C. T. (2001). The development of cognitive and academic abilities: Growth curves from an early childhood educational experiment. *Developmental Psychology, 37*(2), 231–242.

Campbell, F. A., & Ramey, C. T. (1995). Cognitive and school outcomes for high-risk African American students in middle adolescence: Positive effects of early intervention. *American Educational Research Journal, 32,* 743–772.

Campbell, J. R., Hombo, C. M., & Mazzeo, J. (2000). *NAEP 1999: Trends in academic progress.* Washington, DC: U.S. Department of Education.

Campbell, P. B. (1995). Redefining the "girl problem in mathematics." In W. G. Secada, E. Fennema, & L. B. Adajian (Eds.), *New directions for equity in mathematics education* (pp. 225–241). Cambridge, UK: Cambridge University Press.

Campbell, S. B. (2002). *Behavior problems in preschool children: Clinical and developmental issues* (2nd ed.). New York: Guilford Press.

Canfield, R. L., Kreher, D. A., Cornwell, C., & Henderson, C. R. Jr. (2003). Low-level lead exposure, executive functioning, and learning in early childhood. *Child Neuropsychology, 9,* 35–53.

Caputi, M., Lecce, S., Pagnin, A., & Banerjee, R. (2011). Longitudinal effects of theory of mind on later peer relations: The role of prosocial behavior. *Developmental Psychology, 48*(1), 257–270.

Cardon, L. R., DiLalla, L. F., Plomin, R., DeFries, J. C., & Fulker, D. W. (1990). Genetic correlations between reading performance and IQ in the Colorado Adoption Project. *Intelligence, 14,* 245–257.

Carey, S. (1978). The child as word learner. In M. Halle, J. Bresnan, & G. A. Miller (Eds.), *Linguistic theory and psychological reality* (pp. 264–273). Cambridge, MA: MIT Press.

Carey, S. (1985). *Conceptual change in childhood.* Cambridge, MA: MIT Press.

Carey, S., Zaitchik, D., & Bascandziev, I. (2015). Theories of development: In dialog with Jean Piaget. *Developmental Review, 38,* 36–54.

Carlisle, J. F. (2004). Morphological processes that influence learning to read. In C. A. Stone, E. R. Silliman, B. J. Ehren, & K. Apel (Eds.), *Handbook of language and literacy* (pp. 318–339). New York: Guilford Press.

Carlo, M. S., August, D., McLaughlin, B., Snow, C. E., Dressler, C., Lippman, D., et al. (2004). Closing the gap: Addressing the vocabulary needs of English language learners in bilingual and mainstream classrooms. *Reading Research Quarterly, 39,* 188–215.

Carlsen, W. S. (1991). Questioning in classrooms: A sociolinguistic perspective. *Review of Educational Research, 61*(2), 157–178.

Carlson, J. F., Geisinger, K. F., & Jonson, J. L. (Eds.). (2014). *The nineteenth mental measurements yearbook.* Lincoln, NE: Buros Center for Testing.

Carlsson, J., Wangqvist, M., & Friesen, A. (2015). Identity development in the late 20's: A never ending story. *Developmental Psychology, 51*(3), 334–345.

Carpendale, J. I. M. (2009). Piaget's theory of moral development. In U. Miller, J. L. M. Carpendale, & L. Smith (Eds.), *The Cambridge companion to Piaget* (pp. 270–286). New York: Cambridge University Press.

Carpendale, J. I. M., & Lewis, C. (2015). The development of social understanding. In R. M. Lerner & M. E. Lamb (Eds.), *Handbook of child psychology and developmental science: Vol. 2. Cognitive processes* (pp. 381–424). New York: Wiley.

Carpenter, T. P., Fennema, E., Peterson, P. L., & Carey, D. A. (1988). Teachers' pedagogical content knowledge of students' problem solving in elementary arithmetic. *Journal for Research in Mathematics Education, 19,* 385–401.

Carr, M., & Borkowski, J. G. (1989). Attributional training and the generalization of reading strategies with underachieving children. *Learning and Individual Differences, 1,* 327–341.

Carr, M., Borkowski, J. G., & Maxwell, S. E. (1991). Motivational components of underachievement. *Developmental Psychology, 27,* 108–118.

Carr, M., Kurtz, B. E., Schneider, W., Turner, L. A., & Borkowski, J. G. (1989). Strategy acquisition and transfer: Environmental influences on metacognitive development. *Developmental Psychology, 25,* 765–771.

Carringer, D. C. (1974). Creative thinking abilities of Mexican youth: The relationship of bilingualism. *Journal of Cross-Cultural Psychology, 5,* 492–504.

Carroll, J. B. (1993). *Human cognitive abilities: A survey of factor analytic studies.* New York: Cambridge University Press.

Case, R. (1985). *Intellectual development: Birth to adulthood.* Orlando, FL: Academic Press.

Case, R. (1991). A developmental approach to the design of remedial instruction. In A. McKeough

& J. L. Lupart (Eds.), *Toward the practice of theory-based instruction* (pp. 117–147). Hillsdale, NJ: Erlbaum.

Case, R. (1999). Neo-Piagetian theories of intellectual development. In H. Beilin & P. B. Pufall (Eds.), *Piaget's theory: Prospects and possibilities* (pp. 61–104). Hillsdale, NJ: Erlbaum.

Casey, B. J., Getz, S., & Galvan, A. (2008). The adolescent brain. *Developmental Review, 28,* 62–77.

Cassidy, J. (2016). The nature of child's ties. In J. Cassidy & P. R. Shaver (Eds.), *Handbook of attachment: Theory, research, and clinical applications* (pp. 3–24). New York: Guilford Press.

Castro, V. L., Halberstadt, A. G., & Garrett-Peters, P. (2016). A three factory structure of emotion understanding in third-grade children. *Social Development, 25*(3), 602–622.

Cattell, R. B. (1987). *Intelligence: Its structure, growth, and action.* Amsterdam, The Netherlands: North-Holland.

Cattell, R. B., & Horn, J. L. (1978). A check on the theory of fluid and crystallized intelligence with description of new subtest designs. *Journal of Educational Measurement, 15,* 139–164.

Cazden, C. B. (1988). *Classroom discourse: The language of teaching and learning.* Portsmouth, NH: Heinemann.

Cazden, C. B., & Beck, S. W. (2003). Classroom discourse. In A. C. Graesser, M. A. Gernsbacher, & S. R. Goldman (Eds.), *Handbook of discourse processes* (pp. 165–197). Mahwah: Erlbaurm.

Ceci, S. J. (1991). How much does schooling influence general intelligence and its cognitive components?: A reassessment of the evidence. *Developmental Psychology, 27,* 703–722.

Ceci, S. J., Williams, W. M., & Barnett, S. M. (2009). Women's underrepresentation in science: Sociocultural and biological considerations. *Psychological Bulletin, 135*(2), 218–261.

Center on Education Policy. (2012). *State exit exams: A policy in transition.* Washington, DC.

Centers for Disease Control and Prevention. (2000). Blood lead levels in young children: United States and selected states, 1996–1999. *Morbidity and Mortality Weekly Report, 49,* 1133–1137.

Cha, C. B., & Nock, M. K. (2014). Suicidal and nonsuicidal self-injurious thoughts and behaviors. In E. J. Mash & R. A. Barkley (Eds.), *Child psychopathology* (3rd ed., pp. 317–344). New York: Guilford Press.

Cha, K., & Goldenberg, C. (2015). The complex relationship between bilingual home language input and kindergarten children's Spanish and English oral proficiencies. *Journal of Educational Psychology, 107*(4), 935–953.

Chalik, L., Rivera, C., & Rhodes, M. (2014). Children's uses of categories and mental states to predict social behavior. *Developmental Psychology, 50*(10), 2360–2367.

Chambers, D. W. (1983). Stereotypic images of the scientist: The draw-a-scientist test. *Science Education, 67,* 255–265.

Chan, C. K. K., Burtis, P. J., Scardamalia, M., & Bereiter, C. (1992). Constructive activity in learning from text. *American Educational Research Journal, 29,* 97–118.

Chan, L. K. S. (1996). Motivational orientations and metacognitive abilities of intellectually gifted students. *Gifted Child Quarterly, 40,* 184–193.

Chang, V. (1999). Lead abatement and prevention of developmental disabilities. *Journal of Intellectual and Developmental Disability, 24,* 161–168.

Chao, R. K. (2001). Extending research on the consequences of parenting style for Chinese Americans and European Americans. *Child Development, 72,* 1832–1843.

Chapman, M., & Lindenberger, U. (1989). Concrete operations and attentional capacity. *Journal of Experimental Child Psychology, 47,* 236–258.

Chapman, M., Skinner, E. A., & Baltes, P. B. (1990). Interpreting correlations between children's perceived control and cognitive performance: Control, agency, or means–ends beliefs? *Developmental Psychology, 26,* 246–253.

Chassin, L., Bountress, K., Haller, M., & Wang, F. (2014). Adolescent substance use disorders. In E. J. Mash & R. A. Barkley (Eds.), *Child psychopathology* (3rd ed., pp. 180–221). New York: Guilford Press.

Chen, J. A., & Usher, E. L. (2013). Profiles of the sources of science self-efficacy. *Learning and Individual Differences, 24,* 11–21.

Chen, P. P. (2002). Exploring the accuracy and predictability of the self-efficacy beliefs of seventh-grade mathematics students. *Learning and Individual Differences, 14,* 77–90.

Cherney, I. D., & Ryalls, B. O. (1999). Gender-linked differences in the incidental memory of children and adults. *Journal of Experimental Child Psychology, 72,* 305–328.

Chess, S., & Thomas, A. (1987). *Origins and evolution of behavior disorders: From infancy to early adult life.* Cambridge, MA: Harvard University Press.

Cheung, C. S.-S., & Pomerantz, E. M. (2015). Value development underlies the benefits of parents' involvement in children's learning: A longitudinal investigation in the United States and China. *Journal of Educational Psychology, 107*(1), 309–320.

Cheyne, J. A., & Walters, R. H. (1969). Intensity of punishment, timing of punishment, and cognitive structure as determinants of response inhibition. *Journal for Experimental Child Psychology, 7,* 231–244.

Chi, M. T. H. (1978). Knowledge structure and memory development. In R. S. Siegler (Ed.), *Children's thinking: What develops?* (pp. 73–96). Hillsdale, NJ: Erlbaum.

Childs, C. P., & Greenfield, P. M. (1980). Informal modes of learning and teaching: The case of Zinecanteco weaving. In N. Warren (Ed.), *Studies in cross-cultural psychology* (Vol. 2, pp. 269–316). London: Academic Press.

Chiu, L., & Yip, K. (2012). From school dropout to school continuation: The importance of attachment in adolescents' education. In K. S. Yip (Ed.), *Psychology research progress: Recovery and resilience of children, adolescents, adults, and elderly with mental problems application and interventions* (pp. 87–110). New York: Nova Science.

Cho, S., & Ahn, D. (2003). Strategy acquisition and maintenance of gifted and nongifted young children. *Exceptional Children, 69*, 497–505.

Chodorow, N. J. (1989). *Feminism and psychoanalytic theory*. New Haven, CT: Yale University Press.

Choe, D. E., Olson, S. L., & Sameroff, A. J. (2013). The interplay of externalizing problems and physical and inductive discipline during childhood. *Developmental Psychology, 49*(11), 2029–2039.

Chomsky, N. (1957). *Syntactic structures*. The Hague, The Netherlands: Mouton.

Chomsky, N. (1959). Review of B. F. Skinner's *Verbal behavior. Language, 35*, 16–58.

Chomsky, N. (1965). *Aspects of the theory of syntax*. Cambridge, MA: MIT Press.

Chomsky, N. (1980a). Initial states and steady states. In M. Paittelli-Palmarini (Ed.), *Language and learning: The debate between Jean Piaget and Noam Chomsky* (pp. 97–130). Cambridge, MA: Harvard University Press.

Chomsky, N. (1980b). Rules and representations. *Behavioral and Brain Sciences, 3*, 1–61.

Chong, S. C. F., Werker, J. F., Russell, J. A., & Carroll, J. M. (2003). Three facial expressions mothers direct to their infants. *Infant and Child Development, 12*, 211–232.

Choukas-Bradley, S., & Prinstein, M. J. (2014). Peer relationships and the development of psychopathology. *Handbook of developmental psychopathology* (pp. 185–204). New York: Springer.

Christopher, M. E., Hulslander, J., Byrne, B., Samuelsson, S., Keenan, J. M., Pennington, B., et al. (2013). The genetic and environmental etiologies of individual differences in early reading growth in Australia, the United States, and Scandinavia. *Journal of Experimental Child Psychology, 115*, 453–467.

Christophersen, E. R. (1989). Injury control. *American Psychologist, 44*, 237–241.

Christophersen, E. R., & Mortweet, S. L. (2001). *Treatments that work with children: Empirically supported strategies for managing childhood problems*. Washington, DC: American Psychological Association.

Cillessen, A. H. N., & Bukowski, W. M. (2000). *Recent advances in the measurement of acceptance and rejection in the peer system*. San Francisco: Jossey Bass.

Clariana, R. B., Wolfe, M. B., & Kim, K. (2014). The influence of narrative and expository text structures on knowledge structures: Alternative measures of knowledge structures. *Education Technology Research Development, 62*, 601–616.

Clark, E. V. (1973). What's in a word?: On the child's acquisition of semantics in his first language. In T. E. Moore (Ed.), *Cognitive development and the acquisition of language* (pp. 65–110). New York: Academic Press.

Clark, J. M., & Paivio, A. (1991). Dual coding theory and education. *Educational Psychology Review, 3*, 149–210.

Clark, R. M. (1983). *Family life and school achievement: Why poor black children succeed or fail*. Chicago: University of Chicago Press.

Clay, M. M., & Cazden, C. B. (1990). A Vygotskian interpretation of Reading Recovery. In L. C. Moll (Ed.), *Vygotsky and education: Instructional implications and applications of sociohistorical psychology* (pp. 206–222). Cambridge, UK: Cambridge University Press.

Cleary, T. J., & Zimmerman, B. J. (2001). Self-regulation differences during athletic practice by experts, non-experts, and novices. *Journal of Applied Sport Psychology, 13*, 186–206.

Clement, J., Brown, D. E., & Zeitsman, A. (1989). Not all preconceptions are misconceptions: Finding "anchoring conceptions" for grounding instruction on students' intuition. *International Journal of Science Education, 11*, 554–565.

Climie, E. A., & Rostad, K. (2011). Test Review: Wechsler Adult Intelligence Scale (4th ed). *Journal of Psychoeducational Assessment, 29*(6), 581–586.

Clinkenbeard, P. R. (2012). Motivation and gifted students: Implications of theory and research. *Psychology in the Schools, 49*(7), 622–630.

Cobb, P., Wood, T., Yackel, E., Nicholls, J., Wheatley, G., Trigatti, B., et al. (1991). Assessment of a problem centered second-grade mathematics project. *Journal for Research in Mathematics Education, 22*, 3–29.

Cohen, A. D., & Horowitz, R. (2002). What should teachers know about bilingual learners and the reading process? In J. A. H. Sullivan (Ed.), *Literacy and the second language learner* (pp. 29–53). Greenwich, CT: Information Age.

Cohen, J. (1977). *Statistical power analyses for the behavioral sciences* (rev. ed.). New York: Academic Press

Cohen, J. (1988). *Statistical power analysis for the behavioral sciences* (rev. ed.). Hillsdale, NJ: Erlbaum.

Colapinto, J. (2001). *As nature made him: The boy who was raised as a girl*. New York: Perennial.

Cole, M. (1998). Cognitive development and

formal schooling: The evidence from cross-cultural research. In D. Faulkner, K. Littleton, & M. Woodhead (Eds.), *Learning relationships in the classroom* (pp. 31–53). London: Routledge.

Cole, M., Gay, J., Glick, J., & Sharp, D. (1971). *The cultural context of learning and thinking*. New York: Basic Books.

Cole, M., & Scribner, S. (1977). Cross-cultural studies of memory and cognition. In R. V. Kail & J. W. Hagen (Eds.), *Perspectives on the development of memory and cognition* (pp. 239–271). Hillsdale, NJ: Erlbaum.

Coles, R. (1970). *Erik H. Erikson: The growth of his work*. Boston: Little, Brown.

Collaer, M. L., & Hines, M. (1995). Human behavioral sex differences: A role for gonadal hormones during early development? *Psychological Bulletin, 118*, 55–107.

Collins, A., Brown, J. S., & Newman, S. E. (1989). Cognitive apprenticeship: Teaching the crafts of reading, writing, and mathematics. In L. B. Resnick (Ed.), *Knowing, learning, and instruction: Essays in honor of Robert Glaser* (pp. 453–494). Hillsdale, NJ: Erlbaum.

Collins, A., & Kapur, M. (2014). Cognitive apprenticeship. In R. K. Sawyer (Ed.), *Cambridge handbook of the learning sciences* (2nd ed., pp. 109–127). New York: Cambridge University Press.

Collins, A. M., & Loftus, E. F. (1975). A spreading-activation theory of semantic processing. *Psychological Review, 82*, 407–428.

Collins, A. M., & Quillian, M. R. (1969). Retrieval time from semantic memory. *Journal of Verbal Learning and Verbal Behavior, 8*, 240–247.

Collins, C. (1991). Reading instruction that increases thinking abilities. *Journal of Reading, 34*(7), 510–516.

Collins, W. A., Maccoby, E. E., Steinberg, L., Hetherington, E. M., & Bornstein, M. H. (2000). Contemporary research on parenting: The case for nature and nurture. *The American Psychologist, 55*, 218–232.

Colman, R. A., & Thompson, R. A. (2002). Attachment security and the problem-solving behaviors of mothers and children. *Merrill–Palmer Quarterly, 48*, 337–359.

Colonnesi, C., Koops, W., & Terwogt, M. M. (2008). Young children's psychological explanations and their relationship to perception and intention understanding. *Infant and Child Development, 17*, 163–179.

Coltheart, M., & Kohnen, S. (2012). Acquired and developmental disorders of reading and spelling. In M. Faust (Ed.), *The handbook of the neuropsychology of language, 1&2* (pp. 892–920). New York: Wiley.

Coltrane, S. (1998). *Gender and families*. Thousand Oaks, CA: Pine Forge Press.

Confrey, J., & Kazak, S. (2006). A thirty-year reflection on constructivism in mathematics education in PME. In A. Gutierrez & P. Boero (Eds.), *Handbook of research on the psychology of mathematics education: Past, present and future* (pp. 305–345). Rotterdam, The Netherlands: Sense.

Conrad, R. (1979). *The deaf school child*. London: Harper & Row.

Constantino, G. (1992). Overcoming bias in the educational assessment of Hispanic students. In K. F. Geisinger (Ed.), *Psychological testing of Hispanics* (pp. 89–98). Washington, DC: American Psychological Association.

Constantino, J. N., & Charman, T. (2016). Diagnosis of autism spectrum disorder: Reconciling the syndrome, its diverse origins, and variation in expression. *Lancet Neurology, 15*, 279–291.

Cook, E. C., Buehler, C., & Henson, R. (2009). Parents and peers as social influences to deter antisocial behavior. *Journal of Youth and Adolescence, 38*, 1240–1252.

Cooper, K. S. (2012). Safe, affirming and productive spaces: Classroom engagement among Latina high school students. *Urban Education, 48*(4), 490–528.

Cooper, K. S. (2014). Eliciting engagement in the high school classroom: A mixed-methods examination of teaching practices. *American Educational Research Journal, 51*(2), 363–402.

Cooper, K. S., & Miness, A. (2014). Co-creation of caring student-teacher relationships: Does teacher understanding matter? *High School Journal, 97*(4), 264–290.

Copeland, W. E., Angold, A., Shanahan, L., & Costello, E. J. (2014). Longitudinal patterns of anxiety from childhood to adulthood: The Great Smoky Mountains study. *Journal of the American Academy of Child and Adolescent Psychiatry, 53*(1), 21–33.

Copeland-Mitchell, J., Denham, S. A., & DeMulder, E. K. (1997). *Q*-sort assessment of child–teacher attachment relationships and social competence in the preschool. *Early Education and Development, 8*, 27–39.

Coplan, R. J., Hughes, K., Bosacki, S., & Rose-Krasnor, L. (2011). Is silence golden?: Elementary school teachers' strategies and beliefs regarding hypothetical shy/quiet and exuberant/talkative children. *Journal of Educational Psychology, 103*(4), 939–951.

Cornelius, G., & Hornett, D. (1990). The play behavior of hearing-impaired kindergarten children. *American Annals of the Deaf, 135*, 316–321.

Cornelius-White, J. (2007). Learner-centered student-teacher relationships are effective: A meta-analysis. *Review of Educational Research, 77*(1), 113–143.

Coscia, J. M., Ris, M. D., Succop, P. A., & Dietrich, K. N. (2003). Cognitive development of lead exposed children from ages 6 to 15 years: An application of growth curve analysis. *Child Neuropsychology, 9,* 10–21.

Costello, E. J., Compton, S. N., Keeler, G., & Angold, A. (2003). Relationships between poverty and psychopathology: A natural experiment. *Journal of the American Medical Association, 290*(15), 2023–2029.

Côté, S. M., Doyle, O., Petitclerc, A., & Timmins, L. (2013). Child care in infancy and cognitive performance until middle childhood in the millennium cohort study. *Child Development, 84*(4), 1191–1208.

Coughlin, J., McCoy, K. M., Kenzer, A., Mathur, S. R., & Zucker, S. H. (2012). Effects of self-monitoring strategy on independent work behavior of students with mild intellectual disability. *Education and Training in Autism and Developmental Disabilities, 47*(2), 154–164.

Courage, M. L., Bakhtiar, A., Fitzpatrick, C., Kenny, S., & Brandeau, K. (2015). Growing up multitasking: The costs and benefits for cognitive development. *Developmental Review, 35,* 5–41.

Courage, M., & Cowan, N. (Eds.). (2009). *The development of memory in infancy and childhood (studies in developmental psychology)* (2nd ed.). New York: Psychology Press.

Covington, M. V. (1987). Achievement motivation, self-attributions, and the exceptional learner. In J. D. Day & J. G. Borkowski (Eds.), *Intelligence and exceptionality* (pp. 355–389). Norwood, NJ: Ablex.

Covington, M. V. (1992). *Making the grade: A self-worth perspective on motivation and school reform.* New York: Cambridge University Press.

Covington, M. V. (1998) *The will to learn: A guide for motivating young people.* New York: Cambridge University Press.

Covington, M. V. (2000). Goal theory, motivation, and school achievement: An integrative review. *Annual Review of Psychology, 51,* 171–200.

Covington, M. V. (2004). Self-worth theory: Goes to college or do our motivation theories motivate? In D. M. McInerney & S. Van Etten (Eds.), *Big theories revisited* (pp. 91–114). Greenwich, CT: Information Age.

Covington, M. V., & Omelich, C. L. (1979a). Effort: The double-edged sword in school achievement. *Journal of Educational Psychology, 71,* 169–182.

Covington, M. V., & Omelich, C. L. (1979b). It's best to be able and virtuous too: Student and teacher evaluative responses to successful effort. *Journal of Educational Psychology, 71,* 688–700.

Covington, M. V., & Omelich, C. L. (1981). As failures mount: Affective and cognitive consequences of ability demotion in the classroom. *Journal of Educational Psychology, 73,* 796–808.

Covington, M. V., & Omelich, C. L. (1984). Task-oriented versus competitive learning structures: Motivational and performance consequences. *Journal of Educational Psychology, 6,* 1038–1050.

Cowan, N. (2014). Short term-and working memory in childhood. In P. J. Bauer & R. Fivush (Eds), *The Wiley handbook on the development of children's memory* (pp. 202–229). New York: Wiley.

Cowan, N., Elliott, E. M., Saults, J. S., Morey, C. C., Mattox, S., Hismjatullina, A., et al. (2005). On the capacity of attention: Its estimation and its role in working memory and cognitive aptitudes. *Cognitive Psychology, 51,* 42–100.

Cowan, N., Saults, J. S., Elliott, E. M., & Moreno, M. V. (2002). Deconfounding serial recall. *Journal of Memory and Language, 46*(1), 153–177.

Cowell, R. A., Cicchetti, D., Rogosch, F. A., & Toth, S. L. (2015). Childhood maltreatment and its effect on neurocognitive functioning: Timing and chronicity matter. *Development and Psychopathology, 27,* 521–533.

Coyle, E. F., & Liben, L. S. (2016). Affecting girls' activity and job interest through play: The moderating roles of personal gender salience and game characteristics. *Child Development, 87*(2), 414–428.

Coyle, T. R., Read, L. E., Gaultney, J. F., & Bjorklund, D. F. (1998). Giftedness and variability in strategic processing on a multitrial memory task: Evidence for stability in gifted cognition. *Learning and Individual Differences, 10,* 273–290.

Coyne, S. M., Linder, J. R., Rasmussen, E. E., Nelson, D. A., & Birkbeck, V. B. (2016). Pretty as a princess: Longitudinal effects of engagement with Disney Princesses on gender stereotypes, body esteem, and prosocial behavior in children. *Child Development, 87*(6), 1909–1925.

Craig, A. B., Brown, E. R., Upright, J., & DeRosier, M. E. (2016). Enhancing children's social emotional functioning through virtual game-based delivery of social skills training. *Journal of Child Family Studies, 25,* 959–968.

Crain-Thoreson, C., & Dale, P. S. (1992). Do early talkers become early readers?: Linguistic precocity, preschool language, and emergent literacy. *Developmental Psychology, 28,* 421–429.

Cratty, B. J. (1986). *Perceptual and motor development in infants and children* (3rd ed.). Englewood Cliffs, NJ: Prentice-Hall.

Crawley, S., Caporino, N. E., Birmaher, B., Ginsburg, G., Piacentini, J. Albano, A. M., et al. (2014). Somatic complaints in anxious youth. *Child Psychiatry and Human Development, 45,* 398–407.

Crick, N. R., & Werner, N. E. (1998). Response decision processes in relational and overt aggression. *Child Development, 69,* 1630–1639.

Crockett, L. J., & Hayes, R. (2011). Parenting practices and styles. In B. B. Brown & M. J. Prinstein (Eds.), *Encyclopedia of adolescence* (Vol. 2, pp. 241–248). London: Elsevier.

Croft, C. (Ed.) (2015). *Environmental hazards and neurodevelopment: Where ecology and well-being connect.* Oakdale, ON, Canada: Apple Academic Press.

Cronbach, L. J. (1951). Coefficient alpha and the

internal structure of tests. *Psychometrica, 16,* 297–334.

Cronbach, L. J. (1990). *Essentials of psychological testing* (5th ed.). New York: Harper & Row.

Cross, W. E., Grant, B. O., & Ventuneac, A. (2012). Black identity and well-being: Untangling race and ethnicity. In J. M. Sullivan & A. M. Esmail (Eds.), *African American identity: Racial and cultural dimensions of the Black experience* (pp. 125–146). Lanham, MD: Lexington Books.

Cross, W., & Vandiver, B. (2001). Nigresence theory and measurement: Introducing the Cross Racial Identity Scale (CRIS). In J. G. Ponterotto, J. M. Casas, L. M. Suzuki, & C. M. Alexander (Eds.), *Handbook of multicultural counseling* (2nd ed., pp. 371–393). Thousand Oaks, CA: SAGE.

Crowell, J. A., Fraley, R. C., & Roisman, G. I. (2016). Measurement of individual differences in adult attachment. In J. Cassidy & P. R. Shaver (Eds.), *Handbook of attachment: Theory, research, and clinical applications* (3rd ed., pp. 598–637). New York: Guilford Press.

Crystal, D. (1987). *The Cambridge encyclopedia of language.* Cambridge, UK: Cambridge University Press.

Crystal, D. (1995). *The Cambridge encyclopedia of the English language.* Cambridge, UK: Cambridge University Press.

Csikszentmihalyi, M., & Larson, R. (1984). *Being adolescent: Conflict and growth in the teenage years.* New York: Basic Books.

Cucina, J. M., & Howardson, G. N. (2016, November 10). Woodcock–Johnson–III, Kaufman Adolescent and Adult Intelligence Test (KAIT), Kaufman Adolescent Battery for Children (KABC), and Differential Ability Scales (DAS) support Carroll but not Cattell–Horn. *Psychological Assessment.* [Epub ahead of print]

Cuevas, K., Swingler, M. M., Bell, M. A., Marcovitch, S., & Calkins, S. D. (2012). Measures of frontal functioning and the emergence of inhibitory control processes at 10 months of age. *Developmental Cognitive Neuroscience, 2,* 235–243.

Culen, C., Ertl, D.-A., Schubert, K., Bartha-Doering, L., & Haeusler, G. (2017, March 23). Care of girls and women with Turner syndrome—beyond growth and hormones. *Endocrine Connections.* [Epub ahead of print]

Cummings, C. M., Caporino, N. E., & Kendall, P. C. (2014). Comorbidity of anxiety and depression in children and adolescents: 20 years after. *Psychological Bulletin, 140*(3), 816–845.

Cunningham, M. (2001). The influence of parental attitudes and behaviors on children's attitudes toward gender and household labor in early adulthood. *Journal of Marriage and Family, 63*(1), 111–122.

Cutting, L. E., & Denckla, M. B. (2003). Attention: Relationships between attention-deficit hyperactivity disorder and learning disabilities. In H. L. Swanson, K. R. Harris, & S. Graham (Eds.), *Handbook of learning disabilities* (pp. 125–139). New York: Guilford Press.

Cvencek, D., Meltzoff, N., & Greenwald, A. G. (2011). Math-gender stereotypes in elementary school children. *Child Development, 82,* 766–779.

Dai, D. Y. (2002). Are gifted girls motivationally disadvantaged?: Review, reflection, and redirection. *Journal for the Education of the Gifted, 25,* 315–358.

Dale, P. S., Dionne, G., Eley, T. C., & Plomin, R. (2000). Lexical and grammatical development: A behavioral genetic perspective. *Journal of Child Language, 27,* 619–642.

d'Anna, C. A., Zechmeister, E. B., & Hall, J. W. (1991). Toward a meaningful definition of vocabulary size. *Journal of Reading Behavior, 23,* 109–122.

Darling, N., & Steinberg, L. (1993). Parenting style as context: An integrative model. *Psychological Bulletin, 113,* 487–496.

Davidov, M., & Grusec, J. E. (2006). Untangling the links of parental responsiveness to distress and warmth to child outcomes. *Child Development, 77*(1), 44–58.

Davidson, E. S., Yasuna, A., & Tower, A. (1979). The effects of television cartoons on sex-role stereotyping in young girls. *Child Development, 50,* 597–600.

Davis, H. A. (2013). Teacher-student relationships. In J. Hattie & E. M. Anderman (Eds.), *International guide to student achievement* (pp. 221–223). New York: Routledge

Dawes, M., & Xie, H. (2014). The role of popularity goal in early adolescents' behaviors and popularity status. *Developmental Psychology, 50*(2), 489–497.

Dawson, T. L. (2002). New tools, new insights: Kohlberg's moral judgement stages revisited. *International Journal of Behavioral Development, 26*(2), 154–166.

Day, J. D., Borkowski, J. G., Dietmeyer, D. L., Howsepian, B. A., & Saenz, D. S. (1994). Possible selves and academic achievement. In L. Winegar & J. Valsiner (Eds.), *Children's development within social contexts* (pp. 181–201). Hillsdale, NJ: Erlbaum.

De Castella, K., Byrne, D., & Covington, M. (2013). Unmotivated or motivated to fail: A cross-cultural study of achievement, fear of failure, and student disengagement. *Journal of Educational Psychology, 105*(3), 861–880.

de Fiorini, L. G. (1998). The feminine in psychoanalysis: A complete construction. *Journal of Clinical Psychoanalysis, 7,* 421–439.

de Houwer, A. (1987). Gender marking in a young Dutch–English bilingual child. In *Proceedings of the 1987 Child Language Seminar* (pp. 53–65). York, UK: University of York.

de Houwer, A. (1990). *Acquisition of two languages from birth: A case study*. New York: Cambridge University Press.

de Houwer, A. (1995). Bilingual language acquisition. In P. Fletcher & B. MacWhinney (Eds.), *The handbook of child language* (pp. 219–250). Oxford, UK: Blackwell.

De Jong, T. (2010). Cognitive load theory, educational research, and instructional design: Some food for thought. *Instructional Science, 38*, 105–134.

De Jong, T., & van Joolingen, W. R. (1998). Scientific discovery learning with computer simulations of conceptual domains. *Review of Educational Research, 68*(2), 179–201.

Dearing, E., McCartney, K., & Taylor, B. A. (2009). Does higher quality early child care promote low-income children's math and reading achievement in middle childhood. *Child Development, 80*(5), 1329–1349.

Deater-Deckard, K., Ivy, L., & Petrill, S. A. (2006). Maternal warmth moderates the link between physical punishment and child externalizing problems: A parent–offspring behavior genetic analysis. *Parenting: Science and Practice, 6*(1), 59–78.

Debowski, S., Wood, R. E., & Bandura, A. (2001). Impact of guided exploration and enactive exploration on self-regulatory mechanisms and information acquisition through electronic search. *Journal of Applied Psychology, 86*, 1129–1141.

DeCasper, A., & Fifer, W. P. (1980). On human bonding: Newborns prefer their mother's voices. *Science, 208*(1), 174–176.

DeCasper, A., Granier-Deferre, C., Fifer, W. P., & Moon, C. M. (2011). Measuring fetal cognitive development: When methods and conclusions don't match. *Developmental Science, 14*, 224–225.

Deci, E. L., & Ryan, R. M. (1985). *Intrinsic motivation and self-determination in human behavior*. New York: Plenum Press.

Deckner, D. F., Adamson, L. B., & Bakeman, R. (2006). Child and maternal contributions to shared reading: Effects on language and literacy development. *Applied Developmental Psychology, 27*, 31–41.

DeFries, J. C., Fulker, D. W., & LaBuda, M. C. (1987). Evidence for a genetic aetiology in reading disability of twins. *Nature, 329*, 537–539.

DeFries, J. C., Olson, R. K., Pennington, B. F., & Smith, S. D. (1991). Colorado Reading Project: An update. In D. Duane & D. Gray (Eds.), *The reading brain: The biological basis of dyslexia* (pp. 53–87). Parkton, MD: York Press.

DeKlyen, M., & Greenberg, M. T. (2016). Attachment and psychopathology in childhood. In J. Cassidy & P. R. Shaver (Eds.), *Handbook of attachment: Theory, research, and clinical applications* (3rd ed., pp. 639–666). New York: Guilford Press.

Delaney-Black, V., Covington, C., Templin, T., Kershaw, T., Nordstrom-Klee, B., Ager, J., et al. (2000). Expressive language development of children exposed to cocaine prenatally: Literature review and report of a prospective cohort study. *Journal of Communication Disorders, 33*, 463–481.

Delgado-Gaitan, C. (1990). *Literacy for empowerment: The role of parents in children's education*. New York: Falmer Press.

DeLoache, J. S., Cassidy, D. J., & Brown, A. L. (1985). Precursors of mnemonic strategies in very young children's memory. *Child Development, 56*, 125–137.

DeMauro, S. B., Douglas, E., Karp, K., Schmidt, B., Patch, J., Kronberger, A., et al. (2013). Improving delivery room management for very preterm infants. *Pediatrics, 132*, e1018–e1025.

Dempster, F. N. (1981). Memory span: Sources of individual and developmental differences. *Psychological Bulletin, 89*, 63–100.

Dempster, F. N. (1985). Short-term memory development in childhood and adolescence. In C. J. Brainerd & M. Pressley (Eds.), *Basic processes in memory development: Progress in cognitive development research* (pp. 209–248). New York: Springer-Verlag.

DeNavas-Walt, C., & Proctor, B. D. (2015). *Income and poverty in the United States: 2014* (United States Census Bureau, Current Population Reports, P60-252). Washington, DC: United States Government Printing Office.

Dennen, V. P., & Hoadley, C. (2013). Designing collaborative learning through computer support. In C. E. Hmelo-Silver, C. A. Chinn, C. K. K. Chan, & A. O'Donnell (Eds.), *The international handbook of collaborative learning* (pp. 389–402). New York: Routledge.

Denzin, N. K., & Lincoln, Y. S. (Eds.). (2000). *Handbook of qualitative research* (2nd ed.). Thousand Oaks, CA: SAGE.

Deoni, S. C. L., O'Muircheartaigh, J., Elison, J. T., Walker, L., Doernberg, E., Waskiewicz, N., et al. (2016). White matter maturation profiles through early childhood predict general cognitive ability. *Brain Structure and Function, 221*, 1189–1203.

Derry, S. J., DuRussel, L. A., & O'Donnell, A. M. (1998). Individual and distributed cognitions in interdisciplinary teamwork: A developing case study and emerging theory. *Educational Psychology Review, 10*(1), 25–56.

Detweiler, M. F., Cromer, J. S., & Albano, A. M. (2014). Social anxiety in children and adolescents: Biological, developmental, and social considerations. In S. G. Hofmann & P. M. DiBartolo (Eds.), *Social anxiety: Clinical, developmental, and social perspectives* (pp. 253–309). Amsterdam, The Netherlands: Elsevier.

Dev, P. C. (1998). Intrinsic motivation and the student

with learning disabilities. *Journal of Research and Development in Education, 31*(2), 98–108.

deVilliers, P. A., & deVilliers, J. G. (1992). Language development. In M. H. Bornstein & M. E. Lamb (Eds.), *Developmental psychology: An advanced textbook* (pp. 337–418). Hillsdale, NJ: Erlbaum.

Dewey, J. (1913). *Interest and effort in education.* Boston: Riverside Press.

Dewey, J. (1933). *How we think: A restatement of the relation of reflective thinking to the education process.* Boston: Heath.

Dexter, C. A., & Stacks, A. M (2014). A preliminary investigation of the relationship between parenting, parent-child shared reading practices, and child development in low-income families. *Journal of Research in Childhood Education, 28,* 394–410.

di Sessa, A. A. (2014). A history of conceptual change research: Threads and fault lines. In R. K. Sawyer (Ed.), *Cambridge handbook of the learning sciences* (2nd ed., pp. 88–108). New York: Cambridge University Press.

Diamond, A. (1985). Development of the ability to use recall to guide action, as indicated by infants' performance on A$\overline{B}$. *Child Development, 56,* 868–883.

Diamond, A., Werker, J. F., & Lalonde, C. (1994). Toward understanding commonalities in the development of object search: Detour navigation, categorization, and speech perception. In G. Dawson & K. W. Fischer, *Human behavior and the developing brain* (pp. 380–426). New York: Guilford Press.

Diamond, M., & Sigmundson, H. K. (1999). Sex reassignment at birth. In S. J. Ceci & W. M. Williams (Eds.), *The nature–nurture debate* (pp. 55–75). Malden, MA: Blackwell.

Diana v. State Board of Education. C-70–37 RFP (N. D. Cal. June 18, 1973). (stipulated settlement.)

Diaz, R. M., Padilla, K. A., & Weathersby, E. K. (1991). The effects of bilingualism on preschoolers' private speech. *Early Childhood Research Quarterly, 6,* 377–393.

Dickinson, D. K., McCabe, A., & Clark-Chiarelli, N. (2004). Cross-language transfer of phonological awareness in low-income Spanish and English bilingual preschool children. *Applied Psycholinguistics, 25*(3), 323–347.

Dijkstra, J. K., Cillessen, A. H. N., & Borch, C. (2013). Popularity and adolescent friendship networks: Selection and influence dynamics. *Developmental Psychology, 49*(7), 1242–1252.

Dimmitt, C., & McCormick, C. B. (2012). Metacognition in education. In K. Harris, S. Graham, & T. Urdan (Eds.), *APA educational psychology handbook: Vol. 1. Theories, constructs and critical issues* (pp. 157–188). Washington, DC: American Psychological Association.

Ding, Y., Xu, X., Wang, Z., Li, H., & Wang, W. (2014). The relation of infant attachment to attachment and cognitive and behavioral outcomes in early childhood. *Early Human Development, 90,* 459–464.

Dirk, J., & Schmiedek, F. (2016). Fluctuations in elementary school children's working memory performance in the school context. *Journal of Educational Psychology, 108*(5), 722–799.

Dobbing. J. (1974). The later growth of the brain and its vulnerability. *Pediatrics, 53,* 2–6.

Dolezal, S. E., Welsh, L. M., Pressley, M., & Vincent, M. (2003). How do grade-3 teachers motivate their students? *Elementary School Journal, 103,* 239–267.

Domitrovich, C. E., Durlak, J. A., Staley, K. C., & Weissberg, R. P. (2017). Social-emotional competence: An essential factor for promoting positive adjustment and reducing risk in school children. *Child Development, 88*(2), 408–416.

Donaldson, J. M., Vollmer, T. R., Yakich, T. M., & Van Camp, C. (2013). Effects of a reduced timeout interval on compliance with time-out instruction. *Journal of Applied Behavioral Analysis, 46*(2), 369–378.

Donlon, T. F. (1992). Legal issues in the educational testing of Hispanics. In K. F. Geisinger (Ed.), *Psychological testing of Hispanics* (pp. 55–78). Washington, DC: American Psychological Association.

Doom, J. R., & Gunnar, M. R. (2013). Stress physiology and developmental psychopathology: Past, present, and future. *Development and Psychopathology, 25,* 1359–1373.

Douglass, S., & Umaña-Taylor, A. (2016). Time-varying effects of family ethnic socialization on ethnic-racial identity among Latino adolescents. *Developmental Psychology, 52*(11), 1904–1912.

Doyle, K. W., Wolchik, S. A., Dawson-McClure, S. R., & Sandler, I. N. (2003). Positive events as a stress buffer for children and adolescents in families in transition. *Journal of Clinical Child and Adolescent Psychology, 32,* 536–545.

Doyle, R. A., & Voyer, D. (2016). Stereotype manipulations on math and spatial test performance: A meta-analysis. *Learning and Individual Differences, 47,* 103–116.

Doyle, W. (1986). Classroom organization and management. In M. C. Wittrock (Ed.), *Handbook of research on teaching* (3rd ed., pp. 392–431). New York: Macmillan.

Dozier, M., & Rutter, M. (2016). Challenges to the development of attachment relationships faced by young children in foster and adoptive care. In J. Cassidy & P. R. Shaver (Eds.), *Handbook of attachment: Theory, research, and clinical applications* (3rd ed., pp. 696–714). New York: Guilford Press.

Drake, K., Belsky, J., & Fearon, R. M. (2014). From early attachment to engagement with learning in school: The role of self-regulation and persistence. *Developmental Psychology, 50*(5), 1350–1361.

Dreyfus, A., Jungwirth, E., & Eliovitch, R. (1990). Applying the "cognitive conflict" strategy for conceptual change: Some implications, difficulties, and problems. *Science Education, 74*, 555–569.

Driver, R., Asoko, H., Leach, J., Mortimer, E., & Scott, P. (1998). Constructing scientific knowledge in the classroom. In D. Faulkner, K. Littleton, & M. Woodhead (Eds.), *Learning relationships in the classroom* (pp. 258–275). London: Routledge.

Duda, J. L., & Nicholls, J. G. (1992). Dimensions of achievement motivation in schoolwork and sport. *Journal of Educational Psychology, 84*, 290–299.

Duit, R. (1991). Students' conceptual frameworks: Consequences for learning science. In S. M. Glynn, R. H. Yeany, & B. K. Britton (Eds.), *The psychology of learning science* (pp. 65–85). Hillsdale, NJ: Erlbaum.

Dulaney, A., Vasilyeva, M., & O'Dwyer, L. (2015). Individual differences in cognitive resources and elementary school mathematics achievement: Examining the roles of storage and attention. *Learning and Individual Differences, 37*, 55–63.

Duncan, H. D., & Phillips, N. A. (2016). The contributions of bilingualism to cognitive reserve in health aging and dementia. In E. Nicoladis & S. Montanari (Eds.), *Bilingualism across the lifespan: Factors moderating language proficiency* (pp. 305–322). Washington, DC: American Psychological Association.

DuPaul, G. J., & Stoner, G. (2015). *ADHD in the schools: Assessment and intervention strategies* (3rd ed.). New York: Guilford Press.

Durik, A. M., Vida, M., & Eccles, J. (2006). Task values and ability beliefs as predictors of high school literacy choices. *Journal of Educational Psychology, 98*(2), 382–393.

Durlak, J. A., Weissberg, R. P., Dymnicki, A. B., Taylor, R. D., & Schellinger, K. B. (2011). The impact of enhancing students' social and emotional learning: A meta-analysis of school-based universal interventions. *Child Development, 82*(1), 405–432.

Dweck, C. S. (1986). Motivational processes affecting learning. *American Psychologist, 41*, 1040–1048.

Dweck, C. S. (2002a). Beliefs that make smart people dumb. In R. Sternberg (Ed.), *Why smart people can be so stupid* (pp. 24–41). New Haven, CT: Yale University Press.

Dweck, C. S. (2002b). Messages that motivate: How praise molds students' beliefs, motivation, and performance (in surprising ways). In J. Aronson (Ed.), *Improving academic achievement: Impact of psychological factors on education* (pp. 37–60). San Diego, CA: Academic Press.

Dweck, C. S., Davidson, W., Nelson, S., & Enna, B. (1978). Sex differences in learned helplessness: II. The contingencies of evaluative feedback in the classroom. III. An experimental analysis. *Developmental Psychology, 14*, 268–276.

Dweck, C. S., & Leggett, E. L. (1988). A social-cognitive approach to motivation and personality. *Psychological Review, 95*, 256–273.

Eccles, J. S. (1989). Bringing young women to math and science. In M. Crawford & M. Gentry (Eds.), *Gender and thought: Psychological perspectives* (pp. 36–58). New York: Springer-Verlag.

Eccles, J. S. (1999). The development of children ages 6 to 14. *The Future of Children, 9*(2), 30–44.

Eccles, J. S., Freedman-Doan, C., Frome, P., Jacobs, J., & Yoon, K. S. (2000). Gender-role socialization in the family: A longitudinal approach. In T. Eckes & H. M. Trautner (Eds.), *The developmental social psychology of gender* (pp. 333–360). Mahwah, NJ: Erlbaum.

Eccles, J. S., & Jacobs, J. (1986). Social forces shape math participation. *Signs, 11*, 367–380.

Eccles, J. S., Midgley, C., & Wigfield, A. (1993). Development during adolescence: The impact of stage-environment fit on young adolescents' experiences in schools and in families. *American Psychologist, 48*, 90–101.

Eccles, J. S., & Roeser, R. W. (2011). Schools as developmental contexts during adolescence. *Journal of Research on Adolescence, 21*(1), 225–241.

Eccles, J. S., Wigfield, A., Flanagan, C., Miller, C., Reuman, D., & Yee, D. (1989). Self-concepts, domain values, and self-esteem: Relationships and changes in early adolescence. *Journal of Personality, 57*, 283–310.

Eccles, J. S., Wigfield, A., Midgley, C., Reuman, D., MacIver, D., & Feldlaufer, H. (1993). Negative effects of traditional middle schools on students' motivation. *Elementary School Journal, 93*, 553–574.

Eccles-Parson, J., Adler, T. F., & Kaczala, C. M. (1982). Socialization of achievement attitudes and beliefs: Parental influences. *Child Development, 53*, 310–321.

Eder, D., with Evans, C. C., & Parker, S. (1995). *School talk: Gender and adolescent culture*. New Brunswick, NJ: Rutgers University Press.

Ehri, L. C. (2004). Teaching phonemic awareness and phonics: An explanation of the National Reading Panel meta-analyses. In P. McCardle & V. Chhabra (Eds.), *The voice of evidence in reading research* (pp. 153–186). Baltimore: Brookes.

Ehri, L. C., Nunes, S., Willows, D., Schuster, B., Yaghoub-Zadeh, Z., & Shanahan, T. (2001). Phonemic awareness instruction helps children learn to read: Evidence from the National Reading Panel's meta-analysis. *Review of Educational Research, 71*, 393–447.

Eid, W., & Biason-Lauber, A. (2016). Why boys will be boys and girls will be girls: Human sex development and its defects. *Birth Defects Research,* *108,* 365–379.

Eimas, P. D., Siqueland, E. R., Jusczyk, P., & Vigorito, J. (1971). Speech perception in infants. *Science,* *171,* 303–306.

Eisenberg, N., Wolchik, S. A., Hernandez, R., & Pasternack, J. F. (1985). Parental socialization of young children's play: A short-term longitudinal study. *Child Development, 56,* 1506–1513.

Ekornes, S. (2015). Teacher perspectives on their role and the challenges of inter-professional collaboration in mental health promotion. *School Mental Health, 7,* 193–211.

Elbert, T., Pantev, C., Wienbruch, C., Rockstroh, B., & Taub, E. (1995). Increased cortical representation of the fingers of the left hand in string players. *Science, 270,* 305–307.

El-Dinary, P. B., Pressley, M., & Schuder, T. (1992). Teachers learning transactional strategies instruction. In C. K. Kinzer & D. J. Leu (Eds.), *Literacy research, theory, and practice: Views from many perspectives: 41st yearbook of the National Reading Conference* (pp. 453–462). Chicago: National Reading Conference.

Eley, T. C., Bishop, D. V. M., Dale, P. S., Oliver, B., Petrill, S. A., Price, T. S., et al. (1999). Genetic and environmental origins of verbal and performance components of cognitive delay in 2-year-olds. *Developmental Psychology, 35,* 1122–1131.

Elfers, T., Martin, J., & Sokol, B. (2008). Perspective taking: A review of research and theory extending Selman's developmental model of perspective taking. In A. M. Columbus (Ed.), *Advances in psychology research* (Vol. 54, pp. 229–262). New York: Nova Science.

Eliot, L. (2011). Single-sex education and the brain. *Sex Roles, 69,* 363–381.

Elkind, D. (2008). Neo-Piagetian or retro behaviorism? *Psych/CRITIQUES, 53*(43).

Elliot, A. J. (1999). Approach and avoidance motivation and achievement goals. *Educational Psychologist, 34,* 169–189.

Elliott, E. S., & Dweck, C. S. (1988). Goals: An approach to motivation and achievement. *Journal of Personality and Social Psychology, 54,* 5–12.

Ellis, N. R. (Ed.). (1979). *Handbook of mental deficiency: Psychological theory and research.* Hillsdale, NJ: Erlbaum.

Else-Quest, N. M., Hyde, J. S., & Linn, M. C. (2010). Cross-national patterns of gender difference in mathematics and gender equity: A meta-analysis. *Psychological Bulletin, 136*(1), 26–43.

Else-Quest, N. M., & Peterca, O. (2015). Academic attitude and achievement in students of urban public single-sex and mixed-sex high schools. *American Educational Research Journal, 52*(4), 693–718.

Emde, R. N. (1992). Individual meaning and increasing complexity: Contributions of Sigmund Freud and Rene Spitz to developmental psychology. *Developmental Psychology, 28,* 347–359.

Emde, R. N. (1998). Individual meaning and increasing complexity: Contributions of Sigmund Freud and Rene Spitz to developmental psychology. *Psychotherapie Psychosomatik Medizinische Psychologie, 53,* 79–82.

Emmer, E. T., Evertson, C. M., & Worsham, M. E. (2006). *Classroom management for middle and high school teachers* (7th ed.). Boston: Pearson/Allyn & Bacon.

Emmerich, W., Goldman, K., Kirsh, B., & Sharabany, R. (1977). Evidence for a transitional phase in the development of gender constancy. *Child Development, 48,* 930–936.

Engle, P. L., & Black, M. M. (2008). The effect of poverty on child development and educational outcomes. *Poverty on Child Development and Education, 1136,* 243–256.

Enright, R. D. (1994) The moral development of forgiveness. In B. Puka (Ed.), *Reaching out: Caring, altruism, and prosocial behavior* (pp. 219–248). New York: Garland.

Enright, R. D. (2001). *Forgiveness is a choice: A step-by-step process for resolving anger and restoring hope.* Washington, DC: American Psychological Association.

Enright, R. D., Lapsley, D. K., & Levy, V. M. (1983). Moral education strategies. In M. Pressley & J. R. Levin (Eds.), *Cognitive strategy research: Educational applications* (pp. 43–83). New York: Springer-Verlag.

Enright, R. D., & The Human Development Study Group. (1994). Piaget on the moral development of forgiveness: Identity or reciprocity? *Human Development, 37,* 63–80.

Entwisle, D., & Hayduk, L. (1978). *Too great expectations: The academic outlook of young children.* Baltimore: Johns Hopkins University Press.

Epstein, S. (1994). Integration of the cognitive and the psychodynamic unconscious. *American Psychologist, 49,* 709–724.

Erdley, C. A., & Day, H. J. (2017). Friendship in childhood and adolescence. In M. Hojjat & A. Moyer (Eds.), *The psychology of friendship* (pp. 3–19). New York: Oxford University Press.

Erickson, F. (1987). Transformation and school success: The politics and culture of educational achievement. *Anthropology and Education Quarterly, 18,* 335–356.

Erickson, F., & Mohatt, G. (1982). Cultural organization of participation structures in two classrooms of Indian students. In G. Spindler (Ed.), *Doing the ethnography of schooling* (pp. 133–174). New York: Holt, Rinehart & Winston.

Erikson, E. (1943). Observations on the Yurok: Childhood and world image. *American Archaeology and Ethnology, 35*, 257–302.

Erikson, E. (1945). Childhood and tradition in two American Indian tribes. In *Psychoanalytic study of the child* (Vol. 1, pp. 319–350). New York: International Universities Press.

Erikson, E. (1963). *Childhood and society*. New York: Norton.

Erikson, E. (1968). *Identity: Youth and crisis*. New York: Norton.

Erikson, E., & Coles, R. (Eds.). (2000). *The Erik Erikson reader*. New York: Norton.

Erikson, M. G. (2007). The meaning of the future: Toward a more specific definition of possible selves. *Review of General Psychology, 11*(4), 348–358.

Erting, C. J., Prezioso, C., & O'Grady Hynes, M. (1990). The interactional context of deaf mother–infant communication. In V. Volterra & C. J. Erting (Eds.), *From gesture to language in hearing and deaf children* (pp. 97–106). Berlin: Springer-Verlag.

Espelage, D. L. (2016). Sexual orientation and gender identity in schools: A call for more research in school psychology—No more excuses. *Journal of School Psychology, 54*, 5–8.

Esposito, E. A., & Gunnar, M. R. (2014). Early deprivation and developmental psychopathology. In M. Lewis & K. D. Rudolph (Eds.), *Handbook of developmental psychopathology* (pp. 371–388). New York: Springer US.

Espy, K. A., Moore, I. M., Kaufmann, P. M., Kramer, J. H., Mattha, K., & Hutter, J. J. (2001). Chemotherapeutic CNS prophylaxis and neuropsychologic change in children with acute lymphoblastic leukemia: A prospective study. *Journal of Pediatric Psychology, 26*, 1–9.

Evans, G. W., Li, D., & Whipple, S. S. (2013). Cumulative risk and child development. *Psychological Bulletin, 139*(6), 1342–1396.

Evans, J. A., & Hamerton, J. L. (1985). Chromosomal anomalies. In A. M. Clarke, A. D. B. Clarke, & J. M. Berg (Eds.), *Mental deficiency: The changing outlook* (pp. 135–213). New York: Free Press.

Evans, M. A. (2001). Shyness in the classroom and home. In R. W. Crozier & L. E. Alden (Eds.), *International handbook of social anxiety: Concepts, research and interventions relating to the self and shyness* (pp. 159–183). New York: Wiley.

Evans, M. A. (2010). Language performance, academic performance, and signs of shyness: A comprehensive review. In K. Rubin & R. J. Coplan (Eds.), *The development of shyness and social withdrawal* (pp. 179–212). New York: Guilford Press.

Evertson, C. M., Emmer, E. T., & Worsham, M. E. (2002). *Classroom management for elementary teachers* (6th ed.). Boston: Pearson/Allyn & Bacon.

Fabes, R. A., Pahlke, E., Martin, C. L., & Hanish, L. D. (2013). Gender-segregated schooling and gender stereotyping. *Educational Studies, 39*(3), 315–319.

Fabiani, M., & Wee, E. (2001). Age-related changes in working memory function: A review. In C. Nelson & M. Luciana (Eds.), *Handbook of developmental cognitive neuroscience* (pp. 473–488). Cambridge, MA: MIT Press.

Fagot, B. I. (1978). The influence of sex of child on parental reactions to toddler children. *Child Development, 49*, 459–465.

Fagot, B. I. (1981). Male and female teachers: Do they treat boys and girls differently? *Sex Roles, 7*, 263–271.

Fagot, B. I. (1985). Changes in thinking about early sex role development. *Developmental Review, 5*, 83–98.

Fagot, B. I., & Hagan, R. (1991). Observation of parent reactions to sex-stereotyped behaviors: Age and sex effects. *Child Development, 62*, 617–628.

Fagot, B. I., & Leinbach, M. D. (1989). The young child's gender schema: Environmental input, internal organization. *Child Development, 60*, 663–672.

Fagot, B. I., & Leinbach, M. D. (1993). Gender role development in young children: From discrimination to labeling. *Developmental Review, 13*, 86–106.

Fakhoury, M. (2015). Autistic spectrum disorders: A review of clinical features, theories and diagnosis. *International Journal of Developmental Neuroscience, 43*, 70–77.

Faldo, T. (2012). Only children: An updated review. *Journal of Individual Psychology, 68*(1), 38–49.

Fan, X., & Chen, M. (2001). Parental involvement and students' academic achievement: A meta-analysis. *Educational Psychology Review, 13*(1), 1–22.

Farkas, G., Sheehan, D., & Grobe, R. P. (1990). Coursework mastery and school success: Gender, ethnicity, and poverty groups within an urban school district. *American Educational Research Journal, 27*, 807–827.

Farland-Smith, D. (2009). How does culture shape students' perceptions of scientists?: Cross-national comparative study of American and Chinese elementary students. *Journal of Elementary Science Education, 21*, 23–42.

Farmer, T. W., Hamm, J. V., Leung, M. C., Lambert, K., & Gravelle, M. (2011). Early adolescent peer ecologies in rural communities: Bullying in schools that do and do not have a transition during the middle grades. *Journal of Youth and Adolescence, 40*, 1106–1117.

Farrant, B. M., & Zubrick, S. R. (2012). Early vocabulary development: The importance of joint attention and parent–child reading. *First Language, 32*(3), 343–364.

Farrell, E., Peguero, G., Lindsey, R., & White, R.

(1988). Giving voice to high school students: Pressure and boredom, ya know what I'm sayin'? *American Educational Research Association, 25,* 489–502.

Faulkner-Bond, M., & Sireci, S. G. (2015). Validity issues in testing linguistic minorities. *International Journal of Testing, 15,* 114–135.

Fearon, R., Bakermans-Kranenburg, M. J., van IJzendoorn, M. H., Lapsley, A. M., & Roisman, G. I. (2010). The significance of insecure attachment and disorganization in the development of children's externalizing behavior: A meta-analytic study. *Child Development, 81*(2), 435–456.

Fearon, R. P., & Belsky, J. (2016). Precursors of attachment security. In J. Cassidy & P. R. Shaver (Eds.), *Handbook of attachment: Theory, research, and clinical applications* (3rd ed., pp. 291–313). New York: Guilford Press.

Feeney, B. C., & Monin, J. K. (2016) Divorce through the lens of attachment theory. In J. Cassidy & P. R. Shaver (Eds.), *Handbook of attachment: Theory, research, and clinical applications* (3rd ed., pp. 941–965). New York: Guilford Press.

Feeney, B. C., & Woodhouse, S. S. (2016). Caregiving. In J. Cassidy & P. R. Shaver (Eds.), *Handbook of attachment: Theory, research, and clinical applications* (3rd ed., pp. 827–851). New York: Guilford Press.

Feinberg, M. E., Solmeyer, A. R., & McHale, S. M. (2012). The third rail of family systems: Sibling relationships, mental and behavioral health, and preventive intervention in childhood and adolescence. *Clinical Child and Family Psychology Review, 15,* 43–57.

Feldhusen, J. F. (1986). A conception of giftedness. In R. J. Sternberg & J. E. Davidson (Eds.), *Conceptions of giftedness* (pp. 112–127). Cambridge, UK: Cambridge University Press.

Feldhusen, J. F., & Kolloff, M. B. (1981). Me: A self-concept scale for gifted students. *Perceptual and Motor Skills, 53,* 319–323.

Feldman, D. H. (1982). *Developmental approaches to giftedness and creativity.* San Francisco: Jossey-Bass.

Feldman, D. H. (1988). *Nature's gambit: Child prodigies and the development of human potential.* New York: Basic Books.

Feldman, D. H. (2013). Cognitive development in childhood: A contemporary perspective. In R. M. Lerner, M. A. Easterbrooks, & J. Mistry (Eds.), *Handbook of developmental psychology* (2nd ed., pp. 197–213). New York: Wiley.

Feltz, D. L., Landers, D. M., & Becker, B. J. (1988). A revised meta-analysis of the mental practice literature on motor skill performance. In D. Druckman & J. A. Swets (Eds.), *Enhancing human performance: Issues, theories and techniques: Background papers* (pp. 1–65). Washington, DC: National Research Council.

Fennema, E., & Franke, M. L. (1992). Teachers' knowledge and its impact. In D. A. Grouws (Ed.), *Handbook of research on mathematics teaching and learning* (pp. 147–164). New York: Macmillan.

Fernald, A. (1991). Prosody in speech to children: Prelinguistic and linguistic features. In R. Vasta (Ed.), *Annals of child development* (Vol. 8, pp. 43–80). Greenwich, CT: JAI Press.

Fernald, A., & Kuhl, P. (1987). Acoustic determinants of infant preference for motherese speech. *Infant Behavior and Development, 10,* 279–293.

Ferrer, E., Shaywitz, B. A., Holahan, J. M., Marchione, K. E., Michaels, R., & Shaywitz, S. E. (2015). Achievement gap in reading is present as early as first grade and persists through adolescence. *Journal of Pediatrics, 167,* 1121–1125.

Feurstein, R. (1980). *Instrumental enrichment: An intervention program for cognitive modifiability.* Baltimore: University Park Press.

Fey, M. E., Windsor, J., & Warren, S. F. (1995). *Language intervention: Preschool through the elementary years.* Baltimore: Brookes.

Fields, R. D. (2008). White matter in learning, cognition and psychiatric disorders. *Trends in Neurosciences, 31,* 361–370.

Fields, R. D. (2010). Change in the brain's white matter. *Science, 330,* 768–769.

Fidalgo, R., Torrance, M., & Garcia, J.-N. (2008). The long-term effects of strategy-focused writing instruction for grade six students. *Contemporary Educational Psychology, 33*(4), 672–693.

Fincham, F. D., Hokoda, A., & Sanders, R., Jr. (1989). Learned helplessness, text anxiety, and academic achievement: A longitudinal analysis. *Child Development, 60,* 138–145.

Finn, J. D., & Cox, D. (1992). Participation and withdrawal among fourth-grade pupils. *American Educational Research Journal, 29,* 141–162.

Fischer, F. T., Schult, J., & Hell, B. (2013). Sex-specific differential prediction of college admission tests: A meta-analysis. *Journal of Educational Psychology, 105*(2), 478–488.

Fischer, K. W. (1980). A theory of cognitive development: The control and construction of hierarchies of skills. *Psychological Review, 87,* 477–531.

Fischer, K. W. (2008). Dynamic cycles of cognitive and brain development: Measuring growth in mind, brain, and education. In A. M. Battro, K. W. Fischer, & P. Léna (Eds.), *The educated brain* (pp. 127–150). Cambridge UK: Cambridge University Press.

Fischer, K. W. (2009). Mind, brain, and education: Building a scientific groundwork for learning and teaching. *Mind, Brain, and Education, 3,* 3–16.

Fischer, K. W., & Rose, S. P. (1994). Dynamic development of coordination of components in brain and behavior: A framework for theory and research. In G. Dawson & K. W. Fischer (Eds.), *Human behavior and the developing brain* (pp. 3–66). New York: Guilford Press.

Fischer, K. W., & van Geert, P. (2014). Dynamic development of brain and behavior. In P. C. M. Molenaar, R. M. Lerner, & K. M. Newell (Eds.), *Handbook of developmental systems and methodology* (pp. 287–315). New York: Guilford Press.

Fitzgerald, J. (1995). English-as-a-second-language learners' cognitive reading processes: A review of the research in the United States. *Review of Educational Research, 65*, 145–190.

Fitzgerald, J., & Markham, L. (1987). Teaching children about revision in writing. *Cognition and Instruction, 4*, 3–24.

Fitzgerald, J., & Relyea-Kim, J. E. (2013). Bilingual education programs and student achievement. In J. Hattie & E. M. Anderman (Eds.), *International guide to student achievement* (pp. 285–288). New York: Routledge.

Flannery, D. J., Rowe, D. C., & Gulley, B. L. (1993). Impact of pubertal status, timing, and age on adolescent sexual experience and delinquency. *Journal of Adolescent Research, 8*, 21–40.

Flavell, J. H. (1971). Stage-related properties of cognitive development. *Cognitive Psychology, 2*, 421–453.

Flavell, J. H. (1972). An analysis of cognitive-developmental sequences. *Genetic Psychology Monographs, 86*, 279–350.

Flavell, J. H. (1985). *Cognitive development.* Englewood Cliffs, NJ: Prentice-Hall.

Flavell, J. H., Beach, D. H., & Chinsky, J. M. (1966). Spontaneous verbal rehearsal in a memory task as a function of age. *Child Development, 37*, 283–299.

Flavell, J. H., Miller, P. H., & Miller, S. M. (1993). *Cognitive development* (3rd ed.). Englewood Cliffs, NJ: Prentice-Hall.

Flensborg-Madsen, T., & Mortensen, E. L. (2015). Infant developmental milestones and adult intelligence: A 34-year follow-up. *Early Human Development, 91*, 393–400.

Fletcher, J. D. (2009). From behaviorism to constructivism: A philosophical journal from drill and practice to situated learning. In S. Tobias & T. M. Duffy (Eds.), *Constructivist instruction: Success or failure?* (pp. 243–263). New York: Routledge.

Flower, L., & Hayes, J. (1980). The dynamics of composing: Making plans and juggling constraints. In L. Gregg & E. Steinberg (Eds.), *Cognitive processes in writing* (pp. 31–50). Hillsdale, NJ: Erlbaum.

Flynn, J. R. (2016). *Does your family make you smarter?: Nature, nurture, and human autonomy.* Cambridge, UK: Cambridge University Press.

Foersterling, F. (1985). Attribution retraining: A review. *Psychological Bulletin, 98*, 495–512.

Foley, J., & Thompson, L. (2003). *Language learning: A lifelong process.* New York: Oxford University Press.

Fombonne, E. (2009). Epidemiology of pervasive developmental disorders. *International Pediatric Research Foundation, 65*(6), 591–598.

Fonagy, P., Target, M., Cottrell, D., Phillips, J., & Kurtz, Z. (2002). *What works for whom?: A critical review of treatments for children and adolescents.* New York: Guilford Press.

Ford, D. Y. (2012). Gifted and talented education: History, issues, and recommendations. In K. Harris, S. Graham, & T. Urdan (Eds.), *APA educational psychology handbook: Vol. 2. Individual differences and cultural and contextual factors* (pp. 83–110). Washington, DC: American Psychological Association.

Ford, D. Y. (2016). Black and Hispanic students: Cultural differences within the context of education. In L. Corno & E. M. Anderman (Eds.), *Handbook of educational psychology* (3rd ed., pp. 364–377). New York: Routledge/Taylor & Francis.

Fordham, S. (1988). Racelessness as a factor in black students' school success: Pragmatic strategy or pyrrhic victory? *Harvard Educational Review, 58*, 54–84.

Fordham, S., & Ogbu, J. U. (1986). Black students' school success: Coping with the burden of "acting white." *Urban Review, 18*, 176–206.

Foundas, A. L. (2001). The anatomical basis of language. *Topics in Language Disorders, 21*, 1–19

Frances, A. J., & Widiger, T. (2012). Psychiatric diagnosis: Lessons from the DSM-IV past and cautions for the DSM-5 future. *Annual Review of Clinical Psychology, 8*, 109–130.

Frank, M. C., Amso, D., & Johnson, S. P. (2014). Visual search and attention to faces during early infancy. *Journal of Experimental Child Psychology, 118*, 13–26.

Franz, L., Angold, A., Copeland, W., Costello, E. J., Towe-Goodman, N., & Egger, H. (2013). Preschool anxiety disorders in pediatric primary care: Prevalence and comorbidity. *Journal of the American Academy of Child and Adolescent Psychiatry, 52*(12), 1294–1303.

Frechette, S., & Romano, E. (2015). Change in corporal punishment over time in a representative sample of Canadian parents. *Journal of Family Psychology, 29*(4), 507–517.

Freedman-Doan, C., Wigfield, A., Eccles, J., Blumenfeld, P., Arbreton, A., & Harold, R. D. (2000). What am I best at?: Grade and gender differences in children's beliefs about ability improvement. *Journal of Applied Developmental Psychology, 21*, 379–402.

Freiberg, H. J., Huzinec, C., & Templeton. S. M. (2009). Classroom management—a pathway to student achievement. *Elementary School Journal, 110*(1), 164–180.

Freud, A. (1936). *The ego and the mechanisms of defense.* New York: International Universities Press.

Frey, K. S., & Ruble, D. N. (1987). What children say about classroom performance: Sex and grade differences in perceived competence. *Child Development, 58,* 1066–1078.

Fried, P. A. (2002). Conceptual issues in behavioral teratology and their application in determining long-term sequelae of prenatal marihuana exposure. *Journal of Child Psychology and Psychiatry and Allied Disciplines, 43,* 81–102.

Fried, P. A., & Watkinson, B. (1990). 36- and 48-month-neurobehavioral follow-up of children prenatally exposed to marijuana, cigarettes, and alcohol. *Journal of Developmental and Behavioral Pediatrics, 11,* 49–58.

Friedman, N. P., Miyake, A., Altamirano, L. J., Corley, R. P., Young, S. E., Rhea, S. A., et al. (2016). Stability and change in executive function abilities from late adolescence to early adulthood: A longitudinal twin study. *Developmental Psychology, 52*(2), 326–340.

Frisancho, A. R. (1995). *Human adaptation and accommodation.* Ann Arbor: University of Michigan Press.

Frisch, H. L. (1977). Sex stereotypes in adult–infant play. *Child Development, 48,* 1671–1675.

Fuchs, D., & Fuchs, L. S. (1986). Test procedure bias: A meta-analysis of examiner familiarity effects. *Review of Educational Research, 56,* 243–262.

Fuchs, L. S., Zumeta, R. O., Schumacher, R. F., Powell, S. R., Seethaler, P. M., Hamlett, C. L., et al. (2010). The effects of schema-broadening instruction on second graders' word-problem performance and their ability to represent words problems with algebraic equations: A randomized control study. *The Elementary School Journal, 110*(4), 440–463.

Fuglestad, A. J., Rao, R., & Georgeiff, M. K. (2008). The role of nutrition in cognitive development. In C. A. Nelson & M. Luciana (Eds.), *Handbook of developmental cognitive neuroscience* (2nd ed., pp. 623–641). Cambridge, MA: MIT Press.

Fuhrmann, D., Knoll, L. J., & Blakemore, S. J. (2015). Adolescence as a sensitive period of brain development. *Trends in Cognitive Sciences, 19,* 558–566.

Fulcher, M. (2011). Individual differences in children's occupational aspirations as a function of parental traditionality. *Sex Roles, 64*(1–2), 117–131.

Fulcher, M., Sutfin, E. L., & Patterson, C. J. (2008). Individual differences in gender development: Associations with parental sexual orientation, attitudes, and division of labor. *Sex Roles, 58*(5–6), 330–341.

Fulk, B. M. (1996a). The effects of combined strategy and attribution training on LD adolescents' spelling performance. *Exceptionality, 6,* 13–27.

Fulk, B. M. (1996b). Reflections on "The effects of combined strategy and attribution training on LD adolescents' spelling performance." *Exceptionality, 6,* 59–63.

Fulton, B. D., Scheffler, R. M., & Hinshaw, S. P. (2015). State variation in increased ADHD prevalence: Links to NCLB school accountability and state medication laws. *Psychiatric Services, 66*(10), 1074–1082.

Furrer, C., & Skinner, E. (2003). Sense of relatedness as a factor in children's academic engagement and performance. *Journal of Educational Psychology, 95,* 148–162.

Furth, H. G. (1964). Research with the deaf: Implications for language and cognition. *Psychological Bulletin, 62,* 145–164.

Furth, H. G. (1966). *Thinking without language.* New York: Free Press.

Fusaro, M., & Nelson, C. A. (2009). Developmental cognitive neuroscience and education practice. In O. A. Barbarian & B. H. Wasik (Eds.), *Handbook of child development and early education: Research to practice* (pp. 57–77). New York: Guilford Press.

Gagné, R. M., & Dick, W. (1983). Instructional psychology. *Annual Review of Psychology, 34,* 261–295.

Galaburda, A. M., Sherman, G. F., Rosen, G. D., Aboitz, F., & Geschwind, N. (1985). Developmental dyslexia: Four consecutive patients with cortical anomalies. *Archives of Neurology, 35,* 812–817.

Galdi, S., Cadinu. M., & Tomasetto, C. (2014). The roots of stereotype threat: When automatic associations disrupt girls' math performance. *Child Development, 85*(1), 250–263.

Gallagher, T. M. (1981). Contingent query sequences within adult–child discourse. *Journal of Child Language, 8*(1), 51–62.

Gallaway, C., & Woll, B. (1994). Interaction and childhood deafness. In C. Galloway & B. Richards (Eds.), *Input and interaction in language acquisition* (pp. 197–218). Cambridge, UK: Cambridge University Press.

Galton, F. (1869). *Hereditary genius: An inquiry into its laws and consequences.* London: Macmillan.

Ganley, C. M., & Vasilyeva, M. (2014). The role of anxiety and working memory in gender differences in mathematics. *Journal of Educational Psychology, 106*(1), 105–120.

Ganley, C. M., Vasilyeva, M., & Dulaney, A. (2014). Spatial ability mediates the gender difference in middle school students' science performance. *Child Development, 85*(4), 1419–1432.

Garcia, E. E. (1993). Curriculum and instruction: Revision for constant relevancy. *Education and Urban Society, 25,* 270–284.

Gardner, H. (1983). *Frame of mind: The theory of multiple intelligences.* New York: Basic Books.

Gardner, H. (1993). *Multiple intelligences: The theory in practice.* New York: Basic Books.

Gardner, H. (1999). *Intelligence reframed: Multiple*

intelligences for the 21st century. New York: Basic Books.

Gardner, W., & Rogoff, B. (1982). The role of instruction in memory development: Some methodological choices. *Quarterly Newsletter of the Laboratory of Comparative Human Cognition, 4,* 6–12.

Garlick, D. (2002). Understanding the nature of the general factor of intelligence: The role of individual differences in neural plasticity as an explanatory mechanism. *Psychological Review, 109,* 116–136.

Garner, R. (1992). Learning from school texts. *Educational Psychologist, 27,* 53–63.

Garner, R., Alexander, P. A., Gillingham, M. G., Kulikowich, J. M., & Brown, R. (1991). Interest and learning from text. *American Educational Research Journal, 28,* 643–660.

Garner, R., Gillingham, M. G., & White, C. S. (1989). Effects of "seductive details" on macroprocessing and microprocessing in adult and children. *Cognition and Instruction, 6,* 41–57.

Gartstein, M. A., Putnam, S. P., & Kliewer, R. (2016). Do infant temperament characteristics predict core academic abilities in preschool-aged children. *Learning and Individual Differences, 45,* 299–306.

Garvey, C. (1974). Requests and responses in children's speech. *Journal of Child Language, 2,* 41–60.

Gaspard, H., Dicke, A.-L., Flunger, B., Schreier, B., Hafner, I., Trautwein, U., et al. (2015). More value through greater differentiation: Gender differences in value beliefs about math. *Journal of Educational Psychology, 107*(3), 663–677

Gassman-Pines, A. (2013). Daily spillover of low-income mothers' perceived workload to mood and mother-child interactions. *Journal of Marriage and Family, 75,* 1304–1318.

Gauvain, M., & Perez, S. (2015). Cognitive development and culture. In L. S. Liben, U. Müller, & R. M. Lerner (Eds.), *Handbook of child psychology and developmental science: Vol. 2. Cognitive process* (7th ed., pp. 854–896). Hoboken, NJ: Wiley.

Gayan, J., & Olson, R. K. (2003). Genetic and environmental influences on individual differences in printed word recognition. *Journal of Experimental Child Psychology, 84,* 97–123.

Ge, X., Conger, R. D., & Elder, G. H., Jr. (1996). Coming of age too early: Pubertal influences on girls' vulnerability to psychological distress. *Child Development, 67,* 3386–3400.

Ge, X., Conger, R. D., & Elder, G. H., Jr. (2001). Pubertal transition, stressful life events, and the emergence of gender differences in adolescent depressive symptoms. *Developmental Psychology, 37,* 404–417.

Ge, X., Kim, I. J., Brody, G. H., Conger, R. D., Simons, R. L., Gibbons, F. X., & Cutrona, C. E. (2003). It's about timing and change: Pubertal transition effects on symptoms of major depression among African American youths. *Developmental Psychology, 39,* 430–439.

Geary, D. C., & Brown, S. C. (1991). Cognitive addition: Strategy choice and speed-of-processing differences in gifted, normal, and mathematically disabled children. *Developmental Psychology, 27,* 398–406.

Geisinger, K. F. (1992). Fairness and selected psychometric issues in the psychological testing of Hispanics. In K. F. Geisinger (Ed.), *Psychological testing of Hispanics* (pp. 17–42). Washington, DC: American Psychological Association.

Geisinger, K. F. (2003). Testing and assessment in cross-cultural psychology. In J. R. Graham & J. A. Naglieri (Vol. Eds.), *Handbook of psychology: Vol. 10. Assessment psychology* (pp. 95–117). New York: Wiley.

Geisinger, K. F. (Ed). (2015a). *Psychological testing of Hispanics (Second edition): Clinical, cultural, and intellectual issues.* Washington, DC: American Psychological Association.

Geisinger, K. F. (2015b). A brief review of Spanish-language adaptions of some English-language intelligence tests. In K. F. Geisinger (Ed.), *Psychological testing of Hispanics: Clinical, cultural, and intellectual issues* (2nd ed., pp. 67–80). Washington, DC: American Psychological Association.

Gelman, R. (1972). Logical capacity of very young children: Number invariance rules. *Child Development, 43*(1), 75–90.

Gelman, R., & Baillargeon, R. (1983). A review of some Piagetian concepts. In J. H. Flavell & E. M. Markman (Eds.), *Handbook of child psychology: Vol. 3. Cognitive development* (pp. 167–230). New York: Wiley.

Gelman, R., Massey, C. M., & McManus, M. (1991). Characterizing supporting environments for cognitive development: Lessons from children in a museum. In L. Resnick, J. M. Levine, & S. D. Teasley (Eds.), *Perspectives on socially shared cognition* (pp. 226–256). Washington, DC: American Psychological Association.

Gelman, S. A., & Koenig, M. A. (2003). Theory-based categorization in early childhood. In D. H. Rakison & L. M. Oakes (Eds.), *Early category and concept development: Making sense of the blooming, buzzing confusion* (pp. 330–359). New York: Oxford University Press.

Gelman, S. A., & Meyer, M. (2011). Child categorization. *WIREs Cognitive Science, 2,* 95–105.

Genesee, F. (1981). Cognitive and social consequences of bilingualism. In R. G. Gardner & R. Kalin (Eds.), *A Canadian social psychology of ethnic relations.* London: Methuen.

Genesee, F., Lindholm-Leary, K., Saunders, W. M., & Christian, D. (Eds.). (2006). *Educating English language learners: A synthesis of research evidence.* New York: Cambridge University Press.

Gentry, M., Gable, R. K., & Rizza, M. (2002). Students' perceptions of classroom activities: Are there grade-level and gender differences? *Journal of Educational Psychology, 94,* 539–544.

George, M., Koss, K. J., McCoy, K. P., Cummings, M. E., & Davies, P. T. (2010). Examining the family context and relations with attitudes to school and scholastic competence. *Advances in School and Mental Health Promotion, 3*(4), 51–62.

Geraerts, E. (2012). Cognitive underpinnings of recovered memories of child abuse. In R. F. Belli (Ed.), *True and false recovered memories: Toward a reconciliation of the debate* (pp. 175–191). New York: Springer.

Gerding, A., & Signorielli, N. (2014). Gender roles in tween television programming: A content analysis of two genres. *Sex Roles, 70*(1–2), 43–56.

Gershoff, E. T. (2002). Corporal punishment by parents and associated child behavior and experiences: A meta-analytic and theoretical review. *Psychological Bulletin, 128,* 539–579.

Gershoff, E. T. (2016). Should parents' physical punishment of children be considered a source of toxic stress that effects brain development? *Family Relations, 65,* 151–162.

Gershoff, E. T., & Grogan-Kaylor, A. (2016). Spanking and child outcomes: Old controversies and new meta-analysis. *Journal of Family Psychology, 30*(4), 453–469.

Gershoff, E. T., Purtell, K. M., & Holas, I. (2015). *Corporal punishment in U.S. public schools: Legal precedents, current practices, and future policy.* New York: Springer.

Gersten, R., & Baker, S. (2001). Teaching expressive writing to students with learning disabilities: A meta-analysis. *Elementary School Journal, 101,* 251–272.

Gersten, R., Fuchs, L. S., Williams, J. P., & Baker, S. (2001). Teaching reading comprehension strategies to students with learning disabilities: A review of research. *Review of Educational Research, 71,* 279–320.

Ghatala, E. S. (1986). Strategy-monitoring training enables young learners to select effective strategies. *Educational Psychologist, 21,* 43–54.

Ghatala, E. S., Levin, J. R., Pressley, M., & Goodwin, D. (1986). A componential analysis of the effects of derived and supplied strategy-utility information on children's strategy selections. *Journal of Experimental Child Psychology, 41,* 76–92.

Gibbs, J. C., Basinger, K. S., Grime, R. L., & Snarey, J. R. (2007). Moral judgement development across cultures: Revisiting Kohlberg's universality claims. *Developmental Review, 27,* 443–500.

Gibson, E. J., & Spelke, E. S. (1983). The development of perception. In J. H. Flavell & E. M. Markman (Eds.), *Handbook of child psychology: Vol. 3. Cognitive development* (4th ed., pp. 1–76). New York: Wiley.

Gibson, M. A., & Ogbu, J. U. (Eds.). (1991). *Minority status and schooling: A comparative study of immigrant and involuntary minorities.* New York: Garland Press.

Gick, M. L., & Holyoak, K. J. (1980). Analogical problem solving. *Cognitive Psychology, 12,* 306–355.

Gick, M. L., & Holyoak, K. J. (1983). Schema induction and analogical transfer. *Cognitive Psychology, 15,* 1–38.

Giedd, J. N. (2012). The digital revolution and adolescent brain evolution. *Journal of Adolescent Health, 51,* 101–105.

Giedd, J. N., Keshavan, M., & Paus, T. (2008). Why do many psychiatric disorders emerge during adolescence? *Nature Reviews Neuroscience, 9,* 947–957.

Giest, H., & Lompscher, J. (2003). Formation of learning activity and theoretical thinking in science teaching. In A. Kozulin, B. Gindia, V. S. Ageyev, & S. M. Miller (Eds.), *Vygotsky's educational theory in cultural context* (pp. 267–288). Cambridge, UK: Cambridge University Press.

Gilger, J. W., & Wise, S. E. (2004). Genetic correlates of language and literacy impairments. In C. A. Stone, E. R. Silliman, B. J. Ehren, & K. Apel (Eds.), *Handbook of language and literacy* (pp. 25–48). New York: Guilford Press.

Gilliam, W. S., & Zigler, E. F. (2000). A critical meta-analysis of evaluations of state-funded preschool from 1997 to 1998: Implications for policy, service delivery and program evaluation. *Early Childhood Research Quarterly, 15,* 441–473.

Gilligan, C. (1982). *In a different voice: Psychological theory and women's development.* Cambridge, MA: Harvard University Press.

Gilmore, L., Cuskelly, M., & Browning, M. (2015). Mastery motivation in children with disability: Is there evidence for a Down syndrome behavioural phenotype? *International Journal of Disability, Development and Education, 62*(3), 265–275.

Gindis, B. (2003). Remediation through education: Sociocultural theory and children with special needs. In A. Kozulin, B. Gindia, V. S. Ageyev, & S. M. Miller (Eds.), *Vygotsky's educational theory in cultural context* (pp. 200–221). Cambridge, UK: Cambridge University Press.

Ginsburg, H. J., & Miller, S. M. (1982). Sex differences in children's risk-taking behavior. *Child Development, 53,* 426–428.

Glaser, B., & Strauss, A. (1967). *The discovery of grounded theory.* Chicago: Aldine.

Gleason, J. B. (1973). Code switching in children's language. In T. E. Moore (Ed.), *Cognitive development and the acquisition of language.* Oxford, UK: Academic Press.

Glocker, M. L., Langleben, D. D., Ruparel, K., Loughead, J. W., Gur, R. C., & Sachser, N. (2009). Baby schema in infant faces induces cuteness perception and motivation for caretaking in adults. *Ethology, 115*(3), 257–263.

Glover, J. A. (1989). The "testing" phenomenon: Not gone but nearly forgotten. *Journal of Educational Psychology, 81,* 392–399.

Goede, I., Branje, S., & Meeus, W. (2009). Developmental changes and gender differences in adolescents' perceptions of friendships. *Journal of Adolescence, 32,* 1105–1123.

Goelman, H. (1986). The language environments of family day care. In S. Kilmer (Ed.), *Advances in early education and day care* (Vol. 4, pp. 153–179). Greenwich, CT: JAI Press.

Goldberg, S. (1995). Introduction. In S. Goldberg, R. Muir, & J. Kerr (Eds.), *Attachment theory: Social, developmental, and clinical perspectives* (pp. 1–11). Hillsdale, NJ: Analytic Press.

Goldfield, B. A., & Reznick, J. S. (1990). Early lexical acquisition: Rate, content, and the vocabulary spurt. *Journal of Child Language, 17,* 171–183.

Goldin-Meadow, S. (1985). Language development under atypical learning conditions. In K. E. Nelson (Ed.), *Children's language* (Vol. 5, pp. 197–245). Hillsdale, NJ: Erlbaum.

Goldin-Meadow, S., & Mylander, C. (1984). Gestural communication in deaf children: The effects and noneffects of parental input on early language development. *Society for Research in Child Development Monographs, 49*(No. 207), 1–121.

Goldstein, E. B. (2015). *Cognitive psychology: Connecting, mind, research and everyday experience (4th edition).* Stamford, CT: Cengage Learning.

Goleman, D. (1990, March 6). As a therapist, Freud fell short. *New York Times,* pp. C1, C12.

Gombert, E. (1991). *Metalinguistic development.* Chicago: University of Chicago Press.

Göncü, A., & Gauvain, M. (2012). Sociocultural approaches to educational psychology: Theory, research and application. In K. Harris, S. Graham, & T. Urdan (Eds.), *APA educational psychology handbook: Vol. 1. Theories, constructs, and critical issues* (pp. 125–154). Washington, DC: American Psychological Association.

González, G., & Dejarnette, A. F. (2015). Teachers' and students' negotiation moves when teachers scaffold group work. *Cognition and Instruction, 33*(1), 1–45.

Gonzales-Bracken, M. A., Bamaca-Colbert, M. Y., & Allen, K. (2016). Ethnic identity trajectories among Mexican-origin girls during early and middle adolescence: Predicting future psychological adjustment. *Developmental Psychology, 52*(5), 790–797.

Gooden, W. E. (1989). Development of black men in early adulthood. In R. L. Jones (Ed.), *Black adult development and aging* (pp. 63–89). Berkeley, CA: Cobb & Henry.

Goodwyn, S. W., & Acredolo, L. P. (1993). Symbolic gesture versus word: Is there a modality advantage for onset of symbol use? *Child Development, 64*(3), 688–701.

Gopnik, A., Meltzoff, A., & Kuhl P. (1999). *The scientist in the crib: Minds, brains, and how children learn.* New York: Morrow.

Gorman, A., Schwartz, D., Nakamoto J., & Mayeux, L. (2011). Unpopularity and disliking among peers: Partially distinct dimensions of adolescents' social experiences. *Journal of Applied Developmental Psychology, 32,* 208–217.

Gorsuch, R. L. (1983). *Factor analysis* (2nd ed.). Mahwah, NJ: Erlbaum.

Goswami, U. (2004). Neuroscience and education. *British Journal of Educational Psychology, 74,* 1–14.

Goswami, U. (2008). Reading, complexity and the brain. *Literacy, 42,* 67–74.

Goswami, U., & Bryant, P. (1992). Rhyme, analogy, and children's reading. In P. B. Gough, L. C. Ehri, & R. Treiman (Eds.), *Reading acquisition* (pp. 49–63). Hillsdale, NJ: Erlbaum.

Gottesman, I. I., & Hanson, D. R. (2005). Human development: Biological and genetic processes. *Annual Review of Psychology, 56,* 263–286.

Gottfredson, D. C., Gottfredson, G. D., & Hybl, L. G. (1993). Managing adolescent behavior: A multiyear, multischool study. *American Educational Research Journal, 30,* 179–215.

Götz, M., & Huttner, W. B. (2005). The cell biology of neurogenesis. *Nature Reviews: Molecular Cell Biology, 6,* 777–788.

Gould, S. J. (1981). *The mismeasure of man.* New York: Norton.

Graf, P., & Schacter, D. L. (1985). Implicit and explicit memory for new associations in normal and amnesic subjects. *Journal of Experimental Psychology: Learning, Memory, and Cognition, 11,* 501–518.

Graham, S. (1990). The role of production factors in learning disabled students' compositions. *Journal of Educational Psychology, 82,* 781–791.

Graham, S., & Harris, K. R. (1987). Improving composition skills of inefficient learners with self-instructional strategy training. *Topics in Language Disorders, 7,* 66–77.

Graham, S., & Harris, K. R. (1988). Instructional recommendations for teaching writing to exceptional children. *Exceptional Children, 54,* 506–512.

Graham, S., & Harris, K. R. (2003). Students with learning disabilities and the process of writing: A meta-analysis of SRSD studies. In H. L. Swanson, K. R. Harris, & S. Graham (Eds.), *Handbook of learning disabilities* (pp. 323–344). New York: Guilford Press.

Graham, S., & MacArthur, C. (1988). Improving learning disabled students' skill at revising essays produced on a word processor: Self-instructional strategy training. *Journal of Special Education, 22,* 133–152.

Graham, S., McKeown, D., Kiuhara, S., & Harris, K. R. (2012). A meta-analysis of writing instruction for students in the elementary grades. *Journal of Educational Psychology, 104*(4), 879–896.

Graham, S., & Perin, D. (2007). A meta-analysis of writing instruction for adolescent students. *Journal of Educational Psychology, 99*(3), 445–476.

Graham, S., & Taylor, A. Z. (2002). Ethnicity, gender, and the development of achievement values. In A. Wigfield & J. S. Eccles (Eds.), *Development of achievement motivation* (pp. 121–146). San Diego, CA: Academic Press.

Graham, S., & Weiner, B. (1996). Theories and principles of motivation. In D. C. Berliner & R. C. Calfee (Eds.), *Handbook of educational psychology* (pp. 63–84). New York: Macmillan.

Graham, S., & Weiner, B. (2012). Motivation: Past, present and future. In K. Harris, S. Graham, & T. Urdan (Eds.), *APA educational psychology handbook: Vol. 1. Theories, constructs, and critical issues* (pp. 257–293). Washington, DC: American Psychological Association.

Granger, K. L., Hanish, L. D., Kornienko, O., & Bradley, R. H. (2017). Preschool teachers' facilitation of gender-typed and gender-neutral activities during free play. *Sex Roles, 76,* 498–510.

Granier-Deferre, C., Ribeiro, A., Jacquet, A. Y., & Bassereau, S. (2011). Near-term fetuses process temporal features of speech. *Developmental Science, 14,* 336–352.

Graves, S. L., & Aston, C. (2016). History of psychological assessment and interventions with minority populations. In S. L. Graves & J. J. Blake (Eds.), *Psychoeducational assessment and intervention for ethnic minority children: Evidence-based approaches* (pp. 9–21). Washington, DC: American Psychological Association.

Graves, S. L., & Blake, J. J. (Eds.). (2016). *Psychoeducational assessment and intervention for ethnic minority children: Evidence-based approaches.* Washington, DC: American Psychological Association.

Graybill, E. C., & Proctor, S. L. (2016). Lesbian, gay, bisexual, and transgender youth: Limited representation in school support personnel journals. *Journal of School Psychology, 54,* 9–16.

Graziano, W. G., Varca, P. E., & Levy, J. C. (1982). Race of examiner effects and the validity of intelligence tests. *Review of Educational Research, 52,* 469–498.

Green, S. K. (2002). Using an expectancy–value approach to examine teachers' motivational strategies. *Teaching and Teacher Education, 18,* 989–1005.

Greenbaum, J., & Graf, P. (1989). Preschool period development of implicit and explicit remembering. *Bulletin of the Psychonomic Society, 27*(5), 417–420.

Greene, N. D., & Copp, A. J. (2014). Neural tube defects. *Annual Review of Neuroscience, 37,* 221–242.

Greenfield, P. M. (1984). A theory of the teacher in the learning activities of everyday life. In B. Rogoff & J. Lave (Eds.), *Everyday cognition: Its development in social context* (pp. 117–138). Cambridge, MA: Harvard University Press.

Greenfield, P. M., & Savage-Rumbaugh, E. S. (1990). Grammatical combination in *Pan paniscus:* Processes of learning and invention in the evolution and development of language. In S. T. Parker & K. R. Gibson (Eds.), *"Language" and intelligence in monkeys and apes* (pp. 540–578). Cambridge, UK: Cambridge University Press.

Greenough, W. T., Black, J. E., & Wallace, C. S. (1987). Experience and brain development. *Child Development, 58*(3), 539–559.

Griffith, P. L. (1991). Phonemic awareness helps first graders invent spellings and third graders remember correct spellings. *Journal of Reading Behavior, 23,* 215–233.

Grigorenko, E. L. (2007a). Understanding the etiology of complex traits: Sybiotic relationships between psychology and genetics. *Mind, Brain and Education, 1*(4), 193–199.

Grigorenko, E. L. (2007b). Triangulating developmental dyslexia: Behavior, brain and genes. In D. Coch, G. Dawson, & K. W. Fischer (Eds.), *Human behavior and learning and the developing brain: Atypical development* (pp. 117–144). New York: Guilford Press.

Groh, A. M., Narayan, A. J., Bakermans-Kranenburg, M. J., Roisman, G. I., Vaughn, B. E., Fearon, R. M. P., et al. (2017). Attachment and temperament in the early life course: A meta-analytic review. *Child Development, 88,* 770–795.

Groh, A. M., Roisman, G. I., Booth-LaForce, C., Fraley, R. C., Owen, M. T., Cox, M. J., et al.(2014). Stability of attachment security from infancy to late adolescence. *Monographs of the Society for Research in Child Development, 79*(3), 51–66

Grolnick, W. S., Raftery-Helmer, J. N., & Flamm, E. S. (2013). Parent involvement in learning. In J. Hattie & E. M. Anderman (Eds.), *International guide to student achievement* (pp. 101–103). New York: Routledge.

Groschwitz, R. M., Munz, L. S., Straub, J. B., Bohnacker, I., & Plener, P. L. (2017). Strong schools against suicidality and self-injury: Evaluation of a workshop for school staff. *School Psychology Quarterly, 32,* 1–11.

Grosjean, F. (1982). *Life with two languages: An introduction to bilingualism.* Cambridge, MA: Harvard University Press.

Grossman, T. (2015). The development of social brain functions in infancy. *Psychological Bulletin, 141*(6), 1266–1287.

Guay, F., Marsh, H. W., & Boiven, M. (2003). Academic self-concept and academic achievement: Developmental perspectives on their causal ordering. *Journal of Educational Psychology, 95,* 124–136.

Guba, E. G. (Ed.). (1990). *Paradigm dialog.* Newbury CA: SAGE.

Guba, E. G., & Lincoln, Y. S. (1982). Epistemological and methodological bases of naturalistic inquiry. *Educational Communication and Technology Journal, 30,* 233–252.

Gunnar, M. R., Doom, J. R., & Esposito, E. A. (2015). Psychoneuroendocrinology of stress: Normative development and individual differences. In R. M. Lerner (Series Eds.) & M. E. Lamb (Vol. Ed.), *Handbook of child psychology and developmental science: Vol. 3. Socioemotional processes* (7th ed., pp. 106–151). New York: Wiley.

Gunnar, M. R., & Herrera, A. M. (2013). The development of stress reactivity: A neurobiological perspective. In P. D. Zelazo (Ed.), *The Oxford handbook of developmental psychology, Vol. 2: Self and other* (pp. 45–80). New York: Oxford University Press.

Haberlandt, K. (1980). Story grammar and reading time of story constituents. *Poetics, 9,* 99–116.

Hadwin, J., & Perner, J. (1991). Pleased and surprised: Children's cognitive theory of emotion. *British Journal of Developmental Psychology, 9,* 215–234.

Haenen, J., Schrijnemakers, H., & Stufkens, J. (2003). Sociocultural theory and the practice of teaching historical concepts. In A. Kozulin, B. Gindia, V. S. Ageyev, & S. M. Miller (Eds.), *Vygotsky's educational theory in cultural context* (pp. 246–266). Cambridge, UK: Cambridge University Press.

Hakuta, K. (1986). *Mirror of language: The debate on bilingualism.* New York: Basic Books.

Hakuta, K., Bialystok, E., & Wiley, E. (2003). Critical evidence: A test of the critical-period hypothesis for second-language acquisition. *Psychological Science, 14*(1), 31–38.

Hale, G. A., & Lewis, M. (1979). *Attention and cognitive development.* New York: Plenum Press.

Hale, N. G., Jr. (1995). *The rise and crisis of psychoanalysis in the United States: Freud and the Americans, 1917–1985.* New York: Oxford University Press.

Halim, M. L., Ruble, D. N., Tamis-LeMonda, C. S., Zosuls, K. M., Lurye, L. E., & Greulich, F. K. (2014). Pink frilly dresses and the avoidance of all things "girly": Children's appearance rigidity and cognitive theories of gender development. *Developmental Psychology, 50*(4), 1091–1101.

Hall, G. S. (1904). *Adolescence: Vol. 1.* New York: Appleton.

Hall, G. S. (1905). *Adolescence: Vol. 2.* New York: Appleton.

Halpern, D. F. (2000). *Sex differences in cognitive abilities* (3rd ed.). Mahwah, NJ: Erlbaum.

Halpern, H., & Perry-Jenkins, M. (2016). Parents' gender ideology and gendered behavior as predictors of children's gender-role attitudes: A longitudinal exploration. *Sex Roles, 74*(11–12), 527–542.

Halpern, M. E., Güntürkün, O., Hopkins, W. D., & Rogers, L. J. (2005). Lateralization of the vertebrate brain: taking the side of model systems. *Journal of Neuroscience, 25,* 10351–10357.

Hamilton, G. J. (2009). Prescription drug abuse. *Psychology in the Schools, 46*(9), 892–898.

Hamm, M. P., Newton, A. S., Chisholm, A., Shulhan, J., Milne, A., Sundar, P., et al. (2015). Prevalence and effect of cyberbullying on children and young people a scoping review of social media studies. *Journal of the American Medical Association: Pediatrics, 169*(8), 770–777.

Hammen, C. L., Rudolph, K. D., & Abaied, J. L. (2014). Child and adolescent depression. In E. J. Mash & R. A. Barkley (Eds.), *Child psychopathology* (pp. 225–263). New York: Guilford Press.

Hammer, C. S., Hoff, E., Uchikoshi, Y., Gillanders, C., Castro, D. C., & Sandilos, L. E. (2014). The language and literacy development of young dual language learners: A critical review. *Early Childhood Research Quarterly, 29,* 715–733.

Han, J., & Neuharth-Pritchett, S. (2015). Meaning-related and print-related interactions between preschoolers and parents during shared book reading and their associations with emergent literacy skills. *Journal of Research in Childhood Education, 29,* 528–550.

Han, W.-J. (2012). Bilingualism and academic achievement. *Child Development, 83*(1), 300–321.

Hannah, C. L., & Shore, B. M. (1995). Metacognition and intellectual ability: Insights from the study of learning disabled gifted students. *Gifted Child Quarterly, 39,* 95–109.

Harkins, J. E., & Bakke, M. (2003). Technologies for communication: Status and trends. In M. Marschark & P. E. Spencer (Eds.), *Oxford handbook of deaf studies, language, and education* (pp. 406–419). New York: Oxford University Press.

Harnishfeger, K. K., & Bjorklund, D. F. (1993). The ontogeny of inhibition mechanisms: A renewed approach to cognitive development. In M. L. Howe & R. Pasnak (Eds.), *Emerging themes in cognitive development: Vol. 1. Foundations* (pp. 28–49). New York: Springer-Verlag.

Haroutunian-Gordon, S. (1991). *Turning the soul: Teaching through conversation in the high school.* Chicago: University of Chicago Press.

Harrell, R., Capp, R., Davis, D., Peerless, J., & Ravitz, L. (1981). Can nutritional supplements help mentally retarded children? *Proceedings of the National Academy of Sciences of the USA, 78,* 574–578.

Harris, K. R. (1988, April). *What's wrong with strategy intervention research?: Intervention integrity.* Paper presented at the annual meeting of the American Educational Research Association, New Orleans, LA.

Harris, K. R., & Graham, S. (1992). Self-regulated strategy development: A part of the writing process. In M. Pressley, K. R. Harris, & J. T. Guthrie (Eds.), *Promoting academic competence and literacy in school* (pp. 277–309). San Diego, CA: Academic Press.

Harris, K., Santangelo, T., & Graham, S. (2010). Metacognition and strategies instruction in writing. In H. S. Salatas & W. Schneider (Eds.), *Reading, writing, and academic performance* (pp. 226–256). New York: Guilford Press.

Harris, P. L., Brown, E., Marriott, C., Whittall, S., & Harmer, S. (1991). Monsters, ghosts, and witches: Testing the limits of the fantasy–reality distinction. *British Journal of Developmental Psychology, 9,* 105–123.

Hart, B., & Risley, T. R. (1995). *Meaningful differences in the everyday experience of young American children.* Baltimore: Brookes.

Hart, B., & Risley, T. R. (1999). *The social world of children: Learning to talk.* Baltimore: Brookes.

Harter, S. (1992). The relationship between perceived competence, affect, and motivational orientation within the classroom: Processes and patterns of change. In A. K. Boggiano & T. S. Pittman (Eds.), *Achievement and motivation: A social-developmental perspective* (pp. 77–114). New York: Cambridge University Press.

Harter, S., Whitesell, N. R., & Kowalski, P. (1992). Individual differences in the effects of educational transitions on young adolescent's perceptions of competence and motivational orientation. *American Educational Research Journal, 29,* 777–807.

Hartman, D. E. (2009). Test review Wechsler Adult Intelligence Scale IV (WAIS IV): Return of the Gold Standard. *Applied Neuropsychology, 16,* 85–87.

Hartup, W. W. (1989). Social relations and their developmental significance. *American Psychologist, 44,* 120–126.

Hay, D. F., Caplan, M., & Nash, A. (2009). The beginnings of peer relations. In K. H. Rubin, W. M. Bukowski, & B. Laursen (Eds.), *Handbook of peer interactions, relationships, and groups* (pp. 121–142). New York: Guilford Press.

Hayden, E. P., & Mash, E. J. (2014). Child psychopathology: A developmental-systems perspective. In E. J. Mash & R. A. Barkley (Eds.), *Child psychopathology* (pp. 3–74). New York: Guilford Press.

Hayes, J. R., Waterman, D. A., & Robinson, C. S. (1977). Identifying relevant aspects of a problem text. *Cognitive Science, 1,* 297–313.

Heath, S. B. (1989). Oral and literate traditions among black Americans living in poverty. *American Psychologist, 44,* 367–373.

Hebb, D. O. (1949). *The organization of behavior.* New York: Wiley.

Heberle, A. E., & Carter, A. S. (2015). Cognitive aspects of young children's experience of economic disadvantage. *Psychological Bulletin, 141*(4), 723–746.

Hebert, M., Bohaty, J. J., Nelson, J. R., & Brown, J. (2016). The effects of text structure instruction on expository reading comprehension: A meta-analysis. *Journal of Educational Psychology, 108*(5), 609–629.

Heckman, J. J. (2006). Skill formation and the economics of investing in disadvantaged children. *Science, 312,* 1900–1902.

Heine, S. J., Kitzyama, S., Lehman, D. R., Takata, T., Ide, E., Leung, C., et al. (2001). Divergent consequences of success and failure in Japan and North America: An investigation of self-improving motivations and malleable selves. *Journal of Personality and Social Psychology, 81,* 599–615.

Henderlong, J., & Lepper, M. R. (2002). The effects of praise on children's intrinsic motivation: A review and synthesis. *Psychological Bulletin, 128*(5), 774–795.

Henderson, S. W. (2013). Sexual healing. *Journal of the American Academy of Child and Adolescent Psychiatry, 52*(6), 655–657.

Henderson, V. L., & Dweck, C. S. (1990). Motivation and achievement. In S. S. Feldman & G. R. Elliott (Eds.), *At the threshold: The developing adolescent* (pp. 308–329). Cambridge, MA: Harvard University Press.

Henrich, C. C., Kuperminc, G. P., Sack, A., Blatt, S. J., & Leadbeater, B. J. (2000). Characteristics and homogeneity of early adolescent friendship groups: A comparison of male and female non-clique members. *Applied Developmental Science, 4*(1), 15–26.

Henry, L. A., & MacLean, M. (2002). Working memory performance in children with and without intellectual disabilities. *American Journal on Mental Retardation, 107*(6), 421–432.

Henry, L. A., & Millar, S. (1991). Memory span increases with age: A test of two hypotheses. *Journal of Experimental Child Psychology, 51,* 459–484.

Herdt, G. H., & Davidson, J. (1988). The Sambia "Turnim-Man": Sociocultural and clinical aspects of gender formation in male pseudohermaphrodites with 5 alpha-reductase deficiency in Papua New Guinea. *Archives of Sexual Behavior, 17,* 33–56.

Herman, L. M. (2002). Exploring the cognitive world of the bottlenosed dolphin. In C. Allen & M. Bekoff (Eds.), *The cognitive animal: Empirical and theoretical perspectives on animal cognition* (pp. 275–283). Cambridge, MA: MIT Press.

Herman, L. M. (2010). What laboratory research has told us about dolphin cognition. *International Journal of Comparative Psychology, 23*(3), 310–330.

Herman, L. M., & Uyeyama, R. R. (1999). The dolphin's grammatical competency: Comments on Kako. *Animal Learning and Behavior, 27*, 18–23.

Herman, P. A., Anderson, R. C., Pearson, P. D., & Nagy, W. E. (1987). Incidental acquisition of word meaning from expositions with varied text features. *Reading Research Quarterly, 22*, 263–284.

Herrnstein, R. J., & Murray, C. (1994). *The bell curve: Intelligence and class structure in American life.* New York: Free Press.

Hertzog, C. (1989). Influences of cognitive slowing on age differences in intelligence. *Developmental Psychology, 25*, 636–651.

Hess, F. M., & Eden, M. (Eds.) (2017). *Every Student Succeeds Act: What it means for schools, systems, and states.* Cambridge, MA: Harvard Education Press.

Hesse, E. (2016). The adult attachment interview: Protocol, method of analysis, and selected empirical studies: 1985–2015. In J. Cassidy & P. R. Shaver (Eds.), *Handbook of attachment: Theory, research, and clinical applications* (pp. 553–597). New York: Guilford Press.

Hetherington, E. M. (1989). Coping with family transitions: Winners, losers, and survivors. *Child Development, 60*, 1–14.

Hetherington, E. M., & Frankie, G. (1967). Effect of parental dominance, warmth, and conflict on imitation in children. *Journal of Personality and Social Psychology, 6*, 119–125.

Hewitt, J., & Scardamalia, M. (1998). Design principles for distributed knowledge building processes. *Educational Psychology Review, 10*(1), 75–96.

Hiatt, C., Laursen, B., Mooney, K. S., & Rubin, K. H. (2015). Forms of friendship: A person-centered assessment of the quality, stability, and outcomes of different types of adolescent friends. *Personality and Individual Differences, 77*, 149–155.

Hidi, S. (1990). Interest and its contribution as a mental resource for learning. *Review of Educational Research, 60*, 549–571.

Hidi, S. (2001). Interest, reading, and learning: Theoretical and practical considerations. *Educational Psychology Review, 13*(3), 191–209.

Hidi, S. (2016). Revisiting the role of rewards in motivation and learning: Implications of neuroscience research. *Educational Psychology Review, 28*(1), 61–93.

Hidi, S., & Baird, W. (1988). Strategies for increasing text-based interest and students' recall of expository text. *Reading Research Quarterly, 23*, 465–483.

Higa-McMillan, C. K., Francis, S. E., & Chorpita, B. F. (2014). Anxiety disorders. In E. J. Mash & R. A. Barkley (Eds.), *Child psychopathology* (pp. 345–428). New York: Guilford Press.

Hilden, K. R., & Pressley, M. (2007). Self-regulation through transactional strategies instruction. *Reading and Writing Quarterly: Overcoming Learning Difficulties, 23*(1), 51–75.

Hill, N. E., & Wang, M. T. (2015). From middle school to college: Developing aspirations, promoting engagement, and indirect pathways from parenting to post high school enrollment. *Developmental Psychology, 51*(2), 224–235.

Hilliard, L. J., & Liben, L. S. (2010). Differing levels of gender salience in preschool classrooms: Effects on children's gender attitudes and intergroup bias. *Child Development, 81*, 1787–1798.

Hills, T. T., Todd, P. M., & Jones, M. N. (2015). Foraging in semantic fields: How we search through memory. *Topics in Cognitive Science, 7*, 513–534.

Hines, H. (2015). Gendered development. In M. E. Lamb & R. M. Lerner (Eds.), *Handbook of child psychology and developmental science: Vol. 3. Socioemotional processes* (7th ed., pp. 842–887). Hoboken: Wiley.

Hines, M., Golombok, S., Rust, J., Johnston, K. J., Golding, J., & Avon Longitudinal Study of Parents and Children Study Team. (2002). Testosterone during pregnancy and gender role behavior of preschool children: A longitudinal, population study. *Child Development, 73*, 1678–1687.

Hinsley, D., Hayes, J. R., & Simon, H. A. (1977). From words to equations. In P. Carpenter & M. Just (Eds.), *Cognitive processes in comprehension* (pp. 84–106). Hillsdale, NJ: Erlbaum.

Hirsh-Pasek, K., & Golinkoff, R. M. (1991). Language comprehension: A new look at some old themes. In N. Krasegnor, D. Rumbaugh, M. Studdert-Kennedy, & R. Schiefelbusch (Eds.), *Biological and behavioral aspects of language acquisition* (pp. 301–320). Hillsdale, NJ: Erlbaum.

Hitch, G. J., Halliday, M. S., Schaafstal, A. M., & Heffernan, T. M. (1991). Speech, "inner speech," and the development of short-term memory: Effects of picture-labeling on recall. *Journal of Experimental Child Psychology, 51*, 220–234.

Hitchcock, G., & Hughes, D. (1989). *Research and the teacher: A qualitative introduction to school-based research.* New York: Routledge.

Hmelo-Silver, C. E., & DeSimone, C. (2013). Problem-based learning: An instructional model of collaborative learning. In C. E. Hmelo-Silver, C. A. Chinn, C. K. K. Chan, & A. O'Donnell (Eds.), *The international handbook of collaborative learning* (pp. 370–385). New York: Routledge.

Hock, M., Schumaker, J., & Deshler, D. (2003). *Possible selves: Nurturing student motivation.* Lawrence, KS: Edge Enterprises.

Hoff, E. (2001). *Language development.* Monterey, CA: Wadsworth Thompson Learning.

Hoff, E., & Naigles, L. (2002). How children use

input to acquire a lexicon. *Child Development, 73*, 418–433.

Hoff, K. E., & Ervin, R. A. (2013). Extending self-management strategies: The use of a classwide approach. *Psychology in the Schools, 50*(2), 151–164.

Hoffman, H. S. (1969). Stimulus factors in conditioned suppression. In B. A. Campbell & R. M. Church (Eds.), *Punishment and aversive behavior* (pp. 185–234). New York: Appleton-Century-Crofts.

Hoffmann, C. (1991). *An introduction to bilingualism.* London: Longman.

Hogan, K., Nastasi, B. K., & Pressley, M. (2000). Discourse patterns and collaborative scientific reasoning in peer- and teacher-guided discussions. *Cognition and Instruction, 17*, 379–432.

Hogan, K., & Pressley, M. (Eds.). (1997). *Scaffolding student instruction.* Cambridge, MA: Brookline Books.

Hoigaard, R., Kovac, V. B., Overby, N. C., & Haugen, T. (2015). Academic self-efficacy mediates the effects of school psychological climate on academic achievement. *School Psychology Quarterly, 30*(1), 64–71.

Holloway, S. D. (1988). Concepts of ability and effort in Japan and the United States. *Review of Educational Research, 58*, 327–345.

Horn, J. L. (1985). Remodeling old models of intelligence. In B. Wolman (Ed.), *Handbook of intelligence* (pp. 267–300). New York: Wiley.

Horn, J. L., & Cattell, R. B. (1967). Age differences in fluid and crystallized intelligence. *Acta Psychologica, 26*, 107–129.

Horn, J. L., & Hofer, S. M. (1992). Major abilities and development in the adult period. In R. J. Sternberg & C. A. Berg (Eds.), *Intellectual development* (pp. 44–99). Cambridge, UK: Cambridge University Press.

Horn, J. L., & Stankov, L. (1982). Auditory and visual factors of intelligence. *Intelligence, 6*, 165–185.

Horner, S. L., & Gaither, S. M. (2004). Attribution retraining with a second-grade class. *Early Childhood Education Journal, 31*(3), 165–170.

Horney, K. (1967). *Feminine psychology.* New York: Norton.

Hort, B. E., Leinbach, M. D., & Fagot, B. I. (1991). Is there coherence among the cognitive components of gender acquisition? *Sex Roles, 24*, 195–207.

Horton, J. C. (2001). Critical periods in the development of the visual system. In J. B. Bailey Jr., J. T. Bruer, F. J. Symons, & J. W. Lichtman (Eds.), *Critical thinking about critical periods* (pp. 45–65). Baltimore: Brookes.

Horton, M. S. (1982). *Category familiarity and taxonomic organization in young children.* Unpublished doctoral dissertation, Stanford University, Stanford, CA.

Hostinar, C. E., & Gunnar, M. R. (2013). The developmental effects of early life stress: An overview of current theoretical frameworks. *Current Directions in Psychological Science, 22*, 400–406.

Houdé, O., Rossi, S., Lubin, A., & Joliot, M. (2010). Mapping numerical processing, reading, and executive functions in the developing brain: An fMRI meta-analysis of 52 studies including 842 children. *Developmental Science, 13*, 876–885.

Housand, B. C., & Housand, A. M. (2012). The role of technology in gifted students motivation. *Psychology in the Schools, 49*(7), 706–715.

Howe, K. R. (1988). Against the quantitative-qualitative incompatibility thesis. *Educational Researcher, 17*(8), 10–16.

Howe, N., Della Porta, S., Recchia, H., & Ross, H. (2016). "Because if you don't put the top on, it will spill": A longitudinal study of sibling teaching in early childhood. *Developmental Psychology, 52*, 1832–1842.

Howes, C., & Spieker, S. (2016). Attachment relationships in the context of multiple caregivers. In J. Cassidy & P. R. Shaver (Eds.), *Handbook of attachment: Theory, research, and clinical applications* (3rd ed., pp. 314–329). New York: Guilford Press.

Hruby, G. G., & Goswami, U. (2011). Neuroscience and reading: A review for reading education researchers. *Reading Research Quarterly, 46*, 156–172.

Hsin, L., & Snow, C. (2017). Social perspective taking: A benefit of bilingualism in academic writing. *Reading and Writing, 30*(6), 1193–1214.

Hua, Y., Morgan, B. S. T., Kaldenberg, E. R., & Goo, M. (2012). Cognitive strategy instruction for functional mathematical skill: Effects for young adults with intellectual disability. *Education and Training in Autism and Developmental Disabilities, 47*(3), 345–358.

Hua, Y., Woods-Groves, S., Ford, J., & Nobles, K. (2014). Effects of the paraphrasing strategy on expository reading comprehension of young adults with intellectual disability. *Education and Training in Autism and Developmental Disabilities, 49*(3), 429–439.

Huang, B. (2014). The effects of age on second language grammar and speech production. *Journal of Psycholinguistic Research, 43*(4), 397–420.

Huang, C. (2011). Achievement goals and achievement emotions: A meta-analysis. *Educational Psychology Review, 23*, 359–388.

Huang, C. (2012). Discriminant and criterion-related validity of achievement goals in predicting academic achievement: A meta-analysis. *Journal of Educational Psychology, 104*(1), 48–73.

Hubel, D. H., & Wiesel, T. N. (2005). *Brain and visual perception: The story of a 25-year collaboration.* New York: Oxford University Press.

Hudley, C., & Irving, M. (2012). Ethnic and racial identity in childhood and adolescence. In K. Harris, S. Graham, & T. Urdan (Eds.), *APA educational psychology handbook: Vol. 2. Individual differences and cultural and contextual factors* (pp. 267–292). Washington, DC: American Psychological Association.

Hudson, J. A. (1990). Constructive processing in children's event memory. *Developmental Psychology, 26,* 180–187.

Hudson, J., & Nelson, K. (1983). Effects of script structure on children's story recall. *Developmental Psychology, 19,* 625–635.

Hudson, J. A., & Shapiro, L. R. (1991). From knowing to telling: The development of children's scripts, stories, and personal narratives. In A. McCabe & C. Peterson (Eds.), *Developing narrative structure* (pp. 89–136). Hillsdale, NJ: Erlbaum.

Hudson, J. A., & Slackman, E. A. (1990). Children's use of scripts in inferential text processing. *Discourse Processes, 13,* 375–385.

Hughes, C., & Devine, R. T. (2015). A social perspective on theory of mind. In R. M. Lerner & M. E. Lamb (Eds.), *Handbook of child psychology and developmental science: Socioemotional processes* (Vol. 3, 7th ed., pp. 564–609). New York: Wiley.

Hughes, E. G., & Appel, B. (2016). The cell biology of CNS myelination. *Current Opinion in Neurobiology, 39,* 93–100.

Hulleman, C. S., & Barron, K. E. (2016). Motivation interventions in education. In L. Corno & E. M. Anderman (Eds.), *Handbook of educational psychology,* (3rd ed., pp. 160–171). New York: Routledge.

Hulleman, C. S., & Harackiewicz, J. M. (2009). Promoting interest and performance in high school science classes. *Science, 326*(5958), 1410–1412.

Hulleman, C. S., Kosovich, J. J., Barron, K. E., & Daniel, D. B. (2017). Making connections: Replicating and extending the utility value intervention in the classroom. *Journal of Educational Psychology, 109*(3), 387–404.

Hulleman, C. S., Schrager, S. M., Bodmann, S. M., & Harackiewicz, J. M. (2010). A meta-analytic review of achievement goal measures: Different labels for the same constructs or different constructs with similar labels? *Psychological Bulletin, 136,* 422–449.

Hulme, C., & MacKenzie, S. (1992). *Working memory and severe learning difficulties.* Hillsdale, NJ: Erlbaum.

Humes, A. (1983). Putting writing research into practice. *Elementary School Journal, 81,* 3–17.

Hunt, E., & Carlson, J. (2007). Considerations relating to the study of group differences in intelligence. *Perspectives on Psychological Science, 2*(2), 194–213.

Hunt, E., Lunneborg, C., & Lewis, J. (1975). What does it mean to be high verbal? *Cognitive Psychology, 7,* 194–227.

Hunter-Blanks, P., Ghatala, E. S., Pressley, M., & Levin, J. R. (1988). Comparison of monitoring during study and during testing on a sentence-learning task. *Journal of Educational Psychology, 80,* 279–283.

Huston, A. C., Bobbitt, K. C., & Bentley, A. (2015). Time spent in child care: How and why does it effect social development. *Developmental Psychology, 51*(5), 621–634.

Huston, A. C., & Wright, J. C. (1998). Mass media and children's development. In I. E. Sigel & K. A. Renninger (Vol. Eds.) & W. Damon (Ed.-in-Chief), *Handbook of child psychology: Vol. 4. Child psychology in practice* (pp. 999–1058). New York: Wiley.

Hutchins, E. (1991). The social organization of distributed cognition. In L. Resnick, J. M. Levine, & S. D. Teasley (Eds.), *Perspectives on socially shared cognition* (pp. 283–307). Washington, DC: American Psychological Association.

Huttenlocher, J., Haight, W., Bryk, A., Seltzer, M., & Lyons, T. (1991). Early vocabulary growth: Relation to language input and gender. *Developmental Psychology, 27,* 236–248.

Huttenlocher, J., Vasilyeva, M., Cymerman, E., & Levine, S. (2001). Language input and child syntax. *Cognitive Psychology, 45,* 337–374.

Huttenlocher, J., Waterfall, H., Vasileya, M., Vevea, J., & Hedges, L. (2010). Sources of variability in children's language growth. *Cognitive Psychology, 61*(4), 343–365.

Huttenlocher, P. R. (2002). *Neural plasticity: The effects of environment on the development of cerebral cortex.* Cambridge, MA: MIT Press.

Hutton, J. S., Horowitz-Kraus, T., Mendelsohn, A. L., DeWitt, T., Holland, S. K., & C-MIND Authorship Consortium. (2015). Home reading environment and brain activation in preschool children listening to stories. *Pediatrics, 136*(3), 466–478.

Hyde, J. S., Fennema, E., & Lamon, S. J. (1990). Gender differences in mathematics performance: A meta-analysis. *Psychological Bulletin, 107,* 139–155.

Hyde, J. S., & Linn, M. C. (1988). Gender differences in verbal ability: A meta-analysis. *Psychological Bulletin, 104,* 53–69.

Hyde, J. S., & Plant, E. A. (1995). Magnitude of psychological gender differences: Another side to the story. *American Psychologist, 50,* 159–161.

Hyman, I. A. (1990). *Reading, writing, and the hickory stick: The appalling story of physical and psychological abuse in American schools.* San Diego, CA: Lexington Books.

Hyman, I. A., & Wise, J. H. (Eds.). (1977). *Corporal punishment in American education.* Philadelphia: Temple University Press.

Hymel, S., Closson, L. M., Caravita, S. C. S., &

Vaillancourt, T. (2010). Social status among peers: From socioeconomic attraction to peer acceptance to perceived popularity. In P. K. Smith & C. H. Hart (Eds.), *The Wiley-Blackwell Handbook of Childhood Social Development* (2nd ed., pp. 375–392). Hoboken, NJ: Blackwell.

Imperato-McGinley, J., Peterson, R. E., Gautier, T., & Sturla, E. (1979). Androgens and the evolution of male-gender identity among male pseudohermaphrodites with 5a-reductase deificiency. *New England Journal of Medicine, 300*, 1233–1237.

Imuta, K., Henry, J. D., Slaughter, V., Selcuk, B., & Ruffman, T. (2016). Theory of mind and prosocial behavior in childhood: A meta-analytic review. *Developmental Psychology, 52*(8), 1192–1205.

Inhelder, B., Sinclair, H., & Bovet, M. (1974). *Learning and the development of cognition.* Cambridge, MA: Harvard University Press.

Institute of Medicine (IOM) and National Research Council (NRC). (2012). *From neurons to neighborhoods: An update: A workshop summary.* Washington, DC: National Academies Press.

Inzlicht, M., & Schmader, T. (2012). *Stereotype threat: Theory, process, and application.* New York: Oxford University Press.

Isabella, R. A., & Belsky, J. (1991). Interactional synchrony and the origins of infant–mother attachment: A replication study. *Child Development, 62*, 373–384.

Jablansky, S., Alexander, P. A., Dumas, D., & Compton, V. (2016). Developmental differences in relational reasoning among primary and secondary students. *Journal of Educational Psychology, 108*(4), 592–608.

Jackson, N. E., & Butterfield, E. C. (1986). A conception of giftedness designed to promote research. In R. J. Sternberg & J. E. Davidson (Eds.), *Conceptions of giftedness* (pp. 151–181). Cambridge, UK: Cambridge University Press.

Jackson, N. E., & Myers, M. G. (1982). Letter naming time, digit span, and precocious reading achievement. *Intelligence, 6*, 311–329.

Jacob, R., & Parkinson, J. (2015). The potential for school-based interventions that target executive function to improve academic achievement: A review. *Review of Educational Research, 85*(4), 512–552.

Jacobs, J. E., Lanza, S., Osgood, W., Eccles, J. S., & Wigfield, A. (2002). Changes in children's self-competence and values: Gender and domain differences across grades one through twelve. *Child Development, 73*, 509–527.

Jacobs, J. E., & Wigfield, A. (1989). Sex equity in mathematics and science education: Research–policy links. *Educational Psychology Review, 1*, 39–56.

Jacobsen, B., Lowery, B., & DuCette, J. (1986).

Attributions of learning disabled children. *Journal of Educational Psychology, 78*, 59–64.

Jacoby, R., & Glauberman, N. (1995). *The bell curve debate: History, documents, and opinion.* New York: Times Books.

Jaffee, S., & Hyde, J. S. (2000). Gender differences in moral orientation: A meta-analysis. *Psychological Bulletin, 126*(5), 703–726.

James, S., & Hale, L. (2017). Sleep duration and child well-being: A nonlinear association. *Journal of Clinical Child and Adolescent Psychology, 46*(2), 258–268.

Jausovec, N. (1994). Can giftedness be taught? *Roeper Review, 16*, 210–214.

Jausovec, N. (1998). Are gifted individuals less chaotic thinkers? *Personality and Individual Differences, 25*, 253–267.

Jeannin, R., & Leeuwin, K. V. (2015). Associations between direct and indirect perceptions of parental differential treatment and child socioemotional adaptation. *Journal of Child Family Studies, 24*, 1838–1855.

Jenkins, L. N., Floress, M. T., & Reinke, W. (2015). Rates and types of teacher praise: A review and future directions. *Psychology in the Schools, 52*(5), 463–476.

Jenlink, P. M. (2013). Situated cognition theory. In B. J. Irby, G. Brown, R. Lara-Alecio, & S. Jackson (Eds.), *The handbook of educational theories* (pp. 185–198). Charlotte, NC: Information Age.

Jensen, A. R. (1969). How much can we boost IQ and scholastic achievement? *Harvard Educational Review, 39*, 1–123.

Jensen, A. R. (1976, December). Test bias and construct validity. *Phi Delta Kappan*, pp. 340–346.

Jensen, A. R. (1992). Understanding *g* in terms of information processing. *Educational Psychology Review, 4*, 271–308.

Jernigan, T. L., Hesselink, J. R., Sowell, E., & Tallal, P. A. (1991). Cerebral structure on magnetic resonance imaging in language- and learning-impaired children. *Archives of Neurology, 48*, 539–545.

Johnson, D. W., & Johnson, R. (1985). Motivational processes in cooperative, competitive, and individualistic learning situations. In C. Ames & R. Ames (Eds.), *Research on motivation in education* (Vol. 2, pp. 249–286). New York: Academic Press.

Johnson, D. W., & Johnson, R. T. (2013). Cooperative, competitive and individualistic learning. In J. Hattie & E. M. Anderman (Eds.), *International guide to student achievement* (pp. 372–374). New York: Routledge.

Johnson, D., Maruyama, G., Johnson, R., Nelson, D., & Skon, L. (1981). Effects of cooperative, competitive, and individualistic goal structures on achievement: A meta-analysis. *Psychological Bulletin, 89*, 47–62.

Johnson, J. S., & Newport, E. L. (1989). Critical period effects in second language learning: The influence of maturational state on the acquisition of English as a second language. *Cognitive Psychology, 21,* 60–99.

Johnson, K. (2015). Reclaiming the relevance of L2 teacher education. *Modern Language Journal, 99*(3), 515–528.

Johnson, M. H., Jones, E. J. H., & Gliga, T. (2015). Brain adaptation and alternative developmental trajectories. *Development and Psychopathology, 27,* 425–442.

Johnson, R. E. (2003). Aging and the remembering of text. *Developmental Review, 23*(3), 261–346.

Johnson, S. B., Blum, R. W., & Giedd, J. N. (2009). Adolescent maturity and the brain: The promise and pitfalls of neuroscience research in adolescent health policy. *Journal of Adolescent Health, 45,* 216–221.

Johnson, W., Deary, I. J., & Iacono, W. G. (2009). Genetic and environmental transactions underlying educational attainment. *Intelligence, 37,* 466–478.

Johnston, L. D., O'Malley, P. M., Miech, R. A., Bachman, J. G., & Schulenberg, J. E. (2017). *Monitoring the Future national survey results on drug use, 1975–2016: Overview, key findings on adolescent drug use.* Ann Arbor: Institute for Social Research, University of Michigan.

Johnston, M. V. (2009). Plasticity in the developing brain: Implications for rehabilitation. *Developmental Disabilities Research Reviews, 15,* 94–101.

Jolles, D. D., & Crone, E. A. (2012). Training the developing brain: A neurocognitive perspective. *Frontiers in Human Neuroscience, 6,* 1–13.

Jonassen, D. H., & Grabowski, B. L. (2011). *Handbook of individual differences, learning, and instruction.* New York: Routledge.

Jones, C. H., Slate, J. R., Blake, P. C., & Sloas, S. (1995). Relationship of study skills, conceptions of intelligence, and grade level in secondary school students. *High School Journal, 79,* 25–32.

Jones, M. G., & Gerig, T. M. (1994). Silent sixth-grade students: Characteristics, achievement, and teacher expectations. *Elementary School Journal, 95,* 169–182.

Jones, M. G., & Wheatley, J. (1988). Factors influencing the entry of women into science and related fields. *Science Education, 72,* 127–142.

Jones, R. (2004). Listen and learn. *Nature Reviews Neuroscience, 4,* 699.

Joseph, L. M., & Konrad, M. (2009). Teaching students with intellectual or developmental disabilities to write: A review of the literature. *Research in Developmental Disabilities, 30*(1), 1–19.

Juel, C. (1988). Learning to read and write: A longitudinal study of 54 children from first through fourth grades. *Journal of Educational Psychology, 80,* 417–447.

Juel, C., Griffith, P. L., & Gough, P. B. (1986). Acquisition of literacy: A longitudinal study of children in first and second grade. *Journal of Educational Psychology, 78,* 243–255.

Jusczyk, P. W., Pisoni, D. B., & Mullenix, J. (1992). Some consequences of talker variability on speech processing by 2-month-old infants. *Cognition, 43*(2), 253–291.

Juvonen, J. (1988). Outcome and attributional disagreements between students and their teachers. *Journal of Educational Psychology, 80,* 330–336.

Kagan, J. (2010). *The temperamental thread: How genes, culture, time and luck make us who we are.* New York: Dana Press.

Kail, R. V. (1992). Processing speed, speech rate, and memory. *Developmental Psychology, 28,* 899–904.

Kail, R. V. (2000). Speed of information processing: Developmental changes and links to intelligence. *Journal of School Psychology, 38,* 51–61.

Kail, R. V., & Park, Y.-S. (1994). Processing time, articulation time, and memory span. *Journal of Experimental Child Psychology, 57,* 281–291.

Kako, E. E. (1999). Elements of syntax in the systems of three language-trained animals. *Animal Learning and Behavior, 27,* 1–14.

Kamil, M. L. (2004). Vocabulary and comprehension instruction: Summary and implications of the National Reading Panel report. In P. McCardle & V. Chhabra (Eds.), *The voice of evidence in reading research* (pp. 213–234). Baltimore: Brookes.

Kamphaus, R. W., Reynolds, C. R., & Vogel, K. K. (2009). Intelligence testing. In J. L. Matson, F. Andrasik, & M. L. Matson (Eds.), *Assessing childhood psychopathology and developmental disabilities* (pp. 91–115). New York: Springer.

Kandel, E. R., Schwartz, J. H., & Jessell, T. M. (1995). *Essentials of neural science and behavior.* Norwalk, CT: Appleton & Lange.

Kandel, E. R., Schwartz, J. H., Jessell, T. M., Siegelbaum, S. A., & Hudspeth, A. J. (2013). *Principles of neural science.* New York: McGraw Hill.

Kanevsky, L. (1995). Learning potentials of gifted students. *Roeper Review, 17,* 157–163.

Kanfer, F., & Zich, J. (1974). Self-control training: The effect of external control on children's resistance to temptation. *Developmental Psychology, 10,* 108–115.

Kann, L., McManus, T., Harris, W. A., Shanklins, S. L., Flint, K. H., Hawkins, J., et al. (2016). Youth risk behavior surveillance—United States, 2015. *MMWR Surveillance Summaries, 65*(6), 1–174.

Karasik, L. B., Tamis-LeMonda, C. S., & Adolph, K. E. (2014). Crawling and walking infants elicit different verbal responses from mothers. *Developmental Science, 17,* 388–395.

Karchmer, M. A., & Mitchell, R. E. (2003). Demographic and achievement characteristics of deaf and hard-of-hearing students. In M. Marschark & P. E. Spencer (Eds.), *Oxford handbook of deaf studies, language, and education* (pp. 21–37). New York: Oxford University Press.

Karrass, J., & Braungart-Rieker, J. M. (2004). Infant negative emotionality and attachment: Implications for preschool intelligence. *International Journal of Behavioral Development, 28*(3), 221–229.

Karrass, J., & Braungart-Rieker, J. M. (2005). Effects of shared parent–infant book reading on early language acquisition. *Applied Developmental Psychology, 26*, 133–148.

Katcher, A. (1955). The discrimination of sex differences by young children. *Journal of Genetic Psychology, 87*, 131–143.

Katzir, T. (2009). How research in the cognitive neuroscience sheds lights on subtypes of children with dyslexia: Implications for teachers. *Cortex, 45*, 558–559.

Katzir, T., & Pare-Blagoev, J. (2006). Applying cognitive neuroscience research to education: The case of literacy. *Educational Psychologist, 41*, 53–74.

Kaufman, A. S. (1990). *Assessing adolescent and adult intelligence.* Boston: Allyn & Bacon.

Kaufman, A. S., & Kaufman, N. L. (1983). *The Kaufmann Assessment Battery for Children (K-ABC).* Circle Pines, MN: American Guidance Services.

Kaufman, A. S., & Kaufman, N. L. (2004). *The Kaufman Assessment Battery for Children, Second Edition (KABC-II).* Circle Pines, MN: American Guidance Services.

Kaufman, A. S., Reynolds, C. R., & McLean, J. E. (1989). Age and WAIS-R intelligence in a national sample of adults in the 20- to 74-year-old age range: A cross-sectional analysis with education level controlled. *Intelligence, 13*, 235–253.

Keating, D. P., & Bobbitt, B. (1978). Individual and developmental differences in cognitive processing components of mental ability. *Child Development, 49*, 155–169.

Keene, E., & Zimmerman, S. (1997). *Mosiac of thought: Teaching comprehension in a reader's workshop.* Portsmouth, NH: Heinemann.

Keeney, F. J., Cannizzo, S. R., & Flavell, J. H. (1967). Spontaneous and induced verbal rehearsal in a recall task. *Child Development, 38*, 953–966.

Kehle, T., Bray, M. A., & Grigerick, S. E. (2007). Infant and child attachment as it relates to school-based outcomes. *Journal of Early Childhood and Infant Psychology, 3*, 47–60.

Keller, H., & Scholmerich, A. (1987). Infant vocalizations and parental reactions during the first four months of life. *Developmental Psychology, 23*, 62–67.

Kellman, P. J., & Arterberry, M. E. (2006). Infant visual perception. In D. Kuhn & R. Siegler (Vol. Eds.) & W. Damon & R. M. Lerner (Eds.-in-Chief), *Handbook of child psychology: Vol. 2. Cognition, perception and language* (6th ed., pp. 109–160). Hoboken, NJ: Wiley.

Kendziora, K., & Osher, D. (2016). Promoting children's and adolescents' social and emotional development: District adaptations of a theory of action. *Journal of Clinical Child and Adolescent Psychology, 45*(6), 797–811.

Kent, R. D., & Miolo, G. (1995). Phonetic abilities in the first year of life. In P. Fletcher & B. MacWhinney (Eds.), *The handbook of child psychology* (pp. 303–334). Oxford, UK: Blackwell.

Kerestes, M., & Youniss, J. E. (2003). Rediscovering the importance of religion in adolescent development. In R. M. Lerner, F. Jacobs, & D. Wereleib (Eds.), *Handbook of applied developmental science: Promoting positive child, adolescent, and family development through research, policies, and programs: Vol. 1. Applying* (pp. 165–184). Thousand Oaks, CA: SAGE.

Kern, M. L., Hampson, S. E., Goldberg, L. R., & Friedman, H. S. (2012). Integrating prospective longitudinal data: Modeling personality and health in the Terman Life Cycle and Hawaii Longitudinal studies. *Developmental Psychology, 50*(5), 1390–1406.

Kerns, K. A., & Brumariu, L. E. (2016). Attachment in middle childhood. In J. Cassidy & P. R. Shaver (Eds.), *Handbook of attachment: Theory, research, and clinical applications* (pp. 349–365). New York: Guilford Press.

Keys, T. D., Farkas, G., Howes, C., Burchinal, M. R., Duncan, G. J., Vandell, D. L., et al. (2013). Preschool center quality and school readiness: Quality effects and variation by demographic and child characteristics. *Child Development, 84*(4), 1171–1190.

Khalfa, J. (1994). *What is intelligence?* Cambridge, UK: Cambridge University Press.

Kieffer-Renaux, V., Bulteau, C., Grill, J., Kalifa, C., Viguier, D., & Jambaque, I. (2000). Patterns of neuropsychological deficits in children with medulloblastoma according to craniospatial irradiation doses. *Developmental Medicine and Child Neurology, 42*, 741–745.

Kiernan, C. (1985). Behaviour modification. In A. M. Clarke, A. D. B. Clarke, & J. M. Berg (Eds.), *Mental deficiency: The changing outlook* (pp. 465–511). New York: Free Press.

Killen, M., Mulvey, K. L., Richardson, C., Jampol, N., & Woodward, A. (2011). The accidental transgressor: Morally-relevant theory of mind. *Cognition, 119*, 197–215.

Killen, M., & Smetana, J. G. (2015). Origins and development of morality. In M. E. Lamb & R. M. Lerner (Eds.), *Handbook of child psychology and developmental science: Vol. 3. Socioemotional processes* (7th ed., pp. 701–749). Hoboken, NJ: Wiley.

Kilpatrick, J., Martin, W. G., & Schifter, D. (2003). *A research companion to principles and standards for school mathematics*. Reston, VA: National Council of Teachers of Mathematics.

Kim, Y., Otaiba, S. A., Wanzek, J., & Gatlin, B. (2015). Toward an understanding of dimensions, predictors, and the gender gap in written composition. *Journal of Educational Psychology, 107*(1), 79–95.

Kimonis, E. V., Frick, P. J., & McMahon, R. J. (2014). Conduct and oppositional defiant disorders. In E. J. Mash & R. A. Barkley (Eds.), *Child psychopathology* (pp. 145–179). New York: Guilford Press.

King, M. D., Jennings, J., & Fletcher, J. M. (2014). Medical adaptation to academic pressure: Schooling, stimulant use, and socioeconomic status. *American Sociological Review, 79*(6), 1039–1066.

King, R. B. (2015). Sense of relatedness boosts engagement, achievement, and well-being: A latent growth model study. *Contemporary Educational Psychology, 42*, 26–38.

King, R. B., & McInerney, D. M. (2014). Culture's consequence on student motivation: Capturing cross-cultural universality and variability through personal investment theory. *Educational Psychologist, 49*(3), 175–198.

Kintsch, W. (1982). Text representations. In W. Otto & S. White (Eds.), *Reading expository material* (pp. 87–102). New York: Academic Press.

Kintsch, W., & Greene, E. (1978). The role of culture-specific schemata in the comprehension and recall of stories. *Discourse Processes, 1*, 1–13.

Kintsch, W., Mandel, T. S., & Kozminsky, E. (1977). Summarizing scrambled stories. *Memory and Cognition, 5*, 547–552.

Kintsch, W., & Yarbrough, C. J. (1982). Role of rhetorical structure in text comprehension. *Journal of Educational Psychology, 74*, 828–834.

Kirschner, P. A. (2009). Epistemology or pedagogy, that is the question. In S. Tobias & T. M. Duffy (Eds.), *Constructivist Instruction: Success or failure?* (pp. 144–157). New York: Routledge.

Kisilevsky, B. S., & Hains, S. M. (2010). Exploring the relationship between fetal heart rate and cognition. *Infant and Child Development, 19*, 60–75.

Kistner, J. A., Osborne, M., & LeVerrier, L. (1988). Causal attributions of learning-disabled children: Developmental patterns and relation to academic progress. *Journal of Educational Psychology, 80*, 82–89.

Kitsantas, A., & Zimmerman, B. J. (2002). Comparing self-regulatory processes among novice, non-expert, and expert volleyball players: A microanalytic study. *Journal of Applied Sport Psychology, 14*, 91–105.

Klassen, R. M. (2004). Optimism and realism: A review of self-efficacy from a cross-cultural perspective. *International Journal of Psychology, 39*(3), 205–230.

Klausmeier, H. J. (1990). Conceptualizing. In B. F. Jones & L. Idol (Eds.), *Dimensions of thinking and cognitive instruction* (pp. 93–138). Hillsdale, NJ: Erlbaum.

Kliegl, R., Smith, J., & Baltes, P. B. (1990). On the locus and process of magnification of age differences during mnemonic training. *Developmental Psychology, 26*, 894–904.

Kline, M., Tschann, J. M., Johnson, J. R., & Wallerstein, J. S. (1989). Children's adjustment in joint and sole physical custody families. *Developmental Psychology, 25*, 430–438.

Klingberg, T. (2008). White matter maturation and cognitive development during childhood. In C. A. Nelson & M. Luciana (Eds.), *Handbook of developmental cognitive neuroscience* (2nd ed., pp. 237–243). Cambridge, MA: MIT Press.

Klinger, L. G., Dawson, G., Barnes, K., & Crissler, M. (2014). Autism spectrum disorder. In E. J. Mash & R. A. Barkley (Eds.), *Child psychopathology* (pp. 531–572). New York: Guilford Press.

Klingner, J. K., Vaughn, S., & Schumm, J. S. (1998). Collaborative strategic reading during social studies in heterogeneous fourth-grade classrooms. *Elementary School Journal, 99*, 3–22.

Klonsky, D. E., Glenn, C. R., Styer, D. M., Olino, T. M., & Washburn, J. J. (2015). The functions of nonsuicidal self-injury: Converging evidence for a two-factor structure. *Child and Adolescent Psychiatry and Mental Health, 9*(1), 44.

Kloosterman, P. (1988). Self-confidence and motivation in mathematics. *Journal of Educational Psychology, 80*, 345–351.

Klostermann, S., Connell, A., & Stormshak, E. A. (2014). Gender differences in the developmental links between conduct problems and depression across early adolescence. *Journal of Research on Adolescence, 26*(1), 76–89.

Knoors, H. (2016). Foundations for language development in deaf children and the consequences for communication choices. In M. Marschark & P. E. Spencer (Eds.), *The Oxford handbook of deaf studies in language* (pp. 19–31). New York: Oxford University Press.

Knoors, H., & Vervloed, M. P. J. (2003). Educational programming for deaf children with multiple disabilities: Accommodating special needs. In M. Marschark & P. E. Spencer (Eds.), *Oxford handbook of deaf studies, language, and education* (pp. 82–94). New York: Oxford University Press.

Kobak, R., Zajac, K., & Madsen, S. (2016). Attachment disruptions, reparative processes, and psychopathology: Theoretical and clinical implications. In J. Cassidy & P. R. Shaver (Eds.), *Handbook of attachment: Theory, research, and clinical applications* (pp. 25–39). New York: Guilford Press.

Koch, J. (2003). Gender issues in the classroom. In W. M. Reynolds (Vol. Ed.), *Handbook of psychology: Vol. 7. Educational psychology* (pp. 259–281). New York: Wiley.

Koenig, P., & Grossman, M. (2007). Process and content in semantic memory. In J. Hart & M. Kraut (Eds.), *Neural basis of semantic memory* (pp. 247–264). Cambridge, UK: Cambridge University Press.

Koger, S. M., Schettler, T., & Weiss, B. (2005). Environmental toxicants and developmental disabilities: A challenge for psychologists. *American Psychologist, 60,* 243–255.

Kohlberg, L. (1966). A cognitive-developmental analysis of children's sex-role concepts and attitudes. In E. E. Maccoby (Ed.), *The development of sex differences* (pp. 82–173). Stanford, CA: Stanford University Press.

Kohlberg, L. (1969). Stage and sequence: The cognitive-developmental approach to socialization. In D. Goslin (Ed.), *Handbook of socialization theory and research* (pp. 347–480). New York: Rand-McNally.

Kohlberg, L. (1981). *The philosophy of moral development: Moral stages and the idea of justice: Essays on moral development: Vol. 1.* San Francisco: Harper & Row.

Kohlberg, L. (1984). *The psychology of moral development: Essays on moral development: Vol. 2.* San Francisco: Harper & Row.

Kohlberg, L., & Mayer, R. (1972). Development as the aim of education: The Dewey view. *Harvard Educational Review, 42,* 449–496.

Kohlberg, L., Yaeger, J., & Hjertholm, E. (1968). Private speech: Four studies and a review of theories. *Child Development, 39,* 691–736.

Kolb, B., Comeau, W., & Gibb, R. (2008). Early brain injury, plasticity, and behavior. In C. A. Nelson & M. Luciana (Eds.), *Handbook of developmental cognitive neuroscience* (2nd ed., pp. 385–398). Cambridge, MA: MIT Press.

Komarovsky, M. (1985). *Women in college: Shaping new feminine identities.* New York: Basic Books.

Koocher, G. P., & Keith-Spiegel, P. C. (1990). *Children, ethics, and the law.* Lincoln: University of Nebraska Press.

Korbach, A., Brunken, R., & Park, B. (2016). Learner characteristics and information processing in multimedia learning: A moderated mediation of the seductive detail effect. *Learning and Individual Differences, 51,* 59–68.

Kosslyn, S. M., Margolis, J. A., Barrett, A. M., Goldknopf, E. J., & Daly, P. F. (1990). Age differences in imagery abilities. *Child Development, 61,* 995–1010.

Kosslyn, S. M., & Miller, G. W. (2013). *Top brain, bottom brain: Surprising insights into how you think.* New York: Simon and Schuster.

Kosslyn, S. M., Thomas, W. L., & Ganis, G. (2006). *The case for mental imagery.* New York: Oxford University Press.

Kovacs, A. M. (2016). Cognitive effects of bilingualism in infancy. In E. Nicoladis & S. Montanari (Eds.), *Bilingualism across the lifespan: Factors moderating language proficiency* (pp. 249–268). Washington, DC: American Psychological Association.

Kovas, Y., & Plomin, R., (2007). Learning abilities and disabilities: Generalist genes, specialist environments. *Current Directions in Psychological Science, 16,* 284–288.

Kowal, A. K., Krull, J. K., & Kramer, L. (2006). Shared understanding of parental differential treatment in families. *Social Development, 15*(2), 276–295.

Kowalski, R. M., Giumetti, G. W., Schroeder, A. N., & Lattanner, M. R. (2014). Bullying in the digital age: A critical review and meta-analysis of cyberbullying research among youth. *Psychological Bulletin, 140*(4), 1073–1137.

Kramer, L., & Conger, K. J. (2009). What we learn from our sisters and brothers: For better or for worse. *New Directions For Child And Adolescent Development, 126,* 1–12.

Krans, E. E., & Davis, M. M. (2012). Preventing low birthweight: 25 years, prenatal risk, and the failure to reinvent prenatal care. *American Journal of Obstetrics and Gynecology, 206,* 398–403.

Kranzler, J. H., & Floyd, R. G. (2013). *Assessing intelligence in children and adolescents: A practical guide.* New York: Guilford Press.

Krapohl, E., Kimfield, K., Shakeshaft, N. G., Trzaskowski, M., McMillan, A., Pingault, J. B., et al. (2014). The high heritability of educational achievement reflects many genetically influenced traits, not just intelligence. *Proceedings of the National Academy of Sciences of the USA, 111*(42), 15273–15278.

Krauss, R. H., & Glucksberg, S. (1969). The development of communication. *Child Development, 40,* 255–266.

Krawec, J., & Montague, M. (2014). The role of teacher training in cognitive strategy instruction to improve math problem solving. *Learning Disabilities Research and Practice, 20*(3), 126–134.

Kremer, K. P., Maynard, B. R., Polanin, J. R., Vaughn, M. G., & Sarteschi, C. M. (2015). Effects of after-school programs with at-risk youth on attendance and externalizing behaviors: A systematic review and meta-analysis. *Journal of Youth Adolescence, 44,* 616–636.

Kroger, J., & Marcia, J. E. (2011). The identity statuses: Origins and interpretations. In S. J.

Schwartz, K. Luyckx, & V. L. Vignoles (Eds.), *Handbook of identity theory and research* (pp. 31–54). New York: Springer.

Kroll, J. F., Gullifer, J., & Zirnstein, M. (2016). Literacy in adulthood: Reading in two languages. In E. Nicoladis & S. Montanari (Eds.), *Bilingualism across the lifespan: Factors moderating language proficiency* (pp. 225–245). Washington, DC: American Psychological Association.

Krueger, C., & Garvan, C. (2014). Emergence and retention of learning in early fetal development. *Infant Behavior and Development, 37*(2), 162–173.

Kuczaj, S. A. (1977). The acquisition of regular and irregular past tense forms. *Journal of Verbal Learning and Verbal Behavior, 16*, 589–600.

Kuhn, D., Amsel, E., & O'Loughlin, M. (1988). *The development of scientific thinking skills.* San Diego, CA: Academic Press.

Kumar, D., & Sherwood, R. (1997). Hypermedia in science and mathematics: Applications in teacher education, problem solving and student testing. *Journal of Educational Computing Research, 17*(3), 249–262.

Kurtz, B. E. (1990). Cultural influences on children's cognitive and metacognitive development. In W. Schneider & F. E. Weinert (Eds.), *Interactions among aptitudes, strategies, and knowledge in cognitive performance* (pp. 177–199). New York: Springer-Verlag.

Kurtz, B. E., Schneider, W., Carr, M., Borkowski, J. G., & Rellinger, E. (1990). Strategy instruction and attributional beliefs in West Germany and the United States: Do teachers foster metacognitive development? *Contemporary Educational Psychology, 15*, 268–283.

Kwon, M. K., Setoodehnia, M., Baek, J., Luck, S. J., & Oakes, L. M. (2016). The development of visual search in infancy: Attention to faces versus salience. *Developmental Psychology, 52*(4), 537.

Kyllonen, P. C. (2016). Human cognitive abilities: Their organization, development and use. In L. Corno & E. M. Anderman (Eds.), *Handbook of educational psychology* (3rd ed., pp. 121–134). New York: Routledge.

Lagattuta, K. (2005). When you shouldn't do what you want to do: Young children's understanding of desires, rules, and emotions. *Child Development, 76*(3), 713–733.

Lakin, J. M. (2012). Sex differences in reasoning abilities: Surprising evidence that male–female ratios in the tails of the quantitative reasoning distribution have increased. *Intelligence, 41*, 263–274.

Lam, A. C., Ruzek, E. A., Schenke, K., Conley, A. M., & Karabenick, S. A. (2015). Student perceptions of classroom achievement goal structure: Is it appropriate to aggregate? *Journal of Educational Psychology, 107*(4), 1102–1115.

Lam, C. B., Solmeyer, A. R., & McHale, S. M. (2012). Sibling relationships and empathy across the transition to adolescence. *Journal of Youth Adolescence, 41*, 1657–1670.

Lambert, W. E. (1974). Culture and language as factors in learning and education. In F. Aboud & R. D. Mead (Eds.), *Cultural factors in learning* (pp. 91–122). Bellingham: Washington State College.

Lambert, W. E. (1977). The effects of bilingualism on the individual: Cognitive and socio-cultural consequences. In P. Hornby (Ed.), *Bilingualism: Psychological, social, and educational implications* (pp. 15–28). New York: Academic Press.

Lamborn, S. D., Mounts, N. S., Steinberg, L., & Dornbusch, S. M. (1991). Patterns of competence and adjustment among adolescents from authoritative, authoritarian, indulgent, and neglectful families. *Child Development, 62*, 1049–1065.

Lampert, M. (2001). *Teaching problems and the problems of teaching.* New Haven, CT: Yale University Press.

Landi, N., Frost, S. J., Mencl, W. E., Sandak, R., & Pugh, K. R. (2013). Neurobiological bases of reading comprehension: Insights from neuroimaging studies of word-level and text-level processing in skilled and impaired readers. *Reading and Writing Quarterly, 29*(2), 145–167.

Landry, S. H., Zucker, T. A., Taylor, H. B., Swank, P. R., Williams, J. M., Assel, M., et al. (2014). Enhancing child care quality and learning for toddlers at risk: The responsive early childhood program. *Developmental Psychology, 50*(2), 526–541.

Laney, C., & Loftus, E. F. (2008). Emotional content of true and false memories. *Memory and Cognition, 16*(5), 500–516.

Lange, G., MacKinnon, C. E., & Nida, R. E. (1989). Knowledge, strategy, and motivational contributions to preschool children's object recall. *Developmental Psychology, 25*, 772–779.

Langeveld, N. E., Ubbink, M. C., Last, B. F., Grootenhuis, M. A., Voute, P. A., & De Haan, R. J. (2003). Educational achievement, employment and living situation in long-term young adult survivors of childhood cancer in the Netherlands. *Psycho-Oncology, 12*, 213–225.

Langlois, J. H., & Downs, C. (1980). Mothers, fathers, and peers as socialization agents of sex-typed play behavior in young children. *Child Development, 51*, 1217–1247.

Lansford, J. E. (2009). Parental divorce and children's adjustment. *Perspectives on Psychological Science, 4*(2), 140–152.

Lansford, J. E., Sharma, C., Malone, P. S., Woodlief, D., Dodge, K. A., Oburu, P., et al., (2014). Corporal punishment, maternal warmth, and child adjustment: A longitudinal study in eight countries.

Journal of Clinical Child and Adolescent Psychology, *43*(4), 670–685.

Lansford, J. E., Yu, T., Pettit, G. S., Bates, J. E., & Dodge, K. A. (2014). Pathways of peer relationships from childhood to young adulthood. *Journal of Applied Developmental Psychology, 35,* 111–117.

Lantolf, J. P. (2003). Intrapersonal communication and internalization in the second language classroom. In A. Kozulin, B. Gindia, V. S. Ageyev, & S. M. Miller (Eds.), *Vygotsky's educational theory in cultural context* (pp. 349–370). Cambridge, UK: Cambridge University Press.

Lapsley, D. K., & Carlo, G. (2014). Moral development at the crossroads. *Developmental Psychology, 50*(1), 1–7.

Lapsley, D. K., & Yeager, D. (2013). Moral-character education. In W. M. Reynolds & G. E. Miller (Eds.), *Handbook of educational psychology* (2nd ed., pp. 147–177). New York: Wiley.

Larry P. v. Riles, 343 F. Supp. 1306 (N. D. Cal. 1979), aff'd 502 F. 2d (9th Cir. 1974); 495 F. Supp. 926 (N. D. Cal. 1979), aff'd. in part and rev'd in part, 793 F. 2d 969 (9th Cir. 1984).

Larsen, J. P., Hoien, T., Lundberg, I., & Ødegaard, S. (1990). MRI evaluation of the size and symmetry of the planum temporale in adolescents with developmental dyslexia. *Brain and Language, 39,* 289–301.

Larzelere, R. (2000). Child Outcomes of nonabusive and customary physical punishment by parents: An updated literature review. *Clinical Child and Family Psychology Review, 3*(4), 199–221.

Larzelere, R. E., Cox, R. B., & Mandara, J. (2013). Responding to misbehavior in young children: How authoritative parents enhance reasoning with firm control. In R. E. Larzelere, A. S. Morris, & A. W. Harris (Eds.), *Authoritative parenting: Synthesizing nurturance and discipline for optimal child development* (pp. 89–111). Washington, DC: American Psychological Association.

Last, C. G. (1989). Anxiety disorders. In T. H. Ollendick & M. Hersen (Eds.), *Handbook of child psychopathology* (pp. 219–227). New York: Plenum Press.

Lauren, L., & Allen, L. (1999). Factors that predict success in an early literacy intervention project. *Reading Research Quarterly, 34*(4), 404–424.

Laurent, H. K., & Ablow, J. C. (2012). The missing link: Mother's neural response to infant cry related to infant attachment behaviors. *Infant Behavior and Development, 35,* 761–772.

LaVoie, J. C. (1973). Punishment and adolescent self-control. *Developmental Psychology, 8,* 16–24.

LaVoie, J. C. (1974). Cognitive determinants of resistance to deviation in seven-, nine-, and eleven-year-old children of low and high maturity of moral judgment. *Developmental Psychology, 10,* 393–403.

Lawlor, S., Richman, S., & Richman, C. L. (1997). The validity of using the SAT as a criterion for black and white students' admission to college. *College Student Journal, 31,* 507–515.

Lazowski, R. A., & Hulleman, C. S. (2016). Motivation interventions in education: A meta-analytic review. *Review of Educational Research, 82*(2), 602–640.

Leaper, C. (2015). Gender and social-cognitive development. In L. S. Liben, U. Müller, & R. M. Lerner (Eds.), *Handbook of child psychology and developmental science: Vol. 2. Cognitive process* (7th ed., pp. 806–853). Hoboken, NJ: Wiley.

Leaper, C., & Brown, C. S. (2014). Sexism in schools. In L. S. Liben & R. S. Bigler (Eds.), *Advances in child development and behavior: The role of gender in educational contexts and outcomes* (Vol. 47, pp. 189–223). New York: Academic Press.

Leaper, C., & Robnett, R. (2011). Women are more likely than men to use tentative language, aren't they?: A meta-analysis testing for gender differences and moderators. *Psychology of Women Quarterly, 35*(1), 129–142.

Leaper, C., Tenenbaum, H. R., & Shaffer, T. G. (1999). Communication patterns of African-American girls and boys from low income urban backgrounds. *Child Development, 70,* 1489–1503.

Lebel, C., Shaywitz, B., Holahan, J., Shaywitz, S., Marchione, K., & Beaulieu, C. (2013). Diffusion tensor imaging correlates of reading ability in dysfluent and non-impaired readers. *Brain and Language, 125,* 215–222.

Lecanuet, J. P., Granier-Deferre, C., & DeCasper, A. J. (2005). Are we expecting too much from prenatal sensory experiences? In B. Hopkins & S. P. Johnson (Eds.), *Prenatal development of postnatal functions* (pp. 31–49). Westport, CT: Praeger.

Lederberg, A. R. (2003). Expressing meaning: From communicative intent to building a lexicon. In M. Marschark & P. E. Spencer (Eds.), *Oxford handbook of deaf studies, language, and education* (pp. 247–260). New York: Oxford University Press.

Lederberg, A. R., & Mobley, C. E. (1990). The effect of hearing impairment on the quality of attachment and mother–infant interaction. *Child Development, 61,* 1596–1604.

Lee, E. A. E., & Troop-Gordon, W. (2011). Peer processes and gender role development: Changes in gender atypicality related to negative peer treatment and children's friendships. *Sex Roles, 64,* 90–102.

Lee, K., & Bull, R. (2016). Developmental changes in WM, updating and math achievement. *Journal of Educational Psychology, 108*(6), 869–882.

Lee, P. A., Nordenstrom, A., Houk, C. P., Ahmed, S. F., Auchus, R., Baratz, A., et al. (2016). Global disorders of sex development update since 2006: Perceptions, approach and care. *Hormone Research in Paediatrics, 85,* I158–1180.

Lee, S. J. (1994). Behind the model-minority stereotype: Voices of high- and low-achieving Asian American students. *Anthropology and Education Quarterly, 25,* 413–429.

Lee, S., Almeida, D. M., Davis, K. D., Hammer, L. B., King, R. B., & Kelly, E. L. (2015). Latent profiles of perceived time adequacy for paid work, parenting, and partner roles. *Journal of Family Psychology, 29*(5), 788–798.

Lee, S. J., Altschul, I., & Gershoff, E. T. (2013). Does warmth moderate longitudinal associations between maternal spanking and child aggression in early childhood. *Developmental Psychology, 49*(11), 2017–2028.

Lee, W., Lee, M.-J., & Bong, M. (2014). Testing interest and self-efficacy as predictors of academic self-regulation and achievement. *Contemporary Educational Psychology, 39,* 86–99.

Lehman, M., & Hasselhorn, M. (2007). Variable memory strategy use in children's adaptive intratask learning behavior: Developmental change and working memory influences on free recall. *Child Development, 78*(4), 1068–1082.

Lehman, M., & Hasselhorn, M. (2012). Rehearsal dynamics in elementary school children. *Journal of Experimental Child Psychology, 111*(3), 552–560.

Lengua, L. J. (2012). Poverty, the development of effortful control, and children's academic, social, and emotional adjustment. In V. Maholmes & R. B. King (Eds.), *The Oxford handbook of poverty and child development* (pp. 490–510). New York: Oxford University Press.

Lenhart, A. (2015). Pew Research Center: Teens, technology and friendships. Available from *www.pewinternet.org/2015/08/06/teens-technology-and-friendships*.

Lenneberg, E. (1967). *Biological foundations of language.* New York: Wiley.

Lenroot, R. K., & Giedd, J. N. (2010). Sex differences in the adolescent brain. *Brain and Cognition, 72,* 46–55.

Leopold, W. (1939). *Speech development of a bilingual child: A linguist's record: Vol. 1. Vocabulary growth in the first two years.* Evanston, IL: Northwestern University Press.

Leopold, W. (1947). *Speech development of a bilingual child: A linguist's record: Vol. 2. Sound learning in the first two years.* Evanston, IL: Northwestern University Press.

Leopold, W. (1949a). *Speech development of a bilingual child: A linguist's record: Vol. 3. Grammar and general problems.* Evanston, IL: Northwestern University Press.

Leopold, W. (1949b). *Speech development of a bilingual child: A linguist's record: Vol. 4. Diary from age 2.* Evanston, IL: Northwestern University Press.

Leos-Urbel, J. (2015). What works after school? The relationship between after-school program quality, program attendance, and academic outcomes. *Youth and Society, 47*(5), 684–706.

Lepina, S. J., & Evers, K. (2017). Neuroscience of childhood poverty: Evidence of impacts and mechanisms as vehicles of dialog with ethics. *Frontiers in Psychology, 8*(61), 1–13.

Lepper, M. R. (1983). Extrinsic reward and intrinsic motivation: Implications for the classroom. In J. M. Levine & M. C. Wang (Eds.), *Teacher and student perceptions: Implications for learning.* Hillsdale, NJ: Erlbaum.

Lepper, M. R. (1995). Theory by the numbers?: Some concerns about meta-analysis as a theoretical tool. *Applied Cognitive Psychology, 9,* 411–422.

Lepper, M. R., Aspinwall, L. G., Mumme, D. L., & Chabey, R. W. (1990). Self-perception and social-perception processes in tutoring: Subtle social control strategies of expert tutors. In J. M. Olson & M. P. Zanna (Eds.), *Self-inference processes: The Ontario Symposium* (pp. 217–237). Hillsdale, NJ: Erlbaum.

Lepper, M. R., Corpus, J. H., & Iyengar, S. S. (2005). Intrinsic and extrinsic motivational orientations in the classroom: Age differences and academic correlates. *Journal of Educational Psychology, 97*(2), 184–196.

Lepper, M. R., Greene, D., & Nisbett, R. E. (1973). Undermining children's intrinsic interest with extrinsic rewards: A test of the "over-justification" hypothesis. *Journal of Personality and Social Psychology, 28,* 129–137.

Lepper, M. R., & Hodell, M. (1989). Intrinsic motivation in the classroom. In C. Ames & R. Ames (Eds.), *Research on motivation in education: Vol. 3. Goals and cognitions* (pp. 73–105). San Diego, CA: Academic Press.

Lepper, M. R., Keavney, M., & Drake, M. (1996). Intrinsic motivation and extrinsic rewards: A commentary on Cameron and Pierce's meta-analysis. *Review of Educational Research, 66,* 5–32.

Lepper, M. R., & Woolverton, M. (2002). The wisdom of practice: Lessons learned from the study of highly effective tutors. In J. Aronson (Ed.), *Improving academic achievement: Impact of psychological factors on education* (pp. 135–158). New York: Academic Press.

Lerner, R. M., & Fisher, C. B. (2013). Evolution, epigenetics and application in developmental science. *Science, Applied Developmental Science, 17*(4), 169–173.

Lesaux, N. K., Kieffer, M. J., Kelley, J. G., & Harris, J.

R. (2014). Effects of academic vocabulary instruction for linguistically diverse adolescents: Evidence from a randomized field trial. *American Educational Research Journal, 51*(6), 1159–1194.

Letcher, P., Sanson, A., Smart, D., & Toumbourou, J. W. (2012). Precursors and correlates of anxiety trajectories from late childhood to late adolescence. *Journal of Clinical Child and Adolescent Psychology, 41*(4), 417–432.

Letouraenu, P. (2008). The formation of axons and dendrites by developing neurons. In C. A. Nelson & M. Luciana (Eds.), *Handbook of developmental cognitive neuroscience*, (2nd ed., pp. 5–21). Cambridge, MA: MIT Press.

Leung, K., Lau, S., & Lam, W. L. (1998). Parenting styles and academic achievement: A cross-cultural study. *Merrill–Palmer Quarterly, 44*, 157–172.

Levine, S. C., Huttenlocher, L., Taylor, A., & Langrock, A. (1999). Early sex differences in spatial skill. *Developmental Psychology, 35*, 940–949.

Levitt, M. J., Guacci-Franco, N., & Levitt, J. L. (1993). Convoys of social support in childhood and early adolescence: Structure and function. *Developmental Psychology, 29*, 811–818.

Levitt, M. J., Guacci-Franco, N., & Levitt, J. L. (1994). Social support and achievement in childhood and early adolescence: A multicultural study. *Journal of Applied Developmental Psychology, 15*, 207–222.

Levy, D. J., Heissel, J. A., Richeson, J. A., & Adam, E. K. (2016). Psychological and biological responses to race-based social stress as pathways to disparities in educational outcomes. *American Psychologist, 71*(6), 455–473.

Levy, G. D. (1999). Gender-typed and non-gender-typed category awareness in toddlers. *Sex Roles, 41*, 851–873.

Levy, G., & Fivush, R. (1993). Scripts and gender: A new approach for examining gender role development. *Developmental Review, 13*, 126–146.

Levy, Y. (1985). Theoretical gains from the study of bilingualism: A case report. *Language Learning, 35*, 541–554.

Lewanski, L. J., & Lovett, B. J. (2014). Learning disabilities. In E. J. Mash & R. A. Barkley (Eds.), *Child psychopathology* (3rd ed., pp. 625–669). New York: Guilford Press.

Lewis, M. D., Koroshegyi, C., Douglas, L., & Kampe, K. (1997). Age-specific associations between emotional responses to separation and cognitive performance in infancy. *Developmental Psychology, 33*, 32–42.

Lewontin, R. C. (1974). *The genetic basis of evolutionary change*. New York: Columbia University Press.

Lewontin, R. C., Rose, S., & Kamin, L. J. (1984). *Not in our genes: Biology, ideology, and human nature*. New York: Pantheon Books.

Lhyle, K. G., & Kulhavy, R. W. (1987). Feedback processing and error correction. *Journal of Educational Psychology, 79*(3), 320–322.

Li, J., Johnson, S. E., Han, W., Andrews, S., Kendall, G., Strazdins, L., et al. (2014). Parents' nonstandard working schedules and child wellbeing: A critical review of the literature. *Journal of Primary Prevention, 35*, 53–73.

Li, Y., & Wright, M. F. (2014). Adolescents social status goals: Relationships to social status insecurity, aggression, and prosocial behavior. *Journal of Youth Adolescence, 43*, 146–160.

Liben, L. S., & Bigler, R. S. (2017). Understanding and undermining the development of gender dichotomies: The legacy of Sandra Lipsitz Bem. *Sex Roles, 76*(9–10), 544–555.

Liben, L. S., & Coyle, E. F. (2014). Developmental interventions to address the STEM gender gap: Exploring intended and unintended consequences. In L. S. Liben & R. S. Bigler (Eds.), *Advances in child development and behavior: The role of gender in educational contexts and outcomes* (Vol. 47, pp. 77–115). New York: Academic Press.

Liben, L. S., & Signorella, M. L. (1993). Gender-schematic processing in children: The role of initial interpretations of stimuli. *Developmental Psychology, 29*, 141–149.

Licht, B. (1983). Cognitive–motivational factors that contribute to the achievement of learning-disabled children. *Journal of Learning Disabilities, 16*, 483–490.

Licht, B. (1992). Achievement-related beliefs in children with learning disabilities. In L. J. Meltzer (Ed.), *Strategy assessment and instruction for students with learning disabilities: From theory to practice* (pp. 195–220). Austin, TX: PRO-ED.

Licht, B. G., & Dweck, C. S. (1984). Determinants of academic achievement: The interaction of children's achievement orientation with skill area. *Developmental Psychology, 20*, 628–636.

Lichtman, J. W. (2001). Developmental neurobiology overview. In J. B. Bailey Jr., J. T. Bruer, F. J. Symons, & J. W. Lichtman (Eds.), *Critical thinking about critical periods* (pp. 27–43). Baltimore: Brookes.

Lickliter, R., & Honeycutt, H. (2015). Biology, development, and human systems. In R. M. Lerner (Series Eds.) & W. F. Overton & P. C. M. Molenaar (Vol. Eds.), *Handbook of child psychology and developmental science: Vol. 1. Theory and method* (7th ed., pp. 162–207). New York: Wiley.

Lickona, T. (1991). *Educating for character: How our schools can teach respect and responsibility*. New York: Bantam Books.

Liderman, J., Kantrowitz, K., & Flannery, K. (2005). Male vulnerability to reading disability is not likely to be a myth: A call for new data. *Journal of Learning Disabilities, 38*(2), 109–129.

Lieberman, P. (1984). *The biology and evolution of language*. Cambridge, MA: Harvard University Press.

Lieberman, P. (1989). Some biological constraints on universal grammar and learnability. In M. L. Rice & R. L. Schiefelbusch (Eds.), *The teachability of language* (pp. 199–225). Baltimore: Brookes.

Lieberman, P. (2015). The evolution of language. In S. Goldstein, D. Princiotta, & J. A. Naglieri (Eds.), *Handbook of intelligence: Evolutionary theory, historical perspective, and current concepts* (pp. 47–64). New York: Springer.

Lillard, A. S., & Kavanaugh, R. D. (2014). The contribution of symbolic skills to the development of explicit theory of mind. *Child Development, 85*(4), 1535–1551.

Lin, H. C., Manuel, J., McFatter, R., & Cech, C. (2016). Changes in empathy-related cry responding as a function of time: A time course study of adult's responses to infant crying. *Infant Behavior and Development, 42*, 45–59.

Lin, S. C., & Bergles, D. E. (2004). Synaptic signaling between neurons and glia. *Glia, 47*(3), 290–298.

Lincoln, Y. S., & Guba, E. G. (1985). *Naturalistic inquiry*. Newbury Park, CA: SAGE.

Lindauer, P., & Petrie, G. (1997). A review of cooperative learning: An alternative to everyday instructional strategies. *Journal of Instructional Psychology, 24*, 183–187.

Lindberg, S. M., Hyde, J. S., Petersen, J. L., & Linn, M. C. (2010). New trends in gender and mathematics performance: A meta-analysis. *Psychological Bulletin, 136*, 1123–1135.

Lindholm, K. J., & Padilla, A. M. (1978). Child bilingualism: Report on language mixing, switching and translations. *Linguistics, 16*, 23–44.

Lindholm-Leary, K. (2016). Bilinguals and academic achievement in children in dual language programs. In E. Nicoladis & S. Montanari (Eds.), *Bilingualism across the lifespan: Factors moderating language proficiency* (pp. 203–223). Washington, DC: American Psychological Association.

Lindsay, D. S., & Read, J. D. (2006). Adults' memories of long-past events. In L. G. Nilsson & N. Ohta (Eds.), *Memory and society: Psychological perspectives* (pp. 51–72). New York: Psychology Press.

Ling, W. N., Enright, R., & Klatt, J. (2011). Forgiveness as character education for children and adolescents. *Journal of Moral Education, 40*(2), 237–253.

Linnenbrink-Garcia, L., Middleton, M. J., Ciani, K. D., Easter, M. A., O'Keefe, P. A., & Zusho, A. (2012). The strength of relation between performance-approach and performance-avoidance goal orientations: Theoretical, methodological, and instructional implications. *Educational Psychologist, 47*(4), 281–301.

Linnenbrink-Garcia, L., & Patall, E. A. (2016). Motivation. In L. Corno & E. M. Anderman (Eds.), *Handbook of educational psychology* (3rd ed., pp. 91–103). New York: Routledge.

Lin-Siegler, X., Ahn, J. N., Chen, J., Fang, F. A., & Luna-Lucero, M. (2016). Even Einstein struggled: Effects of learning about great scientists' struggles on high school students' motivation to learn science. *Journal of Educational Psychology, 108*(3), 314–328.

Lipka, J., & McCarty, T. L. (1994). Changing the culture of schooling: Navajo and Yup'ik cases. *Anthropology and Education Quarterly, 25*, 266–284.

Lipsey, M., Puzio, K., Yun, C., Hebert, M. A., Steinka-Fry, K., Cole, M. W., et al. (2012). *Translating statistical representation of the effects of education interventions into more readily interpretable forms*. (NCSER 2013-3000). Washington, DC: U.S. Government Printing Office.

Liu, D., Gelman, S. A., & Wellman, H. M. (2007). Components of young children's trait understanding: Behavior-to-trait inferences and trait-to-behavior predictions. *Child Development, 78*(5), 1543–1558.

Lloyd, M. E., & Miller, J. K. (2014). Implicit memory. In P. J. Bauer & R. Fivush (Eds.), *The Wiley handbook on the development of children's memory* (Vol. 1, pp. 336–359). New York: Wiley.

Lloyd, M. E., & Newcome, N. S. (2009). Implicit memory in childhood: Re-assessing developmental invariance. In M. L. Courage & N. Cowan (Eds.), *The development of memory in infancy and childhood* (pp. 93–113). New York: Taylor & Francis.

Loades, M. E., & Mastroyannopoulou, K. (2010). Teachers' recognition of children's mental health problems. *Child and Adolescent Mental Health, 15*(3), 150–156.

Lobel, T. E., Bempechat, J., Gewirtz, J. C., Shoken-Topaz, T., & Bashe, E. (1993). The role of gender-related information and self-endorsement of traits in preadolescents' inferences and judgments. *Child Development, 64*, 1285–1294.

Locke, J. L. (2002). Vocal development in the human infant: Functions and phonetics. In M. L. Kelly & F. Windsor (Eds.), *Investigations in clinical phonetics and linguistics* (pp. 243–256). Mahwah, NJ: Erlbaum.

Locke, J. L., & Mather, P. L. (1989). Genetic factors in the ontogeny of spoken language: Evidence from monozygotic and dizygotic twins. *Journal of Child Language, 16*, 553–559.

Lockhart, P. J. (2001). Fetal alcohol spectrum disorders for mental health professionals—A brief review. *Current Opinion in Psychiatry, 14*, 463–469.

Locurto, C. (1988). On the malleability of IQ. *The Psychologist, 11*, 431–435.

Locurto, C. (1990). The malleability of IQ as judged from adoption studies. *Intelligence, 14*, 275–292.

Locurto, C. (1991a). Beyond IQ in preschool programs? *Intelligence, 15,* 295–312.

Locurto, C. (1991b). Hands on the elephant: IQ, preschool programs, and the rhetoric of innoculation—A reply to commentaries. *Intelligence, 15,* 335–349.

Locurto, C. (1991c). *Sense and nonsense about IQ: The case for uniqueness.* New York: Praeger.

Lomawaima, K. T. (1995). Educating native Americans. In J. A. Banks & C. A. M. Banks (Eds.), *Handbook of research on multicultural education* (pp. 331–347). New York: Macmillan.

Lonigan, C. J., & Whitehurst, G. J. (1998). Relative efficacy of parent and teacher involvement in a shared-reading intervention for preschool children from low-income backgrounds. *Early Childhood Research Quarterly, 13,* 263–290.

Lopez, R. (1997). The practical impact of current research and issues in intelligence test interpretation and use for multicultural populations. *School Psychology Review, 26,* 249–254.

Lord, H., & Mahoney, J. L. (2007). Neighborhood crime and self-care: Risks for aggression and lower academic performance. *Developmental Psychology, 43*(6), 1321–1333.

Lorsbach, T. C., & Morris, A. K. (1991). Direct and indirect testing of picture memory in second and sixth grade children. *Contemporary Educational Psychology, 16,* 18–27.

Loveland, K. K., & Olley, J. G. (1979). The effect of external reward on interest and quality of task performance in children of high and low intrinsic motivation. *Child Development, 50,* 1207–1210.

Lu, J., Bridges, S., & Hmelo-Silver, C. E. (2014). Problem-based learning. In R. K. Sawyer (Ed.), *Cambridge handbook of the learning sciences* (2nd ed., pp. 298–318). New York: Cambridge University Press.

Lubinski, D., Benbow, C. P., & Kell, H. J. (2014). Life paths and accomplishments of mathematically precocious males and females four decades later. *Psychological Science, 25*(2), 2217–2232.

Luby, J., Belden, A., Botteron, K., Marrus, N., Harms, M. P., Babb, C., et al. (2013). The effects of poverty on childhood brain development: The mediating effect of caregiving and stressful life events. *Journal of the American Medical Association: Pediatrics, 167*(12), 1135–1142.

Lucas, N., Nicholson, J. M., & Erbas, B. (2013). Child mental health after parental separation: The impact of resident/non-resident parenting, parent mental health, conflict and socioeconomics. *Journal of Family Studies, 19*(1), 53–69.

Luciana, M. (2003). Cognitive development in children born preterm: Implications for theories of brain plasticity following early injury. *Development and Psychopathology, 15,* 1017–1047.

Luciana, M. (2013). Adolescent brain development in normality and psychopathology *Development and Psychopathology, 25,* 1325–1345.

Ludeke, R. J., & Hartup, W. W. (1983). Teaching behaviors of 9- and 11-year-old girls in mixed-age and same-age dyads. *Journal of Educational Psychology, 75,* 909–914.

Lueptow, L. B., Garovich, L., & Lueptow, M. B. (2001). Social change and the persistence of sex typing, 1974–1997. *Social Forces, 80,* 1–36.

Lui, A. M., & Bonner, S. M. (2016). Preservice and inservice teachers' knowledge, beliefs, and instructional planning in primary school mathematics. *Teaching and Teacher Education, 56,* 1–13.

Lundberg, I. (1991). Phonemic awareness can be developed without reading instruction. In S. A. Brady & D. P. Shankweiler (Eds.), *Phonological processes in literacy: A tribute to Isabelle Y. Liberman* (pp. 47–53). Hillsdale, NJ: Erlbaum.

Luo, W., Paris, S. G., Hogan, D., & Luo, Z. (2011). Do performance goals promote learning?: A pattern analysis of Singapore students' achievement goals. *Contemporary Educational Psychology, 36*(2), 165–176.

Luria, A. R. (1982). *Language and cognition.* New York: Wiley.

Lynch, D. J. (2007). "I've studied so hard for this course but don't get it!": Differences between student and faculty perceptions. *College Student Journal, 41*(1), 22–24.

Lynn, R. (2006). *Race differences in intelligence: An evolutionary analysis.* Augusta, GA: Washington Summit.

Lyons-Ruth, K., & Jacobvitz, D. (2016). Attachment disorganization from infancy to adulthood: Neurobiological correlates, parenting contexts and pathways to disorder. In J. Cassidy & P. R. Shaver (Eds.), *Handbook of attachment: Theory, research, and clinical applications* (pp. 667–695). New York: Guilford Press.

Lytton, H., & Romney, D. M. (1991). Parents' differential socialization of boys and girls: A meta-analysis. *Psychological Bulletin, 109,* 267–296.

Ma, W., Adesope, O., Nesbit, J. C., & Liu, Q. (2014). Intelligent tutoring systems and learning outcomes: A meta-analysis. *Journal of Educational Psychology, 106*(4), 901–918.

MacArthur, C., Phillippakos, Z. A., & Ianetta, M. (2015). Self-regulated strategy instruction in college developmental writing. *Journal of Educational Psychology, 107*(3), 855–867.

MacArthur, C., Schwartz, S., & Graham, S. (1991). Effects of a reciprocal peer revision strategy in special education classrooms. *Learning Disabilities Research and Practice, 6*(4), 201–210.

Maccoby, E. E. (1988). Gender as a social category. *Developmental Psychology, 24,* 755–765.

Maccoby, E. E. (1998). *The two sexes: Growing up apart, coming together.* Cambridge, MA: Belknap Press.

Maccoby, E. E. (2002). Perspectives on gender development. In W. W. Hartup & R. K. Silbereisen (Eds.), *Growing points in developmental science: An introduction* (pp. 202–222). Philadelphia: Psychology Press.

Maccoby, E. E., & Jacklin, C. N. (1974). *The psychology of sex differences.* Stanford, CA: Stanford University Press.

Maccoby, E. E., & Martin, J. A. (1983). Socialization in the context of the family: Parent–child interaction. In P. H. Mussen & E. M. Hetherington, *Manual of child psychology: Vol. 4. Social development* (pp. 1–101). New York: Wiley.

MacKenzie, M. J., Liu, D., & Sameroff, A. J. (2013). Moving beyond the child care debate toward implications for social and political agendas. *Children and Youth Services Review, 35,* 3–6.

MacMillan, D. L., & Knopf, E. D. (1971). Effects of instructional set on perceptions of event outcomes by EMR and nonretarded children. *American Journal of Mental Deficiency, 76,* 185–189.

MacNeilage, P. F., Rogers, L. J., & Vallortigara, G. (2009). Origins of the left & right brain. *Scientific American, 301,* 60–67.

MacPherson, E. M., Candee, B. L., & Hohman, R. J. (1974). A comparison of three methods for eliminating disruptive classroom behavior. *Journal of Applied Behavior Analysis, 7,* 287–297.

MacSwan, J. (2016). Code-switching in adulthood. In E. Nicoladis & S. Montanari (Eds.), *Bilingualism across the lifespan: Factors moderating language proficiency* (pp. 183–200). Washington, DC: American Psychological Association.

MacWhinney, B. (2015). Language development. In L. S. Liben, U. Müller, & R. M. Lerner (Eds.), *Handbook of child psychology and developmental science: Vol. 2. Cognitive process* (7th ed., pp. 296–338). Hoboken, NJ: Wiley.

Madigan, S., Brumariu, L. E., Villani, V., Atkinson L., & Ruth-Lyons, K. (2016). Representational and questionnaire measures of attachment: A meta-analysis of relations to child internalizing and externalizing problems. *Psychological Bulletin, 142*(4), 367–399.

Madison, P. (1969). *Personality development in college.* Reading, MA: Addison-Wesley.

Maeda, Y., & Yoon, S. Y. (2013). A meta-analysis on gender differences in mental rotation ability measured by the Purdue Spatial Visualization Tests: Visualizations of Rotations (PSVT-R). *Educational Psychology Review, 25*(1), 69–94.

Maeda, Y., & Yoon, S. Y. (2016). Are gender differences in spatial ability real or an artifact?: Evaluation of measurement invariance on the Revised PSVT: R. *Journal of Psychoeducational Assessment, 34*(4), 397–403.

Maehr, M. L., & Anderman, E. M. (1993). Reinventing schools for early adolescents: Emphasizing task goals. *Elementary School Journal, 93,* 593–610.

Magai, C., Frias, M. T., & Shaver, P. R. (2016). Attachment in middle and later life. In J. Cassidy & P. R. Shaver (Eds.), *Handbook of attachment: Theory, research, and clinical applications* (pp. 534–552). New York: Guilford Press.

Magnuson, K. A., Ruhm, C., & Waldfogel, J. (2007). The persistence of preschool effects: Do subsequent classroom experiences matter? *Early Childhood Research Quarterly, 22,* 18–38.

Maguire, E. A., Spiers, H. J., Good, C. D., Hartley, T., Frackowiak, R. S. J., & Burgess, N. (2003). Navigation expertise and the human hippocampus: A structural brain imaging analysis. *Hippocampus, 13,* 250–259.

Maguire-Jack, K., Gromoske, A. N., & Berger, L. M. (2012). Spanking and child development during the first 5 years of life. *Child Development, 83*(6), 1960–1977.

Mahn, H., & John-Steiner, V. (2013). Vygotsky and sociocultural approaches to teaching and learning. In W. M. Reynolds & G. E. Miller (Eds.), *Handbook of educational psychology* (2nd ed., pp. 117–145). New York: Wiley.

Maisto, S. A., Carey, K. B., & Bradizza, C. M. (1999). Social learning theory. In K. E. Leonard & H. T. Blane (Eds.), *Psychological theories of drinking and alcoholism* (2nd ed., pp. 106–163). New York: Guilford Press.

Makinodan, M., Rosen, K. M., Ito, S., & Corfas, G. (2012). A critical period for social experience-dependent oligodendrocyte maturation and myelination. *Science, 337,* 1357–1360.

Malakoff, M., & Hakuta, K. (1991). Translation skill and metalinguistic awareness in bilinguals. In E. Bialystok (Ed.), *Language processing in bilingual children* (pp. 141–166). Cambridge, UK: Cambridge University Press.

Maldonado-Carreño, C., & Votruba-Drzal, E. (2011). Teacher–child relationships and the development of academic and behavioral skills during elementary school: A within-and-between-child analysis. *Child Development, 82*(2), 601–616.

Malinowski, B. (1927). *Sex and repression in savage society.* New York: Humanities Press.

Mallory, M. E. (1989). *Q*-sort definition of ego identity status. *Journal of Youth and Adolescence, 18,* 399–412.

Malone, J. C., Liu, S. R., Vaillant, G. E., Rentz, D., & Waldinger, R. J. (2016). Mid-life Eriksonian psychosocial development: Setting the stage for late live cognitive and emotional health. *Developmental Psychology, 52*(3), 496–508.

Mammarella, I. C., & Cornoldi, C. (2014). An analysis of the criteria used to diagnose children with nonverbal learning disability (NLD). *Child Neuropsychology, 20*(3), 255–280.

Mancillas, A. (2006). Challenging the stereotypes about only children: A review of the literature and implications for practice. *Journal of Counseling and Development, 84,* 268–275.

Mandelman, S. D., & Grigorenko, E. L. (2011). Genes, environments, and their interactions. In R. J. Sternberg & S. B. Kaufman (Eds.), *The Cambridge handbook of intelligence* (pp. 85–106). New York: Cambridge University Press.

Mandler, J. M. (1978). A code in the node: The use of a story schema in retrieval. *Discourse Processes, 1,* 14–35.

Mandler, J. M. (1984). *Stories, scripts, and scenes: Aspects of schema theory.* Hillsdale, NJ: Erlbaum.

Mandler, J. M. (1987). On the psychological reality of story structure. *Discourse Processes, 10,* 1–29.

Mandler, J. M., & DeForest, M. (1979). Is there more than one way to recall a story? *Child Development, 50,* 886–889.

Mandler, J. M., & Goodman, M. S. (1982). On the psychological validity of story structure. *Journal of Verbal Learning and Verbal Behavior, 21,* 507–523.

Mandler, J. M., & Johnson, N. S. (1977). Remembrance of things parsed: Story structure and recall. *Cognitive Psychology, 9,* 111–151.

Mandler, J. M., Scribner, S., Cole, M., & DeForest, M. (1980). Cross-cultural invariance in story recall. *Child Development, 51,* 19–26.

Mangin, J. M., & Gallo, V. (2011). The curious case of NG2 cells: Transient trend or game changer? *ASN Neuro, 3,* 37–49.

Manning, B. H. (1988). Application of cognitive behavior modification: First and third graders' self-management of classroom behaviors. *American Educational Research Journal, 25,* 193–212.

Manning, B. H. (1990). Cognitive self-instruction for an off-task fourth grader during independent academic tasks: A case study. *Contemporary Educational Psychology, 15,* 36–46.

Manning, B. H. (1991). *Cognitive self-instruction for classroom processes.* Albany: State University of New York Press.

Manning, B. H., Glasner, S. E., & Smith, E. R. (1996). The self-regulated learning aspect of metacognition: A component of gifted education. *Roeper Review, 18,* 217–223.

Maratsos, M. (1989). Innateness and plasticity in language acquisition. In M. Rice & R. L. Shiefelbusch (Eds.), *The teachability of language* (pp. 105–125). Baltimore: Brookes.

Marceau, K., Ram, N., Houts, R. M., Grimm, K. J., & Susman, E. J. (2011). Individual differences in boys' and girls' timing and tempo of puberty: Modeling development with nonlinear growth models. *Developmental Psychology, 47*(5), 1389–1409.

Marcia, J. E. (1966). Development and validation of ego-identity status. *Journal of Personality and Social Psychology, 3,* 551–558.

Marcia, J. E. (1994). The empirical study of ego identity. In H. A. Bosma, T. L. G. Graafsma, H. D. Grotevant, & D. J. De Levita (Eds.), *Identity and development: An interdisciplinary approach* (pp. 67–80). Thousand Oaks, CA: SAGE.

Marcia, J. E. (2002). Identity and psychosocial development in adulthood. *Identity, 2,* 7–28.

Marcus, D. E., & Overton, W. F. (1978). The development of cognitive gender constancy and sex-role preferences. *Child Development, 49,* 434–444.

Marcus, G. F., Pinker, S., Ullman, M., Hollander, M., Rosen, T. J., & Xu, F. (1992). Overregulation in language acquisition. *Monographs of the Society for Research in Child Development, 57*(4), 1–182.

Markham, J. A., & Greenough, W. T. (2004). Experience-driven brain plasticity: beyond the synapse. *Neuron Glia Biology, 1*(4), 351–363.

Markman, E. M., & Callanan, M. A. (1983). An analysis of hierarchical classification. In R. Sternberg (Ed.), *Advances in the psychology of human intelligence* (Vol. 2, pp. 325–365). Hillsdale, NJ: Erlbaum.

Markon, K. E., Krueger, R. F., Bouchard, T. J., Jr., & Gottesmann, I. I. (2002). Normal and abnormal personality traits: Evidence for genetic and environmental relationships in the Minnesota Study of Twins Reared Apart. *Journal of Personality, 70,* 661–693.

Markovits, H., Benenson, J., & Dolenszky, E. (2001). Evidence that children and adolescents have internal models of peer interactions that are gender differentiated. *Child Development, 72,* 879–886.

Markus, H., & Nurius, P. (1986). Possible selves. *American Psychologist, 41,* 954–969.

Marmor, G. (1975). Development of kinetic images: When does the child first represent movement in mental images. *Cognitive Psychology, 7*(4), 548–549.

Marois, R., & Ivanoff, J. (2005). Capacity limits of information processing in the brain. *Trends in Cognitive Sciences, 9*(6), 296–305.

Marr, M. B. (1997). Cooperative learning: A brief review. *Reading and Writing Quarterly, 13,* 7–20.

Marschark, M. (1993). *Psychological development of deaf children.* New York: Oxford University Press.

Marsh, H. W. (1990a). Causal ordering of academic self-concept and academic achievement: A multiwave, longitudinal panel analysis. *Journal of Educational Psychology, 82,* 646–656.

Marsh, H. W. (1990b). The structure of academic self-concept: The Marsh/Shavelson model. *Journal of Educational Psychology, 82,* 623–636.

Marsh, H. W. (1992). Content specificity of relations

between academic achievement and academic self-concept. *Journal of Educational Psychology, 84,* 35–42.

Marsh, H. W., Abduljabbar, A. S., Morin, A. J. S., Parker, P., Abdelfattah, F., Nagengast, B., et al. (2015). The big-fish–little-pond effect: Generalizability of social comparison processes over two age cohorts from Western, Asian, and Middle Eastern Islamic cultures. *Journal of Educational Psychology, 107*(1), 258–271.

Marsh, H. W., & Ayotte, V. (2003). Do multiple dimensions of self-concept become more differentiated with age?: The differential distinctiveness hypothesis. *Journal of Educational Psychology, 95*(4), 687–706.

Marsh, H. W., Chessor, D., Craven, R., & Roche, L. (1995). The effects of gifted and talented programs on academic self-concept: The big fish strikes again. *American Educational Research Journal, 32,* 285–319.

Marsh, H. W., & Craven, R. G. (1991). Self–other agreement on multiple dimensions of preadolescent self-concept: Inferences by teachers, mothers, and fathers. *Journal of Educational Psychology, 83,* 393–404.

Marsh, H. W., Craven, R. G., & Debus, R. (1991). Self-concepts of young children 5 to 8 years of age: Measurement and multidimensional structure. *Journal of Educational Psychology, 83,* 377–392.

Marsh, H. W., Craven, R. G., & Debus, R. (1999). Separation of competency and affect components of multiple dimensions of academic self-concept: A developmental perspective. *Merrill–Palmer Quarterly, 45,* 567–601.

Marsh, H. W., & Hau, K. T. (2003). Big-fish–little-pond effect on academic self-concept: A cross-cultural (26-country) test of the negative effects of academically selective schools. *The American Psychologist, 58,* 364–376.

Marsh, H. W., Seaton, M., Trautwein, U., Ludtke, O., Hau, K. T., O'Mara, A. J., et al. (2008). The big-fish–little-pond-effect stands up to critical scruitiny: Implications for theory, methodology and future research. *Educational Psychology Review, 20,* 319–350.

Marsh, H. W., & Yeung, A. S. (1997a). Causal effects of academic self-concept on academic achievement: Structural equation models of longitudinal data. *Journal of Educational Psychology, 89,* 41–54.

Marsh, H. W., & Yeung, A. S. (1997b). Coursework selection: Relations to academic self-concept and achievement. *American Educational Research Journal, 34,* 691–720.

Marshall, P. J. (2015) Neuroscience, embodiment, and development. In R. M. Lerner (Series Eds.) & W. F. Overton & P. C. M. Molenaar (Vol. Eds.), *Handbook of child psychology and developmental science: Vol. 1. Theory and method* (7th ed., pp. 244–283). New York: Wiley.

Marshall, P. J., & Kenney, J. W. (2009). Biological perspectives on the effects of early psychosocial experience. *Developmental Review, 29*(2), 96–119.

Marshark, M., & Spencer, P. E. (2016). *The Oxford Handbook on deaf studies in language.* New York: Oxford University Press.

Martin, A. J. (2013). Family–school partnership and academic achievement. In J. Hattie & E. M. Anderman (Eds.), *International guide to student achievement* (pp. 98–100). New York: Routledge.

Martin, A., Schurz, M., Kronblichler, M., & Richlan, F. (2015). Reading in the brain of children and adults: A meta-analysis of 40 functional magnetic resonance imaging studies. *Human Brain Mapping, 36*(5), 1963–1981.

Martin, C. L. (1989). Children's use of gender-related information in making social judgments. *Developmental Psychology, 25,* 80–88.

Martin, C. L. (1993). New directions for investigating children's gender knowledge. *Developmental Reiew, 13,* 184–204.

Martin, C. L., Eisenbud, L., & Rose, H. (1995). Children's gender-based reasoning about toys. *Child Development, 66,* 1453–1471.

Martin, C. L., Fabes, R. A., & Hanish, L. D. (2014). Gendered-peer relationships in educational contexts. In L. S. Liben & R. S. Bigler (Eds.), *Advances in child development and behavior: The role of gender in educational contexts and outcomes* (Vol. 47, pp. 151–187). New York: Academic Press.

Martin, C. L., & Halverson, C. F. (1981). A schematic processing model of sex typing and stereotyping in children. *Child Development, 52,* 1119–1134.

Martin, C. L., & Halverson, C. F. (1983). The effect of sex-typing schemas on young children's memory. *Child Development, 54,* 563–574.

Martin, C. L., & Halverson, C. F. (1987). The roles of cognition in sex-roles and sex-typing. In D. B. Carter (Ed.), *Current conceptions of sex roles and sex-typing: Theory and research* (pp. 123–137). New York: Praeger.

Martin, C. L., Kornienko, O., Schaefer, D. R., Hanish, L. D., Fabes, R. A., & Goble, P. (2013). The role of sex of peers and gender-typed activities in young children's peer affiliative networks: A longitudinal analysis of selection and influence. *Child Development, 84*(3), 921–937.

Martin, C. L., Ruble, D. N., & Szjrybalo, J. (2002). Cognitive theories of early gender development. *Psychological Bulletin, 128,* 903–933.

Martin, C. L., Wood, C. H., & Little, J. K. (1990). The development of gender stereotype components. *Child Development, 61,* 1861–1904.

Martin, G., Richardson, A. S., Bergen, H. A., Roeger L., & Allison S. (2005). Perceived academic performance, self-esteem and locus of control as indicators of need for assessment of adolescent suicide risk: Implications for teachers. *Journal of Adolescence, 28*, 75–87.

Martin, L. T., Burns, R. M., & Schonlau, M. (2010). Mental disorders among gifted and non-gifted youth: A selected review of the epidemiologic literature. *Gifted Child Quarterly, 54*(1), 31–41.

Martin, R. P., & Dombrowski, S. (2008). *Prenatal exposures: Psychological and educational consequences for children.* New York: Springer Science & Business Media.

Martindale, C. (1991). *Cognitive psychology: A neural-network approach.* Pacific Grove, CA: Brooks/Cole.

Martinez, M. E. (1992). Interest enhancements to science experiments: Interactions with student gender. *Journal of Research in Science Teaching, 29*, 167–177.

Martinez, M. E. (2000). *Education as the cultivation of intelligence.* Mahwah, NJ: Erlbaum.

Marvin, R. S., Britner, P. A., & Russell, B. S. (2016). Normative development: The ontogeny of attachment in childhood. In J. Cassidy & P. R. Shaver (Eds.), *Handbook of attachment: Theory, research, and clinical applications* (pp. 273–291). New York: Guilford Press.

Mascolo, M. F., Li, J., Fink, R., & Fischer, K. (2002). Pathways to excellence: Value presuppositions and the development of academic and affective skills in educational contexts. In M. Ferrari (Ed.), *The pursuit of excellence through education* (pp. 113–146). Mahwah, NJ: Erlbaum.

Mascolo, M. P., & Fischer, K. W. (2010). The dynamic development of thinking, feeling, and acting over the life-span. In W. F. Overton & R. M. Lerner (Eds.), *The handbook of life-span development: Vol. 1. Cognition, biology, and methods* (pp 149–194). Hoboken, NJ: Wiley.

Mason, C. L., & Kahle, J. B. (1988). Student attitudes toward science and science-related careers: A program designed to promote a stimulating gender-free learning environment. *Journal of Research in Science Teaching, 26*, 25–39.

Master, A., Cheryan, S., & Meltzoff, A. N. (2016). Computing whether she belongs: Stereotypes undermine girls' interest and sense of belonging in computer science. *Journal of Educational Psychology, 108*(3), 424–437.

Mastropieri, M. A., Sweda, J., & Scruggs, T. E. (2000). Putting mnemonic strategies to work in an inclusive classroom. *Learning Disabilities Research and Practice, 15*, 69–74.

Mather, N., & Goldstein, S. (2002). Learning disabilities and challenging behaviors: A guide to intervention and classroom management. *Education and Treatment of Children, 25*(3), 366–370.

Mathison, S. (1988). Why triangulate? *Educational Researcher, 17*(2), 13–17.

Matsuzawa, T. (1990). Spontaneous sorting in human and chimpanzee. In S. T. Parker & K. R. Gibson (Eds.), *"Language" and intelligence in monkeys and apes* (pp. 451–468). Cambridge, UK: Cambridge University Press.

Mattanah, J. F. (2005). Authoritative parenting and the encouragement of autonomy. In P. A. Cowan, C. P. Cowan, J. C. Ablow, V. K. Johnson, & J. R. Measelle (Eds.), *The family context of parenting in children's adaptation to elementary school* (pp. 119–138). Abingdon, UK: Routledge.

Mattson, S. N., Fryer, S. L., McGee, C. L., & Riley, E. P. (2008). Fetal alcohol syndrome. In C. A. Nelson & M. Luciana (Eds.), *Handbook of developmental cognitive neuroscience* (2nd ed., pp. 643–652). Cambridge, MA: MIT Press.

May, H., Gray, A., Sirnides, P., Goldsworthy, H., Armijo, M., Sam, C., et al. (2015). Year one results from the multisite randomized evaluation of the i3 Scale-Up of Reading Recovery. *American Educational Research Journal, 52*(3), 547–581.

Mayer, M. J., VanAcker, R., Lochman, J. E., & Gresham, F. M. (2009). *Cognitive-behavioral interventions for emotional and behavioral disorders: School-based practice.* New York: Guilford Press.

Mayer, R. E. (1981). Frequency norms and structural analysis of algebra story problems into families, categories, and templates. *Instructional Science, 10*, 135–175.

Mayer, R. E. (2012). Information processing. In K. Harris, S. Graham, & T. Urdan (Eds.), *APA educational psychology handbook: Vol. 1. Theories, constructs and critical issues* (pp. 85–99). Washington, DC: American Psychological Association.

McCabe, J. (2010). Metacognitive awareness of learning strategies in undergraduates. *Memory and Cognition, 39*, 462–476.

McCabe, S. E., & West, B. T. (2013). Medical and nonmedical use of prescription stimulants: Results from a national multicohort study. *Journal of the American Academy of Child and Adolescent Psychiatry, 52*(12), 1272–1280.

McCall, R., Beach, S. R., & Lan, S. (2000). The nature and correlates of underachievement among elementary school children in Hong Kong. *Child Development, 71*, 785–801.

McCall, R. B., Evahn, C., & Kratzer, L. (1992). *High school underachievers: What do they achieve as adults?* Newbury Park, CA: SAGE.

McCarthy, K. A., & Nelson, K. (1981). Children's use of scripts in story recall. *Discourse Processes, 4*, 59–70.

McCartney, K., Clarke-Stewart, A., Owen, M. T., Burchinal, M., Bub, K. L., Belsky, J., et al. (2010). Testing a series of casual propositions relating time in child care to children's externalizing behavior. *Developmental Psychology, 46*(1), 1–17.

McCarty, T. L., Lynch, R. H., Wallace, S., & Benally, A. (1991). Classroom inquiry and Navajo learning styles: A call for reassessment. *Anthropology and Education Quarterly, 22*, 42–59.

McCauley, C., Kellas, G., Dugas, J., & DeVillis, R. F. (1976). Effects of serial rehearsal training of memory search. *Journal of Educational Psychology, 68*, 474–481.

McClelland, J. L., & Rumelhart, D. E. (1981). An interactive activation model of context effects in letter perception: Part 1. An account of basic findings. *Psychological Review, 88*, 375–407.

McConaghy, M. J. (1979). Gender permanence and the genital basis of gender: Stages in the development of constancy of gender identity. *Child Development, 50*, 1223–1226.

McConnell, K., Ryser, G., & Higgins, J. (2000). *Practical ideas that really work for students with ADHD*. Austin, TX: PRO-ED.

McCormick, C. B., Dimmitt, C., & Sullivan, F. R. (2013). Metacognition, learning, and instruction. In W. M. Reynolds & G. E. Miller (Eds.), *Handbook of educational psychology* (2nd ed., pp. 69–97). New York: Wiley.

McCormick, C. B., & Pressley, M. (1997). *Educational psychology: Learning, instruction, and assessment*. New York: Longman.

McCormick, M. P., & O'Connor, E. E. (2015). Teacher–child relationship quality and academic achievement in elementary school: Does gender matter? *Journal of Educational Psychology, 107*(2), 502–516.

McCormick, M. P., O'Connor, E. E., & Barnes, S. P. (2016). Mother–child attachment styles and math and reading skills in middle childhood: The mediating role of children's exploration and engagement. *Early Childhood Research Quarterly, 36*, 295–306.

McCrudden, M. T., & Corkill, A. (2010). Verbal ability and the processing of text with seductive detail sentences. *Reading Psychology, 31*(3), 282–300.

McDaniel, M. A., Agarwal, P. K., Huesler, B. J., McDermott, K. B., & Roediger, H. L. (2011). Test-enhanced learning in a middle school classroom: The effects of quiz frequency and placement. *Journal of Educational Psychology, 103*(2), 399–414.

McDaniel, M. A., Cahill, M. J., Robbins, M., & Wiener, C. (2014). Individual differences in learning and transfer: Stable tendencies for learning exemplars versus abstracting rules. *Journal of Experimental Psychology: General, 143*(2), 668–693.

McDonald, K. L., Baden, R. E., & Lochman, J. E. (2013). Parenting influences on the social goals of aggressive children. *Applied Developmental Science, 17*(1), 29–38.

McDonald, S. M. (1989). Sex bias in the representation of male and female characteristics in children's picture books. *Journal of Genetic Psychology, 150*, 389–401.

McElhaney, K. B, Antonishak, J., & Allen, J. P. (2008). "They like me, they like me not": Popularity and adolescents' perceptions of acceptance predicting social functioning over time. *Child Development, 79*(3), 720–731.

McFarland, J., Hussar, B., de Brey, C., Snyder, T., Wang, X., Wilkinson-Flicker, S., et al. (2017). *The condition of education 2017* (NCES 2017-144). U.S. Department of Education. Washington, DC: National Center for Education Statistics. Retrieved January 19, 2018, from *https://nces. ed.gov/pubsearch/pubsinfo.asp?pubid=2017144*.

McGoldrick, M., & Shibusawa, T. (2012). The family life cycle. In F. Walsh (Ed.), *Normal family processes: Growing diversity and complexity* (4th ed., pp. 375–398). New York: Guilford Press.

McGowan, P. O., & Roth, T. L. (2015). Epigenetic pathways through which experiences become linked with biology. *Development and Psychopathology, 27*(2), 637–648.

McGregor, K. K. (2004). Developmental dependencies between lexical semantics and reading. In C. A. Stone, E. R. Silliman, B. J. Ehren, & K. Apel (Eds.), *Handbook of language and literacy* (pp. 302–317). New York: Guilford Press.

McGrew, K. S. (2009). CHC theory and the human cognitive abilities project: Standing on the shoulders of the giants of psychometric intelligence research. *Intelligence, 37*, 1–10.

McGuire, J. K., Anderson, C. R., Toomey, R. B., & Russell, S. T. (2010). School climate for transgender youth: A mixed method investigation of student experiences and school responses. *Journal of Youth Adolescence, 39*, 1175–1188.

McIntire, M. (1974). *A modified model for the description of language acquisition in a deaf child*. Unpublished master's thesis, California State University, Northridge, CA.

McKeown, M. G. (1985). The acquisition of word meaning from context by children of high and low ability. *Reading Research Quarterly, 20*, 482–496.

McKeown, M. G., & Beck, I. L. (2006). Issues in the advancement of vocabulary instruction: Response to Stahl and Fairbanks's meta-analysis. In K. A. Dougherty Stahl & M. C. McKenna (Eds.), *Reading research at work: Foundations of effective practice* (pp. 262–271). New York: Guilford Press.

McKone, E., Crookes, K., Jeffery, L., & Dilks, D. D. (2012). A critical review of the development of face recognition: Experience is less important than previously believed. *Cognitive Neuropsychology, 29*(1–2), 174–212.

McKoon, G., & Ratcliff, R. (1979). Priming in episodic and semantic memory. *Journal of Verbal Learning and Verbal Behavior, 18*, 463–480.

McLaughlin, B. (1978). *Second-language acquisition in childhood*. Hillsdale, NJ: Erlbaum.

McLaughlin, B. (1984). *Second-language acquisition in childhood: Vol. 1. Preschool children* (2nd ed.). Hillsdale, NJ: Erlbaum.

McLoyd, V. C. (1979). The effects of extrinsic rewards of differential value on high and low intrinsic interest. *Child Development, 50*, 1010–1019.

McLoyd, V., Mistry, S., & Hardaway, C. (2014). Poverty and children's development. In E. T. Gershoff, R. S. Mistry, & D. A. Crosby (Eds.), *Societal contexts of child development: Pathways of influence and implications for practice and policy* (pp. 109–124). New York: Oxford University Press

McNally, R. J. (2012). Searching for repressed memory. In R. F. Belli (Ed.), *True and false recovered memories: Toward a reconciliation of the debate* (pp. 121–147). New York: Springer.

McNeely, C. (2013). School connectedness. In J. Hattie & E. M. Anderman (Eds.), *International guide to student achievement* (pp. 149–151). New York: Routledge

Meadow-Orlans, K. P. (1987). An analysis of the effectiveness of early intervention programs for hearing-impaired children. In M. J. Guralnick & F. C. Bennett (Eds.), *The effectiveness of early intervention for at-risk and handicapped children* (pp. 325–362). New York: Academic Press.

Meaney, M. J. (2010). Epigenetics and the biological definition of gene × environment interactions. *Child Development, 81*(1), 41–79.

Mechling, L. (2007). Assistive technology as a self-management tool for prompting students with intellectual disabilities to initiate and complete daily tasks: A literature review. *Education and Training in Developmental Disabilities, 42*(3), 252–269.

Meece, J. L. (1987). The influence of school experiences on the development of gender schemata. *New Directions for Child Development, 38*, 57–73.

Meece, J. L., & Askew, K. J. S. (2012). Gender, motivation, and educational attainment. In K. Harris, S. Graham, & T. Urdan (Eds.), *APA educational psychology handbook: Vol. 2, Individual differences and cultural and contextual factors* (pp. 139–161). Washington, DC: American Psychological Association.

Meece, J. L., Blumenfeld, P. C., & Hoyle, R. H. (1988). Students' goal orientations and cognitive engagement in classroom activities. *Journal of Educational Psychology, 80*, 514–523.

Meeus, W., Iedema, J., Helsen, M., & Vollebergh, W. (1999). Patterns of adolescent identity development: Review of literature and longitudinal analysis. *Developmental Review, 19*, 419–461.

Mehan, H. (1979). *Social organization in the classroom*. Cambridge, MA: Harvard University Press.

Mehler, J., & Christophe, A. (1995). Maturation and learning of language in the first year of life. In M. S. Gazzaniga (Ed.), *The cognitive neurosciences* (pp. 943–954). Cambridge, MA: MIT Press.

Mehler, J., Jusczyk, P., Lambertz, G., Halsted, N., Bartonici, J., & Amiel-Tison, C. (1988). A precursor of language acquisition in young infants. *Cognition, 29*, 143–178.

Meichenbaum, D. (1977). *Cognitive behavior modification*. New York: Plenum Press.

Meichenbaum, D., & Goodman, J. (1971). Training impulsive children to talk to themselves: A means of developing self-control. *Journal of Abnormal Child Psychology, 77*, 115–126.

Meier, R. P., & Newport, E. L. (1990). Out of the hands of babes: On a possible sign advantage in language acquisition. *Language, 66*, 1–23.

Meisel, J. (1984). *Zum Erwerb von Worstellungsregularitäten und Kasusmarkierungen*. Hamburg, Germany: Universität Hamburg Romanisches Seminar.

Meisel, J. M. (1995). Parameters in acquisition. In P. Fletcher & B. MacWhinney (Eds.), *The handbook of child language* (pp. 10–35). Oxford, UK: Blackwell.

Melby-Lervåg, M., & Hulme, C. (2013). Is working-memory training effective?: A meta-analytic review. *Developmental Psychology, 49*, 270–291.

Meltzer, L. J. (2017). Sleep and developmental psychopathology: Introduction to the special issue. *Journal of Clinical Child and Adolescent Psychology, 46*(2), 171–174.

Meltzoff, A. N. (1985). Immediate and deferred imitation in fourteen- and twenty-four-month-old infants. *Child Development, 56*, 62–72.

Meltzoff, A. N. (2002). Imitation as a mechanism of social cognition: Origins of empathy, theory of mind, and the representation of action. In U. Goswami (Ed.), *Blackwell handbook of childhood cognitive development* (pp. 6–25). Malden, MA: Blackwell.

Meltzoff, A. N., & Moore, M. K. (1977). Imitation of facial and manual gestures by human neonates. *Science, 198*, 75–78.

Meltzoff, A. N., & Moore, M. K. (1983). Newborn infants imitate adult facial gestures. *Child Development, 54*, 702–709.

Meltzoff, A. N., & Prinz, W. (Eds.). (2002). *The imitative mind: Development, evolution, and brain bases*. New York: Cambridge University Press.

Menting, B., Koot, H., & van Lier, P. (2015). Peer acceptance and the development of emotional and behavioral problems: Results from a preventive intervention study. *International Journal of Behavioral Development, 39*(6), 530–540.

Merighi, J., Edison, M., & Zigler, E. (1990). The role of motivational factors in the functioning of mentally retarded individuals. In R. M. Hodapp, J. A. Burack, & E. Zigler (Eds.), *Issues in the developmental approach to retardation* (pp. 114–134). New York: Cambridge University Press.

Merikangas, K. R., & He, J. P. (2014). Epidemiology of mental disorders in children and adolescents: Background and U.S. studies. In J. P. Raynaud, S. S. F. Gau, & M. Hodes (Eds.), *From research to practice in child and adolescent mental yealth* (pp. 19–45). Lanham, MD: Rowman & Littlefield.

Merikangas, K. R., He, J. P., Brody, D., Fisher, P. W., Bouron, K., & Koretz, D. S. (2010). Prevalence and treatment of mental disorders among US children in the 2001–2004 NHANES. *Pediatrics, 125*(1), 75–81.

Merolla, D. M. (2013). The net black advantage in educational transitions: An education careers approach. *American Educational Research Journal, 50*(5), 895–924.

Meyer, B. J. F. (1985). Prose analysis: Purposes, procedures, and problems. In B. K. Britton & J. B. Back (Eds.), *Understanding expository text* (pp. 11–65). Hillsdale, NJ: Erlbaum.

Meyer, D., Schvaneveldt, R. W., & Ruddy, M. G. (1975). Loci of contextual effects on word recognition. In P. M. A. Rabbitt & S. Dornic (Eds.), *Attention and performance* (Vol. 5, pp. 98–118). London: Academic Press.

Meyer, D. K., Turner, J. C., & Spencer, C. A. (1997). Challenge in a mathematics classroom: Students' motivation and strategies in project-based learning. *Elementary School Journal, 97*, 501–521.

Mezzacappa, E., Buckner, J. C., & Earls, F. (2011). Prenatal cigarette exposure and infant learning stimulation as predictors of cognitive control in childhood. *Developmental Science, 14*(4), 881–891.

Mian, N. D., Carter, A. S., Pine, D. S., Wakschlag, L. S., & Briggs-Gowan, M. J. (2015). Development of a novel observational measure for anxiety in young children: The anxiety dimensional observation scale. *Journal of Child Psychology and Psychiatry, 56*(9), 1017–1025.

Midgley, C., Anderman, E., & Hicks, L. (1995). Differences between elementary and middle school teachers and students: A goal theory approach. *Journal of Early Adolescence, 15*, 90–113.

Miles, H. L. W. (1990). The cognitive foundations for reference in a signing orangutan. In S. T. Parker & K. R. Gibson (Eds.), *"Language" and intelligence in monkeys and apes* (pp. 511–539). Cambridge, UK: Cambridge University Press.

Miller, D. I., Eagly, A. H., & Linn, M. C. (2015). Women's representation in science predicts national gender-science stereotypes: Evidence from 66 nations. *Journal of Educational Psychology, 107*(3), 631–644.

Miller, D. N., & Eckert, T. L. (2009). Youth suicidal behavior: An introduction and overview. *School Psychology Review, 38*(2), 153–167.

Miller, G. A. (1956). The magical number seven, plus or minus two: Some limits on our capacity to process information. *Psychological Review, 63*, 81–97.

Miller, G. A. (1977). *Spontaneous apprentices: Children and language.* New York: Seabury Press.

Miller, M. D., Linn, R. L., & Gronlund, N. (2013). *Measurement and assessment in teaching* (11th ed.). New York: Pearson.

Miller, P. H., Woody-Ramsey, J., & Aloise, P. A. (1991). The role of strategy effortfulness in strategy effectiveness. *Developmental Psychology, 27*, 738–745.

Miller, S. A. (1987). *Developmental research methods.* Englewood Cliffs, NJ: Prentice-Hall.

Miller, S. M. (2003). How literature discussion shapes thinking: ZPDs for teaching/learning habits of the heart and mind. In A. Kozulin, B. Gindia, V. S. Ageyev, & S. M. Miller (Eds.), *Vygotsky's educational theory in cultural context* (pp. 289–316). Cambridge, UK: Cambridge University Press.

Miller, S. M., Boyer, B. A., & Rodoletz, M. (1990). Anxiety in children: Nature and development. In M. Lewis & S. M. Miller (Eds.), *Handbook of developmental psychopathology* (pp. 191–207). New York: Plenum Press.

Mills, K. L. (2014). Effects of Internet use on the adolescent brain: Despite popular claims, experimental evidence remains scarce. *Trends in Cognitive Sciences, 18*(8), 385–387.

Mistry, J., Contreras, M., & Dutta, R. (2013). Culture and child development. In R. M. Lerner, M. A. Easterbrooks, & J. Mistry (Eds.), *Handbook of developmental psychology* (2nd ed., pp. 265–285). New York: Wiley.

Mody, M. (2004). Neurobiological correlates of language and reading impairments. In C. A. Stone, E. R. Silliman, B. J. Ehren, & K. Apel (Eds.), *Handbook of language and literacy* (pp. 49–72). New York: Guilford Press.

Moely, B. E., Olson, F. A., Halwes, T. G., & Flavell, J. H. (1969). Production deficiency in young children's clustered recall. *Developmental Psychology, 1*, 26–34.

Molinari, L., Mameli, C., & Gnisci, A. (2012). A sequential analysis of classroom discourse in Italian primary schools: The many faces of the IRF pattern. *British Journal of Educational Psychology, 83*, 414–430.

Money, J., & Ehrhardt, A. (1972). *Man and woman, boy and girl.* Baltimore: Johns Hopkins University Press.

Money, J., & Tucker, P. (1975). *Sexual signatures: On being a man or a woman.* Boston: Little, Brown.

Montague, M., Enders, C., & Dietz, S. (2011). Effects of cognitive strategy instruction on math problem solving of middle school students with disabilities. *Learning Disability Quarterly, 34*(4), 262–272.

Montague, M., Krawec, J., Enders, C., & Dietz, S.

(2014). The effects of cognitive strategy instruction on math problem solving of middle-school students of varying ability. *Journal of Educational Psychology, 106*(2), 469–481.

Moon, C. R., Panneton-Cooper, T., & Fifer, W. P. (1993). Two-day-olds prefer their native language. *Infant Behavior and Development, 16*, 495–500.

Moore, D. S. (2013). Behavioral genetics, genetics, and epigenetics. In P. D. Zelazo (Ed.), *The Oxford handbook of developmental psychology: Vol. 1. Body and mind* (pp. 91–128). New York: Oxford University Press.

Moore, J. L., & Rocklin, T. R. (1998). The distribution of distributed cognition: Multiple interpretations and uses. *Educational Psychology Review, 10*(1), 97–113.

Morgan, M. (1987). Television, sex-role attitudes, and sex-role behavior. *Journal of Early Adolescence, 7*, 269–282.

Morrow, L. M. (1989). *Literacy development in the early years: Helping children read and write.* Boston: Allyn & Bacon.

Morrow, L. M., Pressley, M., Smith, J. K., & Smith, M. (1997). The effect of a literature-based program integrated into literacy and science instruction with children from diverse backgrounds. *Reading Research Quarterly, 32*(1), 54–76.

Moses, J. O., & Villodas, M. T. (2017). The potential protective role of peer relationships on school engagement in at-risk adolescents. *Journal of Youth Adolescence, 46*(11), 2255–2272.

Moshman, D. (1982). Exogenous, endogenous, and dialectical constructivism. *Developmental Review, 2*, 371–384.

Mowrer, D. E. (1980). Phonological development during the first year of life. In N. J. Lass (Ed.), *Speech and language advances in basic research and practice* (Vol. 4, pp. 99–137). New York: Academic Press.

Mrazek, M. D., Chin, J. M., Schmader, T., Hartson, K. A., Smallwood, J., & Schooler, J. W. (2011). Threatened to distraction: Mind-wandering as a consequence of stereotype threat. *Journal of Experimental Social Psychology, 47*(6), 1243–1248.

Muir-Broaddus, J. E. (1995). Gifted underachievers: Insights from the characteristics of strategic functioning associated with giftedness and achievement. *Learning and Individual Differences, 7*, 189–206.

Müller, U., & Kerns, K. (2015). The development of executive function. In L. S. Liben, U. Müller, & R. M. Lerner (Eds.), *Handbook of child psychology and developmental science: Vol. 2. Cognitive processes* (7th ed., pp. 571–623). Hoboken, NJ: Wiley.

Mulvey, K. L., & Killen, M. (2015). Challenging gender stereotypes: Resistance and exclusion. *Child Development, 86*(3), 681–694.

Muniz-Swicegood, M. (1994). The effects of metacognitive reading strategy training on the reading performance and fluent reading analysis strategies of third grade bilingual students. *Bilingual Research Journal, 18*, 83–97.

Murphy, G. L. (2002). *The big book of concepts.* Cambridge, MA: MIT Press.

Murphy, G. L. (2016). Is there an exemplar theory of concepts? *Psychonomic Bulletin Review, 23*, 1035–1042.

Murphy, G. L., Hampton, J. A., & Milovanovic, G. S. (2012). Semantic memory redux: An experimental test of hierarchical category representation. *Journal of Memory and Language, 67*, 521–539.

Murphy, K., McKone, E., & Slee, J. (2003). Dissociations between implicit and explicit memory in children: The role of strategic processing and the knowledge base. *Journal of Experimental Child Psychology, 84*, 124–165.

Murray, B. A. (2006). Hunting the elusive phoneme: A phoneme-direct model for learning phoneme awareness. In K. A. Dougherty Stahl & M. C. McKenna (Eds.), *Reading research at work: Foundations of effective practice* (pp. 114–125). New York: Guilford Press.

Nader-Grosbois, N. (2014). Self-perception, self-regulation and metacognition in adolescents with intellectual disability. *Research in Developmental Disabilities, 35*, 1334–1348.

Nagy, W., & Anderson, R. (1984). How many words are there in printed school English? *Reading Research Quarterly, 19*, 304–330.

Nagy, W., Anderson, R., & Herman, P. (1987). Learning word meanings from context during normal reading. *American Educational Research Journal, 24*, 237–270.

Nagy, W., Herman, P., & Anderson, R. (1985). Learning words from context. *Reading Research Quarterly, 20*, 233–253.

Naito, M. (1990). Repetition priming in children and adults: Age-related dissociation between implicit and explicit memory. *Journal of Experimental Child Psychology, 50*, 462–484.

Nandagopal, K., & Ericsson, K. A. (2012). Enhancing students' performance in traditional education: Implications from the expert performance approach and deliberate practice. In K. Harris, S. Graham, & T. Urdan (Eds.), *APA educational psychology handbook: Vol. 1. Theories, constructs and critical issues* (pp. 257–293). Washington, DC: American Psychological Association.

Naruse, I., & Keino, H. (1995). Apoptosis in the developing CNS. *Progress in Neurobiology, 47*(2), 135–155.

Nasir, N. S., McLaughlin, M. W., & Jones, A. (2009). What does it mean to be African American?: Constructions of race and academic identity in an urban public high school. *American Educational Research Journal, 46*(1), 73–114.

Nasir, N. S., Rowley, S. J., & Perez, W. (2016). Cultural, racial/ethnic, and linguistic diversity and identity. In L. Corno & E. M. Anderman (Eds.), *Handbook of educational psychology* (3rd ed., pp. 186–212). New York: Routledge/Taylor & Francis.

National Academies of Sciences, Engineering, and Medicine. (2016). *Preventing bullying through science, policy, and practice*. Washington, DC: National Academies Press.

National Center on Addiction and Substance Abuse at Columbia University. (2012). *National survey of American attitudes on substance abuse XVII: Teens*. New York: CASAColumbia, QEV Analytics.

National Council of Teachers of Mathematics. (2000). *Principles and standards for school mathematics*. Reston, VA: Author.

National Reading Panel. (2000). *Report of the National Reading Panel: Teaching children to read: An evidence-based assessment of the scientific research literature on reading and its implications for reading instruction: Reports of the subgroups*. Washington, DC: National Institutes of Health, National Institute of Child Health and Human Development.

National Science Foundation, National Center for Science and Engineering Statistics. (2017). *Women, minorities, and persons with disabilities in science and engineering: 2017* (Special Report NSF 17-310). Arlington, VA. Available from *www.nsf.gov/statistics/wmpd*.

Needleman, H. L. (1992). Childhood exposure to lead: A common cause of school failure. *Phi Delta Kappan, 74*, 35–37.

Needleman, H. L., & Bellinger, D. (1991). The health effects of low level exposure to lead. *Annual Review of Public Health, 12*, 111–140.

Neely, J. H. (1976). Semantic priming and retrieval from lexical memory: Evidence for facilitatory and inhibitory processes. *Memory and Cognition, 4*, 648–654.

Neely, J. H. (1977). Semantic priming and retrieval from lexical memory: Roles of inhibitionless spreading activation and limited capacity attention. *Journal of Experimental Psychology, 106*, 226–254.

Neill, A. S. (1960). *Summerhill: A radical approach to child rearing*. New York: Hart.

Nelson, C. A. (1995). The ontogeny of human memory: A cognitive neuroscience perspective. *Development Psychology, 31*(5), 723–738.

Nelson, C. A., Zeanah, C. H., Fox, N. A., Marshall, P. J., Smyke, A. T., & Guthrie, D. (2007). Cognitive recovery in socially deprived young children: The Bucharest Early Intervention Project. *Science, 318*, 1937–1940.

Nelson, K. (1978). How children represent their world in and out of language. In R. S. Siegler (Ed.), *Children's thinking: What develops?* (pp. 255–273). Hillsdale, NJ: Erlbaum.

Nelson, K., & Gruendel, J. (1981). Generalized event representations: Basic building blocks of cognitive development. In A. Brown & M. Lamb (Eds.), *Advances in developmental psychology* (Vol. 1, pp. 231–247). Hillsdale, NJ: Erlbaum.

Neppl, T. K., Senia, J. M., & Donnellson, B. M. (2016). Effects of economic hardship: Testing the family stress model over time. *Journal of Family Psychology, 30*(1), 12–21.

Nettelbeck, T., & Wilson, C. (1997). Speed of information processing and cognition. In W. E. MacLean, Jr. (Ed.), *Ellis' handbook of mental deficiency, psychological theory and research* (pp. 245–274). Mahwah, NJ: Erlbaum.

Neves, D. M., & Anderson, J. R. (1981). Knowledge compilation: Mechanisms for the automatization of cognitive skills. In J. R. Anderson (Ed.), *Cognitive skills and their acquisition* (pp. 251–272). Hillsdale, NJ: Erlbaum.

Newman, P., & Newman, B. (1978). Identity formation and the college experience. *Adolescence, 13*, 311–326.

Newport, E. L. (1990). Maturational constraints on language learning. *Cognitive Science, 14*, 11–28.

Newton, E. K., Laible, D., Carlo, G., Steele, J. S., & McGinley, M. (2014). Do sensitive parents foster kind children or vice versa?: Bidirectional influences between children's prosocial behavior and parental sensitivity. *Developmental Psychology, 50*(6), 1808–1816.

NICHD Early Child Care Research Network. (2005a). *Child care and child development: Results from the NICHD Study of Early Child Care and Youth Development*. New York: Guilford Press.

NICHD Early Child Care Research Network. (2005b). Early child care and children's development in the primary grades: Follow-up results from the NICHD study of early child care. *American Educational Research Journals, 42*(3), 537–570.

Nicholls, J. G. (1978). The development of the concepts of effort and ability, perception of academic attainment, and the understanding that difficult tasks require more than ability. *Child Development, 49*, 800–814.

Nicholls, J. G. (1984). Achievement motivation: Conceptions of ability, subjective experience, task choice, and performance. *Psychological Review, 91*(3), 328–346.

Nicholls, J. G. (1989). *The competitive ethos and democratic education*. Cambridge, MA: Harvard University Press.

Nicholls, J. G. (1990). What is ability and why are we mindful of it?: A developmental perspective. In R. Sternberg & J. Kolligian (Eds.), *Competence considered* (pp. 11–40). New Haven, CT: Yale University Press.

Nicholls, J. G., & Miller, A. (1983). The differentiation

of the concepts of difficulty and ability. *Child Development, 54,* 951–959.

Nicholls, J. G., & Miller, A. (1985). Differentiation of the concepts of luck and skill. *Developmental Psychology, 21,* 76–82.

Nicholls, J. G., & Thorkildsen, T. A. (1987, October). *Achievement goals and beliefs: Individual and classroom differences.* Paper presented at the annual meeting of the Society for Experimental Social Psychology, Charlotte, NC.

Nicoladis, E. (2016). Bilingual speakers' cognitive development in childhood. In E. Nicoladis & S. Montanari (Eds.), *Bilingualism across the lifespan: Factors moderating language proficiency* (pp. 269–284). Washington, DC: American Psychological Association.

Nicoladis. E., & Montanari, S. (2016). *Bilingualism across the lifespan: Factors moderating language proficiency.* Washington, DC: American Psychological Association.

Nievar, A., Moske, A. K., Johnson, D. J., & Chen, Q. (2014). Parenting practices in preschool leading to later cognitive competence: A family stress model. *Early Education and Development, 25*(3), 318–337.

Nigg, J. T., & Barkley, R. A. (2014). Attention-deficit/hyperactivity disorder. In E. J. Mash & R. A. Barkley (Eds.), *Child psychopathology* (pp. 75–144). New York: Guilford Press.

Nikolić, M., Gardner, H. A. R., & Tucker, K. L. (2013). Postnatal neuronal apoptosis in the cerebral cortex: Physiological and pathophysiological mechanisms. *Neuroscience, 254,* 369–378.

Ninio, A. (1980). Picture-book reading in mother–infant dyads belonging to two subgroups in Israel. *Child Development, 51,* 587–590.

Niparko, J. K., & Blankenhorn, R. (2003). Cochlear implants in young children. *Mental Retardation and Developmental Disabilities Research Reviews, 9,* 267–275.

Nisbett, R. E., Aronson, J., Blair, C., Dickens, W., Flynn, J., Halpern, D. F., et al. (2012). Intelligence: New findings and theoretical developments. *American Psychologist, 67*(2), 130–159.

Nobes, G., & Pawson, C. (2003). Children's understanding of social rules and social status. *Merrill–Palmer Quarterly, 49*(1), 77–99.

Noddings, N. (1984). *Caring: A feminine approach to ethics and moral education.* Berkeley: University of California Press.

Noddings, N. (1996). Learning to care and to be cared for. In A. M. Hoffman (Ed.), *Schools, violence, and society* (pp. 185–198). Westport, CT: Praeger/Greenwood Press.

Noggle, C. A., & Dean, R. S. (2013). *The neuropsychology of psychopathology.* New York: Springer .

Nokes-Malach, T. J., Richey, J. E., & Gadgil, S. (2015). When is it better to learn together?: Insights from research on collaborative learning. *Educational Psychology Review, 27*(4), 645–656.

Nolen, S. B. (1988). Reasons for studying: Motivational orientations and study strategies. *Cognition and Instruction, 5,* 269–287.

Nolte, R. Y., & Singer, H. (1985). Active comprehension: Teaching a process of reading comprehension and its effects on reading achievement. *The Reading Teacher, 39,* 24–31.

Nomaguchi, K., & Johnson, W. (2016). Parenting stress among low-income and working-class fathers: The role of employment. *Journal of Family Issues, 37*(11), 1535–1557.

Nosek, B. A., & Smyth, F. L. (2011). Implicit social cognitions predict sex difference in math engagement and achievement. *American Educational Research Journal, 48*(5), 1125–1156.

Numminen, H., Service, E., & Ruoppila, I. (2002). Working memory, intelligence and knowledge base in adult persons with intellectual disability. *Research in Developmental Disabilities, 23,* 105–118.

Oakes, J. (1985). *Keeping track: How schools structure inequality.* New Haven, CT: Yale University Press.

Oakland, T., & Gallegos, E. M. (2005). Selected legal issues affecting students from multicultural backgrounds. In C. L. Frisby & C. R. Reynolds (Eds.), *Comprehensive handbook of multicultural school psychology* (pp. 1048–1078). New York: Wiley.

Oakland, T., & Joyce, D. (2004). Temperament-based learning styles and school-based applications. *Canadian Journal of School Psychology, 19,* 59–74.

Oakland, T., & Parmelee, R. (1985). Mental measurement of minority-group children. In B. B. Wolman (Ed.), *Handbook of intelligence: Theories, measurements, and applications* (pp. 699–736). New York: Wiley.

Ochoa, S. H. (2003). Assessment of culturally and linguistically diverse children. In C. R. Reynolds & R. W. Kamphaus (Eds.), *Handbook of psychological and educational assessment of children* (pp. 563–583). New York: Guilford Press.

Ochs, E., & Schieffelin, B. (1995). The impact of language socialization on grammatical development. In P. Fletcher & B. MacWhinney (Eds.), *The handbook of child psychology* (pp. 73–94). Oxford, UK: Blackwell.

O'Connor, E. E., Capella, E., McCormick, M. P., & McClowry, S. G. (2014). Enhancing the academic development of shy children: A test of the efficacy of INSIGHTS. *School Psychology Review, 43*(3), 239–259.

O'Donnell, A. M. (2012). Constructivism. In K. Harris, S. Graham, & T. Urdan (Eds.), *APA educational psychology handbook: Vol. 1. Theories, constructs and critical issues* (pp. 61–84). Washington, DC: American Psychological Association.

O'Donnell, A. M., & King, A. (Eds.). (1999). *Cognitive perspectives on peer learning.* New York: Erlbaum.

Ogbu, J. U. (1978). *Minority education and caste: The American system in cross-cultural perspective.* New York: Academic Press.

Ogbu, J. U. (1981). Origins of human competence: A cultural–ecological perspective. *Child Development, 52,* 413–429.

Ogbu, J. U. (1987). Variability in minority school performance: A problem in search of an explanation. *Anthropology and Education Quarterly, 18,* 312–334.

Ogbu, J. U. (1997). Understanding the school performance of urban blacks: Some essential background knowledge. In H. J. Walberg & O. Reyes (Eds.), *Children and youth: Interdisciplinary perspectives: Issues in children's and families' lives* (Vol. 7, pp. 190–222). Thousand Oaks, CA: SAGE.

Ogbu, J. U. (2004). Collective identity and the burden of "acting white" in black history, community, and education. *Urban Review, 36*(1), 1–35.

Ogbu, J. U., & Stern, P. (2001). Caste status and intellectual development. In R. J. Sternberg & E. L. Grigorenko (Eds.), *Environmental effects on cognitive abilities* (pp. 3–37). Mahwah, NJ: Erlbaum.

Ogbu, J. U., with Davis, A. (2003). *Black American students in an affluent suburb: A study of academic disengagement.* Mahwah, NJ: Erlbaum.

Oksaar, E. (1977). On becoming trilingual. In C. Molony (Ed.), *Deutsch in Kontaki mit anderen Sprachen* (pp. 296–306). Kronberg, Germany: Scriptor Verlag.

Oller, D. K., & Eilers, R. E. (1988). The role of audition in babbling. *Child Development, 59,* 441–449.

Olson, G. M., & Olson, J. S. (2003). Human-computer interaction: Psychological aspects of the human use of computing. *Annual Review of Psychology, 54,* 491–516.

Olson, R. K. (2006). Genes, environment and dyslexia: The 2005 Norman Geschwind Memorial Lecture. *Annals of Dyslexia, 56*(2), 205–238.

Olweus, D. (2013). School bullying: Development and some important challenges. *Annual Review of Clinical Psychology, 9,* 751–780.

107th Congress. (2002). *The No Child Left Behind Act of 2001.* Washington, DC: U.S. Congress.

Ornstein, P. A., Grammer, J. K., & Coffman, J. L. (2010). Teachers' "mnemonic style" and the development of skilled memory. In H. S. Walters & W. Schneider (Eds.), *Metacognition, strategy use, and instruction* (pp. 23–53). New York: Guilford Press.

Ornstein, P. A., Naus, M. J., & Liberty, C. (1975). Rehearsal and organizational processes in children's memory. *Child Development, 46,* 818–830.

Ornstein, R. (1977). *The psychology of consciousness.* New York: Harcourt, Brace, Jovanovich.

Ornstein, R. (1978). The split and whole brain. *Human Nature, 1,* 76–83.

Osterman, K. (2000). Students' need for belonging in the school community. *Review of Educational Research, 70,* 323–367.

O'Sullivan, J. T., & Pressley, M. (1984). Completeness of instruction and strategy transfer. *Journal of Experimental Child Psychology, 38,* 275–288.

Oyama, S. (1976). Sensitive period for the acquisition of a nonnative phonological system. *Journal of Psycholinguistic Research, 5,* 261–283.

Oyserman, D., Brickman, D., & Rhodes, M. (2007). School success, possible selves and parent school involvement. *Family Relations: An Interdisciplinary Journal of Applied Family Studies, 56,* 479–489.

Oyserman, D., Bybee, D., & Terry, K. (2006). Possible selves and academic outcomes: How and when possible selves impel action. *Journal of Personality and Social Psychology, 91*(1), 188–204.

Oyserman, D., Destin, M., & Novin, S. (2016). The context-sensitive future self: Possible selves motivate in context, not otherwise. *Self and Identity, 14*(2), 173–188.

Paas, F., Van Gog, T., & Sweller, J. (2010). Cognitive load theory: New conceptualizations, specifications, and integrated research perspectives. *Educational Psychology Review, 22*(2), 115–121.

Padilla-Walker, L. M., Carlo, G., Christensen, K. J., & Yorgason, J. B. (2012). Bidirectional relations between authoritative parenting and adolescents' prosocial behavior. *Journal of Research on Adolescents' Prosocial Behavior, 22*(3), 400–408.

Pahlke, E., & Hyde, J. S. (2016). The debate over single-sex schooling. *Child Development Perspectives, 10*(2), 81–86.

Pahlke, E., Shibley Hale, J., & Mertz, J. E. (2013). The effects of single-sex compared with coeducational schooling on mathematics and science achievement: Data from Korea. *Journal of Educational Psychology, 105*(2), 444–452.

Paivio, A. (1971). *Imagery and verbal processes.* New York: Holt, Rinehart & Winston.

Paivio, A. (1986). *Mental representations: A dual-coding approach.* New York: Oxford University Press.

Palincsar, A. S. (1998). Social constructivist perspectives on teaching and learning. *Annual Review of Psychology, 49,* 345–375.

Palincsar, A. S. (2013). Reciprocal teaching. In J. Hattie & E. M. Anderman (Eds.), *International guide to student achievement* (pp. 369–371). New York: Routledge.

Palincsar, A. S., & Brown, A. L. (1984). Reciprocal teaching of comprehension-fostering and monitoring activities. *Cognition and Instruction, 1,* 117–175.

Palladino, P., Poli, P., Masi, G., & Marcheschi, M. (2000). The relation between metacognition and depressive symptoms in preadolescents with learning disabilities: Data in support of Borkowski's model. *Learning Disabilities Research and Practice, 15*, 142–148.

Pallini, S., & Barcaccia, B. (2014). A meeting of the minds: John Bowlby encounters Jean Piaget. *Review of General Psychology, 18*(4), 287–292.

Pallini, S., Biaocco, R., Schneider, H. H., Madigan, S., & Atkinson, L. (2014). Early child–parent attachment and peer relations: A meta-analysis of recent research. *Journal of Family Psychology, 28*(1), 118–123.

Palmer, S. L., Gajjar, A., Reddick, W. E., Glass, J. O., Kun, L. E., Wu, S., et al. (2003). Predicting intellectual outcome among children treated with 35–40 Gy craniospinal irradiation for medulloblastoma. *Neuropsychology, 17*, 548–555.

Panetta, S. M., Somers, C. L., Ceresnie, A. R., Hillman, S. B., & Partridge, R. T. (2014) Maternal and paternal parenting style patterns and adolescent emotional and behavioral outcomes. *Marriage and Family Review, 50*, 342–359.

Papanicolaou, A. C., Pugh, K. R., Simos, P. G., & Mencl, W. E. (2004). Functional brain imaging: An introduction to concepts and applications. In P. McCardle & V. Chhabra (Eds.), *The voice of evidence in reading research* (pp. 383–416). Baltimore: Brookes.

Parents in Action on Special Education v. Hannon et al. (1980, July). No. 74 C 3586, United States District of Illinois, Eastern Division, slip opinion.

Pargulski, J. R., & Reynolds, M. R. (2017). Sex differences in achievement: Distributions matter. *Personality and Individual Differences, 104*, 272–278.

Paris, D. (2009). "They're in my culture, they speak the same way": African American language in multiethnic high schools. *Harvard Educational Review, 79*(3), 428–447.

Paris, S. G., Lipson, M. Y., & Wixson, K. K. (1983). Becoming a strategic reader. *Contemporary Educational Psychology, 8*, 293–316.

Park, B., Flowerday, T., & Brunken, R. (2015). Cognitive and affective effects of seductive details in multimedia learning. *Computers in Human Behavior, 44*, 267–278.

Park, D., Gunderson, E. A., Tsukayama, E., Levine, S. C., & Beilock, S. L. (2016). Young children's motivational frameworks and math achievement: Relation to teacher-reported instructional practices but not teacher theory of intelligence. *Journal of Educational Psychology, 108*(3), 300–313.

Parke, R. D. (1969). Effectiveness of punishment as an interaction of intensity, timing, agent nurturance and cognitive structuring. *Child Development, 40*, 213–236.

Parke, R. D. (1974). Rules, roles, and resistance to deviation in children: Explorations in punishment, discipline and self-control. In A. D. Pick (Ed.), *Minnesota Symposium on Child Psychology* (Vol. 8, pp. 111–144). Minneapolis: University of Minnesota Press.

Parke, R. D. (2002). Fathers and families. In M. H. Bornstein (Ed.), *Handbook of parenting: Vol. 3. Being and becoming a parent* (2nd ed., pp. 27–73). Mahwah, NJ: Erlbaum.

Parke, R. D. (2012). Punishment revisited—Science, values and the right question: Commentary on Gershoff (2002). *Psychological Bulletin, 128*(4), 596–601.

Parke, R. D., Coltrane, S., Duffy, S., Buriel, R., Dennis, J., Powers, J., et al. (2004). Economic stress, parenting, and child adjustment in Mexican American and European American families. *Child Development, 75*(6), 632–1656.

Parker, J. G., Rubin, K. H., Erath, S. A., Wojslawowicz, J. C., & Buskirk, A. A. (2006). Peer relationships, child development, and adjustment: A developmental psychopathology perspective. In D. Cicchetti & D. J. Cohen (Eds.), *Developmental psychopathology* (pp. 419–493). Hoboken, NJ: Wiley.

Parker, P. D., Schoon, I., Tsai, Y.-M., Nagy, G., Trautwein, U., & Eccles, J. S. (2012). Achievement agency, gender, socioeconomic background as predictors of post-school choices: A multicontext study. *Developmental Psychology, 48*(6), 1629–1642.

Parker, S. T., & Gibson, K. R. (Eds.). (1990). *"Language" and intelligence in monkeys and apes*. Cambridge, UK: Cambridge University Press.

Parkin, A. J., & Streete, S. (1988). Implicit and explicit memory in young children and adults. *British Journal of Psychology, 79*, 361–369.

Parsons, J., & Ruble, D. N. (1977). The development of achievement-related expectancies. *Child Development, 48*, 1075–1079.

Pascarella, E. T., & Terenzini, P. T. (1991). *How college affects students*. San Francisco: Jossey-Bass.

Pascual-Leone, J. (1970). A mathematical model for the transition rule in Piaget's developmental stages. *Acta Psychologica, 32*, 301–345.

Patall, E., Cooper, H., & Wynn, S. R. (2010). The effectiveness and relative importance of choice in the classroom. *Journal of Educational Psychology, 102*(4), 896–915.

Patrick, B. C., Skinner, E. A., & Connell, J. A. (1993). What motivates children's behavior and emotion?: Joint effects of perceived control and autonomy in the academic domain. *Journal of Personality and Social Psychology, 65*, 781–791.

Patrick, R. B., & Gibbs, J. C. (2012). Inductive discipline, parental expression of disappointed expectation, and moral identity in adolescence. *Journal of Youth Adolescence, 41*, 973–983.

Paul, P. V. (2003). Processes and components of reading. In M. Marschark & P. E. Spencer (Eds.), *Oxford handbook of deaf studies, language, and education* (pp. 97–109). New York: Oxford University Press.

Paulesu, E., Danelli, L., & Berlingeri, M. (2014). Reading the dyslexic brain: Multiple dysfunctional routes revealed by a new meta-analysis of PET and fMRI activation studies. *Frontiers in Human Neuroscience, 8*, 1–20.

Paus, T. (2010). Growth of white matter in the adolescent brain: Myelin or axon? *Brain and Cognition, 72*, 26–35.

Paus, T., Keshavan, M., & Giedd, J. N. (2008). Why do many psychiatric disorders emerge during adolescence? *Nature Reviews Neuroscience, 9*, 947–957.

Payne, A. C., Whitehurst, G. J., & Angell, A. L. (1994). The role of home literacy environment in the development of language ability in preschool children from low-income families. *Early Childhood Research Quarterly, 9*, 427–440.

Peal, E., & Lambert, W. E. (1962). The relation of bilingualism to intelligence. *Psychological Monographs, 546*, 1–23.

Pearson, B. Z. (1993). Predictive validity of the Scholastic Aptitude Test (SAT) for Hispanic bilingual students. *Hispanic Journal of the Behavioral Sciences, 15*, 342–356.

Pekrun, R., & Stephens, E. J. (2012). Academic emotions. In K. Harris, S. Graham, & T. Urdan (Eds.), *APA educational psychology handbook: Vol. 2. Individual differences and cultural and contextual factors* (pp. 3–31). Washington, DC: American Psychological Association.

Peng, P., & Fuchs, D. (2016). A meta-analysis of working memory deficits in children with learning difficulties: Is there a difference between verbal domain and numerical domain. *Journal of Learning Disabilities, 49*(1), 3–20.

Peng, P., Namkung, J., Barnes, M., & Sun, C. (2016). A meta-analysis of mathematics and working memory: Moderating effects of working memory domain, type of mathematics skill, and sample characteristics. *Journal of Educational Psychology, 108*(4), 455–473.

Pennington, B. F. (1989). Using genetics to understand dyslexia. *Annals of Dyslexia, 39*, 81–93.

Pennington, B. F. (2001). Early reading development in children at family risk for dyslexia. *Child Development, 72*(3), 816–833.

Pennington, B. F., Groisser, D., & Welsh, M. C. (1993). Contrasting cognitive deficits in attention deficit hyperactivity disorder versus reading disability. *Developmental Psychology, 29*, 511–523.

Pennington, B. F., Van Orden, G. C., Smith, S. D., Green, P. A., & Haith, M. M. (1990). Phonological processing skills and deficits in adult dyslexics. *Child Development, 61*, 1753–1778.

Pennock-Román, M. (1992). Interpreting test performance in selective admissions for Hispanic students. In K. F. Geisinger (Ed.), *Psychological testing of Hispanics* (pp. 99–136). Washington, DC: American Psychological Association.

Perdue, N. H., Manzeske, D. P., & Estell, D. B. (2009). Early predictors of school engagement: Exploring the role of peer relationships. *Psychology in the Schools, 46*(10), 1084–1097.

Perez, B. (2004). *Becoming biliterate: A study of two-way bilingual immersion education*. Mahwah, NJ: Erlbaum.

Perfetti, C. A. (1992). The representation problem in reading acquisition. In P. B. Gough, L. C. Ehri, & R. Treiman (Eds.), *Reading acquisition* (pp. 145–174). Hillsdale, NJ: Erlbaum.

Perfetti, C. A., Beck, I., Bell, L., & Hughes, C. (1987). Phonemic knowledge and learning to read are reciprocal: A longitudinal study of first grade children. *Merrill–Palmer Quarterly, 33*, 283–319.

Perlman, S. M. (1973). Cognitive abilities of children with hormone abnormalities: Screening by psychoeducational tests. *Journal of Learning Disabilities, 6*, 21–29.

Perry, D. G., & Bussey, K. (1979). The social learning theory of sex differences: Imitation is alive and well. *Journal of Personality and Social Psychology, 37*, 1699–1712.

Perry, R. P., Stupnisky, R. H., Hall, N., Chippefield, J. G., & Weiner, B. (2010). Bad starts and better finishes: Attribution retraining and initial performance in competitive achievement settings. *Journal of Social and Clinical Psychology, 29*(6), 6689–7000.

Perry-Jenkins, M., Goldberg, A. E., Pierce, C. P., & Sayer, A. G. (2007). Shift work, role overload, and the transition to parenthood. *Journal of Marriage and Family, 69*, 123–138.

Perry-Jenkins, M., Smith, J. Z., Goldberg, A. E., & Logan, J. (2011). Working-class jobs and new parents' mental health. *Journal of Marriage and Family, 73*, 1117–1132.

Pessoa, L. (2014). Understanding brain networks and brain organization. *Physics of Life Reviews, 11*(3), 400–435.

Petersen, J., & Hyde, J. S. (2014). Gender-related academic and occupational interests and goals. In L. S. Liben & R. S. Bigler (Eds.), *Advances in child development and behavior: The role of gender in educational contexts and outcomes* (Vol. 47, pp. 43–76). New York: Academic Press.

Petersen, S. E., & Sporns, O. (2015). Brain networks and cognitive architectures. *Neuron, 88*(1), 207–219.

Petitto, L. A., Holowka, S., Sergio, L. E., Levy, B., & Ostry, D. J. (2004). Baby hands that move to the rhythm of language: Hearing babies acquiring sign languages babble silently on the hands. *Cognition, 93*, 43–73.

Petitto, L. A., Holowka, S., Sergio, L. E., & Ostry, D.

J. (2001). Language rhythms in baby hand movements. *Nature, 413*, 35–36.

Petitto, L. A., & Marantette, P. F. (1991). Babbling in the manual mode: Evidence for the ontogeny of language. *Science, 251*, 299–322.

Petrosini, L., Cutuli, D., & de Bartolo, P. (2013). Environmental influences on development of the nervous system. In R. J. Nelson, S. J. Y. Mizumori, & I. B. Weiner (Eds.), *Handbook of psychology* (2nd ed., pp. 461–479). New York: Wiley.

Pezzella, F. S., Thornberry, T. P., & Smith, C. A. (2016). Race socialization and parenting styles: Links to delinquency for African American and white adolescents. *Youth Violence and Juvenile Justice, 14*(4), 448–467.

Pfundt, H., & Duit, R. (1991). *Bibliography: Students' alternative frameworks and science education* (3rd ed.). Kiel, Germany: IPN.

Phelps, L. (1999). Low-level lead exposure: Implications for research and practice. *School Psychology Review, 28*, 477–492.

Philips, S. U. (1983). *The invisible culture: Communication in classroom and community on the Warm Springs Indian reservation*. New York: Longman.

Phillips, D. A., & Shonkoff, J. P. (Eds.). (2000). *From neurons to neighborhoods: The science of early childhood development*. Washington, DC: National Academies Press.

Phinney, J. S. (1989). Stages of ethnic identity development in minority group adolescents. *Journal of Early Adolescence, 9*, 34–49.

Piaget, J. (1926). *The language and thought of the child*. London: Routledge & Kegan Paul.

Piaget, J. (1929). *The child's conception of the world*. London: Routledge & Kegan Paul.

Piaget, J. (1965). *The moral judgment of the child*. New York: Free Press. (Original work published in 1932)

Piaget, J. (1967). *Biologie et connaissance*. Paris: Gallimard.

Piaget, J. (1970). Piaget's theory. In P. H. Mussen (Ed.), *Carmichael's manual of child psychology* (Vol. 1, 3rd ed., pp. 703–732). New York: Wiley.

Piaget, J. (1972). Intellectual evolution from adolescence to adulthood. *Human Development, 15*, 1–12.

Piaget, J. (1983). Piaget's theory. In W. Kesson (Vol. Ed.) & P. H. Mussen (Gen. Ed.), *History, theory, and methods: Vol. 1. Handbook of child psychology* (pp. 103–128). New York: Wiley.

Piaget, J. (1995). *Sociological studies*. New York: Routledge.

Piaget, J., & Inhelder, B. (1973). *Memory and intelligence*. New York: Basic Books.

Pike, A., & Oliver, B. R. (2016). Child behavior and sibling relationship quality: A cross-lagged analysis. *Journal of Family Psychology, 31*(2), 1–6.

Pinel, P., & Dehaene, S. (2010). Beyond hemispheric dominance: Brain regions underlying the joint lateralization of language and arithmetic to the left hemisphere. *Journal of Cognitive Neuroscience, 22*, 48–66.

Pinker, S. (1994). *The language instinct: How the mind creates language*. New York: Morrow.

Pinquart, M. (2016). Associations of parenting styles and dimensions with academic achievement in children and adolescents: A meta-analysis. *Educational Psychology Review, 28*, 475–493.

Planalp, E. M., & Braungart-Rieker, J. M. (2013). Temperamental precursors of infant attachment with mothers and fathers. *Infant Behavior and Development, 36*, 796–808.

Pleiss, M. K., & Feldhusen, J. F. (1995). Mentors, role models, and heroes in the lives of gifted children. *Educational Psychologist, 30*(3), 159–169.

Plomin, R., & Deary, I. J. (2015). Genetics and intelligence differences: Five special findings. *Molecular Psychiatry, 20*(1), 98–108.

Plomin, R., DeFries, J. C., Knopik, V. S., & Neiderhiser, J. (2013). *Behavioral genetics* (6th ed.). New York: Worth.

Plomin, R., Defries, J. C., McClearn, G. E., & McGuffin, P. (Eds.). (2000). *Behavioral genetics*. San Francisco: Freeman.

Plomin, R., Kovas, Y., & Haworth, C. (2007). Generalist genes: Genetic links between brain, mind, and education. *Mind, Brain, and Education, 1*(1), 11–19.

Plomin, R., & Spinath, F. M. (2004). Intelligence: Genetics, genes, and genomics. *Journal of Personality and Social Psychology, 86*(1), 112–129.

Plutchik, R. (1995). A theory of ego defenses. In H. R. Conte & R. Plutchik (Eds.), *Ego defenses: Theory and measurement* (pp. 13–37). New York: Wiley.

Polan, H. J., & Hofer, M. A. (2016). Psychobiological origins of infant attachment and its role in development. In J. Cassidy & P. R. Shaver (Eds.), *Handbook of attachment: Theory, research, and clinical applications* (pp. 117–132). New York: Guilford Press.

Pollitt, E. (1990). *Malnutrition and infection in the classroom*. Paris: UNESCO.

Polya, G. (1954a). *Mathematics and plausible reasoning: Induction and analogy in mathematics*. Princeton, NJ: Princeton University Press.

Polya, G. (1954b). *Mathematics and plausible reasoning: Induction and analogy in mathematics: Patterns of plausible inference*. Princeton, NJ: Princeton University Press.

Poole, I. R., & Evertson, C. M. (2013). Elementary classroom management. In J. Hattie & E. M. Anderman (Eds.), *International guide to student achievement* (pp. 188–191). New York: Routledge.

Poorthuis, A. M. G., Juvonen, J., Thomaes, S., Denissen, J. J. A., Orobio de Castro, B., et al. (2015). Do grades shape students' school engagement?: The psychological consequence of report card grades at the beginning of secondary school. *Journal of Educational Psychology, 107*(3), 842–854.

Popham, W. J. (2017). *Classroom assessment: What teachers need to know* (8th ed.). New York: Pearson.

Posada, G., Gao, Y., Wu, F., Posada, R., Tascon, M., et al. (1995). The secure-base phenomenon across cultures: Children's behavior, mothers' preferences, and experts' concepts. *Monographs of the Society for Research in Child Development, 60*(Nos. 2–3, Serial No. 244), 27–48.

Posner, J. (2014). A different approach to rising rates of ADHD diagnosis. *Journal of the American Academy of Child and Adolescent Psychiatry, 53*(6), 697.

Posner, M. I. (2001). The developing human brain. *Developmental Science, 4*(3), 253–387.

Posner, M. I., & Rothbart, M. K. (2005). Influencing brain networks: Implications for education. *Trends in Cognitive Sciences, 9*(3), 99–103.

Poteat, V. P., Heck, N. C., Yoshikawa, H., & Calzo, J. P. (2017). Greater engagement among members of Gay-Straight Alliances: Individual and structural contributors. *American Educational Research Association, 53*(6), 1732–1758.

Poteat, V. P., Scheer, J. R., & Mereish, E. H. (2014). Factors affecting academic achievement among sexual minority and gender-variant youth. In L. S. Liben & R. S. Bigler (Eds.), *Advances in child development and behavior: The role of gender in educational contexts and outcomes* (Vol. 47, pp. 261–300). New York: Academic Press.

Potter, D. (2010). Psychosocial well-being and the relationship between divorce and children's academic achievement. *Journal of Marriage and Family, 72*, 933–946.

Poulin, F., & Chan, A. (2010). Friendship stability and change in childhood and adolescence. *Developmental Review, 30*, 257–272.

Powell, S. R. (2011). Solving word problems using schemas: A review of the literature. *Learning Disabilities Research and Practice, 26*(2), 94–108.

Power, D., & Leigh, G. R. (2003). Curriculum: Cultural and communicative contexts. In M. Marschark & P. E. Spencer (Eds.), *Oxford handbook of deaf studies, language, and education* (pp. 38–51). New York: Oxford University Press.

Power, J. D., Fair, D. A., Schlaggar, B. L., & Petersen, S. E. (2010). The development of human functional brain networks. *Neuron, 67*(5), 735–748.

Powlishta, K. K., Sen, M. G., Serbin, L. A., Poulin-Dubois, D., & Eichstedt, J. A. (2001). From infancy through middle childhood: The role of cognitive and social factors in becoming gendered. In R. K. Inger (Ed.), *Handbook of psychology of women and gender* (pp. 116–132). New York: Wiley.

Pratt, A. C., & Brady, S. (1988). Relation of phonological awareness to reading disability in children and adults. *Journal of Educational Psychology, 80*, 319–323.

Preckel, F., Baudson, T. G., Krolak-Schwerdt, S., & Glock, S. (2015). Gifted and maladjusted?: Implicit attitudes and automatic associations related to gifted children. *American Educational Research Journal, 52*(6), 1160–1184.

Preckel, F., Goetz, T., Pekrun, R., & Kleine, M. (2008). Gender differences in gifted and average-ability students: Comparing boys' and girls' self-concept, interest and motivation in mathematics. *Gifted Child Quarterly, 52*(2), 146–159.

Pressley, G. M. (1976). Mental imagery helps eight-year-olds remember what they read. *Journal of Educational Psychology, 68*, 355–359.

Pressley, M. (1977). Imagery and children's learning: Putting the picture in developmental perspective. *Review of Educational Research, 47*, 586–622.

Pressley, M. (1979). Increasing children's self-control through cognitive interventions. *Review of Educational Research, 49*, 319–370.

Pressley, M., & Afflerbach, P. (1995). *Verbal protocols of reading: The nature of constructively responsive reading.* Hillsdale, NJ: Erlbaum.

Pressley, M., Allington, R. L., Wharton-McDonald, R., Block, C. C., & Morrow, L. M. (2001). *Learning to read: Lessons from exemplary first-grade classrooms.* New York: Guilford Press.

Pressley, M., Borkowski, J. G., & O'Sullivan, J. T. (1984). Memory strategy instruction is made of this: Metamemory and durable strategy use. *Educational Psychologist, 19*, 94–107.

Pressley, M., Borkowski, J. G., & O'Sullivan, J. T. (1985). Children's metamemory and the teaching of strategies. In D. L. Forrest-Pressley, G. E. MacKinnon, & T. G. Waller (Eds.), *Metacognition, cognition, and human performance* (pp. 111–153). Orlando, FL: Academic Press.

Pressley, M., Dolezal, S. E., Raphael, L. M., Mohan, L., Roehrig, A. D., & Bogner, K. (2003). *Motivating primary-grade students.* New York: Guilford Press.

Pressley, M., & El-Dinary, P. B. (1997). What we know about translating comprehension-strategies instruction research into practice. *Journal of Learning Disabilities, 30*(5), 486–488, 512.

Pressley, M., El-Dinary, P. B., Gaskins, I., Schuder, T., Bergman, J. L., Almasi, J., et al. (1992). Beyond direct explanation: Transactional instruction of reading comprehension strategies. *Elementary School Journal, 92*, 513–556.

Pressley, M., Gaskins, I. W., Wile, D., Cunicelli, E. A., & Sheridan, J. (1991). Teaching literacy strategies across the curriculum: A case study at Benchmark School. In S. McCormick & J. Zutell (Eds.), *40th yearbook of the National Reading Conference* (pp. 219–228). Chicago: National Reading Conference.

Pressley, M., & Ghatala, E. S. (1989). Metacognitive benefits of taking a test for children and young adolescents. *Journal of Experimental Child Psychology, 47,* 430–450.

Pressley, M., & Ghatala, E. S. (1990). Self-regulated learning: Monitoring learning from text. *Educational Psychologist, 25,* 19–34.

Pressley, M., & Levin, J. R. (1977a). Developmental differences in subjects' associative learning strategies and performance: Assessing a hypothesis. *Journal of Experimental Child Psychology, 24,* 431–439.

Pressley, M., & Levin, J. R. (1977b). Task parameters affecting the efficacy of a visual imagery learning strategy in younger and older children. *Journal of Experimental Child Psychology, 24,* 53–59.

Pressley, M., Levin, J. R., & Ghatala, E. S. (1984). Memory strategy monitoring in adults and children. *Journal of Verbal Learning and Verbal Behavior, 23,* 270–288.

Pressley, M., & MacFadyen, J. (1983). The development of mnemonic mediator usage at testing. *Child Development, 54,* 474–479.

Pressley, M., Raphael, L., Gallagher, J. D., & DiBella, J. (2004). Providence–St. Mel School: How a school that works for African-American students works. *Journal of Educational Psychology, 96,* 216–235.

Pressley, M., Ross, K. A., Levin, J. R., & Ghatala, E. S. (1984). The role of strategy utility knowledge in children's strategy decision making. *Journal of Experimental Child Psychology, 38,* 491–504.

Prinstein, M. J., & Giletta, M. (2016). Peer relations and developmental psychopathology. In D. Cicchetti & D. J. Cohen (Eds.), *Developmental psychopathology* (pp. 527–579). Hoboken, NJ: Wiley.

Purcell-Gates, V. (1995). *Other people's worlds: The cycle of low literacy.* Cambridge, MA: Harvard University Press.

Qin, Z., Johnson, D. W., & Johnson, R. T. (1995). Cooperative versus competitive efforts and problem solving. *Review of Educational Research, 65,* 129–143.

Quigley, S. P., & Paul, P. V. (1984). *Language and deafness.* San Diego, CA: College Hill Press.

Rabinowitz, M., Freeman, K., & Cohen, S. (1992). Use and maintenance of strategies: The influence of accessibility to knowledge. *Journal of Educational Psychology, 84,* 211–218.

Radford, J. (1990). *Child prodigies and exceptional early achievers.* New York: Free Press.

Rais-Bahrami, K., Short, B. L., & Batshaw, M. L. (2002). Premature and small-for-dates infants. In M. L. Batshaw (Ed.), *Children with disabilities* (5th ed., pp. 85–106). Baltimore: Brookes.

Rambaran, A. J., Hopmeyer, A., Schwartz, D., Steglich, C., Badaly, D., & Veenstra, R. (2017). Academic functioning and peer influences: A short-term longitudinal study of network-behavior dynamic in middle adolescence. *Child Development, 88*(2), 523–543.

Ramdoss, S., Machalicek, W., Rispoli, M., Mulloy, A., Lang, R., & O'Reilly, M. (2012). Computer-based interventions to improve social and emotional skills in individuals with autism spectrum disorders: A systematic review. *Developmental Neurehabilitation, 15*(2), 119–135.

Ramey, C. T., Ramey, S. L., & Lanzi, R. G. (2001). Intelligence and experience. In R. J. Sternberg & E. L. Grigorenko (Eds.), *Environmental effects on cognitive abilities* (pp. 83–115). Mahwah, NJ: Erlbaum.

Ramsdal, G., Bergvik, S., & Wynn, R. (2015). Parent–child attachment, academic performance and the process of high-school dropout: A narrative review. *Attachment and Human Development, 17*(5), 522–545.

Rawson, K. A., & Dunlosky, J. (2016). How effective is example generation for learning declarative concepts? *Educational Psychology Review, 28,* 649–672.

Rawson, K. A., Thomas, R. C., & Jacoby, L. L. (2015). The power of examples: Illustrative examples enhance conceptual learning of declarative concepts. *Educational Psychology Review, 27*(3), 483–504.

Redick, T. S., Shipstead, Z., Wiemers, E. A., Melby-Lervåg, M., & Hulme, C. (2015). What's working in working memory training?: An educational perspective. *Educational Psychology Review, 27*(4), 617–633.

Redlinger, W., & Park, T. Z. (1980). Language mixing in young bilinguals. *Journal of Child Language, 3,* 449–455.

Reid, M. K., & Borkowski, J. G. (1987). Causal attributions of hyperactive children: Implications for teaching strategies and self-control. *Journal of Educational Psychology, 79,* 296–307.

Reilly, D., Neumann, D. L., & Andrews, G. (2015). Sex differences in mathematics and science achievement: A meta-analysis of National Assessment of Educational Progress Assessments. *Journal of Educational Psychology, 107*(3), 645–662.

Reiner, W. G., & Reiner, D. T. (2011). Thoughts on the nature of identity: Disorders of sex development and gender identity. *Child and Adolescent Psychiatric Clinics of North America, 20*(4), 627–638.

Reinke, W. M., Stormont, M., Herman, K. C., Puri, R., & Goel, N. (2011). Supporting children's mental health in schools: Teacher perceptions of needs, roles, and barriers. *School Psychology Quarterly, 26*(1), 1–13.

Reis, S. M., & Renzulli, J. S. (2004). Current research on the social and emotional development of gifted and talented students: Good news and future possibilities. *Psychology in the Schools, 41,* 119–130.

Reiser, B. J., & Tabak, I. (2014). Scaffolding. In R. K. Sawyer (Ed.), *Cambridge handbook of the learning sciences* (2nd ed., pp. 44–62). New York: Cambridge University Press.

Renick, M. J., & Harter, S. (1989). Impact of social comparisons on the developing self-perceptions of learning disabled students. *Journal of Educational Psychology, 81,* 631–638.

Renner, L. M., & Boel-Studt, S. (2017, March 13). Physical family violence and externalizing and internalizing behaviors among children and adolescents. *American Journal of Orthopsychiatry.* [Epub ahead of print]

Renninger, K. A., & Hidi, S. (2011). Revisiting the conceptualization, measurement, and generation of interest. *Educational Psychologist, 46*(3), 168–184.

Renninger, K. A., & Wozniak, R. H. (1985). Effect of interest on attentional shift, recognition, and recall in young children. *Developmental Psychology, 21,* 624–632.

Resnick, L. B., Levine, J. M., & Teasley, S. D. (Eds.). (1991). *Perspectives on socially shared cognition.* Washington, DC: American Psychological Association.

Resnick, S. M., Berenbaum, S. A., Gottesman, I. I., & Bouchard, T. J. (1986). Early hormonal influences on cognitive functioning in congenital adrenal hyperplasia. *Developmental Psychology, 22,* 191–198.

Rest, J. (1968). *Developmental hierarchy in preference and comprehension of moral judgment.* Unpublished doctoral dissertation, University of Chicago, Chicago, IL.

Retelsdorf, J., Schwartz, K., & Asbrock, F. (2015). "Michael can't read!": Teachers' gender stereotypes and boys' reading self-concept. *Journal of Educational Psychology, 107*(1), 186–194.

Reyna, V. F., & Brainerd, C. J. (1995). Fuzzy-trace theory: An interim synthesis. *Learning and Individual Differences, 7,* 1–75.

Reynolds, A. J. (2000). *Success in early intervention: The Chicago Child–Parent Centers.* Lincoln: University of Nebraska Press.

Reynolds, C. R., & Kaiser, S. M. (2003). Bias in assessment of aptitude. In C. R. Reynolds & R. W. Kamphaus (Eds.), *Handbook of psychological and educational assessment of children: Intelligence, aptitude, and achievement* (2nd ed., pp. 519–562). New York: Guilford Press.

Reynolds, C. R., & Kamphaus, R. W. (Eds.). (2003). *Handbook of psychological and educational assessment of children: Intelligence, aptitude, and achievement.* New York: Guilford Press.

Reynolds, C. R., & Ramsay, M. C. (2003). Bias in psychological assessment: An empirical review and recommendations. In J. R. Graham & J. A. Naglieri (Vol. Eds.) & I. B. Weiner (Ed.-in-Chief), *Handbook of psychology: Vol. 10. Assessment psychology* (pp. 67–94). New York: Wiley.

Rice, E., Petering, R., Rhoades, H., Winetrobe, H., Goldbach, J., Plant, A., et al. (2015). Cyberbullying perpetration and victimization among middle-school students. *American Journal of Public Health, 105*(3), 66–72.

Richardson, K. (2013). The eclipse of heritability and the foundations of intelligence. *New Ideas in Psychology, 31,* 122–129.

Richert, E. S. (1991). Rampant problems and promising practices in identification. In N. Colangelo & G. A. Davis (Eds.), *Handbook of gifted education* (pp. 81–96). Boston: Allyn & Bacon.

Rief, S. F. (2003). *The ADHD book of lists: A practical guide for helping children and teens with attention deficit disorders.* San Francisco: Jossey-Bass.

Riegle-Crumb, C., King, B., Grodsky, E., & Muller, C. (2012). The more things change: the more they stay the same?: Prior achievement fails to explain gender inequality in entry into STEM college majors over time. *American Educational Research Journal, 49,* 1048–1073.

Ring, M. M., & Reetz, L. (2000). Modification effects on attributions of middle school students with learning disabilities. *Learning Disabilities Research and Practice, 15,* 34–42.

Ringness, T. A. (1961). Self concept of children of low, average, and high intelligence. *American Journal of Mental Deficiency, 65,* 453–461.

Ripple, C. H., & Zigler, E. (2003). Research, policy, and the federal role in prevention initiatives for children. *American Psychologist, 58,* 482–490.

Rips, L. J., Shoben, E. J., & Smith, E. E. (1973). Semantic distance and the verification of semantic relations. *Journal of Verbal Learning and Verbal Behavior, 12,* 1–20.

Risberg, J. (1986). Regional cerebral blood flow in neuropsychology. *Neuropsychologia, 24,* 135–140.

Rispoli, K. M., McGoey, K. E., Koziol, N. A., & Schreiber, J. B. (2013). The relation of parenting, child temperament, and attachment security in early childhood to social competence at school entry. *Journal of School Psychology, 51,* 643–658.

Rist, R. C. (1970). Student social class and teacher expectations: The self-fulfilling prophecy in ghetto education. *Harvard Educational Review, 40,* 411–451.

Ritter, K. (1978). The development of knowledge of an external retrieval cue strategy. *Child Development, 49,* 1227–1230.

Rittle-Johnson, B., Schneider, M., & Star, J. R. (2015). Not a one-way street: Bidirectional relations between procedural and conceptual knowledge of mathematics. *Educational Psychology Review, 27,* 587–597.

Rivas-Drake, D., Seaton, E. K., Markstrom, C.,

Quintana, S., Syed, M., Lee, R. M., et al. (2014a). Ethnic and racial identity in adolescence: Implications for psychosocial, academic and health outcomes. *Child Development, 85*(1), 40–57.

Rivas-Drake, D., Syed, M., Umaña-Taylor, A., Markstrom, C., French, S., Schwartz, S. J., et al. (2014b). Feeling good, happy, and proud: A meta-analysis of positive ethnic-racial affect and adjustment. *Child Development, 85*(1), 77–102.

Rivera v. City of Wichita Falls, 665 F. 2d 531 (1982).

Roberton, M. A. (1984). Changing motor patterns during childhood. In J. R. Thomas (Ed.), *Motor development during childhood and adolescence* (pp. 48–90). Minneapolis, MN: Burgess.

Roberts, R. D., & Lipnevich, A. A. (2012). From general intelligence to multiple intelligences: Meanings, models, and measures. In K. Harris, S. Graham, & T. Urdan (Eds.), *APA educational psychology handbook: Vol. 2. Individual differences and cultural and contextual factors* (pp. 33–57). Washington, DC: American Psychological Association.

Roberts, T. A., & Kraft, R. H. (1989). Developmental differences in the relationship between reading comprehension and hemispheric alpha patterns: An EEG study. *Journal of Educational Psychology, 81*, 322–328.

Robertson, D. A. (2013). Teacher talk: One teacher's reflections during comprehension strategies instruction. *Reading Psychology, 34*, 523–549.

Robinson, C. S., & Hayes, J. R. (1978). Making inferences about relevance in understanding problems. In R. Revlin & R. E. Mayer (Eds.), *Human reasoning* (pp. 195–206). Washington, DC: Winston.

Robinson, J. A., & Kingsley, M. E. (1977). Memory and intelligence: Age and ability differences in strategies and organization of recall. *Intelligence, 1*, 318–330.

Robinson, T. R., Smith, S. W., Miller, M. D., & Brownell, M. T. (1999). Cognitive behavior modification of hyperactivity–impulsivity and aggression: A meta-analysis of school-based studies. *Journal of Educational Psychology, 91*, 195–203.

Rodriguez, O. (1992). Introduction to technical and societal issues in the psychological testing of Hispanics. In K. F. Geisinger (Ed.), *Psychological testing of Hispanics* (pp. 11–16). Washington, DC: American Psychological Association.

Roebers, C. M. (2014). Memory development: The contribution of strategies and metacognitive processes. In P. J. Bauer & R. Fivush, R. (Eds), *The Wiley handbook on the development of children's memory* (pp. 866–894). New York: Wiley.

Roediger, H. L., III. (1990). Implicit memory: Retention without remembering. *American Psychologist, 45*, 1043–1056.

Roediger, H. L., & Karpicke, J. D. (2006). The power of testing memory: Basic research and implications for educational practice. *Perspectives on Psychological Science, 1*, 181–210.

Roelle, J., Schmidt, E. M., Buchau, A., & Berthold, K. (2017). Effects of informing learners about the dangers of making overconfident judgments of learning. *Journal of Educational Psychology, 109*(1), 99–117.

Roen, K. (2015). Intersex/DSD. In C. Richards & M. J. Barker (Eds.), *The Palgrave handbook of the psychology of sexuality and gender* (pp. 183–197). London: Palgrave Macmillan.

Roeser, R. W., Eccles, J. S., & Sameroff, A. J. (2000). School as a context of early adolescents' academic and social–emotional development. *Elementary School Journal, 100*, 443–479.

Rogat, T. K., Linnenbrink-Garcia, L., & DiDonato, N. (2013). Motivation in collaborative groups. In C. E. Hmelo-Silver, C. A. Chinn, C. K. K. Chan, & A. O'Donnell (Eds.), *The international handbook of collaborative learning* (pp. 250–267). New York: Routledge.

Rogers, H., & Saklofske, D. H. (1985). Self-concept, locus of control and performance expectations of learning disabled children. *Journal of Learning Disabilities, 18*, 273–278.

Rogers, T. T., & McClelland, J. L. (2014). Parallel distributed processing at 25: Further explorations in the microstructure of cognition. *Cognitive Science: A Multidisciplinary Journal, 38*, 1024–1077.

Rogers, T. T., & Wolmetz, M. (2016). Conceptual knowledge representation: A cross-section of current research. *Cognitive Neuropsychology, 33*(3–4), 121–129.

Rogoff, B. (1990). *Apprenticeship in thinking: Cognitive development in social context.* New York: Oxford University Press.

Rogoff, B. (1998). Cognition as a collaborative process. In W. Damon (Ed.-in-Chief) & D. Kuhn & R. S. Siegler (Vol. Eds.), *Handbook of child psychology* (pp. 679–744). New York: Wiley.

Rogoff, B. (2003). *The cultural nature of human development.* New York: Oxford University Press.

Rogoff, B., & Waddell, K. J. (1982). Memory for information organized in a scene by children from two cultures. *Child Development, 53*(5), 1224–1228.

Rogol, A. D., Roemmich, J. N., & Clark, P. A. (2002). Growth at puberty. *Journal of Adolescent Health, 31*(6), 192–200.

Rohwer, W. D., Jr. (1980). An elaborative conception of learner differences. In R. E. Snow, P. A. Federico, & W. E. Montague (Eds.), *Aptitude, learning, and instruction: Vol. 2. Cognitive process analysis of learning and problem solving* (pp. 23–46). Hillsdale, NJ: Erlbaum.

Rohwer, W. D., Jr., Ammon, P. R., & Cramer, P. (1974). *Understanding intellectual development.* Hinsdale, IL: Dryden Press.

Rohwer, W. D., Jr., & Litrownik, J. (1983). Age and individual differences in the learning of a memorization procedure. *Journal of Educational Psychology, 75*, 799–810.

Roid, G. H. (2003). *Stanford–Binet Intelligence Scales* (5th ed.). Dale, IL: Stoelting.

Roizen, N. J. (2002). Down syndrome. In M. L. Batshaw (Ed.), *Children with disabilities* (5th ed., pp. 307–320). Baltimore: Brookes.

Romaine, S. (1995). *Bilingualism* (2nd ed.). Oxford, UK: Blackwell.

Roodenrys, S., Hulme, C., & Brown, G. (1993). The development of short-term memory span: Separable effects of speech rate and long-term memory. *Journal of Experimental Child Psychology, 56*, 431–442.

Roorda, D. L., Koomen, H. M. Y., Split, J. L., & Oort, F. J. (2011). The influence of affective teacher–student relationships on students' school engagement and achievement. *Review of Educational Research, 81*, 493–529.

Rosch, E. (1973). On the internal structure of perceptual and semantic categories. In T. Moore (Ed.), *Cognitive development and the acquisition of language* (pp. 111–144). New York: Academic Press.

Rosch, E. (1975). Cognitive representations of semantic categories. *Journal of Experimental Psychology: General, 104*, 192–233.

Rosch, E. (1978). Principles of categorization. In E. Rosch & B. Lloyd (Eds.), *Cognition and categorization* (pp. 9–31). Hillsdale, NJ: Erlbaum.

Rosch, E., & Mervis, C. (1975). Family resemblance studies in the internal structure of categories. *Cognitive Psychology, 7*, 575–605.

Rose, S. A., Feldman, J. F., & Jankowski, J. J. (2011). Modeling a cascade of effects: The role of speed and executive functioning in preterm/full-term differences in academic achievement. *Developmental Science, 14*(5), 1161–1175.

Rose, S. A., Feldman, J. F., Jankowski, J. J., & Van Rossem, R. (2008). A cognitive cascade in infancy: Pathways from prematurity to later mental development. *Intelligence, 36*(4), 367–378.

Rosenberg, J., Pennington, B. F., Willcutt, E. G., & Olson, R. K. (2012). Gene by environment interactions influencing reading disability and the inattentive symptoms of attention deficit/hyperactivity disorder. *Journal of Child Psychology and Psychiatry, 53*(3), 243–251.

Rosenblatt, L. M. (1978). *The reader, the text, the poem: The transactional theory of the literary work.* Carbondale: Southern Illinois University Press.

Rosenquist, C., Conners, F. A., & Roskos-Ewoldsen, B. (2003). Phonological and visuo-spatial working memory in individuals with intellectual disability. *American Journal of Mental Retardation, 108*, 403–413.

Rosenshine, B. V. (1979). Content, time, and direct instruction. In P. L. Peterson & H. J. Walberg (Eds.), *Research on teaching: Concepts, findings, and implications* (pp. 28–56). Berkeley, CA: McCutchan.

Rosenshine, B., & Meister, C. (1994). Reciprocal teaching: A review of nineteen experimental studies. *Review of Educational Research, 64*(4), 479–530.

Rosenthal, R., & Jacobson, L. (1968). *Pygmalion in the classroom: Teacher expectation and pupils' intellectual development.* New York: Holt, Rinehart & Winston.

Rosenthal, S. M. (2016). Transgender youth: Current concepts. *Annals of Pediatric Endocrinology and Metabolism, 21*, 85–192.

Rosenthal, T. L., & Zimmerman, B. J. (1978). *Social learning and cognition.* New York: Academic Press.

Roseth, C. (2016). Character education, moral education, and moral-character education. In L. Corno & E. M. Anderman (Eds.), *Handbook of educational psychology* (3rd ed., pp. 213–255). New York: Routledge.

Ross, B. H. (1984). Remindings and their effects in learning a cognitive skill. *Cognitive Psychology, 16*, 371–416.

Ross, B. M., & Millson, C. (1970). Repeated memory of oral prose in Ghana and New York. *International Journal of Psychology, 5*, 173–181.

Roth, J. L., Malone, L. M., & Brooks-Gunn, J. (2010). Does the amount of participation in afterschool programs relate to developmental outcomes?: A review of the literature. *American Journal of Community Psychology, 45*, 310–324.

Rothbart, M. K. (2012). Advances in temperament: History, concepts, and measures. In M. Zetner & R. L. Shiner (Eds.), *Handbook of Temperament* (pp. 3–20). New York: Guilford Press.

Rothganger, H. (2003). Analysis of the sounds of the child in the first year of age and a comparison to the language. *Early Human Development, 75*, 55–69.

Rotter, J. B. (1954). *Social learning and clinical psychology.* Englewood Cliffs, NJ: Prentice-Hall.

Rovet, J., & Netley, C. (1982). Processing deficits in Turner's syndrome. *Developmental Psychology, 18*, 77–94.

Rubin, K. H., Chen, X., Coplan, R., Buskirk, A. A., & Wojslawowicz, J. C. (2011). Peer relationships in childhood. In M. H. Bornstein & M. E. Lamb (Eds.), *Developmental science: An advanced textbook* (pp. 519–570). New York: Psychology Press.

Ruble, D. N. (1983). The development of social-comparison processes and their role in achievement-related self-socialization. In E. T. Higgins, D. N. Ruble, & W. Hartup (Eds.), *Social cognition and social development* (pp. 134–157). New York: Cambridge University Press.

Ruble, D. N., Boggiano, A. K., Feldman, N. S., & Loebl, J. H. (1980). Developmental analysis of the role of social comparison in self-evaluation. *Developmental Psychology, 16,* 105–115.

Ruble, D. N., & Martin, C. L. (1998). Gender development. In N. Eisenberg (Vol. Ed.) & W. Damon (Ed.-in-Chief), *Handbook of child psychology: Vol. 3. Social, emotional, and personality development* (5th ed., pp. 933–1016). New York: Wiley.

Rudasill, K. M., Gallagher, K. C., & White, J. M. (2010). Temperamental attention and activity, classroom emotional support, and academic achievement in third grade. *Journal of School Psychology, 48,* 113–134.

Rustic, J., & Ennis, J. T. (2015). Attentional development. In L. S. Liben, U. Müller, & R. M. Lerner (Eds.), *Handbook of child psychology and developmental science: Vol. 2. Cognitive process* (7th ed., pp. 158–201). Hoboken, NJ: Wiley.

Rutter, D. R., & Durkin, K. (1987). Turn-taking in mother–infant interaction: An examination of vocalizations and gaze. *Developmental Psychology, 23,* 54–61.

Rutter, M. (2002a). The interplay of nature, nurture, and developmental influences. *Archives of General Psychiatry, 59,* 996–1000.

Rutter, M. (2002b). Nature, nurture, and development: From evangelism through science toward policy and practice. *Child Development, 73,* 1–21.

Ryan, C. M., van Duinkerken, E., & Rosano, C. (2016). Neurocognitive consequences of diabetes. *American Psychologist, 71*(7), 563–576.

Sabar, N., & Levin, T. (1989). Still waters run deep. *Journal of Research in Science Teaching, 26,* 727–735.

Sabol, T. J., & Pianta, R. C. (2012). Recent trends in research on teacher–child relationships. *Attachment and Human Development, 14*(3), 213–231.

Sabol, T. J., & Pianta, R. C. (2013). Relationship between teachers and children. In W. M. Reynolds & G. E. Miller (Eds.), *Handbook of educational sychology* (2nd ed., pp. 199–231). New York: Wiley.

Saccuzzo, D. P., Johnson, N. E., & Guertin, T. L. (1994). Information processing in gifted versus nongifted African Americans, Latino, Filipino, and white children: Speeded versus nonspeeded paradigms. *Intelligence, 19,* 219–243.

Sadker, M., & Sadker, D. (1994). *Failing at fairness: How America's schools cheat girls.* New York: Scribners.

Sadler, P. M., Sonnert, G., Coyle, H. P., Cook-Smith, N., & Miller, J. L. (2013). The influence of teachers' knowledge on student learning in middle school physical science classrooms. *American Educational Research Journal, 50*(5), 1021–1049.

Sadler, T. W. (2012) *Langman's medical embryology.* Baltimore: Lippincott, Williams & Wilkins.

Sadoski, M. (1983). An exploratory study of the relationship between reported imagery and the comprehension and recall of a story. *Reading Research Quarterly, 19,* 110–123.

Sadoski, M. (1985). The natural use of imagery in story comprehension and recall: Replication and extension. *Reading Research Quarterly, 20,* 658–667.

Sadoski, M. (2001). Resolving the effects of concreteness on interest, comprehension, and learning important ideas from text. *Educational Psychology Review, 13*(3), 263–281.

Sadoski, M. (2016). *Safe is not enough: Better schools for LBGTQ students.* Cambridge, MA: Harvard Education Press.

Sadoski, M., & Paivio, A. (2001). *Imagery and text: A dual coding theory of reading and writing.* Mahwah, NJ: Erlbaum.

Sadoski, M., Paivio, A., & Goetz, E. T. (1991). A critique of schema theory in reading and a dual coding alternative. *Reading Research Quarterly, 26*(4), 463–484.

Safer, D. J. (2016). Recent trends in stimulant usage. *Journal of Attention Disorders, 20*(6), 471–477.

Safyer, A. W., & Hauser, S. T. (1995). A developmental view of defenses: Empirical approaches. In H. R. Conte & R. Plutchik (Eds.), *Ego defenses: Theory and measurement* (pp. 120–138). Oxford, UK: Wiley.

Sailors, M., & Price, L. R. (2010). Professional development that supports the teaching of cognitive strategy reading instruction. *The Elementary School Journal, 110*(3), 201–322.

Salili, F., Chiu, C.-Y., & Lai, S. (2001). The influence of culture and context on students' motivational orientation and performance. In F. Salili & C.-Y. Chiu (Eds.), *Student motivation: The culture and context of learning* (pp. 221–247). Dordrecht, The Netherlands: Kluwer.

Salma, R. B. (2012). A longitudinal analysis of academic language proficiency outcomes for adolescent English Language Learners in the United States. *Journal of Educational Psychology, 104*(2), 265–285.

Salmivalli, C., & Peets, K. (2009). Bullies, victims, and bully-victim relationships in middle childhood and early adolescence. In K. H. Rubin, W. M. Bukowski, & B. Laursen (Eds.), *Handbook of peer interactions, relationships, and groups* (pp. 322–340). New York: Guilford Press.

Salmivalli, C., Peets, K., & Hodges, E. V. E. (2011). Bullying. In P. K. Smith & C. H. Hart (Eds.), *The Wiley–Blackwell handbook of childhood social development* (2nd ed., pp. 510–528). Hoboken, NJ: Blackwell.

Salthouse, T. A. (1982). *Adult cognition: An experimental psychology of human aging.* New York: Springer-Verlag.

Salthouse, T. A. (1985). Speed of behavior and its

implications for cognition. In J. E. Birren & K. W. Schaie (Eds.), *Handbook of the psychology of aging* (2nd ed., pp. 400–426). New York: Van Nostrand Reinhold.

Salthouse, T. A. (1988). The role of processing resources in cognitive aging. In M. I. Howe & C. J. Brainerd (Eds.), *Cognitive development in adulthood* (pp. 185–239). New York: Springer-Verlag.

Salthouse, T. A. (1992). The information-processing perspective on cognitive aging. In R. J. Sternberg & C. A. Berg (Eds.), *Intellectual development* (pp. 261–277). Cambridge, UK: Cambridge University Press.

Salthouse, T. A. (2009). When does age-related cognitive decline begin? *Neurobiology of Aging, 30*(4), 507–514.

Sameroff, A. J. (1975). Early influences on development: Fact or fancy? *Merrill–Palmer Quarterly, 21,* 267–294.

Sameroff, A. (2010). A unified theory of development: A dialectic integration of nature and nurture. *Child Development, 81*(1), 6–22.

Sandnabba, N. K., & Ahlberg, C. (1999). Parents' attitudes and expectations about children's cross-gender behavior. *Sex Roles, 40,* 249–262.

Sandoval, J. H., & Mille, M. P. W. (1980). Accuracy judgments of WISC-R items' difficulty for minority groups. *Journal of Consulting and Clinical Psychology, 48,* 249–253.

Santos, C. E., & Umaña-Taylor, A. J. (Eds.). (2015). *Studying ethnic identity: Methodological and conceptual approaches across disciplines.* Washington, DC: American Psychological Association.

Saracho, O. N. (2017). Parents' shared storybook reading: Learning to read. *Early Childhood Development and Care, 187*(3–4), 554–567.

Sattler, J. M. (2002). *Assessment of children.* La Mesa, CA: Author.

Sawyer, J. (2016). In what language do you speak to yourself?: A review of private speech and bilingualism. *Early Childhood Research Quarterly, 36,* 489–505.

Sayfan, L., & Lagattuta, K. H. (2008). Grownups are not afraid of scary stuff, but kids are: Young children's and adults' reasoning about children's, infants', and adults' fears. *Child Development, 79*(4), 821–835.

Sayfan, L., & Lagattuta, K. H. (2009). Scaring the monster away: What will children know about managing fears of real and imaginary creatures. *Child Development, 80*(6), 1756–1774.

Scarborough, H. S. (1989). Prediction of reading disability from familial and individual differences. *Journal of Educational Psychology, 81,* 101–108.

Scarborough, H. S. (2001). Connecting early language and literacy to later reading (dis)abilities:

Evidence, theory, and practice. In S. B. Neuman & D. K. Dickinson (Eds.), *Handbook of early literacy research* (pp. 97–110). New York: Guilford Press.

Scardamalia, M., & Bereiter, C. (1986). Research on written composition. In M. C. Wittrock (Ed.), *Handbook of research on teaching* (3rd ed., pp. 778–803). New York: Macmillan.

Schachter, E. P., & Rich, Y. (2011). Identity education: A conceptual framework for educational researchers and practitioners. *Educational Psychologist, 46*(4), 222–238.

Schacter, D. L. (1987). Implicit memory: History and current status. *Journal of Experimental Psychology: Learning, Memory, and Cognition, 13,* 501–518.

Schacter, D. L. (1992). Understanding implicit memory: A cognitive neuroscience perspective. *American Psychologist, 47,* 559–569.

Schacter, D. L., Chiu, C. Y. P., & Ochsner, K. N. (1993). Implicit memory: A selective review. *Annual Review of Neuroscience, 16,* 159–182.

Schaie, K. W. (1990). Intellectual development in adulthood. In J. E. Birren & K. W. Schaie (Eds.), *Handbook of the psychology of aging* (3rd ed., pp. 291–309). San Diego, CA: Academic Press.

Schaie, K. W. (2009). When does age-related cognitive decline begin?: Salthouse again reifies the "cross-sectional fallacy." *Neurobiology of Aging, 30*(4), 528–529.

Schaie, K. W. (2013). *Developmental influences on adult intelligence: The Seattle Longitudinal Study* (2nd ed.). New York: Oxford University Press.

Schaie, K. W., & Labouvie-Vief, G. (1974). Generational versus ontogenetic components of change in adult cognitive behavior: A fourteen year cross sequential study. *Developmental Psychology, 10,* 305–320.

Schaie, K. W., & Parham, I. A. (1977). Cohort-sequential analyses of adult intellectual development. *Developmental Psychology, 13,* 649–653.

Schatz, E. K., & Baldwin, R. S. (1986). Context clues are unreliable predictors of word meanings. *Reading Research Quarterly, 21,* 439–453.

Schau, C. G., Kahn, L., Diepold, J. H., & Cherry, F. (1980). The relationship of parental expectations and preschool children's verbal sex-typing to their sex-typed toy play behavior. *Child Development, 51,* 607–609.

Schick, B. (2003). The development of American sign language and manually coded English system. In M. Marschark & P. E. Spencer (Eds.), *Oxford handbook of deaf studies, language, and education* (pp. 219–231). New York: Oxford University Press.

Schiefelbusch, R. L., & Bricker, D. D. (1979). *Early language: Acquisition and intervention.* Baltimore: University Park Press.

Schirmer, B. R., & Williams, C. (2003). Approaches

to teaching reading. In M. Marschark & P. E. Spencer (Eds.), *Oxford handbook of deaf studies, language, and education* (pp. 110–122). New York: Oxford University Press.

Schlyter, S. (1990). The acquisition of tense and aspect. In J. Meisel (Ed.), *Two first languages: Early grammatical development in bilingual children* (pp. 87–122). Dordrecht, The Netherlands: Foris.

Schmader, T., & Beilock, S. (2012). An integration of processes that underlie stereotype threat. In M. Inzlicht & T. Schmader, *Stereotype threat: Theory, process, and application* (34–47). New York: Oxford University Press.

Schmader, T., Johns, M., & Forbes, C. (2008). An integrated process model of stereotype threat effects on performance. *Psychological Review, 115*(2), 336–356.

Schmeiser, C. B. (1992). Reactions to technical and societal issues in testing Hispanics. In K. F. Geisinger (Ed.), *Psychological testing of Hispanics* (pp. 79–88). Washington, DC: American Psychological Association.

Schmidt, C. R., Ollendick, T. H., & Stanowicz, L. B. (1988). Developmental changes in the influence of assigned goals on cooperative and competition. *Developmental Psychology, 24*, 574–579.

Schmittau, J. (2003). Cultural-historical theory and mathematics education. In A. Kozulin, B. Gindia, V. S. Ageyev, & S. M. Miller (Eds.), *Vygotsky's educational theory in cultural context* (pp. 225–245). Cambridge, UK: Cambridge University Press.

Schneider, W. (2010). Metacognition, and memory development in childhood and adolescence. In H. S. Waters & W. Schneider (Eds.), *Metacognition, strategy use and instruction* (pp. 54–81). New York: Guilford Press.

Schneider, W. (2015). *Memory development from early childhood through emerging adulthood*. Switzerland: Springer.

Schneider, W., & Ornstein, P. A. (2015). The development of children's memory. *Child Development Perspectives, 9*(3), 190–195.

Schneider, W., & Pressley, M. (1997). *Memory development between two and twenty* (2nd ed.). Mahwah, NJ: Erlbaum.

Schneirla, T. C. (1957). The concept of development in developmental psychology. In D. B. Harris (Ed.), *The concept of development: An issue in the study of human behavior* (pp. 78–108). Minneapolis: University of Minnesota Press.

Schoenfeld, A. H. (1992). Learning to think mathematically: Problem solving, metacognition and sense making in mathematics. In D. A. Grouws (Ed.), *Handbook of research on mathematics teaching and learning: A project of the National Council of Teachers of Mathematics*. New York: Macmillan.

Schraw, G., Flowerday, T., & Lehman, S. (2001). Increasing situational interest in the classroom. *Educational Psychology Review, 13*(3), 211–224.

Schraw, G., & Lehman, S. (2001). Situational interest: A review of the literature and directions for future research. *Educational Psychology Review, 13*(1), 23–52.

Schuchardt, K., Gebhardt, M., & Maehler, C. (2010). Working memory functions in children with different degrees of disability. *Journal of Intellectual Disability Research, 54*(4), 346–353.

Schult, C. A. (2002). Children's understanding of the distinction between intentions and desires. *Child Development, 73*(6), 1727–1747.

Schünemann, N., Spörer, N., & Brunstein, J. C. (2013). Integrating self-regulation in whole-class reciprocal teaching: A moderator-mediator analysis of incremental effects on fifth graders' reading comprehension. *Contemporary Educational Psychology, 38*, 289–305.

Schunk, D. H. (1990). Goal setting and self-efficacy during self-regulated learning. *Educational Psychologist, 25*, 71–86.

Schunk, D. H. (1991). Self-efficacy and academic motivation. *Educational Psychologist, 26*, 207–232.

Schunk, D. (2012). Social cognitive theory. In K. Harris, S. Graham, & T. Urdan (Eds.), *APA educational psychology handbook: Vol. 1. Theories, constructs and critical issues* (pp. 101–123). Washington, DC: American Psychological Association.

Schunk, D. H., Hanson, A. R., & Cox, P. D. (1987). Peer-model attributes and children's achievement behaviors. *Journal of Educational Psychology, 79*, 54–61.

Schunk, D. H., & Mullein, C. A. (2013). Motivation. In J. Hattie & E. M. Anderman (Eds.), *International guide to student achievement* (pp. 67–69). New York: Routledge.

Schunk, D. H., & Pajares, F. (2004). Self-efficacy in education revisted: Empirical and applied evidence. In D. M. McInerney & S. Van Etten (Eds.), *Big theories revisited* (pp. 115–138). Greenwich, CT: Information Age.

Schunk, D. H., & Zimmerman, B. J. (2013). Self-regulation and learning. In W. M. Reynolds & G. E. Miller (Eds.), *Handbook of educational psychology* (2nd ed., pp. 45–68). New York: Wiley.

Schwaighofer, M., Fischer, F., & Bühner, M. (2015). Does working memory training transfer?: A meta-analysis including training conditions as moderators. *Educational Psychologist, 50*(2), 136–166.

Schwartz, D., Gorman, A. H., Nakamoto, J., & McKay, T. (2006). Popularity, social acceptance, and aggression in adolescent peer groups: Links with academic performance and school attendance. *Developmental Psychology, 42*(6), 1116–1127.

Schwartz, S. J. (2001). The evolution of Eriksonian

and neo-Eriksonian identity theory and research: A review and integration. *Identity, 1,* 7-58.

Schwartz, S. J., Donnellan, M. B., Ravert, R. D., Luyckx, K., & Zamboanga, B. (2013). Identity development, personality, and well-being in adolescence and emerging adulthood. In R. M. Lerner, M. A. Easterbrooks, & J. Mistry (Eds.), *Handbook of developmental psychology* (2nd ed., pp. 339–364). New York: Wiley.

Scott, C. M. (2004). Syntactic contributions to literacy learning. In C. A. Stone, E. R. Silliman, B. J. Ehren, & K. Apel (Eds.), *Handbook of language and literacy* (pp. 340–362). New York: Guilford Press.

Scribner, S., & Cole, M. (1981). *The psychology of literacy.* Cambridge, MA: Harvard University Press.

Seaton, M., Marsh, H. W., & Craven, R. G. (2010). Big-fish–little-pond effect: Generalizability and moderation-Two sides of the same coin. *American Educational Research Journal, 47*(2), 390–433.

Seidman, E., Allen, L., Aber, J. L., Mitchell, C., & Feinman, J. (1994). The impact of school transitions in early adolescence on the self-system and perceived social context of poor urban youth. *Child Development, 65,* 507–522.

Selfridge, O. G. (1959). Pandemonium: A paradigm for learning. In D. V. Blake & A. M. Uttley (Eds.), *Proceeding of the symposium on the mechanization of thought processes.* London: H. M. Stationery Office.

Seli, H., Dembo, M. H., & Crocker, S. (2009). Self in self-worth protection: The relationship of possible selves and self-protective strategies. *College Student Journal, 43*(3), 832–842.

Sellers, R. M., Smith, M. A., Shelton, J. N., Rowley, S. A. J., & Chavous, T. M. (1998). Multidimensional model of racial identity: A reconceptualization of African American racial identity. *Personality and Social Psychology Review, 2*(1), 18–39.

Selman, R. L. (1976). Socio-cognitive understanding: A guide to educational and clinical practice. In T. Lickona (Ed.), *Moral development and behavior: Theory, research, and social issues* (pp. 299–316). New York: Holt.

Selman, R. L. (1981). The child as a friendship philosopher. In S. R. Asher & J. M. Gottman (Eds.), *The development of children's friendships* (pp. 242–272). New York: Cambridge University Press.

Semrud-Clikeman, M., Walkowiak, J., Wilkinson, A., & Christopher, G. (2010a). Neuropsychological differences among children with Asperger syndrome, nonverbal learning disabilities, attention deficit disorder, and controls. *Developmental Neuropsychology, 35*(5), 582–600.

Semrud-Clikeman, M., Walkowiak, J., Wilkinson, A., & Minnie, E. P. (2010b). Direct and indirect measures of social perception, behavior, and emotional functioning in children with Asperger's disorder, nonverbal learning disability, or ADHD. *Journal of Abnormal Child Psychology, 38,* 509–519.

Senko, C., Hulleman, C. S., & Harackiewicz, J. M. (2011). Achievement and goal theory at the crossroads: Old controversies, current challenges, and new directions. *Educational Psychologist, 46,* 26–47.

Sentse, M., Ormel, J., Veenstra, R., Verhulst, F. C., & Oldehinkel, A. J. (2015). Child temperament moderates the impact of parental separation on adolescent mental health: The TRAILS study. *Journal of Family Psychology, 25*(1), 97–106.

Serenius, F., Källén, K., Blennow, M., Ewald, U., Fellman, V., Holmström, G., et al. (2013). Neurodevelopmental outcome in extremely preterm infants at 2.5 years after active perinatal care in Sweden. *Journal of the American Medical Association, 309*(17), 1810–1820.

Setlik, J., Bond, G. R., & Ho, M. (2009). Adolescent prescription ADHD medication abuse is rising along with prescriptions for these medications. *Pediatrics, 124*(3), 875–880.

Sharp, D., Cole, M., & Lave, C. (1979). Education and cognitive development: The evidence from experimental research. *Monographs of the Society for Research in Child Development, 44*(Serial No. 178).

Shatz, M. (1983). Communication. In J. H. Flavell & E. M. Markman (Eds.), *Handbook of child psychology: Vol. 3. Cognitive development* (4th ed., pp. 841–889). New York: Wiley.

Shatz, M., & Gelman, R. (1973). The development of communication skills: Modification in the speech of young children as a function of listener. *Monographs of the Society for Research in Child Development, 38*(5, Serial No. 152).

Shaywitz, B. A., Weiss, L. G., Saklofske, D. H., & Shaywitz, S. E. (2016). Translating scientific progress in dyslexia into twenty-first century diagnoses and interventions. In L. G. Weiss, D. H. Saklofske, J. A. Holdnack, & A. Prifitera, *WISC-V assessment and interpretation: Scientist-practitioner perspectives. A volume in practical resources for the mental health professional* (pp. 269–286). Amsterdam: Elsevier.

Shaywitz, S. E. (2003). *Overcoming dyslexia: A new and complete science-based program for overcoming reading problems at any level.* New York: Knopf.

Shaywitz, S. E., Mody, M., & Shaywitz, B. A. (2006). Neural mechanisms in dyslexia. *Current Directions in Psychological Science, 15*(6), 278–281.

Shaywitz, S. E., & Shaywitz, B. A. (2004). Neurobiologic basis for reading and reading disability. In P. McCardle & V. Chhabra (Eds.), *The voice of evidence in reading research* (pp. 417–442). Baltimore: Brookes.

Shaywitz, S. E., & Shaywitz, B. A. (2005). Dyslexia (specific reading disability). *Biological Psychiatry, 57,* 1301–1309.

Shaywitz, S. E., & Shaywitz, B. A. (2008). Paying attention to reading: The neurobiology of reading and dyslexia. *Development and Psychopathology, 20,* 1329–1349.

Shaywitz, S. E., & Shaywitz, B. A. (2014). Making a hidden disability visible: What has been learned from neurobiological studies of dyslexia. In L. H. Swanson, K. R. Harris, & S. Graham (Eds.), *Handbook of learning disabilities* (2nd ed., pp. 643–657). New York: Guilford Press.

Shea, D. L., Lubinski, D., & Benbow, C. P. (2001). Importance of assessing spatial ability in intellectually talented young adolescents: A 20-year longitudinal study. *Journal of Educational Psychology, 93,* 604–614.

Sheehan, M. J., & Watson, M. W. (2008). Reciprocal influences between maternal discipline techniques and aggression in children and adolescents. *Aggressive Behavior, 34,* 245–255.

Sheehy, A., Gasser, T., Molinari, L., & Largo, R. H. (1999). An analysis of variance of the pubertal and midgrowth spurts for length and width. *Annals of Human Biology, 26,* 309–331.

Shepard, R. N., & Metzler, J. (1971). Mental rotation of three-dimensional objects. *Science, 171,* 701–703.

Shepard, T. H. (1998). *Catalog of teratogenic agents* (9th ed.). Baltimore: Johns Hopkins University Press.

Sherman, L. J., Rice, K., & Cassidy, J. (2015). Infant capacities related to building internal working models of attachment figures: A theoretical and empirical review. *Developmental Review, 37,* 109–141.

Shi, B., & Xie, H. (2012). Popular and nonpopular subtypes of physically aggressive preadolescence: Continuity of aggression and peer mechanisms during the transition to middle school. *Merrill–Palmer Quarterly, 58*(4), 530–553.

Shiffrin, R. M. (2010). Perspectives on modeling in cognitive science. *Topics in Cognitive Science, 2,* 736–750.

Shirey, L. L., & Reynolds, R. E. (1988). Effect of interest on attention and learning. *Journal of Educational Psychology, 80,* 159–166.

Shiverick, S. M., & Moore, C. F. (2013). Fulfilment of intention and desire in children's judgements of emotion for sociomoral events. *British Journal of Developmental Psychology, 31,* 395–407.

Shonkoff, J. P., & Phillips, D. A. (2000). *From neurons to neighborhoods: The science of early childhood development.* Washington, DC: National Academy Press.

Short, E. J., & Ryan, E. B. (1984). Metacognitive differences between skilled and less skilled readers: Remediating deficits through story grammar and attribution training. *Journal of Educational Psychology, 76,* 225–235.

Shpancer, N. (2006). The effects of daycare: Persistent questions, elusive answers. *Early Childhood Research Quarterly, 21,* 227–237.

Shurkin, J. N. (1992). *Terman's kids: The groundbreaking study of how the gifted grow up.* Boston: Little, Brown.

Sigman, M., Neumann, C., Jansen, A. A. J., & Bwibo, N. (1989). Cognitive abilities of Kenyan children in relation to nutrition, family characteristics, and education. *Child Development, 60,* 1463–1474.

Signorella, M. L., Bigler, R. S., & Liben, L. (1993). Developmental differences in children's gender schemata about others: A meta-analytic review. *Developmental Review, 13,* 106–126.

Signorella, M. L., & Liben, L. S. (1984). Recall and reconstruction of gender-related pictures: Effects of attitude, task difficulty, and age. *Child Development, 55,* 393–405.

Signorielli, N., & Lears, M. (1992). Children, television, and conceptions about chores: Attitudes and behavior. *Sex Roles, 27,* 157–170.

Silver, E. A. (1987). Foundations of cognitive theory and research for mathematics problem solving instruction. In A. Schoenfeld (Ed.), *Cognitive science and mathematics education* (pp. 33–60). Hillsdale, NJ: Erlbaum.

Simmons, R. G., Blyth, D. A., & McKinney, K. L. (1983). The social and psychological effects of puberty on white females. In J. Brooks-Gunn & A. C. Pertersen (Eds.), *Girls at puberty: Biological and psychosocial aspects* (pp. 229–272). New York: Plenum Press.

Simon, D. A. (2013). Spaced and massed practice. In J. Hattie & E. M. Anderman, *International guide to student achievement* (pp. 411–413). New York; Routledge.

Simon, H. A. (1974). How big is a chunk? *Science, 183,* 482–488.

Simpson, J. A., & Belsky, J. (2016). Attachment theory within a modern evolutionary framework. In J. Cassidy & P. R. Shaver (Eds.), *Handbook of attachment: Theory, research, and clinical applications* (pp. 91–116). New York: Guilford Press.

Sims, P. H. M, van Joolingen, W. R., Savelsbergh, E. R., & van Hout-Walters, B. (2008). Motivation and performance in a collaborative computer-based modeling task: Relations between students' achievement goal orientation, self-efficacy, cognitive processing, and achievement. *Contemporary Educational Psychology, 33,* 58–77.

Singer, D., & Singer, J. (2001). *Handbook of children and the media.* Thousand Oaks, CA: SAGE.

Skinner, B. F. (1953). *Science and human behavior.* New York: Free Press.

Skinner, B. F. (1977). Corporal punishment. In I. A. Hyman & J. H. Wise (Eds.), *Corporal punishment in American education* (pp. 335–336). Philadelphia: Temple University Press.

Skinner, E. A., & Belmont, M. J. (1993). Motivation in the classroom: Reciprocal effects of teacher behavior and student engagement across the school year. *Journal of Educational Psychology, 85*, 571–581.

Skuse, D. H. (1984). Extreme deprivation in early childhood: II. Theoretical issues and a comparative review. *Journal of Child Psychology and Psychiatry, 25*, 543–572.

Slaby, R. G., & Frey, K. S. (1975). Development of gender constancy and selective attention to same sex models. *Child Development, 46*, 849–856.

Slaughter, V., Imuta, K., Peterson, C. C., & Henry, J. D. (2015). Meta-analysis of theory of mind and peer popularity in the preschool and early school years. *Child Development, 86*(4), 1159–1174.

Slavin, R. E. (1991). Synthesis of research on cooperative learning. *Educational Leadership*, 71–77.

Slavin, R. (1995). *Cooperative learning*. Boston: Allyn & Bacon.

Slavin, R. E. (2013). Cooperative learning and achievement: Theory and research. In W. M. Reynolds & G. E. Miller (Eds), *Handbook of educational psychology* (2nd ed., pp. 179–198). New York: Wiley.

Slavin, R. E. (2014). Making cooperative learning powerful: Five key practices bring about the tremendous potential of this approach. *Educational Leadership, 72*(2), 22–26.

Slavin, R. E., Karweit, N. L., & Wasik, B. A. (1994). *Preventing early school failure: Research, policy, and practice*. Boston: Allyn & Bacon.

Smelding, A., Dumas, F., Loose, F., & Regner, I. (2013). Order of administration of math and verbal tests: An ecological intervention to reduce stereotype threat on girls' math performance. *Journal of Educational Psychology, 105*(3), 850–860.

Smetana, J. G. (1993). Understanding of social rules. In M. Bennett (Ed.), *The child as psychologist: An introduction to the development of social cognition* (pp. 111–141). New York: Harvester Wheatsheaf.

Smetana, J. G., Jambon, M., Conry-Murray, C., & Sturge-Apple, M. L. (2012). Reciprocal associations between young children's developing moral judgments and theory of mind. *Developmental Psychology, 48*(4), 1144–1155.

Smith, C., & Lloyd, B. (1978). Maternal behavior and perceived sex of infant: Revisited. *Child Development, 49*, 1263–1265.

Smith, C. L., & Tager-Flusberg, H. (1982). Metalinguistic awareness and language development. *Journal of Experimental Child Psychology, 34*, 449–468.

Smith, E. E., & Medin, D. L. (1981). *Categories and concepts*. Cambridge, MA: Harvard University Press.

Smith, G., Spiker, D., Peterson, C., Cicchetti, D., & Justice, P. (1984). Use of megadoses of vitamins with minerals in Down syndrome. *Journal of Pediatrics, 105*, 228–234.

Smith, K. A., Shepley, S. B., Alexander, J. L., & Ayres, K. M. (2015). The independent use of self-instructions for the acquisition of untrained multi-step tasks for individuals with an intellectual disability: A review of the literature. *Research in Developmental Disabilities, 40*, 19–30.

Smith, M. L., & Glass, G. V. (1987). *Research and evaluation in education and the social sciences*. Englewood Cliffs, NJ: Prentice-Hall.

Smith-Hefner, N. J. (1993). Education, gender, and generational conflict among Khmer refugees. *Anthropology and Education Quarterly, 24*, 135–158.

Snarey, J. R. (1985). Cross-cultural universality of social-moral development: A critical review of Kohlbergian research. *Psychological Bulletin, 97*, 202–232.

Sneider, J. T., & Silveri, M. M. (2015). Neurobiology of teen brain development and the digital age. In M. Grabowski (Ed.), *Neuroscience and media: New understandings and representations* (pp. 29–45). New York: Routledge.

Snow, C. E. (2002). Second language learners and understanding the brain. In S. M. Kosslyn & A. M. Galaburda (Eds.), *The languages of the brain* (pp. 151–165). Cambridge, MA: Harvard University Press.

Snow, C. E., Barnes, W. S., Chandler, J., Goodman, I. F., & Hemphill, L. (1991). *Unfulfilled expectations: Home and school influences on literacy*. Cambridge, MA: Harvard University Press.

Snow, C. E., & Hoefnagel-Hohle, M. (1978). The critical period for language acquisition: Evidence from second language learning. *Child Development, 49*, 1114–1128.

Snow, M. E., Jacklin, C. N., & Maccoby, E. E. (1983). Sex-of-child differences in father–child interaction at one year of age. *Child Development, 54*, 227–232.

Snyder, K. E., & Linnenbrink-Garcia, L. (2013). A developmental, person-centered approach to exploring multiple motivational pathways in gifted underachievement. *The Educational Psychologist, 48*(4), 209–228.

Snyder, K. E., Nietfeld, J. L., & Linnenbrink-Garcia, L. (2011). Giftedness and metacognition: A short longitudinal investigation of metacognitive monitoring in the classroom. *Gifted Child Quarterly, 55*(3), 181–193.

Snyder, T. D., & Dillow, S. A. (2012). *Digest of Educational Statistics 2001* (NCES 2012-001). Washington, DC: Center for Education Statistics, Institute of Education Sciences, U.S. Department of Education.

Sodian, B., Licata, M., Kristen-Antonow, S., Paulus, M., Killen, M., & Woodward, A. (2016). Understanding of goals, beliefs, and desires predicts morally relevant theory of mind: A longitudinal investigation. *Child Development, 87*(4), 1221–1232.

Sodian, B., & Schneider, W. (1990). Children's understanding of cognitive cuing: How to manipulate cues to fool a competitor. *Child Development, 61,* 697–704.

Solomon, J., & George, C. (2016). The measurement of attachment security and related constructs in infancy and early childhood. In J. Cassidy & P. R. Shaver (Eds.), *Handbook of attachment: Theory, research, and clinical applications* (pp. 366–389). New York: Guilford Press.

Son, L. K., & Simon, D. A. (2012). Distributed learning: Data, metacognition and educational implications. *Educational Psychology Review, 24,* 379–399.

Sosinsky, L., & Kim, S. (2013). A profile approach to child care quality, quantity, and type of setting: Parent selection of infant child care arrangements. *Applied Developmental Science, 17*(1), 39–56.

Sosinsky, L. S., Lord, H., & Zigler, E. (2007). For-profit/nonprofit differences in center-based child care quality: Results from the National Institute of Child Health and Human Development Study of Early Child Care and Youth Development. *Journal of Applied Developmental Psychology, 28,* 390–410.

Souto-Manning, M. (2009). Acting out and talking back: Negotiating discourses in American early educational settings. *Early Childhood Development and Care, 179*(8), 1083–1094.

Spear, L. P. (2007). Brain development and adolescent behavior. In D. Coch, G. Watson, & K. W. Fischer (Eds.), *Human behavior, learning, and the developing brain: Typical development* (pp. 362–396). New York: Guilford Press.

Spear, L. P. (2010). *The behavioral neuroscience of adolescence.* New York: Norton.

Spear, L. P. (2013). Adolescent neurodevelopment. *Journal of Adolescent Health, 52*(2), S7–S13.

Spearman, C. (1904). "General intelligence" objectively determined and measured. *American Journal of Psychology, 15,* 201–293.

Spence, J. T. (2011). Off with the old, on with the new. *Psychology of Women Quarterly, 35*(3), 504–509.

Spencer, M. B., Dupree, D., Tinsley, B., McGee, E. O., Hall, J., Fegley, S. G., et al. (2012). Resistance and resiliency in a color-conscious society: Implications for learning and teaching. In K. Harris, S. Graham, & T. Urdan (Eds.), *APA educational psychology handbook: Vol. 1. Theories, constructs and critical issues* (pp. 461–494). Washington, DC: American Psychological Association.

Spencer, P. E. (2016). It seems like only yesterday . . . In M. Marshark & P. E. Spencer (Eds.), *The Oxford handbook on deaf studies in language* (pp. 3–18). New York: Oxford University Press.

Spencer, P. E., & Marschark, M. (2003). Cochlear impants: Issues and implications. In M. Marschark & P. E. Spencer (Eds.), *Oxford handbook of deaf studies, language, and education* (pp. 434–448). New York: Oxford University Press.

Spera, C. (2005). A review of the relationship among parenting practices, parenting styles, and adolescent school achievement. *Educational Psychology Review, 17*(2), 125–146.

Spiegel, H. M. L., & Bonwit, A. M. (2002). HIV infection in children. In M. L. Batshaw (Ed.), *Children with disabilities* (5th ed., pp. 123–139). Baltimore: Brookes.

Spies Shapiro, L. A., & Margolin, G. (2014). Growing up wired: Social networking sites and adolescent psychosocial development. *Clinical Child and Family Psychology Review, 17,* 1–18.

Spitz, H. H. (1986). Preventing and curing mental retardation by behavioral intervention: An evaluation of some claims. *Intelligence, 10,* 197–207.

Spitz, H. H. (1991). Commentary on Locurto's "Beyond IQ in preschool programs?" *Intelligence, 15,* 327–334.

Spitz, H. H. (1992). Does the Carolina Abecedarian Early Intervention Project prevent sociocultural mental retardation? *Intelligence, 16,* 225–237.

Spörer, N., Brunstein, J. C., & Kieschke, U. (2009). Improving students' reading comprehension: Effects of strategy instruction and reciprocal teaching. *Learning and Instruction, 19,* 272–286.

Springer, S. P., & Deutsch, G. (1989). *Left brain, right brain* (3rd ed.). New York: Freeman.

Squire, L. R. (1992). Memory and hippocampus: A synthesis from findings with rats, monkeys and humans. *Psychological Review, 99*(2), 195–231.

Squire, L. R. (2004). Memory systems of the brain: A brief history and current perspective. *Neurobiology of Learning and Memory, 82*(3), 171–177.

Srinivas, S. K., Epstein, A. J., Nicholson, S., Herrin, J., & Asch, D. A. (2010). Improvements in US maternal obstetrical outcomes from 1992 to 2006. *Medical Care, 48*(5), 487–493.

Sroufe, L. A. (2016). The place of attachment in development. In J. Cassidy & P. R. Shaver (Eds.), *Handbook of attachment: Theory, research, and clinical applications* (pp. 997–1011). New York: Guilford Press.

Sroufe, L. A., Carlson, E., & Schulman, S. (1993). Individuals in relationships: Development from infancy through adolescence. In D. C. Funder, R. D. Parke, C. Tomlinson-Keasey, & K. Widaman (Eds.), *Studying lives through time: Personality and development* (pp. 315–342). Washington, DC: American Psychological Association.

Stabler, F., Dumont, H., Becker, M., & Baumert, J. (2017). What happens to the fish's achievement in a little pond?: A simultaneous analysis of class-average achievement effects on achievement and academic self-concept. *Journal of Educational Psychology, 109*(2), 191–207.

Stanovich, K. E. (1986). Matthew effects in reading: Some consequences of individual differences in the acquisition of literacy. *Reading Research Quarterly, 21,* 360–407.

Stanovich, K. E. (1988). Explaining the differences between the dyslexic and the garden-variety poor reader: The phonological–core variable-difference model. *Journal of Learning Disabilities, 21,* 590–604.

Stanovich, K. E., & Cunningham, A. E. (1993). Where does knowledge come from: Specific associations between print exposure and information acquisition. *Journal of Educational Psychology, 85,* 211–229.

Starr, C. R., & Zurbriggen, E. L. (2017). Sandra Bem's schema theory after 34 years: A review of its reach and impact. *Sex Roles, 76*(9–10), 566–578.

Steele, C. M. (2004). Through the back door to theory. *Psychological Inquiry, 14,* 314–317.

Steele, C. M., & Aronson, J. (1995). Stereotype threat and the intellectual test performance of African Americans. *Journal of Personality and Social Psychology, 69,* 797–811.

Steele, C. M., & Aronson, J. (2004). Stereotype threat does not live by Steele and Aronson (1995) alone. *American Psychologist, 59,* 47–48.

Steele, J. L., Slater, R. O., Zamarro, G., Miller, T., Li, J., Burhauser, S., & Bacon, M. (2017). Effects of dual-language immersion programs on student achievement: Evidence from lottery data. *American Educational Research Journal, 54*(1), 282S–306S.

Steenbergen-Hu, S., & Cooper, H. (2013). A meta-analysis of the effectiveness of intelligent tutoring systems on K–12 students' mathematical learning. *Journal of Educational Psychology, 105,* 970–987.

Steenbergen-Hu, S., & Cooper, H. (2014). A meta-analysis of the effectiveness of intelligent tutoring systems on college students' academic learning. *Journal of Educational Psychology, 106*(2), 331–347.

Stein, J., Schettler, T., Wallinga, D., & Valenti, M. (2002). In harm's way: Toxic threats to child development. *Journal of Developmental and Behavioral Pediatrics, 23,* 13–22.

Stein, N. L., & Glenn, C. G. (1979). An analysis of story comprehension in elementary school children. In R. O. Freedle (Ed.), *New directions in discourse processing* (Vol. 2, pp. 53–120). Norwood, NJ: Ablex.

Stein, N. L., & Nezworski, G. (1978). The effects of organization and instructional set on story memory. *Discourse Processes, 1,* 177–193.

Steinberg, L. (1997). *You and your adolescent, Revised edition: A parent's guide for ages 10–20.* New York: HarperResource.

Steinberg, L. (2001). We know some things: Parent–adolescent relationships in retrospect and prospect. *Journal of Research on Adolescence, 11,* 1–19.

Steinberg, L. (2010). Commentary: A behavioral scientist looks at the science of adolescent brain development. *Brain and Cognition, 72*(1), 160–164.

Steinberg, L. (2014). *Age of opportunity: Lessons from the new science of adolescence.* New York: Houghton, Mifflin, Harcourt.

Steiner, H. H., & Carr, M. (2003). Cognitive development in gifted children: Toward a more precise understanding of emerging differences in intelligence. *Educational Psychology Review, 15,* 215–246.

Steinhauer, K. (2014). Event-related potentials in second language research: A brief introduction to the technique, a selected review, and an invitation to reconsider critical periods in L2. *Applied Linguistics, 35*(4), 393–417.

Stern, J. (1985). Biochemical aspects. In A. M. Clarke, A. D. B. Clarke, & J. M. Berg (Eds.), *Mental deficiency: The changing outlook* (pp. 135–212). New York: Free Press.

Stern, M., & Karraker, K. H. (1989). Sex stereotyping of infants: A review of gender labeling studies. *Sex Roles, 20,* 501–522.

Sternberg, R. J. (1981). A componential theory of intellectual giftedness. *Gifted Child Quarterly, 25,* 86–93.

Sternberg, R. J. (1985). *Beyond IQ: A triarchic theory of human intelligence.* Cambridge, UK: Cambridge University Press.

Sternberg, R. J. (1987). Most vocabulary is learned from context. In M. G. McKeown & M. E. Curtis (Eds.), *The nature of vocabulary acquisition* (pp. 89–105). Hillsdale, NJ: Erlbaum.

Sternberg, R. J. (1994). *Encyclopedia of human intelligence.* New York: Macmillan.

Sternberg, R. J. (2013). Contemporary theories of intelligence. In W. M. Reynolds & G. E. Miller (Eds.), *Handbook of educational psychology* (2nd ed., pp. 23–44). New York: Wiley.

Sternberg, R. J., & Davidson, J. E. (1983). Insight in the gifted. *Educational Psychologist, 18,* 51–57.

Sternberg, R. J., & Detterman, D. K. (Eds.). (1986). *What is intelligence?: Contemporary viewpoints on its nature and definition.* Norwood, NJ: Ablex.

Sternberg, R. J., Grigorenko, E. L., & Kidd, K. K. (2005). Intelligence, race and genetics. *American Psychologist, 60*(1), 46–59.

Sternberg, R. J., Jarvin, L., Birney, D. P., Naples, A., Stemler, S. E., Newman, T., et al. (2014). Testing the theory of successful intelligence in teaching grade 4 language arts, mathematics, and science. *Journal of Educational Psychology, 106*(3), 881–899.

Sternberg, R. J., & Powell, J. S. (1983). Comprehending verbal comprehension. *American Psychologist, 38,* 878–893.

Stevens, L. J., & Price, M. (1992). Meeting the challenges of educating children at risk. *Phi Delta Kappan, 74,* 18–23.

Stevenson-Hinde, J., & Shouldice, A. (1995). Maternal

interactions and self-reports related to attachment classifications at 4.5 years. *Child Development, 66,* 583–596.

Stewart, K. (2007). *Helping a child with nonverbal learning disorder or Asperger's disorder: A parent's guide.* Oakland, CA: New Harbinger.

Stice, E., Presnell, K., & Bearman, S. K. (2001). Relation of early menarche to depression, eating disorders, substance abuse, and comorbid psychopathology among adolescent girls. *Developmental Psychology, 37*(5), 608–619.

Stieff, M., Dixon, B. L., Ryu, M., Kumi, B., & Hegarty, M. (2014). Strategy training eliminates sex differences in spatial problem solving in a STEM domain. *Journal of Educational Psychology, 106*(2), 390–402.

Stiles, J., Brown, T. T., Haist, F., & Jernigan, T. L. (2015). Brain and cognitive development. In R. M. Lerner (Series Ed.) & L. Liben & U. Müller (Vol. Eds.), *Handbook of child psychology and developmental science: Vol. 2. Cognitive processes* (7th ed., pp. 9–62). New York: Wiley.

Stipek, D. J., & Daniels, D. H. (1988). Declining perceptions of competence: A consequence of changes in the child or in the educational environment? *Journal of Educational Psychology, 80,* 352–356.

Stipek, D. J., & Gralinski, J. H. (1991). Gender differences in children's achievement-related beliefs and emotional responses to success and failure in mathematics. *Journal of Educational Psychology, 83,* 361–371.

Stipek, D. J., & Hoffman, J. M. (1980). Children's achievement-related expectancies as a function of academic performance histories and sex. *Journal of Educational Psychology, 72,* 861–865.

Stipek, D., & MacIver, D. (1989). Developmental change in children's assessment of intellectual competence. *Child Development, 60,* 521–538.

Storfer, M. D. (1990). *Intelligence and giftedness: The contributions of heredity and early environment.* San Francisco: Jossey-Bass.

Stormshak, E. A., Bullock, B. M., & Falkenstein, C. A. (2009). Harnessing the power of sibling relationships as a tool for optimizing social-emotional development. In L. Kramer & K. J. Conger (Eds.), *Siblings as agents of socialization. New directions for child and adolescent development* (Vol. 126, pp. 61–77). San Francisco: Jossey-Bass.

Strange, W., & Jenkins, J. (1978). Role of linguistic experience in the perception of speech. In R. D. Walk & H. L. Pick (Eds.), *Perception and experience.* New York: Plenum Press.

Strauss, A. L., & Corbin, J. (1998). *Basics of qualitative research: Techniques and procedures for developing grounded theories* (2nd ed.). Thousand Oaks, CA: SAGE.

Strauss, M. S. (1979). Abstraction of prototypical information by adults and 10-month-olds. *Journal of Experimental Psychology: Human Learning and Memory, 5,* 618–632.

Strazdins, L., Obrien, L. V., Lucas, N., & Rodgers, B. (2013). Combining work and family: Rewards or risks for children's mental health. *Social Science and Medicine, 87,* 99–107.

Streeck, J., & Mehus, S. (2005). Microethnography: The study of practices. In K. L. Fitch & R. E. Sanders (Eds.), *Handbook of language and social interaction* (pp. 381–404). Mahwah, NJ: Erlbaum.

Stromswold, K. (1995). The cognitive and neural bases of language acquisition. In M. S. Gazzaniga (Ed.), *The cognitive neurosciences* (pp. 855–870). Cambridge, MA: MIT Press.

Stromswold, K. (1998). The genetics of spoken language disorders. *Human Biology, 70,* 297–324.

Stromswold, K. (2001). The heritability of language: A review and metaanalysis of twin, adoption, and linkage studies. *Language, 77*(4), 647–723.

Stronach, I., & Piper, H. (2008). Can liberal education make a comeback?: The case of "relational touch" at Summerhill school. *American Educational Research Journal, 45*(1), 6–37.

Stuart, M., & Masterson, J. (1992). Patterns of reading and spelling in 10-year old children related to prereading phonological abilities. *Journal of Experimental Child Psychology, 54,* 168–187.

Su, R., Rounds, J., & Armstrong, P. I. (2009). Men and things, women and people: A meta-analysis of sex differences in interests. *Psychological Bulletin, 135*(6), 859–884.

Sugarman, S. (1983). *Children's early thought: Developments in classification.* Cambridge, MA: Cambridge University Press.

Sulloway, F. J. (1992). *Freud: Biologist of the mind.* Cambridge, MA: Harvard University Press.

Sun, Y., & Li, Y. (2009). Postdivorce family stability and changes in adolescents' academic performance: A growth curve model. *Journal of Family Issues, 30*(11), 1527–1555.

Sussman, S., Pokhrel, P., Ashmore, R. D., & Brown, B. B. (2007). Adolescent peer group identification and characteristics: A review of the literature. *Addictive Behaviors, 32,* 1602–1627.

Swain, M., & Lapkin, S. (1982). *Evaluating bilingual education: A Canadian case study.* Clevedon, UK: Multilingual Matters.

Swain, M., & Wesche, M. (1973). Linguistic interaction: Case study of a bilingual child. *Working Papers on Bilingualism, 1,* 10–34.

Swaminathan, N. (2007). Fact or fiction: Babies exposed to classical music end up smarter. *Scientific American Online.*

Swanson, H. L. (2003). Age-related differences in learning disabled and skilled readers' working memory. *Journal of Experimental Child Psychology, 85*, 1–31.

Swanson, H. L. (2014). Does cognitive strategy training on word problems compensate for working memory capacity in children with math difficulties? *Journal of Educational Psychology, 106*(3), 831–848.

Swanson, H. L. (2016). Cognition and cognitive disabilities. In L. Corno & E. M. Anderman (Eds.), *Handbook of educational psychology* (3rd ed., pp. 135–145). New York: Routledge.

Swanson, H. L., & Alloway, T. P. (2012). Working memory, learning, and academic achievement. In K. Harris, S. Graham, & T. Urdan (Eds.), *APA educational psychology handbook: Vol. 1. Theories, constructs and critical issues* (pp. 327–365). Washington, DC: American Psychological Association.

Swanson, H. L., & Fung, W. (2016). Working memory components and problem-solving accuracy: Are there multiple pathways. *Journal of Educational Psychology, 108*(8), 1153–1177.

Swanson, H. L., & Hsieh, C. J. (2009). Reading disabilities in adults: A selective meta-analysis of the literature. *Review of Educational Research, 79*(4), 1362–1390.

Swanson, H. L., & Sáez, L. (2003). Memory difficulties in children and adults with learning disabilities. In H. L. Swanson, K. R. Harris, & S. Graham (Eds.), *Handbook of learning disabilities* (pp. 182–198). New York: Guilford Press.

Sweller, J. (2009). What human cognitive architecture tells us about constructivism. In S. Tobias & T. M. Duffy (Eds.), *Constructivist instruction: Success or failure?* (pp. 127–143). New York: Routledge.

Sweller, J. (2016). Working memory, long-term memory, and instructional design. *Journal of Applied Research in Memory and Cognition, 5*(4), 360–367.

Symons, D., Clark, S., Isaksen, G., & Marshall, J. (1998). Stability of Q-sort attachment security from age two to five. *Infant Behavior and Development, 21*, 785–791.

Tamis-LeMonda, C. S., Bornstein, M. H., Kahana-Kalman, R., Baumwell, L., & Cyphers, L. (1998). Predicting variation in the timing of linguistic milestones in the second year: An event-history approach. *Journal of Child Language, 28*, 127–152.

Tamis-LeMonda, C. S., & Song, L. (2013). Parent–infant communicative interactions in cultural context. In R. M. Lerner, M. A. Easterbrooks, & J. Mistry (Eds.), *Handbook of developmental psychology* (2nd ed., pp. 143–170). New York: Wiley.

Tang, S., & Davis-Kean, P. E. (2015). The association of punitive parenting practices and adolescent achievement. *Journal of Family Psychology, 29*(6), 873–883.

Tannen, D. (1990). *You just don't understand: Women and men in conversation.* New York: Macmillan.

Tannenbaum, A. J. (1983). *Gifted children: Psychological and educational perspectives.* New York: Macmillan.

Tannenbaum, A. J. (1986). Giftedness: A psychosocial approach. In R. J. Sternberg & J. E. Davidson (Eds.), *Conceptions of giftedness* (pp. 21–52). Cambridge, UK: Cambridge University Press.

Tappan, M. B. (1998). Sociocultural psychology and caring pedagogy: Exploring Vygotsky's "hidden curriculum." *Educational Psychologist, 33*, 23–33.

Tarver, S. G., Hallahan, D. P., Kauffman, J. M., & Ball, D. W. (1976). Verbal rehearsal and selective attention in children with learning disabilities: A developmental lag. *Journal of Experimental Child Psychology, 22*, 375–385.

Tashakkori, A., & Teddlie, C. (Eds.). (2003). *Handbook of mixed methods in social and behavioral sciences.* Thousand Oaks, CA: SAGE.

Tavris, C., & Wade, C. (1984). *The longest war: Sex differences in perspective* (2nd ed.). San Diego, CA: Harcourt, Brace, Jovanovich.

Taylor, G. H., Klein, N., & Hack, M. (2000). School-age consequences of birth weight less than 750 g: A review and update. *Developmental Neuropsychology, 17*, 289–321.

Tepper, C. A., & Cassidy, K. W. (1999). Gender differences in emotional language in children's picture books. *Sex Roles, 40*, 265–280.

Terman, L. M. (1925). *Genetic studies of genius: Mental and physical traits of a thousand gifted children.* Stanford, CA: Stanford University Press.

Terman, L. M., & Childs, H. G. (1912). A tentative revision and extension of the Binet–Simon Measuring Scale of Intelligence. *Journal of Educational Psychology, 3*, 61–74, 133–143, 198–208, 277–289.

Terman, L. M., & Oden, M. H. (1947). *The gifted child grows up: Twenty-five years' followup of a superior group.* Stanford, CA: Stanford University Press.

Terman, L. M., & Oden, M. H. (1959). *The gifted group in midlife: Thirty years followup of the superior child.* Stanford, CA: Stanford University Press.

Tharp, R. G. (1982). The effective instruction of comprehension: Results and description of the Kamehameha Early Education Program. *Reading Research Quarterly, 27*, 503–527.

Tharp, R. G., & Gallimore, R. (1988). *Rousing minds to life: Teaching, learning, and schooling in social context.* New York: Cambridge University Press.

Thomas, A. (2017). Gender differences in students' physical science motivation: Are teachers' implicit cognitions another piece of the puzzle? *American Educational Research Journal, 54*(1), 35–58.

Thomas, A., & Chess, S. (1977). *Temperament and development.* New York: Brunner/Mazel.

Thomas, J. R. (1984). Children's motor skill development. In J. R. Thomas (Ed.), *Motor development during childhood and adolescence* (pp. 91–104). Minneapolis, MN: Burges.

Thomas, J. R., & French, K. E. (1985). Gender differences across age in motor performance: A meta-analysis. *Psychological Bulletin, 98,* 260–282.

Thomas, M. S. (2003). Essay review: Limits on plasticity. *Journal of Cognition and Development, 4*(1), 99–125.

Thompson, R. A. (2016). Early attachment and later development: Familiar questions, new answers. In J. Cassidy & P. R. Shaver (Eds.), *Handbook of attachment: Theory, research, and clinical applications* (pp. 330–348). New York: Guilford Press.

Thompson, S. K., & Bentler, P. M. (1971). The priority of cues in sex discrimination by children and adults. *Developmental Psychology, 5,* 181–185.

Thyer, B. A., & Myers, L. L. (1998). Social learning theory: An empirically-based approach to understanding human behavior in the social environment. *Journal of Human Behavior in the Social Environment, 1,* 33–52.

Tobias, S., & Duffy, T. M. (2009). *Constructivist instruction: Success or failure?* New York: Routledge.

Todorov, T. (1984). *Mikhail Bakhtin: The dialogical principle.* Minneapolis: University of Minnesota Press.

Tomasello, M. (1994). Can an ape understand a sentence?: A review of *Language comprehension in ape and child,* by E. S. Savage-Rumsbaugh et al. *Language and Communication, 14,* 377–390.

Tomasello, M. (2000). Do young children have adult syntactic competence? *Cognition, 74,* 209–253.

Tomasello, M. (2003). *Constructing a language: A usage-based theory of language acquisition.* Cambridge, MA: Harvard University Press.

Tomasello, M., & Farrar, M. J. (1986). Joint attention and early language. *Child Development, 57,* 1454–1463.

Tomasello, M., & Mannle, S. (1985). Pragmatics of sibling speech to one-year-olds. *Child Development, 56,* 911–917.

Tomasello, M., & Todd, J. (1983). Joint attention and lexical acquisition style. *First Language, 4,* 197–212.

Tomasetto, C., Mirisola, A., Galdi, S., & Cadinu, M. (2015). Parents' math gender stereotypes, children's self-perceptions, and children's appraisal of parents evaluations in 6 year olds. *Contemporary Educational Psychology, 42,* 186–198.

Tombu, M. N., Asplund, C. L., Dux, P. E., Godwin, D., Martin, J. W., & Marois, R. (2011). A unified attentional bottleneck in the human brain. *Proceedings of the National Academy of Sciences, 108*(33), 13426–13431.

Toomey, R. B., Ryan, C., Diaz, R. M., Card, N. A., & Russell, S. T. (2010). Gender-noncomforming, lesbian, gay, bisexual, and transgender youth: School victimization and young adult psychosocial development. *Developmental Psychology, 46*(6), 1580–1589.

Topping, K., Dekhinet, R., & Zeedyk, S. (2011). Hindrances for parents in enhancing child language. *Educational Psychology Review, 23,* 413–455.

Topping, K., Dekhinet, R., & Zeedyk, S. (2013). Parent–infant interaction and children's language development. *Educational Psychology, 33,* 391–426.

Toppino, T. C., Kasserman, J. E., & Mracek, W. A. (1991). The effect of spacing repetitions on the recognition memory of young children and adults. *Journal of Experimental Child Psychology, 51,* 123–138.

Torgesen, J. K. (1975). Problems and prospects in the study of learning disabilities. In M. Hetherington & J. Hagen (Eds.), *Review of research in child development* (Vol. 5, pp. 385–440). Chicago: University of Chicago Press.

Torgesen, J. K. (1977). Memorization processes in reading-disabled children. *Journal of Educational Psychology, 69,* 571–578.

Torgesen, J. K., & Goldman, T. (1977). Verbal rehearsal and short-term memory in reading disabled children. *Child Development, 48,* 56–60.

Tosto, M. G., Hanscombe, K. B., Haworth, C. M. A., Davis, O. S. P., Petrill, S. A., Dale, P. S., et al. (2014). Why do spatial abilities predict mathematics performance? *Developmental Science, 17*(3), 462–470.

Trautwein, U., & Köller, O. (2003). The relationship between homework and achievement: Still much of a mystery. *Educational Psychology Review, 15,* 115–145.

Troia, G. A. (2004). Phonological processing and its influence on literacy learning. In C. A. Stone, E. R. Silliman, B. J. Ehren, & K. Apel (Eds.), *Handbook of language and literacy* (pp. 271–301). New York: Guilford Press.

Trousdale, K., Martin, J., Abulafia, L., Barnett, C., & Westinghouse, C. (2010). Children's environmenal health: The school environment. *Intellectual and Developmental Disabilities, 48*(2), 135–144.

Tsao, F. M., Liu, H. M., & Kuhl, P. K. (2004). Speech perception in infancy predicts language development in the second year of life: A longitudinal study. *Child Development, 75,* 1067–1084.

Tsitsika, A. K., Tzavela, E. C., Janikian, M., Ólafsson, K., Iordache, A., Schoenmakers, T. M., et al. (2014). Online social networking in adolescence: Patterns of use in six European countries and links with psychological functioning. *Journal of Adolescent Health, 55,* 141–147.

Tucker, C. J., & Updegraf, K. (2009). The relative contributions of parent and siblings to child and adolescent development. In L. Kramer & K. J. Conger (Eds.), *Siblings as agents of socialization. New directions for child and adolescent development* (Vol. 126, pp. 13–28). San Francisco: Jossey-Bass.

Tucker-Drob, E. M., & Bates, T. C. (2016). Large cross-national differences in gene × socioeconomic status interaction on intelligence. *Psychological Science, 27*(2), 138–149.

Tulving, E. (1983). *Elements of episodic memory.* Oxford, UK: Oxford University Press.

Tunmer, W. E., & Arrow, A. W. (2013). Reading: Phonics instruction. In J. Hattie & E. M. Anderman (Eds.), *International guide to student achievement* (pp. 316–319). New York: Routledge.

Turati, C., Valenza, E., Leo, I., & Simion, F. (2005). Three-month-olds' visual preference for faces and its underlying visual processing mechanisms. *Journal of Experimental Child Psychology, 90*(3), 255–273.

Turiel, E. (2015). Moral development. In R. M. Lerner, W. F. Overton, & P. C. M. Molenaar (Eds.), *Handbook of child psychology and developmental science: Vol. 1. Theory and method* (7th ed., pp. 1–39). Hoboken, NJ: Wiley.

Turner, J. C., Christensen, A., Kackar-Cam, H. Z., Trucano, M., & Fulner, S. M. (2014). Enhancing students' engagement: Report of a 3-year intervention with middle school teachers. *American Educational Research Journal, 51*(6), 1195–1226.

Turner, J. C., Midgley, C., Meyer, D. K., Gheen, M., Anderman, E. M., Kang, Y., et al. (2002). The classroom environment and students' reports of avoidance strategies in mathematics: A multimethod study. *Journal of Educational Psychology, 94*, 88–106.

Turner, P. J., & Gervai, J. (1995). A multidimensional study of gender typing in preschool children and their parents: Personality, attitudes, preferences, behavior, and cultural differences. *Developmental Psychology, 31*, 759–772.

Turner-Bowker, D. M. (1996). Gender stereotyped descriptions in children's picture books: Does "Curious Jane" exist in literature? *Sex Roles, 35*, 461–488.

Tuss, P., Zimmer, J., & Ho, H. Z. (1995). Causal attributions of underachieving fourth grade students in China, Japan, and the United States. *Journal of Cross-Cultural Psychology, 26*, 408–425.

Twenge, J. M. (2011). Generational differences in mental health: Are children and adolescents suffering more, or less? *American Journal of Orthopsychiatry, 81*(4), 469–472.

Tychsen, L. (2001). Critical periods for development of visual acuity, depth perception, and eye tracking. In J. B. Bailey Jr., J. T. Bruer, F. J. Symons, & J. W. Lichtman (Eds.), *Critical thinking about critical periods* (pp. 67–80). Baltimore: Brookes.

Tyson, P., & Tyson, R. L. (1990). *Psychoanalytic theories of development.* New Haven, CT: Yale University Press.

Umaña-Taylor, A. J., Quintana, S. M., Lee, R. M., Cross, W. E., Rivas-Drake, D., Schwartz, S. J., et al. (2014). Ethnic and racial identity during adolescence and adulthood. *Child Development, 85*(1), 21–39.

Uncapher, M. R., Thieu, M. K., & Wagner, A. D. (2016). Media multitasking and memory: Differences in working memory and long-term memory. *Psychonomic Bulletin and Review, 23*(2), 483–490.

Underwood, M. K. (2002). Sticks and stones and social exclusion: Aggression among girls and boys. In P. K. Smith & C. H. Hart (Eds.), *Blackwell handbook of childhood social development* (pp. 533–548). Oxford, UK: Blackwell.

Underwood, M., & Ehrenreich, S. E. (2017). The power and the pain of adolescents' digital communication: Cyber victimization and the perils of lurking. *The American Psychologist, 72*, 144–158.

Underwood, M. K., Schockner, A. E., & Hurley, J. C. (2001). Children's responses to same- and other-gender peers: An experimental investigation with 8-, 10-, and 12-year-olds. *Developmental Psychology, 37*, 262–272.

United Nations Office of the High Commissioner for Human Rights. (1989). Convention on the Rights of the Child. Available from *www.ohchr.org/EN/ProfessionalInterest/Pages/CRC.aspx.*

United States of America v. State of South Carolina, 434 U.S. 1026 (1978).

Urdan, T. (2012). Factors affecting the motivation and achievement of immigrant students. In K. Harris, S. Graham, & T. Urdan (Eds.), *APA educational psychology handbook: Vol. 2. Individual differences and cultural and contextual factors* (pp. 293–313). Washington, DC: American Psychological Association.

Urdan, T., & Midgley, C. (2001). Academic self-handicapping: What we know, what more there is to learn. *Educational Psychology Review, 13*(2), 115–138.

Urdan, T., & Midgley, C. (2003). Changes in the perceived classroom goal structure and pattern of adaptive learning during early adolescence. *Contemporary Educational Psychology, 28*(4), 524–551.

U.S. Census Bureau. (2014). Young adults then and now: American Community Survey. 2009–2013. Available from *http://nces.ed.gov/programs/coe/indicator_cgf.asp.*

U.S. Department of Health and Human Services, Administration for Children and Families, Administration on Children, Youth and Families, Children's Bureau. (2013). *Child maltreatment 2012.* Available from *http://www.acf.hhs.gov/programs/cb/research-data-technology/statistics-research/child-maltreatment.*

U.S. Department of Labor, Bureau of Labor Statistics. (2017). *The Economics Daily*, Women in architecture and engineering occupations in 2016. Retrieved January 19, 2018, from *https://www.bls.*

gov/opub/ted/2017/women-in-architecture-and-engineering-occupations-in-2016.htm.

Usher, E. L. (2016). Personal capacity beliefs. In L. Corno & E. M. Anderman (Eds.), *Handbook of educational psychology* (3rd ed., pp. 146–159). New York: Routledge.

Usher, E. L., & Pajares, F. (2008). Sources of self-efficacy in school: Critical review of the literature and future directions. *Review of Educational Research, 78*(4), 751–796.

Uttal, D. H., Meadow, N. G., Tipton, E., Hand. L. L., Alden, A. R., Warren, C., et al. (2013). The malleability of spatial skills: A meta-analysis of training studies. *Psychological Bulletin, 139*, 352–402.

Valdez-Menchaca, M. C., & Whitehurst, G. J. (1992). Accelerating language development through picture book reading: A systematic extension to Mexican day care. *Developmental Psychology, 28*, 1106–1114.

Valencia, R. R., & Suzuki, L. A. (2001). *Intelligence testing and minority students: Foundation, performance factors, and assessment issues.* Thousand Oaks, CA: SAGE.

Valent, J., & Newark, D. A. (2016). The politics of achievement gaps: U.S. public opinion on race-based and wealth-based differences in test scores. *Educational Researcher, 45*(6), 331–346.

Valkenburg, P. M., & Peter, J. (2011). Online communication among adolescents: An integrated model of its attraction, opportunities, and risks. *Journal of Adolescent Health, 48*, 121–127.

van Daalen-Kapteijns, M. M., & Elshout-Mohr, M. (1981). The acquisition of word meanings as a cognitive learning process. *Journal of Verbal Learning and Verbal Behavior, 20*, 386–389.

van Dellen, M. R., & Hoyle, R. H. (2008). Possible selves as behavioral standards in self-regulation. *Self and Identity, 7*(3), 295–304.

Van Laar, C. (2000). The paradox of low achievement but high self-esteem in African-American students: An attributional account. *Educational Psychology Review, 12*, 33–61.

van Loon, M. H., Dunlosky, J., van Gog, T., van Merriënboer, J. J. G., & De Bruin, A. B. H. (2015). Refutations in science texts lead to hypercorrection of misconceptions held with high confidence. *Contemporary Educational Psychology, 41*, 39–48.

Van Merrienboer, J. J., & Sweller, J. (2005). Cognitive load theory and complex learning: Recent developments and future directions. *Educational Psychology Review, 17*(2), 147–177.

Van Ness, H. (1981). Social control and social organization in an Alaskan Athabaskan classroom: A microethngraphy of "getting ready" for reading. In H. Trueba, G. Guthrie, & K. Au (Eds.), *Culture and the bilingual classroom* (pp. 120–138). Rowley, MA: Newbury House.

Vance, Y. H., & Eiser, C. (2002). The school experience of the child with cancer. *Child Care, Health and Development, 28*, 5–19.

Vandell, D. L., Burchinal, M., & Pierce, K. M. (2016). Child care and adolescent functioning at the end of high school: Results from the NICDH study of early child care and youth development. *Developmental Psychology, 52*(10), 1634–1654.

Vandell, D. L., Burchinal, M., Vandergrift, N., Belsky, J., Steinberg, L., & the NICHD Early Child Care Research Network. (2010). Do effects of early child care extend to age 15 years?: Results from the NICHD Study of Early Child Care and Youth Development. *Child Development, 81*(3), 737–756.

Vandermosten, M., Boets, B., Wouters, J., & Ghesquière, P. (2012). A qualitative and quantitative review of diffusion tensor imaging studies in reading and dyslexia. *Neuroscience and Biobehavioral Reviews, 36*(6), 1532–1552.

Vargo, F. E. (2015). *Neurodevelopmental disorders: A definitive guide for educators.* New York: Norton.

Vaughn, B. E., & Bost, K. K., (2016). Attachment and temperament as intersecting developmental products and interacting developmental contexts throughout infancy and childhood. In J. Cassidy & P. R. Shaver (Eds.), *Handbook of attachment: Theory, research, and clinical applications* (3rd ed., pp. 202–222). New York: Guilford Press.

Vellutino, F. R., & Fletcher, J. M. (2005). Developmental dyslexia. In M. J. Snowling & C. Hulme (Eds.), *The science of reading: A handbook* (pp. 362–378). Malden, MA: Blackwell.

Venta, A., Schmueli-Goetz, Y., & Sharp, C. (2014). Assessing attachment in adolescence: A psychometric study of the child attachment interview. *Psychological Assessment, 26*(1), 238–255.

Vernon, P. A. (1991). Studying intelligence the hard way. *Intelligence, 15*, 389–395.

Verschueren, K., & Koomen, H. M. Y. (2012). Teacher–child relationships from an attachment perspective. *Attachment and Human Development, 14*(3), 205–211.

Vetter, A. (2013). "You need some laugh bones!": Leveraging AAL in a high school English class. *Journal of Literacy Research, 45*(2), 173–206.

Vieira, J. M., Matias, M., Ferriera, T., Lopez, F. G., & Matos, P. M. (2016). Parents' work-family experiences and children's problem behaviors: The mediating role of parent-child relationship. *Journal of Family Psychology, 30*(4), 419–430.

Vihman, M. M. (1992). Early syllables and the construction of phonology. In C. A. Ferguson, L. Menn, & C. Stoel-Gammon (Eds.), *Phonological development: Models, research, and implications* (pp. 393–422). Timonium, MD: York Press.

Vilain, E. (2006). Genetics of intersexuality. *Journal of Gay and Lesbian Psychotherapy, 10*(2), 9–26.

Visser, S. N., Danielson, M. L., Bitsko, R. H.,

Holbrook, J. R., Kogan, M. D., Ghandour, R. M., et al. (2014). Trends in the parent-report of health care provider-diagnosed and medicated attention-deficit/hyperactivity disorder: United States, 2003–2011. *Journal of the American Academy of Child and Adolescent Psychiatry, 53*(1), 34–46.

Vitaro, F., Boivan, M., & Bukowski, W. M. (2009). The role of friendship in child and adolescent psychosocial development. In K. H. Rubin, W. M. Bukowski, & B. Laursen (Eds.), *Handbook of peer interactions, relationships, and groups* (pp. 568–585). New York: Guilford Press.

Volling, B. L. (2012). Family transitions following the birth of sibling: An empirical review of changes in the firstborn's adjustment. *Psychological Bulletin, 138*(3), 497–528.

von Glaserfeld, E. (1995). *Radical constructivism: A way of knowing and learning.* Bristol, PA: Falmer Press.

Vosniadou, S., & Mason, L. (2012). Conceptual change induced by instruction: A complex interplay of multiple factors. In K. Harris, S. Graham, & T. Urdan (Eds.), *APA educational psychology handbook: Vol. 2. Individual differences and cultural and contextual factors* (pp. 221–246). Washington, DC: American Psychological Association.

Vouloumanos, A., & Werker, J. F. (2004). Tuned to the signal: The privileged status of speech for young infants. *Developmental Science, 7,* 270–276.

Voyer, D. (2011). Time limits and gender differences on paper-and-pencil tests of mental rotation: A meta-analysis. *Psychonomic Bulletin and Review, 18*(2), 267–277.

Voyer, D., & Voyer, S. D. (2014). Gender differences in academic achievement: A meta-analysis. *Psychological Bulletin, 140*(4), 1174–1204.

Voyer, D., Voyer, S. D., & Saint-Aubin, J. (2017). Sex differences in visual–spatial working memory: A meta-analysis. *Psychonomic Bulletin Review, 24*(2), 307–334.

Vygotsky, L. S. (1962). *Thought and language.* Cambridge, MA: MIT Press.

Vygotsky, L. S. (1978). *Mind in society: The development of higher psychological processes.* Cambridge, MA: Harvard University Press.

Vygotsky, L. S. (1981). The genesis of higher mental functioning. In J. V. Wertsche (Ed.), *The concept of activity in Soviet psychology* (pp. 144–188). Armonk, NY: Sharpe.

Vygotsky, L. S. (1987). *Thinking and speech* (N. Minick, Ed. & Trans.). New York: Plenum Press.

Waddington, C. H. (1961). Genetic assimilation. *Advances in Genetics, 10,* 257–293.

Wade, S. (2001). Research on importance and interest: Implications for curriculum development and future research. *Educational Psychology Review, 13*(3), 243–261.

Wade, S. E., & Adams, R. B. (1990). Effects of importance and interest on recall of biographic text. *Journal of Reading Behavior, 22,* 331–353.

Waggoner, D. (1991). *Undereducation in America.* New York: Auburn House.

Wagmiller, R. L. (2015). The temporal dynamics of childhood economic deprivation and children's achievement. *Child Development Perspectives, 9*(3), 158–163.

Wagner, D. A. (1974). The development of short-term and incidental memory: A cross-cultural study. *Child Development, 45,* 389–396.

Wagner, D. A. (1978). Memories of Morocco: The influence of age, schooling, and environment on memory. *Cognitive Psychology, 10,* 1–28.

Wagner, D. A., & Spratt, J. E. (1987). Cognitive consequences of contrasting pedagogies: The effects of Quranic preschooling in Morocco. *Child Development, 58,* 1207–1219.

Wagner, L., & Hoff, E. (2013). Language development. In R. M. Lerner, M. A. Easterbrooks, & J. Mistry (Eds.), *Handbook of developmental psychology* (2nd ed., pp. 173–196). New York: Wiley.

Walker, L. J. (2006). Gender and morality. In M. Killen & J. G. Smetna (Eds.), *Handbook of moral development* (pp. 93–15). Hillsdale, NJ: Erlbaum.

Walkup, J. T., Stossel, L., & Rendleman, R. (2014). Beyond rising rates: Personalized medicine and public health approaches to the diagnosis and treatment of attention-deficit/hyperactivity disorder. *Journal of the American Academy of Child and Adolescent Psychiatry, 53*(1), 14–16.

Wallace, T. L., & Chhuon, V. (2014). Proximal processes in urban classrooms: Engagement and disaffection in urban youth of color. *American Educational Research Journal, 51*(5), 937–974.

Walters, G. C., & Grusec, J. E. (1977). *Punishment.* San Francisco: Freeman.

Walters, G. D. (2016). The parent–peer interface: Does inductive parenting reduce the criminogenic effect of delinquent peers? *Youth Violence and Juvenile Justice, 14*(4), 411–425.

Walton, G. M., Logel, C., Peach, J. M., Spencer, S. J., & Zanna, M. P. (2015). Two brief interventions to mitigate a "chilly climate" transform women's experience, relationships, and achievement in engineering. *Journal of Educational Psychology, 107*(2), 468–485.

Wandell, B. A., & Yeatman, J. D. (2013). Biological development of reading circuits. *Current Opinion in Neurobiology, 23*(2), 261–268.

Wang, L., & Carr, M. (2014). Working memory and strategy use contribute to gender differences in spatial ability. *The Educational Psychologist, 49*(4), 261–282.

Wang, M. T., & Kenny, S. (2014). Parental physical punishment and adolescent adjustment: Bidirectionality and the moderation effects of child ethnicity and parental warmth. *Journal of Abnormal Child Psychology, 42,* 717–730.

Wang, Y., Cottler, L. B., & Striley, C. W. (2015). Differentiating patterns of prescription stimulant medical and nonmedical use among youth 10–18 years of age. *Drug and Alcohol Dependence, 157,* 83–89.

Wang, Z. (2016). Exploring the effects of seductive details with the 4-phase model of interest. *Learning and Motivation, 55,* 65–77.

Ward, L. P., & McCune, S. K. (2002). The first weeks of life. In M. L. Batshaw (Ed.), *Children with disabilities* (5th ed., pp. 69–84). Baltimore: Brookes.

Wark, G. R., & Krebs, D. L. (1996). Gender and dilemma differences in real-life moral judgment. *Developmental Psychology, 32*(2), 220–230.

Warmuth, K. A., & Cummings, M. E. (2015). Examining developmental fit of the adult attachment interview in adolescence. *Developmental Review, 36,* 200–218.

Washington v. Davis, 426 U.S. 229 (1976).

Wasik, B. A., & Slavin, R. E. (1993). Preventing early reading failure with one-to-one tutoring: A review of five programs. *Reading Research Quarterly, 28,* 178–200.

Wassenberg, R., Feron, F. J., Kessels, A. G., Hendriksen, J. G., Kalff, A. C., Kroes, M., et al. (2005). Relation between cognitive and motor performance in 5- to 6-year-old children: Results from a large-scale cross-sectional study. *Child Development, 76*(5), 1092–1103.

Wasserman, G. A., Factor-Litvak, P., Liu, X., Todd, A. C., Kline, J. K., Slavkovich, V., et al. (2003). The relationship between blood lead, bone lead and child intelligence. *Child Neuropsychology, 9,* 22–34.

Waterman, A., & Goldman, J. (1976). A longitudinal study of ego identity development in a liberal arts college. *Journal of Youth and Adolescence, 5,* 361–369.

Waters, E. (1995). The attachment Q-set. *Monographs of the Society for Research in Child Development, 60*(Nos. 2–3, Serial No. 244), 234–246.

Watson, J. B. (1927, March). What to do when your child is afraid [Interview with Beatrice Black]. *Children,* pp. 25–27.

Watts, W. J. (1979). The influence of language on the development of quantitative, spatial, and social thinking in deaf children. *American Annals of the Deaf, 12,* 45–56.

Waxman, S. R., & Booth, A. E. (2000). Principles that are invoked in the acquisition of words, but not facts. *Cognition, 77*(2), B33–B43.

Weaver, J. M., & Schofield, T. J. (2015). Mediation and moderation of divorce effects on children's behavior problems. *Journal of Family Psychology, 29*(1), 39–48.

Webb, N. M. (1984). Sex differences in interaction and achievement in cooperative small groups. *Journal of Educational Psychology, 76,* 33–34.

Webb, N. M. (1989). Peer interaction and learning in small groups. *International Journal of Educational Research, 13,* 21–39.

Webb, N. M. (2013a). Collaboration in the classroom. In J. Hattie & E. M. Anderman (Eds.), *International guide to student achievement* (pp. 215–217). New York: Routledge.

Webb, N. M. (2013b). Information processing approaches to collaborative learning. In C. E. Hmelo-Silver, C. A. Chinn, C. K. K. Chan, & A. O'Donnell (Eds.), *The international handbook of collaborative learning* (pp. 19–40). New York: Routledge.

Weeda, J. (2013). Summerhill: A call for significance in a world of irrelevance. In T. S. Poetter (Ed.), *Curriculum windows: What curriculum theorists of the 60's can teach us about schools and society today* (pp. 247–264). Charlotte, NC: Information Age.

Weeks, T. E. (1971). Speech registers in young children. *Child Development, 42,* 1119–1131.

Weiner, B. (1979). A theory of motivation for some classroom experiences. *Journal of Educational Psychology, 71,* 3–25.

Weiner, B. (2001). Intrapersonal and interpersonal theories of motivation from an attribution perspective. In F. Salili & C.-Y. Chiu (Eds.), *Student motivation: The culture and context of learning* (pp. 17–30). Dordrecht, The Netherlands: Kluwer.

Weiner, B. (2003). The classroom as courtroom. *Social Psychology of Education, 6,* 3–15.

Weinstein, R. S. (2002). *Reaching higher: The power of expectations in schooling.* Cambridge, MA: Harvard University Press.

Weisner, T. S., & Garnier, H. (1992). Nonconventional family life-styles and school achievement: A 12-year longitudinal study. *American Educational Research Journal, 29,* 605–632.

Weiss, L. G., Prifitera, A., & Munoz, M. R. (2015). Issues related to intelligence testing with Spanish-speaking clients. In K. F. Geisinger (Ed.), *Psychological testing of Hispanics: Clinical, cultural, and intellectual issues* (2nd ed., pp. 81–107). Washington, DC: American Psychological Association.

Weiss, L. G., Saklofske, D. H., & Prifitera, A. (2003). Clinical interpretation of the Wechsler Intelligence Scale for Children—Third edition (WISC-III) index scores. In C. R. Reynolds & R. W. Kamphaus (Eds.), *Handbook of psychological and educational assessment of children: Intelligence, aptitude, and achievement* (2nd ed., pp. 115–146). New York: Guilford Press.

Wellman, H. M. (2014). *Making minds.* New York: Oxford University Press.

Wellman, H. M., & Liu, D. (2004). Scaling of theory-of-mind tasks. *Child Development, 75*(2), 523–541.

Wells, A. S., & Crain, R. L. (1997). *Stepping over the color line: African-American students in white suburban schools*. New Haven, CT: Yale University Press.

Wells, G., & Mejia Arauz, R. (2006). Dialogue in the classroom. *Journal of the Learning Sciences, 15*(3), 379–428.

Wen, X., Bulotsky-Shearer, R. J., Hahs-Vaughn, D. L., & Korfmacher, J. (2012). Head Start program quality: Examination of classroom quality and parent involvement in predicting children's vocabulary, literacy, and mathematics achievement trajectories. *Early Childhood Research Quarterly, 27*, 640–653.

Wentzel, K. R. (1998). Social relationships and motivation in middle school: The role of parents, teachers, and peers. *Journal of Educational Psychology, 90*, 202–209.

Wentzel, K. R. (2003). Sociometric status and adjustment in middle school: A longitudinal study. *Journal of Early Adolescence, 23*, 5–28.

Wentzel, K. R. (2009). Peers and academic functioning at school. In K. H. Rubin, W. M. Bukowski, & B. Laursen (Eds.), *Handbook of peer interactions, relationships, and groups* (pp. 531–547). New York: Guilford Press.

Wentzel, K. (2013). School adjustment. In W. M. Reynolds & G. E. Miller (Eds.), *Handbook of educational psychology* (2nd ed., pp. 213–231). New York: Wiley.

Wentzel, K. R. (2014). Prosocial behavior and peer relations in adolescence. In L. M. Padilla-Walker & G. Carlo (Eds.), *Prosocial development: A multidimensional approach* (pp. 178–200). New York: Oxford University Press.

Wentzel, K. R., Russell, S., & Baker, S. (2016). Emotional support and expectations from parents, teachers, and peers predict adolescent competence at school. *Journal of Educational Psychology, 108*(2), 242–255.

Werker, J. F. (1995). Exploring developmental changes in cross-language speech perception. In L. R. Gleitman & M. Liberman (Eds.), *Language: An invitation to cognitive science* (pp. 87–106). Cambridge, MA: MIT Press.

Werker, J. F., & Pegg, J. E. (1992). Infant speech perception and phonological acquisition. In C. A. Ferguson, L. Menn, & C. Stoel-Gammon (Eds.), *Phonological development: Models, research, and implications* (pp. 285–311). Timonium, MD: York Press.

Werner, H., & Kaplan, E. (1952). The acquisition of word meanings: A developmental study. *Monographs of the Society for Research in Child Development, 15*(1, Serial No. 51).

Wertsch, J. V. (1979). From social interaction to higher psychological processes: A clarification and application of Vygotsky's theory. *Human Development, 22*, 1–22.

Wertsch, J. V. (1985). *Vygotsky and the social formation of mind*. Cambridge, MA: Harvard University Press.

Wertsch, J. V. (1991). *Voices of the mind: A sociocultural approach to mediated action*. Cambridge, MA: Harvard University Press.

White, D. S., & Le Cornu, A. (2011). Visitors and residents: A new typology for online engagement. *First Monday, 16*(9).

White, R. W. (1959). Motivation reconsidered: The concept of competence. *Psychological Review, 66*, 297–333.

Whitehurst, G. J., Arnold, D. S., Epstein, J. N., Angel, A. L., Smith, M., & Fischel, J. E. (1994). A picture book reading intervention in day care and home for children from low-income families. *Developmental Psychology, 30*, 679–689.

Whitehurst, G. J., Epstein, J. N., Angel, A. L., Payne, A. C., Crone, D. A., & Fischel, J. E. (1994). Outcomes of an emergent literacy intervention in Head Start. *Journal of Educational Psychology, 86*, 542–555.

Whitehurst, G. J., Falco, F. L., Lonigan, C. J., Fischel, J. E., DeBaryshe, B. D., Valdez-Menchaca, M. C., et al. (1988). Accelerating language development through picturebook reading. *Developmental Psychology, 24*, 552–559.

Whitehurst, G. J., & Valdez-Menchaca, M. C. (1988). What is the role of reinforcement in early language acquisition? *Child Development, 59*, 430–440.

Whiteman, S. D., Becerra, J. M., & Killoren, S. E. (2009). Mechanisms of sibling socialization in normative family development. In L. Kramer & K. J. Conger (Eds.), *Siblings as agents of socialization. New Directions for Child and Adolescent Development* (Vol. 126, pp. 29–43). San Francisco: Jossey-Bass.

Wigfield, A. (1994). Expectancy-value theory of achievement motivation: A developmental perspective. *Educational Psychology Review, 6*, 49–78.

Wigfield, A., & Eccles, J. (1992). The development of achievement task values: A theoretical analysis. *Developmental Review, 12*, 265–310.

Wigfield, A., & Eccles, J. S. (2000). Expectancy-value theory of achievement motivation. *Contemporary Educational Psychology, 25*, 68–81.

Wigfield, A., Eccles, J. S., Fredriks, S. S., Roeser, R. W., & Schiefele, U. (2015). Development of achievement motivation and engagement. In M. E. Lamb & R. M. Lerner (Eds.), *Handbook of child psychology and developmental science: Vol. 3. Socioemotional processes* (7th ed., pp. 657–700). Hoboken, NJ: Wiley.

Wigfield, A., Eccles, J. S., MacIver, D., Reuman, D. A., & Midgley, C. (1991). Transitions during early adolescence: Changes in children's domain-specific self-perceptions and general self-esteem across the transition to junior high school. *Developmental Psychology, 27*, 552–565.

Wiig, E. H. (1992). Linguistic transitions in children and adolescents with language learning disabilities: Characteristics and training. In S. A. Vogel (Ed.), *Educational alternatives for students with learning disabilities* (pp. 43–63). New York: Springer-Verlag.

Wilder, S. (2015). Impact of problem-based learning on academic achievement in high school: A systematic review. *Educational Review, 67*(4), 414–435.

Wilkinson, L. C., & Marrett, C. B. (Eds.). (1985). *Gender influences on classroom interaction*. Orlando, FL: Academic Press.

Williams, J. P., Kao, J. C., Pao, L. S., Ordynans, J. G., Atkins, J. G., Cheng, R., et al. (2016). Close analysis of texts with structure (CATs): An intervention to teach reading comprehension to at-risk second graders. *Journal of Educational Psychology, 108*(8), 1061–1077.

Williford, A. P., Carter, L. M., & Pianta, R. C. (2016). Attachment and school readiness. In J. Cassidy & P. R. Shaver (Eds.), *Handbook of attachment: Theory, research, and clinical applications* (pp. 966–982). New York: Guilford Press.

Wilmer, H. H., Sherman, L. E., & Chein, J. M. (2017). Smartphones and cognition: A review of research exploring the links between mobile technology habits and cognitive functioning. *Frontiers in Psychology, 8*, 605.

Wilson, P. (1991). Trauma of Sioux Indian high school students. *Anthropology and Education Quarterly, 22*, 367–383.

Wimmer, H., Landerl, K., Linortner, R., & Hummer, P. (1991). The relationship of phonemic awareness to reading acquisition: More consequence than precondition but still important. *Cognition, 40*, 219–249.

Winne, P. H., & Azevedo, R. (2014). Metacognition. In R. K. Sawyer (Ed.), *Cambridge handbook of the learning sciences* (2nd ed., pp. 63–87). New York: Cambridge University Press.

Winne, P. H., Woodlands, M. H., & Wong, B. Y. L. (1982). Comparability of self-concept among learning disabled, normal, and gifted students. *Journal of Learning Disabilities, 15*, 470–475.

Winsler, A. (2009). Still talking to ourselves after all these years: A review of current research on private speech. In A. Winsler, C. Fernyhough, & I. Montero (Eds.), *Private speech, executive functioning, and the development of verbal self-regulation* (pp. 3–41). New York: Cambridge University Press.

Winsler, A., & Naglieri, J. (2003). Overt and covert verbal problem-solving strategies: Developmental trends in use, awareness, and relations with task performance in children aged 5 to 17. *Child Development, 74*(3), 659–678.

Wirkala, C., & Kuhn, D. (2011). Problem-based learning in K–12 education: Is it effective and how does

it achieve its effects? *American Educational Research Journal, 48*, 1157–1186.

Witwer, A. N., Lawton, K., & Aman, M. G. (2014). Intellectual disability. In E. J. Mash & R. A. Barkley (Eds.), *Child psychopathology* (3rd ed., pp. 593–624). New York: Guilford Press.

Wohlwill, J. F. (1973). *The study of behavioral development in children*. New York: Academic Press.

Woll, B., & Ladd, P. (2003). Deaf communities. In M. Marschark & P. E. Spencer (Eds.), *Oxford handbook of deaf studies, language, and education* (pp. 151–163). New York: Oxford University Press.

Wollheim, R. (1989). *Sigmund Freud*. Cambridge, UK: Cambridge University Press.

Woloshyn, V. E., Paivio, A., & Pressley, M. (1994). Using elaborative interrogation to help students acquire information consistent with prior knowledge and information inconsistent with prior knowledge. *Journal of Educational Psychology, 86*, 79–89.

Wong, B. Y. L., Harris, K. R., Graham, S., & Butler, D. L. (2003). Cognitive strategies instruction research in learning disabilities. In H. L. Swanson, K. R. Harris, & S. Graham (Eds.), *Handbook of learning disabilities* (pp. 1383–1402). New York: Guilford Press.

Wood, E., Petkovski, M., De Pasquale, D., Gottardo, A., Evans, M. A., & Savage, R. (2016, May 10). Parent scaffolding of young children when engaged with mobile technology. *Frontiers in Psychology*. [Epub ahead of print]

Wood, R., & Bandura, A. (1989). Impact of conceptions of ability on self-regulatory mechanisms and complex decision-making. *Journal of Personality and Social Psychology, 56*, 407–415.

Wood, S. S., Bruner, J. S., & Ross, G. (1976). The role of tutoring in problem solving. *Journal of Child Psychology and Psychiatry, 17*, 89–100.

Woodhouse, S. S., Dykus, M. J., & Cassidy, J. (2012). Loneliness and peer relations in adolescence. *Social Development, 21*(2), 273–293.

Workman, J. (2016). Sibling additions, resource dilution, and cognitive development during early childhood. *Journal of Marriage and Family, 79*, 1–13.

Worrell, F. C., & Roberson, C. C. B. (2016). Standards for educational and psychological testing: Implications for ethnic minority youth. In S. L. Graves & J. J. Blake (Eds.), *Psychoeducational assessment and intervention for ethnic minority children: Evidence-based approaches* (pp. 41–57). Washington, DC: American Psychological Association.

Wright, R. J. (2009). Moving towards making social toxins mainstream in children's environmental health. *Current Opinions in Pediatrics, 21*(2), 222–229.

Wunsch, M. J., Conlon, C. J., & Scheidt, P. C. (2002). Substance abuse: A preventable threat to development. In M. L. Batshaw (Ed.), *Children with disabilities* (5th ed., pp. 107–122). Baltimore: Brookes.

Wyatt, T. (1995). Language development in African American English child speech. *Linguistics and Education, 7*, 7–22.

Yeager, D. S., & Dweck, C. S. (2012). Mindsets that promote resilience: When students believe that personal characteristics can be developed. *The Educational Psychologist, 47*(4), 302–315.

Yeager, D. S., Henderson, M. D., Paunesku, D., Walton, G. M., D'Mello, S., Spitzer, B. J., et al. (2014). Boring but important: A self-transcendent purpose for learning fosters academic self-regulation. *Journal of Personality and Social Psychology, 107*(4), 559–580.

Yeager, D. S., Romero, C., Paunesku, D., Hulleman, C. S., Schneider, B., Hinojosa, C., et al. (2016). Using design thinking to improve psychological interventions: The case of the growth mindset during the transition to high school. *Journal of Educational Psychology, 108*(3), 374–391.

Yee, E., Chrysikou, E. G., & Thompson-Schill, S. L. (2014). Semantic memory. In K. N. Ochsner & S. M. Kosslyn (Eds.), *Oxford handbook of cognitive neuroscience* (pp. 353–374). New York: Oxford University Press.

Yeh, L-H., Schwarz, A. L., & Baule, A. L. (2011). The impact of text-structure strategy instruction on the text recall and eye movements of second language English readers. *Reading Psychology, 32*, 495–519.

Yeung, W. J. (2012). Explaining the black-white achievement gap: An intergenerational stratification and developmental perspective. In K. Harris, S. Graham, & T. Urdan (Eds.), *APA educational psychology handbook: Vol. 2. Individual differences and cultural and contextual factors* (pp. 315–336). Washington, DC: American Psychological Association.

Yip, T. (2014). Ethnic identity in everyday life: The influence of identity development status. *Child Development, 85*(1), 205–219.

Yip, T., Douglass, S., & Sellers, R. M. (2014). Ethnic and racial identity. In F. T. L. Leong, L. Comas-Diaz, G. C. Nagayama Hall, V. C. McLoyd, & J. E. Trimble (Eds.), *APA handbook of multicultural psychology: Vol. 1. Theory and research* (pp. 179–205). Washington, DC: American Psychological Association.

Yoakum, C. S., & Yerkes, R. M. (1920). *Army mental tests*. New York: Holt.

Yoshikawa, H., Aber, J., & Beardslee, W. R. (2012). The effects of poverty on the mental, emotional, and behavioral health of children and youth. *American Psychologist, 67*(4), 272–284.

Youngstrom, E. A., & Algorta, G. P. (2014). Pediatric bipolar disorder. In E. J. Mash & R. A. Barkley (Eds.), *Child psychopathology* (pp. 264–316). New York: Guilford Press.

Youngstrom, E. A., Glutting, J. J., & Watkins, M. W. (2003). Stanford–Binet Intelligence Scale: Fourth edition (SB4): Evaluating the empirical bases for interpretation. In C. R. Reynolds & R. W. Kamphaus (Eds.), *Handbook of psychological and educational assessment of children: Intelligence, aptitude, and achievement* (2nd ed., pp. 217–242). New York: Guilford Press.

Yu, J., Cheah, C., & Calvin, G. (2016). Acculturation, psychological adjustment, and parenting styles of Chinese immigrant mothers in the United States. *Cultural Diversity and Ethnic Minority Psychology, 22*(4), 504–516.

Zabalia, M. (2002). Action et imagerie mentale chez l'enfant [Action and mental imagery in children]. *L'année Psychologique, 102*(3), 409–422.

Zauche, L. H., Thul, T. A., Mahoney, A. E. D., & Stapel-Wax, J. L., (2016). Influence of language nutrition on children's language and cognitive development: An integrated review. *Early Childhood Research Quarterly, 36*, 318–333.

Zebrack, B. J., & Chesler, M. A. (2002). Quality of life in childhood cancer survivors. *Psycho-Oncology, 11*, 132–141.

Zeffiro, T., & Eden, G. (2001). The cerebellum and dyslexia: Perpetrator or innocent bystander? *Trends in Neuroscience, 24*, 512–513.

Zepeda, C. D., Richey, J. E., Ronevich, P., & Nokes-Malach, T. J. (2015). Direct instruction of metacognition benefits adolescent science learning, transfer, and motivation: An in vivo study. *Journal of Educational Psychology, 107*(4), 954–970.

Zetlin, A., & Murtaugh, M. (1990). Whatever happened to those with borderline IQs? *American Journal of Mental Deficiency, 94*, 463–469.

Zevenbergen, A. A., Whitehurst, G. J., & Zevenbergen, J. A. (2003). Effects of a shared-reading intervention on the inclusion of evaluative devices in narratives of children from low-income families. *Journal of Applied Developmental Psychology, 24*, 1–15.

Zigler, E. F., & Balla, D. (Eds.). (1982). *Mental retardation: The developmental-difference controversy*. Hillsdale, NJ: Erlbaum.

Zigler, E. F., & Hodapp, R. M. (1986). *Understanding mental retardation*. Cambridge, UK: Cambridge University Press.

Zimmerman, B. J. (1989). A social cognitive view of self-regulated academic learning. *Journal of Educational Psychology, 81*, 329–339.

Zimmerman, B. J., & Bandura, A. (1994). Impact of self-regulatory influences on writing course attainment. *American Educational Research Journal, 31*, 845–862.

Zimmerman, B. J., Bandura, A., & Martinez-Pons, M.

(1992). Self-motivation for academic attainment: The role of self-efficacy beliefs and personal goal setting. *American Educational Research Journal, 29,* 663–676.

Zimmerman, B. J., & Schunk, D. H. (2003). Albert Bandura: The scholar and his contributions to educational psychology. In B. J. Zimmerman & D. H. Schunk (Eds.), *Educational psychology: A century of contributions* (pp. 431–457). Mahwah, NJ: Erlbaum.

Zirkel, S., & Johnson, T. (2016). Mirror, mirror on the wall: A critical examination of the conceptualization of the study of Black racial identity in education. *Educational Researcher, 45*(5), 301–311.

Zisenwine, T., Kaplan, M., Kushnir, J., & Sadeh, A. (2013). Nighttime fears and fantasy-reality differentiation in preschool children. *Child Psychiatry Human Development, 44,* 186–199.

Zucker, K. J. (2001). Biological influences on psychosexual differentiation. In R. K. Unger (Ed.), *Handbook of psychology of women and gender* (pp. 101–115). New York: Wiley.

Index

Note. *f* or *t* following a page number indicates a figure or a table.
Page numbers in **bold** refer to entries in the Glossary.